Futures, Options, and Swaps
Second Edition

Futures, Options, and Swaps
Second Edition

Robert W. Kolb

Blackwell Publishers Inc.
350 Main Street
Malden, MA
02148

Blackwell Publishers Ltd.
108 Cowley Road
Oxford OX4 1JF
UK

Library of Congress Cataloging-in-Publication Data

Kolb, Robert W.
  Futures, options, and swaps / Robert W. Kolb—2nd ed.
    p. cm.
  Includes index.
  ISBN 1-57718-063-1 (hc)
  1. Derivative securities. 2. Financial futures. 3. Options (Finance) 4. Swaps (Finance) 5. Option!, (Computer file) 6. Options (Finance)—Prices—Problems, exercises, etc.—Computer programs. I. Title.
  HG6024.A3K649   1997
  332.64'5—dc20   96-34129
                                                                                              CIP

British Library of Congress Cataloging-in-Publication Data

Typeset by AM Marketing.

This book is printed on acid-free paper.

CONTENTS

Contents

PREFACE

Futures, Options, and Swaps, 2e, brings together in one text a comprehensive treatment of the three most important types of financial derivatives. These three types of derivatives are linked by a common pricing framework – the proposition that rational prices preclude arbitrage profits. This guiding principle is introduced in the first chapter and pursued throughout the text.

The text also emphasizes the use of futures, options, and swaps in risk management. While the book features ample examples of speculative strategies that can be implemented with these instruments, the focus of the application examples is the management of preexisting risk.

To integrate the understanding of these instruments, the discussion emphasizes the relationships among futures, options, and swaps. For example, various parity conditions are derived and illustrated. Also, an interest rate swap is analyzed as a portfolio of forward contracts or futures contracts.

The treatment in this text emphasizes financial derivatives, but it does not neglect traditional commodity futures. From years of teaching this material, I have found that futures can be understood best when the discussion begins with a tangible good having no cash flows, such as gold. Accordingly, the book is organized as follows.

ORGANIZATION OF THE TEXT

Chapter 1, *Introduction,* introduces the key concept of arbitrage that will be used in all subsequent pricing discussions. The chapter also defines and illustrates the various derivatives that will be considered in the text and explains the various uses of these instruments.

Futures

Chapters 2–9 focus on futures markets. Chapter 2, *Futures Markets,* provides an introduction to the institutional framework of the market, including margin, the clearinghouse, and daily settlement. Chapter 3, *Futures Prices,* explores the cost-of-carry model in depth, relating it to the no-arbitrage principle introduced in Chapter 1. Chapter 4, *Using Futures Markets,* discusses the role of speculators in providing market liquidity and in aiding price discovery. Chapter 4 also explores techniques of hedging with futures. Chapters 2–4 provide a comprehensive overview of the market and set the stage for the explicit discussion of financial futures.

Chapters 5–9 consider interest rate futures, stock index futures, and foreign currency futures. Chapter 5, *Interest Rate Futures: Introduction,* and Chapter 6, *Interest Rate Futures: Refinements,* provide detailed coverage of interest rate futures. Chapter 5 introduces the contracts and covers the basic pricing principles, while Chapter 6 explores key issues (such as the features of the T-bond contract and the implicit options in the contract) in more detail. Chapter 6 can be omitted without loss of continuity. Chapter 7, *Stock Index Futures: Introduction,* and Chapter 8, *Stock Index Futures: Refinements,* follow a similar strategy in treating stock index futures. Chapter 9, *Foreign Exchange Futures,* discusses the contracts, pricing principles, and applications of foreign exchange futures. It also includes basic material on interest rate parity and purchasing power parity conditions.

Options

Chapters 10–18 cover options in detail. Chapter 10, *The Options Market,* introduces the essential institutional features of the U.S. options market, while Chapter 11, *Option Payoffs and Option Strategies,* begins the analytical treatment of options by exploring popular trading strategies and their payoffs at expiration using familiar no-arbitrage conditions. Chapter 12, *Bounds on Option Prices,* continues to use no-arbitrage arguments to place rational bounds on option prices before expiration.

To specify the exact price that an option should have requires a model of how stock prices can move. Chapter 13, *European Option Pricing,* develops formal pricing models for European options. The price of an option depends on the characteristics of the underlying instrument, notably upon the way in which the price of the underlying instrument can vary. We consider the binomial model and eventually elaborate this model into the Black-Scholes model. Chapter 13 also explores the Merton model. Chapter 14, *Option Sensitivities and Option Hedging,* is a companion to Chapter 13 in that it explores the option sensitivities of the Black-Scholes and Merton models. These sensitivities (DELTA, THETA, VEGA, GAMMA, and RHO) are extremely important in using options to hedge or in controlling the risk of speculative strategies.

Chapter 15, *American Option Pricing,* develops an extensive treatment of American options. It includes coverage of American puts, the exact American call option pricing formula, the analytic approximation approach to pricing American options, and the binomial model as it applies to options with and without dividends. Chapter 16, *Options on Stock Indexes, Foreign Currency, and Futures,* explores stock index options, foreign currency options, and options on futures for both European and American options. Chapter 17, *The Options Approach to Corporate Securities,* shows that the principles of option pricing can be extended to analyze corporate securities. The chapter considers the option features of common stock, straight bonds, convertible bonds, callable bonds, and warrants. One of the most useful features of this chapter is to illustrate the power of the option approach to the world of finance. Chapter 18, *Exotic Options,* is a new chapter in this edition. It details the payoffs for a wide variety of exotic options, presents the valuation formulas, and includes a detailed computational example.

Swaps

The swaps market is the subject of Chapter 19, *The Swaps Market: Introduction,* and Chapter 20, *The Swaps Market: Refinements.* Chapter 19 introduces the institutional features of the market and considers plain vanilla interest rate and foreign currency swaps. Chapter 20 extends the analysis "beyond plain vanilla," and it also illustrates how to use swaps to manage more complicated risk situations.

OPTION! SOFTWARE

Each copy of the text is accompanied by an IBM PC-compatible diskette, including the program **OPTION!**, which can compute virtually every option value discussed in this book, including a comprehensive module for pricing exotic options. Further, **OPTION!** can graph many of the relationships among different option prices discussed in the chapters that follow. Exploring the option concepts of the text with the software can greatly enhance an understanding of option pricing. Instructions for **OPTION!** are found in an appendix at the end of this text. The text also includes more than 60 exercises designed to enhance the understanding of option pricing principles and applications. These exercises can all be solved using **OPTION!** software.

FUTURES DATA

The diskette that accompanies this text also includes a variety of data from the futures market. These data include daily prices on many different futures contracts, with an emphasis on financial futures. The *Futures Data Guide* at the end of this book explains how the data are organized. These data provide an opportunity for analyzing actual futures pricing relationships.

CHANGES IN THE SECOND EDITION

For the second edition of *Futures, Options, and Swaps,* all time-sensitive material has been updated as appropriate. The major change to this edition is the inclusion of a new Chapter 18 on "Exotic Options." This chapter reflects the emergence of an important new class of options. It considers these options in detail, including detailed pricing formulas and worked-out computational examples of each type of option. In addition, the **OPTION!** Software that accompanies this book has been expanded to provide full coverage of all of the exotic options covered in the new Chapter 18.

New topics have been added to reflect changes in the markets. Specific examples are: Chapter 2, which now provides a discussion of the new FASB proposals for accounting for futures contracts and also analyzes the current state of electronic trading with an emphasis on the competing systems of the Chicago Mercantile Exchange (GLOBEX) and the Chicago Board of Trade (Project A); Chapter 5, which focuses greater attention on Eurodollar futures, reflecting their growth in importance for the markets; and Chapter 7, which features a discussion of the demise of Barings Bank in the context of index arbitrage. As with the first edition, the second edition is accompanied by futures data that have been expanded and updated.

ACKNOWLEDGMENTS

As a second edition, much of the material contained here is tried and proven. In writing this book, I have drawn heavily on all five editions of *Understanding Futures Markets* and three editions of *Options: An Introduction.* Thus, most of the material here has been class-tested in many universities.

Over all of these editions, I have received the assistance of numerous people, ranging from hundreds of professors to many hundred students. This book has grown out of their contributions and insights, and I am deeply grateful for their efforts. For this edition, I am particularly indebted to George Wang of the Commodity Futures Trading Commission, Peter Alonzi of the Chicago Board of Trade, Tom Gosnell of Oklahoma State University, and Raffaella Cremonesi and Suk Hun Lee of Loyola University of Chicago.

Producing *Futures, Options, and Swaps, 2e,* required the dedicated efforts of a professional production staff. I would like to thank Rolf Janke, Editorial Director, Mary Beckwith, Assistant Editor, Jan Phillips, Production Manager, Megan Zuckerman, Graphic Designer, and Diane McCree, Production Editor, for their assistance and expertise in putting this project together. Of course, I alone am responsible for any remaining deficiencies.

Robert W. Kolb

<table>
<tr><td>

CHAPTER

1

</td><td>

INTRODUCTION

</td></tr>
</table>

OVERVIEW

This chapter begins by defining a derivative instrument and distinguishing financial derivatives from derivatives in general. As the word implies, a **derivative instrument** is one whose value depends on (i.e., is *derived* from) the value of something else.

The major derivatives considered in this book are forward contracts, futures contracts, options contracts, options on futures, and swap contracts. This chapter briefly introduces each of these instruments and explains their key features. Later chapters consider each instrument in detail. After introducing these instruments, this chapter gives a brief explanation of why financial derivatives are so critically important in finance today. As we will see throughout this text, these instruments have grown from trivial importance to playing a key role in virtually all financial markets. Compared with the fundamental securities on which they are based, financial derivatives afford numerous benefits to both speculators and risk managers. In addition, derivatives offer some surprising advantages in reducing transaction costs and other forms of trading efficiency.

Throughout this text, we will be concerned with the principles that determine the prices of the financial derivatives we consider. The text consistently employs a no-arbitrage principle to illuminate the pricing principles for each instrument. An **arbitrage opportunity** is a chance to make a riskless profit with no investment. In essence, finding an arbitrage opportunity is like finding free money, as we explain in more detail later in this chapter. The **no-arbitrage principle** states that any rational price for a financial instrument must exclude arbitrage opportunities. This is a minimal requirement for a feasible or rational price for any financial instrument. As we will see in detail in the chapters that follow, this no-arbitrage principle is extremely powerful in helping understand what prices can reasonably prevail for forwards, futures, options, options on futures, and swaps.

The chapter then turns to explain how the text is organized. Two software items accompany this text. The first is a computer program called **OPTION!**, which allows the reader to compute option prices with ease. In addition, the accompanying diskette contains a variety of futures market data, which this chapter also briefly explains.

FINANCIAL DERIVATIVES

In the financial marketplace, some securities and some instruments are regarded as fundamental, while others are regarded as derivative. In a corporation, for example, the stock and bonds issued by the firm are fundamental securities and form the bedrock of financial geology. Every corporation must have stock, and stock ownership gives rights of ownership to the firm. Owning a bond issued by a firm gives the bondholder the first claim on the firm's cash flows.

In contrast with fundamental securities, such as stocks and bonds, there is an entirely distinct class of financial instruments called derivatives. In finance, a **derivative** is a financial instrument or security whose payoffs depend on a more primitive or fundamental good. For example, a gold futures contract is a derivative instrument, because the value of the futures contract depends upon the value of the gold that underlies the futures contract. The value of the gold is the key, while the value of a gold futures contract derives from the value of the underlying gold.

A **financial derivative** is a financial instrument or security whose payoffs depend on another financial instrument or security. For example, an option on a share of stock depends on the value of the underlying share. Because the underlying good for a stock option is a financial instrument, a stock option is a type of financial derivative. Similarly, a futures contract on a Treasury bond is a financial derivative, because the value of the T-bond futures depends on the value of the underlying Treasury bond.

This book considers four types of financial derivatives: forwards, futures, options, and swaps. In this section, we briefly introduce each instrument and discuss its basic features. Subsequent chapters focus on futures, options, and swaps in detail, while forward contracts are considered in passing throughout the text.

Forwards

A **forward contract**, as it occurs in both forward and futures markets, always involves a contract initiated at one time; performance in accordance with the terms of the contract occurs at a subsequent time. Further, the type of forward contracting to be considered here always involves an exchange of one asset for another. The price at which the exchange occurs is set at the time of the initial contracting. Actual payment and delivery of the good occur later. So defined, almost everyone has engaged in some kind of forward contract.

The following example illustrates a very simple, yet frequently occurring, type of forward contract. Having heard that a highly prized St. Bernard has just given birth to a litter of pups, a dog fancier rushes to the kennel to see the pups. After inspecting the pedigree of the parents, the dog fancier offers to buy a pup from the breeder. The exchange, however, cannot be completed at this time, since the pup is too young to be weaned. The fancier and breeder thus agree that the dog will be delivered in six weeks and that the fancier will pay the $400 in six weeks upon delivery of the puppy. This contract is not a conditional contract; both parties are obligated to complete it as agreed upon.[1] The puppy example represents a very basic type of forward contract. The example could have been made more complicated by the breeder requiring a deposit, but that would not change the essential character of the transaction.

For example, a foreign currency forward contract calls for the exchange of some quantity of a foreign currency at a future date in exchange for a payment at that later date. At the time of contracting, the forward contract stipulates the price to be paid at the time of delivery of the good. As an example, billions of dollars of foreign currencies change hands daily in a very sophisticated forward market that trades contracts for German marks and English pounds. While forward markets for some goods are highly developed and have standardized market features, a forward contract can be unique, as in the commitment between two individuals to deliver a unique good at a later date in exchange for a price that is established at the time of contracting.

From the simplicity of the contract and its obvious usefulness in resolving uncertainty about the future, it is not surprising that forward contracts have had a very long history. The origin of forward contracting is not clear. Some authors trace the practice to Roman and even classical Greek times. Strong evidence suggests that Roman emperors entered forward contracts to provide the masses with their supply of Egyptian grain. Others have traced the origin of forward contracting to India.[2]

Futures

While the historical origins of forward contracts are obscure, organized futures markets began in Chicago with the opening of the Chicago Board of Trade in 1848.[3] Despite the loss of records in the great Chicago fire of 1871, it appears that futures contracts, as opposed to forward contracts, were being traded on the Board of Trade by the 1860s. Since then, the basic structure of futures contracts has been adopted by a number of other exchanges, both in the United States and abroad.

A **futures contract** is a type of forward contract with highly standardized and closely specified contract terms. As in an all forward contracts, a futures contract calls for the exchange of some good at a future date for cash, with the payment for the good to occur at that future date. The purchaser of a futures contract undertakes to receive delivery of the good and pay for it, while the seller of a futures promises to deliver the good and receive payment. The price of the good is determined at the initial time of contracting.

It is important to understand how futures contracts differ from other forms of forward contracts. First, futures contracts always trade on an organized exchange. Second, futures contracts are always highly standardized with a specified quantity of a good, and with a specified delivery date and delivery mechanism. Third, performance on futures contracts is guaranteed by a **clearinghouse** – a financial institution associated with the futures exchange that guarantees the financial integrity of the market to all traders. Fourth, all futures contracts require that traders post margin in order to trade. **Margin** is a good faith deposit made by the prospective futures trader to indicate his or her willingness and ability to fulfill all financial obligations that may arise from trading futures. Fifth, futures markets are regulated by an identifiable government agency, while forward contracts in general trade in an unregulated market.

While these important features of futures markets will be explored in more detail in Chapter 2, we must bear in mind that forwards and futures are essentially similar contracts. In fact, they differ only in the institutional setting in which they trade, and the principles for pricing and using forwards and futures are almost identical.

Options

Everyone has options. When buying a car we can add more equipment to the automobile that is "optional at extra cost." In this sense, an option is a choice. This book examines options in financial markets. These are a very specific type of option – an option created through a financial contract.

Options have played a role in security markets for many years, although no one can be certain how long. Initially, options were created by individualized contracts between two parties. However, until recently, there was no organized exchange for trading options. The development of option exchanges stimulated greater interest and more active trading of options. In many respects, the recent history of option trading can be regarded as an option revolution.

Every option is either a **call option** or a **put option**.[4] The owner of a call option has the right to purchase the underlying good at a specific price, and this right lasts until a specific date. The owner of a put option has the right to sell the underlying good at a specific price, and this right lasts until a specific date. In short, the owner of a call option can call the underlying good away from someone else. Likewise, the owner of a put option can put the good to someone else by making the opposite party buy the good. To acquire these rights, owners of options buy them from other traders by paying the price, or premium, to a seller.

Options are created only by buying and selling. Therefore, for every owner of an option, there is a seller. The seller of an option is also known as an **option writer**. The seller receives payment for an option from the purchaser. In exchange for the payment received, the seller confers rights to the option owner. The seller of a call option receives payment and, in exchange, gives the owner of a call option the right to purchase the underlying good at a specific price, with this right lasting for a specific time. The seller of a put option receives payment from the purchaser and promises to buy the underlying good at a specific price for a specific time, if the owner of the put option chooses.

In these agreements, all rights lie with the owner of the option. In purchasing an option, the buyer makes payments and receives rights to buy or sell the underlying good on specific terms. In selling an option, the seller receives payment and promises to sell or purchase the underlying good on specific terms – at the discretion of the option owner. With put and call options and buyers and sellers, four basic positions are possible. Notice that the owner of an option has all the rights. After all, that is what the owner purchases. The seller of an option has all the obligations, because the seller undertakes obligations in exchange for payment.

Options on Futures

An **option on a futures** contract or a **futures option** is an option that takes a futures contract as its underlying good. It contrasts with an **option on the physical** – an option on the good itself rather than an option on a futures contract. For example, in the gold market, the physical gold trades. In addition, options on gold and futures contracts on gold trade as well. The option on gold itself is an option on the physical, while the option on the gold futures contract is a futures option. Similarly, in the equity market options trade on a stock index (an option on a physical) and options trade on stock index futures (a futures option).

The structure of a futures option is very similar to an option on the physical. For both instruments, the option owner has the right to exercise, and the seller has a duty to perform upon exercise. Upon exercising a futures option, however, the call owner receives a long position in the underlying futures at the settlement price prevailing at the time of exercise. The call owner also receives a payment that equals the settlement price minus the exercise price of the futures option. (The call owner would not exercise if the futures settlement price did not exceed the exercise price.) When a call option is exercised against her, a call seller receives a short position in the underlying futures at the settlement price prevailing at the time of exercise. In addition, the short call trader pays the long trader the futures settlement price minus the exercise price.

When the owner of a futures put option exercises, he receives a short position in the underlying futures contract at the settlement price prevailing at the time of exercise. In addition, the put owner receives a payment that equals the exercise price minus the futures settlement price. (The put owner would not exercise unless the exercise price exceeded the futures settlement price.) Upon exercise, the put seller receives a long position in the underlying futures contract, and the put seller must pay the exercise price minus the settlement price.

Swaps

A **swap** is an agreement between two or more parties to exchange sets of cash flows over a period in the future. For example, Party A might agree to pay a fixed rate of interest on $1 million each year for five years to Party B. In return, Party B might pay a floating rate of interest on $1 million each year for five years. The parties that agree to the swap are known as **counterparties**. The cash flows that the counterparties make are generally tied to the value of debt instruments or to the value of foreign currencies. Therefore, the two basic kinds of swaps are **interest rate swaps** and **currency swaps**.

As we will see in considerable detail, the principal futures and options markets are regulated markets, and they are dominated by the exchanges where trading takes place. The futures and options contracts are highly standardized, they are limited to relatively few goods, and they have a few fixed expirations per year. In addition, the horizon over which they trade is often much shorter than the risk horizon that businesses face.

In large part, the swap market has emerged because swaps escape many of the limitations inherent in futures and exchange-traded options markets. Swaps, of course, have some limitations of their own. Swaps are custom tailored to the needs of the counterparties. If they wish, the potential counterparties can start with a blank sheet of paper and develop a contract that is completely dedicated to meeting their particular needs. Thus, swap agreements are more likely to meet the specific needs of the counterparties than exchange-traded instruments. The counterparties can select the dollar amount that they wish to swap, without regard to some fixed contract terms, such as those that prevail in exchange-traded instruments. Similarly, the swap counterparties choose the exact maturity that they need, rather than having to fit their needs to the offerings available on an exchange. This is very important in the swap market, because this flexibility allows the counterparties to deal with much longer horizons than can be addressed through exchange-traded instruments. Because the market does not operate on an exchange, participants have far greater privacy, and they also escape regulation to a considerable degree.

APPLICATIONS OF FINANCIAL DERIVATIVES

Financial derivatives have attained their overwhelming popularity and rapid growth for a variety of reasons. This section briefly introduces some of the main benefits that financial derivatives bring to the market. Not all financial derivatives have the same virtues or the same limitations. Therefore, the benefits of derivatives explored in this section do not apply equally to all of the instruments that we will consider. However, subsequent chapters explore the specific applications of forwards, futures, options, and swaps in detail. Here we consider how financial derivatives help make markets more nearly complete, how speculators and risk managers can uses derivatives for their specific ends, and how many traders have been attracted to financial derivatives because of their trading efficiency, particularly their low transaction costs and highly liquid markets.

Market Completeness

In the theory of finance, a **complete market** is a market in which any and all identifiable payoffs can be obtained by trading the securities available in the market. For example, a complete market would allow a trader to purchase a security or set of securities that would pay off if and only if the Dow Jones Industrial Average rose by 99 to 100 points over the next month. It is quite difficult to trade any combination of stocks and bonds that would have a payoff in this circumstance and no other. If the financial instruments available in a market were not sufficiently rich and diverse to permit such a speculation, the market is deemed to be incomplete.

From this definition of market completeness, we see that a complete market is an idealization that is most likely always unobtainable in practice. Nonetheless, completeness is a desirable characteristic of a financial market, because it can be shown that access to a complete market increases the welfare of the agents in the economy. Even if an actual market can never be truly complete, the more closely the market approaches completeness, the better off are the economic agents in the economy.

Financial derivatives play a valuable role in financial markets because they help move the market closer to completeness. If we consider two financial markets that are the same, except one includes financial derivatives, the market with financial derivatives will allow traders to more exactly shape the risk and return characteristics of their portfolios, thereby increasing the welfare of traders and the economy in general.

Speculation

Financial derivatives have a reputation for being risky. Without doubt, these instruments can prove tremendously risky in the hands of uninformed traders. However, the risks associated with financial derivatives are not necessarily evil, because they provide very powerful instruments for knowledgeable traders to expose themselves to calculated and well-understood risks in pursuit of profit.

In the hands of a knowledgeable trader, a position in one or more financial derivatives can permit a careful and artful speculation on a rise or fall in interest rates, on a change in the riskiness of the entire stock market or a single stock, on changing values of the German mark versus the Japanese yen, or on a host of other specific propositions.

The precision and speculative power of derivatives stems largely from the fact that financial derivatives help make the financial market more nearly complete. Although serving as a speculative tool is not the only use (and probably not the most important use) of financial derivatives, they are ideally suited for this purpose.

Risk Management

While financial derivatives are undeniably risky in some applications, they also provide a powerful tool for limiting risks that individuals and firms face in the ordinary conduct of their business. For example, a corporation that is planning to issue bonds faces considerable interest rate risk. If interest rates rise before the bond is issued, the firm will have to pay considerably more over the life of the bond. As we will see, such a firm could use interest rate futures to control its exposure to this risk.

Similarly, a pension fund with widely diversified holdings in the stock market faces considerable risk from general fluctuations in stock prices. The pension fund manager could use options on a stock index to reduce or virtually eliminate that risk exposure.

Even though financial derivatives are risky in the sense that their prices are subject to substantial fluctuations, they can be extremely powerful tools for limiting risk as well. While we consider some of the speculative strategies that financial derivatives facilitate, the text emphasizes using financial derivatives to control risk in the types of situations just discussed. Successful risk management with derivatives requires a thorough understanding of the principles that govern the pricing of financial derivatives.

Trading Efficiency

In many applications, traders can use a position in one or more financial derivatives as a substitute for a position in the more fundamental underlying instruments. For example, we will see that an option position can mimic the profit or loss performance of an underlying stock index. Similarly, an interest rate futures contract can serve as a substitute for investment in a portfolio of Treasury securities.

In many instances, traders find financial derivatives to be a more attractive instrument than the more fundamental underlying security. Often the transaction costs associated with trading a financial derivative are substantially lower than the costs of trading the underlying instrument. For example, a corporation might use the futures market to take a million dollar position in Treasury bonds for a transaction cost of about $100. In other situations, financial derivatives might be more attractive than the underlying securities because of greater liquidity in the market for financial derivatives. For example, a trader might want to hold a well-diversified stock market position. One way of obtaining such a position might be to buy a variety of stocks. Such a strategy would surely incur substantial transaction costs, but might involve the trader in buying or selling some stocks that were not very liquid. (A **liquid market** is a market with enough trading activity to allow traders to readily trade a good for a price that is close to its true value.) Faced with such a situation, the trader might prefer to use a stock index futures contract or options on a stock index to save on transaction costs and to enjoy the benefits of trading in a liquid market.

THE CONCEPT OF ARBITRAGE

There are many alternative definitions of "arbitrage." We begin our analysis with a strict definition of what we call **academic arbitrage**. In academic arbitrage it is possible to trade to generate a riskless profit without investment. An **arbitrageur** is a person who engages in arbitrage. For example, shares of IBM trade on both the New York Stock Exchange and the Pacific Stock Exchange. Suppose shares of IBM trade for $110 on the New York market and for $105 on the Pacific Exchange. A trader could make the following two transactions simultaneously:

Buy 1 share of IBM on the Pacific Exchange for $105.

Sell 1 share of IBM on the New York Exchange for $110.

These two transactions generate a riskless profit of $5. Because both trades are assumed to occur simultaneously, there is no investment. Therefore, such an opportunity qualifies as an academic arbitrage opportunity – it affords riskless profits without investment.

In a well-functioning market, such opportunities cannot exist. If they did exist, they would make all of us fabulously wealthy. The existence of such academic arbitrage opportunities is equivalent to money being left on the street without being claimed. If you have ever been to Wall Street, you know that there is no money lying around there. To understand the pricing of derivative instruments, we assume that there are no arbitrage opportunities. This is our no-arbitrage principle. We apply this principle to determine what we can about prices of financial derivatives on the assumption that there are no arbitrage opportunities.

In our example of the IBM share, we assume that there are no transaction costs. We always begin our exploration of pricing relationships under this assumption of perfect markets, so we assume there are no taxes, no transaction costs, and no frictions of any kind. After developing an understanding of pricing relationships in this simple environment, we go on to consider the more realistic world of transaction costs and other market imperfections.

ORGANIZATION OF THE TEXT

The remainder of this text is organized as follows. Chapters 2–9 focus on futures, Chapters 10–17 consider options and options on futures, and Chapters 18–19 discuss the swaps market. In addition, the text contains material describing and explaining how to use the software that accompanies this book, and the text also includes a variety of computer exercises designed to increase your understanding of options.

Futures

Chapter 2 introduces the futures market and discusses the types of futures available. Although the text mentions futures on physical commodities, the text emphasizes financial futures. Chapter 3 considers the no-arbitrage pricing principles that govern futures in general and financial futures in particular. Chapter 4 discusses the variety of futures market participants and shows how they use the futures market for speculation and risk management.

Chapters 5–9 focus on specific financial futures. Interest rate futures are the focus of Chapters 5–6, while Chapters 7–8 analyze stock index futures, and Chapter 9 considers foreign currency futures.

Options and Options on Futures

Chapter 10 introduces the institutional framework of the options market in the United States. Chapter 11 analyzes a variety of option strategies and shows the power of options for tailoring risk to specific expectations. Chapter 12 approaches option pricing by asking the question: ''What option prices are consistent with the absence of arbitrage opportunities?'' This key idea of no-arbitrage pricing turns out to be an extremely powerful analytical tool that we employ throughout the text.

Option pricing inescapably involves some rather complicated mathematics. But the mathematics are much simpler for a **European option**, an option which can be exercised only at its expiration. Chapter 13 extends the no-arbitrage approach to analyze the pricing of European options and explains the famous Black-Scholes option pricing model. As we will see, it gives extremely accurate results. Chapter 14 explores in detail the exact way in which option prices respond to the various parameters in the Black-Scholes model. These sensitivities can be used to shape the risk and return characteristics of option positions with great precision.

Chapter 15 explores the pricing of American options. An **American option** is an option that can be exercised at any time prior to expiration. The principles of European option pricing still hold, but American option pricing involves some special considerations. Chapter 16 applies the conceptual apparatus developed in earlier chapters to three special instruments: options on indexes, options on foreign currencies, and options on futures. The pricing of these instruments requires applying the concepts already developed to the particular institutional features of these underlying goods. Chapter 17 shows the power of option pricing and analysis in a very different application. The concepts of option pricing can be used to analyze corporate securities as having option characteristics. Therefore, the option approach to corporate securities gives a totally new and very powerful way of thinking about common stock, bonds, convertible debt, and other corporate securities.

Swaps

Chapter 19 introduces the swaps market and chronicles its fantastic growth. In little more than 10 years, the swaps market has come to be a multi-trillion dollar market. Chapter 19 presents the basic features of this major new market for financial derivatives, while Chapter 20 considers some more advanced techniques for using swap agreements to manage risk.

OPTION! Software

As we have mentioned, option pricing is mathematically challenging. While it is critical to understand the formulas (and to compute each different formula by hand at least once!), it is not necessary or useful to compute repeatedly the same formulas. **OPTION!** software can compute virtually every option value discussed in this book. Further, **OPTION!** can graph many of the relationships among different option prices discussed in the chapters that follow. Exploring the option concepts of the text with the software can greatly enhance understanding of option pricing. Instructions for **OPTION!** are found in an appendix at the end of this text.

Exercises for *OPTION!*

This section of the text includes more than 50 exercises designed to enhance your understanding of option pricing principles and applications. These exercises can all be solved using the **OPTION!** software that accompanies this text.

Futures Market Data

The diskette that accompanies this text also includes a variety of data from the futures market. These data include daily prices on many different futures contracts, with an emphasis on financial futures. An appendix at the end of this book explains how the data are organized. These data provide an opportunity for analyzing actual futures pricing relationships.

QUESTIONS AND PROBLEMS

1. If an arbitrage opportunity did exist in a market, how would traders react? Would the arbitrage opportunity persist? If not, what factors would cause the arbitrage opportunity to disappear?

2. Explain why it is reasonable to think that prices in a financial market will generally be free of arbitrage opportunities.
3. Explain the difference between a derivative instrument and a financial derivative.
4. What is the essential feature of a forward contract that makes a futures contract a type of forward contract?
5. Explain why the purchaser of an option has rights and the seller of an option has obligations.
6. In a futures contract, explain the rights and obligations of the buyer or seller. How does this compare with an option contract?
7. Explain the difference between an option on a physical good and an option on a futures.
8. What is the essential feature of a swap agreement?
9. Distinguish between interest rate swaps and currency swaps.
10. What is a complete market? Can you give an example of a truly complete market? Explain.
11. Explain how the existence of financial derivatives enhances speculative opportunities for traders in our financial system.
12. If financial derivatives are as risky as their reputation indicates, explain in general terms how they might be used to reduce a preexisting risk position for a firm.

NOTES

[1] The mutual obligation of both buyer and seller of a futures contract is an important feature of the futures market that helps distinguish futures contracts from options. If you buy a call option, then you buy the right to obtain a good at a certain price, but you have no obligation. Instead, as the term implies, you have an option to buy something but no obligation to do anything. The buyer of a futures contract, by contrast, undertakes an obligation to make a payment at a subsequent time and to take delivery of the good that is contracted. The initiation of any futures contract implies a set of future obligations.

[2] For a discussion of the historical origins of futures contracting, see A. Loosigian, *Interest Rate Futures*, Princeton, NJ: Dow Jones Books, 1980. L. Venkataramanan also discusses the origins of forward contracting in his book, *The Theory of Futures Trading*, New York: Asia Publishing House, 1965.

[3] For an account of the early days of the Chicago Board of Trade, see *The Commodity Trading Manual*, Chicago: Chicago Board of Trade, 1989.

[4] There are also some other more complicated types of options that are not traded on exchanges. For example, an **exchange option** is an option to exchange one asset for another. As we will see when we discuss options on futures, there is a **delivery option** that gives a trader the right to choose which of several assets to surrender. There are still other types of options, but the most important market for options is the option exchange, where just put and call options trade.

<table>
<tr><td>CHAPTER
2</td><td># FUTURES MARKETS</td></tr>
</table>

OVERVIEW

This chapter lays the foundations for understanding how futures markets function. Futures markets originated to trade agricultural commodities, and it is only in the last 20 years that financial futures have come to play an important role in these markets. Accordingly, this chapter considers financial futures in the broad context of the futures markets, while later chapters focus on financial futures more exclusively.

We focus on futures markets in the United States, where they are currently the most complete and provide the widest range of trading opportunities. Futures markets, as they now exist in the United States, are a fairly recent development, but understanding their origins helps us understand both the role these markets play today and likely future changes in that role.

Before entering the arena of the futures market, a prospective trader must understand the organizational form of the futures exchanges, the types of contracts that are traded, and the ways in which futures exchanges compete with each other for business.

The chapter discusses the purposes that futures markets serve and the participants in the markets. Because regulation is important in determining whether futures markets can serve their social function and the interests of the trading parties, the chapter next discusses the regulatory framework, closing with a description of the taxation of futures markets.

The futures industry is large and growing. Such a large industry requires specialization among brokers, trading advisors, and other professionals. In this chapter, we examine some of these specialized functions to show more completely how futures trading functions.

Futures were once a virtual U.S. monopoly. In the 1980s, the industry moved toward true international status. Foreign exchanges developed rapidly, and exchanges around the world began to trade commodities associated with other countries. This process of internationalization will shape the futures industry for the 1990s and beyond. Internationalization is intimately tied to electronic trading. Today, electronic systems allow traders in New York to trade Japanese markets as if they were sitting in Tokyo. The chapter explores this trend toward globalization and the impact of electronic trading.

FUTURES MARKETS

Figure 2.1 shows the growth of trading volume on U.S. futures exchanges. When a contract is first listed for trading, there has been no volume. Assume that the first trade is for one contract, leaving one trader long one contract and one trader short one contract. In this example, there is a buyer and a seller. The buyer is said to have a **long position**, while the seller has a **short position**. The act of buying is also called **going long**, and the act of selling is called **going short**. In order for the contract to trade, there must be a long position and a short position. When one trader buys and another sells a forward contract, the transaction generates one contract of trading **volume**. At any moment in time, there is some number of futures contracts obligated for delivery; this number is called the **open interest**. (As we will see later in this chapter, most futures contracts do not actually lead to delivery.)

The Organized Exchange

As we have noted, futures contracts always trade on an organized exchange. The organization of the Chicago Board of Trade, the oldest and largest futures exchange in the world, is typical. We will use its organizational features to illustrate the institutional characteristics of the other exchanges. The exchange is a voluntary, nonprofit association of its members. **Exchange memberships**, also called **seats**, may be held only by individuals, and these memberships are traded in an active market like other assets. Table 2.1 shows recent membership prices for major futures and security exchanges in the United States. As the prices indicate, these seats are valuable capital assets. Also, the value of these seats fluctuates dramatically, depending mainly on recent and anticipated trading volume.

| **Figure 2.1** | **The Growth of Trading Volume on U.S. Exchanges** |

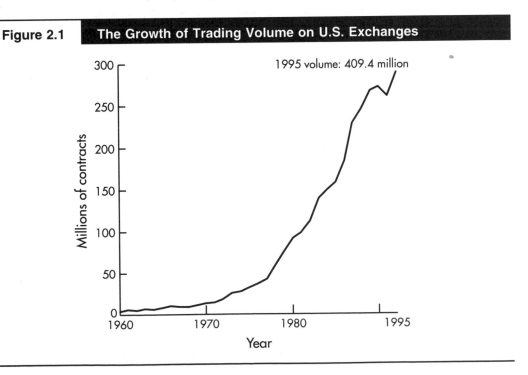

Membership Prices of Major U.S. Futures Exchanges	Table 2.1
Exchange	**Membership Price**
Chicago Mercantile Exchange	$585,000
Chicago Board of Trade	625,000
New York Mercantile Exchange	500,000
Coffee, Sugar and Cocoa Exchange	140,000
New York Cotton Exchange	86,000

Source: From *Futures and Options World*, March 1996. Reprinted by permission.

Exchange members have a right to trade on the exchange and to have a voice in the exchange's operation. Members also serve on committees to regulate the exchange's operations, rules, audit functions, public relations, and legal and ethical conduct of members. Often administrative officers of the exchange manage the ordinary operation of the exchange and report to the membership.

According to federal law and the rules of the exchange, trading may take place only during official trading hours in a designated trading area called a **pit**. This is a physical location on the floor of the exchange. Each commodity trades in a designated pit. In contrast to the specialist system used on stock exchanges, futures contracts trade by a system of **open outcry**. In this system, a trader must make any offer to buy or sell to all other traders present in the pit. Traders also use an unofficial (but highly developed) system of hand signals to express their wishes to buy or sell. Officially, however, all offers to buy or sell must be made through open outcry.

Traders in the pit fall into two groups that we can distinguish by their function. First, a trader can trade for his or her own account and bear the losses or enjoy the profits stemming from this trading. Often, these traders are members of the exchange. Second, a trader could be a broker acting on behalf of his or her own firm or on behalf of a client outside the exchange. For example, the brokers trading on the exchange often represent large brokerage houses such as Merrill Lynch or Prudential Bache. Having distinguished between traders who execute trades for their own accounts and those who execute trades for others, we must realize that certain individuals exercise both functions simultaneously.

Members of the exchange who trade in the pits are typically speculators. A **speculator** is a trader who enters the futures market in pursuit of profit, accepting risk in the endeavor. Some of the traders in the pit that trade for their own account may not be full exchange members themselves. It is possible to lease a seat on the exchange from a full member. Also, some exchanges have created special licenses allowing nonmembers to trade in certain contracts in which the exchanges are anxious to build volume. For the most part, a trader in the pit trading for his or her own account is a speculator.

In addition to speculators, many traders are **hedgers**, traders who trade futures to reduce some preexisting risk exposure. Hedgers are often producers or major users of a given commodity. For example, hedgers in wheat might include wheat farmers and large baking firms. Notice that these hedgers do not necessarily need to own the wheat when they hedge. A farmer might hedge by selling his anticipated harvest through the futures market. This could occur even before the farmer plants. Similarly, the baker who will eventually bake the farmer's wheat harvest into bread may hedge an expected need for wheat months before the wheat is actually required. Therefore, hedging is the purchase or sale of futures as a temporary substitute for a transaction in the cash market. For the most part, hedgers are not themselves located on the floor of the exchange. Instead, they trade through a brokerage firm. The brokerage firm communicates the order to the pit and has it executed by a broker in the pit.

Thus, there are two different kinds of brokers. An **account executive** for a brokerage firm is often called a broker. The account executive could be located in any town or city and the account executive deals with his or her customers, conveying their orders to the exchange. A second type of broker is a **floor broker**, a broker on the floor of the exchange who executes orders for other customers. For a typical transaction entered by a trader off-the-floor of the exchange, the order will be given to the customer's broker (account executive), who will transmit the order to the brokerage firm's representatives at the exchange. There a floor broker, often employed by the brokerage firm, will execute the order on the floor of the exchange.

This organized structure for trading futures contracts differs from the organization of forward markets. Forward markets are loosely organized and have no physical location devoted to the trading.[1] Perhaps the best-developed forward market is the market for foreign exchange. It is a worldwide network of participants, largely banks and brokers, who communicate with each other electronically. In the forward market for foreign exchange, there is no organized exchange and no central trading point.

Standardized Contract Terms

A second major difference between forward and futures contracts is that futures contracts always have standardized contract terms. Futures contracts are highly uniform and well-specified commitments for a carefully described good to be delivered at a certain time and in a certain manner. Generally, the futures contract specifies the quantity and quality of the good that can be delivered to fulfill the futures contract. The contract also specifies the delivery date and method for closing the contract, and the permissible minimum and maximum price fluctuations permitted in trading.

As an example, consider the Chicago Board of Trade wheat contract. One wheat contract consists of 5,000 bushels of wheat that must be of one of the following types: No. 2 Soft Red, No. 2 Hard Red Winter, No. 2 Dark Northern Spring, or No. 1 Northern Spring. The wheat contract trades for expiration in the following months of each year: July, September, December, March, and May. The Board of Trade also stipulates the delivery terms for completing the contract. To deliver wheat in completion of the contract, the wheat must be in a warehouse approved by the Chicago Board of Trade. These warehouses must be in the Chicago Switching District or the Toledo, Ohio, Switching District. The buyer transmits payment to the seller, and the seller delivers a warehouse receipt to the buyer. The holder of a warehouse receipt has title to the wheat in the warehouse. Delivery can occur on any business day in the delivery month.

The contract also stipulates the minimum price fluctuation, or **tick** size. For wheat, one tick is ¼ cent per bushel. With 5,000 bushels per contract, this gives a tick size of $12.50 per contract. The contract also specifies a **daily price limit**, which restricts the price movement in a single day. For wheat, the trading price on a given day cannot differ from the preceding day's closing price by more than 20 cents per bushel, or $1,000 per contract. When the contract is trading in its delivery month, this price limit is not in effect. Also, when a commodity enters a particularly volatile period, price limits are generally expanded over successive days. For example, when Iraq invaded Kuwait in 1990, oil prices skyrocketed for several days. On the first day, the futures price was allowed to rise only by the limit. Because the price rose to the limit in one day, the price limit was expanded for the next day. For most commodities, price limits expand over several days until there is no limit on how much the price can change in a day. Also, some commodities do not have price limits. Finally, the exchange also controls the trading times for each futures contract. Wheat trades from 9:30 A.M. to 1:15 P.M. Chicago time on each trading day, except for the last day of trading when trading in the expiring contract ceases at noon. The last trading day for the wheat contract is seven business days before the last business day of the delivery month.

Although these rules may appear highly restrictive, they actually stimulate trading. Because the good being traded is so highly standardized, all the participants in the market know exactly what is being offered for sale, and they know the terms of the transactions. This uniformity helps promote liquidity. All futures contracts have such a highly developed framework, which specifies all phases of the transaction. As we saw for wheat, these rules regulate all phases of the market, from the amounts the prices can move to the appropriate ways of making delivery. The prospective trader should consult a given contract for these exact details before initiating any trading. Each exchange publishes contract terms.

The Clearinghouse

To ensure that futures contracts trade in a smoothly functioning market, each futures exchange has an associated clearinghouse. The clearinghouse may be constituted as a separate corporation or it may be part of the futures exchange, but each exchange is closely associated with a particular clearinghouse. The clearinghouse guarantees that all of the traders in the futures market will honor their obligations. The clearinghouse serves this role by adopting the position of buyer to every seller and seller to every buyer. This means that every trader in the futures markets has obligations only to the clearinghouse and has expectations that the clearinghouse will maintain its side of the bargain as well. Thus, the clearinghouse substitutes its own credibility for the promise of each trader in the market.

The clearinghouse takes no active position in the market, but instead interposes itself between all parties to every transaction. In the futures market, the number of contracts bought must always equal the number of contracts sold. So, for every party expecting to receive delivery of a commodity, the opposite trading partner must be prepared to make delivery. If we sum all outstanding long and short futures market positions, the total always equals zero.[2]

Table 2.2 shows the typical trading situation. In the table, we assume that all transactions occur on a single day, say, May 1. Party 1 trades on the futures exchange to buy one oats contract of 5,000 bushels for delivery in September. In order for Party 1 to buy the contract, some other participant must sell. In panel (a) of the table it is apparent that Party 1 and Party 2 have exactly complementary positions in the futures market. One party has bought exactly what the other has sold. Notice that the time of delivery, the amount of oats to be delivered, and the price all match. Without a perfect match in all these respects, there could not have been a transaction. In all probability, the two trading parties will not even know each other. It is perfectly possible that each will have traded through a broker from different parts of the country. In such a situation, problems of trust may arise. How can either party be sure that the other will fulfill the agreement?

The clearinghouse exists to solve that problem. As panels (b) and (c) indicate, the clearinghouse guarantees fulfillment of the contract to each of the trading parties. After the initial sale is made, the clearinghouse steps in and acts as the seller to the buyer and acts as the buyer to the seller. In panel (b), the clearinghouse guarantees the buyer of the futures contract, Party 1, that it will deliver at the

Table 2.2	Futures Market Obligations

The oat contract is traded by the Chicago Board of Trade. Each contract is for 5,000 bushels, and prices are quoted in cents per bushel.

(a) **Party 1**	**Party 2**
Buys 1 SEP contract for oats at 171 cents per bushel.	Sells 1 SEP contract for oats at 171 cents per bushel.

(b) **Party 1**	**Clearinghouse**
Buys 1 SEP contract for oats at 171 cents per bushel.	Agrees to deliver to Party 1 a SEP contract for oats at a price of 171 cents per bushel.

(c) **Party 2**	**Clearinghouse**
Sells 1 SEP contract for oats at 171 cents per bushel.	Agrees to receive from Party 2 a SEP contract for oats and to pay 171 cents per bushel.

initially agreed-upon time and price. To the seller, Party 2, the clearinghouse guarantees that it will accept delivery at the agreed-upon time and price, as panel (c) shows. Figure 2.2 illustrates the same idea graphically. Without a clearinghouse, both parties must deal with each other, and they have direct obligations to one another. With a clearinghouse, each party has obligations to the clearinghouse and the clearinghouse will ensure that they perform.

Because of the clearinghouse, the two trading parties do not need to trust each other or even know each other's identity. Instead, the two traders only have to be concerned about the reliability of the clearinghouse. However, the clearinghouse is a large, well-capitalized financial institution. Its failure to perform on its guarantee to the two trading parties would bring the futures market to ruin. In the history of U.S. futures trading, the clearinghouse has always performed as promised, so the risk of a future default by the clearinghouse is very small.

A more careful examination of panels (b) and (c) from Table 2.2 gives further confidence that the clearinghouse will perform as promised. In total, the clearinghouse has no independent position in oats. It is obligated to receive oats and pay 171 cents per bushel, but it is also obligated to deliver oats and receive 171 cents per bushel. These two obligations net out to zero. Since it maintains no futures market position of its own, the riskiness of the clearinghouse is less than it may appear.[3]

Margin and Daily Settlement

In addition to the clearinghouse, there are other safeguards for the futures market. Chief among these are the requirements for margin and daily settlement. Before trading a futures contract, the prospective trader must deposit funds with a broker. These funds serve as a good-faith deposit by the trader and are referred to as **margin**. The main purpose of margin is to provide a financial safeguard to ensure that traders will perform on their contract obligations. The margin requirement restricts the activity of traders, so the exchanges and brokers are anxious that the margin requirements not be unreasonably high. The amount of this margin varies from contract to contract and may vary by broker as well.

The Function of the Clearinghouse in Futures Markets   Figure 2.2

Obligations without a clearinghouse

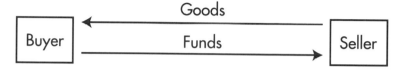

Obligations with a clearinghouse

The margin may be posted in cash, a bank letter of credit, or in short-term U.S. Treasury instruments. The trader who posts this margin retains title to it.

Types of Margin. In this section, we consider the different types of margins and show how margin requirements would affect a trader holding a single futures position. In the next section, we consider margin rules for more complicated positions.

There are three types of margin. The initial deposit just described is the **initial margin** – the amount a trader must deposit before trading any futures. The initial margin approximately equals the maximum daily price fluctuation permitted for the contract being traded. Upon proper completion of all obligations associated with a trader's futures position, the initial margin is returned to the trader. If one has deposited a security as the margin, then the trader earns the interest that accrues while the security has served as the margin.

For most futures contracts, the initial margin may be 5 percent or less of the underlying commodity's value. It may seem strange that the initial margin is so small relative to the value of the commodity underlying the futures contract. The smallness of this amount is reasonable, however, because there is another safeguard built into the system in the form of **daily settlement** or **marking-to-market**. In the futures market, traders are required to realize any losses in cash on the day they occur. In the parlance of the futures market, the contract is marked-to-the-market.

To understand the process of daily settlement, consult Table 2.2 again and consider Party 1, who bought one contract for 171 cents per bushel. Assume that the contract closes on May 2 at 168 cents per bushel. This means that Party 1 has sustained a loss of 3 cents per bushel. Since there are 5,000 bushels in the contract, this represents a loss of $150, which is deducted from the margin deposited with the broker. When the value of the funds on deposit with the broker reaches a certain level, called the **maintenance margin**, the trader is required to replenish the margin, bringing it back to its initial level. This demand for more margin is known as a **margin call**. The additional amount the trader must deposit is called the **variation margin**. The maintenance margin is generally about 75 percent of the amount of the initial margin. For example, assume that the initial margin was $1,400, that Party 1 had deposited only this minimum initial margin, and that the maintenance margin is $1,100. Party 1 has already sustained a loss of $150, so the equity in the margin account is $1,250. The next day, assume that the price of oats drops 4 cents per bushel, generating an additional loss for Party 1 of $200. This brings the value of the margin account to $1,050, which is below the level of the required maintenance margin. This means that the broker will require Party 1 to replenish the margin account to $1,400, the level of the initial margin. To restore the margin account, the trader must pay $350 variation margin. Variation margin must always be paid in cash.

Figure 2.3 uses the initial margin level of $1,400 and the maintenance margin level of $1,100 to illustrate this process. At the outset, the value of the margin deposited with the broker is $1,400. First the trader has mixed results with some small gains and small losses, with losses predominating. Before long, losses drop the value of the account below $1,100. As the figure shows, the trader must then restore the value, or equity, in the account to $1,400. This is shown in Figure 2.3 by the large dot. After this first margin call, the trader has mixed results for a while, followed by large losses. These losses generate a second margin call. Figure 2.3 shows only the required cash flows. The trader could have withdrawn cash whenever the value of the equity exceeded $1,400. However, a trader cannot withdraw funds that would leave the account's equity value below the level of the initial margin.

Figure 2.3   **Account Equity and Margin Requirements**

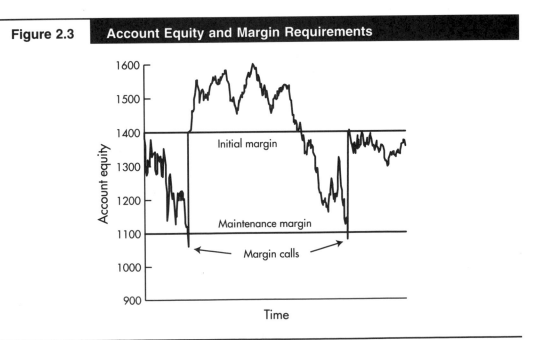

Because futures prices change almost every day, each account will have frequent gains and losses. The losses can require a variation margin payment, and the gains may entitle the trader to withdraw cash. For convenience, traders do not want to face a daily margin call in many cases. There are two basic ways to avoid a margin call. First, a trader can deposit securities with a value well in excess of the initial margin. Second, a trader can deposit funds in excess of the initial margin into an interest-bearing account. In either case, such a deposit provides a liquidity pool that will protect the trader from untimely demands for variation margin payments. Similarly, the trader can instruct the broker to sweep profits from his account into an interest-bearing investment. Those funds can be held ready to meet margin calls as required.

This practice of posting maintenance or variation margin and daily settlement helps make the futures market safer. Assume that Party 1 in Table 2.2 posted only the initial margin, the bare minimum to have the trade executed. Also assume that the trader suffered a loss requiring more margin and that the trader was unable or refused to post the required additional margin. The broker in such a situation is empowered to close the futures position by deducting the loss from the trader's initial margin and returning the balance, less commission costs, to the trader. The broker would also close the trader's entire brokerage account as well. Failure to post the required maintenance margin is a violation of a trader's agreement with the broker. Now it becomes apparent why the initial margin is so small. The initial margin needs to cover only one day's price fluctuation, because any losses will be covered by the posting of additional variation margin. Failure to pay variation margin will lead to the futures position being closed out.

Margin Cash Flows. This section traces the flow of margin funds from the trader to the clearinghouse. The margin system functions through a hierarchy of market participants that links the clearinghouse with the individual trader. The members of an exchange may be classified as clearing members or nonclearing members. A **clearing member** is a member of the exchange that is also a member of the clearinghouse. The clearinghouse deals only with clearing members. As a consequence, any nonclearing member must clear his or her trades through a clearing member.

The clearinghouse demands margin deposits from clearing members to cover all futures positions that are carried by that clearing member. For example, a clearing member might be a large broker who executes orders for individual traders and who provides clearing services for some nonclearing members of the exchange. Therefore, the clearing member will impose margin requirements on all of the accounts that it represents to the clearinghouse.

Figure 2.4 shows the margin flows for an individual trader who might trade through a clearing member or a nonclearing member. In the figure, Trader A trades through a broker who is a clearing member. In this case, Trader A deposits margin funds with the clearing member, who makes margin deposits with the clearinghouse. As a second alternative in Figure 2.4, Trader B trades through a broker who is a nonclearing member of the exchange. This broker must arrange to clear all trades with a clearing member. In this situation, Trader B deposits margin funds with his or her broker. This broker deposits margin funds with a clearing member, and the clearing member deposits margin funds with the clearinghouse.

It is not very important whether Traders A and B trade directly through a clearing member or a nonclearing member. Most large brokerage firms are clearing members, so most individual traders who trade through their local broker will be trading through a clearing member. However, many members of each exchange trade for their own account as speculators. Few of them are clearing members, so they need to clear their trades through a clearing member.

Figure 2.4   **Margin Cash Flows**

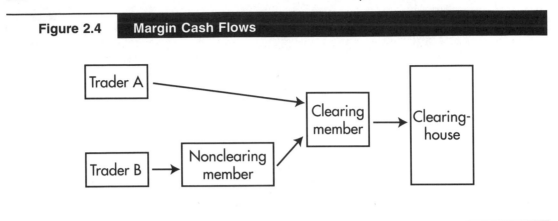

Closing a Futures Position

Initially, we discussed the completion of a futures contract through delivery. However, in the discussion of variation margin we noted that the broker might close the position after trading on May 2. The careful reader might remember that the initial trade shown in Table 2.2 called for a September delivery. In view of that fact, it may not seem that the futures position could be closed in May. There are, however, three ways to close a futures position: delivery, offset, and an exchange-for-physicals (EFP).

Delivery. Most futures contracts are written to call for completion of the futures contract through the physical delivery of a particular good. As we have seen in our discussion of the wheat contract, delivery takes place at certain locations and at certain times under rules specified by a futures exchange. In recent years, exchanges have introduced futures contracts that allow completion through **cash settlement**. In cash settlement, traders make payments at the expiration of the contract to settle any gains or losses, instead of making physical delivery. Both physical delivery and cash settlement close the contract in the expiration period. However, few futures contracts are actually closed through either physical delivery or cash settlement. For example, in the fiscal year ending September 30, 1995, only about three-fourths of 1 percent of all contracts traded were settled by either physical delivery or cash settlement. Table 2.3 shows the commodity groups and the percentage of contracts completed by delivery or cash settlement within each group. Only currencies had more than 2 percent of its contracts settled by delivery or cash settlements, but these are both less than 2 percent. In the energy, livestock, and wood groups, delivery is extremely rare. Therefore, the vast majority of all contracts initiated must be completed by some means other than delivery or cash settlement.[4]

Offset. By far, most futures contracts are completed through **offset** or via a **reversing trade**. To complete a futures contract obligation through offset, the trader transacts in the futures market to bring his or her net position in a particular futures contract back to zero. Consider again the situation depicted in Table 2.2. The first party has an obligation to the clearinghouse to accept 5,000 bushels of oats in September and to pay 171 cents per bushel for them at that time. Perhaps the trader does not wish to actually receive the oats and wants to exit the futures market earlier, say May 10. The trader can fulfill the commitment by entering the futures market again and making the reversing trade depicted in Table 2.4.

Completion of Futures Contracts via Delivery or Cash Settlement		Table 2.3

October 1, 1994–September 30, 1995

Commodity Group	Volume	Delivered or Settled in Cash	
		Contracts	**Percentage**
Grains	21,093,886	70,548	0.33
Oilseeds	20,687,820	158,003	0.76
Livestock	6,238,509	12,900	0.21
Other agricultural	12,742,515	60,302	0.47
Energy/wood	47,941,379	74,978	0.16
Metals	17,393,317	157,323	0.90
Financial instruments	259,029,356	1,940,293	0.75
Currencies	24,293,644	521,611	2.15
All commodities	409,420,426	2,995,958	0.73

Source: From Commodity Futures Trading Commission, Annual Report, 1995.

The Reversing Trade	Table 2.4

	Party 1's Initial Position	**Party 2**
May 1	Bought 1 SEP contract for oats at 171 cents per bushel.	Sold 1 SEP contract for oats at 171 cents per bushel.
	Party 1's Reversing Trade	**Party 3**
May 10	Sells 1 SEP contract for oats at 180 cents per bushel.	Buys 1 SEP oats contract at 180 cents per bushel.

The first line of Table 2.4 merely repeats the initial trade that was made on May 1. On May 10, Party 1 takes exactly the opposite position by selling 1 SEP contract for oats at the current futures price of 180 cents per bushel. This time the trader transacts with a new entrant to the market, Party 3. After this reversing trade, Party 1's net position is zero. The clearinghouse recognizes this, and Party 1 is absolved from any further obligation. In this example, the price of September oats rose 9 cents per bushel during this period, happily yielding Party 1 a profit of $450. Party 2, the original seller, is not affected by Party 1's reversing trade. Party 2 still has the same commitment, because the clearinghouse continues to stand ready to complete this transaction described in Table 2.2. Now the clearinghouse also assumes a complementary obligation to the new market entrant, Party 3. Note that the position of the clearinghouse has not really changed due to the transactions on May 10. Also, Party 2 and Party 3 have complementary obligations after the new trades, just as Party 1 and Party 2 had complementary obligations after the initial transactions on May 1.

In entering the reversing trade, it is crucial that Party 1 sell exactly the same contract that was bought originally. Note in Table 2.4 that the reversing trade matches the original transaction in the good traded, the number of contracts, and the maturity. If it does not, then the trader undertakes a new obligation instead of canceling the old. If Party 1 had sold one DEC contract on May 10 instead of selling the SEP contract, for example, he or she would be obligated to receive oats in September and to deliver oats in December. Such a transaction would result in holding two positions instead of a reversing trade.

Exchange-for-Physicals (EFP). A trader can complete a futures contract by engaging in an **exchange-for-physicals (EFP)**. In an EFP, two traders agree to a simultaneous exchange of a cash commodity and futures contracts based on that cash commodity. For example, assume that Trader A is long one wheat contract and genuinely wishes to acquire wheat. Also, assume that Trader B is short one wheat contract and owns wheat. The two traders agree on a price for the physical wheat and agree to cancel their complementary futures positions against each other. Table 2.5 shows this initial position in the first panel. Trader A buys the wheat from Trader B and they report their desire to cancel their futures position to the futures exchange. The exchange notes that their positions match (one short and one long) and cancels their futures obligations. The bottom panel of Table 2.5 illustrates the positions of Traders A and B in completing the EFP.

In this example, the result is much like an offsetting trade, because both futures traders have completed their obligations and are now out of the market. However, the EFP differs in certain respects from an offsetting trade. First, the traders actually exchange the physical good. Second, the futures contract was not closed by a transaction on the floor of the exchange. Third, the two traders privately negotiated the price and other terms of the transaction. Because an EFP transaction takes place away from the trading floor of the exchange, it is sometimes known as an **ex-pit** transaction. Federal law and exchange rules generally require all futures trading to take place in the pit. However, the EFP is the one recognized exception to this general rule. EFPs are also known as **against actuals** or **versus cash** transactions.

EXCHANGES AND TYPES OF FUTURES

Since the founding of the Chicago Board of Trade in 1848, futures markets have flourished. The past decade has been a period of extraordinary growth for futures markets, due largely to the development

Table 2.5	An Exchange-for-Physicals Transaction

Before the EFP

Trader A	Trader B
Long 1 wheat futures.	Short 1 wheat futures.
Wants to acquire actual wheat.	Owns wheat and wishes to sell.

EFP Transaction

Trader A	Trader B
Agrees with Trader B to purchase wheat and cancel futures.	Agrees with Trader A to sell wheat and cancel futures.
Receives wheat; pays Trader B.	Delivers wheat; receives payment from Trader A.
Reports EFP to exchange; exchange adjusts books to show that Trader A is out of the market.	Reports EFP to exchange; exchange adjusts books to show that Trader B is out of the market.

of entirely new types of contracts in foreign exchange, interest rates, and stock indexes. Within the last few years, several new types of contracts have been developed, including futures on stock indexes and options on futures contracts. The future promises to be a period of continued explosive growth for the industry.

Worldwide Exchanges

Table 2.6 lists the major U.S. futures exchanges, the date they began trading, and the principal types of contracts they trade. Recent years have seen considerable consolidation in the industry. One of the largest mergers was the union of the Commodity Exchange of New York (COMEX) and the New York Mercantile Exchange (NYME) into the New York Mercantile Exchange with NYMEX and COMEX divisions. Table 2.7 covers some major foreign exchanges. The oldest of these is more than 140 years old. Differences in size among these exchanges are striking, ranging from the New York Cotton Exchange, which by state law can trade only cotton futures, to the very large exchanges, such as the Chicago Board of Trade (CBOT) and the Chicago Mercantile Exchange (CME), which have more than 1,000 members each and trade a wide variety of futures. The futures markets of Chicago alone directly employ more than 40,000 people.

Types of Futures Contracts

The types of futures contracts that are traded fall into four fundamentally different categories. The underlying good traded may be a physical commodity, a foreign currency, an interest-earning asset, or an index, usually a stock index. Contracts for more than 50 different goods are currently available. While later chapters focus on financial futures, it is useful to have some appreciation for the range of goods that trade on futures markets.

U.S. Futures Exchanges				Table 2.6
	Principal Types of Contracts			
Exchange and Year Founded	**Physical**	**Currencies**	**Interest Rates**	**Index**
Chicago Board of Trade (CBOT) 1848	♦		♦	♦
Chicago Mercantile Exchange (CME) 1919	♦	♦	♦	♦
Coffee, Sugar and Cocoa Exchange (New York) 1882	♦			
Kansas City Board of Trade (KCBT) 1856	♦			♦
Mid-America Commodity Exchange (Chicago) 1880	♦	♦	♦	
Minneapolis Grain Exchange 1881	♦			
New York Cotton Exchange, Inc. 1870	♦	♦		♦
New York Mercantile Exchange 1872	♦			♦

Source: From *Futures (1996 Source Book)*. Reprinted with permission of *Futures* Magazine.

Table 2.7	Non-U.S. Futures Exchanges			
	Principal Types of Contracts			
Exchange	**Physical**	**Currencies**	**Interest Rates**	**Stock Index**
Bolsa de Mercadorios de São Paulo	♦	♦	♦	♦
London International Financial Futures Exchange (LIFFE)	♦	♦	♦	♦
International Petroleum Exchange (London)	♦			
London Futures & Options Exchange (FOX)	♦			
Tokyo International Financial Futures Exchange (TIFFE)		♦	♦	
Osaka Securities Exchange				♦
Tokyo Commodity Exchange	♦			
Tokyo Stock Exchange			♦	♦
Singapore International Monetary Exchange (SIMEX)	♦	♦	♦	♦
Deutsche Boerse			♦	♦
Marche a Terme International de France (MATIF)	♦	♦	♦	♦
Hong Kong Futures Exchange	♦	♦	♦	♦
New Zealand Futures Exchange		♦	♦	♦
Sydney Futures Exchange	♦	♦	♦	♦
Toronto Futures Exchange				♦
Montreal Exchange			♦	♦
Winnipeg Commodity Exchange	♦			
Kuala Lumpur Commodity Exchange	♦			

Source: From *The Wall Street Journal, Futures* Magazine, *Intermarket* Magazine, *various issues.*

Agricultural and Metallurgical Contracts. In the agricultural area, contracts are traded in grains (corn, oats, and wheat), oil and meal (soybeans, soymeal, and soyoil, and sunflower seed and oil), livestock (live hogs, cattle, and pork bellies), forest products (lumber and plywood), textiles (cotton), and foodstuffs (cocoa, coffee, orange juice, rice, and sugar). For many of these commodities, several different contracts are available for different grades or types of the commodity. For most of the goods, there are also a number of months for delivery. The months chosen for delivery of the seasonal crops generally fit their harvest patterns. The number of contract months available for each commodity also depends on the level of trading activity. For some relatively inactive futures contracts, there may be trading in only one or two delivery months in the year.[5] By contrast, an active commodity, such as soybean meal, may have trading in eight delivery months. The metallurgical category includes the genuine metals, as well as petroleum contracts. Among the metals, contracts are traded on gold, silver, platinum, palladium, and copper. Of the petroleum products, heating oil, crude oil, gasoline, and propane are traded on futures markets.

Interest-Earning Assets. Futures trading on interest-bearing assets started only in 1975, but the growth of this market has been tremendous. Contracts are traded now on Treasury bills, notes, and bonds, on Eurodollar deposits, and on municipal bonds. The existing contracts span almost the entire yield curve, so it is possible to trade instruments with virtually every maturity. The CME trades two contracts with three-month maturities – T-bills and Eurodollar time deposits. This makes possible trading based on anticipated interest rate differentials for the same maturity. In addition, contracts on foreign debt instruments are traded on foreign futures exchanges. For example, major contracts on government bonds are traded on exchanges in London, Paris, Frankfurt, and Tokyo.

Foreign Currencies. Active futures trading of foreign currencies dates back to the inception of freely floating exchange rates in the early 1970s. Contracts trade on the British pound, the Canadian dollar, the Japanese yen, the Swiss franc, and the German mark. Contracts are also listed on French francs, Dutch guilders, and the Mexican peso, but these have met with only limited success and are no longer traded. The foreign exchange futures market represents the one case of a futures market existing in the face of a truly active forward market. The forward market for foreign exchange is many times larger than the futures market. Many people believe that the presence of the forward market deterred the introduction and slowed the growth of futures trading in foreign exchange. Contracts on different currencies are also traded on a number of foreign futures exchanges, as Table 2.7 shows.

Indexes. The last major group of futures contracts is for indexes. Most, but not all, of these contracts are for stock indexes. Beginning only in 1982, these contracts have been quite successful, with trading on market indexes in full swing. Exchanges trade contracts on four different U.S. stock indexes: the Standard and Poor's 500, a Major Market Index, the New York Stock Exchange Index, and the Value Line Index. Foreign exchanges trade futures on foreign stock indexes, such as the trading of the Japanese Nikkei index on the Tokyo Futures Exchange and on the Singapore International Monetary Exchange (SIMEX) as well.

In September 1990, the Chicago Board of Trade and the Chicago Mercantile Exchange began trading futures contracts based on Japanese financial markets. The Chicago Mercantile Exchange trades a contract based on the Nikkei 225 stock index and the Chicago Board of Trade launched a contract based on the TOPIX index of major firms traded on the Tokyo Stock Exchange. Neither contract has met expectations, due in part to the poor performance of the Japanese stock market in recent years. One of the most striking things about these stock index contracts is that they do not admit the possibility of actual delivery. A trader's obligation must be fulfilled by a reversing trade or a cash settlement at the end of trading. Other types of indexes also are traded in futures markets, including a foreign exchange index and an index of municipal bonds.

Relative Importance of Commodity Types

Figure 2.5 presents another division of futures contracts into eight categories and shows the relative importance of trading in these different categories in the United States in 1995. As Figure 2.5 shows, over half of the trading volume stems from financial instruments. These include futures contracts based on underlying instruments such as Treasury securities and stock indexes. As we have noted, trading in these contracts began in 1975, so growth in this area has been dramatic. Figure 2.6 shows how the portions of futures trading volume have shifted among these commodity groups over recent years.

Figure 2.5   **Market Share by Commodity Type**

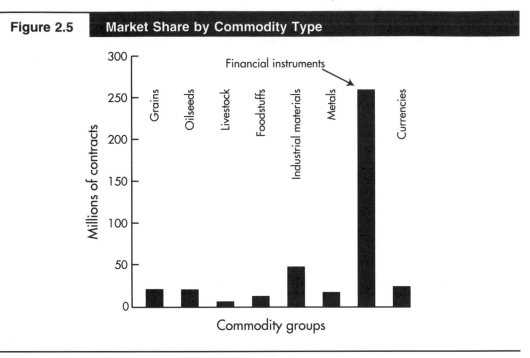

Figure 2.6   **Changing Commodity Trading Volume**

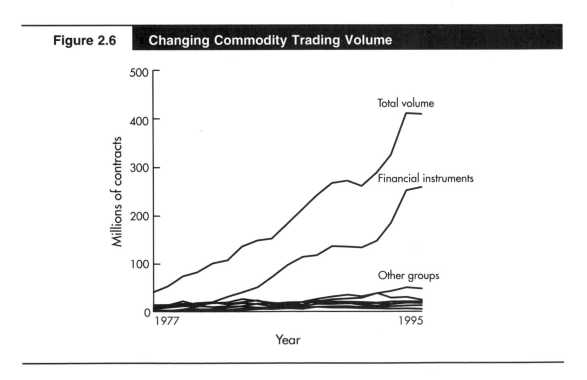

PURPOSES OF FUTURES MARKETS

Any industry as old and as large as the futures market must serve some social purpose. If it did not, it would most likely have passed from existence some time ago. Traditionally, futures markets have been recognized as meeting the needs of three groups of futures market users: those who wish to discover information about future prices of commodities, those who wish to speculate, and those who wish to hedge. While Chapter 4 discusses the uses that these three groups make of futures markets in detail, it is important to have some understanding of the social function of futures markets before proceeding. Traditionally, speculation is not regarded as socially useful by itself, although it may have socially useful by-products. Thus, there are two main social functions of futures markets – price discovery and hedging.

Price Discovery

Price discovery is the revealing of information about future cash market prices through the futures market. As discussed earlier, in buying or selling a futures contract, a trader agrees to receive or deliver a given commodity at a certain time in the future for a price that is determined now. In such a circumstance, it is not surprising that there is a relationship between the futures price and the price that people expect to prevail for the commodity at the delivery date specified in the futures contract. While the exact nature of that relationship will be considered in detail in Chapter 3, the relationship is predictable to a high degree. By using the information contained in futures prices today, market observers can form estimates of what the price of a given commodity will be at a certain time in the future. The forecasts of future prices that can be drawn from the futures market compare in accuracy quite favorably with other types of forecasts. Futures markets serve a social purpose by helping people make better estimates of future prices, so that they can make their consumption and investment decisions more wisely.

As an example of price discovery and its benefits, consider a mine operator who is trying to decide whether to reopen a marginally profitable silver mine. The silver ore in the mine is not of the best quality, so the yield from the mine will be relatively low. The financial wisdom of operating the mine will depend on the price the miner can obtain for the silver once it is mined and refined. However, the miner must make the decision about the mine today, and the silver will not be ready for market for 15 months. The crucial element in the miner's decision is the future price of silver.

While the price of silver 15 months from now cannot be known with certainty, it is possible to use the futures market to estimate that future price. The price quoted in the futures market today for a silver futures that expires in 15 months can be a very useful estimate of the future price. As we will see in Chapter 3, for some commodities an estimate of the future price of a good drawn from the futures market is one of the best estimates possible. In our example, let us assume that the futures price for silver is high enough to justify operating the mine again. The miner figures that the new mine will be profitable if he can obtain the futures price for the silver when it becomes available in 15 months. In this situation, the miner has used the futures market as a vehicle of price discovery. Farmers, lumber producers, cattle ranchers, and other economic agents can use futures markets the same way. They all use futures market estimates of future cash prices to guide their production or consumption decisions.

Hedging

Many futures market participants trade futures as a substitute for a cash market transaction. For example, we considered a farmer who sold wheat futures in anticipation of a harvest, and we noted that the farmer used futures as an alternative to the sale of wheat through the cash market. We now consider this classic kind of hedge in more detail. At planting time, the farmer bears a risk associated with the uncertain harvest price his wheat will command. The farmer might use the futures market to hedge by selling a futures contract. If the farmer expects to harvest 100,000 bushels of wheat in nine months, the farmer could establish a price for that harvest by selling 20 wheat futures contracts. (Each wheat contract is for 5,000 bushels.) By selling these futures contracts, the farmer seeks to establish a price today for the wheat that will be harvested in the future. With certain qualifications, this futures transaction protects the farmer from wheat price fluctuations that might occur between the present and the future harvest. The futures transaction served as a substitute for a cash market sale of wheat. A cash market sale was impossible, because the wheat did not actually exist. In this example, the farmer sells wheat in the futures market as a temporary substitute for a future anticipated cash market transaction. Therefore, **anticipatory hedging** is a futures market transaction used as a substitute for an anticipated future cash market transaction.

Hedging transactions can take other forms. For example, consider an oil wholesaler who holds a substantial inventory of gasoline. The wholesaler needs the inventory as a stock from which to service retail customers. If the wholesaler simply holds the stock of gasoline, she must bear the price risk of fluctuating gasoline prices. As an alternative, she can sell crude oil futures as a substitute for selling the gasoline itself. By holding gasoline in her business inventory and selling crude oil futures to offset the risk associated with the gasoline, the wholesaler can reduce her business risk. The wholesaler could have used the cash market directly to reduce risk by simply selling her entire inventory in the cash market. Unfortunately, this method of reducing business risk eliminates the business, because the wholesaler would no longer have the gasoline inventory that is essential to her entire business. Selling futures substitutes for the risk-reducing transaction of selling her entire inventory.

For both of our examples, the hedger uses the futures market as a substitute for a cash market transaction. Both hedgers had a preexisting risk associated with the commodity being sold. The farmer anticipated harvesting and selling wheat, and he used the futures market as a substitute for a cash market sale of wheat. Even though the farmer did not have wheat on hand when he sold futures, he did have a preexisting risk in wheat. The risk arose from the anticipated holding of the cash wheat at harvest. For the oil wholesaler, the risk was immediate. As prices of oil fluctuate, the value of her gasoline inventory would fluctuate as well. Thus, the wholesaler had a preexisting risk associated with the price of oil, and she used the futures market transaction to reduce that risk.

Because hedgers are traders that use futures transactions as substitutes for cash transactions, hedgers are almost always business concerns that deal with a specific commodity. Almost without exception, individual traders are speculators because they enter the futures market in pursuit of profit and increase their risk in the process. By contrast, hedgers have a preexisting risk exposure of some form that leads them to use futures transactions as a substitute for a cash market transaction. Hedging is the prime social rationale for futures trading and, therefore, we will give hedging a great deal of attention throughout the discussion of futures. Chapter 4 explains the use that the hedger makes of the futures markets, while the techniques and applications of hedging are elaborated for specific markets in Chapters 5 through 9.

Traders in the futures markets are either speculators or hedgers, or the agents of one of these two groups. Yet the benefits provided by the futures market extend to many other sectors of society. The individual interested in forecasts of futures prices need not enter the market to benefit. For example, our silver miner did not need to trade any futures to capture the benefits of price discovery. The forecasts are available for the price of the daily newspaper. The chance for hedgers to avoid unacceptable risks by entering the futures market also has wide implications for social welfare. Some individuals would not engage in certain clearly beneficial forms of economic activity if they were forced to bear all of the risk of the activity themselves. Being able to transfer risk to other parties via the futures market enhances economic activity in general. Of course, a general stimulation of economic activity benefits society as a whole.

REGULATION OF FUTURES MARKETS

There are four identifiable tiers of regulation in the futures market: the broker; the exchange and clearinghouse; an industry self-regulatory body, the National Futures Association (NFA); and a federal government agency, the Commodities Futures Trading Commission (CFTC). To a large extent, these tiers overlap, but each regulatory body has its specific duties.

The Broker

As we have seen in our discussion of the margin system, the broker essentially represents his or her customers to the exchange and clearinghouse. In the margin system, the clearinghouse holds the clearing member responsible for all of the accounts that clearing member carries. Because of the representations to the industry that the broker makes on behalf of its client, the broker has a duty to keep informed about the activities of its customer and to ensure that those activities are proper. Among futures market participants, the often-repeated rule for brokers is "know your customer." The broker is the industry representative in the best position to know a given customer, because the customer gains access to trading directly through the broker.

As we will see in more detail, some kinds of futures trading are not permitted to any traders. Other traders have restrictions on the kind of trading that they should engage in. As an example, let us consider a **position limit**. For a commodity with a position limit, no single trader is allowed to hold more than a certain number of contracts. This rule limits the influence of a single trader on the market and aims to prevent the trader from controlling the futures price.[6] On occasion, some traders have tried to circumvent this rule by trading through different accounts. Often, the broker can detect such a maneuver and has a duty to report such activity. As this example shows, the broker is often in the best position to detect some abuses, because he or she is closest to the customer. The trading of some customers is restricted due to the nature of the customer's business. For example, some financial institutions are allowed to trade only certain types of futures for hedging purposes. The broker for such an institution should not allow prohibited trading.

In general terms, the broker is responsible for knowing the customer's position and intentions, for ensuring that the customer does not disrupt the market or place the system in jeopardy, and for keeping the customer's trading activity in line with industry regulations and legal restrictions.

Futures Exchanges and Clearinghouses as Regulators

The futures exchanges and clearinghouses have specific regulatory duties. Many of these duties require the exchange and clearinghouse to control the conduct of exchange and clearing members. To do so, the exchanges formulate and enforce rules for their members and rules for trading on the exchange. Generally, the rules of each exchange are designed to create a smoothly functioning market in which traders can feel confident that their orders will be executed properly and at a fair price. Thus, all exchanges prohibit fraud, dishonorable conduct, and defaulting on contract obligations.

More specifically, exchange rules prohibit **fictitious trading** – trading that merely gives the appearance of transacting without actually changing ownership. Exchange rules prohibit circulating rumors to affect price, disclosing a customer's order, trading with oneself, taking the opposite side of a customer's order, making false statements to the exchange, and failing to comply with a legitimate order by the exchange.

The rules also prohibit **prearranged trading**. A prearranged trade occurs when two futures market participants consult in advance and agree to make a certain trade at a given price. Instead, the rules require that all orders be offered to the entire market through open outcry. The rules prohibit prearranged trading because a prearranged trade is noncompetitive and can be abusive. For example, assume that a floor broker receives an order to buy wheat and that the fair market price for the wheat contract is $4.20 per bushel. In a prearranged trade, the floor broker might agree with a friendly floor trader to buy the contract from him or her at $4.21. With the true market value at $4.20, this practice cheats the customer by $.01 per bushel or $50 per contract. Had the order been offered to the market as the rules require, the order would have been filled at the prevailing price of $4.20. Thus, the prohibition of prearranged trading aims at ensuring that each order is executed at a fair market price.

The rules also prohibit a broker from trading for his or her own account at the customer's requested price before filling a customer's order. The broker who trades for himself or herself before filling a customer's order engages in the prohibited practice called **front running**. To see why this practice is prohibited, assume that market prices are rising rapidly due to some new information. Assume also that the broker holds a customer order to buy. If the broker executes his or her own order first, the broker's own order will be executed at a more favorable price, because of the quickly rising prices. Thus, front running gives the broker an unfair advantage. As a second example, assume that a broker receives a very large customer order to sell. The broker knows that placing this order will depress the futures price temporarily. The front running broker would enter his or her own order to sell first. The broker's order would be executed at the high price, and the broker would then execute the customer's order. Upon execution of the customer's order, the price falls as the broker anticipated. Now the broker can buy and close his or her position. This gives the broker a profit from front running. In front running, the broker uses his or her special knowledge of order flow or market movement to obtain an unethical and prohibited personal advantage.

In **dual trading**, a single individual fulfills the function of a floor trader and a floor broker simultaneously. That is, a single individual trades for his or her own account, while executing orders for traders off-the-floor of the exchange. Although permitted for many decades, dual trading does offer potential for abuse, and the practice has come under heightened scrutiny. Because dual trading creates a situation in which a single individual has his or her own orders in hand along with orders from an outside customer, dual trading can also facilitate front running and other questionable trading practices.

Traders maintain that dual trading serves the market in several ways. First, defenders maintain that dual trading helps promote liquidity in the market. If a trader can only execute orders for his or her own account or only execute orders for others, there will be less potential trading volume at any given time. Second, this lack of liquidity may lead to larger spreads between bid and asked prices, thereby making the market less efficient than it would be otherwise. Finally, defenders of dual trading maintain that the practice keeps trading costs low, because a dual trader needs to make only a portion of his or her income by acting as a floor broker.

In late 1993, the CFTC banned dual trading, but allowed a number of significant exceptions. For example, dual trading continues to be permitted for commodities with daily trading volume of fewer than 8,000 contracts, for exchanges with very well-developed audit systems, and where the banning of dual trading would adversely affect the public interest. In recent years, it appears that formerly dual traders on the CME have not gained a greater share of customers now that the traders' personal trading is restricted, and these traders have not shifted their trading to other commodities.[7]

Futures exchanges also set daily price limits, position limits, and margin requirements, although the CFTC has a role in each of these types of rules. In addition, each exchange has rules that govern membership on the exchange. For example, exchange rules establish membership requirements and specify how customer complaints are to be resolved. For each of these categories, the rules of the exchange are subject to review by the CFTC. However, the CFTC generally provides broad guidelines within which the exchanges and clearinghouses form their own specific rules.

National Futures Association (NFA)

In 1974, Congress passed a new law for the regulation of futures markets. Part of that law authorized the futures industry to create one or more self-regulatory bodies "... to prevent fraudulent and manipulative acts and practices, to promote just and equitable principles of trade, in general, to protect the public interest, and to remove impediments to and perfect the mechanism of free and open futures trading." While the law has contemplated more than a single self-regulatory body, the National Futures Association is the only such body in existence.

The following parties are required to be members of the NFA: Futures Commission Merchants, Commodity Pool Operators, Introducing Brokers, Commodity Trading Advisors, and Associated Persons. Exchanges, banks, and commodity business firms may join the NFA, but membership is not compulsory. Floor traders and floor brokers are not required to be members, because they are subject to exchange regulation. One must be a member of the NFA in order to do commodity-related business with the public.

The NFA screens and tests applicants for registration, and reviews personal background information before allowing individuals to register in the various categories of futures professionals. The NFA also requires FCMs and Introducing Brokers to maintain adequate capital and accurate trading records and can audit member firms' records and capital adequacy. For serious violations, the NFA can suspend or expel violators from the futures industry. Finally, the NFA operates an arbitration process for resolving trading disputes.

As the NFA states, it seeks to prevent infractions before they occur. By doing so, the NFA helps the futures industry remain viable by keeping the public trust. However, in assessing the NFA, it is wise to remember that it is an industry self-regulatory body, designed to protect the integrity of the industry and to promote the interests of the industry.

Commodity Futures Trading Commission (CFTC)

The Commodity Futures Trading Commission Act of 1974 established the commission. Before this act, commodity futures markets were regulated solely under the Commodity Exchange Act administered through the Department of Agriculture. The new act supplemented, rather than replaced, the Commodity Exchange Act. The CFTC Act brought currency and metal futures under federal regulation.

The CFTC has specific powers under the CFTC Act. One important area of CFTC jurisdiction concerns the approval of new contracts. Before trading, an exchange must submit the newly designed contract to the CFTC for approval. The CFTC is responsible for determining whether trading in such a contract is contrary to the public interest. To receive approval, the contract must show promise of serving an economic purpose, such as making for fairer pricing of the commodity in some way or in making hedging possible. Providing an arena for speculation is not enough justification to show that a futures contract would serve an economic function.

The CFTC also regulates futures market trading rules, including the daily permitted maximum price fluctuation, certain features of the delivery process, and minimum price fluctuation limits. Generally, the CFTC is not involved in determining membership in the exchanges, but it can review complaints of membership exclusion or other unfair treatment by the exchanges. Perhaps the most striking power of the CFTC is the emergency power to intervene in the conduct of the market itself when the commission believes manipulation is present. Also, the CFTC has the power to require competency tests of brokers and commodity representatives.

Aims of Regulation

Futures market regulations today control both entry into and the operation of futures markets. Before a new contract can be traded, the CFTC must approve the contract for trading. Another dimension of current regulatory practice focuses not on entry but on the operation or performance of futures markets. On the operational side, futures market regulation aims to provide a marketplace in which the social functions of futures markets can be fulfilled. Practices that interfere with the process of price discovery or the efficient transfer of unwanted risk make futures markets perform poorly. For example, practices that make futures prices behave as poor indicators of future spot prices reduce the usefulness of the futures market for price discovery. Also, practices that distort prices can increase the cost of transferring risk. To see more clearly the point of regulation, we consider one of the most feared aspects of futures trading abuse, **price manipulation**.

"It is a felony for a person to manipulate or attempt to manipulate the price of any commodity in commerce or for future delivery."[8] To prove manipulation, the manipulator must be shown to have the ability to set an artificial futures price, must have intended to set an artificial price, and must have succeeded in setting such a price. In essence, an artificial price is a price that does not reflect free demand and supply conditions. By trading in certain ways, it may be possible for a trader or group of traders to move the price in the market from its economically sound or justified price. The basic way of accomplishing this feat is through a market corner or a market squeeze. In a corner or squeeze, a trader or group of traders gains effective control over the pricing mechanism in the futures market. These are discussed in more detail later in this chapter.

Given these problems created by price manipulation, it may seem clear that there is a need for government regulation of futures markets. Some observers argue that such governmental regulation is not needed. According to these authors, the exchanges have a strong incentive for self-regulation.

Only by attracting the public for trading can the exchange make money as a whole. Therefore, according to this argument, the exchange left to its own devices will be self-regulating, obviating the need for governmental regulation.[9]

In addition to the issue of price manipulation, other areas of concern to regulators include: insider trading, front running, capital formation concerns, and the effect of futures trading on the riskiness of the cash market for commodities. Insider trading is trading on information not available to the public at large. For example, a government clerk working on a forecast of the size of the corn crop has access to information that could be valuable in futures trading. Using such information to guide trading would be a case of insider trading. Recently, insider trading scandals in the stock market have attracted a great deal of public attention. Insider trading in futures markets is not subject to the same limitations as those found in the stock market. Nonetheless, most exchanges have some restrictions on insider trading. Some observers argue that prohibitions against insider futures trading would actually be harmful. Under this view, insider trading contributes to liquidity and to market efficiency.

New Regulatory Initiatives

In early 1996, the Securities Exchange Commission (SEC) and the Financial Accounting Standards Board (FASB) were both proposing new rules for disclosure of risk positions in firms' derivatives positions. These proposals were being disseminated in the wake of several major scandals involving significant losses resulting from derivatives trading. The SEC proposal would require firms to disclose quantitative information about market risks in tabular form, would require firms to present sensitivity analyses of their risk positions, would require firms to present qualitative risk information, and would permit firms to disclose value-at-risk information.

The FASB proposal would require all derivatives to be recognized in the firms' financial statements at fair value. For reporting purposes, derivatives would be divided into those that stand alone and those that hedge some other instrument. The hedging derivatives would be divided into those that hedge asset, liabilities, or forecasted transactions. This FASB proposal has come under strong attack by the derivatives industry as failing to allow deferral of gains and losses on hedging transactions. Almost certainly, the SEC and FASB proposals will be revised and the implementation of the resulting rules will be deferred for a few years.[10]

TAXATION OF FUTURES TRADING

In 1981, Congress passed a law regarding the taxation of gains and losses in futures trading that had dramatic effects on the ways in which futures contracts could be used. The new law stipulated that all paper gains and losses on futures positions must be treated as though they were realized at the end of the tax year. For tax purposes, this new law meant that the futures positions must be marked-to-market at the end of the year. Forty percent of any gains or losses are to be treated as short-term gains; 60 percent are to be treated as long-term capital gains or losses. Prior to the passage of the Tax Reform Act of 1986, long-term capital gains were taxed at a lower rate than ordinary income or short-term capital gains. The 1986 law stipulates that all income is taxed at one rate. This change removes the protection of the long-term rates, but the new law also reduced overall tax rates. As a net result, the 1986 law seems to have had little effect on profits from futures trading.

BROKERS, ADVISORS, AND COMMODITY FUND MANAGERS

We have already seen that speculators and hedgers are traders who trade for their own accounts. Also, we have mentioned that the market utilizes brokers, those individuals who execute trades for a customer, whether a speculator or a hedger. Since there are a number of different types of brokers, in this section we consider brokers in more detail.

In discussing brokers earlier in this chapter, we focused on an individual who executes orders on the floor of the exchange. We mentioned that such a broker is often the employee of a brokerage firm, such as Merrill Lynch. In the futures market, there are special names for the individuals and firms that execute orders on behalf of others.

Floor Broker (FB)

When an individual off the floor of the exchange places an order, he or she usually does so through an account executive with a brokerage firm. The order is transmitted to the floor of the exchange where it is executed by a **floor broker** – an individual who executes an order for the purchase or sale of a futures contract for another person. There are about 7,500 floor brokers on the floor all together.

Many floor brokers are members of **broker associations** or **broker groups**. A broker group is an association of floor brokers who band together to fill orders for their customers. The group might be as small as two brokers who cover for each other during vacations or as large as groups of brokers who operate in several markets and who share profits and expenses. These broker groups have become an important force among the trading community. For example, there are more than 200 broker groups at the Chicago Mercantile Exchange and more than 100 at the New York Mercantile Exchange.

Broker groups provide some services to the futures community. First, they provide a training ground for new brokers. Second, they provide a flexible pool of manpower to respond to radical fluctuations in trading volume. Third, they provide an easy way for large brokerage houses to achieve execution in several pits simultaneously. Fourth, the capital of the association stands behind each of the members of the group. Thus, there is less chance of any single broker defaulting.

These broker groups have become the object of criticism for several reasons. First, the existence of an association might encourage members to trade with each other preferentially, instead of offering a trade to the entire market as the rules require. Second, broker groups were accused of dishonesty in fulfilling customer orders in some important recent legal actions. For example, one member of a broker group might trade for his own account, while another member of the same group might act as a floor broker in executing an order for someone outside the broker group. The temptation exists to give a preferential price to the other member of the broker group at the expense of the outside party. In 1993, the CFTC increased its monitoring of these broker groups and required identification of such cooperative relationships.

Futures Commission Merchant (FCM)

A **futures commission merchant** is a firm or individual that accepts orders to trade futures on behalf of another party and who accepts money to support such an order. Thus, a brokerage firm that accepts orders to trade futures is a futures commission merchant or FCM. In many cases, the FCM will be a large firm with offices in many cities that accepts orders from individuals and other firms. The

FCM transmits these orders to the floor of the exchange where they are executed by a floor broker. The floor broker may be an employee of the FCM, although this is not always the case. Since the mid-1980s, the number of FCMs has declined due to consolidation in the industry and stiff competition. In 1984, there were approximately 400 FCMs, but that number declined to about 275 by 1996.

Introducing Broker (IB)

An **introducing broker** is an individual or firm that accepts orders to trade futures, but who does not accept the funds to support such orders. Thus, the FCM accepts money to support the orders (such as margin deposits), but the introducing broker does not. Essentially, the IB finds a customer and solicits that customer's business. However, the IB does not process the trade or hold monies for margin. Instead, the IB works with another broker, called a **carrying broker**, who processes the trade, holds the margin deposit, and provides accounting and documentation of the trades to the customer. The introducing broker and carrying broker share the commissions earned for executing trades. In 1989, the number of IBs peaked at about 1,800. By late 1996, then number of IBs had fallen to about 1,300.

Associated Person (AP)

An **associated person** is an individual who solicits orders, customers, or customer funds, or an individual who supervises anyone who makes such solicitations. Thus, a floor broker or an introducing broker is also an associated person, as is the manager of a branch office of an FCM. This broad category includes most of the professional individuals who make their livings in the futures industry. There were more than 55,000 APs in 1990, but that number fell to about 48,000 by 1996.

Commodity Trading Advisor (CTA)

A **commodity trading advisor** is a person who directly or indirectly advises others regarding their futures trading. This category also applies to individuals who advise the public through written publications or other mass media. Thus, the writer of a futures newsletter that recommends certain positions in the futures market would be a CTA. In 1993, there were more than 2,700 CTAs.

Commodity Pool Operator (CPO)

A **commodity pool operator** is an individual or firm that operates or solicits funds for a commodity pool. A **commodity pool** consists of a collection of funds used to engage in futures trading activities. Typically, a number of individuals contribute funds to form the commodity pool. The pool operator uses those funds to engage in speculative futures trading. The individuals who contributed monies to the pool own a share of the entire pool. Thus, a commodity pool is similar to a mutual fund in which individuals contribute funds for investment in stocks and bonds. There are approximately 1,325 commodity pool operators in the United States.

THE CHANGING ENVIRONMENT OF FUTURES MARKETS

Rapid changes confront the futures markets in the United States. Most notable among these are competition from foreign futures markets and the emergence of electronic trading systems.

The Internationalization of Futures Markets

For decades, the United States has dominated the futures industry. Until recently, the totality of foreign exchanges generated a relatively insignificant trading volume compared to that of the United States. This has changed in the last five years, and all indications suggest that foreign futures exchanges will continue to grow much more rapidly than U.S. exchanges. This growing foreign competition brings with it additional challenges to U.S. markets in the form of around-the-clock trading and international competition in trading costs.

Growing Foreign Exchanges. Table 2.8 lists the top ten futures exchanges around the world. While U.S. exchanges continue to enjoy a commanding lead over the exchanges of any other nation, U.S. futures volume now accounts for less than half of total world volume. The decline in preeminence has been continuing for some time. Only a few years ago, the United States accounted for much more than half of world futures volume. For example, in 1988 U.S. volume was 69.11 percent of the world's total.

Most foreign exchanges are quite new. In spite of their recent start and relatively small size, the foreign exchanges present new competitive challenges to the dominating Chicago-based exchanges. This competition arises in virtually all types of futures contracts. Table 2.9 lists the most successful contracts traded on foreign exchanges.

Around-the-Clock Trading. With the emergence of foreign futures exchanges, futures trading on some goods continues almost 24 hours a day. In this respect, the three most popular contracts are Treasury bills, Eurodollars, and Treasury bonds. For Treasury bills and Eurodollars, futures contracts trade in Singapore, London, Chicago, and Tokyo. Because these markets trade during local daylight hours, they cover different periods of time. Among them, these futures exchanges offer trading for more than 20 hours of each 24-hour period. In many instances, the trading hours overlap. First, Tokyo

Table 2.8	Top Ten Futures Exchanges for 1995	
Exchange	**1995 Volume**	**Percentage of Top 10 Volume**
Chicago Board of Trade, U.S.A.	165,616,177	0.2035
Chicago Mercantile Exchange, U.S.A.	146,662,764	0.1802
Bolsa de Mercadorias e Futuros, Brazil	130,832,733	0.1608
London International Financial Futures Exchange, U.K.	107,397,420	0.1320
New York Mercantile Exchange, U.S.A.	63,636,046	0.0782
MATIF, Paris	56,691,754	0.0697
London Metal Exchange, U.K.	43,397,381	0.0533
Tokyo International Financial Futures Exchange, Japan	36,360,296	0.0447
Tokyo Commodity Exchange for Industry, Japan	35,125,427	0.0432
Meff Renta Variable, Spain	28,096,699	0.0345
Total Top 10 1995 Volume	813,818,692	

Source: From *Futures Industry*, February 1995. Reprinted by permission.

Top Five Futures Contracts Traded Abroad		Table 2.9
Contract	**Exchange**	**1995 Volume (millions)**
Average Interest Rate on Interbank Deposits	BBF, Brazil	8.6
U.S. Dollar	BM&F, Brazil	6.1
Interest Rate	BM&F, Brazil	4.6
Notionnel (Govt. bond)	MATIF, France	3.0
Bund (German bond)	LIFFE, London	2.8

Source: From *Futures Industry*, December 1995/January 1996. Rankings and volume are based on first 11 months of 1995.

and Singapore have almost identical trading hours, which one might expect because they are in similar time zones. Before Singapore closes, the London market opens. The Chicago markets open during London's afternoon trading. Virtually the entire day witnesses trading in some market, and trading hours continue to expand.

For U.S. Treasury bonds, similar trading hours are available. Contracts on U.S. bonds trade in London, Chicago, New York, and Tokyo. The Chicago Board of Trade has two sessions per day. One session occurs during regular business hours, while the other covers the evening hours in Chicago. Taken together, these exchanges offer futures trading on Treasury bonds 18.5 hours of each 24-hour period.

International Competition in Trading Costs. With the ability of many traders to choose the country in which they wish to trade, exchange fees become a matter of competitive concern. For example, we have seen that Eurodollars trade in a number of markets worldwide. As a result, exchanges compete for Eurodollar trading volume. One element of this competition is the fee the exchange charges for executing an order. The large exchanges with well-established contracts have the most latitude in setting fees. Traders need those contracts and would likely feel forced to pay even excessively high fees to trade those markets.

Ironically, the largest exchanges, those in the United States, have the lowest fees. These lower fees may reflect economies of scale in operating a futures exchange. European exchanges are somewhat higher, and the highest fees are found in Asian markets. For example, a member of the Chicago Board of Trade can trade a contract for substantially less than $1. By contrast, a member of the Tokyo Commodity Exchange may face a fee as large as $20. Many observers see exchange fees as an important point of future competition among exchanges.

In the uncertain U.S. budget environment of the 1990s, some administration officials floated the idea of a tax on futures transactions. Few countries impose a tax on futures transactions. Only Finland, Hong Kong, France, and Japan tax these transactions. The tax in Finland is only about $.02 per round turn, but in Japan the tax can be over $15.00 per round turn. This Japanese tax and other restrictions in the Japanese market have led to a downturn in Japanese market activity, and many individuals in the futures industry fear that taxes in the U.S. could destroy the competitiveness of U.S. markets.

ELECTRONIC FUTURES TRADING

From the beginning of organized futures exchanges in the mid-1800s until a few years ago, the system of open outcry has been the only method of futures trading. While open outcry continues to dominate futures trading, we are now seeing the emergence of automated trading systems that may eventually change the entire face of the futures markets.

The advent of electronic trading systems also promises to be an important element in global competition among futures exchanges. In futures trading, the U.S. markets are the oldest and best established. In some ways, the members of the U.S. exchanges are the most conservative and wedded to tradition, particularly the tradition of trading in pits through open outcry. Exchange policies are controlled by exchange members. In the Chicago markets, a high proportion of members are individuals who trade for their own accounts. Their livelihood depends upon the trading acumen that they have developed through their years in the trading pits. Electronic trading systems threaten to make those open outcry skills obsolete. Not surprisingly, these members have resisted any threats to the system of open outcry.

New and smaller exchanges have little tradition to confront. Compared to pit trading with open outcry, electronic trading is definitely cheaper to launch. Many traders also believe that electronic systems are operationally superior to pit trading. Further, there are many different electronic trading systems, all of which have their own features. No matter what one believes about the virtues of open outcry versus electronic trading, it is clear that electronic trading is here to stay. Because electronic trading is largely technologically driven, we can expect accelerating change in this area. Some smaller foreign exchanges have a much larger commitment to electronic trading than do the major exchanges. The four largest systems are: GLOBEX, sponsored by the CME and the French exchange MATIF; Project A, sponsored by the CBOT; Access, sponsored by NYMEX; and APT sponsored by the LIFFE of London. Table 2.10 shows recent volume for these major systems. The remainder of this section provides a brief description of GLOBEX and Project A.

GLOBEX

Because of initial resistance by U.S. traders, exchanges in the United States have been relatively slow to develop electronic trading systems. However, because the U.S. exchanges dominate world futures markets, any system that prevails in the United States will have an extremely good chance of being the dominant electronic trading system in the world. After many delays, GLOBEX began trading in

Table 2.10	Electronic Futures Trading		
System	**Exchange**	**Country**	**Recent Monthly Volume**
GLOBEX	CME	United States	725,000
APT	LIFFE	United Kingdom	370,000
Access	NYMEX	United States	140,000
Project A	CBOT	United States	117,000

Source: From "Any Time, Any Place," *Risk* 9:3, March 1996, pp. 27–31. Reprinted by permission of Risk Magazine Ltd.

June 1992. GLOBEX was initially developed by the Chicago Mercantile Exchange. The Paris exchange, MATIF, also trades through GLOBEX, and GLOBEX continues to court other exchanges.

Initially, GLOBEX was created to augment open outcry. Currently, trading on GLOBEX is restricted to hours when the Chicago Mercantile Exchange is not open. However, when one considers the success of electronic trading systems at other exchanges, it seems clear that electronic trading has a future that goes far beyond a mere supplement to pit trading. That future remains obscure, however. In its first year of trading, GLOBEX traded just slightly more than one million contracts. (This is less than one-half of 1 percent of industry volume.) Ironically, MATIF accounts for more volume on GLOBEX than the CME. At one point, the CBOT was a partner in the GLOBEX venture, but it has now abandoned that venture and instead launched its own electronic trading system called Project A.

Project A

Project A is an electronic order-entry and matching system operated by the CBOT for off-hours trading of CBOT contracts. The system operates from 2:30 to 4:30 P.M. and from 10:30 P.M. to 6:00 A.M. Chicago time. During the regular trading day, all trading takes place in pits using open-outcry. Initially the system allowed for trading of financial futures and options, but it has now been expanded to include agricultural contracts. Trades entered in open-outcry sessions can be offset on Project A, and vice versa.

With its expanded hours, traders can trade CBOT products during the entire time the cash Treasury market is open. Also, overseas traders can trade CBOT contracts during their daylight hours, and the ability to trade CBOT contracts during the Chicago night allows real-time spread trading of CBOT contracts against foreign markets.

MARKET CORNERS AND SQUEEZES

The most dramatic dislocation in a futures market occurs in a corner or squeeze. While various commentators use somewhat different definitions, we will define a **corner** as a successful effort by a trader or group of traders to manipulate the price of a futures contract by gaining effective control over trading in the futures and the supply of the deliverable good. In a market **squeeze**, a trader achieves effective control over the price of a futures contract due to disruptions in the supply of the cash commodity. The manipulative part of a squeeze arises when the trader uses this circumstance to control the price of the good. These disruptions need not be due to actions of the controlling trader, but might originate from other forces, such as the weather.

Manipulating the price of a futures contract is a violation of the Commodity Exchange Act. Such price manipulation not only cheats other traders, but it also impairs the marketplace. First, other traders are cheated because the manipulation forces them to trade at a price that is not economically justified. In general, markets function properly when prices in the market represent the true equilibrium value of the good being traded. By definition, in a corner or squeeze, the price is manipulated, so it cannot be at its equilibrium level. Second, a manipulation also impairs the market because honest traders flee markets in which prices do not correspond to the true economic value of the good being traded. If honest traders abandon the futures market, the market cannot serve its social functions. The market will not serve its price discovery function because the prices in the market are manipulated prices. Also, the market does not provide a means for transferring risk, because honest traders are afraid to participate in the market. For these reasons, the price manipulation associated with a corner or squeeze is the worst fate that can befall a market.

This section discusses one proven manipulation and one alleged manipulation. First, we consider a manipulation in silver by the Hunt brothers of Dallas and their co-conspirators. This manipulation occurred in 1979–1980. Second, we examine an alleged manipulation of soybeans that occurred in 1989. At that time, the large grain-trading firm Ferruzzi Finanziaria held seven million bushels of soybeans, and the exchanges and the CFTC moved to force Ferruzzi to liquidate. In Federal Court, the Hunt brothers were found to have manipulated silver prices. However, Ferruzzi has never been brought to trial, and the manipulation in soybeans has not been proven, although Ferruzzi has paid the Chicago Board of Trade in settlement of the dispute.

The Hunt Silver Manipulation

With little doubt, the Hunt manipulation of silver in 1979–1980 was the grandest futures manipulation of the twentieth century. At one time, the Hunts and their co-conspirators controlled silver worth more than $14 billion. Figure 2.7 shows the price of silver for 1979 and 1980. At the beginning of 1979, an ounce of silver was worth about $6. In January 1980, the price briefly exceeded $50 during one trading day. In March 1980, the price of silver crashed, and silver fell to the $12 per ounce range. In 1996, silver traded for about $5–6 per ounce.

In some ways, the silver manipulation was very simple, while in other ways it was incredibly complex. The manipulative efforts involved many other participants besides the flamboyant and well-known Hunts. These other conspirators included a number of very wealthy Saudis. In outline, the

Figure 2.7   Silver Prices in 1979–1980

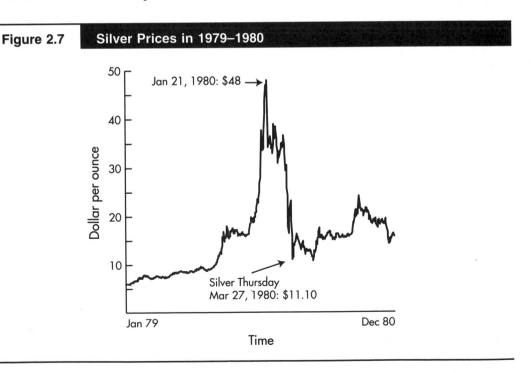

Hunts operated a corner on the silver market. They amassed gigantic futures positions and demanded delivery on those contracts as they came due. At the same time, they bought tremendous quantities of physical silver and held the physical silver off the market. Thus, they accelerated demand through the futures market as they restricted supply through the cash market. As a result the price of silver shot up.

As silver approached $50 per ounce in January 1980, the exchanges and the CFTC took effective action by imposing liquidation-only trading. Under **liquidation-only trading**, traders are allowed to trade only to close an existing futures position; they are not allowed to establish any new positions. (This rule forces traders to exit the market as any existing positions come to expiration; they cannot roll those positions forward to a later contract maturity.) The next day, the price of silver dropped by $12 per ounce in one day. From January through February and into March, the manipulators struggled to support the price of silver. However, the exchanges also increased margins on silver. On March 19, the Hunts defaulted on their margin obligations. In a final desperate attempt to support the price of silver, the manipulators announced a plan on March 26, 1980, to issue bonds backed by their physical silver holdings. The market interpreted this ploy as an act of desperation and the market crashed again the next day. March 27, 1980, has become known as Silver Thursday because of this famous crash that ended the Hunts' effective domination of silver.

Minpeco, S.A., a Peruvian government-sponsored minerals marketing firm, was a major short trader in the silver market during 1979–1980. They sued the Hunts, their co-conspirators, and their brokers for $90 million of actual losses plus interest, plus trebled punitive damages. Minpeco won about $200 million in settlements and judgments against the defendants. This sum included a pre-judgment settlement payment of $34 million by Merrill Lynch and Bache, two of the conspirators' largest brokers. The jury found that the three Hunt brothers, Bunker, Herbert, and Lamar, had indeed manipulated the silver market. After the verdict, Lamar Hunt, owner of the Kansas City Chiefs NFL team, paid $17 million in settlement. The full settlement was never collected from Bunker and Herbert, who sought protection in bankruptcy. Thus, these two brothers, who began the 1980s among the world's richest men, were bankrupt by 1990.

The Alleged Soybean Manipulation of 1989

The Soybean crisis of 1989 had its origins at least as far back as the preceding year. In 1988, the Midwest suffered a severe drought, which greatly reduced soybean yields. Thus, the market entered the 1989 crop year with greatly diminished supplies. Figure 2.8 shows the price of soybeans for 1989. Through early 1989, Central Soya, a wholly-owned grain subsidiary of the Italian firm Ferruzzi, amassed large holdings of physical soybeans and took large long positions in the May 1989 soybean contract. As late as May 16, Ferruzzi held 16.2 million bushels of May soybean futures. The Chicago Board of Trade revoked Ferruzzi's status as a hedger on May 18. This meant that Ferruzzi was forced to reduce its futures position to the 3 million bushel speculative position limit. As a result, the May contract liquidated in an orderly manner.

However, instead of merely offsetting its May positions, Ferruzzi **rolled its position forward**. That is, Ferruzzi sold May contracts and bought July soybean futures. This action set the stage for a larger problem in July. By early June, Ferruzzi held a long position of 32 million bushels in the July futures contract. In addition, by July 1, Ferruzzi had achieved effective control over the deliverable supply of soybeans. Ferruzzi controlled seven million bushels, while all other traders controlled only

Figure 2.8   Soybean Prices in 1989

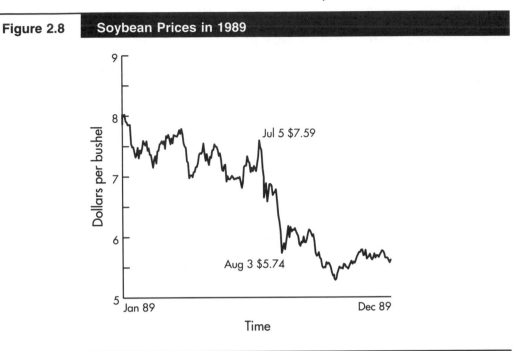

1.6 million. With Ferruzzi holding 32 million bushels in long futures and only 1.6 million bushels available for delivery by other traders, Ferruzzi clearly had a dominant market position.

On July 11, 1989, the Chicago Board of Trade declared that an emergency existed. Effective on July 12, the Board of Trade revoked Ferruzzi's status as a hedger. This meant that Ferruzzi was once again subject to the 3 million bushel position limit. Further, the CBOT ordered liquidation of at least 20 percent of futures positions for each of the next several trading days down to an absolute limit of no more than 1 million bushels at the close of trading on July 20. These actions helped avert the crisis, and the July contract traded without further disruptions. On September 15, 1989, Ferruzzi announced that its major grain and oilseed traders in Paris had resigned due to "differences over trading strategies."[11]

Ferruzzi later filed suit against the CBOT, and the CBOT imposed fines on Ferruzzi. In 1992, the dispute was laid to rest when Ferruzzi paid $2 million to the CBOT and dropped its suit. The CBOT viewed this payment as a fine, but Ferruzzi has disputed this characterization. The aftermath of this mess lingered into 1993, when the chairman of Ferruzzi committed suicide and deep losses of about $350 million, apparently stemming from the trading debacle, were discovered.[12]

CONCLUSION

This chapter has explored the basic institutional features of the futures markets, focusing on the United States. We have seen that futures contracts are a type of forward contract traded on organized exchanges and featuring highly standardized contract terms. The institutional environment includes a clearinghouse to guarantee performance to all trades and a margin system designed to protect the financial integrity of the marketplace. This system allows the futures market to provide two key social benefits: price discovery and risk transference through hedging.

Futures markets trade contracts on a variety of goods, ranging from the traditional agricultural commodities to metals, interest rate contracts, contracts on stock indexes, and foreign currency futures. The market has a complex regulatory environment, with brokers, exchanges, an industry organization, and a federal agency all playing a role. These regulatory bodies govern the activities of a variety of futures market participants, including: floor brokers, introducing brokers, futures commission merchants, advisors, and commodity pool operators.

Today, the futures industry in the United States faces challenges from emerging foreign futures markets and a movement toward electronic trading accelerated by technological change. These trends in the market threaten to end the dominance of futures trading long enjoyed by U.S. exchanges, but these same developments broaden the range and scope of futures trading available in the increasingly worldwide economy.

QUESTIONS AND PROBLEMS

1. Explain the different roles of a floor broker and an account executive.
2. At a party, a man tells you that he is an introducing broker. He goes on to explain that his job is introducing prospective traders such as yourself to futures brokers. He also relates that he holds margin funds as a service to investors. What do you make of this explanation?
3. Assume that you are a floor broker and a friend of yours is a marketmaker who trades soybeans on the floor of the Chicago Board of Trade. Beans are trading at $6.53 per bushel. You receive an order to buy beans and you buy one contract from your friend at $6.54, one cent above the market. Who wins, who loses, and why? Explain the rationale for making such practice illegal.
4. Back at the party after several more hours. Your buddy from Question 2 buttonholes you again and starts to explain his great success as a dual trader, trading both beans and corn. What do you think?
5. You are having trouble escaping from your friend in Question 4. He goes on to explain that liquidation-only trading involves trading soybean against soyoil to profit from the liquidation that occurs when beans are crushed. Explain how your understanding of "liquidation-only trading" differs from your friend's.
6. In purchasing a house, contracting to buy the house occurs at one time. Typically, closing occurs weeks later. At the closing the buyer pays the seller for the house and the buyer takes possession. Explain how this transaction is like a futures or forward transaction.
7. In the futures market, a widget contract has a standard contract size of 5,000 widgets. What advantage does this have over the well-known forward market practice of negotiating the size of the transaction on a case-by-case basis? What disadvantages does the standardized contract size have?
8. What factors need to be considered in purchasing a commodity futures exchange seat? What are all the possible advantages that could come from owning a seat?
9. Explain the difference between initial and maintenance margin.
10. Explain the difference between maintenance and variation margin.
11. On February 1, a trader is long the JUN wheat contract. On February 10, she sells a SEP wheat futures, and sells a JUN wheat contract on February 20. On February 15, what is her position in

wheat futures? On February 25, what is her position? How would you characterize her transaction on February 20?

12. Explain the difference between volume and open interest.
13. Define "tick" and "daily price limit."
14. A trader is long one SEP crude oil contract. On May 15, he contracts with a business associate to receive 1,000 barrels of oil in the spot market. The business associate is short one SEP crude oil contract. How can the two traders close their futures positions without actually transacting in the futures market?
15. Explain how a trader closes a futures market position via cash settlement.
16. Explain "price discovery."
17. Contrast anticipatory hedging with hedging in general.
18. What is "front running"?
19. Explain the difference in the roles of the National Futures Association and the Commodity Futures Trading Commission.

NOTES

[1] There are some exceptions to this general rule. For example, the London Metals Exchange trades metals forwards, but has a physical trading floor.

[2] Notice that this is different from the stock market. Stocks represent title to the real assets of the firms, and these are owned by someone at every point in time. The long and short positions in the stock market, when "netted out," always equal the number of shares actually in existence, not zero, as in the futures market.

[3] We might say that the clearinghouse is "perfectly hedged." No matter whether futures prices rise or fall, the wealth of the clearinghouse will not be affected. This is the case since the clearinghouse holds both long and short positions that perfectly balance each other.

[4] For some commodities, such as wheat, delivery is permitted in more than one location. This feature saves transportation costs and helps prevent market irregularities such as corners. Stephen Craig Pirrong, Roger Kormendi, and Philip Meguire, "Multiple Delivery Points, Pricing Dynamics, and Hedging Effectiveness in Futures Markets for Spatial Commodities," *Journal of Futures Markets*, 14:5, August 1994, pp. 545–73, find that this delivery option is priced and that the value of this option can be substantial. Pirrong, Kormendi, and Meguire find that additional delivery points increase the hedging effectiveness of the contract.

[5] Often there may be a number of delivery months on which trading is permitted, but contracts with little trading volume will actually have an active market in only one or two delivery months at a time.

[6] Position limits do not apply in the same way to hedgers.

[7] See Eric C. Chang, Peter R. Locke, and Steven C. Mann, "The Effect of CME Rule 552 on Dual Traders," *Journal of Futures Markets*, 14:4, June 1994, pp. 493–510. Other studies are quite skeptical regarding the benefits of restrictions on dual trading: Tom Smith and Robert E. Whaley, "Assessing the Costs of Regulation: The Case of Dual Trading," *Journal of Law & Economics*, 37:1, April 1994, pp. 215–46; Sugato Chakravarty, "Should Actively Traded Futures Contracts Come Under the Dual-Trading Ban?" *Journal of Futures Markets*, 14:6, September 1994, pp. 661–84. Hun Y. Park, Asani Sarkar, and Lifan Wu, "The Costs and Benefits of Dual Trading," Federal Reserve Bank of New York, *Staff Reports*, Number 2, June 1995, find that dual traders attain better execution for their customers than pure brokers. But, they also find that this performance is pit specific, with this superior performance not being characteristic of trading in all commodities.

[8] G. D. Koppenhaver, "Futures Market Regulation," *Economic Perspectives*, 11:1, January/February 1987.

[9] See F. Easterbrook, "Monopoly, Manipulation, and the Regulation of Futures Markets," *Journal of Business*, 59:2, Part 2, April 1986, pp. S103–S127, who argues against such regulation. By contrast, A. Kyle, in "A Theory of Futures Market Manipulations," in R. Anderson (ed.), *The Industrial Organization of Futures Markets*, Lexington, MA: D. C. Heath, 1984, argues that squeezes increase the cost of hedging and should therefore be regulated to make them more difficult.

[10] See Donald L. Horwitz, "SEC Proposes Rules for Derivatives Disclosure, "*Futures Industry*, March/April 1996, pp. 33–35; Phoebe Mix, "FASB Struggles with Derivatives Accounting," *Futures Industry*, March/April 1996, pp. 31–32; and Pat Arbor, "Does FASB Control the Future of Futures?" *Risk*, 9:1, January 1996, p. 19.

[11] This account relies on F. Bailey, "Emergency Action: July 1989 Soybeans," Chicago: Chicago Board of Trade, 1990. See also K. Schap and C. Flory, "Ferruzzi vs. CBOT: Who Is Right?" *Futures*, September 1989, and K. Pierog, "Report Vindicates CBOT Action in July Soybeans," *Futures*, October 1989.

[12] See "Ferruzzi's Problems May Be Italy's Too," *The Wall Street Journal*, August 12, 1993.

FUTURES PRICES

OVERVIEW

Having explored the basic institutional features of the futures market in Chapter 2, we now consider futures prices. In an important sense, the study of the prices in a market provides the essential key to understanding all features of the market. Prices and the factors that determine those prices will ultimately influence every use of the market.

This chapter examines the fundamental factors that affect futures prices. There is little doubt that the determinants of foreign exchange futures prices and orange juice futures prices, for example, are very different. We must also recognize, however, that a common thread of understanding links futures contracts of all types. This chapter follows that common thread, while subsequent chapters explore the individual factors that affect prices for financial futures. Perhaps the most basic and most common factor affecting futures prices is the way in which their prices are quoted. Our discussion of futures prices begins with reading the price quotations that are available every day in *The Wall Street Journal*.

Futures market prices bear economically important relationships to other observable prices as well. An important goal of this chapter is to understand those relationships. The futures price for delivery of coffee in three months, for example, must be related to the spot price, or the current cash price, of coffee at a particular physical location. The **spot price** is the price of a good for immediate delivery. In a restaurant, for example, you buy a cup of coffee at the spot price. The spot price is also called the **cash price** or the **current price**.

This important difference between the cash price and the futures price is called the **basis**. Likewise, the futures price for delivery of coffee in three months must be related in some fashion to the futures price for delivery of coffee in six months. The difference in price for two futures contract expirations on the same commodity is an intracommodity spread. As we will see, the time spread can also be an economically important variable.

Because futures contracts call for the delivery of some good at a particular time in the future, we can be sure that the expectations of market participants help determine futures prices. If people believe that gold will sell for $50 per ounce in three months, then the price of the futures contract for delivery of gold in three months cannot be $100. The connection between futures prices and expected future spot prices is so strong that some market observers believe that they must be, or at least should be, equal.

Similarly, the price for storing the good underlying the futures contract helps determine the relationships among futures prices and the relationship between the futures price and the spot price. By storing goods, it is possible, in effect, to convert corn received in March into corn that can be delivered in June. The difference in price between the March corn futures and the June corn futures must, therefore, be related to the cost of storing corn.

All of these futures pricing issues are interconnected. The basis, the spreads, the expected future spot price, and the cost of storage all form a system of related concepts. This chapter describes the linkages among these concepts that are common to all futures contracts. The discussion begins with the futures prices themselves.

READING FUTURES PRICES

One of the most complete and widely available sources for futures prices is *The Wall Street Journal* (WSJ), which publishes futures prices daily. These prices are reported in a standardized format, as Figure 3.1 shows. The date shown near the top of Figure 3.1 is the day for which the prices were recorded. The publication date of the WSJ is the next business day. As the heading states, the open interest (to be discussed later) pertains to the preceding trading day. Figure 3.1 shows quotations for agricultural and metallurgical futures. In later chapters, we present quotations for financial futures. For each contract, the listing shows the commodity, the exchange where it is traded, the amount of the good in one contract, and the units in which prices are quoted. For example, the very first contract is for the corn contract traded by the CBOT. One contract is for 5,000 bushels and the prices are quoted in cents per bushel.

At this point a word of warning is appropriate. The information about the contracts shown with the prices is useful, but incomplete. For corn, the type of corn that is traded is not mentioned, nor is the delivery procedure. Further, the WSJ does not give information about daily price limits and it does not report the tick size. With so much information omitted, a trader should not trade based just on what the WSJ shows. To have a good insight into the price behavior and the price fluctuations of a contract requires additional information, such as that found in the *Commodity Trading Manual* published by the Chicago Board of Trade.

For each of the delivery months, the price listings have a row of data, with the first line going to the contract that matures next, also called the **nearby contract**. Each succeeding line pertains to another maturity month. Contracts that mature later are called **distant** or **deferred contracts**. The first three columns of prices give the opening, high, and low prices for each contract for the day of trading being reported.

The next price column records the **settlement price**, which is the price at which contracts are settled at the close of trading for the day. The settlement price is not always the last trade price of the day, as it would be with stocks. In Chapter 2, we examined the feature of daily settlement. All margin flows are based on the settlement price. If the settlement price brings a trader's equity below the level required for maintenance margin, then the trader will receive a margin call and will have to pay variation margin.

Futures Price Quotations **Figure 3.1**

FUTURES PRICES

Tuesday, April 23, 1996

Open Interest Reflects Previous Trading Day

GRAINS AND OILSEEDS

CORN (CBT) 5,000 bu.; cents per bu.

	Open	High	Low	Settle	Change	Lifetime High	Lifetime Low	Open Interest
May	473	479	469½	478½	+ 8½	479	259½	74,519
July	453	461	450	460½	+ 10¼	461	254	163,163
Sept	371½	375	369½	373¾	+ 3¾	391	260	55,979
Dec	335½	338	330	334	....	354	239	125,662
Mr97	341	342¼	336	339¾	− ½	357	279¼	12,932
May	343	343	339	341½	− ½	356	306	1,229
July	343	343	339½	340¾	− ¾	355	284	3,478
Dec	293	294	289	292½	+ ½	302	249¾	3,632

Est vol 100,000; vol Mn 94,934; open int 440,594, −8,850.

OATS (CBT) 5,000 bu.; cents per bu.

	Open	High	Low	Settle	Change	Lifetime High	Lifetime Low	Open Interest
May	252	258¾	249¼	258¾	+ 10	258¾	153½	1,858
July	248½	257½	248½	257½	+ 10	257½	165	4,884
Sept	226½	231	223	231	+ 8½	231½	163	3,663
Dec	227½	232½	223½	232¼	+ 8	232½	160	3,121
Mr97	227½	233½	227½	233½	+ 7	233½	197	214

Est vol 2,400; vol Mn 2,907; open int 13,740, +118.

SOYBEANS (CBT) 5,000 bu.; cents per bu.

	Open	High	Low	Settle	Change	Lifetime High	Lifetime Low	Open Interest
May	818	820	802	812¼	− 1¼	824	602	29,005
July	821½	829½	811½	822	+ ½	832½	599½	80,862
Aug	825	825½	811	820½	+ ½	829½	626	9,778
Sept	805	807	795	804	+ ¾	810	623	5,672
Nov	790	800	784	794	+ 2½	806	585	69,364
Ja97	800	800½	789	799¾	+ 4½	813	650	5,511
Mar	804	804	796	803	+ 2¾	816	679	1,702
May	800	805	798	805	+ 1	818	735	1,443
July	808	808	796	803¼	+ 1¼	820	633	1,966
Nov	719	720	713	717½	+ 4	734	601	1,592

Est vol 65,000; vol Mn 73,929; open int 206,895, +1,664.

SOYBEAN MEAL (CBT) 100 tons; $ per ton.

	Open	High	Low	Settle	Change	Lifetime High	Lifetime Low	Open Interest
May	257.10	259.80	254.00	256.90	....	259.80	181.50	18,766
July	262.00	263.40	258.00	260.90	− .10	263.90	183.00	50,879
Aug	262.50	263.00	258.20	261.00	− .70	263.00	189.50	9,944
Sept	258.20	258.50	255.00	258.00	+ .30	259.00	188.00	6,117
Oct	254.00	254.00	251.00	253.00	+ .30	255.00	190.00	3,542
Dec	253.50	254.00	250.50	253.40	+ .70	254.50	178.00	15,009
Ja97	253.50	254.00	250.50	252.70	+ 1.20	255.50	215.00	795
Mar	254.00	254.00	250.70	252.30	− .40	255.50	227.00	669
May	251.50	251.50	250.00	250.00	− 1.50	256.00	237.50	399

Est vol 25,000; vol Mn 23,759; open int 106,166, +1,698.

SOYBEAN OIL (CBT) 60,000 lbs.; cents per lb.

	Open	High	Low	Settle	Change	Lifetime High	Lifetime Low	Open Interest
May	26.85	26.85	26.38	26.62	− .10	27.85	23.50	17,065
July	27.18	27.24	26.75	27.06	− .03	27.90	23.88	46,493
Aug	27.35	27.37	27.00	27.21	− .06	27.90	24.28	8,449
Sept	27.55	27.55	27.15	27.40	− .04	27.85	24.49	4,256
Oct	27.50	27.53	27.20	27.49	− .03	28.02	24.65	2,908
Dec	27.90	27.92	27.48	27.79	− .02	28.25	24.45	15,188
Ja97	27.75	27.80	27.60	27.80	− .05	28.25	25.12	678
Mar	28.12	28.12	27.80	28.05	− .02	28.40	25.45	454
May		....	....	28.20	+ .03	28.45	25.65	201

Est vol 15,000; vol Mn 15,577; open int 95,713, −786.

WHEAT (CBT) 5,000 bu.; cents per bu.

	Open	High	Low	Settle	Change	Lifetime High	Lifetime Low	Open Interest
May	635	654	635	653½	+ 25½	654	379	9,109
July	609½	619½	602	615½	+ 21	619½	325	60,180
Sept	604	621	601	611	+ 18½	621	374	13,715
Dec	601	619	601	617½	+ 22½	619	362	15,119
Mr97	592	609	592	599	+ 17	609	456½	1,088
July	456	457	450	453	− 2½	465	365	1,081

Est vol 30,000; vol Mn 12,312; open int 100,388, −1,545.

WHEAT (KC) 5,000 bu.; cents per bu.

	Open	High	Low	Settle	Change	Lifetime High	Lifetime Low	Open Interest
May	684½	684½	676	684½	+ 25	684½	368	7,017
July	658¼	658¼	659	658¼	+ 25	658¼	330	21,987
Sept	640	645	631	644½	+ 24¼	645	387	6,776
Dec	630	637	620	630	+ 17	637	437	4,446
Mr97	610	620	610	615½	+ 16½	620	468½	788

Est vol 10,472; vol Mn 5,109; open int 41,022, −428.

WHEAT (MPLS) 5,000 bu.; cents per bu.

	Open	High	Low	Settle	Change	Lifetime High	Lifetime Low	Open Interest
May	82.65	82.90	82.65	82.80	− .10	82.90	73.50	1,223
July	82.65	82.80	82.50	82.80	− .10	82.80	73.75	572
Oct		....	....	79.55	+ .45	79.50	75.50	286
Dec	77.75	78.50	78.50	78.50	+ .15	78.50	75.00	1,510

Est vol 25,000; vol 12,658; open int 59,855, +788.

ORANGE JUICE (CTN) 15,000 lbs.; cents per lb.

	Open	High	Low	Settle	Change	Lifetime High	Lifetime Low	Open Interest
May	132.80	133.90	132.50	133.85	+ .65	138.00	106.50	7,797
July	131.35	132.50	130.60	132.45	+ 1.00	135.00	110.00	7,517
Sept	129.75	130.00	129.25	130.25	+ .35	137.00	113.00	2,952
Nov	126.00	126.00	125.50	125.80	− .10	135.50	117.00	946
Ja97	122.50	122.75	122.30	122.95	+ .15	135.50	117.50	3,065
Mar	124.50	124.50	123.50	124.95	− .05	138.00	120.00	188
May		....	....	126.95	− .05	131.00	119.60	136

Est vol 6,800; vol 5,187; open int 22,603, +311.

METALS AND PETROLEUM

COPPER-HIGH (Cmx.Div.NYM) 25,000 lbs.; cents per lb.

	Open	High	Low	Settle	Change	Lifetime High	Lifetime Low	Open Interest
Apr	123.70	123.70	123.10	123.25	− .45	127.80	110.50	1,540
May	122.05	123.20	121.60	121.70	− 1.05	126.00	107.00	16,250
June	121.70	121.70	120.90	120.60	− .65	122.00	109.00	1,274
July	120.10	120.60	119.30	119.50	− .65	122.90	105.50	16,174
Aug	118.80	118.80	118.80	118.30	− .70	119.50	108.00	565
Sept	118.30	118.30	117.00	117.20	− .75	121.00	105.25	3,885
Oct	116.40	116.40	116.40	116.10	− .65	119.00	108.00	492
Nov	115.00	115.00	115.00	115.50	− .65	116.30	107.00	362
Dec	114.70	114.70	113.80	114.00	− .65	118.80	106.00	5,772
Ja97		....	....	113.10	− .60	118.50	106.00	310
Feb		....	....	112.20	− .55	112.90	106.00	177
Mar	111.80	111.80	111.00	111.20	− .45	115.30	104.75	990
Apr		....	....	110.35	− .40	113.70	104.00	148
May		....	....	109.45	− .35	112.50	103.80	531
June		....	....	108.45	− .30	113.65	103.60	173
July		....	....	107.45	− .25	113.70	103.00	263
Sept		....	....	105.55	− .15	113.70	103.00	232

Est vol 13,000; vol Mn 8,593; open int 49,410, +282.

GOLD (Cmx.Div.NYM) 100 troy oz.; $ per troy oz.

	Open	High	Low	Settle	Change	Lifetime High	Lifetime Low	Open Interest
Apr	392.00	392.00	391.50	391.30	− .20	430.20	385.00	47
June	393.60	394.50	393.30	393.40	− .20	447.00	370.90	102,127
Aug	395.80	396.60	395.70	395.70	− .20	423.00	393.90	20,837
Oct	398.30	398.30	398.30	398.10	− .20	432.20	395.50	5,556
Dec	400.60	401.40	400.50	400.50	− .20	447.50	379.60	24,474
Fb97		....	....	402.90	− .20	428.00	403.50	5,125
Apr	406.00	406.00	406.00	405.40	− .20	428.00	403.50	4,899
June	408.60	408.60	408.60	407.90	− .30	456.00	407.00	6,721
Aug		....	....	410.40	− .30	414.50	414.50	1,005
Oct		....	....	412.90	− .30	426.50	413.30	211
Dec		....	....	415.40	− .30	477.00	402.00	7,401
Ju98		....	....	423.20	− .30	489.50	421.50	5,521
Dec		....	....	431.20	− .30	505.00	424.30	4,867
Ju99		....	....	439.30	− .30	520.00	442.00	3,701
Dec		....	....	455.10	− .30	506.00	439.00	3,520
Ju00		....	....	455.40	− .30	473.50	445.50	3,788
Dec		....	....	463.10	− .30	474.50	451.00	2,585

Est vol 16,000; vol Mn 20,789; open int 202,661, +2,993.

PLATINUM (NYM) 50 troy oz.; $ per troy oz.

	Open	High	Low	Settle	Change	Lifetime High	Lifetime Low	Open Interest
Apr	415.50	415.50	414.50	412.70	− 2.30	467.50	399.00	15
July	408.00	409.50	407.00	407.70	− 0.30	451.90	402.00	19,962
Oct	412.00	412.00	411.00	410.90	− 0.30	441.00	403.50	3,354
Ja97		....	....	413.70	− 0.30	442.00	408.00	1,077

Est vol 1,602; vol Mon 2,716; open int 25,362, −444.

SILVER (Cmx.Div.NYM) 5,000 troy oz.; cnts per troy oz.

	Open	High	Low	Settle	Change	Lifetime High	Lifetime Low	Open Interest
Apr		....	....	531.2	− 0.9	551.0	551.0	1
May	533.0	535.5	531.0	531.5	− 1.0	646.0	475.0	36,482
July	537.5	540.5	536.0	536.7	− 0.8	642.0	480.0	37,584
Sept	542.0	546.0	540.5	541.5	− 0.7	602.0	488.0	11,876
Dec	550.0	552.5	550.0	548.8	− 0.6	670.0	454.0	8,535
Mr97	557.0	561.0	556.0	556.4	− 0.5	611.0	544.0	3,320
May		....	....	561.3	− 0.5	606.0	557.0	779
Jly	569.5	569.5	569.5	566.3	− 0.5	655.0	550.0	1,248
Dec		....	....	579.5	− 0.5	695.0	502.0	1,331
Jl98		....	....	597.7	− 0.5	700.0	700.0	175
Dec	610.0	610.0	610.0	611.7	− 0.5	734.0	584.0	245
Jl99		....	....	633.7	− 0.5	660.0	637.0	297

Source: From *The Wall Street Journal,* April 24, 1996, p. C16. Reprinted by permission of *The Wall Street Journal,*

Typically, the settlement price will equal the last trading price for the day, but they are not always the same. Most exchanges have a settlement committee for each commodity, usually comprised of members of the exchange who trade that commodity. This committee meets immediately at the close of trading to establish the settlement price. The committee is responsible for establishing a settlement price that fairly indicates the value of the futures contract at the close of trading. When trading is active and prices are stable at the end of the day, the settlement committee has an easy job. The prices recorded from trades will be continuous, fluctuating little from trade to trade. In such cases the committee may simply allow the final trading price to be the settlement price. Therefore, in many cases the price for the last trade and the settlement price are the same price, but they are conceptually distinct.

Difficulties arise for the settlement committee, however, when a contract has little trading activity. Imagine that the last trade for a particular maturity of a given commodity occurred three hours before the close of trading and that significant information pertaining to that commodity was discovered after that last trade. In this example, the last actual trade price for the contract does not represent what the true economic price would be at the close of trading. In such a case, the settlement committee performs an important function by establishing a settlement price that differs from the price on the last recorded trade.

To establish a settlement price, the members use information on other maturity months for the same commodity. The difference between prices of contracts for different delivery months is very stable, at least relative to the futures prices themselves. So the settlement committee will use that price difference, or spread, to establish the settlement price on the contract that was not recently traded. Even more drastic situations might arise from time to time, but the settlement committee must establish a settlement price even when there is very little information to go on. Having this function performed by a committee helps rule out the possibility that an inaccurate settlement price might be chosen to generate a windfall gain for the person choosing the settlement price.

The next column, after the settlement price, is denoted as "Change." The value in this column is the change in the settlement price from the preceding day to the current day, the day for which prices are reported. The next two columns show the lifetime high and low prices for each contract. Figure 3.1 indicates how radically prices may differ for some contracts over their lives. For the contracts about to mature, the difference between the lifetime highs and lows can be enormous. For the contracts that have just been listed, there has been little time for the lifetime high and low prices to diverge radically.

The final column in Figure 3.1 is headed by the title of "Open Interest," which shows the total number of contracts outstanding for each maturity month. **Open interest** is the number of futures contracts for which delivery is currently obligated. To understand the meaning of this more clearly, assume that the December 1997 widget contract has just been listed for trading, but that the contract has not traded yet. At this point, the open interest in the contract is zero. Trading begins and the first contract is bought. This purchase necessarily means that some other trader sold. This transaction creates one contract of open interest, because there is one contract now in existence for which delivery is obligated.

Subsequent trading can increase or decrease the open interest, as Table 3.1 shows for trading in the incredibly popular widget contract. At $t = 0$, trading opens on the widget contract. The open interest is zero as is volume to date. At $t = 1$, Trader A buys and Trader B sells one widget contract. This transaction creates one contract of volume. After the transaction, the open interest is one contract, because one contract is obligated for delivery, as Table 3.1 shows. At $t = 2$, Trader C buys and Trader

	How Trading Affects Open Interest	Table 3.1
Time	**Action**	**Open Interest**
$t = 0$	Trading opens for the popular widget contract.	0
$t = 1$	Trader A buys and Trader B sells 1 widget contract.	1
$t = 2$	Trader C buys and Trader D sells 3 widget contracts.	4
$t = 3$	Trader A sells and Trader D buys 1 widget contract.	3
	(Trader A has offset 1 contract and is out of the market.	
	Trader D has offset 1 contract and is now short 2 contracts.)	
$t = 4$	Trader C sells and Trader E buys 1 widget contract.	3

Ending Positions	**Trader**	**Long Position**	**Short Position**
	B		1
	C	2	
	D		2
	E	1	
	All Traders	3	3

D sells three widget contracts. The volume resulting from these trades is three contracts and the open interest is now four contracts. At $t = 3$, Trader A sells and Trader D buys one widget contract, creating one more contract of volume. Notice here that Trader A offsets his one contract through a reversing trade. After this offsetting transaction, Trader A is out of the market. Trader D has reversed one of her three contracts. This reduces the open interest by one contract. At $t = 4$, Trader C sells and Trader E buys one widget contract, for one contract of volume. With this transaction, Trader C reverses one contract, but Trader E enters the market. Because Trader E, in effect, takes the place of Trader C for this one contract, the open interest remains at three. The bottom panel of the table summarizes each trader's position and shows how the open interest remains at three contracts.

When a contract is distant from maturity, it tends to have relatively little open interest. As the contract approaches maturity, the open interest increases. Most often the contract closest to delivery, the nearby contract, has the highest level of open interest. As the nearby contract comes very close to maturity, however, the open interest falls. This is due to the fact that traders close their positions to avoid actual delivery. As we saw in Chapter 2, actual delivery is fairly unusual. When the futures contract matures, all traders with remaining open interest must make or take delivery, and the open interest goes to zero. Recall, also, that the open interest figures reported in the WSJ pertain to the day preceding the day for which prices are reported. Figure 3.2 shows the pattern of open interest for the December 1989 S&P 500 futures contract over its life, and Figure 3.3 shows the pattern of trading volume for the same contract. (This contract was the nearby contract at the time of the mini-crash of October 13, 1989.) The open interest and volume of trading follow a predictable pattern, such as the one shown in these two figures. Notice that the peak open interest occurs when the contract has about two to three months remaining until expiration.

In Figure 3.1, beneath the lines for each of the contract maturities, the WSJ reports more trading information. The figure shows the estimated volume for all maturities for a given commodity, followed by the actual volume for the preceding day. Next, the open interest for all contract maturities is shown. Finally, the last number reports the change in the open interest since the preceding day. We

Figure 3.2   DEC 1989 S&P 500 Futures Open Interest

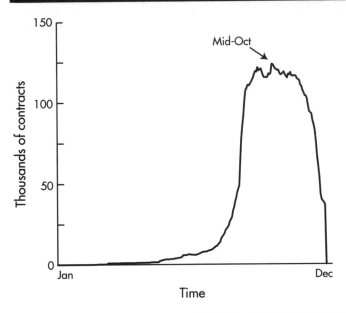

Figure 3.3   DEC 1989 S&P 500 Futures Trading Volume

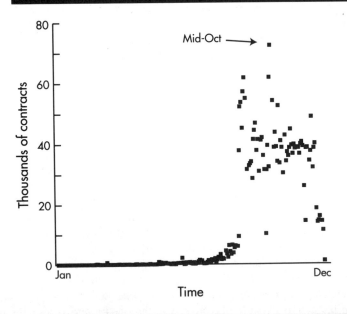

may also note that it is possible for the volume of trading to exceed the number of contracts of open interest. This occurs when trading activity is particularly heavy for a given commodity on a certain day.

THE BASIS AND SPREADS

In this section, we analyze relationships between two prices. The **basis** is the relationship between the cash price of a good and the futures price for the same good. We also consider spreads. A **spread** is the difference between two futures prices. If the two prices are for futures contracts on the same underlying good, but with different expiration dates, the spread is an **intracommodity spread**. If the two futures prices that form a spread are futures prices for two underlying goods, such as a wheat futures and a corn futures, then the spread is an **intercommodity spread**.

The Basis

The basis receives a great deal of attention in futures trading. The **basis** is the current cash price of a particular commodity at a specified location minus the price of a particular futures contract for the same commodity:

$$\text{Basis} = \text{Current Cash Price} - \text{Futures Price}$$

Several features of this definition require explanation. First, the definition of the basis depends upon a cash price of a commodity at a specific location. The cash price of corn, for example, might differ between Kansas City and Chicago, so the basis for those two locations will also differ. Normally, one good cannot sell for different prices in two markets. If such a good had two prices, a trader could buy the commodity in the cheaper market and sell it in the market with the higher price, thereby reaping an arbitrage profit. Prices for corn in Chicago and Kansas City can differ, of course, because of the expense of transporting corn from one location to another. If corn is grown near Chicago, then we might reasonably expect the price of corn in Chicago to be lower than the price of corn in Kansas City. So the basis calculated in considering futures prices may differ, depending upon the geographic location of the spot price that is used to compute the basis.

Usually people speaking of the basis are referring to the difference between the cash price and the nearby futures contract. There is, however, a basis for each outstanding futures contract, and this basis will often differ in systematic ways, depending upon the maturities of the individual futures contracts. Table 3.2 shows spot and futures gold prices for July 11, and illustrates this phenomenon. The cash, or spot, price is the London A.M. fix, or morning quotation, so the basis pertains to London. The futures prices are from the COMEX. The right column shows the basis for each futures contract. The basis is negative for all delivery months in this example. The chart of the basis shows that it is possible to contract for the future sale or purchase of gold at a price that exceeds the current cash price. The difference between the current cash price of $353.70 per ounce and the price of the more distant futures contracts is striking, as much as $37.80 per ounce for the most distant DEC contract.

Futures markets can exhibit a pattern of either normal or inverted prices. In a **normal market**, prices for more distant futures are higher than for nearby futures. For example, the gold prices in Table 3.2 represent a normal market. In an **inverted market**, distant futures prices are lower than the prices for contracts nearer to expiration. The interpretation of the basis can be very important,

Table 3.2	Gold Prices and the Basis (July 11)	
Contract	Prices	The Basis
CASH	353.70	
JUL (this year)	354.10	−.40
AUG	355.60	−1.90
OCT	359.80	−6.10
DEC	364.20	−10.50
FEB (next year)	368.70	−15.00
APR	373.00	−19.30
JUN	377.50	−23.80
AUG	381.90	−28.20
OCT	386.70	−33.00
DEC	391.50	−37.80

particularly for agricultural commodities. For many commodities, the fact that the harvest comes at a certain time each year introduces seasonal components into the series of cash prices. Many traders believe that understanding these seasonal factors can be very beneficial for speculation and hedging. Also, as will become clear, the basis, such as that shown in Table 3.2, can be used as a valuable information source to predict future spot prices of the commodities that underlie the futures contracts.

A further point about the basis emerges from a consideration of Table 3.2. Notice that the basis for the nearby contract is only −$.40, about one-thousandth of the cash price. There is good reason that it should be so small. The JUL contract is extremely close to delivery on the date in question, July 11. At delivery the futures price and the cash price must be equal, except for minor discrepancies due to transportation and other transaction costs. If someone were to trade the JUL contract on the day in question, the trade would be for the delivery of gold within three weeks. The price of gold for delivery within three weeks must closely approximate the current spot price of gold.

When the futures contract is at expiration, the futures price and the spot price of gold must be the same. The basis must be zero, again subject to the discrepancy due to transaction costs. This behavior of the basis over time is known as **convergence**, as Figures 3.4 and 3.5 illustrate. In Figure 3.4, the cash price lies above the futures price. As time progresses, and the futures contract approaches maturity, the basis narrows. At the maturity of the futures contract, the basis is zero, consistent with the no-arbitrage requirement that the futures price and cash price be equal at the maturity of the futures contract. Figure 3.5 shows the basis itself, corresponding to the prices in Figure 3.4. The basis is positive, but declines to zero as the futures contract approaches maturity.

Figures 3.6a and b illustrates one other feature of the basis that is very important for futures trading. Figure 3.6a shows prices for the MAR S&P 500 futures contract. The graph covers the range from 300 to 400, a 100-point range within which the contract traded between July and its expiration in March of the next year. Figure 3.6b illustrates how the basis for this contract behaved over the same time interval. This bottom panel also covers a 100-point scale to make the two graphs comparable.

As the graph dramatically reveals, the fluctuation in the basis was much less than the range of fluctuation in the futures price itself. This is almost always the case. The basis is almost always much more stable than the futures price or the cash price, when those prices are considered in isolation. The futures price may oscillate and the cash price may swing widely, but the basis (cash − futures

Converging Cash and Futures Prices   **Figure 3.4**

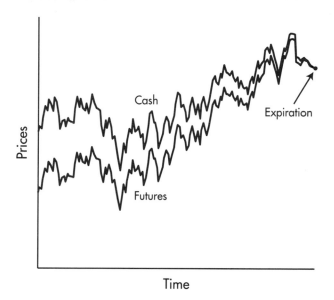

Convergence of the Basis to Zero   **Figure 3.5**

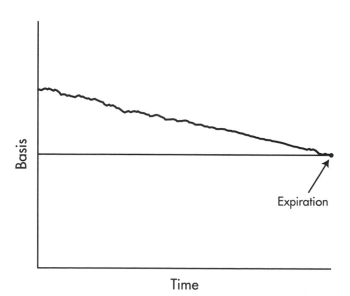

Figure 3.6a   S&P 500 Cash and Basis Cash Market Value of S&P 500

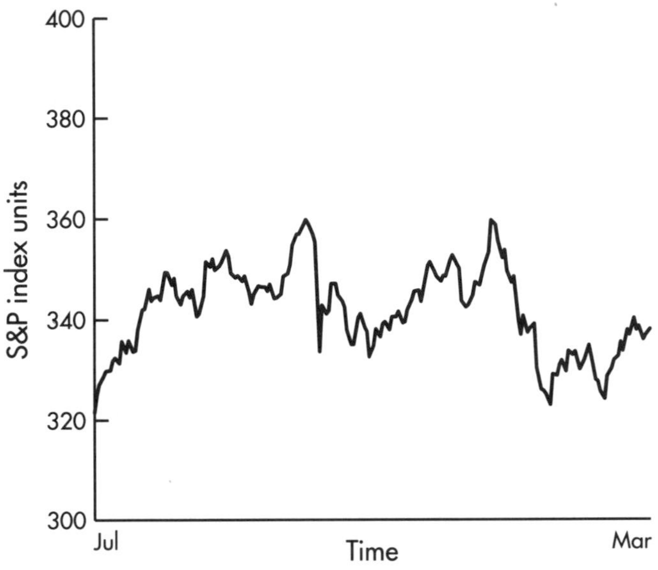

Figure 3.6b   S&P 500 Basis

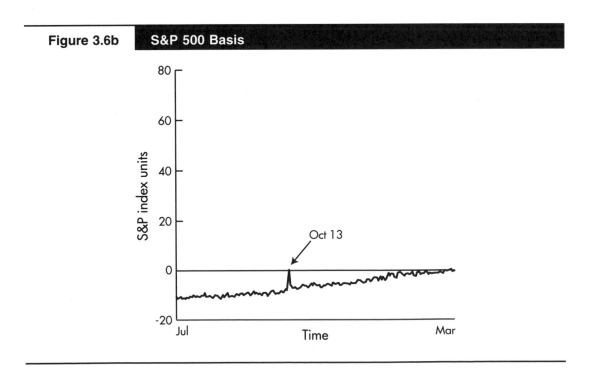

price) tends to be relatively steady. The relatively low variability of the basis is very important for hedging and for certain types of speculation, as will be discussed in Chapter 4.

Spreads

Just as there is an important relationship between each futures contract and the cash price of the commodity, the relationship among futures prices on the same good, an intracommodity spread, is also important, because it indicates the relative price differentials for a commodity to be delivered at two points in time. As we will see, there are strong economic relationships that govern the permissible time spreads that may exist between any two futures contracts.

Spread relationships are important for speculators. Much speculation involves some kind of spread position – the holding of two or more related futures contracts. If a trader hopes to use futures markets to earn speculative profits, an understanding of spread relationships is essential. Since most speculation uses spreads, the search for a profit turns on an ability to identify spread relationships that are economically unjustified. While the understanding of the spread relationships in a particular commodity requires considerable knowledge about the commodity itself, certain general principles apply to all spreads.

Figure 3.7 shows the spread between the S&P 500 futures contract for JUN of this year and the MAR contract for next year, computed here as the June price minus the March price. The time period here is the same used in Figures 3.6a and b. Thus, we can see the stability of the spread in Figure 3.7 compared to the price itself in Figures 3.6a and b.

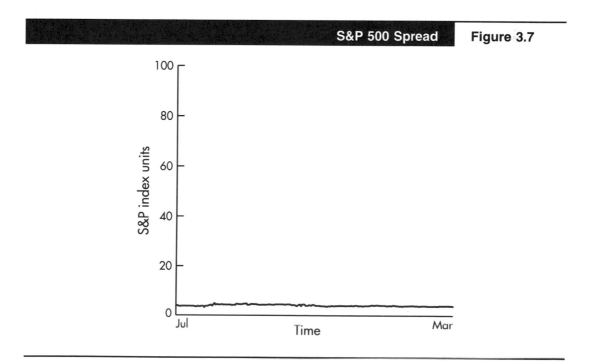

S&P 500 Spread   **Figure 3.7**

MODELS OF FUTURES PRICES

In this section, we consider two models of futures prices. The first of these is the cost-of-carry model. According to this model, futures prices depend on the cash price of a commodity and the cost of storing the underlying good from the present to the delivery date of the futures contract. The second model is the expectations model. According to this view, the futures price today equals the cash price that traders expect to prevail for the underlying good on the delivery date of the futures contract. For example, the futures price in January for the JUL contract is the market's January estimate of what the price of corn will be in July when the futures contract expires.

To explore these models, we employ the concept of arbitrage. We begin by assuming that prices in the market do not allow any arbitrage profits. Under this assumption, we ask what futures pricing relationships are permissible. For the sake of simplicity, we begin by assuming that futures markets are perfect. A **perfect market** is a market with no transaction costs and no restrictions on free contracting between two parties. Thus, the analysis begins under the assumptions of an idealized world – a world that allows no arbitrage and that includes no market frictions. Gradually, we develop a more realistic analysis by relaxing these assumptions. This approach allows us to start the analysis within a fairly simple environment and to add complications after we explore the most essential features of the pricing relationships.

The Cost-of-Carry Model in Perfect Markets

In this section, we use the concept of arbitrage introduced in Chapter 1 to explore the cost-of-carry model or carrying charge theory of futures prices. The **cost-of-carry** or **carrying charge** is the total cost to carry a good forward in time. For example, wheat on hand in June can be carried forward to, or stored until, December.

Carrying charges fall into four basic categories: storage costs, insurance costs, transportation costs, and financing costs. Storage costs include the cost of warehousing the commodity in the appropriate facility. While storage seems to apply most clearly to physical goods, such as wheat or lumber, it is also possible to store financial instruments. In many cases, the owner of a financial instrument will leave the instrument in a bank vault. For many goods in storage, insurance is also necessary. For example, stored lumber should be protected against fire, and stored wheat should be insured against water damage.

The carrying charges also include, in some cases, transportation costs. Wheat in a railroad siding in Kansas must be carried to delivery in two senses. It must be stored until the appropriate delivery time for a given futures contract, but it must also be physically carried to the appropriate place for delivery. As will become obvious, transportation costs between different locations determine price differentials between those locations. Without question, transportation charges play different roles for different commodities. Transporting wheat from Kansas to Chicago could be an important expense. By contrast, delivery of Treasury bills against a futures contract is accomplished by a wire transfer costing only a few dollars. In almost all cases, the most significant carrying charge in the futures market is the financing cost. For most situations, financing the good under storage overwhelms the other costs.

The carrying charge reflects only the charges involved in carrying a commodity from one time or one place to another. The carrying charges do not include the value of the commodity itself. So, if gold costs $400 per ounce and the financing rate is 1 percent per month, the financing charge for carrying the gold forward is $4 per month (1% × $400).

Most participants in the futures markets face a financing charge on a short-term basis that is equal to the repo rate. The **repo rate** is the interest rate on repurchase agreements. In a **repurchase agreement** a person sells securities at one point in time, with the understanding that they will be repurchased at a certain price at a later time. Most repurchase agreements are for one day only and are known, accordingly, as overnight repos. The repo rate is relatively low, exceeding the rate on Treasury bills by only a small amount.[1] The financing cost for such goods is so low because anyone wishing to finance a commodity may offer the commodity itself as collateral for the loan. Further, most of the participants in the market tend to be financial institutions of one type or another who have low financing costs anyway, at least for very short-term obligations.

Cash and Futures Pricing Relationships. The carrying charges just described are important because they play a crucial role in determining pricing relationships between spot and futures prices as well as the relationships among prices of futures contracts of different maturities. For present purposes, we will assume that the only carrying charge is the financing cost at an interest rate of 10 percent per year. As an example, consider the prices and the accompanying transactions shown in Table 3.3.

The transactions in Table 3.3 represent a successful cash-and-carry arbitrage. This is a **cash-and-carry arbitrage** because the trader buys the cash good and carries it to the expiration of the futures contract. The trader traded at $t = 0$ to guarantee a riskless profit without investment. There was no investment, because there was no cash flow at $t = 0$. The trader merely borrowed funds to purchase the gold and to carry it forward. The profit in these transactions was certain once the trader made the transactions at $t = 0$. As these transactions show, to prevent arbitrage the futures price of the gold should have been $440 or less. With a futures price of $440, for example, the transactions in Table 3.3 would yield a zero profit. From this example, we can infer the following general rule:

Cash-and-Carry Gold Arbitrage Transactions	Table 3.3

Prices for the Analysis

Spot price of gold	$400
Future price of gold (for delivery in 1 year)	$450
Interest rate	10%

Transaction		Cash Flow
$t = 0$	Borrow $400 for one year at 10%.	+$400
	Buy 1 ounce of gold in the spot market for $400.	−400
	Sell a futures contract for $450 for delivery of 1 ounce in 1 year.	0
	Total Cash Flow	$0
$t = 1$	Remove the gold from storage.	$0
	Deliver the ounce of gold against the futures contract.	+450
	Repay loan, including interest.	−440
	Total Cash Flow	+$10

Cost-of-Carry Rule 1:

The futures price must be less than or equal to the spot price of the commodity plus the carrying charges necessary to carry the spot commodity forward to delivery.

We can express Rule 1 mathematically as follows:

$$F_{0,t} \leq S_0(1 + C) \tag{3.1}$$

where:

$F_{0,t}$ = the futures price at $t = 0$ for delivery at time = t
S_0 = the spot price at $t = 0$
C = the cost-of-carry, expressed as a fraction of the spot price, necessary to carry
     the good forward from the present to the delivery date on the futures

As we have seen, if prices do not conform to cost-of-carry rule 1, a trader can borrow funds, buy the spot commodity with the borrowed funds, sell the futures contract, and carry the commodity forward to deliver against the futures contract. These transactions would generate a certain profit without investment, or an arbitrage profit. There would be a certain profit, because it is guaranteed by the sale of the futures contract. Also, there would be no investment, since the funds needed to carry out the strategy were borrowed and the cost of using those funds was included in the calculation of the carrying charge. Such opportunities cannot exist in a rational market. The cash-and-carry arbitrage opportunity arises because the spot price is too low relative to the futures price.

We have seen that an arbitrage opportunity arises if the spot price is too low relative to the futures price. As we now see, the spot price might also be too high relative to the futures price. If the spot price is too high, we have a reverse cash-and-carry arbitrage opportunity. As the name implies, the steps necessary to exploit the arbitrage opportunity are just the opposite of those in the cash-and-carry arbitrage strategy. As an example of the reverse cash-and-carry strategy, consider the prices for gold and the accompanying transactions in Table 3.4.

In these transactions, the arbitrageur sells the gold short. As in the stock market, a short seller borrows the good from another trader and must later repay it. Once the good is borrowed, the short seller sells it and takes the money from the sale. (The transaction is called short selling because one sells a good that he or she does not actually own.) In this example, the short seller has the use of all of the proceeds from the short sale, which are invested at the interest rate of 10 percent. The trader also buys a futures contract to ensure that he or she can acquire the gold needed to repay the lender at the expiration of the futures in one year.

Notice that these transactions guarantee an arbitrage profit. Once the transactions at $t = 0$ are completed, the $12 profit at $t = 1$ year is certain. Also, the trader had no net cash flow at $t = 0$, so the strategy required no investment. To make this arbitrage opportunity impossible, the spot and futures prices must obey cost-of-carry rule 2.

Cost-of-Carry Rule 2:

The futures price must be equal to or greater than the spot price plus the cost of carrying the good to the futures delivery date.

Reverse Cash-and-Carry Gold Arbitrage Transactions	Table 3.4

Prices for the Analysis

Spot price of gold	$420
Future price of gold (for delivery in 1 year)	$450
Interest rate	10%

Transaction		Cash Flow
$t = 0$	Sell 1 ounce of gold short.	+$420
	Lend the $420 for 1 year at 10%.	−420
	Buy 1 ounce of gold futures for delivery in 1 year.	0
	Total Cash Flow	$0
$t = 1$	Collect proceeds from the loan ($420 × 1.1).	+$462
	Accept delivery on the futures contract.	−450
	Use gold from futures delivery to repay short sale.	0
	Total Cash Flow	+$12

Expressing this rule mathematically with the notation we introduced earlier:

$$F_{0,t} \geq S_0(1 + C) \tag{3.2}$$

If prices do not obey this rule, there will be an arbitrage opportunity. Table 3.5 summarizes the transactions necessary to conduct the cash-and-carry and the reverse cash-and-carry strategies.

To prevent arbitrage, we have seen that the two following rules must hold:

To prevent cash-and-carry arbitrage	$F_{0,t} \leq S_0(1 + C)$	(3.1)
To prevent reverse cash-and-carry arbitrage	$F_{0,t} \geq S_0(1 + C)$	(3.2)

Together, Equations 3.1 and 3.2 imply cost-of-carry rule 3:

Transactions for Arbitrage Strategies	Table 3.5

Market	Cash-and-Carry	Reverse Cash-and-Carry
Debt	Borrow funds.	Lend short sale proceeds.
Physical	Buy asset and store; deliver against futures.	Sell asset short; secure proceeds from short sale.
Futures	Sell futures.	Buy futures; accept delivery; return physical asset to honor short sale commitment.

Cost-of-Carry Rule 3:

The futures price must equal the spot price plus the cost of carrying the spot commodity forward to the delivery date of the futures contract.

Expressing rule 3 mathematically, we have:

$$F_{0,t} = S_0(1 + C) \qquad (3.3)$$

Notice that the relationship of Equation 3.3 was derived under the following assumptions: Markets are perfect; that is, they have no transaction costs and no restrictions on the use of proceeds from short sales. It must be acknowledged that this argument explicitly excludes transaction costs. Transaction costs exist on both sides of the market, for purchase or sale of the futures. In many markets, however, transaction costs for short selling are considerably more expensive, which limits the applicability of the reverse cash-and-carry strategy.

Spreads and the Cost-of-Carry. These same cost-of-carry relationships also determine the price relationships that can exist between futures contracts on the same good that differ in maturity. As an example, consider the prices and accompanying arbitrage transactions shown in Table 3.6.

As this example shows, the spread between two futures contracts cannot exceed the cost of carrying the good from one delivery date forward to the next, as cost-of-carry rule 4 states.

Cost-of-Carry Rule 4:

The distant futures price must be less than or equal to the nearby futures price plus the cost of carrying the commodity from the nearby delivery date to the distant delivery date.

Table 3.6	Gold Forward Cash-and-Carry Arbitrage

Prices for the Analysis

Futures price for gold expiring in 1 year	$400
Futures price for gold expiring in 2 years	$450
Interest rate (to cover from year 1 to year 2)	10%

Transaction		Cash Flow
$t = 0$	Buy the futures expiring in 1 year.	+$0
	Sell the futures expiring in 2 years.	0
	Contract to borrow $400 at 10% for year 1 to year 2.	0
	Total Cash Flow	$0
$t = 1$	Borrow $400 for 1 year at 10% as contracted at $t = 0$.	+$400
	Take delivery on the futures contract.	−400
	Begin to store gold for 1 year.	0
	Total Cash Flow	$0
$t = 2$	Deliver gold to honor futures contract.	+450
	Repay loan ($400 × 1.1).	−440
	Total Cash Flow	+$10

Expressing rule 4 mathematically, we have:

$$F_{0,d} \leq F_{0,n}(1 + C), \qquad d > n \tag{3.4}$$

where:

$F_{0,d}$ = the futures price at $t = 0$ for the distant delivery contract maturing at $t = d$
$F_{0,n}$ = the futures price at $t = 0$ for the nearby delivery contract maturing at $t = n$
C = the percentage cost of carrying the good from $t = n$ to $t = d$

As we have seen, if this relationship did not hold, a trader could buy the nearby futures contract and sell the distant contract. The trader would then accept delivery on the nearby contract and carry the good until the delivery of the distant contract, thereby making a profit.

To complete our argument, we analyze what happens if the nearby futures price is too high relative to the distant futures price. To conduct the arbitrage in this case, consider the gold prices and arbitrage transactions shown in Table 3.7.

Thus, forward reverse cash-and-carry arbitrage is possible if the nearby futures price is too high relative to the distant futures price. To exclude this arbitrage opportunity, prices must conform to cost-of-carry rule 5.

Gold Forward Reverse Cash-and-Carry Arbitrage	Table 3.7

Prices for the Analysis

Futures price for gold expiring in 1 year	$440
Futures price for gold expiring in 2 years	$450
Interest rate (to cover from year 1 to year 2)	10%

Transaction		Cash Flow
$t = 0$	Sell the futures expiring in 1 year.	+$0
	Buy the futures expiring in 2 years.	0
	Contract to lend $440 at 10% from year 1 to year 2.	0
	Total Cash Flow	$0
$t = 1$	Borrow 1 ounce of gold for 1 year.	$0
	Deliver gold against the expiring futures.	+440
	Invest proceeds from delivery for 1 year.	−440
	Total Cash Flow	$0
$t = 2$	Accept delivery on expiring futures.	−$450
	Repay 1 ounce of borrowed gold.	0
	Collect on loan of $440 made at $t = 1$.	+484
	Total Cash Flow	+$34

Cost-of-Carry Rule 5:
   The nearby futures price plus the cost of carrying the commodity from the nearby delivery date to the distant delivery date cannot exceed the distant futures price.

Expressing cost-of-carry rule 5 mathematically, we have:

$$F_{0,d} \geq F_{0,n}(1 + C), \qquad d > n \tag{3.5}$$

   From our two arbitrage arguments in Tables 3.6 and 3.7, we have derived the rules expressed in Equations 3.4 and 3.5. To exclude forward:

Cash-and-Carry Arbitrage	$F_{0,d} \leq F_{0,n}(1 + C), \qquad d > n$	(3.4)
Reverse Cash-and-Carry Arbitrage	$F_{0,d} \geq F_{0,n}(1 + C), \qquad d > n$	(3.5)

Following the same pattern of argument we used for spot prices and futures prices, we see that Equations 3.4 and 3.5 imply cost-of-carry rule 6.

Cost-of-Carry Rule 6:
   The distant futures price must equal the nearby futures price plus the cost of carrying the commodity from the nearby to the distant delivery date.

We can express cost-of-carry rule 6 mathematically as follows:

$$F_{0,d} = F_{0,n}(1 + C), \qquad d > n \tag{3.6}$$

If these relationships were ever violated, profit-hungry traders would immediately recognize the chance and trade until prices adjusted to eliminate all of the arbitrage opportunities.

Summary. All of the cost-of-carry relationships explored to this point assumed that markets are perfect. In particular, we assumed that they allowed unrestricted short selling. We made heavy use of these assumptions. For example, we assumed that the borrowing and lending rates were equal, that we could sell gold short and use 100 percent of the proceeds from the short sale, and that it was possible to contract to borrow and lend at forward rates. All of these assumptions require qualifications, which the next section will develop.
   The basic rules developed in this section provide a very useful framework for analyzing relationships between cash and futures prices, on the one hand, and spreads between futures prices, on the other. Cost-of-carry rule 3 and Equation 3.3 express the basic cash-futures relationship:

$$F_{0,t} = S_0(1 + C) \tag{3.3}$$

Cost-of-carry rule 6 and Equation 3.6 express the relationship for two futures prices:

$$F_{0,d} = F_{0,n}(1 + C), \qquad d > n \tag{3.6}$$

Notice that these two equations have the same form. We therefore use Equation 3.3 to make a final point to summarize the cost-of-carry model in perfect markets. Equation 3.7 says that the cost-of-carry in the perfect market we have been considering equals the ratio of the futures price to the spot price minus 1. In Equation 3.7, the "C" is the **implied repo rate** – the interest rate implied by the difference between the cash and futures prices. Solving Equation 3.3 for the cost-of-carry C, we have:

$$C = F_{0,t}/S_0 - 1 \qquad\qquad\qquad (3.7)$$

In a well-functioning market, the implied repo rate must equal the actual repo rate. As we have seen in this section, deviations from this relationship lead to arbitrage opportunities in a perfect market. We now turn to consider the qualifications to the basic conclusion that are required by market imperfections.

The Cost-of-Carry Model in Imperfect Markets

In real markets, four market imperfections operate to complicate and disturb the relationships of Equations 3.3 and 3.6. First, traders face transaction costs. Second, restrictions on short-selling frustrate reverse cash-and-carry strategies. Third, borrowing and lending rates are not generally equal as the assumption of perfect markets would imply. Finally, some goods cannot be stored, so they cannot be carried forward to delivery. This section considers each of these in turn.

The main effect of these market imperfections is to require adjustments in the identities expressed by Equations 3.3 and 3.6. Market imperfections do not invalidate the basic framework we have been building. Instead of being able to state an equality as we did in the perfect markets framework leading to Equations 3.3 and 3.6, we will find that market imperfections introduce a certain indeterminacy into the relationship.

Direct Transaction Costs. In actual markets, traders face a variety of direct transaction costs. First, the trader must pay a fee to have an order executed. For a trader off the floor of the exchange, these fees include brokerage commissions and various exchange fees. Even members of the exchange must pay a fee to the exchange for each trade. Second, in every market, there is a bid-asked spread. A market maker on the floor of the exchange must try to sell at a higher price (the **asked price**) than the price at which he or she is willing to buy (the **bid price**). The difference between the asked price and the bid price is the **bid-asked spread**. In our discussion, we will assume that these transaction costs are some fixed percentage of the transaction amount, T. For simplicity, we assume that the transaction costs apply to the spot market, but not to the futures market.

To illustrate the impact of transaction costs, we use the same prices with which we began our analysis in perfect markets. Now, however, we consider transaction costs of 3 percent. With transaction costs, our previous arbitrage strategy of buying the good and carrying it to delivery will not work. Table 3.8 shows the results of this attempted arbitrage. With transaction costs, the attempted arbitrage results in a certain loss, not an arbitrage profit.

We would have to pay $400 as before to acquire the good, plus transaction costs of 3 percent for a total outlay of $400(1 + T) = \$412$. We would then have to finance this total until delivery for a cost of $\$412(1.1) = \$453.20$. In return, we would only receive $450 upon the delivery of the futures contract. Given these prices, it clearly does not pay to attempt this cash-and-carry arbitrage. As Table 3.8 shows, these attempted arbitrage transactions generate a certain loss of $3.20. With transaction

Table 3.8	Attempted Cash-and-Carry Gold Arbitrage Transactions

Prices for the Analysis

Spot price of gold	$400
Future price of gold (for delivery in 1 year)	$450
Interest rate	10%
Transaction cost (T)	3%

Transaction		Cash Flow
$t = 0$	Borrow $412 for 1 year at 10%.	+$412
	Buy 1 ounce of gold in the spot market for $400 and pay 3% transaction costs, to total $412.	−412
	Sell a futures contract for $450 for delivery of 1 ounce in 1 year.	0
	Total Cash Flow	$0
$t = 1$	Remove the gold from storage.	$0
	Deliver the ounce of gold to close futures contract.	+450.00
	Repay loan, including interest.	−453.20
	Total Cash Flow	−$3.20

costs of 3 percent and the same spot price of $400, the futures price would have to exceed $453.20 to make the arbitrage attractive. To see why this is so, consider the cash outflows and inflows. We pay the spot price plus the transaction costs, $S_0(1 + T)$, to acquire the good. Carrying the good to delivery costs $S_0(1 + T)(1 + C)$. These costs include acquiring the good and carrying it to the delivery date of the futures. In our example, the total cost is:

$$S_0(1 + T)(1 + C) = \$400(1.03)(1.1) = \$453.20$$

Thus, to break even, the futures transaction must yield $453.20. We can write this more formally as:

$$F_{0,t} \leq S_0(1 + T)(1 + C) \tag{3.8}$$

If prices follow Equation 3.8, the cash-and-carry arbitrage opportunity will not be available. Notice that Equation 3.8 has the same form as Equation 3.1, but Equation 3.8 includes transaction costs.

In our discussion of the cost-of-carry model in perfect markets, we saw that futures prices could not be too high relative to spot prices. Otherwise, arbitrage opportunities would be available, as we saw in Table 3.4. We now explore the transactions as shown in Table 3.4, except we include the transaction costs of 3 percent. Table 3.9 shows these transactions.

Including transaction costs in the analysis gives a loss on the same transactions that were profitable with no transaction costs. In the original transactions of Table 3.4 with the same prices, the profit was $12. For perfect markets, Equation 3.2 gave the no-arbitrage conditions for the reverse cash-and-carry arbitrage strategy.

Attempted Reverse Cash-and-Carry Gold Arbitrage	Table 3.9

Prices for the Analysis

Spot price of gold	$420
Future price of gold (for delivery in 1 year)	$450
Interest rate	10%
Transaction costs (T)	3%

Transaction		Cash Flow
$t = 0$	Sell 1 ounce of gold short, paying 3% transaction costs.	+$407.40
	Receive $420(.97) = $407.40.	
	Lend the $407.40 for 1 year at 10%.	−407.40
	Buy 1 ounce of gold futures for delivery in 1 year.	0
	Total Cash Flow	$0
$t = 1$	Collect loan proceeds ($407.40 × 1.1).	+$448.14
	Accept gold delivery on the futures contract.	−450.00
	Use gold from futures delivery to repay short sale.	0
	Total Cash Flow	−$1.86

$$F_{0,t} \geq S_0(1 + C) \tag{3.2}$$

Including transaction costs, we have:

$$F_{0,t} \geq S_0(1 - T)(1 + C) \tag{3.9}$$

Combining Equations 3.8 and 3.9 gives:

$$S_0(1 - T)(1 + C) \leq F_{0,t} \leq S_0(1 + T)(1 + C) \tag{3.10}$$

Equation 3.10 defines the **no-arbitrage bounds** – bounds within which the futures price must remain to prevent arbitrage. In general, transaction costs force a loosening of the price relationship in Equation 3.3. In perfect markets, Equation 3.3 gave an exact equation for the futures price as a function of the spot price and the cost-of-carry. If the futures price deviated from that no-arbitrage price, traders could transact to reap a riskless profit without investment. For a market with transaction costs, Equation 3.10 gives bounds for the futures price. If the futures price goes beyond these boundaries, arbitrage is possible. The futures price can wander within the bounds without offering arbitrage opportunities, however. As an example, consider the bounds implied by the transactions in Table 3.8. If there are no transaction costs, the futures price must be exactly $440 to exclude arbitrage. With the 3 percent transaction costs on spot market transactions, the futures price is free to wander within the range $426.80 to $453.20 without creating any arbitrage opportunity, as Table 3.10 shows.

Figure 3.8 illustrates the concept of arbitrage boundaries. The vertical axis graphs futures prices and the horizontal axis shows the time dimension. The solid horizontal line in the graph shows the no-arbitrage condition for a perfect market. In a perfect market, the futures price must exactly equal

Table 3.10	Illustration of No-Arbitrage Bounds

Prices for the Analysis

Spot price of gold	$400
Interest rate	10%
Transaction costs (T)	3%

No-Arbitrage Futures Price in Perfect Markets

$$F_{0,t} = S_0(1 + C) = \$400(1.1) = \$440$$

Upper No-Arbitrage Bound with Transaction Costs

$$F_{0,t} \leq S_0(1 + T)(1 + C) = \$400(1.03)(1.1) = \$453.20$$

Lower No-Arbitrage Bound with Transaction Costs

$$F_{0,t} \geq S_0(1 - T)(1 + C) = \$400(.97)(1.1) = \$426.80$$

Figure 3.8	No-Arbitrage Bounds

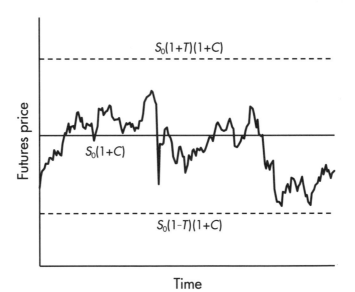

the spot price times 1 plus the cost-of-carry, $F_{0,t} = S_0(1 + C)$. With transaction costs, however, we have a lower and an upper bound. If the futures price goes above the upper no-arbitrage bound, there will be a cash-and-carry arbitrage opportunity. This occurs when $F_{0,t} > S_0(1 + T)(1 + C)$. Likewise, if the futures price falls too low, it will be less than the lower no-arbitrage bound. Futures prices that are too low relative to the spot price give rise to a reverse cash-and-carry arbitrage. This opportunity arises when $F_{0,t} < S_0(1 - T)(1 + C)$. Figure 3.8 shows these no-arbitrage boundaries as dotted lines.

If the futures price stays between the bounds, no arbitrage is possible. If the futures price crosses the boundaries, arbitrageurs will flock to the market to exploit the opportunity. For example, if the futures price is too high, traders will buy the spot commodity and sell the futures. This action will raise the price of the spot good relative to the futures price, thereby driving the futures price back within the no-arbitrage boundaries. If the futures price stays within the boundaries, no arbitrage is possible, and the arbitrageurs will not be able to affect the futures price.

From Figure 3.8, we can note three important points. First, the greater the transaction costs, T, the farther apart will be the bounds. With higher transaction costs, the arbitrage relationships we have been exploring are less binding on possible prices. Second, we have been assuming that all traders in the market face the same percentage transaction costs, T. Clearly, different traders face different transaction costs. For example, a retail trader, who is not an exchange member, can face transaction costs that are much higher than those for a floor trader. It is easily possible for the retail trader to pay as much as 100 times the exchange and brokerage fees paid by a floor trader. Therefore, Figure 3.8 really pertains to a particular trader, not to every trader in the market. Consider a trader facing higher transaction costs of $2T$ instead of T. For this trader, the no-arbitrage bounds would be twice as wide as those in Figure 3.8. Third, we have seen that market forces exist to keep the futures price within the no-arbitrage bounds, and that each trader faces his or her own particular bounds, depending on that trader's transaction costs.

Differences in transaction costs give rise to the concept of **quasi-arbitrage**. Some traders, such as small retail customers, face full transaction costs. Other traders, such as large financial institutions, have much lower transaction costs. For example, exchange members pay much lower transaction costs than do outside traders. Therefore, the quasi-arbitrageur is a potential cash-and-carry or reverse cash-and-carry trader with relatively lower transaction costs. The futures price should stay within the bounds of the lowest transaction cost trader. Once the futures price drifts beyond the bounds of the lowest transaction cost trader, he or she will exploit the arbitrage opportunity. As we have seen, arbitrage activity will drive the futures price back within the no-arbitrage bounds for that trader.

Thus, in the actual market, we expect to see futures prices within the no-arbitrage bounds of the lowest transaction cost trader. This means that traders with higher transaction costs will not be able to exploit any arbitrage opportunities. If prices start to drift away from the perfect markets equality of Equation 3.3, they will be exploited first by the traders with low transaction costs. This exploitation will take place through quasi-arbitrage, because the low transaction cost trader does not face the full transaction costs of an outside trader.

Unequal Borrowing and Lending Rates. In perfect markets, all traders can borrow and lend at the risk-free rate. This is not true in real markets. Generally, traders face a borrowing rate that exceeds the lending rate. In our examples of cash-and-carry and reverse cash-and-carry arbitrage, we have assumed that the two rates were the same. For the cash-and-carry arbitrage, the trader borrows funds, while the trader lends funds in the reverse cash-and-carry arbitrage. Throughout our examples, we assumed that traders could both borrow and lend at a 10 percent rate. If the borrowing and lending rates are not equal, Equation 3.10 requires adjustment to reflect that fact. In Equation 3.10, the upper bound on the futures price comes from the cash-and-carry arbitrage possibility, as shown in Figure 3.8. In the cash-and-carry arbitrage, the trader borrows funds so the borrowing rate is the appropriate rate in the expression for the upper bound. Analogously, the reverse cash-and-carry trade uses a strategy of lending to fix the lower bound. Thus, the lending rate is appropriate for the expression giving the lower bound. Equation 3.11 reproduces Equation 3.10, but reflects the different borrowing and lending rates:

$$S_0(1 - T)(1 + C_L) \le F_{0,t} \le S_0(1 + T)(1 + C_B) \qquad (3.11)$$

where:

C_L = the lending rate
C_B = the borrowing rate

These differential borrowing and lending rates serve to widen the no-arbitrage boundaries that we have been exploring, because generally $C_L < C_B$. We can illustrate the effect of the differential rates by extending the example of Table 3.10 to include unequal borrowing and lending rates. Table 3.11 illustrates the effect of these unequal rates on the no-arbitrage bounds. As the table shows, including differential borrowing and lending rates widens the no-arbitrage boundaries.

Restrictions on Short Selling. In our analysis, we have so far assumed that traders can sell assets short and use the proceeds from the short sale. In all of our examples, we have also assumed that the short seller has the unrestricted use of all funds arising from the short sale. Consider for a moment, however, the position of the broker who facilitates a short sale. In the stock market, for example, the prospective short seller asks his or her broker to borrow a share from another customer and to sell it on behalf of the short seller. If the short seller received all of the funds from the short sale, the broker would be in a precarious position. The broker has borrowed the share from another customer and must return the share upon demand. If the broker allows the short seller to have all of the proceeds of the short sale, the broker runs a significant risk. The short seller might, for instance, take all of the funds and abscond. Alternatively, the price might move against the short seller and the short seller might not be able to pay to reacquire the stock.

Table 3.11	Illustration of No-Arbitrage Bounds with Differential Borrowing and Lending Rates

Prices for the Analysis

Spot price of gold	$400
Interest rate (borrowing)	12%
Interest rate (lending)	8%
Transaction costs (T)	3%

Upper No-Arbitrage Bound with Transaction Costs and a Borrowing Rate

$$F_{0,t} \le S_0(1 + T)(1 + C_B) = \$400(1.03)(1.12) = \$461.44$$

Lower No-Arbitrage Bound with Transaction Costs and a Lending Rate

$$F_{0,t} \ge S_0(1 - T)(1 + C_L) = \$400(.97)(1.08) = \$419.04$$

Because of these inherent risks, there are restrictions on short selling in virtually all markets. These restrictions are important, because we found that short selling was a necessary technique for the reverse cash-and-carry arbitrage strategy. If a trader sells the spot good short, Equation 3.2 must hold to prevent arbitrage. Further, from 3.1 and 3.2, we were able to derive the no-arbitrage condition of 3.3 for a perfect market.

In actual markets, there are serious impediments to short selling. First, for some goods, there is virtually no opportunity for short selling. This is particularly true for many physical goods. Second, even when short selling is permitted, restrictions limit the use of funds from the short sale. Often these restrictions mean that the short seller does not have the use of all of the proceeds from the short sale. A typical percentage for the broker to retain is 50 percent, meaning that the short seller would have the use of only 50 percent of the funds.

In the arbitrage relationship of Expression 3.2, we concluded that:

$$F_{0,t} \geq S_0(1 + C)$$

This result assumes unrestricted short selling, so that the short seller has full use of the short sale proceeds, S_0. As we saw, the reverse cash-and-carry transaction employs the short sale, and this arbitrage strategy determines the lower bound for the futures price. To reflect the fact that the short seller does not have use of the proceeds, but only some fraction f, we can recast Equation 3.2 to say:

$$F_{0,t} \geq S_0(1 + fC)$$

where:

f = the fraction of usable funds derived from the short sale

This fraction must lie between zero and one. In a perfect market, $f = 1.0$, and it effectively drops out of the equation. With restricted short selling, we can now rewrite our no-arbitrage conditions. First, for a market that is perfect except for restricting short sales, we have a modification of Equation 3.3:

$$S_0(1 + fC) \leq F_{0,t} \leq S_0(1 + C) \tag{3.12}$$

We can also integrate restricted short selling into our imperfect markets framework of Equation 3.11. Taking into account transaction costs, differential borrowing and lending rates, and restricted short selling, the no-arbitrage bounds are:

$$S_0(1 - T)(1 + fC_L) \leq F_{0,t} \leq S_0(1 + T)(1 + C_B) \tag{3.13}$$

The restrictions on short selling widen the no-arbitrage bounds. Notice now, however, that restricted short selling affects only the reverse cash-and-carry strategy, so restricted short selling affects only the lower bound. The effects are substantial, however. Table 3.12 shows the lower no-arbitrage bounds for restrictions on the use of short sale proceeds. When traders face large restrictions on short selling, there is little chance for reverse cash-and-carry arbitrage. If traders can use only half of the short sale proceeds, the lower no-arbitrage bound is so low that it can have little effect on the futures price. We will see, however, that different traders face different restrictions on using proceeds from a short

Table 3.12	Illustration of No-Arbitrage Bounds with Various Short-Selling Restrictions

Prices for the Analysis

Spot price of gold	$400
Interest rate (borrowing)	12%
Interest rate (lending)	8%
Transaction costs (T)	3%

Upper No-Arbitrage Bound with Transaction Costs and a Borrowing Rate

$$F_{0,t} \leq S_0(1 + T)(1 + C_B) = \$400(1.03)(1.12) = \$461.44$$

Lower No-Arbitrage Bound with Transaction Costs and a Lending Rate, $f = 1.0$

$$F_{0,t} \geq S_0(1 - T)(1 + fC_L) = \$400(.97)[1 + (1.0)(.08)] = \$419.04$$

Lower No-Arbitrage Bound with Transaction Costs and a Lending Rate, $f = 0.75$

$$F_{0,t} \geq S_0(1 - T)(1 + fC_L) = \$400(.97)[1 + (.75)(.08)] = \$411.28$$

Lower No-Arbitrage Bound with Transaction Costs and a Lending Rate, $f = 0.5$

$$F_{0,t} \geq S_0(1 - T)(1 + fC_L) = \$400(.97)[1 + (0.5)(.08)] = \$403.52$$

sale. The differential use of these short sale proceeds is related to the concept of quasi-arbitrage. Traders with better access to short sale proceeds have less than full transaction costs to pay when they engage in cash-and-carry or reverse cash-and-carry trading strategies.

Equation 3.13 expresses the final results of our cost-of-carry model analysis and it includes transaction costs, differential borrowing and lending rates, and restrictions on short selling. In complexity, it is a far cry from our simple perfect markets/no-arbitrage relationship of Equation 3.3. The two are closely related, however. In terms of Equation 3.13, the perfect markets assumptions can be expressed as:

$T = 0$ so there are no transaction costs;
$C_B = C_L = C$ so borrowing and lending rates are equal;
$f = 1.0$ so traders have full use of short sale proceeds.

If these three conditions hold, we are back to our perfect market assumptions, and Equation 3.13 becomes:

$$(1.0)S_0(1 - 0)(1 + C) \leq F_{0,t} \leq S_0(1 + 0)(1 + C)$$

which reduces to:

$$S_0(1 + C) \leq F_{0,t} \leq S_0(1 + C)$$
$$F_{0,t} = S_0(1 + C)$$

This final expression is simply Equation 3.3, the perfect markets version of our cost-of-carry model.

Limitations to Storage. Of all commodities, gold is perhaps the most storable. It is chemically stable, it has a high value relative to weight and volume, and so on. Some other commodities cannot be stored very well at all, however. The storability of a commodity is important to futures pricing because the arbitrage strategies that we have been considering depend on being able to store the underlying good. For example, the cash-and-carry arbitrage strategy assumes that a trader can buy a commodity today and store it until a later delivery date on a futures contract. If a commodity cannot be stored, some of the arbitrage strategies that we have been considering will not be available. Therefore, the no-arbitrage bounds we have developed will have to be altered to reflect the actual limitations to storage.

In the cash-and-carry arbitrage strategy, the ability to store the commodity limits the futures price relative to the cash price. As we saw in Equation 3.1, the futures price cannot exceed the cash price by more than the cost-of-carry. To see the importance of this point, imagine a tasty tropical fruit that can be harvested on only one day per year, and assume that the fruit spoils in one day if it is not eaten. These physical characteristics of the fruit make it impossible to store. This limitation to storage means that a cash-and-carry strategy cannot link futures and cash prices. Because the fruit is not storable, we could say that the storage cost is infinite. Thus, Equation 3.1 would merely say that the futures price must be less than infinity. This we already know without a business degree.

While the tropical fruit example is quite fanciful, there are also commodities with very practical limits to storage. The Chicago Mercantile Exchange traded a futures contract on fresh eggs for many years. While eggs can be stored for a while, there are definite limits that cannot be exceeded. Grains and oilseeds play an important role in agricultural futures. While wheat, oats, corn, soybeans, soymeal, and soyoil all store well, they cannot be stored indefinitely. Therefore, when storage is limited, the cash-and-carry strategy is also limited. The importance of these limitations to storage varies across commodities. As we noted, they are not important for gold, but they can be important for perishable assets.

How Traders Deal with Market Imperfections. We have seen that transaction costs, differential borrowing rates, and restrictions on short selling all act to widen the no-arbitrage bounds that link cash and futures prices. It is also important to realize that these factors have vastly different effects on different traders. Also, they differ widely across markets. This section considers these market imperfections in a practical light.

There are two critical points about transaction costs. First, every trader faces transaction costs on every trade. Second, these costs differ widely across traders. Let us consider two extreme cases. In both instances, we are interested in the marginal transaction cost, because the marginal transaction cost determines whether the trade takes place. Imagine a professor in Miami who occasionally dabbles in the futures market. Such a trader will trade through a brokerage firm. The broker will charge a commission, the floor broker who executes the order will face a bid-asked spread, and the trader will have to pay exchange fees as well. Together these costs could be as low as $15–20 or they could be much higher. In addition, the professor incurs substantial search costs to determine how to trade. These are difficult to quantify. In contrast with our dabbling professor, consider a major gold trading firm, such as Handy and Harmon or Engelhard. Such firms refine silver and gold and trade it worldwide. As part of their commercial enterprise, they operate a futures trading desk to hedge their own risk exposure in the gold market. In addition, the traders on the desk actively trade in the market, searching for the arbitrage opportunities that we have been considering. A large trading firm faces a very low marginal transaction cost.

These differences in transaction costs stem from several sources. First, the firm is already in the market for other business purposes. Unlike the professor who studies the market merely looking for a good trading opportunity, these commercial concerns are already in the market in support of their physical metals business. This presence makes their information-gathering cost much lower than that faced by the professor who trades only occasionally. Second, the commercial concern will typically own an exchange membership and have its own people on the floor. If so, the firm faces no brokerage commission, which is a large cost of each trade for the professor.

A third and major factor is the difference in the chance to sell short. Short selling of metals is effectively closed to the professor, but it is virtually wide open for the metals trading firm. For the professor, selling short, if it is possible at all, will involve substantial limitations on the use of the short sale proceeds. The metals trading firm, by contrast, will hold an inventory of gold. Thus, the trading firm can simulate short selling by merely selling some of its inventory. From a trading perspective, the sale of the gold that the firm already owns is identical to selling gold short. As long as the firm has access to a supply of gold it can sell, it can replicate the trading effect of selling short. For firms with substantial gold stocks, there is virtually no limitation to replicating a short sale. In sum, for many markets, large commercial concerns in the business face very low transaction costs. For them, the market imperfections we have examined are of little practical importance. Thus, in some markets, prices closely approximate the perfect markets pricing relationship of Equation 3.3.

The Concept of a Full Carry Market

In the price quotations of Figure 3.1, we can readily observe different patterns of prices for different commodities. In general, for some commodities, the futures price rises with the maturity of the futures contract. For some commodities, the prices are inversely related to the futures maturity. For yet other commodities, the prices rise and fall, showing no obvious relationship to maturity.

We can group commodities into different types by the degree to which their prices approximate full carry. In a **full carry market**, futures prices conform to Equations 3.3 and 3.6. If prices match the relationships specified in the equation, the market is said to be at full carry. If the futures price is higher than Equations 3.3 and 3.6 indicate, then the market is **above full carry**. If the futures price is less than the fully carry price, the market is **below full carry**.

As an example, consider the following data for August 16:

Gold September	410.20
Gold December	417.90
Banker's Acceptance Rate – 90 days	7.80%

Is gold at full carry? In addition to financing, warehousing and insuring gold also has costs. These amounts are negligible for gold in percentage terms, so we ignore them for the present. We begin by annualizing the percentage difference between the two gold prices:[2]

$$\left(\frac{F_{0,d}}{F_{0,n}}\right)^4 = 1.0772$$

Thus, the implied annual percentage difference between the two gold prices is 7.72 percent. This corresponds almost exactly to our interest rate estimate. In fact, this is not surprising because gold is almost always at full carry. From this example, we can see that in a full carry market, prices should be normal. That is, the more distant futures price should exceed the nearby price. Other markets are not at full carry. Some markets are normal at times and near full carry, while they diverge radically from full carry at other times.

We have already seen that a well-developed market for short sales is important in keeping the no-arbitrage bounds tight, so that prices will more closely conform to the full carry relationship. There are five main factors that affect market prices and move them toward or away from full carry: short selling conditions, supply, seasonality of production, seasonality of consumption, and ease of storage.

Ease of Short Selling. We have already seen in our discussion of the cost-of-carry model that short selling restrictions widen the no-arbitrage bounds on futures prices. In the extreme case, where short selling is not permitted, there can be no reverse cash-and-carry arbitrage, so the futures price has no lower no-arbitrage bound. In markets for physical goods, short selling is highly restricted, even though some commercial interests can replicate short selling by reducing their inventories. By contrast, it is very easy to sell financial assets short. For this reason, and for others, financial assets tend to be full carry assets.

Large Supply. If the supply of an asset is large relative to its consumption, the market for the good will more closely approximate a full carry market. On the side of cash-and-carry arbitrage, a large supply makes it easier for traders to acquire the physical good to store for future delivery. Relative to consumption for jewelry or industrial uses, for example, the supply of gold is very large. This factor helps keep gold near full carry. By contrast, the world supply of copper is low relative to consumption. Typical supplies of copper on hand roughly equal three months of production. Markets for copper and other industrial metals are not full carry markets.

Nonseasonal Production. Temporary imbalances in supply and demand tend to cause distortions in normal price relationships. If production is highly seasonal, the stock of a good will be subject to large shifts. Many agricultural commodities have highly seasonal production due to their harvest cycles. In these markets, prices tend to be high for periods immediately prior to the harvest and low for the post-harvest months.

Nonseasonal Consumption. Foodstuffs, such as soybeans, may have seasonal production, but consumption is fairly steady. People like to eat all year. For other goods, production is fairly continuous, but consumption is highly seasonal. For example, contract prices for heating oil often show a seasonal pattern of high prices in winter, while gasoline prices are often relatively high for summer months.

High Storability. The tropical fruit that must be harvested and eaten in a single day is the perfect example of a nonstorable commodity. If the good is nonstorable, cash-and-carry arbitrage strategies cannot link the cash price with the futures price. Thus, the cost-of-carry model is unlikely to apply to a good with poor storage characteristics. To a great extent, most physical commodities traded on futures exchanges have good storage characteristics. Some commodities that were less storable (such as fresh eggs and potatoes) have passed from futures trading. To the extent that a commodity has poor storage characteristics, however, the cost-of-carry model is unlikely to apply.

Convenience Yield

We have seen in the preceding section that various factors cause the array of futures prices to vary from full carry for many commodities. In general, the cost-of-carry model fails to apply when an asset has a **convenience yield** – a return on holding the physical asset. When holding an asset has a convenience yield, the futures price will be below full carry. In an extreme case, the market can be so far below full carry that the cash price can exceed the futures price. When the cash price exceeds the futures price, or when the nearby futures price exceeds the distant futures price, the market is in **backwardation**. An asset has a convenience yield when traders are willing to pay a premium to hold the physical asset at a certain time. For example, natural gas prices tend to be high in the winter – just when people need heat. Likewise, soybean prices are high right before harvest – just when supplies are low and people still want to eat.

To explore the concept of the convenience yield more fully, assume that this is October and the cash price of soybeans is $6.00 per bushel. Harvest is one month away, and a trader owns 5,000 bushels of soybeans. The futures price of soybeans for November is $5.50. In this example, the market is in backwardation, because the cash price exceeds the futures price. Under these circumstances, the trader will hold the soybeans from October to November only if he or she has some clear need for owning the beans during this period.

If the trader does not need the physical beans for the next month, he or she can sell the beans and buy a NOV futures contract. This strategy will yield a profit of $.50 per bushel, and it will save a month of carrying costs. Clearly, only a person with a need for physical beans will hold them given the price structure. For example, consider a food processor who still wants beans in October. The food processor might derive a convenience yield from owning beans, but only persons with a business need for the beans, such as a food processor, could derive a convenience yield.

If the bean market is below full carry, it might seem that there is an opportunity for a reverse cash-and-carry arbitrage. This strategy requires selling beans short, but it is clear that short selling will not be possible. Short selling involves borrowing beans from someone else. Because the market is below full carry, no one will lend beans costlessly. Anyone who owns the beans holds them because of the convenience yield they derive. If they owned the beans and received no convenience yield, they would sell them outright in the market and buy the cheaper SEP futures to replace their beans in two months. Lending the beans to someone else so that other party can make money is the last application the holder of the physical beans would consider. Thus, if an asset has a convenience yield, the market can be below full carry, or even in backwardation. Such a situation will not provide a field day for reverse cash-and-carry arbitrage strategies, however, because short selling opportunities will not be available.

Summary

In our exploration of the cost-of-carry model, we have seen that cash-and-carry and reverse cash-and-carry strategies place no-arbitrage bounds on futures prices. Transaction costs, differential borrowing and lending rates, restrictions on short selling, and limitations to storage all act to widen those bounds. Therefore, while the cost-of-carry model reveals much about the determinants of futures prices, it does not provide a complete determination of futures prices.

As we have seen, some commodities have characteristics that promote full carry. These include easy short selling, a large supply of the good, nonseasonal production and consumption, and high storability. Related to these, and also contributing to the applicability of the cost-of-carry model, is the lack of a convenience yield. Because market imperfections and the characteristics of the commodities themselves sometimes combine to force the no-arbitrage bounds apart, other factors help determine where within the no-arbitrage bounds the futures price will lie. Within the no-arbitrage bounds, the market's expectation plays a large role in futures price determination.

FUTURES PRICES AND EXPECTATIONS

Earlier we considered a tropical fruit that can be harvested on only one day per year, say, July 4. The fruit is so delicate that it must also be consumed on that day or it will spoil. How would a futures contract on such a fruit be priced? As we explore in this section, the cost-of-carry model breaks down for the pricing of such a futures contract.

Cash-and-carry arbitrage strategies do not apply to this fruit, because it cannot be carried. The fruit spoils in one day. Therefore, the cash price and the futures price are not linked by the opportunity to carry the fruit forward. Another way of making the same point is to say that the cost-of-carry is infinite. Thus, any positive cash price is consistent with any positive futures price, no matter how high.

Reverse cash-and-carry strategies also do not apply. For example, assume that the cash price of the fruit is $2 on July 4, and the futures price for delivery in one year is $1. From our discussion of convenience yield, we know that this backwardation is due to the benefit that holding the cash fruit conveys. Therefore, no one would lend the fruit for short selling. Anyone who does not need the fruit for immediate consumption would merely sell it in the cash market and buy the cheaper futures. In sum, short selling would not be possible, so reverse cash-and-carry strategies will not serve to link the cash and futures prices. Because both the cash-and-carry and reverse cash-and-carry strategies fail for this fruit, they impose no-arbitrage bounds on the futures price.

The Role of Speculation

What does determine the futures price? Assume that market participants expect the price of the fruit in the next harvest to be $10 each. This price is the **expected future spot price**. In this event, the futures price must equal, or at least closely approximate, the expected future spot price. If this were not the case, profitable speculative strategies would arise.

As an example, if the futures price were $15, exceeding the expected future spot price of $10, speculators would sell the futures contract and then plan to buy the fruit for $10 on the harvest date. They would then be able to deliver the fruit and collect $15, for a $5 profit, if all went according to plan. By contrast, if the futures price were below the expected future spot price, say at $7, speculators would buy the futures contract, take delivery on the harvest date paying $7, and plan to sell the fruit at the market price of $10.

In short, the presence of speculators in the marketplace ensures that the futures price approximately equals the expected future spot price. Too great a divergence between the futures price and the expected future spot price creates attractive speculative opportunities. In response, profit-seeking speculators will trade as long as the futures price is sufficiently far away from the expected future spot price. We can express this basic idea by introducing the following notation.

$$F_{0,t} \approx E_0(S_t) \tag{3.14}$$

where:

$E_0(S_t)$ = the expectation at $t = 0$ of the spot price to prevail at time t

Equation 3.14 states that the futures price approximately equals the spot price currently expected to prevail at the delivery date. If this relationship did not hold, there would be attractive speculative opportunities.

Limits to Speculation

With Equation 3.14, we have said that the futures price and the expected future spot price should be approximately equal. Why does this relationship hold only approximately? There are two basic answers to this question, one of which is fairly obvious and the second of which is fairly profound. First, the relationship holds only approximately because of transaction costs. Second, if some participants in the market are more risk averse than others, the futures price can diverge sharply from the expected future spot price.

Transaction Costs. Assume that the fruit has a futures price of $9 and an expected future spot price of $10, and assume that the cost of transacting to take advantage of this discrepancy is $2. With these prices, a trader cannot buy the futures for $9 and plan to make a $1 profit by selling the fruit at its expected future spot price. This opportunity is not profitable with the transaction costs, because the total cost of acquiring the fruit would be the $9 delivery on the futures plus the $2 transaction cost. Transaction costs can keep the futures price from exactly equaling the expected future spot price. This parallels our discussion of transaction costs and their effect on the cost-of-carry model.

Risk Aversion. Traders in futures markets can be classified, at least roughly, into hedgers and speculators. Hedgers have a preexisting risk associated with a commodity and sometimes enter the market to reduce that risk, while speculators trade in the hope of profit. Entering the futures market as a speculator is a risky venture. If people are risk averse, however, they incur risk willingly only if the expected profit from bearing the risk will compensate them for the risk exposure. Without doubt, most participants in financial markets are risk averse, so they seek compensation to warrant their taking a risky position. In the futures markets, speculative profits can come only from a favorable movement in the price of a futures contract.

Assume that the expected future spot price of the fictional fruit is $10.00 and that the corresponding futures price is $10.05. Assume also that there is tremendous uncertainty about what the actual price of the fruit will be. The market expects a cash price of $10 upon harvest, but the fruit is very susceptible to weather conditions, and it is also subject to the dread fictional fruit weevil. For a speculator, there appears to be a $.05 profit available from the strategy of selling the futures, buying fruit for $10.00 at harvest, and delivering against the futures contract. This strategy subjects the speculator to considerable risk if the weather is bad or if the weevil strikes, however. Speculators may decide that the expected profit of $.05 is not worth the risk exposure. If the speculators do not pursue the $.05 expected profit, there will be no market forces to drive the futures price into exact equality with the expected future spot price. Thus, the futures price can differ from the expected future spot price if traders are risk averse.

Summary. The strong principles of the cost-of-carry model place no-arbitrage bounds on futures prices in many instances. In some cases those bounds are very wide, or even nonexistent, due to transaction costs, restrictions on short selling, or the characteristics of the physical commodity. Within the bounds placed by cash-and-carry and reverse cash-and-carry strategies, expectations play a major role in establishing futures prices. We have seen that speculative strategies are available when the futures price does not equal the expected future spot price. Still, these speculative strategies do not ensure exact equality between the futures price and the expected future spot price. The futures price can diverge from the expected future spot price due to transaction costs or due to risk aversion on the part of traders. Of the two, risk aversion is much more important and deserves extended consideration.

FUTURES PRICES AND RISK AVERSION

In this section, we explore in detail two theories of how risk aversion can affect futures prices. We have already seen that risk aversion among speculators can allow the futures price to diverge from the expected future spot price. According to the theory of normal backwardation, this divergence occurs in a systematic way. As a second theory, the **Capital Asset Pricing Model** (CAPM) relates market prices to a measure of systematic risk. Some scholars have applied the CAPM to futures markets to understand the differences that might exist between futures prices and expected future spot prices.

The Theory of Normal Backwardation

Assume for the moment that speculators are rational; that is, they make assessments of expected future prices based on available information. In assessing this information, rational speculators occasionally make mistakes, but on the whole, they process the information efficiently. As a result, their expectations, on average, are realized. This does not imply that they are mistake free. Instead, they make errors of assessment that are not biased. The expectational errors are randomly distributed around the true price that the commodity will have in the future. Assume also that speculators have "homogeneous expectations," that is, they expect the same future spot price.

Such a group of speculators might confront the prices prevailing in a futures market and find that those prices match the expected future spot prices. If the futures price reaches the expected price of the commodity when the futures contract matures, then there is no reason to speculate in futures. If the futures price matches a speculator's expectation of subsequent cash prices for the commodity, then the speculator must expect neither a profit nor a loss by entering the futures market. Yet, by entering the market under such conditions, the speculator would certainly incur additional risk. After all, the trader's expectations might be incorrect. Faced with such a situation, no risk averse speculator would trade, because the speculator would face additional risk without compensation.

Hedgers, taken as a group, need to be either long or short in the futures market to reduce the risk they face in their businesses. For example, a wheat farmer has a long position in cash wheat because he or she grows wheat. The farmer can reduce risk by selling wheat futures. If hedgers are net short, for example, speculators must be net long. For the sake of simplicity, consider a single speculator who is considering whether to take a long position. As just noted above, the rational speculator takes a long futures position only if the expected future spot price exceeds the current futures price. Otherwise, the speculator must expect not to make any profit.

The hedger, we assume, needs to be short to avoid unwanted risk. According to this line of reasoning, he must be willing to sell the futures contract at a price below the expected future spot price of the commodity. Otherwise, the hedger cannot induce the speculator to accept the long side of the contract. From this point of view, he, in effect, buys insurance from the speculator. The hedger transfers his unwanted risk to the speculator and pays an expected profit to the speculator for bearing the risk. The payment to the speculator is the difference between the futures price and the expected future spot price. Even so, the speculator does not receive any sure payment. The speculator must still wait for the expected future spot price to materialize to capture the profit expected for bearing the risk.

Thus far, the discussion has focused on a single hedger and a single speculator. It is necessary, however, to try to do justice to the fact that the marketplace is peopled by many individuals with different needs, different levels of risk aversion, and different expectations (heterogeneous expectations) about future spot prices.

Figure 3.9 depicts the situation that might prevail in the futures market for a commodity. It shows the relevant positions of hedgers and speculators as two groups. As the futures price varies, the number of contracts desired by the two groups will vary as well. We assume that hedgers are net short. At no futures price will hedgers, taken as a group, desire a long position in the futures.[3] This is reasonable given the definition of a hedger as one who enters the futures market to reduce a preexisting risk. Line WX shows the hedgers' desired position in the futures market for various futures prices. At higher prices, hedgers want to sell more futures contracts, as the downward slope for line WX indicates. Lines WX and YZ are drawn as straight lines, but that is only for convenience. Also, note that the hedgers hedge different amounts depending on the futures price. With low prices, they sell fewer contracts, thereby hedging less of their preexisting risk than they would if futures prices were high.

Figure 3.9   Hypothetical Net Positions

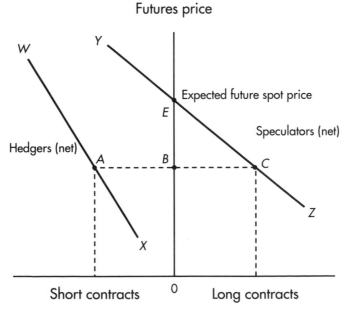

In Figure 3.9, speculators are willing to hold either long or short net positions as the situation demands. Assuming that the speculators, as a group, correctly assess the appropriate expected future spot price, they will be neither long nor short when the futures price equals the expected future spot price. At that point, speculators hold a zero net position in the futures market. (In such a situation, some speculators would be long, others short, reflecting their divergent opinions. But, in the aggregate, they would hold a net zero position.) Line YZ shows the speculators' desired positions as a function of the futures price. If the futures price exceeds the expected future spot price, the speculators will desire to be net short as well as the hedgers. If the futures price lies below the expected future spot price, speculators will want to be net long, holding some position between E and Z on line YZ.

Not all positions shown on the graph are feasible. If the futures price lies above point E, then both the hedgers and speculators desire to be short. Yet, the number of outstanding short contracts must equal the number of long contracts. As the figure is drawn, there is only one price at which the market can clear: point B. With a price of B, the net short position desired by the hedgers exactly offsets the net long position desired by the speculators. This is reflected graphically by the fact that the distance AB equals the distance BC. Through the typical process by which markets reach equilibrium, the futures market may reach an equilibrium price at B, with the futures price lying below the expected future spot price.

Notice that the slope of WX (the hedgers' line) is steeper than that of YZ (the speculators' line). The more gentle slope of YZ expresses the greater risk tolerance of the speculators. For any drop in the futures price below the expected future spot price, E, the increase in the speculators' demand for long contracts exceeds the drop in the hedgers' desire to hold the short contracts. Indeed, this must be the case. Economically, the speculators must be more risk tolerant than the hedgers. After all, the speculators in this model accept the risk that the hedgers are unwilling to bear, so the speculators must be more risk tolerant.

This account explains how the futures price can diverge from the expected future spot price, even with no transaction costs. Likewise, if hedgers want to be net long, speculators must be net short. If the speculators are net short, then they can hope to earn a return for their risk-bearing services only if the futures price lies above the expected future spot price. Again, the futures price need not equal the expected future spot price. Instead, the relationship between the futures price and the expected future spot price depends in part on whether the hedgers need to be net short or net long.

Clearly, in this model, the futures price will be below the expected future spot price if the hedgers are net short, as in Figure 3.9. The amount of the discrepancy depends upon the risk aversion of the two groups. For example, assume that the speculators are more risk averse than Figure 3.9 depicts. Higher risk aversion is represented in the graph by the steepness of the hedgers' or speculators' line. If the speculators were more risk averse, their line would be steeper. As a result, at price B the speculators would be willing to hold fewer long contracts and the market would not clear at that price. Instead, the market clearing price would be below B, the exact price depending upon the steepness of the speculators' line. In that case, the market clearing price would be below B and fewer hedgers would be able to hedge.

This approach to determining futures prices originated with John Maynard Keynes and John Hicks. The view that hedgers are net short, as shown in Figure 3.9, is associated with Keynes and Hicks. Over the life of the futures contract, the futures price must move toward the cash price. (This is already clear, since the basis must equal zero at the maturity of the futures contract, as was discussed earlier.) If expectations about the future spot price are correct, and hedgers are net short, then the futures price must lie below the expected future spot price. In such a case, futures prices can be expected to rise over the life of a contract.

The view that futures prices tend to rise over the contract life due to the hedgers' general desire to be net short is known as **normal backwardation**. (Normal backwardation should not be confused with a market that is in backwardation. A market is in backwardation at a given moment if the cash price exceeds the futures price or if a nearby futures price exceeds a distant futures price.) Conversely, if hedgers are net long, then the futures price would lie above the expected future spot price, and the price of the futures contract would fall over its life. This pattern of falling prices is known as a **contango**. Figure 3.10 depicts these price patterns.[4]

Figure 3.10 illustrates the price patterns for futures that we might expect under different scenarios. In considering the figure, assume that market participants correctly assess the future spot price, so that the expected future spot price in the figure turns out to be the actual spot price at the maturity of the futures contract. If the futures price equals the expected future spot price, then the futures price will lie on the dotted line, which equals the expected future spot price. With initially correct expectations, and no information causing a revision of expectations, the futures price should remain constant over its entire trading life.

Alternative conceptions certainly exist, such as the theory of normal backwardation and the contango. If speculators are net long, as Keynes and Hicks believed, then futures prices must rise over the life of the contract if the speculators are to receive their compensation for bearing risk. Prices then follow the path that is labeled "Normal backwardation" in Figure 3.10. With the futures price rising over its life, the speculator earns a return for bearing risk. Notice that the line for normal backwardation terminates at the expected future spot price. This is necessary since the futures price and the spot price must be equal at the maturity of the futures contract, and the figure is drawn assuming that the expected future spot price turns out to be the subsequently observed spot price.

Figure 3.10	Patterns of Futures Prices

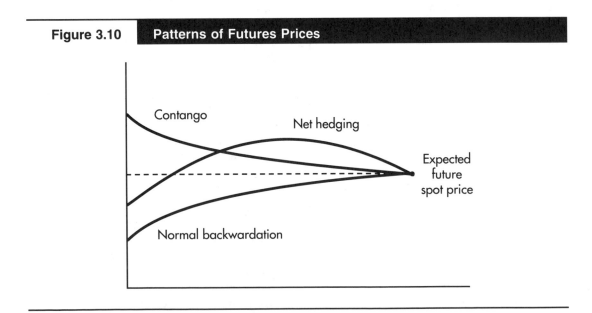

If speculators are net short and are to receive compensation for bearing risk, futures prices must follow a contango, as Figure 3.10 also illustrates. The fall in futures prices, as the contract approaches maturity, gives the short speculators the compensation that induced them to enter the market.

One final possibility, also shown in Figure 3.10, is known as the **net hedging hypothesis**. According to this view, the net position of the hedgers might change over the life of the futures contract. When the contract begins trading, the hedgers are net short and the speculators are net long. In such a situation, the futures price lies below the expected future spot price. Over time, the hedgers gradually change their net position. Eventually, the hedgers are net long, requiring the speculators to be net short. For the speculators to receive their compensation in this case, the futures price must lie above the expected future spot price, as it did in the contango.

Perhaps this account of hedgers changing from being net short to net long over the life of the contract appears dubious, but it is certainly conceivable. Consider grain farmers who wish to hedge the crop that they will produce. To hedge the price risk associated with harvest, they need to be short. Cereal producers have a need for the grain, and they hedge their price risk by being long. To show how the price could follow the pattern suggested by the net hedging hypothesis, imagine that the farmers hedge first. This makes the hedgers net short. Later, the cereal producers begin to hedge their future need for the grain, and the net hedging position of the farmers and cereal producers taken together begins to move toward zero. When it reaches zero, the farmers and cereal producers in the aggregate are neither short nor long. Time passes, and still more cereal producers hedge by going long. Eventually, the long hedgers come to predominate and all hedgers taken together are net long. Under such a condition, the futures price must lie above the expected future spot price if the speculators are to receive compensation for bearing risk.

Even though the theory of normal backwardation originated in about 1920, there is still no broad consensus on whether the theory is true. While the issue has been well-studied, different studies focus on different commodities and different time periods, and this has, perhaps, led to widely differing results. In general, it might be too optimistic to assume that all commodities would share the same characteristics. Perhaps the most accurate generalization of these studies is to conclude that there is no overwhelming evidence in support of normal backwardation.[5]

Futures Prices and the Capital Asset Pricing Model

The Capital Asset Pricing Model (CAPM) has been widely applied to all kinds of financial instruments, including futures contracts. Equation 3.15 expresses the basic relationship of the CAPM:

$$E(R_j) = r + \beta_j [E(R_m) - r] \qquad (3.15)$$

where:

r = the risk-free rate
$E(R_j)$ = expected return on asset j
$E(R_m)$ = expected return on the market portfolio
β_j = the ''beta'' of asset j

The CAPM measures the systematic risk of an asset by β, and β is usually estimated from a regression equation of the following form:

$$r_{j,t} = \alpha_j + \beta_j r_{m,t} + \epsilon_{j,t} \qquad\qquad (3.16)$$

where:

$r_{j,t}$ = the return on asset j in the tth period
$r_{m,t}$ = the return on the market portfolio j in the tth period
α_j = the constant term in the regression
$\epsilon_{j,t}$ = the residual error for day t

According to the CAPM, only unavoidable risk should be compensated in the marketplace, and traders can avoid much risk through diversification. Even after diversification, risk remains for some assets because the returns of the asset are correlated with the market as a whole. This remaining risk is systematic. In essence, β_j measures the systematic risk of asset j relative to the market portfolio. According to Equation 3.15, an asset with $\beta = 1$ has the same degree of systematic risk as does the market portfolio, and the asset should earn the same return as the market. The risk-free asset has $\beta = 0$, and it should earn the risk-free rate of interest.

As we have seen, futures market trading does not require any investment. However, trading futures does require margin payments, but these are not investments. With no funds invested, there is no capital to earn the risk-free interest rate. Therefore, a futures position should have zero return if $\beta = 0$. If the beta of a futures position exceeds zero, a long position in the futures contract should earn a positive return. For example, for futures position j, assume the following values hold:

$$E(R_m) = .09$$
$$r = .06$$
$$\beta_j = .7$$

According to Equation 3.15, a long position in futures contract j should earn:

$$E(R_j) = \beta_j[E(R_m) - r] = .7(.09 - .06) = .021$$

Thus, positive betas for futures contracts lead to the expectation of rising futures prices. Zero betas would be consistent with futures prices that neither rise nor fall. A negative beta would imply that futures prices should fall.

As with the theory of normal backwardation, approximately equal numbers of studies support and oppose the CAPM as it applies to futures markets. This untidy irresolution may be due to the fact that futures returns are very close to zero. Thus, some studies find average returns significantly different from zero, while others do not. Most studies do seem to find that futures contracts have betas near zero, at least when these betas are measured using conventional techniques. Final resolution of these issues will require more comprehensive data sets and analyses than have been employed to date.

CHARACTERISTICS OF FUTURES PRICES

In this section, we consider four characteristics of futures prices and changes in futures prices. First, we consider the relationship between futures prices and forward prices for the same good. Theoretically, these prices could differ even when they depend on the same underlying good. This is possible because of the feature of daily settlement on the futures contract, but not on the forward contract. Second, we consider the forecasting ability of futures prices. If futures prices equal expected future spot prices, the process of price discovery is aided substantially. Third, we consider the distribution of futures price changes. If the distribution of price changes is non-normal, statistical tests become more difficult, because most popular tests assume that the distribution of price changes is normal. As we will see, the distribution is generally not normal. This has important implications in many areas. For example, a test of whether the average change in futures prices is positive depends on the normality of the changes being tested. Fourth, we consider the volatility of futures prices and the effect of futures price volatility on the volatility of cash market prices.

Futures Prices versus Forward Prices

In Chapters 1 and 2, we considered the differences between forward and futures markets. Here we analyze the factors that can cause forward and futures prices to diverge, even when the contracts have the same underlying commodities and the same time to expiration. Forward and futures prices can differ because of different tax treatments, different transaction costs, or different margin rules. Also, the chance of a default may be higher on a forward contract, due to the lack of a clearinghouse in forward markets. The main conceptual reason for a possible difference in prices stems from the daily settlement that characterizes futures markets, however.

To see the potential difference between forward and futures prices, consider the following example. A gold futures and a gold forward both expire in one year, and the current price of both contracts is $500. We assume that the spot price of gold in one year will also be $500. Thus, there will be no profit or loss on either contract. Also, when the contracts expire, the forward price, the futures price, and the cash price must all be equal. We have explored arbitrage arguments to show that this result must obtain. There are about 250 trading days in a year, so we consider two very simple possible price paths that gold might follow over that year. First, we assume that the futures price rises by $2 each day for 125 days and then falls by $2 per day for 125 days. Second, we assume that the gold price falls by $2 per day for 125 days and then rises by $2 per day for 125 days. Figure 3.11 illustrates the two price paths. Under either scenario, the price will be $500 at expiration in one year. Thus, there is no profit or loss on either contract.

The forward trader is indifferent between the two possible price paths. The forward trader has no cash flow at the beginning and none at the end. Because of daily settlement, however, the futures trader has definite preferences. For example, a long futures trader would much prefer the price to rise first and fall later. Each day the price rises, the long futures trader receives a settlement payment that can be invested. Getting the cash inflows early in the holding period means that the futures trader can earn more interest than otherwise.

Assuming a 10 percent interest rate, the difference in these two price paths is about $25 for the futures trader. If the price rises first, the long futures trader receives payments that can be invested. Later in the year, however, the futures trader must make daily settlement payments. Nonetheless, in Figure 3.11, the trader makes $12.48 in interest by year end if the price rises first.[6] Similarly, the trader loses $12.48 in interest if prices fall first. Notice that these differences stem strictly from the interest gains or losses on the daily settlement payments. This is clear from the example, because there are no profits or losses on the futures position. Therefore, we can see that the futures trader can be better or worse off than the forward trader.

Figure 3.11   **Possible Futures Price Paths**

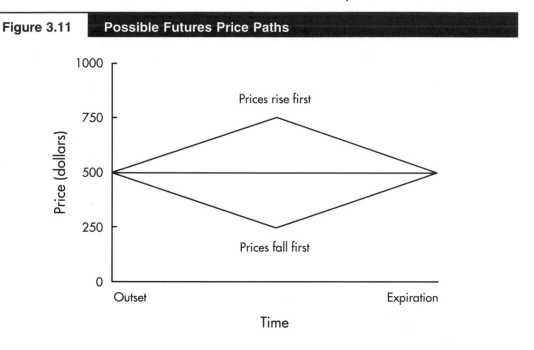

Of course, traders do not know which will be more attractive until after the event, because no one knows what course prices will take. After all, interest rate movements are subject to chance. This makes it impossible to know at the outset which price path will occur, so the gold trader would not know which contract to take in our example, the forward or the futures.

It is possible to draw a general rule from this analysis. If the futures price is positively correlated with interest rates, then a long trader will prefer a futures position over a forward position. This result has been proven rigorously in a number of studies. While the proof of this proposition is quite mathematical, we can follow the intuition that underlies it.

If the futures price and interest rates rise together, then the long futures trader will receive settlement payments that can be invested at the higher interest rate. If futures prices and interest rates both fall, the futures trader must make settlement payments, but the trader can finance those payments at the new lower interest rate. In this argument, the trader does not need to forecast interest rates to have a preference for futures over forwards. Instead, the preference for a futures over a forward depends only on the correlation between the futures price and the interest rate.

Both the futures and the forward will have the same profit in the end, exclusive of the settlement payments. If the futures position is likely to have more favorable interim cash flows due to its positive correlation with interest rates, the futures price should exceed the forward price. By the same token, if the futures price is negatively correlated with interest rates, then the futures price should be lower than the forward price. This conclusion follows, because the long futures trader will then tend to experience losses just as interest rates rise. Finally, if the price of a commodity is uncorrelated with interest rates, then the forward and futures prices should be equal. Notice that all these conclusions arise strictly from economic reasoning.

While most studies find a statistical difference between forward and futures prices, the difference is generally too small to be important economically. Thus, we can generally assume that forward and futures prices are approximately equal for most practical purposes.

Statistical Characteristics of Futures Prices

This section considers three statistical characteristics of futures prices.[7] First, we explore whether the price changes of futures contracts are normally distributed. Second, we consider whether successive price changes are correlated, and finally we consider whether the volatility of futures contracts varies with the time remaining until the contract expires.

The Distribution of Futures Prices. As we noted earlier, most statistical tests of futures prices rely on the assumption that the underlying price changes are normally distributed. If futures price changes are not normally distributed, then these tests become more difficult to conduct. Almost all studies in this area agree that changes in futures prices are not normally distributed, but that the distribution of percentage changes in futures price is leptokurtic. Figure 3.12 illustrates **leptokurtosis** – the tendency for a distribution to have too many extreme observations relative to a normal distribution. In the figure, the solid line shows a normal distribution. The dotted line shows a leptokurtic distribution. The greater frequency of extreme observations makes the leptokurtic distribution have ''fat tails.''

As a second major theme, many of these papers try to determine what distribution futures prices follow if they are not normal. Two candidates dominate. First, the distribution may be stable Paretian.

Normality and Leptokurtosis   **Figure 3.12**

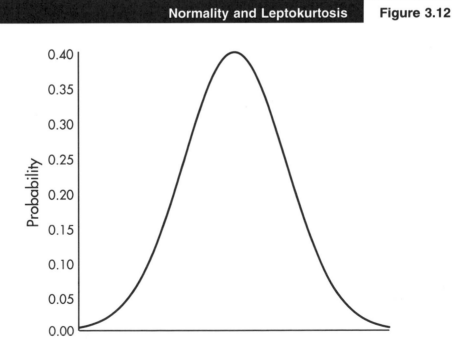

This distribution is symmetrical, like the normal distribution, but it is leptokurtic relative to a normal distribution. Second, some studies find that the distribution of futures price changes seems to be similar to a mixture of two or more normal distributions. Thus, these studies find that the distribution is not normal, but that it can be approximated by a mixture of normal distributions. Both camps agree that this non-normalcy requires extra caution in making statistical inferences about futures prices.

Autocorrelation. In addition to testing the distribution of futures price changes, several studies have examined whether the times series of futures price changes is autocorrelated. A time series is **autocorrelated** if the value of one observation in the series is statistically related to another. In **first-order autocorrelation**, for example, one observation is related to the immediately preceding observation. This question has considerable practical importance. For example, if futures prices exhibit positive first-order autocorrelation, then positive returns in one period tend to be followed by positive returns in the next period. Similarly, negative returns tend to be followed by subsequent negative returns.

If the correlation were strong enough, it would be possible to devise trading strategies to profit from this follow-on tendency. For example, with positive first-order autocorrelation, one could devise a trading rule to buy the futures immediately following a price rise. Then, the second price rise would generate a profit.

Almost all studies find that futures prices exhibit statistically significant first-order autocorrelation. While the autocorrelation appears to be significant statistically, it does not appear to be important economically. In other words, the autocorrelation is not strong enough to allow profitable trading strategies after we consider transaction costs.

The Volatility of Futures Prices. In a paper now regarded as a classic, Paul Samuelson argued that the volatility of futures prices should increase as the contract approaches expiration.[8] This is the **Samuelson hypothesis**. In his analysis, Samuelson assumed that competitive forces in the futures market keep the futures price at a level equal to the expected future spot price at the contract's termination. Under this assumption, futures prices should follow a **martingale** – a price process in which the expected value of the next price equals the current price, so the expected price change is zero. Therefore, this conclusion implies that the futures price equals the expected future spot price.

While the mathematics of Samuelson's model are somewhat complex, the intuition is clear. High price volatility implies big price changes. Price changes are large when more information is being revealed about a commodity. Early in a futures contract's life, little information is known about the future spot price for the underlying commodity. Later, as the contract nears maturity, the rate of information acquisition increases. For example, little is known about a corn harvest a full year before harvest time. As the harvest approaches, the market gets a much better idea of the ultimate price that corn will command. For a futures contract expiring near the harvest, Samuelson's model implies that the futures price should be more volatile as the harvest approaches, and most studies support the hypothesis.

CONCLUSION

While futures markets have a reputation for high risk and wild price swings, this chapter has stressed the underlying rationality of futures prices. We cannot deny that prices vary suddenly and sharply in the futures market, but it is quite possible that these price movements accurately reflect the arrival of new information at the market. Further, it is also apparent that futures prices observe the economic laws detailed earlier. Both the cost-of-carry model and the expected future price framework provide rational procedures for thinking about the behavior of futures prices. It must also be admitted that futures prices, on the whole, conform to these theories.

If the conclusions reached about futures pricing above are correct, then a picture of the usefulness of the market begins to emerge. If prices react rationally to new information, and if spread relationships are strongly interconnected, and if futures prices are good estimates of expected future spot prices, it is possible to understand the uses that can be made of the market by different elements of society. These different groups in society were identified as those who wish to discover price information by observing futures markets, as speculators and as hedgers. If futures prices closely approximate expected future spot prices, then the price discovery function is well served. Speculators, on the other hand, will have a difficult life, because profitable opportunities will not be abundant. Hedgers, for their part, have an apparent opportunity to reduce their risk exposure with relatively little cost.

Chapter 4 explores how these different groups use the futures market. The difficulties facing speculators are examined more closely, along with the benefits that the futures markets provide to hedgers and to society as a whole.

QUESTIONS AND PROBLEMS

1. Explain the function of the settlement committee. Why is the settlement price important in futures markets in a way that the day's final price in the stock market is not so important?
2. Open interest tends to be low when a new contract expiration is first listed for trading, and it tends to be small after the contract has traded for a long time. Explain.
3. Explain the distinction between a normal and an inverted market.
4. Explain why the futures price converges to the spot price and discuss what would happen if this convergence failed.
5. Is delivery, or the prospect of delivery, necessary to guarantee that the futures price will converge to the spot price? Explain.
6. As we have defined the term, what are the two key elements of "academic arbitrage"?
7. Assume that markets are perfect in the sense of being free from transaction costs and restrictions on short selling. The spot price of gold is $370. Current interest rates are 10 percent, compounded monthly. According to the cost-of-carry model, what should the price of a gold futures contract be if expiration is six months away?
8. Consider the information in Question 7. Round trip futures trading costs are $25 per 100 ounce gold contract, and buying or selling an ounce of gold incurs transaction costs of $1.25. Gold can be stored for $.15 per month per ounce. (Ignore interest on the storage fee and the transaction costs.) What futures prices are consistent with the cost-of-carry model?
9. Consider the information in Questions 7 and 8. Restrictions on short selling effectively mean that the reverse cash-and-carry trader in the gold market receives the use of only 90 percent of the value of the gold that is sold short. Based on this new information, what is the permissible range of futures prices?
10. Consider all of the information about gold in Questions 7–9. The interest rate in Question 7 is 10 percent per annum, with monthly compounding. This is the borrowing rate. Lending brings only 8 percent, compounded monthly. What is the permissible range of futures prices when we consider this imperfection as well?

11. Consider all of the information about gold in Questions 7–10. The gold futures expiring in six months trades for $375 per ounce. Explain how you would respond to this price, given all of the market imperfections we have considered. Show your transactions in a table similar to Table 3.8 or 3.9. Answer the same question, assuming that gold trades for $395.

12. Explain the difference between pure and quasi-arbitrage.

13. Assume that you are a gold merchant with an ample supply of deliverable gold. Explain how you can simulate short selling and compute the price of gold that will bring you into the market for reverse cash-and-carry arbitrage.

14. Assume that silver trades in a full carry market. If the spot price is $5.90 per ounce and the futures that expires in one year trades for $6.55, what is the implied cost-of-carry? Under what conditions would it be appropriate to regard this implied cost-of-carry as an implied repo rate?

15. What is "normal backwardation"? What might give rise to normal backwardation?

16. Assume that the CAPM beta of a futures contract is zero, but that the price of this commodity tends to rise over time very consistently. Interpret the implications of this evidence for normal backwardation and for the CAPM.

17. Explain why futures and forward prices might differ. Assume that platinum prices are positively correlated with interest rates. What should be the relationship between platinum forward and futures prices? Explain.

18. Consider the life of a futures contract from inception to delivery. Explain two fundamental theories on why the futures prices might exhibit different volatility at different times over the life of the contract.

NOTES

[1] For a very informative and readable account of repurchase agreements, see M. Bowsher, "Repurchase Agreements," *Instruments of the Money Market,* Richmond: Federal Reserve Bank of Richmond, 1981.

[2] The ratio of the distant to the nearby futures price defines the interest rate between the two dates $t = n$ and $t = d$. In this example, $d - n$ is 90 days, so we raise the expression to the 4th power to account for the quarterly compounding.

[3] By assuming that hedgers will be net short no matter what the futures price, we are merely assuming that their preexisting risk requires a short position. Some potential hedgers would, of course, abandon their risk-reducing short position if the futures price were low enough. However, in so doing, the potential hedger would have abandoned the intention of hedging and would be speculating. This is clear if we recall that the risk-reducing futures trade is to go short.

[4] A normal market gives rise to "normal backwardation" and an inverted market is consistent with prices following a "contango." (In the French futures market, you may sometimes encounter the "Last Contango in Paris." Sorry.)

[5] For a more extended summary of these studies, see R. Kolb, *Understanding Futures Markets,* 5e, Malden, MA: Blackwell Publishers, 1997, Chapter 3.

[6] This calculation assumes that the interest rate is 10 percent per annum and there are 250 trading periods, for a daily interest factor of 1.000381. Thus, the first day, the price rises by $2 so this gives interest of $2(1.000381)^{250} - \$2 = \$.20$, and so on. Later, when the losses start, those losses must also be compounded out to the horizon.

[7] For a more complete discussion and summary of the studies in this area, including detailed references, see R. Kolb, *Understanding Futures Markets,* 5e, Malden, MA: Blackwell Publishers, 1997.

[8] P. Samuelson, ''Proof That Properly Anticipated Prices Fluctuate Randomly,'' *Industrial Management Review,* 6:2, Spring 1965, pp. 41–49.

USING FUTURES MARKETS

OVERVIEW

In the two preceding chapters, we discussed the institutional setting of futures markets and the determination of futures prices. This chapter explores three different ways that futures markets serve different elements of society. As we have already noted, futures markets provide a means of price discovery. Second, futures markets provide an arena for speculation. Third, futures markets provide a means for transferring risk, or hedging. This chapter explores each of these contributions of futures markets.

First we will analyze the function of **price discovery** – the revelation of information about the prices of commodities in the future. Because prices in the futures markets provide information that is not readily available elsewhere, the markets serve societal needs. We note that price discovery is open to everyone, the first group of beneficiaries from these markets.

Speculators comprise the second major group to benefit from futures markets. A **speculator** is a trader who enters the futures market in pursuit of profit, thereby accepting an increase in risk. It may seem strange to list an opportunity for speculation as a service to society, but consider the following examples. Casinos provide speculative opportunities for citizens, and that might be reckoned as a public service. Professional and college sports teams also provide a way for people to speculate by betting, illegally in some states and legally in others.

Clearly, sports teams do not exist so that people can bet on them, but the chance to bet is a side effect, and perhaps a side benefit, of the existence of sports. The situation is similar in the futures markets. Futures markets do not exist in order to provide the chance to speculate, but they do provide speculative opportunities. Less obvious is the way in which speculators themselves contribute to the smooth functioning of the futures market. As we show, the speculator pursues profits. As a side effect, the speculator provides liquidity to the market that helps the market function more effectively.

Hedgers are a third major group of futures market users. A **hedger** is a trader with a preexisting risk who enters the futures market in order to reduce that risk. For example, a wheat farmer has price risk associated with the future price of wheat at harvest. By trading in the futures market, the farmer may be able to reduce that preexisting risk. This opportunity to transfer risk is perhaps the greatest contribution of futures markets to society. In many cases, businesses face risks that result from the ordinary conduct of business. Often these risks are undesired, and the futures market provides a way in which risk may be transferred to other individuals willing to bear it. If people know that unwanted risks may be avoided by transacting in the futures market at a reasonable cost, then they will not be afraid to make decisions that will expose them initially to certain risks. They know that they can hedge that risk.

From the point of view of society, hedging has important advantages. Enterprises that are profitable, but that involve more risk than their principals wish to bear, can still be pursued. The unwanted risk can then be transferred in the futures market, and society benefits economically. This is the strongest argument for the existence of futures markets. By providing an efficient means of transferring risk to those individuals in society willing to bear it cheaply, futures markets contribute to the economy.

PRICE DISCOVERY

In Chapter 3, we explored the connection between futures prices and expected future spot prices, focusing on the relationship between futures prices and expected future spot prices. This relationship is crucial for the futures market's ability to fulfill the social function of price discovery. In this section, we consider this issue in more detail.

Students of futures markets admit a close connection between futures prices and expected future spot prices. The question is how the futures market can be used to reveal information about subsequent commodity prices. The usefulness of price forecasts based on futures prices depends on three factors:

1. The need for information about future spot prices.
2. The accuracy of the futures market forecasts of those prices.
3. The performance of futures market forecasts relative to alternative forecasting techniques.

Information

Many individuals and groups in society need information about the future price of various commodities. For example, with information about the price of gold one year from now, it would be relatively simple to make a fortune. Certainly, speculation would be much more rewarding if one had a private and infallible source of information about future spot prices. Aside from such dreams of wealth, information about future spot prices is also needed for more mundane purposes, such as the planning of future investment and consumption by individuals, corporations, and governmental bodies.

Consider an underpaid college professor who wants to buy a house. Interest rates are high, so taking a long-term mortgage in such times would commit him to a lifetime of large payments. On the other hand, if he does not buy a house, then he cannot take advantage of the tax deduction that the interest portion of the house payments would provide. If interest rates were to drop soon, then it would be reasonable to wait to buy the house. By consulting the financial pages of the newspaper, the professor could find out what the market believed about the future level of interest rates. Futures contracts on long-term Treasury bonds are traded on the Chicago Board of Trade. If the interest rate for a bond to be delivered in six months is three percentage points lower than current interest rates, then there is good reason to expect interest rates will fall over the next six months. In such a situation, the college professor might do well to wait a few months to buy his house.

Another example concerns a furniture manufacturer who makes wooden furniture. Assume that she is printing her catalog now for the next year and must include the prices of the different items of furniture. Setting prices in advance is always a very tricky affair. In addition to other problems, the price she charges will depend upon the expected future price of lumber. The cost of lumber varies greatly, depending largely on the health of the construction industry, so it is difficult for her to know how to include that cost factor in her calculations. One way in which she might deal with this is to use the prices from the lumber futures market to estimate the costs of the wood that she will have to purchase later on. In doing so, she uses the futures markets for their **price discovery** benefit.

In both of these examples, individuals use futures prices to estimate the spot price at some future date. The advisability of such a technique depends on the accuracy of the forecasts drawn from the futures market. Futures prices may, of course, differ from subsequently observed spot prices. If there is a large discrepancy, the futures forecasts may not be very useful. Errors could result from two sources: inaccurate but unbiased forecasts and bias in the forecast itself.

Accuracy

A forecasting estimator is unbiased if the average value of the forecast equals the value of the variable to be forecasted.[1] Thus, futures prices might provide unbiased forecasts with very large errors. The situation is reminiscent of the joke about the two economists who predicted the unemployment rate for the next year. The first economist predicted that 12 percent of the work force would be unemployed, while the second put the figure at full employment, or zero percent unemployed. The actual rate turned out to be 6 percent, from which the economists cheerfully concluded that, on average, they were exactly right. In forecasting the unemployment rate, one could say that the economists had provided an unbiased forecast but one that had large errors.

As is typical for many commodities, the forecasts from the futures market have large errors. Futures prices fluctuate radically, which means that most of the time they provide an inaccurate forecast of the underlying commodity's spot price at the time of delivery. Without question, the large size of the forecast errors from the futures markets limits the forecasts' reliability.

One might reasonably wonder why there should be such large errors. According to the theory of finance, prices in well-developed markets reflect all available information. As new information becomes available, futures prices adjust themselves very swiftly. As a consequence, futures prices tend to exhibit radical fluctuations, which means that the prices will be inaccurate as estimates of subsequent spot prices.

In addition to the large errors that one can observe in futures market forecasts, futures prices may be biased. One possible reason for this was considered in Chapter 3. Futures prices may embody a risk premium that keeps the futures price from equaling the expected future spot price. In general, the possibility of bias is not too great a concern, at least for practical matters. Further, while there is still no real agreement about their existence, there is agreement that, if biases do exist, they are small. In general, the errors in futures forecasts are so large that they tend to drown out any biases that may also be present.

Performance

Since forecasts based on futures prices seem to be so poor, why would anyone care about them? Before discarding the forecasts, consider the alternatives. What other forecast might be more accurate?

A considerable amount of study on this topic has failed to lead to any final answer. Nonetheless, evidence suggests that forecasts based on futures prices are not excelled by other forecasting techniques. Futures forecasts have been compared to other techniques and have not been found to be inferior. The current situation in forecasts of the foreign exchange rate is typical. For example, compared to professional foreign exchange forecasting firms, some of which charge large fees, the futures price of foreign currency predicts very well. Many professional firms have recently turned in forecasting records with results worse than those of chance.[2]

In spite of the large errors in forecasts based on futures market prices, the futures market seems better than the alternatives. To summarize, the accuracy of futures forecasts is not that good, but it is certainly better than the alternatives, and futures market forecasts are free. Someone needing a forecast of future spot prices should not rely too heavily on any forecast. When relying on some forecasting technique, however, it should be the forecast freely available in the futures market.

SPECULATION

Defining speculation or identifying the speculator in the futures market is always difficult. For our purposes, the following definition of a speculator will prove useful. A **speculator** is a trader who enters the futures market in search of profit and, by so doing, willingly accepts increased risk.[3]

Most individuals have no heavy risk exposure in most commodities. Consider an individual who is neither a farmer nor a food processor, but who has an interest in the wheat market. If she trades a wheat futures contract, then she most likely is speculating in the sense defined previously. She enters the futures market, willingly increases her risk, and hopes for profit.

One might object that this individual does not have a preexisting risk exposure in wheat. In fact, everyone who eats bread does. One's plans for consuming bread may change if wheat prices rise too high. This objection makes a good point. In order to know whether a particular action in the futures market is a speculative trade requires knowledge about the trader's current assets and future consumption plans. For an individual, however, entry into the futures market is most likely to be for speculation. For the woman who traded a wheat futures contract, the size of the wheat contract (5,000 bushels) is so large relative to her needs for wheat that the transaction increases her overall risk. Assuming that she, like most people, is risk averse, she will not expose herself to the additional risk of entering the futures market unless she hopes to profit by doing so. This is what classifies her as a speculator.

Earlier, we also noted that speculators use futures transactions as a substitute for a cash market transaction. For an individual, trading a 5,000 bushel futures contract is unlikely to be a substitute for a cash market transaction, and this criterion also identifies the individual trading wheat as a speculator. Different types of speculators may be categorized by the length of time they plan to hold a position. Traditionally, there are three kinds of speculators: scalpers, day traders, and position traders.

Scalpers

Of all speculators, scalpers have the shortest horizon over which they plan to hold a futures position. Scalpers aim to foresee the movement of the market over a very short interval, ranging from the next few seconds to the next few minutes. Many scalpers describe themselves as psychologists trying to sense the feel of the trading among the other market participants. In order to do this, they must be in the trading pit; otherwise, they could not hope to see buying or selling pressure building up among the other traders.[4]

Since their planned holding period is so short, scalpers do not expect to make a large profit on each trade. Instead, they hope to make a profit of one or two ticks – the minimum allowable price movement. Many trades by scalpers end in losses or in no profit. If the prices do not move in the scalper's direction within a few minutes of assuming a position, the scalper will likely close the position and begin looking for a new opportunity.

This type of trading strategy means that the scalper will generate an enormous number of transactions. Were he or she to make these transactions through a broker as an off-the-floor participant, the scalper would lose any anticipated profit through high transaction costs. Since scalpers are members of the exchange, or lease a seat from a member, their transaction costs are very low. Scalpers probably pay less than $1 per round turn in most futures markets, compared to about $25–80 for an off-the-floor trader who trades through a regular broker. Without these very low transaction costs, the scalper's efforts would be hopeless. To sense the direction of the market and to conserve on transaction costs, a scalper needs to be on the floor of the exchange.

In his book, *The New Gatsbys,* Bob Tamarkin explores the personalities of futures traders based on his own experience. Writing about scalpers, he says:

> Many traded by feel rather than by fundamentals, forgetting about things like leading economic indicators, government policies, and even supplies of commodities. They simply tried to catch the market on the way up and ditch it on the way down. In the trading pits they could do it faster and better than any outside speculators because they were squarely in the heart of the action.

Discussing scalpers in general and describing an individual scalper named Paul, Tamarkin tells us:

> Each trader had a theory about what was happening in the next five minutes. If everyone thought the market was going to open higher, but it opened lower, the psychology in the pit changed immediately. It was a herd mentality fed on raw emotion. It was the easy way. Get the trading feel of the crowd in the pit; then jump on board for the move. By the time the public got in, the market ticked that quarter or half cent, and Paul had his profit. The ultimate price of a commodity may have been determined by supply and demand, Paul thought, but in the interim, emotional factors reigned supreme.[5]

Although it may not be apparent at first glance, scalpers provide a valuable service to the market by their frenzied trading activity. By trading so often, scalpers help supply the market with liquidity. Their trading activity increases the ease with which other market participants may find trading partners. Without high liquidity, some outside traders would avoid the market, which would decrease its usefulness. A high degree of liquidity is necessary for the success of a futures market, and scalpers play an important role in providing this liquidity. We might say that scalpers provide the opportunity for other traders to trade immediately.

To illustrate the role played by scalpers in providing liquidity, consider the following example. An off-the-floor trader might see the most recently quoted price on a ticker machine and desire to trade at that price. If the market is not liquid, then it may be difficult to trade at or near that price for at least two reasons. First, if the market is not liquid, the observed transaction might have occurred some time ago and there may not be anyone willing to trade at that last reported price. Second, without the willing pool of potential traders represented by the scalpers in the pit, the bid-asked spread could be quite wide, making it difficult to trade near the last reported price. The scalpers in the pit are there to seek profit, but they compete with each other to trade. As a result, the presence of the scalpers helps keep the bid-asked price narrow, keep the market more active and price quotations more current, and attract outside traders to the market because they know their orders can be executed near the equilibrium price for the commodity.

In an interesting article, Professor William Silber explores the behavior of scalpers. He arranged to observe all of the transactions of a scalper he identifies only as Mr. X. Mr. X was a trader on the New York Futures Exchange, trading New York Stock Exchange Composite index futures. For 31 trading days in late 1982 and early 1983, Silber tracked all of Mr. X's trading. Table 4.1 presents some of Silber's results. During this period, Mr. X traded 2,106 times, or about 70 times per day. These transactions involved the purchase and sale (round turn) of 2,178 contracts.

Table 4.1 also shows the number of trades, which Silber defines as going from a zero net position and returning to a zero net position. Fewer than half (48 percent) of these trades were profitable, while 22 percent generated losses. Thirty percent were scratch trades – those with neither a profit nor a loss. The trades generated an average profit of $10.56, or a total trading profit of $7,698.24 over the period. On average a trade took 116 seconds. So the average length of time that Mr. X had a risk exposure was two minutes. The longest trade, hence the longest period of risk exposure, took 547 seconds, or a little over nine minutes. Clearly, Mr. X is reluctant to maintain positions for very long.

Table 4.2 presents one-half hour of Mr. X's trading. During this period, Mr. X made 19 transactions. Notice how Mr. X opens a position, either long or short, and then moves quickly back to a zero position in the market. During this half-hour, Mr. X goes through five trading cycles, beginning and ending the half-hour with a net zero position.

As Silber concludes, the major function that Mr. X provides to the market is liquidity. As a scalper, Mr. X takes the other side of trades coming in from traders off the floor of the exchange. Also, Silber found that Mr. X's trades tended to be more profitable when they were held for a shorter time. For instance, Mr. X's trades taking longer than three minutes were losing trades on average. As Silber concludes: ''Scalper earnings compensate for the skill in evaluating market conditions in

Table 4.1	Mr. X's Trades Over 31 Trading Days
Total Transactions	2,106
Number of Contracts Traded (Round turns – buy and sell 1 contract)	2,178
Number of Trades (Zero net position to a zero net position)	729
Profitable	353 (48%)
Unprofitable	157 (22%)
Scratch	219 (30%)

Source: From William L. Silber, "Marketmaker Behavior in an Auction Market: An Analysis of Scalpers in Futures Markets," *Journal of Finance* 39:4, September 1984, pp. 937–53. Reprinted by permission of the American Finance Association.

	One-Half Hour of Mr. X's Trading		Table 4.2
Transaction	Time	Contracts Traded (Buy +/Sell −)	Net Position
1	10:05:29	2	2
2	10:06:47	−2	0
3	10:08:10	5	5
4	10:09:15	−1	4
5	10:09:49	−2	2
6	10:10:25	−1	1
7	10:11:20	−1	0
8	10:12:56	6	6
9	10:13:29	−3	3
10	10:15:38	−1	2
11	10:16:58	−1	1
12	10:17:23	−1	0
13	10:22:25	−5	−5
14	10:23:11	3	−2
15	10:23:23	2	0
16	10:25:26	5	5
17	10:26:12	−1	4
18	10:26:18	−1	3
19	10:28:12	−3	0

Source: From William L. Silber, "Marketmaker Behavior in an Auction Market: An Analysis of Scalpers in Futures Markets," *Journal of Finance* 39:4, September 1984, pp. 937–53. Reprinted by permission of the American Finance Association.

the very short run and for providing liquidity to the market over the time horizon."[6] This accords with the excerpts from Tamarkin.

Day Traders

Compared to scalpers, day traders take a very farsighted approach to the market. Day traders attempt to profit from the price movements that may take place over the course of one trading day. The day trader closes his or her position before the end of trading each day so that he or she has no position in the futures market overnight. Day traders may trade on or off the floor.

A day trader might follow a strategy such as concentrating activity around announcements from the U.S. government. The Department of Agriculture releases production figures for hogs at intervals that are well known in advance. The day trader may think that the hog figures to be released on a certain day will indicate an unexpectedly high level of production. If so, such an announcement will cause the futures prices for hogs to fall, due to the unexpectedly large future supply of pork. To take advantage of this insight, the day trader would sell the hog contract prior to the announcement and then wait for prices to fall after the announcement. Such a strategy could be implemented without holding a futures market position overnight. Therefore, it is a suitable strategy for a day trader to pursue. (To avoid drastic effects on markets, government announcements are often made late in the day, after the affected market closes.)

The scalper's strategy of holding a position for a very short interval is clearly motivated, but it is not so apparent why day traders limit themselves to price movements that will occur only during the interval of one day's trading. The basic reason is risk. Day traders believe that it is too risky to hold a speculative position overnight; too many disastrous price movements could occur.

To see the danger of maintaining a position overnight, consider a position in orange juice concentrate traded by the Citrus Associates of the New York Cotton Exchange. In late November, a trader holds a short position in orange juice futures. The weather in Florida is crucial for orange juice prices, and the trader checks the weather forecast for Florida that day before trading closes. There seems to be no possibility of damaging weather in the next few days, so he maintains his position overnight. Unexpectedly, a strong cold front pushes into Florida and destroys a large portion of the orange crop, which, in November, is still on the trees and not yet mature. Naturally, futures prices soar on the opening of trading the next day, and the trader who held his position overnight suffers a large loss. In fear of such sudden developments, day traders close their positions each day before trading stops.

The overwhelming majority of speculators are either scalpers or day traders, which indicates just how risky it can be to take a position home overnight. As the close of trading approaches each day, the pace of trading increases. Typically, 25 percent of the day's trading volume occurs in the last half hour of trading. The last five minutes are particularly frenetic as traders attempt to close all of their open positions.

Position Traders

A **position trader** is a speculator who maintains a futures position overnight. On occasion they may hold them for weeks or even months. There are two types of position traders, those holding an **outright position** and those holding a **spread position**. Of the two strategies, the outright position is far riskier.

Outright Positions. An outright position trader might adopt the following strategy if she believed that long-term interest rates were going to rise more than the market expected over the next two months. As interest rates rise, the futures prices, representing the price of bonds, must fall. However, the trader does not really know when during the next two months the rise in rates will occur. To take advantage of her belief about the course of interest rates, she could sell the futures contract on U.S. Treasury bonds traded at the Chicago Board of Trade and hold that position over the next two months. If she is correct, there will be a sharp rise in rates not correctly anticipated by the market, and futures prices will fall. She can then offset and reap her profit.

The danger in this trader's outright position is clear. If she has made a mistake, and interest rates fall unexpectedly, then she will suffer a large loss. The outright position offers a chance for very large gains if she is correct, but it carries with it the risk of very large losses as well. For most speculators, the risks associated with outright positions are too large. The expected trading life of a new trader is about six months, but it is much shorter for outright position traders.

Spread Positions. More risk-averse position traders may trade spreads. Intracommodity spreads involve differences between two or more contract maturities for the same underlying deliverable good. In contrast, intercommodity spreads are price differences between two or more contracts written on different, but related, underlying goods. For example, the difference between the July wheat and corn contracts would be an intercommodity spread. The spread trader trades two or more contracts with related price movements, the goal being to profit from changes in the relative prices.

Consider the case of a spread speculator who believes that the difference between the futures price of wheat and corn is too high. Such a trader believes that the intercommodity spread between wheat and corn is inconsistent with the justifiable price differential between the two goods. Wheat normally sells at a higher price per bushel than corn, but for this trader the differential in prices is too large. On February 1, the following closing prices could be observed for the JUL wheat and corn contracts, quoted in cents per bushel.

JUL Wheat	329.50
JUL Corn	229.00

The trader believes that this difference of more than one dollar is too large and is willing to speculate that the price of corn will rise relative to the price of wheat. Accordingly, the trader transacts as shown in the top panel of Table 4.3.

Figure 4.1 shows the prices for the JUL corn and wheat contracts for the relevant period. Prices are expressed in cents per bushel. As the figure shows, prices of both corn and wheat did not change dramatically, but both prices fell after February 1, with wheat prices falling more than corn. Because the trader was short wheat and long corn, the price movements gave a profit on the wheat side of the trade and a loss on the corn side. However, the drop in wheat prices was greater than the drop in corn prices, giving an overall profit on the spread position. Figure 4.2 tracks the profits that the trader enjoyed from February 1 to June 1.

In this example, the trader correctly bet that the price of corn would rise relative to the price of wheat. As it happened, both prices fell, but the price of wheat fell more, giving an overall profit on the transaction. However, this result is not necessary for the trader to have a profit. For example, if wheat and corn both rose, but corn rose more, the trade would still be profitable. In a spread trade, only the relative prices matter, not the absolute prices.

An Intercommodity Spread	Table 4.3

The wheat and corn contracts are both for 5,000 bushels.

Date	Futures Market
February 1	Sell 1 JUL wheat contract at 329.50 cents per bushel. Buy 1 JUL corn contract at 229.00 cents per bushel.
June 1	Buy 1 JUL wheat contract at 282.75 cents per bushel. Sell 1 JUL corn contract at 219.50 cents per bushel.

	Corn Loss:
	     −$.095 per bushel × 5,000 bushels = −$475.00
	 Wheat Profit:
	     $.4675 per bushel × 5,000 bushels = $2,337.50
	         Total Profit: $1,862.50

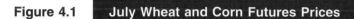

Figure 4.1   **July Wheat and Corn Futures Prices**

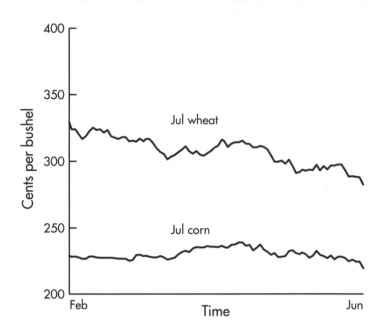

Other types of spread strategies are also possible. In an intracommodity spread, a trader takes a position in two or more maturity months for the same good. The belief behind this strategy is that the relative prices between delivery dates for the same commodity will change, generating a profit for the trader. Whereas an outright position only requires a belief about the price movement of one commodity, a spread position focuses on the relative price movements between two or more commodities, or contract maturities.

The spread example considered previously was relatively simple, but spreads can be quite complex. One frequently mentioned complex spread is known as a **butterfly spread**, which is best illustrated by an example. Assume that today is November 10 and the prices for copper are as shown in Table 4.4. In comparing the price for September delivery, 67.5 cents per pound, with the prices on the adjacent delivery months of July and December, it seems that the September price is out of line. To this speculator, it appears that the September price should be about halfway between the July and December prices, but it is seriously below that level. Since the speculator does not really know whether copper prices are going to rise or fall in general, she only wants to attempt to take advantage of this apparent pricing discrepancy between different maturities.

To do this, she initiates a futures transaction known as a butterfly spread, such as the one illustrated in Table 4.5. Since she expects the price of the September contract to rise relative to the July and December contracts, she sells one contract of each of the July and December maturities. To offset the sale of these two contracts, she buys two contracts for the September delivery. By April 15, the prices of all of the contracts have fallen, but their price relationships are much closer to what

Wheat/Corn Spread Profits (February 1–June 1)   **Figure 4.2**

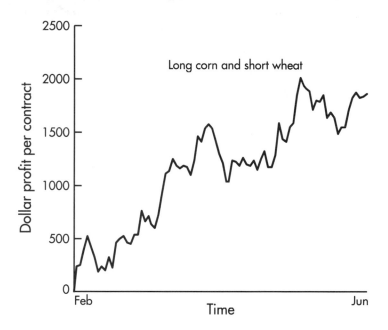

Copper Futures Prices on November 10	Table 4.4

Delivery Month (of following year)	Price (cents per pound)
JUL	67.0
SEP	67.5
DEC	70.5

the speculator believed was correct. On April 15, the September price has risen, relative to the other contracts, to a point about halfway between them. This is exactly what she expected to happen. The wings of the butterfly spread (the July and December contracts) have flapped, bringing all of the prices into line. As Table 4.5 reveals, this generates a total profit of $750 on the spread.

The classification of speculators into scalpers, day traders, and position traders is useful, but it should not obscure the fact that individuals can have multiple speculative strategies. A particular trader can easily merge his or her activities as a scalper and a position trader. Those individuals actively trading in the pits take advantage of all types of opportunities that might become available.

Table 4.5	A Butterfly Spread in Copper

The copper contract trades on the Commodity Exchange, Inc. Each contract is for 25,000 pounds.

Date	Futures Market
November 10	Sell 1 JUL copper contract at 67 cents per pound. Buy 2 SEP copper contracts at 67.5 cents per pound. Sell 1 DEC copper contract at 70.5 cents per pound.
April 15	Buy 1 JUL copper contract at 65 cents per pound. Sell 2 SEP copper contracts at 67 cents per pound. Buy 1 DEC copper contract at 68.5 cents per pound.

Profits and Losses:
JUL: +\$.02 × 25,000 pounds = +\$500
SEP: −\$.005 × 2 contracts × 25,000 pounds = −\$250
DEC: +\$.02 × 25,000 pounds = +\$500
Total Profit: \$750

SPECULATIVE PROFITS

In this section, we review several dimensions of speculative trading. First, we consider the available evidence on speculator success and failure for individuals. We have already seen that scalpers seem to make speculative profits. Here, we examine the results of several studies of overall trader performance. Second, we evaluate the practices and profits for some technical trading systems. Third, we consider the aims and performance of commodity pools. Finally, we analyze speculative profits in an efficient markets setting.

Evidence on Speculative Profits

For the most part, speculative profits and losses are difficult to observe. Most traders cherish the privacy of their brokerage accounts. This privacy allows them to enjoy their profits and lick their trading wounds in private and also to tell ''fish stories'' about their trading prowess. Nonetheless, there are several studies that assess the trading results of speculators. A prime source of this information comes from the CFTC report in which traders with large positions are required to report those positions. This information is made public, although it is presented only in aggregate form. Therefore, it is possible to determine what large (above the reporting requirements) and small (below the reporting requirements) traders are doing in the aggregate. Note that this is not the same as being able to examine a sample of actual trading for particular individuals.

The studies on the magnitude of speculative profits do not reach a consensus, and some of the methodologies employed have been criticized. Nonetheless, there appears to be little reason to think that speculators make large profits, particularly after considering transaction costs. Rather, the results of some gains and some losses might be broadly consistent with speculators trading futures contracts that are fairly priced.

Technical Trading Systems

In futures markets, more than any other segment of the financial markets, technical trading systems seem to find favor. This can be verified by browsing through a recent issue of *Futures* and noting the many advertisements for various technical trading systems. **Technical analysis** is a method of analyzing markets that uses only market data (prices, volume, open interest, and similar information) to predict future price movements. For example, technical analysts believe certain price formations suggest that futures prices will rise. Other formations, according to technical analysis, portend a price decline. We do not explore the methods of technical analysis here, but many books cover the subject.[7] Instead, we want to explore the evidence on whether technical analysis can generate speculative profits.

To have any chance of success, technical analysis depends on the existence of patterns in futures prices. In most markets, scholars find that price patterns do exist, but that these patterns are not sufficiently strong to permit technical trading strategies to generate a profit. To make a trading profit, including covering transaction costs, would require very significant patterns. Many studies are based on simulations of trading systems, instead of systems that are in actual use. While many of these studies suggest that technical analysis may have some merit, this is a very controversial area, and the final word has not yet been written on the subject. If technical analysis is useful in futures trading, that result would stand in contrast to findings for other financial markets.[8]

Commodity Funds

A **commodity fund** or a **commodity pool** is a financial institution that accepts funds from a variety of participants and uses those funds to speculate in the futures market. As such, its organization is similar to a mutual fund. We have noted that trading futures does not require investment as such. Thus, the commodity funds use their customers' funds for two purposes: margin deposits and earning interest. The interest-earning portion provides a pool of funds for future margin calls. Gains and losses for the funds come from futures trading and from the interest that is being earned. Most funds rely strongly on technical analysis for their trading strategies.

What performance can we expect from commodity funds? To analyze this question, we make two initial assumptions. First, we assume that patterns in futures prices are not sufficient to allow technical analysis to generate profits. Second, we assume that the futures price equals the expected future spot price. Under these two restrictions, we would expect the futures trading portion of the commodity fund to neither lose nor profit. Under our assumptions, the fund might trade, but the expected payoff on each trade would be zero. For the interest-earning portion of their assets, we would expect the invested assets to earn the money market rate of interest. Under these assumptions, we expect a commodity fund to underperform a buy-and-hold money market investment, due to the transaction costs that the fund incurs in its trading strategy. To succeed, the commodity fund must be able to earn speculative profits, presumably through technical trading systems, since most funds rely largely on those systems.

Typically, commodity funds use only about 30 percent of invested funds as margin deposits. Thus, the bulk of the money received sits in a money market investment. Second, returns are often negative. Third, even when funds earn positive returns, they typically do not outperform their inherent level of systematic risk. That is, they do not beat the market. Fourth, even if funds are not attractive as investments in themselves, they might be useful in reducing risk when added to a portfolio of stocks and bonds. Evidence on this point is mixed. Fifth, past performance is not a good guide to future performance. In sum, the evidence seems fairly consistent with an efficient markets perspective. Funds do not seem to be an exciting investment vehicle, but they may be a useful tool in some circumstances.

"Normal" Speculative Returns

We have seen several examples of apparently successful speculation. First, we saw that Mr. X in Silber's study earned positive returns by scalping. Second, we considered several studies that reported on speculative profits. Third, we noted that some technical trading systems seem to earn positive returns, while evidence suggests that other systems do not. Finally, we examined commodity pools and found some evidence that some pools make speculative profits. In this section, we want to consider futures market speculation from an efficient markets perspective. To do this, we will review the concept of a "normal profit," and then consider Mr. X's trading in more detail.

An **efficient market** is a market in which prices fully reflect the information contained in a specified information set. To differentiate versions of the efficient markets hypothesis, we can specify different information sets. The traditional versions of the efficient markets hypothesis are known as the weak, semi-strong, and strong versions.[9] The **weak form** of the efficient markets hypothesis claims that prices in a market fully reflect all information contained in the history of volume and price. The **semi-strong** version claims that market prices fully reflect all publicly available information. The **strong** version states that market prices reflect all information, whether public or private. Private information includes information possessed only by corporate insiders and governmental officials.[10] The strong version is almost certainly false, so we will be concerned only with the weak and semi-strong forms.

If the weak form version is true, then no information about past or present prices or volume is useful for guiding a speculative strategy. If the futures market is weakly efficient, there will be no cash-and-carry arbitrage opportunities of the type we analyzed in Chapter 3. Additionally, technical trading strategies will not work. If the semi-strong version is true, then studying information about the determinants of prices will also not be useful in guiding a trading strategy.

Unlike investing in stocks or bonds, trading futures requires no actual investment, because of the system of margin and daily settlement. This suggests that any steady profits in futures trading would be inconsistent with an efficient market. Thus, the scalping profits of about $10 per contract reviewed earlier seem to fly in the face of the efficient markets hypothesis. We now want to examine some additional costs that the scalper faces.

To trade futures on a major exchange, one must own a seat, or secure the use of a seat from one who does own one. Second, trading on the exchange involves a commitment of time and energy. Since the time and energy is being committed to trading, it cannot be applied elsewhere to earn a return. Third, trading futures necessarily involves risk. Most people are unwilling to risk money unless the expected returns from those risks are high enough to justify the risk. With these ideas in mind, consider Mr. X, who we assume owns a seat on a major exchange. What income does he need to make trading worthwhile from a financial point of view, and how does this compare with his actual trading results?

The first consideration is the value of the seat that is required in order to trade. As mentioned in Chapter 2, seats on the exchanges are bought and sold in a market and CME and CBOT seats have recently sold in the range of $450,000 to $600,000. Taking a conservative figure of $500,000, it is clear that our trader loses the use of $500,000 by virtue of buying his seat. Assume that an equally risky investment would return a modest 10 percent. To cover the cost of his seat, Mr. X must make $50,000 per year. Second, Mr. X commits his time to trading, and he could hold another job if he were not trading. Most of the traders are people of competence and executive ability, and trading is grueling and nerve-wracking work with long hours that go beyond the limited trading times. Mr. X, having exhibited a willingness to work as hard as a trader must work and with the talents necessary to succeed as a trader, could expect to earn a relatively handsome salary in some other capacity. Perhaps $60,000 per year would be realistic and conservative. As most salaried positions have fringe benefits for medical, dental, and life insurance, this is extremely conservative.

In addition to the foregone opportunities of investing the price of his seat elsewhere and of taking alternative employment, the high risk of trading must also be acknowledged. Relative to trading, a salaried position is very secure. Being risk averse, Mr. X would reasonably expect some compensation for his additional risk exposure. The amount of compensation is very difficult to quantify and clearly depends on his personal risk tolerance. Finally, the character of a trader's work needs to be considered somewhat more fully. Trading is extremely demanding – physically, emotionally, and mentally. A casual survey of the trading pits reveals few elderly participants. From conversations with many traders, it is clear that they do not generally expect to be trading past the age of 40.[11] As another indicator of the level of stress one need only consult *The Wall Street Journal,* which has frequent articles on the problems of traders. They lose their voices from shouting and need voice coaches, they occasionally sustain physical injuries, and they sometimes suffer anxiety as a result of the stress in their work.[12] While many traders are attracted by the excitement of the pits, many people would demand high compensation for working under such conditions. The extreme physical and psychic demands are difficult to value in terms of dollars, but they are real costs.

Table 4.6 shows that Mr. X should make at least $110,000 per year without there being the slightest hint that supernormal profits are being captured. Many traders make very handsome incomes and live quite well – when they are not on the trading floor. This fact alone does not warrant the conclusions that trading futures contracts is an easy way to get rich quickly. The traders have high costs to cover before they reach the point at which they start to make supernormal profits. The chance to speculate on futures may not be the way to easy street.

The real-world data from Silber's study reveal the difficulties traders face. As Silber notes, Mr. X earned relatively little during this period. During the 31 trading days of Silber's sample, Mr. X had average profits of $742 per day. This was before commissions, which averaged $1.22 per contract traded. After commissions, Mr. X had daily profits of $672.00 per day. With approximately 250 trading days per year, Mr. X would earn about $168,000 per year. Silber reports that these results

Hypothetical Alternative Income for Mr. X	Table 4.6
Resource	**Annual Amount**
Use of money to secure seat	$50,000
Foregone alternative employment	60,000
Additional risk undertaken	?
Additional stress and strain	?
	Total: $110,000 + ?

place Mr. X in the upper quartile of scalpers on the NYFE. When we compare these results with the opportunity cost computed in Table 4.6, we can see that Mr. X does well, but not wonderfully. If we consider the risks he takes, the stress and strain he bears, and the out-of-pocket costs he faces, Mr. X will have to do better than he did in this period to convince us that he can beat the market.

HEDGING

In contrast to the speculator, the **hedger** is a trader who enters the futures market in order to reduce a preexisting risk. If a trader trades futures contracts on commodities in which he or she has no initial position, and in which he or she does not contemplate taking a cash position, then the trader cannot be a hedger. The futures transaction cannot serve as a substitute for a cash market transaction. Having a position, in this case, does not mean that the trader must actually own a commodity. An individual or firm who anticipates the need for a certain commodity in the future or a person who plans to acquire a certain commodity later also has a position in that commodity. In many cases, a hedger has a certain **hedging horizon** – the future date when the hedge will terminate. For example, a farmer can anticipate that he or she will want to hedge from planting to the harvest. In other cases, there will be no specific horizon. We begin with two examples in which hedgers have definite hedging horizons.

A Long Hedge

The idea that you may be at risk in a certain commodity without actually owning it may be a confusing idea to some. Yet consider the following example. Silver is an essential input for the production of most types of photographic films and papers, and the price of silver is quite volatile. For a film manufacturer, there is considerable risk that profits could be dramatically affected by fluctuations in the price of silver. If production schedules are to be maintained, it is absolutely essential that silver be acquired on a regular basis in large quantities. Assume that the film manufacturer needs 50,000 troy ounces of silver in two months and confronts the silver prices shown in Table 4.7 on May 10. The current spot price is 1052.5 cents per ounce, and the price of the JUL futures contract lies above that at 1068.0, with the SEP futures contract trading at 1084.0.

Fearing that silver prices may rise unexpectedly, the film manufacturer decides that the price of 1068.0 is acceptable for the silver that he will need in July. He realizes that it is hopeless to buy the silver on the spot market at 1052.5 and to store the silver for two months. The price differential of 15.5 cents per ounce would not cover his storage costs. Also, the manufacturer will receive an

Table 4.7	Silver Futures Prices on May 10	

The COMEX trades a silver contract for 5,000 troy ounces.

Contract	Price (cents per troy ounce)
Spot	1052.5
JUL	1068.0
SEP	1084.0

acceptable level of profits even if he pays 1068.0 for the silver to be delivered in July. To pay a price higher than 1068.0, however, could jeopardize profitability seriously. With these reasons in mind, he decides to enter the futures market to hedge against the possibility of future unexpected price increases, and accordingly, he enters the trades shown in Table 4.8.

Taking the futures price as the best estimate of the future spot price, the manufacturer expects to pay 1068.0 cents per ounce for silver in the spot market two months from now in July. At the same time, he buys ten 5,000 ounce JUL futures contracts at 1068.0 cents per ounce. Since he buys a futures contract in order to hedge, this transaction is known as a **long hedge**. The trader is also purchasing a futures contract in anticipation of needing the silver at a future date, so these transactions also represent an **anticipatory hedge**. Time passes, and by July the spot price of silver has risen to 1071.0 cents per ounce, three cents higher than expected. Needing the silver, the manufacturer purchases the silver on the spot market, paying a total of $535,500. This is $1,500 more than expected. Since the futures contract is about to mature, the futures price must equal the spot price, so the film manufacturer is able to sell his ten futures contracts at the same price of 1071.0 cents per ounce, making a three cent profit on each ounce, and a total profit of $1,500 on the futures position. The cash and futures results net to zero. In the cash market, the price was $1,500 more than expected, but there was an offsetting futures profit of $1,500, which generated a net wealth change of zero.

The Reversing Trade and Hedging

One peculiar feature of these transactions is that the manufacturer did not accept delivery on the futures contract but offset the contract instead. Rather than accepting delivery on a contract, it usually is better to reverse the trade because offsetting saves on transaction costs and administrative difficulties. The short trader has the right to choose the delivery destination and the long trader must fear that the short trader will select an unpalatable destination. Instead of taking delivery, the long trader can acquire the physical commodity from normal suppliers. The hedger in this example could have achieved the same result by accepting delivery. If delivery were accepted on the futures contract, the silver would have been secured at a price of 1068.0, which is what happened when the reversing trade was used.

	A Long Hedge in Silver	Table 4.8
Date	**Cash Market**	**Futures Market**
May 10	Anticipates the need for 50,000 troy ounces in two months and expects to pay 1068 cents per ounce, or a total of $534,000.	Buys ten 5,000 troy ounce JUL futures contracts at 1068 cents per ounce.
July 10	The spot price of silver is now 1071 cents per ounce. The manufacturer buys 50,000 ounces, paying $535,500.	Since the futures contract is at maturity, the futures and spot prices are equal, and the ten contracts are sold at 1071 cents per ounce.
	Opportunity loss: −$1,500	Futures profit: $1,500
	Net Wealth Change = 0	

A Short Hedge

Although the long silver hedge involved the purchase of a futures contract, hedges do not necessarily involve long futures positions. A **short hedge** is a hedge in which the hedger sells a futures contract. As an example, we assume the same silver prices and a date of May 10, as shown in Table 4.7. A Nevada silver mine owner is concerned about the price of silver, since she wants to be able to plan for the profitability of her firm. If silver prices fall, she may be forced to suspend production. Given the current level of production, she expects to have about 50,000 ounces of silver ready for shipment in two months. Considering the silver prices shown in Table 4.7, she decides that she would be satisfied to receive 1068.0 cents per ounce for her silver.

To establish the price of 1068.0 cents per ounce, the miner decides to enter the silver futures market. By hedging, she can avoid the risk that silver prices might fall in the next two months. Table 4.9 shows the miner's transactions. Notice that these are exactly the mirror image of the film manufacturer's transactions. Anticipating the need to sell 50,000 ounces of silver in two months, the mine operator sells ten 5,000 ounce futures contracts for July delivery at 1068.0 cents per ounce. On July 10, with silver prices at 1071.0 cents per ounce, the miner sells the silver and receives $535,000. This is $1,500 more than she originally expected. In the futures market, however, the miner suffers an offsetting loss. The futures contracts she sold at 1068.0, she offsets in July at 1071.0 cents per ounce. Once again, the profits and losses in the two markets offset each other, and produce a net wealth change of zero.

Viewing the results from the vantage point of July, it is clear that the miner would have been $1,500 richer if she had not hedged. She would have received $1,500 more than originally expected in the physicals market, and she would have incurred no loss in the futures market. However, it does not follow that she was unwise to hedge. In hedging, the miner and the film manufacturer both decided that the futures price was an acceptable price at which to complete the transaction in July.

Do Hedgers Need Speculators?

Hedging is often viewed as the purchasing of insurance. According to this view, hedgers trade in the futures market and speculators bear the risk that the hedgers try to avoid. Naturally, the speculators

Table 4.9	A Short Hedge in Silver	
Date	**Cash Market**	**Futures Market**
May 10	Anticipates the sale of 50,000 troy ounces in two months and expects to receive 1068 cents per ounce, or a total of $534,000.	Sells ten 5,000 troy ounce July futures contracts at 1068 cents per ounce.
July 10	The spot price of silver is now 1071 cents per ounce. The miner sells 50,000 ounces, receiving $535,500.	Buys 10 contracts at 1071.
	Profit: $1,500	Futures loss: –$1,500
	Net Wealth Change = 0	

demand some compensation for this service. In Chapter 3, the theories of normal backwardation and the contango were considered as explanations of the way in which speculators might receive compensation for bearing risk. In considering the two sides of the silver example, however, no speculators were needed to assume position trades. The long and short hedgers balanced each other out perfectly.

While the example is artificial, it illustrates an important point. Hedgers, as a group, need speculators to take positions and bear risk only for the mismatch in contracts demanded by the long and short hedgers. To the extent that their positions match, position trading speculators are not needed for the job of bearing risk. This helps explain why the risk premiums, if there are any, are not large. In this example, the hedgers do not need speculators to act as position traders. However, even if long and short hedgers were always in balance, the market would still need the liquidity provided by scalpers, such as Mr. X, the scalper we studied earlier.

Cross-Hedging

In the examples of a long and short hedge in silver, the hedgers' needs were perfectly matched with the institutional features of the silver markets. The goods in question were exactly the same goods traded on the futures market, the cash amounts matched the futures contract amounts, and the hedging horizons of the miner and film manufacturer matched the delivery date for the futures contract. In actual hedging applications, it will be rare for all factors to match so well. In most cases the hedged and hedging positions will differ in (1) time span covered, (2) the amount of the commodity, or (3) the particular characteristics of the goods. In such cases, the hedge will be a **cross-hedge** – a hedge in which the characteristics of the spot and futures positions do not match perfectly.

As an example, consider the problem faced by a film manufacturer who uses silver, a key ingredient in manufacturing photographic film. Film production is a process industry, with more or less continuous production. However, COMEX silver futures trade for delivery in January, March, May, July, September, and December. The film manufacturer will also need silver in February, April, and so on. Thus, the futures expiration dates and the hedging horizon for the film manufacturer do not match perfectly. Second, consider the differences in quantity between the futures contract and the film manufacturer's needs. The COMEX contract is for 5,000 troy ounces of silver. The film manufacturer will likely need many thousands of ounces, so it will be fairly easy for the manufacturer to choose and trade a number of contracts that will bring the quantity of silver futures close to the actual need. However, if a hedger needed to hedge 7,500 ounces, he or she might have a problem choosing between one or two contracts. Finally, consider the differences in the physical characteristics of the silver underlying the futures contract and the silver used in manufacturing film. To produce film, silver needs to be in pellet form, and it does not need to be as pure as silver bullion. Also, the pellets contain other metals besides silver. The COMEX silver contract specifies that deliverable silver must be in 1,000 ounce ingots that are 99.9 percent pure. In other words, the silver in the futures contract is extremely pure and refined, not like the adulterated silver products that are typically used in industry. Thus, the film manufacturer will have to hedge his or her industrial silver with pure silver bullion. Cross-hedging is often particularly problematic in the interest rate futures market. Financial instruments are extremely varied in their characteristics, such as risk level, maturity, and coupon rate. By contrast, really active futures contracts are only traded on a few different types of interest-bearing securities.

When the characteristics of the position to be hedged do not perfectly match the characteristics of the futures contract used for the hedging, the hedger must be sure to trade the right number and kind of futures contract to control the risk in the hedged position as much as possible. In general, we cannot expect a cross-hedge to be as effective in reducing risk as a direct hedge. We consider cross-hedging in more detail in later chapters.

Risk-Minimization Hedging

In our first examples, we considered hedges when the hedger had a definite horizon in view. Often, the hedger will not want to hedge for a specific future date. Instead, the hedger may want to control a continuing risk on an indefinite basis. Consider, for example, a soy dealer who holds an inventory of soybeans. From this inventory, the dealer meets orders from her customers. As her inventory becomes low, she periodically replenishes her own inventory from cash market sources. The inventory that she holds will fluctuate in value with the price of soybeans. However, she can reduce the fluctuations in the value of her inventory by selling futures contracts, as the following case study shows.

Assume that today is June 19, 1989, and that the dealer's inventory is one million bushels. The cash price of beans has been very volatile in recent months and is near a high, as Figure 4.3 shows. Therefore, the dealer decides to hedge by selling soybean futures. After she sells futures, she will be long the physical soybeans in her inventory and short soybean futures. If the hedge works, the risk of the combined cash/futures position should be less than the cash position alone.

With an inventory of one million bushels, and a soybean contract calling for 5,000 bushels, it might seem wise to sell one bushel in the futures market for each bushel in the cash market. This

| **Figure 4.3** | **Soybean Cash Prices (March 27, 1989–June 4, 1990)** |

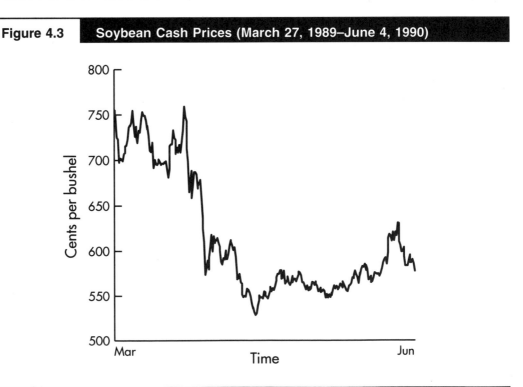

would call for selling 200 soybean contracts. However, a 1:1 hedge may not be optimal. In our example, the dealer wants to minimize her preexisting risk that comes from holding her soybean inventory. We assume that she holds a given bean inventory for business reasons, and we treat that inventory decision as fixed. The dealer's problem is to choose the number of futures contracts that will minimize her risk. Thus, we define the **hedge ratio** (HR) as the number of futures contracts to hold for a given position in the commodity:

$$HR = \frac{\text{Futures Position}}{\text{Cash Market Position}} \tag{4.1}$$

The dealer will trade HR units of the futures to establish the futures market hedge. After establishing the hedge, the trader has a portfolio, P, that consists of the spot position plus the futures position. The profits and losses on the portfolio for one day will be:

$$P_{t+1} - P_t = S_{t+1} - S_t + HR(F_{t+1} - F_t) \tag{4.2}$$

Note that in our initial discussion we considered that the dealer might hedge each bushel in her cash position with one bushel of futures. In that case, the hedge ratio would be -1.0, the negative sign indicating a short position. Generally, if the trader is long the cash commodity, the futures position will be short. Likewise, if the trader is short the cash good, the futures position will be long.

Now, however, the dealer wants to choose the hedge ratio that will minimize the risk of the portfolio of the spot beans and the futures position. The variance of the combined position depends on the variance of the cash price, the variance of the futures price, and the covariance between the two prices. It is a basic statistical rule that the variance of returns on a portfolio, P, of one unit of the spot asset and HR units of a futures contract is given by Equation 4.3:

$$\sigma_P^2 = \sigma_S^2 + HR^2\sigma_F^2 + 2\ HR\rho_{SF}\sigma_S\sigma_F \tag{4.3}$$

where:

σ_P^2 = variance of the portfolio, P_t
σ_S^2 = variance of S_t
σ_F^2 = variance of F_t
ρ_{SF} = correlation between S_t and F_t

The dealer minimizes the variance by choosing a hedge ratio defined as follows:[13]

$$HR = \frac{\rho_{SF}\sigma_S\sigma_F}{\sigma_F^2} = \frac{COV_{SF}}{\sigma_F^2} \tag{4.4}$$

where:

COV_{SF} = the covariance between S_t and F_t

As a practical matter, the easiest way to find the risk-minimizing hedge ratio is to estimate the following regression:

$$S_t = \alpha + \beta F_t + \epsilon_t \tag{4.5}$$

where:

    α = the constant regression parameter
    β = the slope regression parameter
    ϵ = an error term with zero mean and standard deviation of 1.0

The estimated β from this regression is the risk-minimizing hedge ratio, because the estimated β equals the sample covariance between the independent (F_t) and dependent (S_t) variables divided by the sample variance of the independent variable. This is exactly the definition we gave of the risk-minimizing hedge ratio in Equation 4.4.

From the regression estimation, we also obtain a measure of hedging effectiveness. The coefficient of determination, or R^2, is provided by the regression estimate. Conceptually:

    R^2 = portion of total variance in the cash price changes statistically related to the futures price changes

Thus the R^2 will always be a number between 0 and 1.0. The closer to 1.0, the better the degree of fit in the regression between the cash and the futures and the better chance for our hedge to work well.

There are at least three possible measures of S_t and F_t that we might be tempted to employ in the regression of Equation 4.5 – price levels, price changes, and percentage price changes. There has been considerable controversy regarding the proper measure. While this controversy is not fully resolved, we recommend using either the change in price or the percentage change in price, not the price level. If the general range of prices over the estimation period is fairly stable, the price change measure will be satisfactory. If the price changes dramatically, using percentage price changes will give better results.

We now apply this regression approach to the problem of our soybean dealer as of June 19, 1989, using 60 days of daily data to estimate the following regression equation:

$$\Delta C_t = \alpha + \beta \Delta F_t + \epsilon_t$$

where:

    ΔC_t = change in cash price on day t
    ΔF_t = change in futures price on day t

Estimating the regression gives the following parameter estimates:

$$\hat{\alpha} = .6976$$
$$\hat{\beta} = .8713$$
$$R^2 = .56$$

With the estimated β = .8713, the model suggests selling .8713 bushels in the futures market for each bushel in inventory. With one million bushels in inventory and a futures contract of 5,000 bushels, the model suggests selling 174 contracts, because:

$$.8713 \times (1,000,000/5,000) = 174.26 \text{ contracts}$$

From the estimation of the model, we see that the regression accounts for 56 percent of the variance of the cash price change during our sample period. This is an important point, because the regression chose an estimate of β to maximize the R^2. This provides no certainty that we can expect similar results beyond the estimation period. To this point in our example, we have used the data that would actually be available to a trader on June 19, 1989. We assume that our soybean dealer estimated her hedge ratio and placed the hedge at the close of business on June 19. Next, we want to evaluate the performance of the hedge.

Figure 4.4 shows how soybeans performed from June 20, 1989, through June 4, 1990, when we assume that the dealer offset in the futures market, thereby ending the hedge. The graph in Figure 4.4 shows the wealth change from June 20 forward for one contract of cash soybeans and for a contract (5,000 bushels) of cash soybeans hedged with .8713 futures contracts. As the figure shows, in late summer 1989, soybean prices fell dramatically. From the time the hedge was placed until

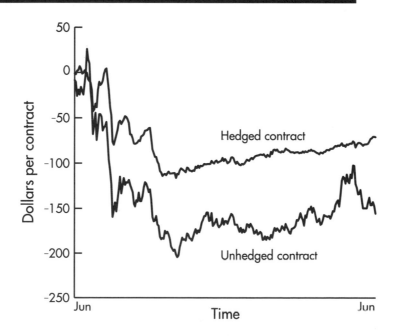

Performance of Hedged and Unhedged Soybean Positions (June 20, 1989–June 4, 1990)   **Figure 4.4**

October 1989, soybean prices fell about $2.00 per bushel. During the same interval, the hedge position lost about $1.00 per bushel. From autumn 1989 through May 1990, prices drifted somewhat higher.

Comparing the unhedged and the hedged strategies, we see that both lost money. However, the hedged strategy avoided about 50 percent of the loss associated with the drop in cash prices. Over the life of the hedge, the unhedged bushel of soybeans lost $1.56 and the hedged bushel lost $.71. On the inventory of one million bushels, this represents a benefit of $850,000 from hedging. From Figure 4.4, we can also see that the hedged position had much less variance than the cash position. For an unhedged bushel, the standard deviation of the price change was $.0815 per day. For the hedged position, the standard deviation was $.0431.

Several special points need to be made about this particular hedge. First, we see that the hedge made money because the short position in the futures gave profits as soybean prices fell. We must realize that bean prices could have risen just as easily. In that event, the futures position in the hedge would have lost money. This brings us to the second point. Hedging aims at reducing risk, not generating profits. In this case, the goal was to reduce variance, which the hedge did. Had bean prices risen, the hedge would also have reduced variance, and would have been successful in attaining its goal. Thus, the hedger must expect an equal chance of monetary gains and losses from placing a hedge. However, with a good hedge, the variance can be reduced substantially.

The period we chose for our analysis was a special time in the bean market. We discussed in Chapter 2 that there may have been an attempted manipulation of the July 1990 soybean futures contract by the Italian grain firm Ferruzzi. Thus, our estimation period consisted of the run-up in prices that culminated in the market crisis of July 1990. The beginning portion of our hedging period includes the price collapse that resulted after Ferruzzi was forced from the market. These events disturbed the normal price relationship between cash and futures prices for soybeans, so this period would be difficult for any hedging model. Nonetheless, the hedge worked fairly well in reducing the volatility of the bean dealer's inventory value. Given the collapsing prices, the hedge also saved her about $850,000.

Costs and Benefits of Hedging

We have defined a hedger as a futures trader with a preexisting risk who enters the futures market to reduce that risk. We have also seen that this definition implies that hedging activities will be restricted to commercial concerns generally. For most individuals, taking a futures position means that risk increases, because the futures commitment is large relative to the trader's preexisting risk in that commodity. Therefore, the costs and benefits of hedging will accrue mainly to business firms. In this section, we explore the rationale for hedging by corporations.

Because the analysis is simpler, we begin by considering the incentives for hedging in a perfect market. As we have seen, hedging is essentially a transaction in a financial market. From the point of view of the firm, the decision to hedge is essentially a financing decision. In perfect markets, the financial policy of the corporation is irrelevant, because shareholders can always transact to undo the actions of the firm's managers. For example, as Miller and Modigliani have shown,[14] managerial decisions regarding the mixture of debt and equity can be unwound by the shareholders to create any capital structure the shareholder desires. Thus, if the firm issues no debt, the shareholder can create homemade leverage by issuing debt on his or her personal account.

In futures hedging, the situation is similar. If the firm fails to hedge, the shareholder in a perfect market can effectively hedge his or her stake in the firm by trading a fractional share in the futures market. Similarly, if the firm hedges by selling futures, for instance, the shareholder can create an unhedged personal stake in the firm by buying a fractional futures contract. While hedging in a perfect market cannot increase the value of the firm, it cannot decrease it either, because shareholders can always transact to offset the firm's action. If corporate hedging in a perfect market is pointless, as this argument suggests, then any real benefit to hedging must come from market imperfections.

We consider five market imperfections that can make hedging important and that may impose real costs on firms: taxes, costs of financial distress, transaction costs, principal-agent problems, and the costliness of diversification.

Taxes as an Incentive to Hedge. In a perfect market, there are no taxes. In real markets, when taxes are levied on annual accounting income, they can provide an incentive for a firm to hedge. Consider a firm that will mine 1,000 ounces of gold bullion this year at a cost of $300 per ounce. The futures price for gold, and thus the firm's expected sale price, is $400 per ounce. This price will give a profit of $100,000. However, this is only an expected price, and the actual price may be $300 or $500 per ounce with equal probability, we assume. We also assume that the tax rate is 20 percent and that the firm has a tax credit of $20,000 that it can apply to offset income taxes. To hedge, the firm would sell futures for its 1,000 ounces of production at the $400 per ounce futures price. Table 4.10 shows the different outcomes depending on the sale price of gold and the firm's decision to hedge or not to hedge.

For both the hedged and the unhedged firm, revenues from selling gold will be either $300,000 or $500,000, depending on whether the gold price is $300 or $500. For the unhedged firm, there is no futures result. If the gold price is $300, the hedged firm has a futures gain of $100,000, because the hedge involved selling 1,000 ounces in the futures market at $400. If the gold price is $500, the hedging firm loses $100,000 in the futures market, because it sold for a futures price of $400 when it could have received $500 by not hedging. Production costs are $300,000 for all scenarios. Pre-tax profits for the unhedged firm will be either zero or $200,000, depending on the price of gold. For the hedged firm, the pre-tax profit will be $100,000 in both cases, due to the hedging.

We can now consider the effect of taxes and the $20,000 tax credit. A tax credit can be used only if the firm owes taxes. For the unhedged firm, the $300 price means that the firm has zero net income and no taxes due. Therefore, the firm cannot use the tax credit, and its after-tax net income is zero. If gold sells for $500, the unhedged firm can use its tax credit fully, and its after-tax net

	How Taxes Provide an Incentive to Hedge		Table 4.10	
	Unhedged Firm		**Hedged Firm**	
Sale Price of Gold	**$300**	**$500**	**$300**	**$500**
Gold Revenue	$300,000	$500,000	$300,000	$500,000
Futures Result	0	0	+100,000	−100,000
Less Production Cost	−300,000	−300,000	−300,000	−300,000
Pre-Tax Profit	0	$200,000	$100,000	$100,000
Tax Obligation	0	−40,000	−20,000	−20,000
Add Tax Credit (if applicable)	0	+20,000	+20,000	+20,000
Net Income	0	$180,000	$100,000	$100,000
Expected After-Tax Net Income	$90,000		$100,000	

income is $90,000. Thus, the unhedged firm has a 50 percent chance of using its tax credit. For the hedging firm, pre-tax income will be $100,000 no matter what the price of gold may be. This means that its tax obligation will be $20,000 in both cases. Thus, the hedged firm uses its tax credit to honor its taxes. This leaves the hedging firm with $100,000 in after-tax net income, no matter what the price of gold may be.

The difference between the unhedged and hedged firms comes down to the following distinction. By hedging, the firm guarantees that it will be able to use its tax credit. By not hedging, the firm runs a 50 percent chance of not being able to use the $20,000 credit. Notice that the difference in the expected after-tax net income between the two firms exactly equals $10,000, which is exactly the expected loss on being unable to use the tax credit for the unhedged firm ($20,000 × .50). Therefore, in our example, taxes create a legitimate incentive to hedge. With hedging, the firm is able to increase its expected after-tax income. With taxes, hedging can increase the value of the firm.

Costs of Financial Distress as an Incentive to Hedge. In Table 4.10, the expected pre-tax profits are the same for both the no-hedging and the hedging strategies. However, hedging reduces the risk inherent in the pre-tax profits. In perfect markets, reducing risk has no value, as long as expected values remain the same. Under perfect market assumptions, investors can diversify costlessly to create any risk position they desire. If a particular firm follows a high risk strategy and goes bankrupt, assets are immediately deployed in an equally useful role. In the real world, by contrast, there are real costs associated with bankruptcy and financial distress. Lawyers and accountants must be paid, for example. In addition, assets cannot be deployed instantly to earn the same return. Therefore, a risk-reducing strategy can help avoid these costs of financial distress, and hedging can consequently increase the value of the firm.

Transaction costs of hedging provide a disincentive for hedging. We have reason to believe that futures prices closely approximate expected future spot prices. If the futures price equals the expected future spot price, the expected profit from trading a futures contract is zero. This holds for both hedging and speculating. Therefore, the expected cost of a hedging transaction is roughly the transaction costs associated with placing and managing the hedge. For any one hedge, the actual result can be wildly favorable or negative, but the expected result is to lose the transaction costs. For the firm that continuously hedges, the law of large numbers comes into play. On some hedges, the firm will win, while it will lose on others. Over many hedges, the law of large numbers assures us that the actual result will more and more closely approximate the theoretical result – no futures gain nor losses, but losses equal to the transaction costs. Therefore, a policy of consistent hedging can be expected to lose the transaction costs in the long run. This high probability of a slightly negative result provides a disincentive for hedging.

Principal-Agent Conflicts as an Incentive to Hedging. In perfect markets, managers of the firm act as pure agents of the shareholders. They operate the firm in the interests of the shareholders, as the shareholders would run the firm for themselves. However, in real firms, managers and shareholders often have conflicting desires. These lead to conflicts between the principals (shareholders) and their agents (managers). For example, managers may like to have sumptuous offices. The shareholders pay for the offices, and the managers use them. In the hedging decision, shareholders may tolerate more risk than managers. Shareholders can hold a portfolio of stocks, so one company may be only a small fraction of the shareholder's portfolio. By contrast, the managers work full-time for the firm and may have a very large portion of their wealth committed to the firm. In this situation, the managers are more anxious than the shareholders to reduce risk. Given the managers' higher risk aversion, they may hedge when shareholders would really prefer that the firm be unhedged.

Lack of Owner Diversification as an Incentive to Hedge. In addition to managers, some shareholders may not be as fully diversified as perfect market conditions would imply. If the shareholders have committed a substantial portion of their wealth to a single firm, they may be as highly risk averse as managers. For example, a farmer may have his or her entire wealth committed to a farm. This lack of diversification on the part of the owner can also create an incentive to hedge.

Summary. In this section, we have considered some of the costs and benefits associated with hedging. We began by observing that, essentially, only firms can hedge, because only firms can reduce their risks by trading futures. In perfect markets, hedging would be pointless, because individual traders could then effectively hedge instead of just the firms. Therefore, incentives to hedge arise from market imperfections. We saw that taxes and the costs of financial distress can both create a situation in which hedging can increase firm value. We also considered the potential conflicts between owners and managers as principals and agents that can lead the managers to hedge more than the shareholders desire. Finally, we saw that incomplete owner diversification can also create an incentive to hedge.

If futures prices equal expected future spot prices, the expected gain or loss from trading a futures contract is zero, except for the transaction costs that must be paid. This means that the expected monetary payoff from hedging is slightly negative. Persistent hedging is very likely to generate a loss equal to the costs of transacting and the costs of managing the hedge. These costs provide a strong disincentive for the firm to hedge.

CONCLUSION

In this chapter, we have explored the three major uses that observers and traders make of futures markets. We began by considering the function of price discovery, a service of futures markets that can be enjoyed by traders and nontraders alike. We considered the way in which producers could use information from the futures market to guide their production decisions. If futures prices provide a good guide to future spot prices, then futures markets reveal price information that helps society allocate capital more efficiently.

The futures market attracts speculators – traders who enter the futures market in pursuit of profit, willingly increasing their risks to do so. We classified speculators according to the length of time they planned to hold a futures position as scalpers, day traders, and position traders. We noted that spread trading is an important form of speculative trading and considered different spread trading techniques.

We examined the available evidence on the profitability of speculative trading. We found that studies disagree considerably on the magnitude and even the existence of speculative trading profits. We briefly considered the performance of technical trading systems, where we once again found different conclusions in the academic literature. Commodity funds have become important speculative trading vehicles in recent years. We analyzed the evidence on the performance of commodity funds, and again found no evidence of overwhelming trading acumen. Finally, we considered the concept of "normal" speculative profits. This was an effort to take into consideration the investment of funds and time that are necessary to speculate as a scalper or other floor trader. We found that the trader must make a substantial income to justify the investment and loss of other job opportunities.

Hedging is one of the most important social functions of futures markets. A hedger is a trader who enters the futures market in an effort to reduce a preexisting risk. We saw that traders can hedge by being either long or short in the futures market. Except for providing liquidity, we noted that hedgers needed speculative position traders only to absorb an imbalance between long and short hedgers. Much hedging activity involves an imperfect match between the characteristics of the asset being hedged and the asset underlying a futures contract. Hedging in such a situation is cross-hedging. We gave examples of how traders might use the market to hedge in such a situation. In many instances, hedgers will want to employ risk-minimization techniques for a given position. We showed that it is possible to derive the correct futures position to minimize a given initial risk using a statistical analysis of historical data. Using actual soybean data, we followed a strategy from beginning to end for hedging soybeans over the 1989–1990 period. Finally, we considered the costs and benefits of hedging.

QUESTIONS AND PROBLEMS

1. Explain how futures markets can benefit individuals in society who never trade futures.
2. A "futures price" is a market-quoted price today of the best estimate of the value of a commodity at the expiration of the futures contract. What do you think of this definition?
3. Explain the concept of an unbiased predictor.
4. How are errors possible if a predictor is unbiased?
5. Scalpers trade to capture profits from minute fluctuations in futures prices. Explain how this avaricious behavior benefits others.
6. Assume that scalping is made illegal. What would the consequences of such an action be for hedging activity in futures markets?
7. A trader anticipates rising corn prices and wants to take advantage of this insight by trading an intracommodity spread. Would you advise that she trade long nearby/short distant or the other way around? Explain.
8. Assume that daily settlement prices in the futures market exhibit very strong first order serial correlation. How would you trade to exploit this strategy? Explain how your answer would differ if the correlation were statistically significant but, nonetheless, small in magnitude.
9. Assume that you are a rabid efficient markets believer. A commodity fund uses 20 percent of its funds as margin payments. The remaining 80 percent are invested in risk-free securities. What investment performance would you expect from the fund?
10. Consider two traders. The first trader is an individual with his own seat who trades strictly for his own account. The other trader works for a brokerage firm actively engaged in retail futures brokerage. Which trader has a lower effective marginal trading cost? Relate this comparison in marginal trading costs to quasi-arbitrage.
11. Consider the classic hedging problems of the farmer who sells wheat in the futures market in anticipation of a harvest. Would the farmer be likely to deliver his harvested wheat against the futures? Explain. If he is unlikely to deliver, explain how he manages his futures position instead.
12. A cocoa merchant holds a current inventory of cocoa worth $10 million at present prices of $1,250 per metric ton. The standard deviation of returns for the inventory is .27. She is considering a risk-minimization hedge of her inventory using the cocoa contract of the Coffee, Cocoa and Sugar Exchange. The contract size is 10 metric tons. The volatility of the futures is .33. For the particular grade of cocoa in her inventory, the correlation between the futures and spot cocoa is

.85. Compute the risk-minimization hedge ratio and determine how many contracts she should trade.

13. A service station operator read this book. He wants to hedge his risk exposure for gasoline. Every week, he pumps 50,000 gallons of gasoline, and he is confident that this pattern will hold through thick and Hussein. What advice would you offer?

NOTES

[1] For a more formal treatment of the property of unbiasedness in estimators, see J. Maddala, *Introduction to Econometrics,* New York: Macmillan, 1988.

[2] See R. Levich, "Currency Forecasters Lose Their Way," *Euromoney,* August 1983, pp. 140–47. Chapter 9 discusses the forecasting accuracy of professional currency forecasters in more detail.

[3] Some authors attempt to distinguish speculators from investors. The usual difference between the two definitions seems to lie in their respective attitudes toward risk and the length of time they expect to hold their positions. Speculators are contrasted only with hedgers, so any investor in the futures market, no matter how conservative, would be regarded as a speculator for the purposes of this book.

[4] On the floor of the exchanges, different commodities are traded in different pits. A pit is really an area of the floor, surrounded by steps or risers, which are usually about five steps high. The arrangement allows traders to see and communicate with each other. The term "pit" is really synonymous with trading in futures, as indicated by the title of Frank Norris' novel, *The Pit,* which is the story of futures trading in wheat.

[5] B. Tamarkin, *The New Gatsbys: Fortunes and Misfortunes of Commodity Traders,* New York: William Morrow, 1985, pp. 26, 43.

[6] W. L. Silber, "Marketmaker Behavior in an Auction Market: An Analysis of Scalpers in Futures Markets," *Journal of Finance,* September 1984, 39:4, p. 937–53.

[7] See, for example, *Commodity Trading Manual,* Chicago: Chicago Board of Trade, 1989, and Martin J. Pring (ed.), *The McGraw-Hill Handbook of Commodities and Futures,* New York: McGraw-Hill, 1985.

[8] For a more complete survey of technical trading systems, see R. Kolb, *Understanding Futures Markets,* 5e, Malden, MA: Blackwell Publishers, 1997, Chapter 4.

[9] These three versions of the efficient markets hypothesis were first articulated by E. Fama in "Efficient Capital Markets: Theory and Empirical Work," *Journal of Finance,* May 1970, pp. 383–417. For a more recent survey of the efficient markets literature, see T. Copeland and F. Weston, *Financial Theory and Corporate Policy,* 3e, Reading, MA: Addison-Wesley, 1988.

[10] The concept of market efficiency entered the popular culture through the back door with the movie *Trading Places,* starring Eddie Murphy and Dan Ackroyd. Murphy and Ackroyd acquire some private information about the size of the orange crop by getting early access to a government crop report. Their use of the crop report constitutes the use of private information to earn a supernormal profit trading orange juice futures and is a violation of strong form market efficiency. This information allows them to bankrupt the "bad guys" and to retire to a Pacific island paradise.

[11] The youthfulness of the traders is particularly apparent in the newer markets, such as the interest rate futures market. Relatively, the older, more traditional commodities are traded by older traders. In his book, *The New Gatsbys* (New York: Morrow, 1985), Bob Tamarkin emphasizes the physical strains and the mental stresses that traders endure. For example, see Chapter 20, "Pit Falls."

[12] Many traders will not leave the trading pit during the six- to seven-hour trading session, even to go to the bathroom. It is simply too risky to leave the trading floor for even a short period of time. This indicates the level of stress in the pits.

[13] To find the risk-minimizing hedge ratio, we take the derivative of the portfolio's risk in Equation 3.3 with respect to HR, set the derivative equal to zero, and solve for HR:

$$\frac{d\ \sigma_P^2}{d\ \text{HR}} = 2\ \text{HR}\ \sigma_F^2 - 2\ \rho_{CF}\sigma_C\sigma_F = 0$$

$$\text{HR} = \rho_{CF}\frac{\sigma_C}{\sigma_F} = \frac{\text{COV}_{CF}}{\sigma_F^2}$$

[14] M. Miller and F. Modigliani, "The Cost of Capital, Corporate Finance, and the Theory of Investment," *American Economic Review*, 48:3, June 1958, pp. 261–97.

CHAPTER 5 | INTEREST RATE FUTURES: INTRODUCTION

OVERVIEW

This chapter explores one of the most successful and exciting innovations in the history of futures markets – the emergence of interest rate futures contracts. Since the first contracts were traded on October 20, 1975, the market has expanded rapidly. In spite of a number of relatively unsuccessful contracts that have been introduced, such as commercial paper and Certificate Delivery GNMA contracts, the market has been a huge success. By fall 1995, open interest exceeded $2.6 trillion (face value) of underlying financial instruments, up from just $800 billion in 1990 and $300 billion in 1987. From inception, the interest rate futures market has come to represent about one-half of the entire futures market, and most industry observers expect the continued growth of the futures market to center around financial instruments.

Almost all of the activity in the U.S. interest rate futures is concentrated in two exchanges, the Chicago Board of Trade (CBOT) and the International Monetary Market (IMM) of the Chicago Mercantile Exchange (CME). The Board of Trade specializes in contracts at the longer end of the maturity spectrum, with active contracts on long-term Treasury bonds and ten-year, five-year, and two-year Treasury notes. In addition, the CBOT trades a municipal bond contract. By contrast, the International Monetary Market has successful contracts with very short maturities, trading contracts for three-month Treasury bills and Eurodollar Deposits. While this chapter discusses features of many different contracts, we focus on the seven most important contracts: the T-bond contract, three T-note contracts, and the municipal bond contract traded on the CBOT, along with the T-bill and Eurodollar contracts traded on the IMM of the CME. For the most part, these are highly active contracts that differ widely in their contract terms and the maturities of the underlying instruments. Figure 5.1 presents price quotations for key contracts.

INTEREST RATE FUTURES CONTRACTS

To understand the interest rate futures market, we need to understand the specifications for the different contracts. Among all the different types of futures contracts, interest rate futures exhibit the most variety, with the characteristics of the futures contracts being tailored to the particular attributes of the underlying instruments. We begin by considering the contract specifications for the major short-maturity contracts.

Treasury Bill Futures

The T-bill futures contract, traded by the International Monetary Market of the Chicago Mercantile Exchange, calls for the delivery of T-bills having a face value of $1,000,000 and a time to maturity of 90 days at the expiration of the futures contract. The contracts trade for delivery in March, June, September, and December. The delivery dates are chosen to make newly issued 13-week T-bills immediately deliverable against the futures contract. Also, a previously issued one-year T-bill will have 13 weeks until maturity, and it can also be delivered against the T-bill futures contract. The IMM permits delivery on the three business days following the last day of trading.

Price quotations for T-bill futures use the IMM Index, which is a function of the discount yield (DY):

$$\text{IMM Index} = 100.00 - \text{DY} \tag{5.1}$$

where:

DY = Discount yield, e.g., 7.1 is 7.1 percent

As an example, a discount yield of 8.32 percent implies an IMM index value of 91.68. The IMM adopted this method of price quotation to ensure that the bid price would be below the asked price, the relationship prevailing in most markets. Price fluctuations may be no smaller than one tick, or one **basis point**. Given the fact that the instruments are priced by using a discount yield and a contract size of $1,000,000, a one basis point movement in the interest rate generates a price change of $25.00. Equation 5.2 gives the price that must be paid at delivery for the cash market bill:

$$\text{Bill Price} = \$1,000,000 - \frac{\text{DY (\$1,000,000)(DTM)}}{360} \tag{5.2}$$

where:

DTM = Days until maturity

With a discount yield of 8.32 percent on the futures contract, the price to be paid for the T-bill at delivery would be $979,200:

$$\text{Bill Price} = \$1,000,000 - \frac{.0832(\$1,000,000)(90)}{360} = \$979,200$$

If the futures yield rose to 8.35 percent, the delivery price would be $979,125, changing $25 for each basis point. Many futures contracts have a daily price limit, a constraint on how much the futures price is allowed to move in a single day of trading. For example, in former times the limit for the T-bill contract was 60 basis points, or $1,500, in either direction from the previous day's settlement price. The contract specifications have been changed and now there is no limit on the daily price fluctuation.

Figure 5.1 presents price quotations for T-bill futures. These quotations are similar in structure to those for other futures contracts. The first four columns of figures give the open, high, low, and settlement quotations in terms of the IMM index. The "Chg" column shows the change in the IMM Index from the previous day's settlement. Under the heading "Discount" are the settlement discount yield and the change in the settlement discount yield. Notice that the settlement discount yield plus the settlement IMM index always sum to 100.0. Similarly, the change in the IMM index and the change in the discount yield are always equal in magnitude but opposite in sign. The last column gives the open interest for each contract maturity. The final line of the quotations reports the volume, open interest across all maturities, and the change in the open interest since the previous day.

Although the contract specifications call for the delivery of a T-bill having 90 days to maturity, delivery of 91- or 92-day bills is also permitted with a price adjustment. The price can be adjusted by substituting the correct number of days until maturity in Equation 5.2. In any event, all of the delivered T-bills must be of the same maturity. Upon delivery, the short trader must deliver the T-bills and the long trader must pay the invoice amount. The invoice amount is:

$$\text{Invoice Amount} = \$1,000,000 - \frac{\text{T-bill Yield } (\$1,000,000)(\text{DTM})}{360} \tag{5.3}$$

The actual delivery process extends over two business days. On the first day, the short trader gives notice to the IMM Clearinghouse that he or she will deliver. The Clearinghouse assigns the delivery to an outstanding long trader. The two traders communicate with their own and the other trader's banks to alert the banks to the impending transactions. To consummate the transaction, the short trader delivers the bills and the long trader pays the short trader. This is accomplished through wire transfers between the banks of the two traders. Figure 5.2 diagrams the delivery process followed by the IMM clearinghouse.

Eurodollar Futures

Eurodollar deposits are U.S. dollar deposits held in a commercial bank outside the United States. These banks may be either foreign banks or foreign branches of U.S. banks. The deposits are normally nontransferable and cannot be used as collateral for loans. London dominates the Eurodollar deposit market, so rates in this market are often based on **LIBOR**, the **London Interbank Offer Rate**. LIBOR is the rate at which banks are willing to lend funds to other banks in the interbank market. LIBOR is an important rate in international finance. For example, many loans to developing countries have been priced as LIBOR plus some number of percentage points.

Eurodollar futures, like T-bill futures, trade on the IMM of the CME. Eurodollar futures have come to dominate the market for short-term contracts and greatly exceed the T-bill contract in volume and open interest. Like the T-bill contract, the instrument underlying the Eurodollar contract has a three-month maturity. Unlike the T-bill contract, the underlying good is not a bond but a time deposit held in a commercial bank. Also, unlike the T-bill contract, there is no actual delivery on the Eurodollar contract. Instead, the contract is fulfilled by cash settlement.

Figure 5.1 | Price Quotations for Major Interest Rate Futures Contracts

INTEREST RATE

TREASURY BONDS (CBT)-$100,000; pts. 32nds of 100%

	Open	High	Low	Settle	Change	Lifetime High	Low	Open Interest
June	110-14	110-17	109-30	110-08	– 8	121-23	93-06	343,237
Sept	109-27	109-27	109-13	109-23	– 8	120-29	102-06	26,095
Dec	109-05	109-07	108-31	109-06	– 8	120-15	107-00	5,344
Mr97	....	....	....	108-25	– 8	120-00	106-20	936

Est vol 255,000; vol Mn 257,787; op int 275,671, –8,669.

TREASURY BONDS (MCE)-$50,000; pts. 32nds of 100%

June	110-11	110-12	109-30	110-05	– 11	121-09	98-10	11,115

Est vol 4,400; vol Mn 5,031; open int 11,167, +625.

TREASURY NOTES (CBT)-$100,000; pts. 32nds of 100%

June	108-06	108-09	107-30	108-05	– 2	114-26	102-10	288,551
Sept	107-25	107-28	107-24	107-28	– 3	114-26	106-09	35,093
Dec	107-07	107-09	107-07	107-09	– 2	113-30	105-29	2,409

Est vol 65,000; vol Mn 61,838; open int 326,073, +3,188.

5 YR TREAS NOTES (CBT)-$100,000; pts. 32nds of 100%

June	106-15	106-15	106-08	106-13	– 1	111-07	05-025	176,873
Sept	....	....	....	06045	– 1	10-305	05-015	11,448

Est vol 31,500; vol Mn 26,405; open int 188,356, +2,218.

2 YR TREAS NOTES (CBT)-$200,000, pts. 32nds of 100%

June	03105	03112	103-09	03112	– 0.7	105-19	102-26	17,379

Est vol 11,100; vol Mn 380; open int 17,386, +66.

30-DAY FEDERAL FUNDS (CBT)-$5 million; pts. of 100%

	Open	High	Low	Settle	Change	Lifetime High	Low	Open Interest
Apr	94.790	94.790	94.780	94.785	+ .05	94.980	94.980	4,201
May	94.73	94.73	94.72	94.73	....	95.05	94.49	4,250
June	94.71	94.71	94.70	94.71	....	95.20	94.48	4,628
July	94.69	94.69	94.69	94.69	– .01	95.34	94.66	2,894
Aug	94.68	94.68	94.67	94.68	– .01	95.39	94.61	1,352
Sept	94.63	94.64	94.62	94.64	– .01	95.43	94.54	1,158
Oct	94.55	94.56	94.54	94.56	– .01	95.51	94.41	907
Nov	....	....	....	94.48	– .02	95.54	94.35	215
Dec	....	....	....	94.43	– .03	94.56	94.37	41
Ja97	....	....	....	94.37	– .04	95.35	94.34	111

Est vol 888; vol Mn 282; open int 19,842, +80.

MUNI BOND INDEX (CBT)-$1,000; times Bond Buyer MBI

	Open	High	Low	Settle	Chg	High	Low	Open Interest
June	112-08	112-10	111-30	112-07	+ 6	120-29	108-23	11,627

Est vol – – 2,300; vol Mn 3,949; open int 11,635, +137.
The index: Close 113-26; Yield 6.42.

TREASURY BILLS (CME)-$1 mil.; pts. of 110%

	Open	High	Low	Settle	Chg	Discount Settle	Chg	Open Interest
June	95.00	95.01	95.00	95.01	....	4.99	....	9,527
Sept	94.85	94.85	94.83	94.84	....	5.16	....	5,087
Dec	....	....	....	94.66	....	5.34	....	793

Est vol 562; vol Mn 619; open int 15,407, +260.

LIBOR-1 MO. (CME)-$3,000,000; points of 100%

May	94.59	94.59	94.58	94.59	....	5.41	....	15,513
June	94.59	94.60	94.59	94.60	....	5.40	....	4,662
July	94.58	94.59	94.58	94.59	....	5.41	....	4,238
Aug	94.57	94.57	94.56	94.57	....	5.43	....	1,383
Sept	94.50	94.50	94.49	94.49	– .01	5.51	+ .01	833
Oct	....	....	....	94.44	– .01	5.56	+ .01	200
Nov	....	....	....	94.37	– .03	5.63	+ .03	320
Dec	94.07	94.09	94.06	94.10	– .02	5.90	+ .02	1,145
Ja97	....	....	....	94.28	– .01	....	+ .01	220

Est vol 1,332; vol Mn 1,735; open int 28,561, +187.

EURODOLLAR (CME)-$1 million; pts of 100%

	Open	High	Low	Settle	Chg	Yield Settle	Chg	Open Interest
May	94.54	94.55	94.54	94.55	....	5.45	....	17,564
June	94.56	94.56	94.53	94.55	....	5.45	....	380,507
July	94.50	94.51	94.49	94.50	– .01	5.50	+ .01	2,130
Sept	94.40	94.41	94.35	94.38	– .01	5.62	+ .01	358,468
Dec	94.14	94.15	94.10	94.14	– .01	5.86	+ .01	344,217
Mr97	93.94	93.97	93.91	93.96	– .01	6.04	+ .01	239,138
June	93.81	93.81	93.75	93.79	– .01	6.21	+ .01	201,494
Sept	93.67	93.67	93.62	93.66	– .02	6.34	+ .02	174,671
Dec	93.51	93.52	93.48	93.52	– .01	6.48	+ .01	134,625
Mr98	93.48	93.48	93.43	93.47	– .01	6.53	+ .01	108,682
June	93.40	93.40	93.36	93.40	– .01	6.60	+ .01	86,446
Sept	93.32	93.32	93.29	93.33	– .01	6.67	+ .01	72,242
Dec	93.21	93.22	93.19	93.22	– .01	6.78	+ .01	57,318
Mr99	93.17	93.18	93.15	93.18	– .01	6.82	+ .01	46,463

Source: From *The Wall Street Journal*, April 24, 1996, p. C16. Reprinted by permission of *The Wall Street Journal*, © 1996 Dow Jones & Company, Inc. All rights reserved worldwide.

Treasury Bill Futures Delivery Procedure   Figure 5.2

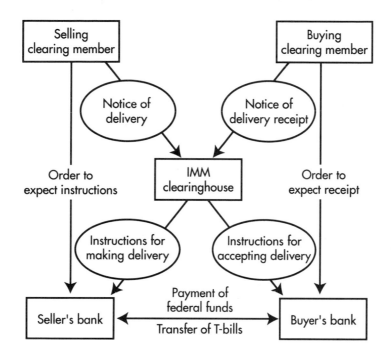

The Eurodollar futures contract was the first contract to use cash settlement rather than the delivery of an actual good for contract fulfillment. We have already noted that Eurodollar deposits are nontransferable, a feature that by itself precludes delivery. As a result, the IMM requires fulfillment of a contract by a cash payment based on its measure of Eurodollar rates. To establish the settlement rate at the close of trading, the IMM determines the three-month LIBOR rate. It then uses this rate indication to establish the final settlement price. The rules of the exchange are quite explicit:

> The final settlement price shall be determined by the Clearing House as follows. On the last day of trading the Clearing House shall determine the London Interbank Offered Rate (LIBOR) for three-month Eurodollar Time Deposit funds both at the time of termination of trading and at a randomly-selected time within the last 90 minutes of trading. The final settlement price shall be 100 minus the arithmetic mean, rounded to the nearest 1/100th of a percentage point, of the LIBOR at these two times.
>
> To determine the LIBOR at either time the Clearing House shall select at random 12 reference banks from a list of no less than 20 participating banks that are major banks in the London Eurodollar

market. Each reference bank shall quote to the Clearing House its perception of the rate at which three-month Eurodollar Time Deposit funds are currently offered by the market to prime banks. These rates must be confirmed in writing by telex before they are accepted as official; only after confirmation will they be used to determine the final settlement price. The two highest and the two lowest quotes shall be eliminated. The arithmetic mean of the remaining eight quotes shall be the LIBOR at that time. If for any reason there is difficulty in obtaining a quote within a reasonable time interval from one of the banks in the sample, that bank shall be dropped from the sample, and another shall be randomly selected to replace it.[1]

The use of a number of banks with polling at two separate times and confirmation required in writing is designed to thwart any attempted manipulation of the final settlement price. Since its inception in 1981, this procedure has worked very well, with Eurodollar futures having grown very rapidly. Once the final settlement price is determined, traders with open positions settle with cash through the normal marking-to-market procedure. This fulfills their obligation and the contract expires.

Prior to the final trading day, the daily settlement price depends on the quotations in the futures market. In a sense, the futures price appears free to wander from the spot market values except for the final day of trading. This is an illusion, however. Consider, for example, the second to last trading day. Traders know that tomorrow the futures settlement price will be set equal to the average LIBOR actually available from banks. Therefore, the price today cannot be very different from today's cash market LIBOR. If it did differ significantly, traders would enter the market to buy or sell futures and would expect to reap their profit when the futures price is pegged to the cash market LIBOR. This same argument holds for every other day prior to expiration as well, so the Eurodollar futures contract must behave as though there will be an actual delivery at the contract's expiration. We will see evidence of this relationship later.

For the Eurodollar contract, the contract size is for $1,000,000, with the yield being quoted on an add-on basis. The add-on yield is given by:

$$\text{Add-on Yield} = \left(\frac{\text{Discount}}{\text{Price}}\right)\left(\frac{360}{\text{DTM}}\right) \tag{5.4}$$

For example, assume the discount yield is 8.32 percent. We have already seen that this discount yield gives a price of $979,200 for a $1 million face value three-month T-bill. Therefore, the dollar discount is $20,800 and 90 days remain until the bill will mature. With these values we have:

$$\text{Add-on Yield} = \left(\frac{\$20,800}{\$979,200}\right)\left(\frac{360}{90}\right) = .0850$$

Add-on yields exceed corresponding discount yields. In our example, the discount yield is 8.32 percent, and the add-on yield equivalent is 8.5 percent. However, for both measures, a shift of one basis point is worth $25 on a $1,000,000 contract. Note also that these yields and relationships vary with maturity, so the statements made here hold only for three-month maturities.

Figure 5.1 shows price quotations for Eurodollar futures from *The Wall Street Journal.* The quotations have the same structure as the T-bill futures examined in the previous section, but the yields are add-on yields. Like the T-bill contract, the Eurodollar contract uses the IMM index. Thus, the quoted price is:

$$\text{IMM Index} = 100.00 - \text{LIBOR} \qquad (5.5)$$

The relationship between the T-bill and Eurodollar futures yields is very stable. Using data on a pair of September contracts, Figure 5.3 shows the settlement yields for both contracts over the lives of the contracts, with Eurodollar yields exceeding T-bill yields. The relationship between the two is very steady. To emphasize this strong correspondence between these yields, we estimated the following regression for this pair of contracts using daily data:

$$\text{Change in Eurodollar Yield}_t = \alpha + \beta \ \text{Change in T-bill Yield}_t + e_t$$

The results were:

$$\text{Change in Eurodollar Yield}_t = -0.00045 + 1.0621 \ \text{Change in T-bill Yield}_t$$

with an R^2 of 0.9119 and a t-statistic for β of 56.00, based on 305 observations. What the graph strongly indicates, the regression confirms: There is an extremely strong relationship between the level of T-bill and Eurodollar yields. Notice also that the Eurodollar yield lies above the T-bill yield. From the regression we can see that Eurodollar yields move just slightly more than 1:1 for a change in T-bill yields, because the estimated $\beta = 1.0621$. Later in this chapter, we explore some speculative strategies based on the relationship between these two yields.

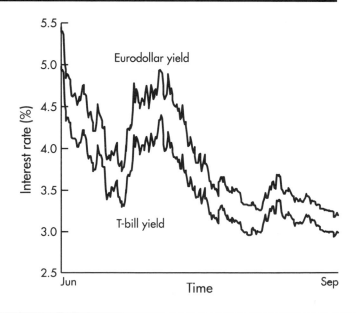

SEP T-Bill and Eurodollar Futures Yields　　**Figure 5.3**

Treasury Bond Futures

Of all futures contracts, the T-bond contract is one of the most complex and most interesting. The complexity of the contract stems from the delivery rules under which it is traded and from the wide variety of bonds that can be delivered to fulfill the contract. For the T-bill contract, delivery takes place within a very narrow span of time, but the Chicago Board of Trade, which trades the T-bond contract, employs a radically different delivery procedure.

In spite of its peculiarities, the T-bond contract is perhaps the single most successful futures contract ever introduced. Starting in August 1977, its success has been amazing. In 1986, for example, more than 52 million T-bond futures contracts were traded, and in 1995 this figure exceeded 88 million. With a face value per contract of $100,000, this represents an underlying value of more than $8.8 trillion. This single contract accounted for more than 50 percent of the CBOT's total volume of futures and options contracts.

Figure 5.1 presented quotations for T-bond futures from *The Wall Street Journal.* The structure of these quotations parallels the others we have already examined. The first four columns of figures give the open, high, low, and settlement price for the contract, with the quotations in "points and 32nds of par." For example, a quoted price of 97-26 means that the contract traded for 97 and 26/32nds of par. The decimal equivalent of this value is 97.8125 percent of par. With a par value of $100,000 per contract, the cash price would be $97,812.50. The next column shows the change since the previous settlement in 32nds. The next column shows the bond yield implied by the futures price, followed by the change in the bond yield since the previous settlement. The final column of figures gives the open interest per contract. The final line in the quotations gives the usual volume and open interest information.

For the T-bond contract, the minimum price fluctuation is 1/32nd of one full percentage point of face value. This means that the minimum price fluctuation per contract is $31.25 [(1/32)(.01)($100,000)]. In normal market conditions, the daily price limit is three full points, or 96 32nds, for a daily price limit of $3,000 per contract, which can be expanded in periods of high volatility.

Delivery against the T-bond contract is a several day process that the short trader can trigger to cause delivery on any business day of the delivery month. Like the T-bill and Eurodollar contracts, the T-bond contract trades for delivery in March, June, September, and December. Delivery can be made on any business day of the delivery month, with the short trader choosing the exact delivery day. To effect delivery, the short trader initiates a delivery sequence that extends over three business days. Figure 5.4 shows the delivery procedure for T-bond futures, a procedure that applies to other Board of Trade contracts, such as the T-note futures contracts.

The **first position day** is the first permissible day for the short trader to declare his or her intention to make delivery, with the delivery taking place two business days later. The first permissible day for such an announcement falls in the month preceding the delivery month, since delivery can occur as soon as the first business day of the delivery month. If the short declares the intention to deliver on any other day besides the first position day, then that day is called **position day**. On position day, the short trader announces the intention to deliver on the second business day thereafter.

The second day in the delivery sequence is the **notice of intention day**. On this day, the Clearing Corporation matches the short trader with the long trader having the longest outstanding position, and identifies the short and long traders to each other. The short trader is then obligated to make delivery to that particular long trader on the next business day. The third and final day of the delivery

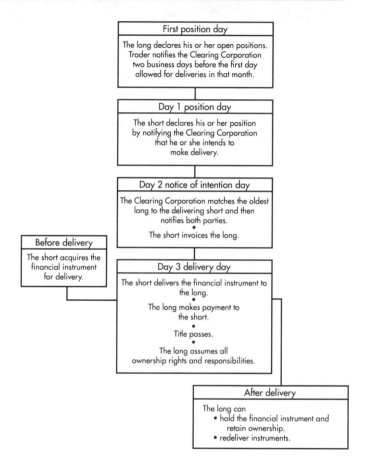

The Delivery Procedure for T-Bond Futures   **Figure 5.4**

Source: Reprinted by permission of the Chicago Board of Trade.

sequence is **delivery day,** when the actual transaction takes place. On this day the short delivers the financial instrument to the long trader and receives payment. The long trader then has all rights of ownership in the T-bonds that were delivered in fulfillment of the contract.

For the T-bond futures contract, a wide variety of bonds may be delivered against the contract at any one time. The rules of the Board of Trade call for the delivery of $100,000 worth of T-bonds having at least 15 years remaining until maturity or to their first permissible call date.

Table 5.1 presents some key dates in the delivery process for both the T-bond and T-note futures contracts, and Table 5.2 shows the T-bonds eligible for delivery in 1996. The first two columns of Table 5.2 list the coupon rate and maturity date. The rest of the table lists conversion factors for each bond and each maturity date. (These conversion factors are explained later.)

Table 5.1	The Delivery Sequence for T-Bond and T-Note Futures Expiring in 1997				
Contract Expiration	First Position	First Notice	First Delivery	Last Trading	Last Delivery
MAR 97	FEB 27	FEB 28	MAR 3	MAR 21	MAR 31
JUN	MAY 29	MAY 30	JUN 2	JUN 20	JUN 30
SEP	AUG 28	AUG 29	SEP 2	SEP 19	SEP 30
DEC	NOV 26	NOV 28	DEC 1	DEC 19	DEC 31

Table 5.2	Deliverable T-Bonds and Conversion Factors			
Coupon	Maturity	JUN 96	SEP 96	DEC 96
6.000	Feb 15, 2026	0.7747	0.7751	0.7757
6.125	Aug 15, 2023	0.8076	0.8079	0.8086
6.875	Aug 15, 2025	0.8738	0.8740	0.8744
7.125	Feb 15, 2023	0.9043	0.9044	0.9049
7.250	May 15, 2016	0.9260	0.9266	0.9268
7.250	Aug 15, 2022	0.9184	0.9185	0.9189
7.500	Nov 15, 2024	0.9441	0.9445	0.9444
7.500	Nov 15, 2016	0.9501	0.9505	0.9506
7.625	Nov 15, 2022	0.9589	0.9592	0.9592
7.625	Feb 15, 2025	0.9581	0.9580	0.9583
7.875	Feb 15, 2021	0.9867	0.9865	0.9868
8.000	Nov 15, 2021	0.9998	1.0000	0.9998
8.125	May 15, 2021	1.0132	1.0133	1.0131
8.125	Aug 15, 2021	1.0134	1.0132	1.0133
8.125	Aug 15, 2019	1.0131	1.0128	1.0130
8.500	Feb 15, 2020	1.0526	1.0522	1.0522
8.750	May 15, 2017	1.0751	1.0750	1.0744
8.750	May 15, 2020	1.0790	1.0789	1.0784
8.750	Aug 15, 2020	1.0795	1.0790	1.0789
8.875	Aug 15, 2017	1.0883	1.0877	1.0875
8.875	Feb 15, 2019	1.0907	1.0901	1.0899
9.000	Nov 15, 2018	1.1030	1.1027	1.1021
9.125	May 15, 2018	1.1149	1.1146	1.1138
9.250	Feb 15, 2016	1.1224	1.1215	1.1210
9.875	Nov 15, 2015	1.1824	1.1816	1.1803
10.625	Aug 15, 2015	1.2542	1.2525	1.2512
11.250	Feb 15, 2015	1.3111	1.3089	1.3073

Source: From Chicago Board of Trade World Wide Web site. Reprinted by permission.

As Table 5.2 shows, more than 25 different bonds could be delivered against the DEC 96 contract. Coupons on these bonds range from 6 percent to 11.25 percent and the maturities range from 2015 to 2026. With all of these bonds outstanding, quite a few different bonds will be deliverable against the T-bond contract for years to come.

The fact that some bonds are cheap, and some expensive, suggests that there may be an advantage to delivering one bond rather than another. If there is such an advantage, why did the CBOT allow several bonds to be delivered against the contract? These considerations are intimately related and have an important impact on the contract design. The significant differences in maturity and coupon rates among these bonds cause large price differences. Because the short trader chooses whether to make delivery, and which bond to deliver, we might expect that only the cheapest bond would ever be delivered.

To eliminate an incentive to deliver just one particular bond, the CBOT initiated a system of conversion factors which alters the delivery values of different bonds as a function of their coupon rate and term-to-maturity. The conversion factors in Table 5.2 are based on a hypothetical bond with 20 years to maturity and an 8 percent coupon rate. A quick glance at Table 5.2 shows only one such bond existed in the fall of 1996.

For purposes of delivery, the CBOT adjusts the price of every bond using a conversion factor that is specific to a given bond and a particular futures contract expiration. The invoice amount is calculated according to Equation 5.6:

$$\text{Invoice Amount} = \text{DSP}(\$100,000)(\text{CF}) + \text{AI} \tag{5.6}$$

where:

DSP = decimal settlement price (e.g., 96-16 = .965)
CF = conversion factor
AI = accrued interest

Each term requires comment. The **decimal settlement price** is simply the decimal equivalent of the quoted price, which is expressed in ''points and 32nds of par.'' The $100,000 reflects the contract amount. The conversion factor attempts to adjust for differences in coupons and maturities among the deliverable bonds.

The conversion factor for any bond can be approximated quite accurately by following two rules:

1. Assume that the face value of the bond to be delivered is $1.
2. Discount the assumed cash flows from the bond at 8 percent using the bond pricing equation.

The result approximates the conversion factor for the bond in question. This will only be an approximation, however, because the official conversion factors reflect quarterly intervals between the present and the delivery date. Exact conversion factors are available in the form shown as Table 5.2 from the Chicago Board of Trade.[2] The conversion factors can also be found from these formulas:

For bonds with an even number of full semiannual periods until maturity:

$$\text{CF} = \sum_{t=1}^{n} \frac{C_t}{1.04^t} + \frac{1}{1.04^n} \tag{5.7}$$

For bonds with an uneven number of full semiannual periods until maturity:

$$CF = \frac{\sum_{t=1}^{n} \frac{C_t}{1.04^t} + \frac{1}{1.04^n} + C_t}{1.04^{.5}} - .5C_t \qquad (5.8)$$

where:

    CF = conversion factor

    C_t = semiannual coupon payment in dollars assuming a \$1 face value bond

    n = the number of full semiannual periods remaining from the bond before
          maturity (or call if the bond is callable)

As examples, we will compute the conversion factors for the SEP 96 and DEC 96 deliveries of the $7\frac{1}{4}$ bond maturing on May 15, 2016. As we have seen, on September 1, 1996, there were 39 full semiannual periods until maturity on this bond, one in May 1996, 38 in the years from November 15, 1996, through November 15, 2015, and one from November 15, 2015, to maturity on May 15, 2016. There were no excess complete quarters, so we can use the simpler formula. Assuming a \$1 face value, the semiannual coupon would be \$.03625 = .5(.0725).

$$CF = \sum_{t=1}^{39} \frac{.03625}{1.04^t} + \frac{1}{1.04^{39}}$$

$$= .709938 + .216621$$

$$= .9266$$

This matches the conversion factor in Table 5.2 of .9266.

As a second example, we compute the conversion factor for the same bond for delivery on the DEC 96 contract. On December 1, 1996, we saw that this bond had 38 full semiannual periods and an excess complete quarter before it matures. Therefore, we use the second version of the conversion factor formula. We have:

$$CF = \frac{\sum_{t=1}^{38} \frac{.03625}{1.04^t} + \frac{1}{1.04^{38}} + .03625}{1.04^{.5}} - .5(.03625)$$

$$= \frac{.702085 + .225285 + .036250}{1.04^{.5}} - .018125$$

$$= .9268$$

This value matches the .9268 of Table 5.2.

Looking closely at the conversion factors in Table 5.2, we can note that the closer the coupon rate is to 8 percent, the closer the conversion factor will be to 1. For a bond with an 8 percent coupon, the conversion factor would equal 1.0. This makes sense, because the conversion factor would be calculated by discounting an 8 percent coupon instrument at 8 percent. For bonds with coupon rates above 8 percent, the shorter the maturity, the closer the conversion factor will be to 1. Just the opposite holds for bonds with coupon rates below 8 percent. In general, if yields are 8 percent across all maturities, the conversion factors will be proportional to the bonds' market prices. This is exactly the desired situation, since the delivery value of a bond should be proportional to its market value.

With a flat term structure and yields at 8 percent, there is no advantage to delivering any bond rather than another. The correlative of this proposition is somewhat disturbing and very important for T-bond futures. If the term structure is not flat, or if yields are not equal to 8 percent, then there is some bond that is better to deliver than the other permissible bonds. This bond is known as the **cheapest-to-deliver**. Among T-bond futures traders, the concept of the cheapest-to-deliver bond is well known. Most brokerage houses have computer systems that show the cheapest-to-deliver T-bonds on a real time basis. Since this feature is well known, futures prices tend to track the cheapest-to-deliver bond, which may change over time.

The interplay of actual bond market prices and the conversion factor biases noted here determine which bond will be the cheapest-to-deliver at any given moment. Prior to actual delivery, some bond will be the cheapest to acquire and to carry to delivery. We have already noted that the cost-of-carry relationship considers the net financing cost of carrying an asset to delivery. In the T-bond futures market, the net financing cost is the price that must be paid for funds less the coupon rate obtained by holding the bond itself. Therefore, at any particular moment, the cheapest-to-deliver bond will be the bond that is most profitable to deliver. In Chapter 6, we explain how to find the cheapest-to-deliver bond in more detail.

Why did the CBOT adopt this cumbersome system of conversion factors, particularly since it introduces biases into the market? As we have seen, a substantial deliverable supply of the spot commodity is a necessary condition for a successful futures contract. If the supply of the deliverable commodity is insufficient, then opportunities for market corners and squeezes can arise. To ensure a large deliverable supply, the CBOT allowed a wide range of bonds to qualify for delivery. With many bonds eligible for delivery, it is necessary to adjust bond prices to reflect their varying market values.

In futures markets, the short trader usually has choices to make in the delivery process. For example, we have noted that the short trader chooses the exact delivery day in the delivery month and chooses which deliverable bond to deliver. Therefore, the short trader has a number of options imbedded in the futures position. These timing and quality options have a value to the seller, so they effectively reduce the prices that we observe in futures markets. Assessing the value of these options for the seller becomes quite complicated. We consider them briefly later in this chapter, and we focus on them in substantial detail in Chapter 6.

Treasury Note Futures

T-bonds and T-notes share a very similar structure, but they differ in the term to maturity at which they are initially offered. Both instruments pay semiannual coupons. Just as the spot market instruments are very similar, the T-bond and T-note futures contracts are very similar as well.

There are three T-note futures contracts trading at the Chicago Board of Trade. While similar in structure, these contracts are based on notes of varying maturities. Nominally, the contracts are designated as ten-, five-, and two-year contracts. However, a range of maturities is deliverable against each contract, with maturity being measured on the first day of the delivery month. Deliverable maturities on 21 months to two years for the two-year contract, four years three months to five years three months for the five-year contract, and six years six months up to ten years for the ten-year contract. The contract size for the five-year and ten-year contracts is $100,000 of face value, but it is $200,000 for the two-year contract. By having a larger denomination for the two-year contract, the CBOT brings the volatilities of the contracts into the same range. This difference in the volatility of the underlying bonds leads to differences in price quotations. For the two-year, the tick size is one quarter of a 32nd, while the five-year contract has a one half of a 32nd tick size. Each contract allows for a range of deliverable maturities, thereby increasing the deliverable supply for each contract.

The T-note and T-bond contracts use the same system of conversion factors as the T-bond contract, and they have the same delivery system. The ten-year and five-year contracts have substantial trading volume and open interest. The two-year contract started trading on June 22, 1990. Although the trading volume and open interest on this contract increased in the years following its inception, it still remains quite small compared to the five-year and ten-year contracts.

Price movements of T-bonds and T-notes are closely related. Figure 5.5 shows T-note and T-bond futures prices for a pair of September contracts. Using these prices we estimated the following regression for the T-bond and the ten-year T-note futures contracts:

$$\text{Change in T-bond Futures } P_t = \alpha + \beta \text{ Change in T-note Futures } P_t + \epsilon$$

The results were:

$$\text{Change in T-bond Futures } P_t = 0.01273 + 1.3511 \text{ Change in T-note Futures } P_t$$

Figure 5.5	SEP T-Bond and T-Note Futures Prices

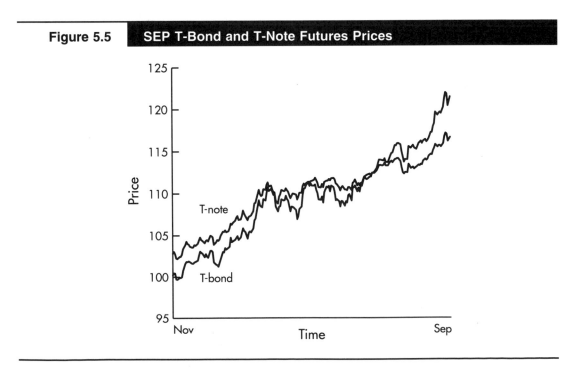

with an R^2 of 0.8253, a t-statistic for β of 30.58, with 200 observations. This simple exercise emphasizes the close relationship between prices of the two instruments. This correspondence is also clearly visible in Figure 5.5.

Municipal Bond Futures

The Chicago Board of Trade began trading a municipal bond futures contract in June 1985. This contract employs cash settlement similar to that used for Eurodollar futures. Among interest rate futures, it is unique in using a bond index as a basis for pricing the contract.

The futures contract is based on *The Bond Buyer* Municipal Bond Index (MBI) of 40 actively traded tax-exempt bonds issued by municipalities in the United States. The bonds may be general obligation or revenue bonds. The collection of bonds in the index is quite diverse, including bonds issued by housing authorities, transportation agencies, or pollution control authorities. Table 5.3 shows the type of bonds included in the index. To be included in the index, a bond must be rated A- or better by Standard & Poor's or A or better by Moody's, with at least $50 million face value outstanding, $75 million for a housing authority bond. The bond must have at least 19 years remaining until maturity, and it must be callable within seven to 16 years. In addition, the bond must pay a fixed semiannual coupon.

Twice monthly the index is updated with some bonds being dropped and others added, keeping the total number of bonds at 40. This updating keeps the index composed of bonds that meet the conditions outlined earlier. For example, if a bond's rating drops below the cutoff or if a default occurs, the bond is dropped. Likewise, if a bond is not actively traded, it will be deleted from the index.

To compute the index value, five municipal bond brokers are polled for each bond. The brokers state the price at which $100,000 face value of a bond would trade. The highest and lowest prices are discarded, and a simple average of the three remaining quotes is taken as the bond price. Each dollar price is then divided by a conversion factor (CF) to give a **converted price**. As we saw with T-bond and T-note futures, this conversion factor represents the price at which each bond would yield 8 percent. Table 5.3 shows this conversion factor for each bond and the bond's converted price. The index value is the average of the 40 adjusted bond prices, multiplied by a **coefficient** (coeff) that corrects for changes in membership among the 40 bonds.

To see how the coefficient works, let us assume that we are at the beginning of the index's life. The coefficient is 1.0 and the average bond price is $101.00, so the index value will be 101.00. Now one bond is deleted from the index, and a new bond is added. Recomputing the index's value with the substituted bond gives 101.50, we assume. Without adjustment, the index value will jump from 101.00 to 101.50 just from switching the bonds in the index. If this were allowed, the replacement of bonds would cause gains and losses without any new information being revealed about interest rates. Therefore, to ensure that the index value before and after substitution of a bond is the same, the index must be computed by adjusting the coefficient. The coefficient needs to change so that the index value is still 101.00 after the substitution. The coefficient (coeff) that keeps the index value the same is given as follows:

$$\text{New Coeff} = \frac{\text{Old Coeff}}{\text{New Mean Converted Bond Price}} \qquad (5.9)$$

Table 5.3	Typical Bonds Included in the Municipal Bond Index	
Issue	**Coupon**	**Maturity Year**
Triborough Bridge	7.125	2019
Ohio Housing Finance	7.650	2029
Florida Board of Education	7.250	2023
California Health Facility	7.000	2020
New York State Energy Research Development	7.250	2024
New York City Municipal Water	7.500	2019
Atlanta Airport	7.900	2018
Brazos River Authority Texas	7.200	2018
Matagorda Navigation	7.200	2018
Maryland Health & Education	6.750	2023
Port Authority of New York & New Jersey	7.250	2025
Michigan State Hospital	7.100	2018
Northern California Transmission	7.000	2024
Massachusetts Port Authority	7.500	2020
Hawaii Airports	7.300	2020
Los Angeles Water & Power	7.125	2030
New York State Energy	7.500	2025
Ohio Housing	7.850	2021
Washington Public Power #3	7.500	2018
Port Authority New York & New Jersey	7.250	2025
Clark County Nevada IDR	7.800	2020
Frankin County Convention	7.000	2019
Los Angeles Wastewater	7.150	2020
Martin County IDA Florida	7.300	2020
Los Angeles California	7.000	2021
Philadelphia Gas Works	7.000	2020

In our example, we would have:

$$\text{New Coeff} = \frac{101.00}{101.50} = .9951$$

Multiplying the new average converted price by the new coefficient, .9951, gives the index value before the substitution, 101.00. Taking all of these factors into account, we can express the value of the MBI as follows:

$$\text{MBI} = \text{Coeff} \; \frac{1}{40} \sum_{j=1}^{40} \frac{P_j}{CF_j} \tag{5.10}$$

where:

P_j = price of the jth bond, average of three usable price quotations
CF_j = conversion factor for the jth bond
Coeff = MBI coefficient

Thus, a futures price of 90-16 indicates 90.50 percent of par. The underlying value of the futures contract is 1,000 times *The Bond Buyer* index value, and a futures price of 90-16 implies a contract size of $90,500. The contract trades for delivery in March, June, September, and December. The tick size is one 32nd or $31.25 per contract. The daily trading limit is three points or $3,000. The contract is settled in cash. Thus, on the final trading day, the settlement price of the futures is set equal to the cash value of the index. This practice ensures that the futures price and the cash market price will converge when the contract expires.

PRICING INTEREST RATE FUTURES CONTRACTS

Introduction

Interest rate futures trade in markets that are virtually always at full carry. In other words, the cost-of-carry model provides a virtually complete understanding of the price structure of interest rate futures contracts. To understand why the cost-of-carry model fits interest rate futures, recall our discussion of Chapter 3. There we identified five features of the underlying good that promote full carry: ease of short selling, large supply of the underlying good, nonseasonal production, nonseasonal consumption, and ease of storage.

The goods that underlie the major interest rate futures contracts meet these conditions very well. First, bonds are created and mature in a nonseasonal way, so the restrictions on seasonality are met virtually perfectly. Second, storage is fairly effortless. Most Treasury securities exist only in computer records, not even being committed to paper. Third, the supply is incredibly ample. For the most important contracts, the underlying instruments are highly liquid debt instruments. For the three T-note contracts, the T-bond contract, and the T-bill contract, the underlying instruments are all issues of the U.S. Treasury. These instruments are available in huge supply and trade in a highly liquid market. The Eurodollar and municipal bond contracts both deal with questions of deliverable supply by avoiding delivery completely. They both use cash settlement. Finally, short selling is very well developed in this market. Because these securities are held in such large amounts by futures market participants, these traders can simulate short selling by selling some of their inventory of Treasury securities. Therefore, it appears that interest rate futures prices should behave like the cost-of-carry model in a perfect market. That is, interest rate futures markets should be at full carry.

In Chapter 3 we considered the cost-of-carry model in perfect markets and concluded that the futures price should equal the spot price plus the cost of carrying the spot good forward to delivery on the futures contract:

$$F_{0,t} = S_0(1 + C) \qquad (3.3)$$

We also concluded that a similar relationship must hold between a nearby futures price and a distant futures price:

$$F_{0,d} = F_{0,n}(1 + C) \qquad\qquad (3.6)$$

where:

$F_{0,t}$ = current futures price for a contract that expires at time t
S_0 = current spot price
C = percentage cost-of-carry between two dates
$F_{0,n}$ = nearby futures price
$F_{0,d}$ = distant futures price

Finally, if we assumed that the only carrying cost is the financing cost, we also concluded that dividing the futures price by the spot price yielded an **implied repo rate**:

$$\frac{F_{0,t}}{S_0} = 1 + C \qquad\qquad (3.7)$$

where:

C = the implied repo rate

As we will see, the model applies very well to interest rate futures. However, we must take account of some of the peculiarities of debt instruments.

The Cost-of-Carry Model in Perfect Markets

In this section, we apply the cost-of-carry model to interest rate futures under the assumption of perfect markets. In addition, we assume that the only carrying charge is the interest rate to finance the holding of a good, and we assume that we can disregard the special features of a given futures contract. For example, we ignore the options that sellers of futures contracts may hold, such as the option to substitute various grades of the commodity at delivery or the option to choose the exact delivery date within the delivery month, and we ignore the differences between forward and futures prices that may result from the daily resettlement cash flows on the futures contract. In summary, we are assuming:

1. Markets are perfect.
2. The financing cost is the only carrying charge.
3. We can ignore the options that the seller may possess.
4. We can ignore the differences between forward and futures prices.

Later in this chapter, we will relax these assumptions.

Each interest rate futures contract that we have considered specifies the maturity of the deliverable bond. For example, the T-bill futures contract requires that a deliverable T-bill must have a maturity of 90–92 days. This requirement applies on the delivery date. As we saw in Chapter 3, the cash-and-carry strategy involves selling a futures contract, buying the spot commodity, and storing it until the futures delivery date. Then the trader delivers the good against the futures contract. For example, if the futures price of gold is too high relative to the cash market price of gold, a trader could engage in a cash-and-carry arbitrage. Part of this strategy would involve buying gold, storing until the futures expiration, and delivering the gold against the futures contract.

To apply this strategy in the interest rate futures market, we must be very careful. For example, if a T-bill futures contract expires in 77 days, we cannot buy a 90-day T-bill and store it for future delivery. If we attempt to do so, we will find ourselves with a 13-day T-bill on the delivery date. This will not be deliverable against the futures contract. Therefore, to apply a cash-and-carry strategy, a trader must buy a bond that will still have or come to have the correct properties on the delivery date. For our T-bill cash-and-carry strategy, the trader must secure a 167-day T-bill to carry for 77 days. Then, the bill will have the requisite 90 days remaining until expiration on the delivery date.

We illustrate the cash-and-carry strategy with an example. Consider the data in Table 5.4. The yields used in Table 5.4 are not the discount yields of the IMM index, but the yields calculated according to the bond pricing formula. The example assumes perfect markets, including the assumption that one can either borrow or lend at any of the riskless rates represented by the T-bill yields. These restrictive assumptions will be relaxed momentarily. The data presented in Table 5.4, and the assumptions just made, mean that an arbitrage opportunity is present. Since the futures contract matures in 77 days, the spot 77-day rate represents the financing cost to acquire the 167-day T-bill, which can be delivered against the MAR futures contract on March 22. This is possible because the T-bill that has 167 days to maturity on January 5 will have exactly 90 days to maturity on March 22.

Transactions presented in Table 5.5 indicate that an arbitrage opportunity exists because the prices and interest rates on the three instruments are mutually inconsistent. To implement a cash-and-carry strategy, a trader can sell the MAR futures and acquire the 167-day T-bill on January 5. The trader then holds the bill for delivery against the futures contract. The trader must finance the holding of the bill during the 77-day interval from January 5 to delivery on March 22. To exploit the rate discrepancy, the trader borrows at the short-term rate of 6 percent and uses the proceeds to acquire the long-term T-bill. At the maturity of the futures, the long-term T-bill has the exactly correct maturity and can be delivered against the futures contract. This strategy generates a profit of $2,235 per contract. Relative to the short-term rate, the futures yield and the long-term T-bill yield were too high. In this example, the trader acquires short-term funds at a low rate (6 percent) and reinvests those funds at a higher rate (10 percent). It may appear that this difference generates the arbitrage profit, but that is not completely accurate, as the next example shows.[3]

Interest Rate Futures and Arbitrage	Table 5.4

Today's Date: January 5

Futures	Yield According to the Bond Pricing Formula
MAR Contract (Matures in 77 days on March 22)	12.50%
Cash Bills:	
167-day T-bill (Deliverable on MAR futures)	10.00
77-day T-bill	6.00

Table 5.5	Cash-and-Carry Arbitrage Transactions

January 5
Borrow $956,750 for 77 days by issuing a 77-day T-bill at 6%.
Buy 167-day T-bill yielding 10% for $956,750.
Sell MAR T-bill futures contract with a yield of 12.50% for $970,984.

March 22
Deliver the originally purchased T-bill against the MAR futures contract and collect $970,984.
Repay debt on 77-day T-bill that matures today for $968,749.

$$
\begin{array}{rr}
\text{Profit:} & \$970,984 \\
- & 968,749 \\
\hline
\$ & 2,235
\end{array}
$$

Consider the same values as shown in Table 5.4, but now assume that the rate on the 77-day T-bill is 8 percent. Now the short-term rate is too high relative to the long-term rate and the futures yield. To take advantage of this situation, we reverse the cash-and-carry procedure of Table 5.5, as Table 5.6 shows. In other words, we now exploit a reverse cash-and-carry strategy. With this new set of rates, the arbitrage is more complicated, since it involves holding the T-bill that is delivered on the futures contract. In this situation, the arbitrageur borrows $955,131 for 167 days at 10 percent and invests these funds at 8 percent for the 77 days until the MAR futures matures. The payoff from the 77-day investment of $955,131 will be $970,984, exactly enough to pay for the delivery of the T-bill on the futures contract. This bill is held for 90 days until June 20 when it matures and pays $1,000,000. On June 20, the arbitrageur's loan on the 167-day T-bill is also due, and equals $998,308. This trader repays this debt from the $1,000,000 received on the maturing bill. The strategy yields a profit of $1,692. Notice in this second example that the trader borrowed at 10 percent and invested

Table 5.6	Reverse Cash-and-Carry Arbitrage Transactions

January 5
Borrow $955,131 by issuing a 167-day T-bill at 10%.
Buy a 77-day T-bill yielding 8% for $955,131 that will pay $970,984 on March 22.
Buy one MAR futures contract with a yield of 12.50% for $970,984.

March 22
Collect $970,984 from the maturing 77-day T-bill.
Pay $970,984 and take delivery of a 90-day T-bill from the MAR futures contract.

June
Collect $1,000,000 from the maturing 90-day T-bill that was delivered on the futures contract.
Pay $998,308 debt on the maturing 167-day T-bill.

$$
\begin{array}{rr}
\text{Profit:} & \$1,000,000 \\
- & 998,308 \\
\hline
\$ & 1,692
\end{array}
$$

the funds at 8 percent temporarily. This shows that it is the entire set of rates that must be consistent and that arbitrage opportunities need not only involve misalignment between two rates.

From our analyses in Chapter 3, we know that the reverse cash-and-carry strategy involves selling an asset short and investing the proceeds from the short sale. In our example of Table 5.6, the short sale is the issuance of debt. By issuing debt, the arbitrageur literally sells a bond. In Chapter 3, we also noted that a trader could simulate a short sale by selling from inventory. The same is true for interest rate futures. For example, a bank that holds investments in T-bills can simulate a short sale by selling a T-bill from inventory.

To this point, we have considered a cash-and-carry strategy in Table 5.5 and a reverse cash-and-carry strategy in Table 5.6. These two examples show that there must be a very exact relationship among these rates on the different instruments to exclude arbitrage opportunities. If the yield on the MAR futures is 12.50 percent and the 167-day spot yield is 10 percent, there is only one yield for the 77-day T-bill that will not give rise to an arbitrage opportunity, and that rate is 7.15 percent. To see why that is the case, consider two ways of holding a T-bill investment for the full 167-day period of the examples:

1. hold the 167-day T-bill, or
2. hold a 77-day T-bill followed by a 90-day T-bill that is delivered on the futures contract.

Since these two ways of holding T-bills cover the same time period and have the same risk level, the two positions must have the same yield to avoid arbitrage. For the examples, the necessary yield on the 77-day T-bill can be found by using an equation expressing the yield on a long-term instrument as being equal to the yield on two short-term positions:

$$(1.10)^{167/360} = (1 + x)^{77/360}(1.1250)^{90/360}$$

This equation holds only if the rate, x, on the 77-day T-bill equals 7.1482 percent.

We can also express the same idea in terms of the prices of the bills. To illustrate this point, consider the prices of three securities. The first is a 167-day bill that yields 10.00 percent and pays $1 upon maturity. Second is a T-bill futures with an underlying bill having a $1 face value. With a yield of 12.50 percent, the futures price will be $.970984. Finally, the third instrument matures in 77 days, has a face value of $.970984, and yields 7.1482 percent.

$$P_{167} = \frac{\$1}{(1 + r_{167})^{167/360}} = \frac{\$1}{1.1^{167/360}} = .956750$$

$$P_F = \frac{\$1}{(1 + r_{fut})^{90/360}} = \frac{\$1}{1.1250^{90/360}} = .970984$$

$$P_{77} = \frac{\$.970984}{(1 + r_{77})^{77/360}} = \frac{\$.970984}{1.071482^{77/360}} = .956750$$

The third instrument is peculiar, with its strange face value. However, this is exactly the payoff necessary to pay for delivery on the futures contract in 77 days. Notice also that the 77-day bill and the 167-day bill have the same price. They should, because both prices of $.956750 are the investment now that is necessary to have a $1 payoff in 167 days. The futures yield and the 167-day yield were taken as fixed. The yield on the 77-day bill, 7.1482 percent, is exactly the yield that must prevail if the two strategies are to be equivalent and to prevent arbitrage.

The Financing Cost and the Implied Repo Rate. With these prices, and continuing to assume that the only carrying cost is the financing charge, we can also infer the implied repo rate. We know that the ratio of the futures price divided by the spot price equals 1 plus the implied repo rate. As we have seen, the correct spot instrument for our example is the 167-day bill, because this bill will have the appropriate delivery characteristics when the futures matures. Thus, we have:

$$1 + C = \frac{P_F}{P_{167}} = \frac{.970984}{.956750} = 1.014878$$

The implied repo rate, C, is 1.4878 percent. This covers the cost-of-carry for 77 days from the present to the expiration of the futures. We can annualize this rate as follows:

$$1.014878^{360/77} = 1.071482$$

The annualized repo rate is 7.1482 percent. This exactly matches the interest rate on the 77-day bill that will prevent arbitrage. Therefore, assuming that the interest cost is the only carrying charge, the cost-of-carry equals the implied repo rate.

This equivalence between the cost-of-carry and the implied repo rate also leads to two rules for arbitrage.

1. If the implied repo rate exceeds the financing cost, then exploit a cash-and-carry arbitrage opportunity: Borrow funds; buy the cash bond; sell futures; hold the bond and deliver against futures.
2. If the implied repo rate is less than the financing cost, then exploit a reverse cash-and-carry arbitrage opportunity: Buy futures; sell the bond short and invest proceeds until futures expires; take delivery on futures; repay short sale obligation.

The Futures Yield and the Forward Rate of Interest. We have seen that the futures price of an interest rate futures contract implies a yield on the instrument that underlies the futures contract. We call this implied yield the futures yield. Now we continue to assume that the financing cost is the only carrying charge, that markets are perfect, that we can ignore the options that the seller of a futures contract may possess, and that the price difference between forward contracts and futures contracts is negligible. Under these conditions, we can show that the futures yield must equal the forward rate of interest.

We continue to use the T-bill futures contract as our example. The T-bill futures, like many other interest rate futures contracts, has an underlying instrument that will be delivered when the contract expires. If we consider a SEP contract, it calls for the delivery of a 90-day T-bill that will mature in December. The futures yield covers the 90-day span of time from delivery in September to maturity in December. Given the necessary set of spot rates, it is possible to compute a forward rate to cover any given period.

To illustrate the equivalence between futures yields and forward rates under our assumptions, we continue to use our example of a T-bill with a 167-day holding period. Let us assume the following spot yields:

For a 167-day bill   10.0000%
For a 77-day bill   7.1482

These two spot rates imply a forward rate to cover the period from day 77 to day 167:

$$(1 + r_{0,167})^{167/360} = (1 + r_{0,77})^{77/360}(1 + r_{77,167})^{90/360}$$

Substituting values for the spot bills and solving for the forward rate, $r_{77,167}$, gives:

$$(1.10)^{167/360} = (1.071482)^{77/360}(1 + r_{77,167})^{90/360}$$
$$(1 + r_{77,167})^{90/360} = \frac{(1.10)^{167/360}}{(1.071482)^{77/360}} = \frac{1.045205}{1.014877} = 1.029884$$
$$1 + r_{77,167} = 1.1250$$
$$r_{77,167} = .1250$$

Therefore, the forward rate, to cover day 77 to day 167, is 12.50 percent. As we saw earlier, the futures yield is also 12.50 percent for the T-bill futures that expires on day 77. Therefore, the futures yield equals the forward rate for the same period. In deriving this result, we must bear our assumptions in mind: markets are perfect, the financing cost is the only carrying charge, and we ignore the seller's options and the difference between forward and futures prices.

The Cost-of-Carry Model for T-Bond Futures

In this section, we apply the cost-of-carry model to the T-bond futures contract. In essence, the same concepts apply, with one difference. The holder of a T-bond receives cash flows from the bond. This affects the cost-of-carry that the holder of the bond actually incurs. For example, assume that the coupon rate on a $100,000 face value T-bond is 8 percent and the trader finances the bond at 8 percent. In this case, the net carrying charge is zero – the earnings offset the financing cost.

To illustrate this idea, let us assume that, on January 5, a T-bond that is deliverable on a futures contract has an 8 percent coupon and costs 100.00. The trader faces a financing rate of 7.1482 percent for the 77 days until the futures contract is deliverable. Because the T-bond has an 8 percent coupon rate, the conversion factor is 1.0 and plays no role. With an 8 percent coupon, the accrued interest from the date of purchase to the delivery date on the futures is:

$$(77/182)(.04)(100,000) = \$1,692$$

Therefore, the invoice amount will be $101,692. If this is the invoice amount in 77 days, the T-bond must cost the present value of that amount, discounted for 77 days at the 77-day rate of 7.1482 percent. This implies a cost for the T-bond of $100,200. If the price is less than $100,200, a cash-and-carry arbitrage strategy will be available. Under these circumstances the cash-and-carry strategy would have the cash flows shown in Table 5.7.

The transactions in Table 5.7 show that the futures price must adjust to reflect the accrual of interest. The bond in Table 5.7 had no coupon payment during the 77-day interval, but the same adjustment must be made to account for cash throwoffs that the bondholder receives during the holding period.

Table 5.7	Cash-and-Carry Transactions for a T-Bond

January 5
Borrow $100,200 for 77 days at the 77-day rate of 7.1482%.
Buy the 8% T-bond for $100,200.
Sell 1 T-bond futures contract for $101,692.

March 22
Deliver T-bond; receive invoice amount of $101,692.
Repay loan of $101,692.

                                                    Profit: 0

The Cost-of-Carry Model in Imperfect Markets

We now relax our assumption of perfect markets and see how the cost-of-carry model applies to interest rate futures. Specifically, we will focus on the possibility that the borrowing and lending rates may differ. We continue to ignore the seller's options and the price differences between forward and futures contracts. Thus, in this section we analyze the cost-of-carry model for the situation in which:

1. The borrowing rate exceeds the lending rate.
2. The financing cost is the only carrying charge.
3. We can ignore the options that the seller may possess.
4. We can ignore the differences between forward and futures prices.

In Chapter 3 we saw that allowing the borrowing and lending rates to differ leads to an arbitrage band around the futures price. For example, let us assume that the borrowing rate is 25 basis points, or one-fourth of a percentage point, higher than the lending rates. Continuing to use our T-bill example, we have:

Instrument	Lending Rate	Borrowing Rate
77-day bill	7.1482	7.3982
167-day bill	10.0000	10.2500

These assumptions approximate real market conditions. For example, a bank might be able to lend funds to the government by buying a T-bill. To borrow, however, the bank might have to transact at a somewhat higher repo rate.

When it was possible to both borrow and lend at the same rate, our earlier examples showed that the futures yield must be 12.50 percent. Now, with these different borrowing and lending rates, we want to determine how the futures yield can vary from 12.50 percent. To do this we apply the cash-and-carry and reverse cash-and-carry strategies. In both cases, we find the futures price that gives exactly a zero gain or loss on the strategy.

In the cash-and-carry strategy, we sell the futures and borrow in order to buy a good that we can deliver on the futures contract. Table 5.8 details the transactions with unequal borrowing and

Cash-and-Carry Transactions with Unequal Borrowing and Lending Rates	Table 5.8

January 5
Borrow $956,750 for 77 days at the 77-day borrowing rate of 7.3982%.
Buy 167-day T-bill yielding 10% for $956,750.
Sell 1 T-bill futures contract with a yield of 12.2760% for $971,468.

March 22
Deliver the originally purchased T-bill against the MAR futures contract and collect $971,468.
Repay debt on 77-day T-bill that matures today for $971,468.

Profit: 0

---

lending rates. The table illustrates the highest futures yield and lowest futures price that gives a zero profit with the unequal borrowing and lending rates. From this example, we see that the futures yield can be as low as 12.2760 percent without generating an arbitrage opportunity. This futures yield implies that the futures price can be as high as $971,468 and still not generate an arbitrage opportunity.

We now consider the reverse cash-and-carry strategy. Here, we will borrow long-term to finance a short-term investment and we purchase the futures. When the futures expires, we accept delivery and hold the delivered good until the bond matures. Table 5.9 illustrates the transactions that show how high the futures yield can be and how low the futures price can be without providing an arbitrage opportunity.

From the transactions in Table 5.9, we see that the futures yield can be as high as 12.9751 percent without providing an arbitrage opportunity. Similarly, the corresponding futures price can be as low as $969,961 without creating an arbitrage opportunity.

Reverse Cash-and-Carry Transactions with Unequal Borrowing and Lending Rates	Table 5.9

January 5
Borrow $955,743 at the 167-day borrowing rate of 10.25%.
Buy a 77-day T-bill yielding 7.1482% for $955,743.
Buy 1 MAR futures contract with a futures yield of 12.9751% for $969,961.

March 22
Collect $969,961 from the maturing 77-day T-bill.
Pay $969,961 and take delivery of a 90-day T-bill on the futures contract.

June
Collect $1,000,000 from the maturing 90-day T-bill that was delivered on the futures contract.
Pay $1,000,000 debt on the maturing 167-day T-bill.

Profit: 0

With equal borrowing and lending rates in our earlier examples, we saw that the futures yield had to be exactly 12.50 percent and the futures price had to be $970,984. The unequal borrowing and lending rates create a no-arbitrage band for the futures. Now the futures yield must fall in the range from 12.2760 to 12.9751 percent, and the futures price must lie in the range $969,961 to $971,468. As long as the futures yield and futures price stay within these respective ranges, arbitrage will not be possible.

A Practical Survey of Interest Rate Futures Pricing. If markets are perfect, if the only carrying charge is the financing cost, if we ignore the seller's options, and if we ignore differences between futures and forward prices, we have seen how the cost-of-carry model specifies an exact futures yield and futures price. If we allow market imperfections in the form of unequal borrowing and lending rates, we have seen that the cost-of-carry model leads to a no-arbitrage band of possible futures prices. Now we provide a practical approach to include other market imperfections in our analysis.

In Chapter 3, we considered transaction costs, a typical market imperfection. There we saw that transaction costs lead to a no-arbitrage band of possible futures prices. In essence, transaction costs increase the no-arbitrage band just as unequal borrowing and lending rates do. In Chapter 3, we also considered impediments to short selling as a market imperfection that would frustrate the reverse cash-and-carry arbitrage strategy. From a practical perspective, restrictions on short selling are relatively unimportant in interest rate futures pricing. First, supplies of deliverable Treasury securities are plentiful and government securities have little (or zero) convenience yield. Second, because Treasury securities are so widely held, many traders can simulate short selling by selling T-bills, T-notes, or T-bonds from inventory. Therefore, restrictions on short selling are unlikely to have any pricing effect.

In our analysis of the cost-of-carry model, we found that the futures yield must equal the forward rate of interest, under our assumptions. By assuming that we could ignore the difference between forward and futures prices, we implicitly assumed that we could ignore the effect of daily resettlement cash flows on pricing. However, in Chapter 3, we saw that daily resettlement cash flows could affect pricing of the futures contract if the price of the cash commodity were correlated with interest rates. In the interest rate futures market, the underlying goods are highly correlated with interest rates. Therefore, we might expect to find differences between futures and forward prices, and between futures and forward yields. In Chapter 3, we saw that a negative correlation between the price of the cash commodity and interest rates would lead to a futures price that is less than the forward price. This is exactly the situation with interest rate futures, because bond prices fall as interest rates rise. Therefore, we would expect the futures price to be less than the forward price for this reason. However, most studies indicate that this is not a serious problem in general. From a practical point of view, this difference is unlikely to be critical. We consider the theoretical ramifications of this relationship in more detail in Chapter 6.

In the construction of interest rate futures contracts, we have seen that the seller of a futures contract possesses timing and quality options that may be valuable. For example, the seller of a T-bond futures possesses a timing option because she can decide which day of the delivery month to deliver. Likewise, the seller possesses a quality option, because she can decide which bond to deliver. The buyer of the futures knows that the seller acquires these options by selling the futures. Therefore, the futures price must adjust to account for those options. This means that the futures price with the seller's options must be less than it would be if it had no options attached.

Studies have shown that the seller's options can have significant value. We consider this issue in detail in Chapter 6. Here we note that these options have sufficient value to be of practical importance in using interest rate futures. As we will see in Chapter 6, it is even possible that these options can account for 15 percent of the futures price.

Interest Rate Futures Pricing: An Example

We conclude our discussion of interest rate futures pricing in this chapter by applying the cost-of-carry model to actual market data. For this illustration, we consider the difference between a JUN and SEP T-bond futures price. Under the simplifying assumptions made earlier, we would expect these two prices to be closely related by the financing cost of carrying a bond from June to September. We know that market imperfections, the difference between futures and forward prices, and the seller's options might all disturb this relationship. Nonetheless, we expect the main component of this price difference to be tied to the financing cost from September to December.

To apply this idea to actual data, we use the JUN T-bill futures contract to provide a proxy for the financing rate to hold a T-bond from June to September. To accept delivery on the JUN T-bond futures and carry the delivered bond forward to the September delivery involves paying the invoice price to acquire the bond, financing the bond for three months at the JUN T-bill rate, receiving the accrued interest on the bond, which we estimate as having an 8 percent coupon rate, and selling the SEP futures. In a perfect market, this strategy should yield a zero profit. In other words, we expect the quantity:

$$F_{0,d} + AI - F_{0,n}(1 + C) = 0 \qquad (5.11)$$

where:

$F_{0,d}$ = SEP T-bond futures price
$F_{0,n}$ = JUN T-bond futures price plus accrued interest due at delivery
C = three month cost-of-carry estimated from JUN T-bill futures
AI = interest accrued from T-bond in September, estimated at $2,000 per contract
    (8 percent per year on $100,000 for one quarter)

Figure 5.6 graphs the value of Equation 5.11 for a one contract position. In an absolutely perfect market, we expect the value to be zero. As Figure 5.6 shows, it is extremely close to zero. The minimum value is −$202, and the maximum value is $48. Thus, the graph of the value of Equation 5.11 ranges from −2/10 of one percent to +1/20 of one percent. These values are all the closer considering the crude estimate of the accrued interest and the fact that we did not even attempt to find the cheapest-to-deliver bond. Presumably, a more exacting analysis would lead to yet smaller discrepancies.

SPECULATING WITH INTEREST RATE FUTURES

In the interest rate futures market, it is possible to speculate by holding an outright position, or by trading a spread. An outright position, such as buying a T-bill futures, is a simple bet on the direction of interest rates. More sophisticated speculative strategies involve trading spreads. As we discussed in Chapter 4, a spread speculation involves a bet on a change in the relationship between two futures prices. In this section we consider some basic speculative strategies and illustrate them with examples.

Figure 5.6   **Cost-of-Carry Model for JUN and SEP T-Bonds**

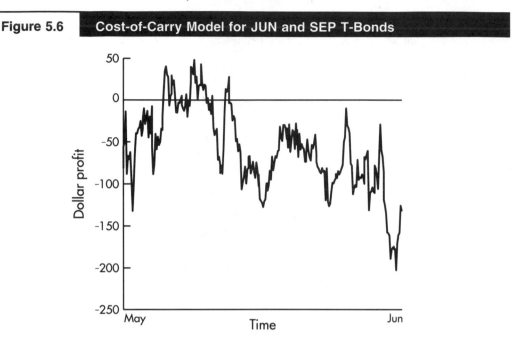

The concept of a speculative profit is a very slippery notion, as we discussed in Chapter 4. A speculator might earn accounting profits that constitute a justifiable return to the application of his capital and energies. This is different from economic profit or an economic rent, which would be a profit in excess of return for the use of capital and the bearing of risk. Accounting profits are consistent with market efficiency, but economic profits are not. As the speculative strategies of this section are considered, it is important to keep these different conceptions of profit in mind.

Speculating with Outright Positions

For a speculator with an outright position in futures, the speculation is very simple. The long trader is betting that interest rates will fall so that the price of the futures will rise. The short trader is betting that interest rates will rise so that the futures price will fall.

As an example of an outright speculation, we consider a trader who anticipated rising interest rates on September 20, 1990, following the Iraqi invasion of Kuwait. In particular, the trader believes that short-term rates will rise, so she trades the Eurodollar contract as shown in Table 5.10. To profit from rising rates, the trader must be short in interest rate futures. Accordingly, she sells one DEC 90 Eurodollar contract at 90.30. Five days later, interest rates have risen and the futures contract trades at 90.12. Satisfied with the profit, she sells, for a gain of 18 basis points. Because each basis point is worth $25, her total profit is $450.

Speculating with Spreads

For the most part, speculation with interest rate futures relies on spread trading. An intracommodity spread is typically a speculation on the term structure of interest rates, for example, a spread between

Speculating with Eurodollar Futures	Table 5.10
Date	**Futures Market**
September 20	Sell 1 DEC 90 Eurodollar futures at 90.30.
September 25	Buy 1 DEC 90 Eurodollar futures at 90.12.

Profit: 90.30 – 90.12 = .18

Total Gain: 18 basis points × $25 = $450

the nearby and distant T-bill futures. An intercommodity spread can be a speculation on the changing shape of the yield curve, or it can be a speculation on shifting risk levels between different instruments. For example, T-bills and T-bonds have the same default risk, so a bond/bill spread is a yield curve speculation. Often, an intercommodity spread is a speculation on changing risk levels between different instruments, for example, a spread between T-bills and Eurodollars. Of course, a given spread could combine features of both term structure and risk structure speculations. This section illustrates various types of spread speculation.

An Intracommodity T-Bill Spread. Table 5.11 presents a series of spot rates and futures rates for T-bills. As the spot rates show, the yield curve slopes upward, with three-month bills yielding 10 percent and 12-month bills yielding 12 percent. The table shows three futures contracts, with the nearby contract maturing in three months. For the futures contracts, the futures yields are consistent with the term structure given by the spot rates, in the sense that the futures yields equal the forward rates from the term structure. Faced with such circumstances, particularly with a very steep upward sloping yield curve, a speculator might believe that the term structure would flatten within six months. Even if one were not sure whether rates were going to rise or fall, the speculator could still profit from a T-bill futures spread by entering the transactions shown in Table 5.12.

If the yield curve flattens, the yield spread between successively maturing futures contracts must narrow. Currently, the yield spread between the DEC and SEP futures contracts is 100 basis points. By buying the more distant DEC contract and selling the SEP contract, the trader bets that the yield differential will narrow. If the yield curve flattens, no matter whether the general level of rates rises or falls, then this spread strategy gives a profit. As Table 5.12 shows, yields have fallen dramatically by April 30. The yield on the DEC contract has fallen from 13.50 percent to 11.86 percent and the SEP yield has moved from 12.50 percent to 10.98 percent. For the profits on this speculative strategy, the important point is that the yield spread has changed from 100 basis points to 88 basis points.

Spot and Futures T-Bill Rates for March 20				Table 5.11
Time to Maturity or Futures Expiration	**Spot Rates**	**Futures Contract**	**Futures Yield**	**IMM Index**
3 months	10.00%	JUN	12.00%	88.00
6 months	11.00	SEP	12.50	87.50
9 months	11.50	DEC	13.50	86.50
12 months	12.00			

Table 5.12	Speculation on T-Bill Futures
Date	**Futures Market**
March 20	Buy the DEC T-bill futures at 86.50. Sell the SEP T-bill futures at 87.50.
April 30	Sell the DEC T-bill futures at 88.14. Buy the SEP T-bill futures at 89.02.

Profits:

DEC	SEP
88.14	87.50
−86.50	−89.02
1.64	− 1.52

Total Gain: 12 basis points × $25 = $300

This generates a profit on the spread of 12 basis points, or $300 because each basis point change represents $25. The same kind of result could have been obtained in a market with rising rates, as long as the yield curve flattens.

This example shows that all interest rate futures intracommodity spreads are speculations on the changing shape of the yield curve. No matter what change in the shape of the yield curve is anticipated, there is a way to profit from that change by trading the correct interest rate futures spread.

A T-Bill/T-Bond Spread. To illustrate the use of spreads more completely, consider a flat yield curve, with the rates shown in Table 5.13. Here all rates, spot and futures, are at 12 percent, representing a perfectly flat yield curve. If a trader believes that the yield curve is going to become upward sloping, two strategies could take advantage of this belief. First, the trader could use an intracommodity spread similar to the spread of Table 5.12. Since the speculator anticipates a positively sloping yield curve, he or she could sell the distant T-bill futures and buy the nearby T-bill futures. This spread would be speculating that the yield curve would become upward sloping for the very low maturity instruments represented by the T-bills.

With an upward sloping yield curve, however, we would expect the greatest difference in yields between short maturity and long maturity instruments, that is, between T-bills and T-bonds. This implies that long-term yields are expected to rise relative to short-term yields. To take advantage of

Table 5.13	Spot and Futures Yields, June 20			
Cash Market	**Yield**	**Futures Market**	**Yield**	**Price**
3-month T-bill	12.00%	SEP T-bill	12.00%	88.00
6-month T-bill	12.00	DEC T-bill	12.00	88.00
10-3/8s 2007-12	12.00	SEP T-bond	12.00	
		DEC T-bond	12.00	

this anticipated change in yields, the trader might use an intercommodity spread, as shown in Table 5.14.

If long-term yields are expected to rise relative to short-term yields, the best spread strategy calls for selling the futures contract on a long-term instrument while buying a futures on a short-term instrument. This is exactly the course pursued by a speculator who transacts as shown in Table 5.14. With yields at 12 percent, the T-bond instrument has a price of 69-29, and the T-bill futures price is 88.00. By October 14, yields have moved as anticipated, with T-bond futures yields at 12.778 percent and the T-bill futures at 12.20 percent. For the T-bond contract, this gives a price change of 4-05. Since each 32nd of a point of par represents $31.25 on a T-bond futures contract, this gives a total profit on the T-bond contract of $4,156.25. On the T-bill side, rates have not risen as rapidly, only 20 basis points. Since each basis point represents $25, there is a loss on the T-bill futures of $500. When the T-bill loss is offset against the T-bond gain, the net profit from the speculation is $3,656.25.

In this example, we assumed that one T-bond and one T-bill contract were traded. Often such a procedure will not be the best, since different futures contracts have different price volatilities. In this case, the T-bond yield moved almost four times as much as the T-bill yield, but the T-bond price moved more than eight times as much in terms of dollars. This difference in the sensitivity of prices can be very important, both for speculating and for hedging. Notice, also, that both contracts were traded for the same futures delivery month. This shows that a speculative strategy focusing on yield curve changes need not employ different futures maturities. It will be necessary, however, to use either different futures expiration months, or different contracts.

A T-Bill/Eurodollar (TED) Spread. Another basic kind of speculation possible in the interest rate futures market is a speculation on the changing risk structure of interest rates. In these days of a continuing international debt crisis, it is a time of danger for banks heavily engaged in international lending, with great fear of widespread default on the part of many third world nations. A speculator might view this situation as offering potential opportunity. If the crisis developed, we might expect to find a widening of the yield spread between T-bill deposits and Eurodollar deposits, for example.

Intercommodity Spread Speculation	Table 5.14
Date	**Futures Market**
June 20	Sell the DEC T-bond futures at 69-29 with a yield of 12%. Buy the DEC T-bill futures at 88.00 with a yield of 12%.
October 24	Buy the DEC T-bond futures at 65-24 with a yield of 12.78%. Sell the DEC T-bill futures at 87.80 with a yield of 12.20%.

Profits:

T-bond	T-bill
69-29	87.80
−65-24	−88.00
4-05	−.20
= $4,156.25	= −$500

Total Profit: $3,656.25

This widening yield spread would reflect the changing perception of the risk involved in holding Eurodollar deposits in the face of potentially very large loan losses. In February, assume that yields for the DEC T-bill and Eurodollar futures contracts are 8.82 and 9.71 percent, respectively. If the full riskiness of the banks' position has yet to be understood, we might expect the yield spread to widen. This would be the case whether interest rates were rising or falling. To take advantage of this belief, a trader could sell the DEC Eurodollar contract and buy the DEC T-bill contract, as Table 5.15 shows.

Since the trader expects the yield spread to widen, he or she sells the Eurodollar contract and buys the T-bill contract for index values of 90.29 and 91.18, respectively. Later, on October 14, the yield spread of the example has, in fact, widened, with T-bill yields having moved up slightly so the spread has widened by 27 basis points, which means a profit of $675 on the speculation.

Perhaps the single most important point about speculation can be emphasized using this example. Virtually everyone is aware of the problems that were faced by banks involved in international lending in the 1980s. Therefore, the futures prices must already have imbedded in them the market's expectation of the future yield spread between T-bills and Eurodollars. By engaging in the speculative strategy discussed here, a trader speculates against the rest of the market. It was not enough to expect yield spreads to widen, but the trader must have expected them to widen more than the market expected. And the trader must have been right to make a profit. This spread relationship is so well known that it has a name – the TED spread (Treasury/Eurodollar).[4]

Notes Over Bonds, the NOB Trade. Like the TED spread, other strategies are sufficiently popular to earn nicknames. The NOB is a speculative strategy for trading T-note futures against T-bond futures. The term ''NOB'' stands for **notes over bonds**. As we have seen, prices of bonds and notes are strongly correlated. Because the T-bonds underlying the T-bond futures contract have a longer duration than the T-notes underlying the T-note futures contract, a given change in yields will cause a greater price reaction for the T-bond futures contract. The NOB spread is designed to exploit that

Table 5.15	Intercommodity Spread in Short-Term Rates
Date	**Futures Market**
February 17	Sell 1 DEC Eurodollar futures contract with an IMM index value of 90.29. Buy 1 DEC T-bill futures contract yielding 8.82% with an IMM index value of 91.18.
October 14	Buy 1 DEC Eurodollar futures contract with an IMM Index value of 89.91. Sell 1 DEC T-bill futures contract yielding 8.93% with an IMM index value of 91.07.

Profits:

Eurodollar	T-bill
90.29	91.07
−89.91	−91.18
.38	−.11

Total Profit: 27 basis points × $25 = $675

fact. Thus, the NOB spread is essentially an attempt to take advantage of either changing levels of yields or a changing yield curve by using an intermarket spread.

If yields rise by the same amount on both instruments, one can expect a greater price change on the T-bond. Assume a trader is long the T-bond futures and short the T-note futures. An equal drop in rates will give a profit on the long T-bond futures that exceeds the loss on the T-note futures, giving a profit on the spread.

The NOB can also be used to trade based on expectations of a changing yield curve shape. For example, assume a trader expects the yield curve to become more steeply upward sloping. This implies that yields on the long maturities (T-bonds) would rise relative to yields on shorter maturities (T-notes). To take advantage of this belief, the trader should sell T-bond futures and buy T-note futures. If a trader expects the yield curve to become more downward sloping, the trader would buy T-bond futures and sell T-note futures. Notice that this speculation only concerns the relative yields, not the levels.

HEDGING WITH INTEREST RATE FUTURES

In this section, we explore the concept of hedging with interest rate futures. We present a series of examples, progressing from simple cases to more complex situations. In essence, the hedger in interest rate futures attempts to take a futures position that will generate a gain to offset a potential loss in the cash market. This also implies that the hedger takes a futures position that will generate a loss to offset a potential gain in the cash market. Thus, the interest rate futures hedger is attempting to reduce risk, not to make profits.

A Long Hedge Example

A portfolio manager learns on December 15 that he will have $972,000 to invest in 90-day T-bills six months from now. Current yields on T-bills stand at 12 percent and the yield curve is flat, so forward rates are all 12 percent as well. The manager finds the 12 percent rate attractive and decides to lock it in by going long in a T-bill futures contract maturing on June 15, exactly when the funds come available for investment. As Table 5.16 shows, the manager anticipates the cash position on December 15 and buys one T-bill futures contract to hedge the risk that yields might fall before the funds are available for investment on June 15. With the current yield and, more importantly, the forward rate on T-bills of 12 percent, the portfolio manager expects to be able to buy $1,000,000 face value of T-bills because:

$$\$972,065.42 = \$1,000,000/(1.12)^{.25}$$

The hedge is initiated and time passes. On June 15, the 90-day T-bill yield has fallen to 10 percent, confirming the portfolio manager's fears. Consequently, $1,000,000 face value of 90-day T-bills is worth:

$$\$976,454.09 = \$1,000,000/(1.10)^{.25}$$

Just before the futures contract matures, the manager sells one JUN T-bill futures contract, making a profit of $4,388.67. But in the spot market, the cost of $1,000,000 face value of 90-day T-bills has

Table 5.16	A Long Hedge with T-Bill Futures	
Date	**Cash Market**	**Futures Market**
December 15	A portfolio manager learns he will receive $972,065 in six months to invest in T-bills. Market Yield: 12% Expected face value of bills to purchase $1,000,000.	The manager buys 1 T-bill futures contract to mature in six months. Futures price: $972,065
June 15	Manager receives $972,065 to invest. Market yield: 10% $1,000,000 face value of T-bills now costs $976,454.	The manager sells 1 T-bill futures contract maturing immediately. Futures yield: 10% Futures price: $976,454
	Loss = –$4,389	Profit = $4,389
	Net wealth change = 0	

risen from $972,065 to $976,454, generating a cash market loss of $4,389. However, the futures profit exactly offsets the cash market loss for a zero change in wealth. With the receipt of the $972,065 that was to be invested, plus the $4,389 futures profit, the original plan may be executed, and the portfolio manager purchases $1,000,000 face value in 90-day T-bills.[5]

By design, this example is extremely artificial in order to illustrate the long hedge. Notice that the yield curve is flat at the outset, and only its level changes. Figure 5.7 portrays the kind of yield curve shift that was assumed. This idealized yield curve shift is unlikely to occur. Also, the assumption of a flat yield curve plays a crucial role in accounting for the simplicity of this example. If the yield curve is flat, spot and forward rates are identical. When one ''locks-in'' some rate via futures trading, it is necessarily a forward rate that is locked-in, as the next example shows. Also, we assumed the portfolio manager received exactly the right amount of funds at exactly the right time to purchase $1,000,000 of T-bills. These unrealistic assumptions are gradually relaxed in the following examples.

A Short Hedge. A government securities dealer agrees to sell another firm $1,000,000 face value of 90-day T-bills in four months for $967,000, a price that implies a yield of 14.37 percent. The forward rate (for a 90-day T-bill beginning in four months) from the yield curve also equals 14.37 percent, and the yield on the futures contract is also 14.37 percent. Assume also that the current 90-day T-bill spot rate is 13 percent. The difference, measured in yields at the outset, is –1.37 percent (13 percent – 14.37 percent). Table 5.17 shows the security dealer's position in the cash and futures markets. If rates fall below the expected 14.37 percent, the security dealer will have to deliver T-bills worth more than the $967,000 he will receive. To protect against this eventuality, the dealer buys one T-bill futures contract with a futures price of $967,000 and a futures yield of 14.37 percent.

Time passes and the market's expectations are realized. Four months after the hedge is opened, the 90-day T-bill yield is 14.37 percent, as implied by the forward rate. In the cash market, the security dealer delivers T-bills worth the anticipated amount of $967,000 and receives $967,000,

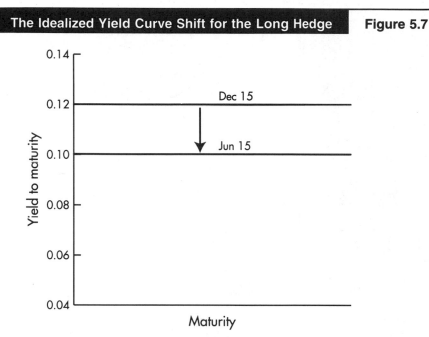

The Idealized Yield Curve Shift for the Long Hedge | **Figure 5.7**

A Short Hedge Using T-Bill Futures | **Table 5.17**

Date	Cash Market	Futures Market
Time = 0	The security dealer commits to selling $1,000,000 face value of 90-day T-bills in 4 months for $967,000. Implied yield: 14.37% Spot yield: 13.00%	The security dealer buys 1 T-bill futures contract that matures in 4 months. Future price: $967,000 Futures yield: 14.37%
Time = 4 mos.	Spot yield is 14.37%. The security dealer delivers $1,000,000 of T-bills and receives $967,000 as expected. Profit = 0	The security dealer sells 1 T-bill futures contract. With yields at 14.37%, the futures price is $967,000. Loss = 0
	Net wealth change = 0	

generating no profit or loss. In the futures market, the futures yield has been constant at 14.37 percent, generating no profit or loss there either.

This example is instructive because of what it reveals about the basis and its role in hedging with interest rate futures. In futures markets for commodities, a constant basis helps to insure an effective hedge. Not so with interest rate futures. Figure 5.8 depicts the movement of the basis over

| **Figure 5.8** | **Changes in the Basis Over Time for the Short Hedge** |

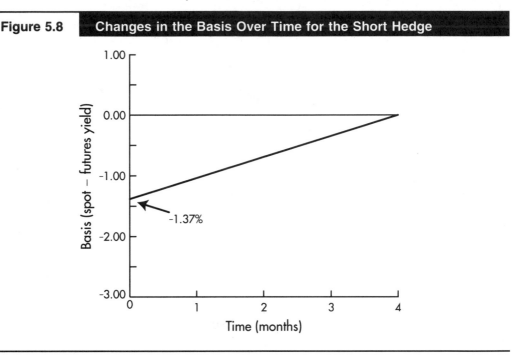

time for this example of a short hedge. Measuring the basis as (Spot Yield – Futures Yield), the basis certainly changed dramatically, –1.37 percent in four months. But this change in the basis did not interfere with the effectiveness of the hedge, because it was completely anticipated by the hedger. The security dealer looked to the forward rate for the time the hedge was to be lifted to determine what price to demand for the T-bills to be sold. Consequently, the hedger using interest rate futures need not be concerned about all changes in the basis, but only unanticipated changes, i.e., changes not consistent with the expectations imbedded in the yield curve at the time the hedge is initiated.

We can make the same point in another way. For the interest rate futures market, we are concerned with the difference between the forward rate and the futures yield. The forward rate is estimated from the term structure at the time the hedge is initiated for the time the hedge is to be terminated. The forward rate of interest is the rate pertaining to the instrument being hedged. For good hedging performance in the interest rate futures market, this difference between the forward rate and the futures yield needs to be constant, as it was in the short hedge example. The next two examples illustrate the importance of changes in this difference between the forward rate and the futures yield.

The Cross-Hedge

The financial vice president of a large manufacturing firm has decided to issue $1 billion worth of 90-day commercial paper in three months. The outstanding 90-day commercial paper of the firm yields 17 percent, or 2 percent above the current 90-day T-bill rate of 15 percent. Fearing that rates might rise, the vice president decides to hedge against the risk of increasing yields by entering the interest rate futures market.

He decides to hedge the firm's commercial paper in the T-bill futures market, because rates on commercial paper and T-bills tend to be highly correlated. Since one type of instrument is being hedged with another, this hedge becomes a **cross-hedge**. In general, a cross-hedge occurs when the hedged and hedging instruments differ with respect to: (1) risk level, (2) coupon, (3) maturity, or (4) the time span covered by the instrument being hedged and the instrument deliverable against the futures contract. This means that the vast majority of all hedges in the interest rate futures markets are cross-hedges. The hedge being contemplated by the vice president is a cross-hedge, because the commercial paper and the T-bill differ in risk. Assuming that the commercial paper is to be issued in 90 days (and that the T-bill futures contract matures at the same time) ensures that the commercial paper and the T-bill delivered on the futures contract cover the same time span.

Therefore, the vice president decides to sell 1,000 T-bill futures contracts to mature in three months. Table 5.18 shows the transactions. The futures price is $963,575, implying a futures yield of 16 percent. Notice that this differs by 1 percent from the current 90-day T-bill yield of 15 percent. Time passes, and in three months the futures yield has not changed, remaining at 16 percent. However, since the futures contract is about to mature, the spot and futures rates are now equal. Consequently, the trade incurs no gain or loss on the futures contract.

In the cash market the 90-day commercial paper spot rate at the end of the hedging period has become 18 percent, not the 17 percent that was the original 90-day spot rate at the initiation date of the hedge. Since the vice president *thought* he was "locking-in" the 17 percent spot rate, he expected to receive $961,509,400 for the commercial paper issue. But the commercial paper rate at the time of issue is 18 percent, so the firm receives only $959,465,798. This appears to be a loss in the cash market of $2,043,602. However, this is only appearance. The vice president may have thought that he was locking in the prevailing spot rate of 17 percent at the time the hedge was initiated, but such

A Cross-Hedge Between T-Bill Futures and Commercial Paper		Table 5.18
Date	**Cash Market**	**Futures Market**
Time = 0	The Financial V.P. plans to sell 90-day commercial paper in 3 months in the amount of $1 billion, at an expected yield of 17%, which should net the firm $961,509,400.	The V.P. sells 1,000 T-bill futures contracts to mature in 3 months with a futures yield of 16%, a futures price per contract of $963,575, and a total futures price of $963,575,000.
Time = 3 mos.	The spot commercial paper rate is now 18%, the usual 2% above the spot T-bill rate. Consequently, the sale of the $1 billion of commercial paper nets $959,465,798, not the expected $961,509,400. Opportunity loss = ?	The T-bill futures contract is about to mature, so the T-bill futures rate = spot rate = 16%. The futures price is still $963,575 per contract, so there is no gain or loss. Gain/loss = 0
	Net wealth change = ?	

a belief was unwarranted. By hedging the issuance of the commercial paper, the vice president should have expected to lock in the three-month forward rate for 90-day commercial paper.

Figure 5.9 clarifies these relationships by presenting yield curves for T-bills and commercial paper. The yield curves are consistent with the data of the preceding discussion. At the outset of the hedge, the 90-day spot T-bill rate is .15, and the commercial paper rate equals .17. The 180-day spot rates are .154989 and .174989 for T-bills and commercial paper, respectively. The shape of the yield curves gives sufficient information to calculate the forward, and hence the futures, rates for the time span covering the period from day 90 to day 180.

Using the following notation:

$$r_{b,e} = \text{the rate on a bond to begin at time } b \text{ and to be held until time } e,$$

it is necessarily the case that:

$$(1 + r_{0,6})^5 = (1 + r_{0,3})^{.25}(1 + r_{3,6})^{.25}$$

From Figure 5.9, it is clear that, for T-bills, $r_{0,6} = .154989$ and $r_{0,3} = .15$. Therefore:

$$(1.154989)^5 = (1.15)^{.25}(1 + r_{3,6})^{.25}$$

and $r_{3,6} = .16$. That is, the T-bill forward rate for the period to cover from three to six months hence must be 16 percent. By exactly analogous reasoning, the corresponding commercial paper forward rate must be 18 percent:

Figure 5.9   **Hypothetical Yield Curves for T-Bills and Commercial Paper**

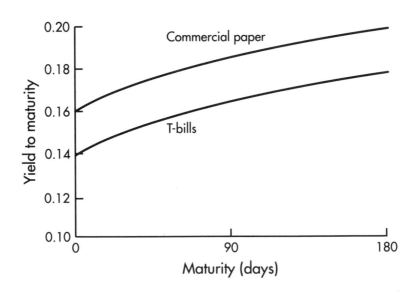

$$(1.174989)^{.5} = (1.17)^{.25}(1 + r_{3,6})^{.25}$$

Therefore, $r_{3,6} = .18$ for commercial paper.

These forward rates, evaluated at time = 0, are the expected future rates to prevail on three-month T-bills and commercial paper beginning in three months. Consequently, the implied yield on the commercial paper of this example is .18, not the .17 that the vice president attempted to lock in.

Now it is possible to understand exactly why the vice president was unable to lock in 17 percent, even though it was the spot rate prevailing at the time the hedge was initiated. The reason is simply this: For the time period over which the commercial paper was to be issued (from three to six months in the future), the market believed the 90-day commercial paper rate would be 18 percent in three months. The futures price and yield reflected this belief. Although the vice president desired a 17 percent rate, the market's expected rate was 18 percent, and by entering the futures contract the vice president locked in the 18 percent rate. Therefore, the opportunity loss of Table 5.18 is only apparent. The vice president's expectation of issuing the commercial paper at 17 percent was completely unwarranted. Instead, the vice president should have expected to issue the commercial paper at the market's expected rate of 18 percent. Then he would have expected to net $959,465,798 for the firm, which is exactly what happened in the example.

A Cross-Hedge with Faulty Expectations

In the preceding example, the vice president misunderstood the nature of the futures market. If the vice-president had understood everything correctly, Table 5.18 would have shown a zero total wealth change. Thus far, all of the examples have been of perfect hedges – hedges leaving total wealth unchanged. Sometimes, however, even when the hedge is properly initiated with the appropriate expectations, those expectations can turn out to be false. In such cases, the hedge will not be perfect; total wealth will either increase or decrease.

To illustrate this possibility, assume the same basic hedging problem as in the cross-hedge example. In particular, assume that the vice president wishes to hedge the same issuance of commercial paper and that the yield curves are as shown in Figure 5.9. The actions and expectations of the vice president, shown in Table 5.19, are exactly correct. The yield curve implies that, in 90 days, the 90-day T-bill and commercial paper rates will stand at 16 and 18 percent, respectively.

However, in this instance, assume that these expectations formed are incorrect. During the 90-day period before the commercial paper was issued, the market came to view the commercial paper as being riskier than was previously thought, and the economy experienced a higher rate of inflation than anticipated. Historically, assume that the yield premium of commercial paper had been 2 percent above the T-bill rate, consistent with Figure 5.9. But now, due to the perception of increased risk for commercial paper, the yield differential widens to 2.25 percent. Then assume that in three months the T-bill rate happens to be 16.25 percent, rising due to greater than anticipated inflation. Under these assumptions, the commercial paper rate is 18.5 percent, not the originally expected 18 percent.

As Table 5.19 reveals, the total gain on the futures position is $519,000. Due to the commercial paper rate being 18.5 percent, and not the originally anticipated 18 percent, there is a loss on the commercial paper of $1,013,700. Since the error in expectation was .5 percent on the commercial paper, but only .25 percent on the T-bills, the gain on the futures does not offset the total loss of the

Table 5.19	A Cross-Hedge With Faulty Expectations	
Date	**Cash Market**	**Futures Market**
Time = 0	The Financial V.P. decides to sell 90-day commercial paper in 3 months in the amount of $1 billion, at an expected yield of 18%, which should net the firm $959,465,798.	The V.P. sells 1,000 T-bill futures contracts to mature in 3 months, with a futures yield of 16%, a futures price per contract of $963,575, and a total futures price of $963,575,000.
Time = 3 mos.	The spot commercial paper rate was expected to be 18% at this time, but is really 18.5%. Consequently, the sale of the $1 billion of commercial paper nets $958,452,098, not the expected $959,465,798.	The T-bill futures contract is about to mature, so the T-bill futures rate = spot rate = .1625. The futures price is $963,056 per contract, so there is a gain per contract of $519, and a total gain on the 1,000 contracts of $519,000.
	Opportunity loss = –$1,013,700	Gain = +$519,000
	Net wealth change = –$494,700	

commercial paper. This results in a net wealth change of –$494,700. However, the loss would have been –$1,013,700 without the futures hedge.

In general, real world hedges will not be perfect. Rates on both sides of the hedge tend to move in the same direction, but by uncertain amounts. On occasion rates can even move in opposite directions generating enormous gains or losses. In the example just discussed, assume that the commercial paper rate turned out to be 18.5 percent, but that the T-bill rate was 15.75 percent – *below* the expected 16 percent. In this case, the loss on the commercial paper would be –$1,013,700, and the loss on the futures would be –$1,568,000 for a total loss of –$2,581,700, because the firm loses on both sides of the hedge. Such an outcome is unlikely, but it is a possible result of which hedgers should be aware.

CONCLUSION

In this chapter, we have considered the contract specifications of the most important interest rate futures contracts. We have explored the proper pricing of futures contracts using the cost-of-carry framework and have seen how interest rate futures are related to the term structure of interest rates.

We have noted some difficulties in applying the simplest form of the cost-of-carry relationship to interest rate futures, particularly to the T-bond futures contract. The breakdown of the arbitrage conditions gives expectations of future interest rates a role in determining of interest rate futures prices.

If interest rate futures prices are not determined by strict cost-of-carry relationships, there may be ample reward to various speculative strategies. The chapter concluded by exploring some simple speculative strategies, as well as more complex relationships involving several instruments. In the next chapter, we continue our exploration of interest rate futures by considering the pricing performance and the hedging use of interest rate futures.

QUESTIONS AND PROBLEMS

1. A 90-day T-bill yields 8.75 percent. What is the price of a $1,000,000 face value bill?
2. The IMM index stands as 88.70. What is the discount yield? If you buy a T-bill futures at that index value and the index becomes 88.90, what is your gain or loss?
3. What is the difference between *position day* and *first position day*?
4. A $100,000 face value T-bond has an annual coupon rate of 9.5 percent and paid its last coupon 48 days ago. What is the accrued interest on the bond?
5. What conditions are necessary for the conversion factors on the CBOT T-bond contract to create favorable conditions for delivering one bond instead of another?
6. The Municipal Bond Index futures does not allow for delivery of bonds. Explain why the futures price must converge to the spot index value nonetheless.
7. The JUN T-bill futures IMM index value is 92.80, while the SEP has a value of 93.00. What is the implied rate to cover the period from June to September?
8. A spot 180-day T-bill has a discount yield of 9.5 percent. If the implied repo rate for the next three months is 9.2 percent, what is the price of a futures that expires in three months?
9. For the next three futures expirations, you observe the following Eurodollar quotations:

MAR	92.00
JUN	91.80
SEP	91.65

What shape does the yield curve have? Explain.
10. Assume that the prices in the preceding problem pertain to T-bill futures and the MAR contract expires today. What should be the spot price of an 180-day T-bill?
11. The cheapest-to-deliver T-bond is a 12 percent bond that paid its coupon 87 days ago and it is priced at 105-16. The conversion factor of the bond is 1.0900. The nearby T-bond futures expires in 50 days and the current price is 98-00. If you can borrow or lend to finance a T-bond for a total outlay of 2 percent over this period, how would you transact? What if you could borrow or lend at 3 percent? What if you could borrow at 3 percent and lend at 2 percent? Explain.
12. You expect a steepening yield curve over the next few months, but you are not sure whether the level of rates will increase or decrease. Explain two different ways you can trade to profit if you are correct.
13. The Iraqi invasion of Alaska has financial markets in turmoil. You expect the crisis to worsen more than other traders suspect. How could you trade short-term interest rate futures to profit if you are correct? Explain.
14. You believe that the yield curve is strongly upward sloping and that yields are at very high levels. How would you use interest rate futures to hedge a prospective investment of funds that you will receive in nine months? If you faced a major borrowing in nine months, how would you use futures?
15. The spot rate of interest on a corporate bond is 11 percent, and the yield curve is sharply upward sloping. The futures rate on the T-bond futures that is just about to expire is 8 percent, but the

yield for the futures contract that expires in six months is 8.75 percent. (You are convinced that this difference is independent of any difference in the cheapest-to-deliver bonds for the two contracts.) In these circumstances, a corporate finance officer wants to lock-in the current spot rate of 11 percent on a corporate bond that her firm plans to offer in six months. What advice would you give her?

NOTES

[1] Chicago Mercantile Exchange, ''Inside Eurodollar Futures,'' p. 19.

[2] The best way to secure a regular source of conversion factors, as well as much other useful information, is to visit the CBOT's site on the World Wide Web.

[3] For studies of this approach to pricing T-bill futures, see I. Kawaller and T. Koch, ''Cash-and-Carry Trading and the Pricing of Treasury Bill Futures,'' *Journal of Futures Markets,* 4:2, Fall 1984, pp. 115–23.

[4] See the Chicago Mercantile Exchange, ''Market Perspectives,'' February 1987, 5:1, pp. 1–4. See also the Chicago Mercantile Exchange, ''The TED Spread,'' *Financial Strategy Paper,* 1987.

[5] For simplicity, we use easier price and yield calculations in many of these hedging examples, abstracting from the full complexity of market yield calculations.

INTEREST RATE FUTURES: REFINEMENTS

OVERVIEW

Chapter 6 builds on the foundation of Chapter 5. Having already explored the fundamental features of interest rate futures, we now turn to refining our understanding of these important markets. Thus, Chapter 6 considers more closely some of the same issues addressed in Chapter 5. In addition, we examine some new issues, such as the informational efficiency of the interest rate futures market.

The T-bond contract is perhaps the most important futures contract ever devised. It also happens to be one of the most complicated. We begin this chapter with a detailed analysis of the T-bond contract. This analysis lays the foundation for a richer understanding of how to apply interest rate futures to speculate and to manage risk. Next, we consider the informational efficiency of the interest rate futures markets. A market is efficient with respect to some set of information if prices in the market fully reflect the information contained in that set. There have been many studies of informational efficiency for interest rate futures, and we review the results of those studies.

In Chapter 5 we saw that interest rate futures should be full carry markets. However, this conclusion requires some qualifications. Taking the T-bond contract as a model, we analyze the special features of the contract and show how those features can make full carry difficult to measure. For example, seller's options have important implications for the theoretically correct futures price.

Many traders use interest rate futures to manage risk. The techniques for risk management are quite diverse and increasingly sophisticated. Essentially, two different sets of techniques apply, depending upon the nature of the risk. Therefore, we consider applications for short-term interest rate futures first and then conclude the chapter by examining the applications of long-term interest rate futures.

THE T-BOND FUTURES CONTRACT IN DETAIL

In Chapter 5 we explored the basic features of the T-bond futures contract. In this section, we first review what we know about the contract from Chapter 5. Then we develop a more complete analysis of the contract. This procedure provides a richer understanding of the contract which helps us to understand how to use interest rate futures for speculation and risk management.

Review of the T-Bond Contract

In our discussion of the T-bond futures contract in Chapter 5, we noted that the contract calls for the delivery of $100,000 principal amount of U.S. Treasury bonds that have at least 15 years to maturity or their first call date at the time of delivery. We noted that the delivery procedure stretched over three business days, with actual delivery occurring on the third day, which could be any business day of the delivery month.

For any particular futures contract expiration, a variety of bonds will be deliverable. These bonds can be of any coupon rate and any maturity above the minimum. In many cases, the bonds that are deliverable will include some recently issued Treasury bonds that may not even have existed when the contract was first listed for trading.

Without some adjustment, one of these bonds is likely to be much better to deliver than the others. For example, if the contract allowed the delivery of any bond without a price adjustment, every trader would want to deliver the cheapest bond. To make the variety of bonds permitted for delivery comparable, the CBOT uses a system of conversion factors. Essentially, the conversion factor for a given bond is found by assuming that the bond has a face value of $1 and discounting all of the bond's cash flows at 8 percent. Chapter 5 gave the exact formulas for finding the conversion factors. While the conversion factors eliminate much of the inequalities between various bonds, they do not do a complete job. As a consequence, there is still a particular bond that is cheapest-to-deliver among the bonds permitted for delivery.

As another complication, we noted in Chapter 5 that the seller of the T-bond futures possesses several options. For example, the seller chooses which bond to deliver and which day to make delivery. These and other options have significant value, as we explore next.

The Cheapest-to-Deliver Bond

In this section we show how to determine which bond will be cheapest-to-deliver, and we show how to find the exact invoice amount, including all the nuances in computing accrued interest. First, we analyze the cheapest-to-deliver bond when some time remains before expiration, but there will be no coupon payment. Second, we consider the case when a coupon payment intervenes between the beginning of the holding period and the futures expiration.

The Case of No Intervening Coupons. Assume today is June 16, 1997, and the JUN 97 T-bond futures settlement price is 93-00. A short trader decides to make today her position day and to deliver against her futures contract. The actual delivery date will be June 18, 1997. She is considering two bonds and wants to know exactly how much she will receive for each and which she should deliver. The two bonds are:

Maturity	Coupon	Price	JUN 97 CF
May 15, 2019	7.25	82-16	.9231
Nov. 15, 2018	9.875	108-16	1.1899

We want to determine the exact invoice amount for each bond and which bond is cheapest-to-deliver.

To answer these questions, we first compute the cash price and invoice amounts for $100,000 face value of these bonds. The total price depends upon the stated price plus the accrued interest (AI). In Chapter 5 we saw that a bond accrues interest for each day based on the coupon rate and the principal amount. In the market, the actual calculation also depends upon the number of days in a half-year, as Table 6.1 shows.

Both bonds have the same coupon dates each year, May 15 and November 15, so both are on the May-November cycle. As Table 6.1 shows, for a regular year, there are 184 days in the May-November half-year. From May 15 to June 18 is 34 days. Therefore, the accrued interest for each bond is:

7.25% bond: $AI = (34/184)(.5)(.0725)(\$100,000) = \$670$
9.875% bond: $AI = (34/184)(.5)(.09875)(\$100,000) = \$912$

From Chapter 5:

$$\text{Invoice Amount} = DFP(\$100,000)(CF) + AI$$

	Days in Half-Years	Table 6.1

	Days in Half-Year			
	Interest Paid on 1st or 15th		Interest Paid on Last Day	
Interest Period	Regular Year	Leap Year	Regular Year	Leap Year
January to July	181	182	181	182
February to August	181	182	184	184
March to September	184	184	183	183
April to October	183	183	184	184
May to November	184	184	183	183
June to December	183	183	184	184
July to January	184	184	184	184
August to February	184	184	181	182
September to March	181	182	182	183
October to April	182	183	181	182
November to May	181	182	182	183
December to June	182	183	181	182
1 year (any 2 consecutive half-years)	365	366	365	366

Source: From Treasury Circular No. 300, 4th Rev.

where:

DFP = decimal futures price (e.g., 96-16 = .965)
CF = conversion factor
AI = accrued interest

With a June 16 futures settlement price of 93-00, invoice amounts are:

7.25% bond: .9300($100,000)(.9231) + $670 = $86,518
9.875% bond: .9300($100,000)(1.1899) + $912 = $111,573

Thus, the two bonds have radically different invoice amounts; the 9.875 percent bond has an invoice amount 29 percent greater than the 7.25 percent bond.

To complete delivery, the short trader must deliver one bond and receive the invoice amount. Which should she deliver? The decision depends upon the difference between the invoice amount and the cash market price, which is the profit from delivery. The bond that is most profitable to deliver is the cheapest-to-deliver bond. In other words, the short trader will select the bond to deliver to maximize profit. For a particular bond I, the profit π_i is:

$$\pi_i = \text{Invoice Amount} - (P_i + \text{AI}_i) = (\text{DFP}_i)(\$100,000)(\text{CF}_i) + \text{AI}_i - (P_i + \text{AI}_i)$$

Because the accrued interest is included in the invoice amount and subtracted as a payment being made by surrendering the bond, the profit simplifies to:

$$\pi_i = \text{DFP}_i(\$100,000)(\text{CF}_i) - P_i \qquad\qquad (6.1)$$

To find the cheapest-to-deliver bond, the short trader will compute the profitability for each deliverable bond. The bond with the maximum profit is the cheapest-to-deliver.[1] For the two bonds, the profit from delivery is:

For the 7.25% bond: π = .9300($100,000)(.9231) − $82,500 = $3,348
For the 9.875% bond: π = .9300($100,000)(1.1899) − $108,500 = $2,161

Thus, delivering the 7.25 percent bond is more profitable, so it is cheaper-to-deliver.

Which bond is cheaper-to-deliver depends on the level of interest rates. Figure 6.1 shows the profits from delivery for three bonds:

25 year; 7% coupon
16 year; 14% coupon
20 year; 8% coupon

The 20-year, 8 percent coupon bond is the nominal bond that underlies the futures contract. It has a conversion factor of 1.0, as do all 8 percent coupon bonds. Therefore, the profit from delivery on an 8 percent coupon bond will always be zero if the futures and bond are priced fairly, as Figure 6.1

Cheapness for Delivery and Bond Yields   **Figure 6.1**

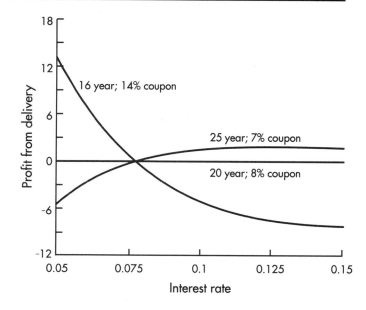

shows. The practice of using conversion factors does not introduce any biases for an 8 percent coupon bond.

As Figure 6.1 shows, bias is possible for the other two bonds with coupon rates that differ from 8 percent. If interest rates are below 8 percent, Figure 6.1 shows that there is an advantage to delivering the 16-year bond. By contrast, if yields exceed 8 percent, it is better to deliver the 25-year bond. At one point in Figure 6.1, a trader can be indifferent about which bond to deliver. Notice that when yields are exactly 8 percent, the profit from delivery for all three bonds is zero.

We can extract a general rule from this analysis. When interest rates are below 8 percent, there is an incentive to deliver short maturity/high coupon bonds. When interest rates exceed 8 percent, there is an incentive to deliver long maturity/low coupon bonds. Expressing the same idea in terms of duration, a trader should deliver low duration bonds when interest rates are below 8 percent and high duration bonds when interest rates are above 8 percent.

The Case of Intervening Coupons. So far, we have dealt with the cheapest-to-deliver bond when there are no coupon payments to consider. We now consider which bond is cheapest-to-deliver when a bond pays a coupon between the beginning of the cash-and-carry holding period and the futures expiration. To find the cheapest-to-deliver bond before expiration, we apply the cash-and-carry strategy. The bond with the greatest profit at delivery from following the cash-and-carry strategy will be the cheapest-to-deliver.

We assume that a trader buys a bond today and carries the bond to delivery. We compare the cash flows associated with that carry relative to the invoice amount based on today's futures price. Of course, we cannot know the future cash flows with certainty. In particular, the futures price might change. However, we make our computation assuming that interest rates and futures prices remain constant. For this analysis, we must consider the estimated invoice amount plus our estimate of the cash flows associated with carrying the bond to delivery.

The estimated invoice amount depends on three factors:

1. Today's quoted futures price.
2. The conversion factor for the bond we plan to deliver.
3. The accrued interest on the bond at the expiration date.

Acquiring and carrying a bond to delivery involves three cash flows as well:

1. Pay today the quoted price plus accrued interest.
2. Finance the bond from today until expiration.
3. Receive and invest any coupons paid between today and expiration.

We can bring all of these factors together by considering the time line in Figure 6.2.

Today we purchase a bond and finance it until delivery. Between today and delivery, we receive and invest a coupon. At delivery, we surrender the bond and receive the invoice amount. Thus, we have:

$$\text{Estimated Invoice Amount} = \text{DFP}_0(\$100{,}000)(\text{CF}) + \text{AI}_2$$

Estimated Future Value of the Delivered Bond =

$$(P_0 + \text{AI}_0)(1 + C_{0,2}) - \text{COUP}_1(1 + C_{1,2})$$

where:

Figure 6.2   **Time Line for Cash-and-Carry Arbitrage**

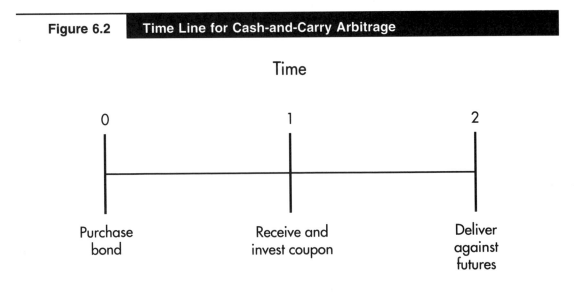

P_0 = quoted price of the bond today, $t = 0$
AI_0 = accrued interest as of today, $t = 0$
$C_{0,2}$ = interest factor for $t = 0$ to expiration at $t = 2$
$COUP_1$ = coupon that will be received before delivery at $t = 1$
$C_{1,2}$ = interest factor from $t = 1$ to $t = 2$
DFP_0 = decimal futures price today, $t = 0$
CF = conversion factor for a particular bond and the specified futures expiration
AI_2 = accrued interest at $t = 2$

The short trader will maximize profit by choosing to deliver the cheapest-to-deliver bond. For bond I, the expected profit from delivery is the estimated invoice amount less the estimated value of what will be delivered:

$$\pi = DFP_0(CF) + AI_2 - \{(P_0 + AI_0)(1 + C_{0,2}) - COUP_1(1 + C_{1,2})\} \tag{6.2}$$

As an illustration, assume that today is April 15, 1997, and we want to find the cheapest-to-deliver bond for the JUN 97 futures expiration. We illustrate the computation with the two bonds we have already considered, with different prices for the different date.

Maturity	Coupon	Price	JUN 97 CF
May 15, 2019	7.25	81-00	.9231
Nov. 15, 2018	9.875	106-16	1.1899

We assume that the bonds will be financed and the coupons invested at the repo rate of 10 percent and that the settlement price of the JUN 97 T-bond futures on April 15 is 91-00. We assume a $100,000 face value and a target delivery date of June 30, 1997. Figure 6.3 shows all of the dates and the number of days between dates.

The semiannual coupons for the two bonds are $3,625 for the 7.25 percent bond and $4,938 for the 9.875 percent bond. Both bonds paid their last coupon on November 15, 1996, 151 days ago. For a regular year, the November-May half-year has 181 days. Therefore, the accrued interest as of April 15 for the bonds is:

For the 7.25% bond: $AI_0 = \$3,625(151/181) = \$3,024$
For the 9.875% bond: $AI_0 = \$4,938(151/181) = \$4,120$

The amount to be financed for each bond is:

For the 7.25% bond: $P_0 + AI_0 = \$81,000 + \$3,024 = \$84,024$
For the 9.875% bond: $P_0 + AI_0 = \$106,500 + \$4,120 = \$110,620$

Next we consider the accrued interest that will accumulate by the delivery date. From May 15, 1997, to June 30, 1997, is 46 days in a half-year of 184 days. Therefore, the bonds will have the following accrued interest on June 30, 1997:

For the 7.25% bond: $AI_2 = \$3,625(46/184) = \$906$
For the 9.875% bond: $AI_2 = \$4,938(46/184) = \$1,235$

Figure 6.3   **Dates for Cash-and-Carry Arbitrage**

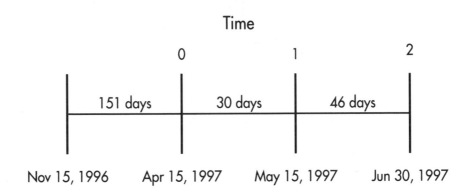

With a futures price of 91-00 on April 15, 1997, the $DFP_0 = .91$. The estimated invoice amount for the two bonds is:

For the 7.25% bond: $.91(\$100,000)(.9231) + \$906 = \$84,908$
For the 9.875% bond: $.91(\$100,000)(1.1899) + \$1,235 = \$109,516$

Next, we compute the financing rates. On April 15, 76 days remain until the projected delivery date, so $C_{0,2} = .10(76/360) = .0211$. From May 15, 1997, until June 30, 1997, is 46 days, so $C_{1,2} = .10(46/360) = .0128$. Finally, we are in a position to compute the profits from delivery. Table 6.2 summarizes all of these intermediate calculations.

Using the values in Table 6.2, we compute the expected profit from delivering each bond. For the 7.25 percent bond:

$$\pi = (.91)(100,000)(.9231) + 906 - [(81,000 + 3,024)(1.0211) - (3,625)(1.0128)]$$
$$= 84,908 - 85,797 + 3,671$$
$$= \$2,782$$

For the 9.875 percent bond:

Table 6.2   **Data for Cheapest-to-Deliver Bonds**

Bond	P_0	AI_0	$C_{0,2}$	$C_{1,2}$	DFP_0	CF	AI_2
7.25%	81,000	$3,024	.0211	.0128	.91	.9231	906
9.875%	106,500	$4,120	.0211	.0128	.91	1.1899	1,235

$$\pi = (.91)(100,000)(1.1899) + 1,235 - [(106,500 + 4,120)(1.0211) - 4,938(1.0128)]$$
$$= 109,516 - 112,954 + 5,001$$
$$= \$1,563$$

For the 7.25 percent bond, the profit from delivery is \$2,782, but delivering the 9.875 percent bond generates only \$1,563. Therefore, the 7.25 percent bond is cheaper-to-deliver.

The Cheapest-to-Deliver Bond and the Implied Repo Rate. We can also analyze the same situation using the implied repo rate. Here the implied repo rate for the given period equals the net cash flow at delivery divided by the net cash flow when the carry starts:

$$\text{Implied Repo Rate} = \frac{\text{Net Cash Flow Over Horizon}}{\text{Net Cash Flow at Inception}}$$

The numerator consists of cash inflows of the invoice amount, plus the future value of the coupons at the time of delivery, less the cost of acquiring the bond initially. The denominator consists of the cost of buying the bond. Therefore, in terms of our notation:

$$\text{Implied Repo Rate} = \frac{DFP_0(100,000)(CF) + AI_2 + COUP_1(1 + C_{1,2}) - (P_0 + AI_0)}{(P_0 + AI_0)}$$

For the 7.25 percent bond we have:

$$\text{Implied Repo Rate} = \frac{.91(100,000)(.9231) + 906 + 3,625(1.0128) - (81,000 + 3,024)}{(81,000 + 3,024)} = .0542$$

For the 9.875 percent bond:

$$\text{Implied Repo Rate} = \frac{.91(100,000)(1.1899) + 1,235 + 4,938(1.0128) - (106,500 + 4,120)}{(106,500 + 4,120)} = .0352$$

Annualizing these rates, for the 7.25 percent bond we have $(.0542)(360/76) = 25.67$ percent, and for the 9.875 percent bond we have $(.0352)(360/76) = 16.67$ percent. Thus, the low coupon 7.25 percent bond has a higher implied repo rate, suggesting that this bond is better than the 9.875 percent bond to carry to delivery. From this example, we can draw the following rule about the cheapest-to-deliver bond before expiration: The cheapest-to-deliver bond has the highest implied repo rate in a cash-and-carry strategy.

If the implied repo rate equals the borrowing rate, the cash-and-carry arbitrage transaction leaves a zero profit. To illustrate this principle, we focus on the 9.875 percent bond and the cash-and-carry transactions of Table 6.3. As the example of Table 6.3 shows, financing a cash-and-carry arbitrage at the implied repo rate yields a zero profit.

To summarize, we state some general rules about how to conduct arbitrage if the cost of funds varies from the implied repo rate. The transactions we have considered assumed that the futures price did not change and that markets were perfect. In particular, for the reverse cash-and-carry arbitrage, the assumption that the trader has full use of the short sale proceeds was critical. Subject to these restrictions, and the elaboration of the next section, the general rules hold:

1. Cash-and-carry arbitrage nets a zero profit if the actual borrowing cost equals the implied repo rate.
2. If the effective borrowing rate is less than the implied repo rate, one can earn an arbitrage profit by cash-and-carry arbitrage, i.e., buy the cash bond and sell the futures.
3. If the effective borrowing rate exceeds the implied repo rate and if one can sell bonds short, then one can earn an arbitrage profit by reverse cash-and-carry arbitrage, i.e., sell the bond short, buy the futures, and cover the short position at the expiration of the futures.

Why They Call It Risk Arbitrage

In this section, we add more realism to our analysis of arbitrage by considering the peculiarities of the T-bond futures contract in still greater detail. As we will show, market realities add a risk component to both the cash-and-carry and reverse cash-and-carry arbitrage. These complications take our arbitrage framework out of the realm of "academic arbitrage" and show why all arbitrage in the T-bond futures market is really "risk arbitrage." The sources of risk are different for the cash-and-carry and reverse cash-and-carry strategies, and the risks stem from three sources: intervening coupon payments that must face reinvestment, the use of conversion factors, and the options that the seller possesses. In this section, we consider the risks generated by the reinvestment problem and the use of conversion factors. We also treat the seller's options in a general way.

Frustrations to Cash-and-Carry Arbitrage. A closer examination of Table 6.3 shows some potentially risky elements of the cash-and-carry arbitrage. First, the debt was financed at a constant rate throughout the 76-day carry period. Second, the trader actually was able to invest the coupon at the expected reinvestment rate of 10 percent. Third, the futures price did not change over the horizon. We consider each of these problems in turn.

Assume that the trader in Table 6.3 finances the acquisition of the T-bond with overnight repos. The overnight repo rate changes each day, so the financing cost could drift upward. With an increasing financing cost, the transactions of Table 6.3 will not end in a zero profit. Instead, they will give a

Table 6.3	Transactions Showing Implied Repo Rates

April 15, 1997
Borrow $110,620 for 76 days at implied repo rate of 16.67%.
Buy $100,000 face value of 9.875 T-bonds maturing on Nov. 15, 2018, for a total price of $110,620 including accrued interest.
Sell 1 JUN 97 T-bond futures contract at the current price of 91-00.

May 15, 1997
Receive coupon payment of $4,938 and invest for 46 days at 10%.

June 30, 1997 (Assuming futures is still at 91-00)
Deliver the bond and receive invoice amount of $109,516.
From the invested coupon receive $4,938 + $4,938(.10)(46/360) = $5,001
Repay debt: $110,620 + $110,620 (.1667) (76/360) = $114,513

Net Profit = $109,516 + $5,001 − $114,513 = $4 ≈ 0 (given rounding error)

loss. Therefore, the transactions in Table 6.3 are potentially risky, depending upon the financing rate for the bond. Second, assume that the bond is financed for the entire period at the implied repo rate of 16.67 percent. Also assume that short-term rates drift lower, so that the coupon can only be invested at 8 percent, not the 10 percent shown in Table 6.3. Now the reinvested coupons will only grow to $4,988, not the $5,001 shown in the table. Therefore, the changing rate will generate a loss. These two examples illustrate the risks that remain inherent in a supposedly riskless cash-and-carry strategy. We now turn to a bigger danger, a change in the futures price that can affect the cash flows from the cash-and-carry strategy.

In the transactions of Table 6.3, we assumed that the futures price did not change over the life of the contract. With the financing rates given, the cash-and-carry transactions yielded a zero profit. Now let us assume that the financing of the bond and the investment of the coupon work out exactly as Table 6.3 shows. However, now we consider a drop in the futures price from 91-00 when the contract is initiated to 89-00 at expiration. Such a change in the futures price is entirely feasible, and we need to consider the effect of this changing price on the cash flows from the cash-and-carry strategy.

Table 6.4 presents the same transactions as the zero profit cash-and-carry transactions of Table 6.3. The only difference between the two tables results from a drop in the futures price from 91-00 to 89-00 over the life of the contract. With a futures expiration price of 89-00, the actual invoice amount is:

$$\text{Invoice Amount} = .89(\$100,000)(1.1899) + \$1,235 = \$109,516$$

The drop in the futures price has generated daily resettlement cash inflows of $2,000 over the life of the contract. With the reduced invoice amount, however, the cash-and-carry transactions generate a loss. As the transactions show, the reason for the loss is that futures price fluctuations generate gains or losses on a $1 for $1 basis. For example, a two point drop in the futures price generates a

Transactions Showing Implied Repo Rates	Table 6.4

April 15, 1997
Borrow $110,620 for 76 days at implied repo rate of 16.67%
Buy $100,000 face value of 9.875 T-bonds maturing on Nov. 15, 2018, for a total price of $110,620 including accrued interest.
Sell 1 JUN 97 T-bond futures contract at the current price of 91-00.

May 15, 1997
Receive coupon payment of $4,938 and invest for 46 days at 10%.

June 30, 1997 (Assuming futures has fallen to 89-00)
Between April and June, the futures price has fallen from 91-00 to 89-00, generating cash inflows of $2,000.
Deliver the bond and receive invoice amount of $107,136.
From the invested coupon receive $4,938 + $4,938(.10)(46/360) = $5,001
Repay debt: $110,620 + $110,620 (.1667) (76/360) = $114,513

Net Profit = $2,000 + $107,136 + $5,001 − $114,513 = −$376

gain of $2,000 in this case. However, when the futures price changes by $1, the delivery value of the bond changes by $1 times the conversion factor, which exceeds 1.0 in our example. This makes it possible for the supposedly riskless transaction to generate a loss. The dropping futures price generates $2,000 in daily resettlement profits, but it reduces the invoice amount from $109,516 to $107,136, a drop of $2,380. Thus, the changing price generates a new profit of $2,000 and a new loss of $2,380, for a net loss of $376, which differs by the rounding error of $4 from the value in Table 6.4.

Frustrations to Reverse Cash-and-Carry Arbitrage. In reverse cash-and-carry transactions, a trader sells an underlying good short and buys a futures contract. The trader then invests the proceeds from the short sale, planning to take delivery on the futures and return the borrowed commodity. Table 6.5 shows the reverse cash-and-carry transactions that are the mirror image of Table 6.3. In Table 6.5, the transactions generate a zero profit. The profit must be zero, because the transactions are exact complements to the transactions in Table 6.3.

We now consider the risk elements inherent in the reverse cash-and-carry transactions. First, all of the same risk elements that plagued the cash-and-carry strategy apply to the reverse cash-and-carry strategy as well. The trader of Table 6.5 could have lost if she had been forced to invest the short sale proceeds at less than the implied repo rate. If she had been forced to pay more than 10 percent on the borrowings to pay the coupon, the transactions would have resulted in a loss also. Finally, if futures prices had risen, she would have had daily resettlement inflows that were less than the rise in the invoice amount, and these would have generated losses as well.

In addition to these sources of risk that plague cash-and-carry and reverse cash-and-carry strategies alike, the reverse cash-and-carry strategy faces other special risks stemming from the seller's options. In Table 6.5, we made several implicit assumptions. We assumed that the short futures trader delivered on June 30, 1997, and that the short trader delivered exactly the same bond that the trader of Table 6.5 sold short.

Table 6.5	Transactions Showing Implied Repo Rates

April 15, 1997
Sell short $100,000 face value of 9.875 T-bonds maturing on Nov. 15, 2018, for a total price of $110,620 including accrued interest.
Buy 1 JUN 97 T-bond futures contract at the current price of 91-00.
Lend $110,620 for 76 days at implied repo rate of 16.67%.

May 15, 1997
Borrow $4,938 for 46 days at 10% and make coupon payment of $4,938.

June 30, 1997 (Assuming futures is still at 91-00)
Collect investment: $110,620 + $110,620 (.1667) (76/360) = $114,513.
Accept delivery of the bond and pay invoice amount of $109,516.
Pay debt from funds borrowed to make coupon payment: $4,938 + $4,938(.10)(46/360) = $5,001

Net Profit = $114,513 − $109,516 − $5,001 = −$4 ≈ 0 (given rounding error)

From Chapter 5, we know that the short trader of a T-bond futures has several options associated with the delivery. First, the short trader holds a **quality option** – the option to choose which bond to deliver. In Chapter 5, we noted that there are typically more than 20 deliverable bonds, and the short trader can deliver any of these. Therefore, the reverse cash-and-carry trader cannot be sure that she will receive a particular bond in the delivery. If the delivered bond is not the same bond that she sold short, she must go into the market to buy the bond that will allow her to cover the short sale. Of course, this exposes her to the risk that the price of the 9.875 percent bond could have changed. The seller of a T-bond futures contract also possesses a second important option. The **timing option** is the seller's option to choose the day of delivery. From Chapter 5 we know that delivery can occur on any business day in the delivery month. Therefore, the reverse cash-and-carry trader cannot be sure that delivery will occur on a particular date. This also exposes the trader of Table 6.5 to risk, because she cannot be sure that the delivery will occur on June 30. In addition to the quality and timing options, the short trader also possesses some other highly specialized options that add to the risk of the reverse cash-and-carry transactions. These options make the reverse cash-and-carry transactions extremely risky. As we discuss in the next section, these options have an important impact on the pricing of T-bond futures.

SELLER'S OPTIONS IN T-BOND FUTURES

The structure of the T-bond futures contract gives the seller timing and quality options. The timing option arises from the seller's right to choose the time of delivery. The quality option stems from the seller's right to select which bond to deliver. Certain features of the T-bond futures contract confer both types of options on the seller. We have already seen that the seller's ability to choose the delivery day impedes the long trader's reverse cash-and-carry trading strategies because the long trader can never know when the short will choose to deliver. However, besides frustrating the long trader, the quality and timing options have specific value for the short trader.

While we may distinguish timing and quality options conceptually, they become entangled in the actual specification of the T-bond futures contract. The two main seller's options in the T-bond futures market are the **wildcard option** and the **end-of-the-month option**. In this section, we analyze the effects of these options on the pricing of the T-bond contract and discuss optimal trading strategies to exploit these options.

The Wildcard Option

In the T-bond futures market, the futures seller chooses the position day by notifying the exchange of an intention to deliver. The actual delivery takes place two business days later. For example, if today is Monday, June 13, the trader may notify the exchange of his intention to deliver and June 13 becomes the position day. Actual delivery occurs in two business days on Wednesday, June 15. By making June 13 the position day, the short seller determines that the settlement price on June 13 will be the settlement price used to determine the invoice amount.

Under the rules of the exchange, the settlement price is determined at 2 P.M. On position day, the short trader has until 8 P.M. Chicago time to notify the exchange of an intention to deliver. The day of notification becomes the position day, with the invoice amount being based on the settlement price that day. Therefore, the short trader has a window from 2 to 8 P.M. for good luck to strike. If interest rates jump between 2 and 8 P.M., the short trader can notify the exchange of an intention to deliver and secure the 2 P.M. settlement price on the futures. The trader can then deliver the bond that fell in price due to a jump in interest rates.

The **wildcard option** is the option for the seller to lock-in the 2 P.M. price by announcing an intention to deliver anytime before 8 P.M. In fact, the seller possesses a series of wildcard options. For example, on first position day, the second-to-last business day of the month preceding expiration, the seller has the wildcard option. If bond prices fall between 2 and 8 P.M. that day, the seller can announce an intention to deliver and capture the 2 P.M. price. If nothing happens between 2 and 8 P.M., the seller need not announce any intention to deliver. Instead, the seller can merely wait until the next day, hoping that something happens between 2 and 8 P.M. to cause a drop in bond prices. The seller can continue to play this game until the third-to-last business day of the month, which is the last position day. In buying a T-bond futures, the long trader has conferred an option to the seller, and the long trader stands at risk each day. The value of the wildcard option depends on the chance that something will happen to cause a drop in bond prices between 2 and 8 P.M. on any possible position day.

Let us explore the effect of changes in interest rates on futures traders by using the June 13 data for two bonds in Table 6.6. Both bonds, we assume, will pay a coupon on June 15, so we ignore accrued interest. Bond A in the table has 30 years to maturity, pays a 7 percent coupon, and sells for 88.69 percent of par. It yields 8.00 percent and has a conversion factor for the June T-bond futures of .8869. Bond B has 20 years to maturity, pays a 12 percent coupon, and sells for 139.59 percent of par. It yields 8.00 percent and has a conversion factor of 1.3959. The settlement price on June 13 for the JUN futures is 100-00. For Bond A, the invoice amount is $88,690, and for Bond B it is $139,590. By construction, both bonds have the zero profit from delivery.

Table 6.6 has been constructed so that neither bond is better to deliver than the other. Each gives a delivery profit of zero, because the price is proportional to the conversion factor and there is no accrued interest to consider. The price is proportional to the conversion factor, because we assume that both bonds yield 8 percent. Let us assume that this is the situation when trading ends on June 20. If yields remain unchanged, the trader will be indifferent about delivering one bond or the other.

We want to explore whether a change in interest rates can affect the desirability of delivering and whether changing rates can affect the choice of delivery instrument. Now assume that late in the Chicago afternoon of June 13, interest rates jump by 1 percent due to an invasion of a Middle East principality. Bond A now yields 9.00 percent and its price falls to 79.36 percent of par. Now there is at least one beneficiary of the invasion, because the short trader can deliver this bond against the futures contract.

To buy $100,000 principal amount of Bond A costs $79,360, and the trader can deliver this bond against the futures contract for the invoice amount of $88,690. This change in rates gives the short trader a profit from delivery of $9,330, the full amount of the bond's price fall. This results from the fact that the invoice amount was set at 2 P.M., but the bond price was free to fall between

Table 6.6	Bond Data at 2 P.M. on June 13				
Bond	Coupon Rate	Price	Conversion Factor	Yield	Profit from Delivery
A: 30-year	.07	88.69	.8869	.0800	0
B: 20-year	.12	139.59	1.3959	.0800	0

2 and 8 P.M. on June 13. The short seller plays his wildcard and announces his intention to deliver. Table 6.7 summarizes this change for Bond A. For Bond B, also shown in Table 6.7, the rise in rates also causes the price to fall from 139.59 to 127.60. This gives a $11,990 profit from delivering Bond B after the rise in rates. Table 6.7 also shows the effect of a fall in rates from 8 to 7 percent. With this fall in rates, the trader shows a loss from delivering, so the trader defers delivery, hoping that rates will rise. In our example of rising rates, the wildcard option paid handsomely. Simply by the good luck of rates rising during the wildcard interval, the short trader was able to secure a delivery profit of $9,330 with Bond A or $11,990 with Bond B.

The chance to wait from 2 to 8 P.M. to play the wildcard is a timing option. However, the wildcard option also involves a quality option. At 2 P.M. on June 10 the trader is indifferent between delivering Bond A and Bond B in Table 6.6, because both have zero delivery profits. When rates rise due to the invasion, the two cash market prices change by different amounts, as Table 6.7 details. With the jump in rates, both bonds are profitable to deliver, but it is clearly better to deliver Bond B for a delivery profit of $11,990, rather than Bond A with a delivery profit of only $9,330. This example illustrates the quality option inherent in the wildcard option.

However, the quality component of the wildcard option is even better than it appears at first. We have seen that the settlement price for computing the invoice amount is fixed at 2 P.M. on position day and that the short trader must announce an intention to deliver by 8 P.M. that same evening. However, the short trader has until 5 P.M. the next business day, notice of intention day, to declare which bond he or she intends to deliver. Thus, the trader has an extra business day to choose the bond that will be best to deliver.

The change in rates gives a clear preference for delivering one bond rather than another. As Table 6.7 shows, for a drop in yields to 7 percent, it is better to deliver Bond A. Of course, the short trader prefers not to deliver if yields fall, but if he must, he prefers to deliver Bond A. This example illustrates how changing interest rates can change the preferred delivery instrument, thereby creating a quality option.

The End-of-the-Month Option

As we have discussed, the seller of a T-bond futures contract may choose to deliver any deliverable bond on any business day of the delivery month. The last trading day for T-bond futures is the eighth to last business day of the delivery month. All contracts open after that time must be satisfied by delivery. The settlement price established on the final trading day is the settlement price used in all

Wildcard Option Results from Sudden Yield Changes		Table 6.7
	Yields Fall to 7%	Yields Rise to 9%
Bond A		
Price	100.00	79.36
Dollar Payoff to Deliver	−$11,310	$9,330
Bond B		
Price	139.59	127.60
Dollar Payoff to Deliver	−$13,800	$11,990

invoice calculations for all deliveries in the remainder of the month. The seller must deliver, but he can still make two choices. First, the seller can choose which remaining day to deliver, and the seller can choose which bond to deliver.

Let us assume that interest rates are certain to be stable for those last few days. If so, the seller has a clear means to determine which day to deliver. Each additional day the seller holds the bond, the bond accrues interest. However, for each additional day the seller holds the bond, the seller must finance the bond, presumably at the overnight repo rate. Thus, the seller's choice is clear. If the coupon yield on the bond exceeds the financing rate to hold the bond, the seller should deliver on the last day. If the financing rate exceeds the coupon yield, the seller should deliver immediately. The choice of when to deliver, based on the rate of accruing interest, is a timing option and is known as the **accrued interest option**. It is a component of the end-of-the-month option.

In general, interest rates will not be constant over the last eight business days of the month. As interest rates change during this period, bond prices will change. However, for any given potential delivery day during this period, the invoice amount for a bond will not change. The invoice amount is determined by the settlement price on the last trading day and the amount of accrued interest to the delivery day. From the seller's point of view, the income to be received from delivery is known for each bond. The seller must deliver one of the deliverable bonds, but he still possesses a quality option. The seller can choose which bond to deliver.

Seller's Options in the Real Market

While the seller's options may be interesting and may give a devilish twist to the T-bond and T-note futures contracts, it remains to be seen how important they really are. First, we will examine estimates of the value of the seller's options and their effects on futures prices. Second, we will consider the extent to which traders seem to pay attention to these options in guiding their own trading.

The Value of the Seller's Options. With all perfect market conditions in place, we are accustomed to the conclusion of the cost-of-carry model that the futures price should equal the spot price times one plus the cost-of-carry:

$$F = S(1 + C)$$

In discussing the seller's options, we have seen how they can have value. However, this formulation of the cost-of-carry model leaves no role for the seller's options. If the seller's options have value, then market equilibrium requires that the following equation should hold:

$$F + SO = S(1 + C)$$

where:

SO = value of seller's options

This implies that:

$$F = S(1 + C) - SO \tag{6.3}$$

If this reformulation of the cost-of-carry model did not hold, the market would not be in equilibrium. This reformulation also implies that the futures prices observable in the market should be below the simple cost-of-carry price by the amount of the seller's options.

In other words, the market bids down the futures price because of the seller's options. The futures price must fall until the futures price plus the seller's options, $(F + SO)$, just equals the spot price times one plus the cost-of-carry, $S(1 + C)$. If the futures price were not bid down, then the seller would, in effect, get the options for free, and this would violate the principles of an efficient market.

This approach to the seller's options has been used by a number of scholars to estimate the value of the seller's options inherent in the T-bond futures contract. One difficulty with estimating the value of these options is that options generally have greater value the more time that remains until expiration. In other words, the seller's options should be worth more one year from delivery than they are worth three months from delivery. Most studies indicate that the seller's options have considerable value.

Seller's Options and Trader Behavior. Thus far we have seen that the seller's options appear to have value. Possessing these options suggests that traders should behave in similar ways. Thus, we would expect to find traders delivering the same bonds on the same days and not delivering on the same days. Further, we expect short traders to be aware of, and follow, the optimal policy for delivering to take advantage of their options.

Table 6.8 summarizes aspects of the delivery behavior for CBOT interest rate futures for a recent expiration. As the table shows, relatively few contracts are filled by delivery. As a general rule for the T-bond contract, there seems to be considerable attention paid to the characteristics of the bonds being delivered. Second, deliveries are infrequent in the early part of the month. Traders seem anxious to wait to exploit their end-of-the-month option. On occasion, however, significant deliveries do occur before the last few trading days. We might expect all traders to follow the exact same delivery strategy of delivering the same bond on the same day. In practice we see departures from that behavior. Some of the early deliveries of just a few contracts appear to be motivated by other concerns. Also, even when deliveries are heavy, traders deliver different bonds. This suggests that some traders may find it cheaper to deliver a bond from their existing inventory rather than to buy the cheapest-to-deliver bond for the express purpose of making delivery.

Gerald D. Gay and Steven Manaster examined the different strategies open to short T-bond traders to determine whether profits were available from optimal delivery strategies and to determine

CBOT Deliveries for Interest Rate Futures December 1995 Contract		Table 6.8
Contract	**Maximum Open Interest**	**Open Interest on First Position Day**	**Deliveries**
T-Bond	408,172	204,065	15,379
10-Year T-Note	251,687	131,922	7,374
5-Year T-Note	174,950	115,420	30,796
2-Year T-Note	23,010	15,821	11,603

Source: From Commodity Futures Trading Commission, Delivery Report.

whether traders followed those optimal strategies.[2] They reached several important conclusions. First, delivery strategies during the 1977–1983 period would have generated profits. This means that futures prices during this period did not fully reflect the value of the options available to the short sellers. Second, they compared an optimal delivery strategy with the actual deliveries during this period. They found that the actual deliveries exploited some, but not all, of the seller's options. In other words, the short traders took advantage of their options to some extent, but they did not fully exploit the options available to them. As Gay and Manaster note, these options may not have been fully understood by traders in this early period. This leaves open the possibility that futures prices will adjust to fully reflect the value of the seller's options as the market moves toward maturity.

INTEREST RATE FUTURES MARKET EFFICIENCY

A market is informationally efficient if prices in that market fully reflect all information in a given information set. If the market is efficient with respect to some information set, then that information cannot be used to direct a trading strategy to beat the market. A trader beats the market by consistently earning a rate of return that exceeds the risk-adjusted market equilibrium rate of return. There are three commonly distinguished forms of the market efficiency hypothesis: the weak form, the semi-strong form, and the strong form. These versions of market efficiency are distinguished by their information sets. The weak form efficiency hypothesis asserts that information contained in the past history of price and volume data cannot be used to beat the market. The semi-strong form asserts that traders cannot rely on public information to beat the market. The strong form asserts that even private information is insufficient to allow a trader to beat the market.

We have seen that cash-and-carry and reverse cash-and-carry arbitrage strategies rely only on observable prices. Thus, successful arbitrage strategies violate weak form efficiency. For example, large divergences between forward and futures rates of interest would generate important academic arbitrage opportunities. Because the futures market is a zero-sum game, in the absence of transaction costs, one participant's profits imply offsetting losses for others.

For these reasons, users of any market should be concerned about market efficiency. This is true whether one is a speculator or hedger. Researchers have long recognized the importance of market efficiency. This section reviews the development of research on interest rate futures market efficiency and draws conclusions about the efficiency based on the state of research to date. In spite of the attention that has been focused on the efficiency question, only T-bill and T-bond futures contracts have been explored well in published works. Almost all of these analyses focus on divergences between forward rates implied by spot market positions and futures market positions. This focus on rate discrepancies means that the tests have sought evidence of academic arbitrage opportunities in the interest rate futures market. Many early tests were based on a less than full understanding of the conditions under which market efficiency could be judged.

Early tests of futures market efficiency focused exclusively on differences between forward rates and futures rates on T-bills. Differences between these rates were sometimes interpreted without further ado as evidence of market inefficiency. Immediate difficulties with this conclusion arose because different researchers arrived at radically different conclusions, some finding efficiency and others finding gross inefficiencies. From preceding chapters, we know that forward and futures rates can differ for at least two basic reasons: market imperfections or the influence of daily resettlement. Many of the earliest researches into efficiency did not take these two factors into adequate consideration, yet both are important.

Attempts to evaluate academic arbitrage opportunities in the T-bill futures market involve taking complementary positions in the futures market and in the spot market. The difference in the futures and forward yields must be sufficiently large to cover considerable transaction costs if there is to be genuine academic arbitrage. While many studies neglect the full magnitude of these transaction charges, more recent studies find potential for arbitrage even after transaction costs.

Depending on the exact way in which the arbitrage attempt is conducted, a trader must incur a variety of transaction costs. To see the full magnitude of these expenses, consider the misaligned futures and cash T-bill prices in Table 6.9. We explored these prices in Chapter 5. The transactions costs incurred to exploit this misalignment depend on the trader's initial position in the spot or futures market. With no position in either market, the trader must pay all transaction costs from the gross trading profits to capture an academic arbitrage profit. If an opportunity is attractive enough to show a profit, even after paying full transaction costs, it can be considered **pure arbitrage**.

If the trader already holds a portfolio of T-bills, for example, then some transaction costs can be avoided. Some of the costs have already been paid, and they should be considered as sunk costs for the analysis of the arbitrage. If a trader with an initial portfolio can successfully engage in arbitrage, then the profitable transaction is regarded as **quasi-arbitrage**. In discussing pure arbitrage and quasi-arbitrage, we refer to academic arbitrage.

To exploit the rate discrepancies in Table 6.9 via pure arbitrage, the trader must be able to pay a variety of transaction costs:

1. Issuing a 77-day T-bill is equivalent to borrowing. The most creditworthy traders can borrow a T-bill for about 50 basis points above its current yield. For $956,750 for 77 days, the borrowing cost is about $1,023. Consider also that the acquisition of the $956,750 might be through the issuance of a term repo agreement.
2. To buy a 167-day T-bill, a trader must pay the asked price for the bill, even if he or she is a market participant, which could involve an additional cost of about $100. If not a participant in the spot T-bill market, the trader must trade through a broker and pay a commission as well.
3. In selling the MAR futures contract, a trader can receive only the bid price, thereby increasing costs about $25. If he or she is not a trader on the IMM, the trader must pay commission costs as well.

Interest Rate Futures and Arbitrage	Table 6.9

Today's Date: January 5

Futures	Yield According to the Bond Pricing Formula
MAR Futures Contract	
(Matures in 77 days on March 22)	12.50%
Cash Bills	
167-Day T-bill	
(Deliverable on MAR Futures)	10.00
77-Day T-bill	6.00

4. Delivering the T-bill also has costs, because the short trader in the futures market bears all costs of delivery. These costs might be about $50.
5. Paying off the due bill also involves transaction costs of the wire transfer and record keeping, which might be $25.

   This list of transaction charges is only an indication of the additional expenses that a trader might face in an arbitrage attempt. Many of the charges shown in the list are difficult to gauge, and different market participants face different levels of expense. Nonetheless, the expenses are large and can offset a substantial difference between forward and futures yields. In addition, a trader also faces a cost not shown in the list. To find an arbitrage opportunity, a trader must search for it, and the cost of searching for the opportunity must be included in the calculation of the arbitrage profit.

   From the list of transaction costs, we see that some market participants are in a much better position than others. If a participant has a portfolio of spot T-bills, has a very good credit rating, is a trader on the futures exchange, and has a network of computerized information sources already in operation, then the transaction costs incurred in attempting to conduct an arbitrage operation are much smaller. This is the difference between pure arbitrage and quasi-arbitrage. For pure arbitrage, the yield discrepancy must be large enough to cover all transaction costs faced by a market outsider. For quasi-arbitrage, the trader faces less than full transaction costs.

   Richard Rendleman and Christopher Carabini conducted one of the most thorough and careful studies of T-bill futures efficiency using daily data for the period from January 6, 1976, to March 31, 1978. The analysis focused on the three futures contracts closest to maturity at any moment. By a careful analysis of the transaction costs faced by a market outsider, Rendleman and Carabini defined a band of difference between the forward rate and the futures rate that would still not support pure arbitrage. In other words, if forward and futures rates diverged only slightly, by 50 basis points or less, the yield difference would not cover transaction costs and pure arbitrage would be impossible. Figure 6.4 shows their results. The divergences between actual and theoretical yields for T-bill futures always fall within the band of 50 basis points, which denotes the no-profit limits. This was true for all 1,606 observations in their sample, supporting their conclusion that the T-bill futures market was efficient, in the sense of excluding opportunities for pure arbitrage.

   Regarding quasi-arbitrage opportunities, Rendleman and Carabini found occasions in which a trader could improve the return on a portfolio of spot T-bills. The quasi-arbitrage opportunities were found only infrequently, and no attempt was made to factor in the search costs needed to discover the opportunities. About these quasi-arbitrage opportunities, Rendleman and Carabini conclude: " . . . the inefficiencies in the Treasury bill futures market do not appear to be significant enough to offer attractive investment alternatives to the short-term portfolio manager."[3]

   In spite of the care with which the Rendleman and Carabini study was conducted, it is subject to one serious limitation: it relies on daily closing prices. In an evaluation of an arbitrage attempt, the purchase and sale of two related goods must be assumed to occur simultaneously. However, the spot and futures markets for T-bills close at different times. This means that the closing prices for each day will not be prices for the same moment on both markets. In academic jargon, the prices are nonsimultaneous or exhibit nonsimultaneity.

   To improve the test of T-bill futures efficiency, Elton, Gruber, and Rentzler (hereafter EGR) observed **intraday prices** – prices from throughout the trading day. With intraday prices on futures and spot T-bills, they matched the times at which the trades occurred to determine simultaneous prices in both markets. Their data set consisted of a sample of intraday spot prices spaced approximately

Pure Arbitrage in T-Bill Futures   **Figure 6.4**

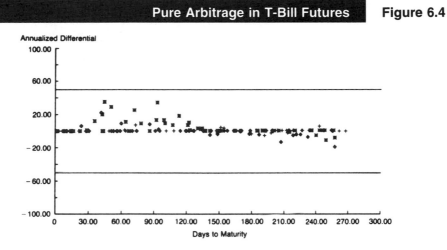

Source: From R. Rendleman and C. Carabini, "The Efficiency of the Treasury Bill Futures Market," *Journal of Finance* 34, 1979, pp. 895–914. Reprinted by permission of the American Finance Association.

an hour apart and every T-bill futures trade during the period from January 6, 1976, through December 22, 1982.

EGR divide the strategies they consider into those that involve immediate and delayed execution. For immediate execution, EGR assume that an arbitrage opportunity is identified from their simultaneous cash/futures price pairs and the trader enters arbitrage transactions at those prices. For delayed execution, EGR assume that an arbitrage opportunity is identified from one cash/futures price pair and the trade is executed at the prices of the next pair. This implies a delay of about one hour between identification and execution. According to EGR's analysis, the immediate execution strategy replicates the situation facing the floor trader, while the delayed execution strategy would be available to a market participant farther removed from the pit.

To analyze pure arbitrage strategies, EGR assume transaction costs on the arbitrage transactions of $175 plus an annual cost of 50 basis points to cover selling a T-bill short. As we have seen, a trader who enters such arbitrage transactions still faces daily resettlement cash flows. Therefore, any planned arbitrage profit can only be an expected profit. The actual profit may differ due to the effect of daily resettlement cash flows. Table 6.10 presents the key results of EGR's study of pure arbitrage for both immediate and delayed execution. EGR assume that these daily resettlement cash flows earn the overnight rate on a certificate of deposit.

The immediate execution results assume that transactions take place immediately upon finding an attractive opportunity, and the expected profit means that the effects of daily resettlement have not yet been considered. However, these results are net of transaction costs. The results are stratified by a filter rule that divides the opportunities by the size of the expected profit. For example, they found a total of 2,304 opportunities with some expected profit. The average expected profit across all of these trades was $894, assuming a transaction of one contract size.

Table 6.10	Pure Arbitrage Results for T-Bill Futures							
		Immediate Execution				**Delayed Execution**		
Size of Filter	**Number of Trades**	**Expected Profit**	**Actual Profit**	**Standard Error**	**Number of Trades**	**Expected Profit**	**Actual Profit**	**Standard Error**
$ 0	2,304	$ 894	$ 889	$15	1,725	$ 893	$ 880	$18
100	2,093	980	975	16	1,569	977	964	19
200	1,902	1,064	1,058	16	1,428	1,059	1,041	19
300	1,738	1,142	1,135	16	1,301	1,137	1,117	20
400	1,595	1,212	1,206	17	1,206	1,199	1,176	20
500	1,469	1,279	1,271	17	1,107	1,267	1,244	21
600	1,332	1,352	1,346	18	1,005	1,339	1,315	22
700	1,190	1,437	1,432	18	890	1,429	1,401	23
800	1,063	1,519	1,516	18	789	1,517	1,490	24

Source: From E. Elton, M. Gruber, and J. Rentzler, "Intra-Day Tests of the Efficiency of the Treasury Bill Futures Market," *The Review of Economics and Statistics* 66, February 1984, pp. 129–37. Reprinted with kind permission of Elsevier Science – NL, Sara Burgerhartstraat 25, 1055 KV Amsterdam, The Netherlands.

Notice that they found many opportunities with very large discrepancies. For example, they found 1,063 opportunities with expected profits exceeding $800. The actual profit differs from the expected profit due to the interest gain or cost incurred on the daily resettlement cash flows. These differences are very small. If execution of the trades is delayed until the next cash market quotation, the expected profits diminish. Yet overall, EGR's results indicate that these arbitrage opportunities persist. Therefore, EGR conclude that the T-bill futures market is not efficient with respect to pure arbitrage opportunities.

In comparing the Rendleman and Carabini study with the later study by EGR, we must give greater weight to the results of EGR. The data employed by EGR are more complete, and they reduce the problems of nonsimultaneous pricing. Recent studies of T-bill futures market efficiency have tended to corroborate the results of EGR.

Having found frequent and significant departures from efficiency in the T-bill futures market, we now turn to the T-bond futures contract. The T-bond futures market has not received nearly the attention devoted to the T-bill futures market. Part of the reason for this difference is the extreme complexity of the T-bond contract, particularly the diversity of deliverable instruments and the seller's options. Since the short trader chooses which bond to deliver in fulfillment of the contract, the long position has no opportunity for arbitrage, as we showed earlier in this chapter. For cash-and-carry arbitrage, the short trader could conduct arbitrage if it were profitable to:

1. buy a bond,
2. sell a futures contract on the bond, and
3. store the bond until delivery.

As we have seen, even such a strategy is limited in its effectiveness. The bond that the short trader might hold will pay a coupon, in most cases, on the 15th of the month preceding delivery. The investment rate for the coupon is uncertain, so the short trader cannot really count on an arbitrage profit if he or she must rely on the cash flow from the reinvested coupons. These conditions drastically restrict the possible arbitrage strategies. Further, we have seen that the futures price is bid down to reflect the seller's options. Capturing profits from the seller's options is risky. As a consequence, the reduction in futures prices to account for the seller's options makes successful arbitrage even less likely.

In their paper on T-bond futures efficiency, Kolb, Gay, and Jordan investigated the possibility of arbitrage for all T-bond futures contracts in existence from December 1977 through June 1981.[4] They analyze just one day for each instrument, the last business day of the month preceding the delivery month. This is the first position day. For this date, and for any position day, arbitrage is possible because the trader knows what invoice amount will be received for a particular deliverable bond. The short trader receives the invoice amount upon delivery, with the invoice amount depending on the futures price, the conversion factor, and the accrued interest as discussed earlier in this chapter. From this cash flow, the short trader must pay the cost of acquiring the bond and the financing cost of holding the bond from the time of acquisition until it can be delivered. Since the short trader chooses which bond to deliver, he need find only one deliverable bond that is profitable to secure an arbitrage opportunity. Figure 6.5 shows the profitability of delivery for all deliverable bonds for 15 contract maturities, as calculated for the last business day of the month preceding the delivery month.

Only three contract maturities had a bond that promised a positive cash flow: SEP 78, SEP 80, and MAR 80. For the SEP 78 contract, the positive cash flow was $49.07 and for the SEP 80 contract,

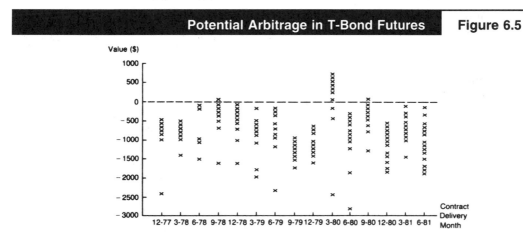

Potential Arbitrage in T-Bond Futures   **Figure 6.5**

Values of eq. (2) for each deliverable bond. Invoice Amount — (Bond Price + Accrued Interest) − Financing Cost
(values less than − $3000 not reported)

Source: From R. Kolb, G. Gay, and J. Jordan, "Are There Arbitrage Opportunities in the Treasury-Bond Futures Market?" *Journal of Futures Markets* 3, 1987, pp. 217–29. Reprinted by permission of John Wiley & Sons, Inc. Journals.

the positive cash flow was $27.57. Out of these potential profits, the arbitrageur would have had to pay transaction and search costs, so these two occasions represent no chance for an arbitrage profit.

For the MAR 80 contract, one bond would have yielded a cash flow as large as $591.34. If there is to be hope of arbitrage, it must rest with this contract. This hope, however, appears to be illusory. Prices reported for this date vary widely from source to source, with reported futures prices differing by as much as $1,625. The uncertainty over the actual prices at which one could contract requires that this apparent arbitrage opportunity be regarded as spurious. Kolb, Gay, and Jordan conclude that their results, while limited, are fully consistent with the efficiency of the T-bond futures market.

Because of difficulty with specifying a tight arbitrage link between the cash market and the T-bond futures contract, most subsequent explorations of T-bond futures efficiency have focused on speculative strategies. Successful speculative strategies would constitute evidence against efficiency if they earn a return too great for the level of speculative risk undertaken. However, the difficulty with evaluating such strategies lies in determining a market standard risk/expected return relationship. As a consequence, tests of speculative efficiency are always simultaneous tests of market efficiency and the adequacy of the risk/expected return measure used. Bearing this limitation in mind, we briefly consider some further tests of T-bond futures efficiency.

An important limitation of the Kolb, Gay, and Jordan methodology was the necessary restriction to a period within the delivery month. Bruce Resnick and Elizabeth Hennigar extended a similar analysis to periods outside the delivery month. Their results support the efficiency of the T-bond futures market.[5] In a separate study, Resnick evaluated the pricing relationship between T-bond futures of different maturities, in effect asking if the spread relationships were efficient. Resnick's findings also support a general conclusion of efficiency.[6]

R. Klemkosky and D. Lasser conducted a study similar to Resnick and Hennigar's, but used a different time period and attempted to adjust for taxes. Noting that any kind of cash-and-carry arbitrage evaluation depends on the estimate of borrowing costs, Klemkosky and Lasser found inefficiencies. While they acknowledged that they were unable to fully adjust for risk, Klemkosky and Lasser judged the divergences between the spot and futures prices to be inconsistent with full efficiency. As they concluded: "... either the borrowing costs are still being underestimated or the T-bond market was inefficient during periods of high interest rates, possibly because of an extraordinarily large risk premium being placed on the variable coupon reinvestment return."[7]

In a test of speculative efficiency, Don Chance examined speculative strategies based on the response of the futures market to announcements of changes in the Consumer Price Index. Chance found that T-bond futures prices rose following an announcement of lower inflation (measured against past inflation or against "expected" inflation). Chance found that the T-bond futures prices adjusted slowly to this information, so that traders could react swiftly to the market and make a speculative profit as the market digested the information over the day following the announcement.[8]

How can we assess the variety of evidence on the efficiency of the interest rate futures market? Several years ago, it appeared the weight of evidence favored efficiency, but today it appears that weight is beginning to shift. The study by Elton, Gruber, and Rentzler is particularly persuasive. The study is extremely rich in observations and every effort was made to adjust for potential discrepancies. Attempts to assess the efficiency of the T-bond futures markets are much more difficult, and the current state of evidence is inconclusive. In attempting to summarize this evidence in a single sentence, it appears that persistent inefficiencies continue to exist in these markets, but the size of the inefficiencies may not be large enough to reward a change in professions. Remember, none of these studies includes the search cost or the use of human capital required to find and exploit the alleged arbitrage opportunity.

We must also remember that most of these studies have focused on the existence of arbitrage opportunities. Arbitrage, however, is the grossest kind of inefficiency. A market may well have no arbitrage opportunities and still be inefficient. If risky positions can be taken in the futures market, and those risky positions earn returns in excess of a risk-adjusted normal return, then the futures market would still be inefficient. Few tests of such possibilities have been conducted, probably due to the difficulty in defining a risk-adjusted normal return. The ones that have been conducted reach divergent conclusions.

APPLICATIONS: EURODOLLAR AND T-BILL FUTURES

In Chapter 5 we considered speculative strategies and some hedging strategies. In this section we explore alternative risk management strategies using short-term interest rate futures. We proceed by considering a series of examples. Taken together, these examples provide a handbook of techniques for a variety of risk management strategies. All of these strategies turn on protection against shifting interest rates.

Changing the Maturity of an Investment

Many investors find themselves with an existing portfolio that may have undesirable maturity characteristics. For example, a firm might hold a six-month T-bill and realize that it will have a need for funds in three months. By the same token, another investor might hold the same six-month T-bill and fear that those funds might have to face lower reinvestment rates upon maturity in six months. This investor might prefer a one-year maturity. Both the firm and the investor could sell the six-month bill and invest for the preferred maturity. However, spot market transaction costs are relatively high, and many investors prefer to alter the maturities of investment by trading futures. The two examples that follow show how to use futures to accomplish both a shortening and lengthening of maturities.

Shortening the Maturity of a T-Bill Investment. Consider a firm that has invested in a T-bill. Now, on March 20, the T-bill has a maturity of 180 days, but the firm learns of a need for cash in 90 days. Therefore, it would like to shorten the maturity so it can have access to its funds in 90 days, around mid-September.

For simplicity, we assume that the short-term yield curve is flat with all rates at 10 percent on March 20. For convenience, we assume a 360-day year to match the pricing conventions for T-bills. The face value of the firm's T-bill is $10 million. With 180 days to maturity and a 10 percent discount yield, the price of the bill is given by:

$$P = \text{FV} - [\text{DY}(\text{FV})(\text{DTM})]/360$$

where:

P = bill price
FV = face value
DY = discount yield
DTM = days until maturity

Therefore, the 180-day bill is worth $9,500,000. If the yield curve is flat at 10 percent, the futures yield must also be 10 percent, and the T-bill futures price must be $975,000 per contract. Starting from an initial position of a six-month T-bill, the firm of our example can shorten the maturity by selling T-bill futures for expiration in three months, as Table 6.11 shows. On March 20, there was no cash flow, because the firm merely sold futures. On June 20, the six-month bill is now a three-month bill and can be delivered against the futures. In Table 6.11, the firm delivers the bills and receives the futures invoice amount of $9,750,000. (Although we have assumed the futures price did not change, this does not limit the applicability of our results. No matter how the futures price changed from March to June, the firm would still receive a total of $9,750,000. We assume that this occurs in June instead of over the period.) The firm has effectively shortened the maturity from six months to three months.

Lengthening the Maturity. Consider now, on August 21, an investor who holds a $100 million face value T-bill that matures in 30 days on September 20. She plans to reinvest for another three months after the T-bill matures. However, she fears that interest rates might fall unexpectedly. If so, she would be forced to reinvest at a lower rate than is now reflected in the yield curve. The SEP T-bill futures yield is 9.8 percent, as is the rate on the current investment. She finds this rate attractive and would like to lengthen the maturity of the T-bill investment. She knows that she can lengthen the maturity by buying a September futures contract and taking delivery. She will then hold the delivered bills until maturity in December.

With a 9.8 percent discount futures yield, the value of the delivery unit is $975,500. With $100 million coming available on September 20, the investor knows she will have enough funds to take delivery of ($100,000,000/$975,500) = 102.51 futures contracts. Therefore, she initiates the strategy presented in Table 6.12.

On August 21, she held a bill worth $99,183,333, assuming a yield of 9.8 percent. With the transactions of Table 6.12, she had no cash flow on August 21. With the maturity of the T-bill in September, the investor received $100,000,000 and used almost all of it to pay for the futures delivery. She also received $499,000, which we assume she invested at 9.8 percent for three months. In December, this investment would be worth $499,000 + $499,000(.098)(90/360) = $511,226. With the T-bills maturing in December, the total proceeds will be $102,511,226, from an investment that was worth $99,183,333 on August 21. This gives her a discount yield of 9.8 percent over the four-month horizon from August to December.

Notice that this transaction "locked in" the 9.8 percent on the futures contract. In this example, this happens to match the spot rate of interest. However, the important point to recognize is that

Table 6.11	Transactions to Shorten Maturities	
Date	**Cash Market**	**Futures Market**
March 20	Holds six-month T-bill with a face value of $10,000,000, worth $9,500,000. Wishes a three-month maturity.	Sell 10 JUN T-bill futures contracts at 90.00, reflecting the 10% discount yield.
June 20		Deliver cash market T-bills against futures; receive $9,750,000.

	Transactions to Lengthen Maturities	Table 6.12
Date	**Cash Market**	**Futures Market**
August 21	Holds 30-day T-bill with a face value of $100,000,000. Wishes to extend the maturity for 90 days.	Buy 102 SEP T-bill futures contracts, with a yield of 9.8%.
September 20	30-day T-bill matures and investor receives $100,000,000. Invest $499,000 in money market fund.	Accept delivery on 102 SEP futures, paying $99,501,000.
December 19	T-bills received on SEP futures mature for $102,000,000.	

lengthening the maturity involves locking into the futures yield, no matter what that yield may be. Thus, for the period covered by the T-bill delivered on the futures contract, the investment will earn the futures yield at the time of contracting.

Fixed and Floating Loan Rates

In recent years, interest rates have fluctuated dramatically. These fluctuating rates generate interest rate risk that few economic agents are anxious to bear. For example, in housing finance, home buyers seek fixed rate loans, because the fixed rate protects the borrower against rising rates. By the same token, lenders may be unwilling to offer fixed rate loans, because they fear that their cost of funds might rise. With fixed rate lending, and a rising cost of funds, the lender faces a risk of paying more to acquire funds than it is earning on its fixed rate lending. Therefore, many lenders want to make floating rate loans.

In this section, we show how the borrower who receives a floating rate loan can effectively convert this loan into a fixed rate loan, thereby protecting against rises in interest rates. Similarly, for a lender who feels compelled to offer fixed rate loans, we show how the lender can use the futures markets to make the investment perform like a floating rate loan. Either the borrower or lender can bear the interest rate risk. Whichever party bears the interest rate risk can hedge the risk through the futures market. In a floating rate loan, the borrower bears or hedges the risk. In a fixed rate loan, the lender bears or hedges the risk.

In this section we consider a single transaction from two points of view, the lender's and the borrower's. First, we assume that the loan is a floating rate loan and that the borrower hedges the interest rate risk associated with the loan. Second, we consider a fixed rate loan in which the lender hedges the interest rate risk.

Converting a Floating Rate to a Fixed Rate Loan. A construction firm plans a project that will take six months to complete at a total cost of $100 million. The bank offers to provide the funds for six months at a rate 200 basis points above the 90-day LIBOR rate. However, the bank insists that the loan rate for the second quarter will be 200 basis points above the 90-day LIBOR rate that prevails at that date. Also, the construction company must pay interest after the first quarter. Principal plus interest are due in six months.

Today is September 20 and the current 90-day LIBOR rate is 7.0 percent. The DEC Eurodollar futures yield is 7.3 percent. Based on these rates and the borrowing plan, the construction company will pay 9 percent for the first three months and 9.3 percent for the second three months. These rates give the following cash flows from the loan:

September 20	Borrow principal	+ $100,000,000
	Make loan to construction company	− $100,000,000
December 20	Pay interest	− $1,750,000
March 20	Receive principal and interest from construction company	+ $104,575,000
	Pay principal and interest	− $101,825,000

The cash flows for September and December are certain. However, the cash flow in March depends upon the LIBOR rate that prevails in December. The firm expects a 9.3 percent rate, which equals the futures yield for the DEC futures plus 200 basis points. However, between September and December, that rate could rise. For example, if the spot 90-day LIBOR rate in December is 7.8 percent, the firm will pay 9.8 percent and the total interest due in March will be $125,000 higher than expected.

The construction firm decides to lock into the 7.3 futures yield and its expected 9.3 borrowing rate so that it will know its borrowing cost. Starting with a floating rate loan and transacting to fix the interest rate is called a **synthetic fixed rate loan**. Table 6.13 shows how the construction company trades to protect itself from a jump in rates. At the outset, the firm accepts the floating rate scheme for its loan and sells 100 DEC Eurodollar futures. If rates rise, the short futures position will give enough profits to pay the additional interest expense on the second quarter's loan.

Table 6.13	Synthetic Fixed Rate Borrowing	
Date	**Cash Market**	**Futures Market**
September 20	Borrow $100,000,000 at 9.00% for three months and commit to extend the loan for three additional months at a rate 200 basis points above the three-month LIBOR rate prevailing at that time.	Sell 100 DEC Eurodollar futures contracts at 92.70, reflecting the 7.3% yield.
December 20	Pay interest of $2,250,000. LIBOR is now at 7.8%, so borrow $100,000,000 for three months at 9.8%.	Offset 100 DEC Eurodollar futures at 92.20, reflecting the 7.8% yield. Produces profit of $125,000 = 50 basis points × $25 per point × 100 contracts.
March 20	Pay interest of $2,450,000 and repay principal of $100,000,000.	
	Total Interest Expense: $4,700,000	Futures Profit: $125,000
	Net Interest Expense After Hedging: $4,575,000	

As Table 6.13 shows, LIBOR rises by 50 basis points to 7.8 percent. This implies a borrowing rate of 9.8 percent for the second quarter, as the table shows. However, the rise in rates has created a futures profit of $125,000 = 50 basis points times $25 per basis point times 100 contracts. The table shows that the firm pays $125,000 more interest in the second quarter than anticipated due to the jump in rates. However, this is exactly offset by the futures profit.[9] In September, the firm expected to pay a total of $4,575,000 in interest for the loan. Counting the futures profit, this is exactly the interest that the firm pays because it hedged. By trading in the futures market, the construction firm changed its floating rate loan into a fixed rate loan.

Converting a Fixed Rate to a Floating Rate Loan. We now consider the same transaction from the lender's point of view. If the construction company really wants a fixed rate loan, let them have it, reasons the bank. The bank's cost of funds equals the 90-day LIBOR rate, we assume. The bank expects to pay 7.0 percent for funds this quarter and 7.3 percent next quarter, or an average rate of 7.15 percent over the six months of the loan. Therefore, the bank decides to make a fixed rate six-month loan to the construction company at 9.15 percent. The bank's expected profit is the 200 basis point spread between the lending rate and the bank's LIBOR-based cost of funds. The bank expects to secure the funds by borrowing:

September 20	Borrow principal	+ $100,000,000
December 20	Receive interest	+ $2,250,000
	Pay interest	– $1,750,000
March 20	Receive principal and interest	+ $102,325,000
	Pay principal and interest	– $101,825,000

If all goes as expected, the bank's gross profit will be $1,000,000. Having made a fixed rate loan, however, the bank is at risk of rising interest rates. For example, if LIBOR rises by 50 basis points to 7.8 percent for the second quarter, the bank will have to pay an additional $125,000 in interest. To avoid this risk, the bank transacts as shown in Table 6.14. Notice how they almost exactly match the transactions of the construction company, except that the bank has a lower borrowing rate. If interest rates rise, the bank's cost of funds rises, just as was the case for the construction company with a floating rate loan. Both the construction company and the bank were able to hedge by selling Eurodollar futures.

With the rise in rates, the bank paid $125,000 more interest than it expected. However, this increased interest was offset by a futures market gain. Originally, the bank wanted to shift the interest rate risk to the construction company. However, as the transactions of Table 6.14 show, the bank is able to give the construction company the fixed rate loan it desires and still avoid the interest rate risk. In essence, the bank creates a **synthetic floating rate loan**. For its customer it offers a fixed rate loan, but the bank transacts in the futures market to make the transaction equivalent to having given a floating rate loan.

Strip and Stack Hedges

In the example of the synthetic fixed rate loan and synthetic floating rate lending, the interest rate risk focused on a single date. Often, the period of the loan covers a number of different dates at which the rate might be reset. For example, the construction company of our previous example makes

Table 6.14	Synthetic Floating Rate Lending	
Date	**Cash Market**	**Futures Market**
September 20	Borrow $100,000,000 at 7.00% for three months and lend it for six months at 9.15%.	Sell 100 DEC Eurodollar futures contracts at 92.70, reflecting the 7.3% yield.
December 20	Pay interest of $1,750,000. LIBOR is now at 7.8%, so borrow $100,000,000 for three months at 7.8%.	Offset 100 DEC Eurodollar futures at 92.20, reflecting the 7.8% yield. Produces profit of $125,000 = 50 basis points × $25 per point × 100 contracts.
March 20	Pay interest of $1,950,000 and repay principal of $100,000,000.	
	Total Interest Expense: $3,700,000	Futures Profit: $125,000
	Net Interest Expense After Hedging: $3,575,000	

a more realistic assessment of how long it will take to complete a project. Instead of six months, the construction firm realizes the project will take a year.

The bank insists on making a floating rate loan for three months at a rate 200 basis points above the LIBOR rate prevailing at the time of the loan. On September 15, the construction company observes the following rates:

Three-month LIBOR	7.00%
DEC Eurodollar	7.30
MAR Eurodollar	7.60
JUN Eurodollar	7.90

For these four quarters, the firm expects to finance the $100,000,000 at 9.00, 9.30, 9.60, and 9.90 percent, respectively. Therefore, the construction company expects to borrow $100,000,000 for a year at an average rate of 9.45 percent. This gives a total expected interest cost of $9,450,000.

A Stack Hedge Example. The construction firm decides to lock in this borrowing rate by hedging with Eurodollar futures. To implement the hedge, the firm sells 300 DEC Eurodollar futures. The firm hopes to protect itself against any changes in interest rates between September and December. In December, the futures will expire and the firm will offset the DEC futures and replace them with MAR futures. This is a **stack hedge**, because all of the futures contracts are concentrated, or stacked, in a single futures expiration.

We now consider how the construction firm fares with a single change in interest rates over the next year. Shortly after the firm enters the hedge, LIBOR rates jump by 50 basis points. Therefore, the firm's borrowing costs for the next three quarters are:

December-March	9.80%
March-June	10.10
June-September	10.40

For simplicity, we consider only one interest rate change, so the firm secures these rates. Table 6.15 shows the construction firm's transactions and the results of the hedge. The firm hedges its $100,000,000 loan with 300 contracts, or $300,000,000 of underlying Eurodollars. After taking the loan, the first quarter's rate is fixed at 9.00 percent. Therefore, the firm is at risk for $100,000,000 for three quarters. Because the maturity of the Eurodollars that underlie the futures is only one quarter, it requires three times as much futures value as its spot market exposure.

With the shift in rates, the firm must pay $9,825,000 in interest, which is more than the expected $9,450,000 when the firm took the loan. This difference is due to the across the board interest rate rise of 50 basis points. The same interest rate rise generates a futures trading profit of $375,000. Thus, the futures profit exactly offsets the increase in interest costs and the construction firm has successfully hedged its interest rate risk using a stack hedge.

		Results of a Stack Hedge	Table 6.15
Date	**Cash Market**	**Futures Market**	
September 20	Borrow $100,000,000 at 9.00% for three months and commit to roll over the loan for three quarters at 200 basis points over the prevailing LIBOR rate.	Sell 300 DEC Eurodollar futures contracts at 92.70, reflecting the 7.3% yield.	
December 20	Pay interest of $2,250,000. LIBOR is now at 7.8%, so borrow $100,000,000 for three months at 9.8%.	Offset 300 DEC Eurodollar futures at 92.20, reflecting the 7.8% yield. Produces profit of $375,000 = 50 basis points × $25 per point × 300 contracts.	
March 20	Pay interest of $2,450,000 and borrow $100,000,000 for three months at 10.10%.		
June 20	Pay interest of $2,525,000 and borrow $100,000,000 for three months at 10.40%.		
September 20	Pay interest of $2,600,000 and principal of $100,000,000.		
	Total Interest Expense: $9,825,000	Futures Profit: $375,000	
	Interest Expense Net of Hedging: $9,450,000		

A Danger in Using Stack Hedges. We now consider a potential danger in using a stack hedge of this type. In the example, the stack hedge worked perfectly because all interest rates changed by the same 50 basis points. As a result, the stack hedge gave a perfect hedge, and the construction firm had no changes in its anticipated total borrowing cost. The same stack hedge might have performed very poorly if interest rates had changed in a somewhat different fashion.

For example, after the loan agreement is signed, the funds are received, and the same stack hedge is implemented, assume there is a single change in futures yields as follows. The DEC futures yield rises from 7.3 to 7.4 percent, the MAR futures yield rises from 7.6 to 8.3 percent, and the JUN futures yield jumps from 7.9 to 8.6 percent, as Figure 6.6 shows. With this change in rates, the construction firm will have the following borrowing costs and interest expenses:

September-December	9.00%	$2,250,000
December-March	9.40	2,350,000
March-June	10.30	2,575,000
June-September	10.60	2,650,000

This change in rates gives the same increase in borrowing costs from the initially expected level of $9,450,000 to $9,825,000. However, there is one important difference. The DEC futures yield changed by only 10 basis points. Therefore, the futures profit on 300 DEC Eurodollar contracts is only $75,000 = 10 basis points times $25 per basis point times 300 contracts. Now the net borrowing cost after hedging is $9,750,000. This is $300,000 more than initially expected.

Figure 6.6   **Yield Curve Shifts**

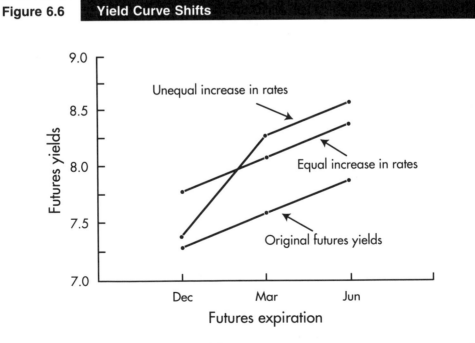

The graph of Figure 6.6 shows the original position for the DEC, MAR, and JUN Eurodollar futures yields. In our first example of a stack hedge, we assumed that all futures yields rose by 50 basis points. The rates after this equal jump are shown in the graph. We then considered an unequal increase in rates and the effectiveness of the stack hedge. Figure 6.6 shows those unequal rates for which the stack hedge was so ineffective. With the unequal increase in rates, the futures yield curve has steepened considerably. The DEC futures yield increased slightly, but the MAR futures yield increased more, as did the JUN futures yield. The poor performance of the stack hedge was due to this unequal change in rates.

A Strip Hedge. The stack hedge of the previous example was really hedging against a change in the DEC futures yield, because all of the contracts were stacked on that single futures expiration. Instead of using a concentration of contracts on a single expiration, a **strip hedge** uses an equal number of contracts for each futures expiration over the hedging horizon.

For our example of a $100,000,000 financing requirement at risk for three quarters, we have seen that a Eurodollar hedge requires 300 contracts. In a strip hedge, the construction firm would sell 100 Eurodollar contracts each of the DEC, MAR, and JUN futures. With the strip hedge in place, each quarter of the coming year is hedged against shifts in interest rates for that quarter. To illustrate the effectiveness of this strip hedge for an unequal increase in rates, Table 6.16 shows the results for the construction firm example.

The strip hedge of Table 6.16 works perfectly. The superior performance of the strip hedge results from aligning the futures market hedges with the actual risk exposure of the construction firm. Because the construction firm faced interest rate adjustments each quarter, it needed to hedge the interest rate risk associated with each quarter. This it could do through a strip hedge, but not through a stack hedge.

Strip versus Stack Hedges. From the example of the strip hedge, it appears that a strip hedge will always be superior to a stack hedge. While there are many circumstances where a strip hedge will be preferred, it is not always better than a stack hedge. Our earlier example of a firm that had a six-month horizon used a stack hedge with great success. Here the stack hedge exactly matched the timing of the firm's interest rate exposure, whereas a strip hedge would not have worked as well. The important point is to use a strip or stack hedge as required to match the timing of the futures hedge to the timing of the cash market risk exposure.

There is also a practical consideration that often leads hedgers to use a stack hedge when theory might favor a strip hedge. To implement a strip hedge requires trading more distant contracts. In our example, the construction firm traded the nearby, second, and third contracts. There is not always sufficient volume and liquidity in distant contracts to make such a strategy viable. Strips work well with Eurodollar futures because Eurodollar futures now have sufficient volume in distant contracts to make them attractive. This has not always been the case, however. When distant contracts lack liquidity, the hedger must trade off the advantages of a strip hedge with the potential lack of liquidity in the distant contracts. For the dominant interest rate futures contracts, strips work well because of the great liquidity in these markets.

Tailing the Hedge

In Chapter 3 we considered the effect of daily resettlement cash flows on futures pricing and the performance of futures positions. There we concluded that a correlation between the futures price

Table 6.16	Results of a Strip Hedge	
Date	Cash Market	Futures Market
September 20	Borrow $100,000,000 at 9.00% for three months and commit to roll over the loan for three quarters at 200 basis points over the prevailing LIBOR rate.	Sell 100 Eurodollar futures for each of: DEC at 92.70, MAR at 92.40, and JUN at 91.90.
December 20	Pay interest of $2,250,000. LIBOR is now at 7.8%, so borrow $100,000,000 for three months at 9.8%.	Offset 100 DEC Eurodollar futures at 92.60. Produces profit of $25,000 = 10 basis points × $25 per point × 100 contracts.
March 20	Pay interest of $2,450,000 and borrow $100,000,000 for three months at 10.10%.	Offset 100 MAR Eurodollar futures at 91.70. Produces profit of $175,000 = 70 basis points × $25 per point × 100 contracts.
June 20	Pay interest of $2,525,000 and borrow $100,000,000 for three months at 10.40%.	Offset 100 JUN Eurodollar futures at 91.40. Produces profit of $175,000 = 70 basis points × $25 per point × 100 contracts.
September 20	Pay interest of $2,600,000 and principal of $100,000,000.	
	Total Interest Expense: $9,825,000	Futures Profit: $375,000
	Interest Expense Net of Hedging: $9,450,000	

and interest rates could justify a difference between forward and futures prices. A positive correlation between the futures price and interest rates will cause the futures price to exceed the forward price. By contrast, a negative correlation between the futures price and interest rates will cause the futures price to fall below the forward price. In interest rate futures, the futures price is strongly negatively correlated with interest rates, because rising interest rates generate falling interest rate futures prices.

Daily resettlement cash flows also have potential importance for hedging. If a futures hedge generates positive daily resettlement cash flows, those funds will be available for investment once they are received. This means that the futures market hedging gain may unintentionally exceed the cash market loss. While unintentional gains on a futures hedge may not seem to be a problem, it is also possible to have the contrary results. For a hedge that is functioning properly, but the futures position is losing money, the futures position may generate losses that exceed the complementary cash market gain.

In **tailing the hedge** the trader slightly adjusts the hedge to compensate for the interest that can be earned from daily resettlement profits or paid on daily resettlement losses. Thus, the tail of the hedge is the slight reduction in the hedge position to offset the effect of daily resettlement interest. Tailing a hedge can work for any kind of hedging. However, because the daily resettlement cash flows are likely to be more important when the futures price is correlated with interest rates, tailing the hedge is most often observed in interest rate futures hedging.

To illustrate the principle behind tailing the hedge, consider the following idealized example. A large financial institution plans to buy $1 billion in 90-day T-bills 91 days from now. The T-bill futures that expires then has a yield of 10.00 percent, so the expected cost of those T-bills is $975 million. The institution hedges that commitment by buying 1,000 T-bill futures contracts. Overnight, interest rates fall by 10 basis points. With this fall in rates, the expected cost of the T-bills increases to $975,250,000, for a cash market loss of $250,000. The drop in rates, however, generates a futures gain of $250 per contract for a total gain of $250,000. Thus, the futures market gain exactly offsets the cash market loss – at least it does before we consider the interest on the $250,000 daily resettlement.

The $250,000 daily resettlement flow can be invested for the next 90 days over the hedging horizon. (The funds are available for investment for 90 days because we started with a 91-day horizon.) We assume an investment rate of 10 percent with daily compounding and a 360-day year. Therefore, the $250,000 will grow to $256,028 = $250,000(1.1)^{(90/360)}$ by the time the hedge is over. For simplicity, we assume that this is the only change in rates. At the end of the hedging period, the financial institution buys its T-bills and still has $6,028 left over. This is the interest from the daily resettlement cash flow.

Consider now the original hedged position and assume that rates rose by 10 basis points instead of falling. This change in rates generates a $250,000 daily resettlement outflow that the institution would have to finance for the next 90 days. Under this scenario, the financial institution would not be able to buy the T-bills because it would lack $6,028 at the termination of the hedge. The institution had to pay the $6,028 as interest to finance the $250,000 daily resettlement outflow. From this example, it is clear that the financial institution traded too many futures contracts. The total effect on the futures – the daily resettlement cash flow plus interest – exceeded the cash market effect. This was true whether rates rose or fell.

To reduce these errors in hedging, the financial institution could have traded slightly fewer futures contracts. With the 10 percent investment rate on the daily resettlement flow and a 90-day investment horizon, every dollar of daily resettlement flow will grow to $1.0241 = $1(1.1)^{(90/360)}$. Therefore, the financial institution can find the tailed hedge position by multiplying the untailed hedge position by the **tailing factor**. In our example, the tailing factor is 1/1.0241. Notice, however, that the tailing factor is nothing other than the present value of $1 at the hedging horizon discounted to the present (plus one day) at the investment rate for the resettlement cash flows.[10] Thus, we define the tailing factor as the present value (as of tomorrow) of $1 to be received at the hedging horizon. The tailed hedge position is:

$$\text{Tailed Hedge} = \text{Untailed Hedge (Tailing Factor)} \tag{6.4}$$

In the untailed hedge of 1,000 contracts in our example, the tailed hedge would be 976.45 = 1000/1.0241 contracts. Had the institution traded exactly that number of contracts, the results of the 10 basis point change in rates would have been a daily resettlement cash flow of $244,112.50 = 10 basis points times 25 basis points per contract times 976.45 contracts. This daily resettlement flow would grow to $250,000 = $244,112.50(1.1)^{(90/360)}$ by the time the hedge is lifted. Now the futures market effect at the hedging horizon exactly matches the cash market effect. In summary, to tail the hedge, we discount the untailed hedge position from the hedging horizon date to the present.

Because the tailed hedge depends on the time from the present to the hedging horizon, the tailed hedge changes constantly even if there is no change in the futures price. In the example of the $1 billion T-bill hedge, assume that the investment rate for daily resettlement cash flows is still 10 percent, but assume that only 31 days remain until the hedge will be terminated. The daily resettlement cash flow will be available for investment over 30 days. The tailing factor in this case is .9921 = $1/(1.1)^{(30/360)}$. This implies that the tailed hedge position on this date would be 992 contracts. For this example, the tailed hedge grew from 976 to 992 contracts over 60 days. This growth in the tailing factor is just the familiar growth in the present value factor as the discounting period gets smaller. For a hedging horizon of one day, the tailing factor is the present value from the hedging horizon to the present (plus one day). This is no time at all, so the tailing factor one day before the hedging horizon is 1.0.

Because futures can only be traded in whole contracts, tailing the hedge requires a large position (such as the 1,000 contracts of our example) to be useful. Also, since the tail depends on the interest rate from the present to the hedging horizon, the tail adjustment can only be as good as the hedger's estimate of the term interest rate from the present to the hedging horizon. In most cases the tail adjustment is fairly small in percentage terms. In our original example of a 10 percent interest rate and a 90-day horizon, the tailed hedge was only 2.35 percent smaller than the untailed hedge. The higher the interest rate and the more distant the hedging horizon, the greater will be the tailing factor. However, even in most illustrative examples, the tail is seldom more than 5 percent of the untailed position.[11]

HEDGING WITH T-BOND FUTURES

This section begins with an example of a cross-hedge of AAA corporate bonds. The example shows that a simple hedging rule of using $1 of futures per $1 of bonds can lead to horrible hedging results. This then leads to a discussion of alternative hedging techniques focusing on hedging with T-bonds.

In all previous hedging examples, the hedged and hedging instruments were very similar. Often, however, the need arises to hedge an instrument very different from those underlying the futures contract. The effectiveness of a hedge depends on the gain or loss on both the spot and futures sides of the transaction. But the change in the price of any bond depends on the shifts in the level of interest rates, changes in the shape of the yield curve, the maturity of the bond, and its coupon rate.

To illustrate the effect of the maturity and coupon rate on hedging performance, consider the following example. A portfolio manager learns on March 1 that he will receive $5 million on June 1 to invest in AAA corporate bonds paying an annual coupon of 5 percent and having ten years to maturity. The yield curve is flat and is assumed to remain so over the period from March 1 to June 1. The current yield on AAA bonds is 9.5 percent. Since the yield curve is flat, the forward rates are also all 9.5 percent, so the portfolio manager expects to acquire the bonds at that yield. However, fearing a drop in rates, he decides to hedge in the futures market to lock-in the forward rate of 9.5 percent.

The next step is to select the appropriate hedging instrument. The manager considers two possibilities: T-bills or T-bonds. However, the AAA bonds have a 5 percent coupon and a ten-year maturity, which do not match the coupon and maturity characteristics of either the T-bills or T-bonds deliverable on the respective futures contracts. The deliverable T-bills have a zero coupon and a maturity of only 90 days, while the deliverable T-bonds have a maturity of at least 15 years and an assortment of coupons. For this example, assume that the deliverable T-bond is a 20-year, 8 percent coupon bond.

To explore fully the potential difficulties of this situation, we consider hedging the AAA position with T-bill and T-bond futures. We ignore T-notes to dramatize the need to match coupon and maturity characteristics. For the bills and bonds, we assume the yields are 8 and 8.5 percent, respectively. Table 6.17 presents the hedging transactions and results for the T-bill hedge.

Because $5 million is becoming available for investment, assume the manager buys $5 million face value of T-bill futures contracts. Time passes, and by June 1 yields have fallen by 42 basis points on both the AAAs and the T-bills, respectively. The price of the corporate bond is $739.08, or $21.63 higher than the anticipated price of $717.45. Since the manager expected to buy 6,969 bonds, this means that the total additional outlay would be $150,739 (6,969 × $21.63), and this represents the loss in the cash market. In the futures market, rates also fell 42 basis points, generating a futures price increase of $956 per contract. Because five contracts were bought, the futures profit is $4,780. However, the loss in the cash market exceeds the gain in the futures market, for a net loss of $145,959. Note that this loss results even though rates changed by the same amount on both investments.

Consider now the same hedging problem, but assume we implement the hedge using $5 million face value of T-bond futures. Table 6.18 presents the transactions and results. Again yields fall by 42 basis points on both instruments. Consequently, the effect on the cash market is the same, but the total futures gain is $193,750, more than offsetting the loss in the cash market and generating a net wealth change = +$43,011.

If the goal of the hedge is to secure a net wealth change of zero, a gain is appropriately viewed as no better than a loss. It is only by accident of rates moving in the appropriate direction that the gain was not a loss anyway. Recall that all of the simplifying assumptions were in place – a flat yield

A Cross-Hedge Between Corporate Bonds and T-Bill Futures	Table 6.17

Date	Cash Market	Futures Market
March 1	A portfolio manager learns he will receive $5 million to invest in 5%, 10-year AAA bonds in three months, with an expected yield of 9.5% and a price of $717.45. The manager expects to buy 6,969 bonds.	The portfolio manager buys $5 million face value of T-bill futures (5 contracts) to mature on June 1 with a futures yield of 8.0% and a futures price, per contract, of $980,944.
June 1	AAA yields have fallen to 9.08%, causing the price of the bonds to be $739.08. This represents a loss, per bond, of $21.63. Since the plan was to buy 6,969 bonds, the total loss is (6,969 × $21.63) = –$150,739. Loss = –$150,739	The T-bill futures yield has fallen to 7.58%, so the futures price = spot price = $981,900 per contract, or a profit of $956 per contract. Since 5 contracts were traded, the total profit is $4,780. Gain = $4,780
	Net wealth change = –$145,959	

Table 6.18	A Cross-Hedge Between Corporate Bonds and T-Bond Futures	
Date	**Cash Market**	**Futures Market**
March 1	A portfolio manager learns he will receive $5 million to invest in 5%, 10-year AAA bonds in three months, with an expected yield of 9.5% and a price of $717.45. The manager expects to buy 6,969 bonds.	The portfolio manager buys $5 million face value of T-bond futures (50 contracts) to mature on June 1 with a futures yield of 8.5% and a futures price, per contract, of $96,875.
June 1	AAA yields have fallen to 9.08%, causing the price of the bonds to be $739.08. This represents a loss, per bond, of $21.63. Since the plan was to buy 6,969 bonds, the total loss is (6,969 × $21.63) = –$150,739.	The T-bond futures yield has fallen to 8.08%, so the futures price = spot price = $100,750 per contract, or a profit of $3,875 per contract. Since 50 contracts were traded, the total profit is $193,750.
	Loss = –$150,739	Gain = $193,750
	Net wealth change = +$43,011	

curve with rates on both instruments moving in the same direction and by the same amount. However, as noted earlier, the coupon and maturity of the hedged and hedging instruments do not match. All three instruments, the bond, the T-bill futures, and the T-bond futures have different durations, reflecting different sensitivities to interest rates. Consequently, for a given shift in yields (e.g., 42 basis points), the prices of the three instruments will change by different amounts. Therefore, a simple hedge of $1 in the futures market per $1 in the cash market is unlikely to produce satisfactory results.

Alternative Hedging Strategies

We have seen that simple approaches to hedging interest rate risk often give unsatisfactory results, due to mismatches of coupon and maturity characteristics. For the best possible hedges, we need strategies that take these coupon and maturity mismatches into consideration. This section chronicles some of the major strategies for hedging interest rate risk, starting from simple models and going on to more complex models.

Face Value Naive (FVN) Model. According to the FVN model, the hedger should hedge $1 of face value of the cash instrument with $1 face value of the futures contract. For example, a hedger wishing to hedge $100,000 face value of bonds would use one T-bond futures contract. The example we just considered used this strategy. The FVN strategy neglects two critically important factors:

1. By focusing on face values, the FVN model completely neglects potential differences in market values between the cash and futures positions. Therefore, keeping face value amounts equal between the cash and futures market can result in poor hedges because the market values of the two positions differ.

2. The FVN model neglects the coupon and maturity characteristics that affect duration for both the cash market good and the futures contract.

Because of these deficiencies, we will not consider the FVN model further.

Market Value Naive (MVN) Model. The MVN model resembles the FVN model, except it recommends hedging $1 of market value in the cash good with $1 of market value in the futures market. For example, if a $100,000 face value bond has a market value of $90,000 and the $100,000 face value T-bond futures contract is priced at 80-00, the MVN model would recommend hedging the cash bonds with $1.125 = (90/80)$ futures contracts.

Because it considers the difference between market and face value, the MVN model escapes the first criticism lodged against the FVN model. However, the MVN model still makes no adjustment for the price sensitivity of the two goods. Therefore, we dismiss the MVN model without further consideration.

Conversion Factor (CF) Model. The CF model applies only to futures contracts that use conversion factors to determine the invoice amount, such as T-bond and T-note futures. The intuition of this model is to adjust for differing price sensitivities by using the conversion factor as an index of the sensitivity.

In particular, the CF model recommends hedging $1 of face value of a cash market security with $1 of face value of the futures good times the conversion factor. As we have seen for T-bond and T-note futures, there are many deliverable instruments with different conversion factors. To apply the CF model, we must determine which instrument is cheapest-to-deliver and use the conversion factor for that instrument. Assuming we have identified the cheapest-to-deliver security, the hedge ratio (HR) is given by:

$$HR = -\left(\frac{\text{Cash Market Principal}}{\text{Futures Market Principal}}\right) (\text{Conversion Factor}) \qquad (6.5)$$

The negative sign indicates that one must take a futures market position opposite to the cash market position. For example, if the hedger is long in the cash market, the hedger should sell futures.

As an example, assume that a bond manager wishes to hedge a long position of $500,000 face value of bonds with T-bond futures. We assume the cheapest-to-deliver bond has a conversion factor of 1.2. In this situation, the manager should sell $600,000 worth of T-bond futures [$500,000(1.2)] or six contracts. The CF model attempts to secure the same amount of principal value of bonds on both the cash and futures sides of the hedge. This method is useful principally when one contemplates delivering a cash market bond against a futures contract.

Basis Point (BP) Model. The BP model focuses on the price effect of a one basis point change in yields. For example, we have seen that a change of one basis point causes a $25 change in the futures price of a T-bill or Eurodollar contract. Assume that today is April 2 and that a firm plans to issue $50 million of 180-day commercial paper in six weeks. For a one basis point yield change, the price of 180-day commercial paper will change twice as much as the 90-day T-bill futures contract, assuming equal face value amounts. In other words, on $1 million of 180-day commercial paper, a one basis point yield change causes a $50 price change. In an important sense, the commercial paper will be twice as sensitive to a change in yields.

To reflect this greater sensitivity, we can use the BP model to compute the following hedge ratio:

$$HR = -\frac{BPC_C}{BPC_F} \tag{6.6}$$

where:

BPC$_C$ = dollar price change for a 1 basis point change in the cash instrument
BPC$_F$ = dollar price change for a 1 basis point change in the futures instrument

The ratio BPC$_C$/BPC$_F$ indicates the relative number of contracts to trade. In our commercial paper example, the cash basis price change (BPC$_C$) is twice as great as the futures basis price change (BPC$_F$), so the hedge ratio is −2.0.

To explore the effect of this weighting, consider the following BP model hedge of the commercial paper. Planning to issue commercial paper, the firm will lose if rates rise, because the firm will receive less cash for its commercial paper. As it needs to sell the commercial paper, it is now long commercial paper and must hedge by selling futures. With a −2.0 hedge ratio and a $50 million face value commitment in the cash market, the firm should sell 100 T-bill futures contracts.

Table 6.19 presents the BP model transactions. After rates on both sides of the contract move by 45 basis points, we have the following result. In the cash market, the firm receives $112,500 less than anticipated for its commercial paper. This loss, however, is exactly offset by the price movement

Table 6.19	Hedging Results with the BP Model for the Commercial Paper Issuance

April 2

Cash Market
Firm anticipates issuing $50 million in 180-day commercial paper in 45 days at a yield of 11%.

Futures Market
Firm sells 100 T-bill June futures contracts yielding 10% with an index value of 90.00.

May 15
Spot market and futures market rates have both risen 45 basis points. The spot rate is now 11.45% and the futures market yield is 10.45%.

Cash Market Effect
Each basis point move causes a price change of $50 per million-dollar face value. Firm will receive $112,500 less for the commercial paper, due to the change in rates. (45 basis points × −$50 × 50 contracts = −$112,500)

Futures Market Effect
Each basis point increase gives a futures market profit of $25 per contract.

Futures Profit = 45 basis points × +$25 × 100 contracts = +$112,500

Net wealth change = 0

on the $100 million of T-bills underlying the futures position. The BP model helped identify the correct number of futures to trade for each unit in the cash market. By contrast, the FVN model would have suggested trading only 50 futures, which would have hedged only half of the loss.

Sometimes the yields may not change by the same amount as they did in Table 6.19. In that case, the hedger may wish to incorporate the relative volatility of the yields into the hedge ratio. For example, assume that the commercial paper rate is 25 percent more volatile than the T-bill futures rate. In other words, a 100 basis point rise in the T-bill futures rate normally might be accompanied by a 125 basis point rise in the commercial paper rate. To give the same total price change in the futures market as in the cash position, we would need to consider that difference in volatility in determining the hedge ratio. In that case, the hedge ratio becomes:

$$HR = -\left(\frac{BPC_C}{BPC_F}\right) RV \qquad (6.7)$$

where:

RV = volatility of cash market yield relative to futures yield, normally found by regressing the yield of the cash market instrument on the futures market yield

If we incorporate RV, assumed to be 1.25, into our commercial paper hedge, the transactions would appear as shown in the top portion of Table 6.20. Now the hedge ratio is:

Hedging Results with the BP Model Adjusted for Relative Yield Variances for the Commercial Paper Issuance	**Table 6.20**

April 2

Cash Market
Firm anticipates issuing $50 million in 180-day commercial paper in 45 days at a yield of 11%.

Futures Market
Firm sells 125 T-bill June futures contracts yielding 10% with an index value of 90.00.

May 15
Spot market rates have risen 56 basis points to 11.56% and futures rates have risen 45 basis points to 10.45%.

Cash Market Effect
Each basis point move causes a price change of $50 per million-dollar face value. Firm will receive $140,000 less for the commercial paper, due to the change in rates. (56 basis points × –$50 × 50 contracts = –$140,000)

Futures Market Effect
Each basis point increase gives a futures market profit of $25 per contract.

Futures Profit = 45 basis points × +$25 × 125 contracts = +$140,625

Net wealth change = +$625

$$HR = -\left(\frac{\$50}{\$25}\right) 1.25 = -2.5$$

Consequently, the hedger sells 125 T-bill futures contracts. Assume again that the T-bill yields rise by 45 basis points. Also, true to its greater relative volatility, the commercial paper yield moves 56 basis points, 1.25 times as much. Because more T-bill futures were sold, the T-bill futures profit still almost exactly offsets the commercial paper loss.

Regression (RGR) Model. One way of calculating a hedge ratio for interest rate futures is the regression technique we considered in Chapter 4. The hedge ratio found by regression minimizes the variance of the combined futures-cash position during the estimation period. This estimated ratio is applied to the hedging period.

For the RGR model the hedge ratio is:

$$HR = \frac{COV_{C,F}}{\sigma_F^2} \tag{6.8}$$

where:

$COV_{C,F}$ = covariance between cash and futures
σ_F^2 = variance of cash and futures

As noted in Chapter 4, this hedge ratio is the regression coefficient found by regressing the change in the cash position on the change in the futures position. These changes can be measured as dollar price changes or as percentage price changes.

$$\Delta C_t = \alpha + \beta \Delta F_t + \epsilon_t$$

The RGR model uses the hedge ratio that gives the lowest sum of squared errors for the data used in the estimation. Using the estimated hedge ratio for an actual hedge assumes that the relationship between the price changes on the futures and cash instruments does not change dramatically between the sample period and the actual hedging period.

This is a practical assumption. If the relationship is basically unchanged, then the estimated hedge ratio will perform well in the actual hedging situation. Fundamental shifts in the relationship between the price of the futures contract and the cash market good can lead to serious hedging errors. This danger is present in all hedging situations, but may be exacerbated in interest rate hedging. Without doubt, the RGR model has proven its usefulness in the market for the traditional futures contracts, and it has been adapted for use in the interest rate futures market by Louis Ederington, Charles Franckle, Joanne Hill, and Thomas Schneeweis.[12]

However, there are some problems in applying the RGR model to interest rate hedging. First, since it involves statistical estimation, the technique requires a data set for both cash and futures prices. This data may sometimes be difficult to acquire, particularly for an attempt to hedge a new security. In such a case, no cash market data would even exist, and a proxy would have to be used. Second, the RGR model does not explicitly consider the differences in the sensitivity of different bond prices to changes in interest rates. As the examples of Tables 6.17 and 6.18 indicate, this can be a very important factor. The regression approach does include the different price sensitivities indirectly, however, since their differential sensitivities will be reflected in the estimation of the hedge ratio. Third, any cash bond will have a predictable price movement over time. The price of any instrument will equal its par value at maturity. The RGR model does not consider this change in the cash bond's price explicitly, but the sample data should reflect this price movement tendency. Fourth, the hedge ratio is chosen to minimize the variability in the combined futures-cash position over the life of the hedge. Since the RGR hedge ratio depends crucially on the planned hedge length, one might reasonably prefer a hedging technique focusing on the wealth position of the hedge when the hedge ends.[13] After all, the wealth change from the hedge depends on the gain or loss when the hedge is terminated, not on the variability of the cash-futures position over the life of the hedge. In spite of these difficulties, the RGR model is a useful way to estimate hedge ratios, both for traditional commodities and, to a lesser extent, for interest rate hedging.

Price Sensitivity (PS) Model. The PS model has been designed explicitly for interest rate hedging.[14] The PS model assumes that the goal of hedging is to eliminate unexpected wealth changes at the hedging horizon, as defined in Equation 6.9:

$$dP_i + dP_F\,(N) = 0 \qquad\qquad (6.9)$$

where:

dP_i = unexpected change in the price of the cash market instrument
dP_F = unexpected change in the price of the futures instrument
N = number of futures to hedge a single unit of the cash market asset

Equation 6.9 expresses the goal that the unexpected change in the value of the spot instrument, denoted by I, and the futures position, denoted by F, should together equal zero. If this is achieved, the wealth change, or hedging error, is zero. Instead of focusing on the variance over the period of the hedge, the PS model uses a hedge ratio to achieve a zero net wealth change at the end of the hedge.

The problem for the hedger is to choose the correct number of contracts, denoted by N in Equation 6.9, to achieve a zero hedging error. Equation 6.10 gives the correct number of contracts to trade (N), per spot market bond:

$$N = -\left(\frac{R_F P_i D_i}{R_i F P_F D_F}\right) \mathrm{RV} \qquad\qquad (6.10)$$

where:

R_F = 1 + the expected futures yield
R_i = 1 + the expected yield to maturity on asset I
FP_F = the futures contract price
P_i = the price of asset I expected to prevail at the hedging horizon
D_i = the duration of asset I expected to prevail at the hedging horizon
D_F = the duration of the asset underlying futures contract F expected to prevail at the hedging horizon
RV = the volatility of the cash market asset's yield relative to the volatility of the futures instrument's yield

In nontechnical terms, Equation 6.10 says that the number of futures contracts to trade for each cash market instrument to be hedged is the number that should give a perfect hedge, assuming that yields on the cash and futures instrument change by the same amount. To explore the meaning and application of this technique, consider again the AAA bond hedges of Tables 6.17 and 6.18. The large hedging errors resulted from the different price sensitivities of the futures instruments and the AAA bonds.

Table 6.21 presents the data needed to calculate the hedge ratios for hedging the AAA bonds with T-bill or T-bond futures. Here we assume that the cash and futures market assets have the same volatilities, so RV = 1.0. For the T-bill hedge:

$$N = -\frac{(1.08)(-\$717.45)(7.709)}{(1.095)(\$980,944)(.25)} = .022244$$

The hedger should sell .022244 T-bill futures per AAA bond to be hedged. Because the portfolio manager plans to buy 6,969 bonds, he should hedge this commitment by trading 155 (actually, 155.02) T-bill futures. For the T-bond hedge:

$$N = -\frac{(1.085)(-\$717.45)(7.709)}{(1.095)(\$96,875)(10.143)} = .005577$$

With 6,969 bonds to hedge, the portfolio manager should sell 39 (actually, 38.8667) T-bond futures.

With either of these hedges, the same shift in yields on the AAA bonds and the futures instrument should give a perfect hedge. Table 6.22 presents the performance of these two hedges for the same 42 basis point drop in rates used in Tables 6.17 and 6.18.

With the given hedges and the same drop in yields, the T-bill hedge gave a futures gain of $148,203 to offset the loss on the AAA bonds of $150,742. The futures gain on the T-bond hedge

Table 6.21	Data for the Price Sensitivity Hedge			
Cash Instrument		**T-Bill Futures**		**T-Bond Futures**
P_i $717.45	FP_i	$980,944	FP_F	$96,875
D_i 7.709	D_F	.25	D_F	10.143
R_i 1.095	R_F	1.08	R_F	1.085
	N	.02224	N	.005577
	Number of Contracts to Trade	155	Number of Contracts to Trade	39

Table 6.22	Performance Analysis of Price Sensitivity Future Hedge		
	Cash Market	**T-Bill Hedge**	**T-Bond Hedge**
Gain/Loss	−$150,742	+$148,203	+$150,608
Hedging Error	—	$2,539	$134
Percentage of Cash Market Loss Hedged		98.32%	99.91%

is $150,608. The next line of Table 6.22 shows the size of the hedging error for the T-bill and T-bond hedges, while the final line gives the percentage of the cash market loss that was hedged. The T-bill hedge was 98.32 percent effective, while the T-bond hedge was 99.91 percent effective. Both hedges were almost perfect. The slight errors were due to rounding error and to the large change in interest rates. In these examples, the PS model worked very effectively. In actual hedging situations, one could not hope for such nearly perfect results, since yields need not change by the same amount on all instruments all of the time.

Conclusion. It is difficult to compare all of the hedging models reviewed in this section, because they differ so much in aim and complexity. The naive hedges, FVN and MVN, are probably appropriate only for hedging short-term instruments with short-term futures contracts. The conversion factor model is essentially a naive model applicable to futures contracts with the structure of T-note or T-bond futures contracts.

The most widely used technique is some version of the PS model, although the regression model also is often employed. In fact, it has been shown that the PS and RGR models are equivalent when the hedging horizon is instantaneous.[15] Because of problems in acquiring data for the RGR model, the PS model appears to be preferred.

In a number of papers, Joanne Hill and Thomas Schneeweis find that the RGR model is an effective hedging tool.[16] However, D. Lasser finds the RGR model to perform no better than various naive models.[17] Raymond Chiang, Gerald Gay, and Robert Kolb find that the PS model is more effective than naive models in hedging the risk of corporate bonds.[18] A. Toevs and D. Jacob offer a useful comparison of a number of hedging strategies, including the naive models and the RGR model, in which they find the PS model to be the most effective.[19] Finally, Ira Kawaller argues that the RGR approach is inferior to the BP or PS approaches to hedging.[20] Table 6.23 summarizes the various approaches to hedging.

Immunization with Interest Rate Futures

In bond investing, duration mismatches result in exposure to interest rate risk. For example, a financial institution such as a bank or savings and loan association might have an asset portfolio with a duration greater than its liability portfolio. A sudden rise in interest rates will cause the value of the assets to fall more than the value of the liability portfolio. As another type of risk, a bond portfolio might be managed to a certain future date, perhaps when a firm's pension liabilities become due. If the duration of the bond portfolio exceeds the time until the horizon date, a swing in interest rates will cause the present value of the bond portfolio to change more than the present value of the liabilities, leaving the entire bond portfolio/pension plan exposed to interest rate risk. By matching the duration of the assets and liabilities, it is possible for the financial institution to immunize itself against interest rate risk, which we call the Bank Immunization Case. For the bond portfolio being managed to a horizon date, a similar immunization can be achieved by setting the duration of a bond portfolio equal to the length of the planning period. We call this the Planning Period Case.[21]

Often such immunization is very difficult to achieve. For example, banks cannot simply turn away depositors because they wish to lengthen the duration of their liabilities. With the development of interest rate futures markets, financial managers have a valuable new tool to use in immunization strategies. This section presents two examples of immunizing with interest rate futures, one for the Planning Period Case and one for the Bank Immunization Case. Table 6.24 presents data on three

Table 6.23	Summary of Alternative Hedging Strategies
Hedging Model	**Basic Intuition**
Face Value Naive (FVN)	Hedge $1 of cash instrument face value with $1 of futures instrument face value.
Market Value Naive (MVN)	Hedge $1 of cash instrument market value with $1 of futures instrument market value.
Conversion Factor (CF)	Find ratio of cash market principal to futures market principal. Multiply this ratio by the conversion factor for the cheapest-to-deliver instrument.
Basis Point (BP)	For a 1 basis point yield change, find the ratio of the cash market price change to the futures market price change. (Sometimes weighted by the relative volatility of interest rates on the cash market instrument compared to the futures instrument interest rate.)
Regression (RGR)	For a given cash market position, use regression analysis to find the futures position that minimizes the variance of the combined cash/futures position.
Price Sensitivity (PS)	Using duration analysis, find the futures market position designed to give a zero wealth change at the hedging horizon. (Sometimes weighted by the relative volatility of interest rates on the cash market instrument compared to the futures instrument interest rate.)

Table 6.24	Instruments for the Immunization Analysis				
	Coupon	**Maturity**	**Yield**	**Price**	**Duration**
Bond A	8%	4 yrs.	12%	885.59	3.475
Bond B	10%	10 yrs.	12%	903.47	6.265
Bond C	4%	15 yrs.	12%	463.05	9.285
T-Bond Futures*	8%	20 yrs.	12%	718.75	8.674
T-Bill Futures*	–	¼ yr.	12%	972.07	.25

*For comparability, face values of $1,000 are assumed for these instruments.

bonds we will use in the immunization examples, along with data for T-bill and T-bond futures contracts. The table reflects the assumption of a flat yield curve and instruments of the same risk level.

The Planning Period Case. Consider a $100 million bond portfolio of Bond C with a duration of 9.285 years. Assume now that a manager wants to shorten the portfolio duration to six years to match a given planning period. The shortening could be accomplished by selling Bond C and buying Bond A until the following conditions are met:

$$W_A D_A + W_C D_C = 6 \text{ years}$$
$$W_A + W_C = 1 \text{ year}$$

where W_I = percent of portfolio funds committed to asset I. This means that the manager must put 56.54 percent of the $100 million in Bond A, the funds coming from the sale of Bond C. Call this Portfolio 1.

Alternatively, the manager could adjust the portfolio's duration to match the six-year planning period by trading interest rate futures. In Portfolio 2, the manager will keep $100,000,000 in Bond C and trade futures to adjust the duration of the combined portfolio of Bond C and futures. If Bond C and T-bill futures comprise Portfolio 2, the T-bill futures position must satisfy the condition:

$$P_P = P_C N_C + FP_{\text{T-bill}} N_{\text{T-bill}}$$

where:

$$P_P = \text{value of the portfolio}$$
$$P_C = \text{price of Bond C}$$
$$FP_{\text{T-bill}} = \text{T-bill futures price}$$
$$N_C = \text{number of C bonds}$$
$$N_{\text{T-bill}} = \text{number of T-bills}$$

Equation 6.10 expresses the change in the price of a bond as a function of duration and the yield on the asset:

$$dP = -D\left(\frac{d(1+r)}{(1+r)}\right)P \tag{6.10}$$

Applying Equation 6.10 to the portfolio value, Bond C, and the T-bill futures we have the following immunization condition:

$$-D_P\left(\frac{d(1+r)}{(1+r)}\right)P_P = -D_c\left(\frac{d(1+r)}{(1+r)}\right)P_C N_c + -D_{\text{T-bill}}\left(\frac{d(1+r)}{(1+r)}\right)FP_{\text{T-bill}} N_{\text{T-bill}}$$

This can be simplified to:

$$D_P P_P = D_C P_C N_C + D_{\text{T-bill}} FP_{\text{T-bill}} N_{\text{T-bill}}$$

Because immunization requires mimicking Portfolio 1, which has a total value of $100,000,000 and a duration of six years, it must be that:

$$P_P = \$100,000,000$$
$$D_P = 6$$
$$D_C = 9.285$$
$$P_C = \$463.05$$
$$N_C = 215,959$$
$$D_{\text{T-bill}} = .25$$
$$FP_{\text{T-bill}} = \$972.07$$

Solving for $N_{\text{T-bill}} = -1,351,747$ indicates that this many T-bills (assuming \$1,000 par value) must be sold short in the futures market. Because a T-bill futures contract has a \$1,000,000 face value, this technique requires selling 1,352 contracts. The same technique used to create Portfolio 2 can be applied using a T-bond futures contract, giving rise to Portfolio 3. Solving:

$$D_P P_P = D_C P_C N_C + D_{\text{T-bond}} FP_{\text{T-bond}} N_{\text{T-bond}}$$

for $N_{\text{T-bond}}$ gives $N_{\text{T-bond}} = -52,691$. Since T-bond futures contracts have a face value denomination of \$100,000, the trader must sell 527 T-bond futures contracts. For each of the three portfolios, Table 6.25 summarizes the relevant data.

Table 6.25		Portfolio Characteristics for the Planning Period Case		
		Portfolio 1 (Bonds Only)	Portfolio 2 (Short T-Bill Fut.)	Portfolio 3 (Short T-Bond Fut.)
Portfolio Weights	W_A	56.54%	–	–
	W_C	43.46%	100%	100%
	W_{Cash}	~0	~0	~0
Number of Instruments	N_A	63,844	0	–
	N_C	93,856	215,959	215,959
	$N_{\text{T-bill}}$	–	(1,351,747)	–
	$N_{\text{T-bond}}$	–	–	(52,691)
Value of Each Instrument	$N_A P_A$	56,539,608	–	–
	$N_C P_C$	43,460,021	99,999,815	99,999,815
	$N_{\text{T-bill}} FP_{\text{T-bill}}$	–	1,313,992,706	–
	$N_{\text{T-bond}} FP_{\text{T-bill}}$	–	–	37,871,656
	Cash	371	185	185
Portfolio Value	$N_A P_A +$ $N_C P_C +$ Cash	100,000,000	100,000,000	100,000,000

Source: From R. Kolb and G. Gay, "Immunizing Bond Portfolios with Interest Rate Futures," *Financial Management*, Summer 1982, pp. 81–89. Reprinted by permission of the Financial Management Association, College of Business Administration #3331, University of South Florida, Tampa, FL 33620-5500, tel. (813) 974-2084.

To see how the immunized portfolio performs, assume that rates drop from 12 to 11 percent for all maturities. Assume also that all coupon receipts during the six-year planning period can be reinvested at 11 percent until the end of the planning period. With the shift in interest rates the new prices are:

$$P_A = \$913.57$$
$$P_C = \$504.33$$
$$FP_{\text{T-bill}} = \$974.25$$
$$FP_{\text{T-bond}} = \$778.13$$

Table 6.26 shows the effect of the interest rate shift on portfolio values, terminal wealth at the horizon (year 6), and on the total wealth position of the portfolio holder. As Table 6.26 reveals, each portfolio responds similarly to the shift in yields. The slight differences are due to either rounding errors or the fact that the duration price change formula holds exactly only for infinitesimal changes in yields. The largest difference (between terminal values for Portfolios 1 and 2) is only .29 percent, which reveals the effectiveness of the alternative strategies.

The Bank Immunization Case. Assume that a bank holds a $100,000,000 liability portfolio in Bond B, the composition of which is fixed. The bank wishes to hold an asset portfolio of Bonds A and C that will protect the wealth position of the bank from any change as a result of a change in yields.

Five different portfolio combinations illustrate different means to achieve the desired result:

Portfolio 1:	Hold Bond A and Bond C (the traditional approach)
Portfolio 2:	Hold Bond C; Sell T-bill futures
Portfolio 3:	Hold Bond A; Buy T-bond futures
Portfolio 4:	Hold Bond A; Buy T-bill futures
Portfolio 5:	Hold Bond C; Sell T-bond futures

Effect of a 1% Drop in Yields on Realized Portfolio Returns			Table 6.26
	Portfolio 1	**Portfolio 2**	**Portfolio 3**
Original Portfolio Value	100,000,000	100,000,000	100,000,000
New Portfolio Value	105,660,731	108,914,787	108,914,787
Gain/Loss on Futures	–0–	(2,946,808)	(3,128,792)
Total Wealth Change	5,660,731	5,967,979	5,785,995
Terminal Value of all Funds at $t = 6$	197,629,369	198,204,050	197,863,664
Annualized Holding Period Return over 6 Years	1.120234	1.120776	1.120455

Source: From R. Kolb and G. Gay, "Immunizing Bond Portfolios with Interest Rate Futures," *Financial Management*, Summer 1982, pp. 81–89. Reprinted by permission of the Financial Management Association, College of Business Administration #3331, University of South Florida, Tampa, FL 33620-5500, tel. (813) 974-2084.

For each portfolio in Table 6.27, the full $100,000,000 is put in a bond portfolio (and is balanced out by cash). Portfolio 1 exemplifies the traditional approach of immunizing by holding only bonds. Portfolios 2 and 5 are composed of Bond C and a short futures position. By contrast, the low volatility Bond A is held in Portfolios 3 and 4. In conjunction with Bond A, the overall interest rate sensitivity is increased by buying interest rate futures.

Now assume an instantaneous drop in rates from 12 to 11 percent for all maturities. Table 6.28 shows the effect of the 1 percent drop on the portfolios. As the rows reporting wealth change reveal, all five methods perform similarly. The small differences stem from rounding errors and the discrete change in interest rates.

One important concern in the implementation of immunization strategies is the transaction cost involved. In immunizing, commission charges, marketability, and liquidity of the instruments involved become increasingly important. These considerations highlight the practical usefulness of interest rate futures in bond portfolio management. Consider as an example the transaction costs associated with the different immunization portfolios for the Planning Period Case. Starting from the initial position of $100,000,000 in Bond C, and shortening the duration to six years, Table 6.29 shows the trades necessary and the estimated costs involved. To implement the ''bonds only'' traditional approach of Portfolio 1, one must sell 122,103 bonds of type C and buy 63,844 bonds of type A. Assuming a commission charge of $5 per bond, the total commission is $929,735. By contrast one could sell 1,352 T-bill futures contracts to immunize Portfolio 2, or sell 527 T-bond futures contracts for Portfolio 3, at total costs of $27,040 and $10,540, respectively. (Additionally one would have to deposit approximately $2,000,000 margin for the T-bill strategy or $800,000 for the T-bond strategy. But this margin deposit can be in the form of interest earning assets.) Table 6.29 presents these transaction costs calculations.

Clearly there is a tremendous difference in transaction costs between trading the cash and futures instruments. In an extreme example of this type, the transaction costs for the ''bonds only'' case is prohibitive, amounting to almost 1 percent of the total portfolio value. It is practically impossible for another reason: the volume of bonds to be traded is enormous, exceeding any reasonable volume for bonds of even the largest issue. The superior marketability and liquidity of the futures market is clearly evident. The 1,352 T-bill futures contracts are a small percentage of the daily volume or recent open interest. Likewise, the 527 T-bond futures constitute only a trivial fraction of the volume and open interest in that market. The evident ability of the futures market to absorb the kind of activity involved in this example demonstrates the practical usefulness of interest rate futures in managing bond portfolios.[22]

Until recently, immunization strategies for bond portfolios have focused on all bond portfolios. Here it has been shown that interest rate futures can be used in conjunction with bond portfolios to provide the same kind of immunization. The method advocated here works equally well for the Planning Period Case and the Bank Immunization Case. Note that all of the examples assumed parallel shifting yield curves. If the change in interest rates brings about nonparallel shifts in the yield curve, then the ''bonds only'' and ''bonds-with-futures'' approaches will give different results. Which method turns out to be superior would depend upon the pattern of interest rate changes that actually occurred.

CONCLUSION

Interest rate futures constitute one of the most exciting and complex financial markets. Only in recent years have the uses of the market begun to mature, and there remain many potential users who could

Liability Portfolio and Five Alternative Immunizing Portfolios — Table 6.27

		Liability Portfolio	Portfolio 1 (Bonds Only)	Portfolio 2 (Short T-Bill Futures)	Portfolio 3 (Long T-Bond Futures)	Portfolio 4 (Long T-Bill Futures)	Portfolio 5 (Short T-Bond Futures)
Portfolio Weights	W_A	0	51.98%	0	100%	100%	0
	W_B	100%	0	0	0	0	0
	W_C	0	48.02%	100%	0	0	100%
	W_{Cash}	~0	~0	~0	~0	~0	~0
Number of Instruments	N_A	0	58,695	0	112,919	112,919	0
	N_B	110,684	0	0	0	0	0
	N_C	0	103,704	215,959	0	0	215,959
	$N_{T\text{-}bill}$	0	0	(1,242,710)	0	1,148,058	0
	$N_{T\text{-}bond}$	0	0	0	44,751	0	(48,441)
	$N_A P_A$	0	51,979,705	0	99,999,937	99,999,937	0
	$N_B P_B$	99,999,673	0	0	0	0	0
	$N_C P_C$	0	48,020,137	99,999,815	0	0	99,999,815
	Cash	327	158	185	63	63	185
	$N_{T\text{-}bill}P_{T\text{-}bill}$	0	0	(1,208,001,110)	0	1,115,992,740	0
	$N_{T\text{-}bond}P_{T\text{-}bond}$	0	0	0	32,164,781	0	(34,816,969)
Portfolio Value		100,000,000	100,000,000	100,000,000	100,000,000	100,000,000	100,000,000

Source: From R. Kolb and G. Gay, "Immunizing Bond Portfolios with Interest Rate Futures," *Financial Management*, Summer 1982, pp. 81–89. Reprinted by permission of the Financial Management Association, College of Business Administration #3331, University of South Florida, Tampa, FL 33620-5500, tel. (813) 974-2084.

	Liability	Portfolio 1	Portfolio 2	Portfolio 3	Portfolio 4	Portfolio 5
Effect of a 1% Drop in Yields on Total Wealth						**Table 6.28**
Original Port. Value	100,000,000	100,000,000	100,000,000	100,000,000	100,000,000	100,000,000
New Port. Value	105,910,526	105,923,188	108,914,788	103,159,474	103,159,474	108,914,788
Profit on Futures	0	—	(2,709,108)	2,657,314	2,502,766	(2,876,427)
Total Wealth Change (Port. and Futures)	5,910,526	5,923,188	6,205,680	5,816,788	5,662,240	6,038,361
Total Wealth Change (Asset-Liability Port.)	—	12,622	295,154	(93,738)	(248,286)	127,835
% Wealth Change	—	.00013	.00295	(.00094)	(.00248)	.00128

Source: From R. Kolb and G. Gay, "Immunizing Bond Portfolios with Interest Rate Futures," *Financial Management*, Summer 1982, pp. 81–89. Reprinted by permission of the Financial Management Association, College of Business Administration #3331, University of South Florida, Tampa, FL 33620-5500, tel. (813) 974-2084.

Transaction Costs for the Planning Period Case		Table 6.29	
	Portfolio 1	Portfolio 2	Portfolio 3
Number of Instruments Traded			
Bond A	63,844	–	–
Bond C	(122,103)	–	–
T-Bill Futures Contracts	–	1,352	–
T-Bond Futures Contracts	–	–	527
One Way Transaction Cost			
Bond A @ $5	319,220	–	–
Bond C @ $5	610,515	–	–
T-Bill Futures $20	–	27,040	–
T-Bond Futures @ $20	–	–	10,540
Total Cost of Becoming Immunized	$929,735	$27,040	$10,540

Source: From R. Kolb and G. Gay, "Immunizing Bond Portfolios with Interest Rate Futures," *Financial Management*, Summer 1982, pp. 81–89. Reprinted by permission of the Financial Management Association, College of Business Administration #3331, University of South Florida, Tampa, FL 33620-5500, tel. (813) 974-2084.

benefit from the market. As we have seen, interest rate futures have many applications, including bond portfolio management. Interest rate futures can also be used to control foreign interest rate risk, to manage public utilities and insurance companies, to hedge mortgage financing risk, and to reduce risk in creative financing arrangements. Other uses abound and are just starting to be explored.

QUESTIONS AND PROBLEMS

Assume today is January 30, 1997. You are considering two bonds as potential bonds for delivery against the JUN 97 T-bond futures contract, which settled at 102-08. First is the $7\frac{1}{4}$ bond that matures on May 15, 2021. Second, you might deliver the $13\frac{1}{4}$ bond that matures on May 15, 2019, but is callable on May 15, 2014. Use this information for Questions 1–8.

1. Using the facts outlined above, find the conversion factors for the two bonds for the JUN 97 futures contract.
2. On January 30, 1997, what is the accrued interest on each bond?
3. Consider a position day of June 15, 1997. What is the accrued interest on each bond?
4. Assuming the settlement price on position day (June 15, 1997) is 114-00, find the invoice amounts for both bonds.
5. The $7\frac{1}{4}$ bond trades for 85-00 and the $13\frac{1}{4}$ is at 137-00. Which bond do you expect to be cheaper to deliver? (Assume a financing rate of 8 percent.)
6. Assume that between now (January 30, 1997) and delivery on June 15, 1997, that you can finance a cash-and-carry transaction at 8 percent. This is your borrowing and lending rate. Further assume that you have full use of all short sale proceeds. Find all possible arbitrage strategies.

7. Find the implied repo rates for both bonds.

8. Continue to assume that you can borrow and lend at 8 percent. However, now you can use only 90 percent of any short sale proceeds on a reverse cash-and-carry strategy. How does this change your trading strategy, if at all?

9. Explain the risks inherent in a reverse cash-and-carry strategy in the T-bond futures market.

10. Explain how the concepts of quasi-arbitrage help to overcome the risks inherent in reverse cash-and-carry trading in T-bond futures.

11. Assume economic and political conditions are extremely turbulent. How would this affect the value of the seller's options on the T-bond futures contract? If they have any effect on price, would they cause the futures price to be higher or lower than it otherwise would be?

12. Explain the difference between the wildcard option and the end-of-the-month option.

13. Some studies find that interest rate futures markets were not very efficient when they first began but that they became efficient after a few years. How can you explain this transition?

14. Assume you hold a T-bill that matures in 90 days, when the T-bill futures expires. Explain how you could transact to effectively lengthen the maturity of the bill.

15. Assume that you will borrow on a short-term loan in six months, but you do not know whether you will be offered a fixed rate or a floating rate loan. Explain how you can use futures to convert a fixed to a floating rate loan and to convert a floating rate to a fixed rate loan.

16. You fear that the yield curve may change shape. Explain how this belief would affect your preference for a strip or a stack hedge.

17. A futures guru says that tailing a hedge is extremely important because it can change the desired number of contracts by 30 percent. Explain why the guru is nuts. How much can the tailing factor reasonably change the hedge ratio?

18. We have seen in Chapter 4 that regression-based hedging strategies are extremely popular. Explain their weaknesses for interest rate futures hedging.

19. You estimate that the cheapest-to-deliver bond on the T-bond futures contract has a duration of 6.5 years. You want to hedge your medium-term Treasury portfolio that has a duration of 4.0 years. Yields are 9.5 percent on the futures and on your portfolio. Your portfolio is worth $120,000,000, and the futures price is 98-04. Using the PS model, how would you hedge?

20. Explain the relationship between the Bank Immunization Case and hedging with the PS model.

21. Compare and contrast the BP model and the RGR model for immunizing a bond portfolio.

NOTES

[1] We ignore the differences between the three day settlement process in futures markets and the one day settlement procedures common in the cash market.

[2] G. Gay and S. Manaster, "Implicit Delivery Options and Optimal Delivery Strategies for Financial Futures Contracts," *Journal of Financial Economics,* 16:1, May 1986, pp. 41–72.

[3] See R. Rendleman and C. Carabini, "The Efficiency of the Treasury Bill Futures Market," *Journal of Finance,* 34:4, 1979, pp. 895–914. In this article, they develop the idea of quasi-arbitrage.

[4] See R. Kolb, G. Gay, and J. Jordan, "Are There Arbitrage Opportunities in the Treasury-Bond Futures Market?" *Journal of Futures Markets,* 2:3, Fall 1982, pp. 217–30.

[5] B. Resnick and E. Hennigar, "The Relationship Between Futures and Cash Prices for U.S. Treasury Bonds," *Review of Research in Futures Markets,* 2:3, 1983, pp. 282–99.

[6] B. Resnick, "The Relationship Between Futures Prices for U.S. Treasury Bonds," *Review of Research in Futures Markets,* 3:1, 1984, pp. 88–104.

[7] R. Klemkosky and D. Lasser, "An Efficiency Analysis of the T-Bond Futures Market," *Journal of Futures Markets,* 5:4, Winter 1985, pp. 607–20. Quoted material is from page 620.

[8] D. Chance, "A Semi-Strong Form Test of the Efficiency of the Treasury Bond Futures Market," *Journal of Futures Markets,* Fall 1985, 5:3, pp. 385–405.

[9] We ignore the daily resettlement feature and the interest that could have been earned on the $125,000 futures profit in the second quarter.

[10] Strictly speaking, it is the discount factor from the hedging horizon to the present plus one day. For example, the hedge was initiated with 91 days to the horizon, the cash flow was generated on that day and became available for investment with 90 days to run until the hedging horizon.

[11] For more on tailing, see I. Kawaller, "Hedging with Futures Contracts: Going the Extra Mile," *Journal of Cash Management,* July-August 1986, pp. 34–36, and I. Kawaller and T. Koch, "Managing Cash Flow Risk in Stock Index Futures: The Tail Hedge," *Journal of Portfolio Management,* 15:1, Fall 1988, pp. 41–44.

[12] See L. Ederington, "The Hedging Performance of the New Futures Market," *Journal of Finance,* 34:1, March 1979, pp. 157–70; C. Franckle, "The Hedging Performance of the New Futures Market: Comment," *Journal of Finance,* 35:5, December 1980, pp. 1272–79; and J. Hill and T. Schneeweis, "Risk Reduction Potential of Financial Futures," in G. Gay and R. Kolb, *Interest Rate Futures: A Comprehensive Introduction,* Richmond, VA: Robert F. Dame, 1982, pp. 307–24.

[13] The dependence of the RGR hedge ratio on the planned length of the hedging period was proven by C. Franckle, "The Hedging Performance of the New Futures Market: Comment," *Journal of Finance,* 35:5, December 1980, pp. 1272–79.

[14] See R. Kolb and R. Chiang, "Improving Hedging Performance Using Interest Rate Futures," *Financial Management,* 10:4, 1981, pp. 72–79; and "Duration, Immunization, and Hedging with Interest Rate Futures," *Journal of Financial Research,* 10:4, Autumn 1982, pp. 161–70.

[15] A. Toevs and D. Jacob, "Futures and Alternative Hedge Ratio Methodologies," *Journal of Portfolio Management,* 12:3, Spring 1986, pp. 60–70.

[16] For an example, see J. Hill and T. Schneeweis, "Risk Reduction Potential of Financial Futures," in G. Gay and R. Kolb, *Interest Rate Futures: Concepts and Issues,* Englewood Cliffs, NJ: Prentice Hall, 1982, pp. 307–24.

[17] D. Lasser, "A Measure of Ex-Ante Hedging Effectiveness for the Treasury-Bill and Treasury-Bond Futures Markets," working paper.

[18] R. Chiang, G. Gay, and R. Kolb, "Interest Rate Hedging: An Empirical Test of Alternative Strategies," *Journal of Financial Research,* 6:3, Fall 1983, pp. 187–97.

[19] A. Toevs and D. Jacob, "Futures and Alternative Hedge Ratio Methodologies," *Journal of Portfolio Management,* 12:3, Spring 1986, pp. 60–70.

[20] See I. G. Kawaller, "Choosing the Best Interest Rate Hedge Ratio," *Financial Analysts Journal,* 48:5, September/October 1992, pp. 74–77.

[21] For a more complete explanation of bank immunization and planning period immunization, see R. Kolb, *Investments,* 4e, Miami: Kolb Publishing, 1995.

[22] This discussion of immunization with futures draws upon G. Gay and R. Kolb, ''Immunizing Bond Portfolios with Interest Rate Futures,'' *Financial Management,* 11:2, Summer 1982, pp. 81–89.

STOCK INDEX FUTURES: INTRODUCTION

OVERVIEW

Everyone who follows the financial news hears predictions about the future of the stock market. Usually these predictions refer to the future movement of some stock market index. With the advent of stock index futures trading in 1982, these pundits can now trade to take advantage of their insights. (Perhaps they should be required to do so.) In addition to providing a chance to speculate, stock index futures also have a role in hedging various kinds of portfolio risk.

Currently, dramatic changes in stock index futures are under way. Previously successful contracts have greatly diminished importance, while new contracts begin to gain ascendancy. This chapter begins our exploration of stock index futures and the indexes upon which they are based. We focus on four stock market indexes and the futures contracts that are based on them. These indexes are: the Major Market Index (MMI), the Standard and Poor's 500 (S&P 500), the New York Stock Exchange (NYSE) index, and the Nikkei index. Several other contracts trade inactively, so this chapter considers only these four most important indexes.[1]

Successful trading of the index contracts requires a thorough understanding of the construction of the indexes. When the differences and interrelationships among the indexes are understood, it is easier to understand the differences among the futures contracts that are based on those indexes. The differences among the indexes should not be exaggerated, however. The kinds of risk and the expected changes in the levels of the indexes are predicted by the **Capital Asset Pricing Model** (CAPM). The CAPM expresses the relationship between the returns of individual stocks and partially diversified portfolios, on the one hand, and the broad indexes on the other.

As is the case with all futures contracts, the exact construction of the contracts is very important for the trader. No-arbitrage conditions constrain the possible deviations between the price of the futures contract and the level of the underlying index. Cash-and-carry strategies keep the futures price from being too high relative to the price of the stock market index. Similarly, the availability of reverse cash-and-carry strategies keeps the futures price from being too low relative to stock prices. In other words, potential arbitrage strategies constrain the basis for stock index futures as these strategies do for other types of futures contracts.

THE FOUR INDEXES

The four indexes, the Major Market Index, the Standard and Poor's 500, the New York Stock Exchange Composite index, and the Nikkei index, are familiar names, but few people are actually acquainted with how these indexes are computed. For an understanding of stock index futures, however, a thorough knowledge of the indexes is indispensable. In general, stock market indexes can be value weighted or price weighted. In a **value weighted index**, each stock in the index affects the index value in proportion to the market value of all shares outstanding, while a **price weighted index** is one that gives a weight to each stock that is proportional to its stock price. In a value weighted index, IBM and Microsoft would have roughly equal weights, because their market values are similar. By contrast, in a price weighted index a small capitalization firm could have a much higher weight than a much larger firm if the small capitalization firm had a high stock price but relatively few outstanding shares. Of the indexes we consider, the MMI and Nikkei indexes are price weighted, while the S&P 500 and NYSE indexes are value weighted.

All four indexes exclude dividends, which means that the indexes do not reflect the full appreciation that the market has enjoyed over any given period. The omission of dividends is very important for understanding the pricing of the futures contracts as well. As we will see in our discussion of pricing, the presence of dividends is a major factor.

The Major Market Index

In the early 1980s, the Chicago Board of Trade attempted to launch a futures contract based on the most famous of all stock market indexes – the **Dow Jones Industrial Average** (DJIA). After prolonged legal maneuvering, Dow Jones succeeded in preventing the futures contract from trading. In response, the American Stock Exchange created the Major Market Index (MMI) and licensed the index to the CBOT to provide the underlying index for a futures contract. Starting in the fall of 1993, the American Stock Exchange licensed the MMI to the Chicago Mercantile Exchange, and MMI stock index futures now trade on the CME.

The MMI consists of 20 stocks chosen so that the MMI behaves as much as possible like the DJIA, which consists of 30 stocks. In fact, most MMI stocks are also included in the DJIA, as Table 7.1 shows. The MMI is computed by adding the share prices of the 20 stocks comprising the index and dividing by the MMI divisor. Similarly, the DJIA is computed by adding the prices of the 30 represented shares and dividing by the Dow Jones divisor. For both indexes, the divisor is used to adjust for stock splits, mergers, stock dividends, and changes in the stocks included in the index. The MMI is constructed so that the MMI value is about one-fifth of the DJIA.

For both the MMI and the DJIA, the index can be computed according to the following formula:

$$\text{Index} = \frac{\sum_{i=1}^{N} P_i}{\text{Divisor}} \qquad (7.1)$$

where:

P_i = price of stock I

	Comparison of the Major Market Index and the Dow Jones Industrial Average	Table 7.1

	Included in	
Firm	**Major Market Index**	**Dow Jones Industrial Average**
Allied Signal		X
Alcoa		X
American Express	X	X
AT&T	X	X
Bethlehem Steel		X
Boeing		X
Caterpillar		X
Chevron	X	X
Coca-Cola	X	X
Disney	X	X
Dow Chemical	X	
DuPont	X	X
Eastman Kodak	X	X
Exxon	X	X
General Electric	X	X
General Motors	X	X
Goodyear		X
IBM	X	X
International Paper	X	X
Johnson & Johnson	X	
McDonald's	X	X
Merck	X	X
Minnesota Mining, Mfg.	X	X
J.P. Morgan		X
Philip Morris	X	X
Procter & Gamble	X	X
Sears Roebuck	X	X
Texaco		X
Union Carbide		X
United Technologies		X
Westinghouse		X
Woolworth		X

Because the indexes depend on the number of dollars from summing all the prices, the MMI and DJIA do not reflect the percentage change in the price of a share. For example, consider a stock that doubles from $1 to $2, and contrast this price change with a stock that moves from $100 to $101. In the first case, a stock has increased 100 percent, while in the latter case, a stock has increased just 1 percent. For the MMI and the DJIA, both stock price changes have the same effect on the index, because the index depends on the sum of the prices, not the percentage price changes of the individual stocks.

Both the MMI and DJIA use a divisor to compute the index value. The divisors used in computing the indexes are designed to keep the index value from changing due to stock splits or stock dividends or due to a substitution of one stock for another in the index. To see how the divisor functions, assume that Dow Jones decides to delete Navistar International from the index and replace it with Dow Chemical. We also assume that Navistar is priced at 6.00, Dow Chemical trades at 47.00, and the current value of the index is 1900.31, with a divisor of .889. Assuming that the sum of the 30 stock prices is $1,689.375, the substitution of Dow for Navistar will generate a new total of prices of $1,730.375, which equals the old sum ($1,689.375) plus the current price of the new stock ($47) minus the current price of the deleted stock ($6). If the divisor is not changed, the new index value will be 1946.43. Thus, the substitution of one stock for another, with no change in the divisor, manufactures a jump in the DJIA of 46 points. Obviously, this cannot be permitted or the index will become meaningless as a barometer of stock prices.

For the index to reflect the level of prices in the market accurately, simply substituting one stock for another should not change the index. The same principle holds for stock dividends and stock splits. Therefore, the divisor must change to accommodate the change in stocks or the stock dividend or the stock split. In our example of substituting Dow Chemical for Navistar, the divisor must change to maintain a constant index value of 1900.31 with the new total of prices of 1730.375. Therefore, the new divisor must satisfy the following equation:

$$1900.31 = \frac{1730.375}{\text{New Divisor}}$$

$$\text{New Divisor} = \frac{1730.375}{1900.31} = .9106$$

Thus, to keep the index value unchanged, the new divisor must be .9106. Generalizing from this example, we see that Equation 7.2 gives the value for the new divisor:

$$\text{New Divisor} = \frac{\text{New Sum of Prices}}{\text{Index Value Before Substitution}} \qquad (7.2)$$

To find the new divisor, compute the new sum of prices that results from substituting one firm for another. Then divide this sum by the original index value.

The Nikkei Index

The Nikkei index is a price weighted index like the MMI. It is the most widely followed and quoted index for the Japanese stock market, and it includes 225 of the largest Japanese firms, including Sony, Fuji Photo Film, Honda, Toyota, Yamaha, NEC, Citizen Watch, and Nippon Telephone and Telegraph. Membership in the 225 stocks occurs only due to special events such as mergers and liquidations. In the 1980s, there were only eight substitutions.

Shares in the Japanese stock market are classified as First Section or Second Section. Stocks in the First Section are the larger and more important firms in the economy, and all Nikkei shares are in the first section. The Nikkei index had a spectacular run-up during the last half of the 1980s, and a serious fall in the early 1990s. In 1980 the Nikkei stood at about 12,000 and increased to over 38,000 by 1990. From 1990 through 1992, it fell dramatically and stood at about 18,000 by the end of 1993. It recovered to the 20,000 range by 1996.

The S&P 500 Index

Of the four indexes, the S&P 500 index is the most widely used in the U.S. finance industry. For example, many managers are judged by comparing the performance of their portfolios to the performance of the S&P 500. The index is based on 500 firms which come from various industries and most of which are listed on the New York Stock Exchange.[2] Together, these 500 firms comprise approximately 80 percent of the total value of the stocks listed on the New York Stock Exchange.

Each of the stocks in the index has a different weight in the calculation of the index, and the weight is proportional to the total market value of the stock (the price per share times the number of shares outstanding). Therefore, the S&P 500 index is a value weighted index. This contrasts with the composition of the MMI, the DJIA, and the Nikkei which assign equal weight to each stock price. The value of the S&P 500 index is reported relative to the average value during the period of 1941–1943, which was assigned an index value of 10. As a simplified example of the way the index is computed, assume that the index consists of only three securities, ABC, DEF, and GHI. Table 7.2 shows how the value of the three firms would be weighted to calculate the index. For each stock, the total market value of the outstanding shares is computed. In the table, the three firms' shares have a total value of $19,000. If the value in the 1941–1943 period had been $2,000, the current level of the index would be calculated as shown in the table, where X is the current index level with a value of 95.00. Mathematically, the calculation of the index is given by:

| | Calculation of S&P 500 | | | Table 7.2 |

	Outstanding Shares		Price		Value
Company ABC	100	×	$50	=	$ 5,000
Company DEF	300	×	40	=	12,000
Company GHI	200	×	10	=	2,000
	Current Market Valuation			=	$19,000

If the 1941–43 value were $2,000, then $19,000 is to $2,000 as X is to 10.

$$\frac{\text{Current Market Valuation}}{\text{1941–43 Market Valuation}} = \frac{\$19,000}{\$2,000} = \frac{X}{10}$$

$$\$190,000 = \$2,000X$$
$$95.00 = X$$

$$\text{S\&P Index}_t = \left(\frac{\sum_{i=1}^{500} N_{i,t} P_{i,t}}{\text{O.V.}} \right) 10 \qquad (7.3)$$

where:

> O.V. = original valuation in 1941–43
> $N_{i,t}$ = number of shares outstanding for firm i
> $P_{i,t}$ = price of shares in firm i

The weights of each firm change as their prices rise and fall relative to other firms represented in the index. Firms such as Exxon, AT&T, and IBM represent large shares of the index, while other firms have only a minuscule impact. The index is computed on a continuous basis during the trading day and reported to the public. There is considerable variability in the performance of the index over time, even though it is a large portfolio of the very largest and most stable firms. As we will see in the next chapter, recent developments in the stock index futures market have given new importance to the volatility of stock market indexes.

The New York Stock Exchange Composite Index

The New York Stock Exchange Composite index is broader than the S&P 500, since it includes all of the approximately 1,700 stocks listed on the New York Stock Exchange. The largest 50 companies account for about 40 percent of the value of the NYSE capitalization.

The weight of each stock in the index is proportional to its value, just as is the case with the S&P 500 index. Therefore, the NYSE index is a value weighted index. The NYSE and S&P 500 indexes use a similar method to calculate the indexes. However, the NYSE Composite index takes its base date as December 31, 1965. At any subsequent point in time, the value of the NYSE index is given by:

$$\text{NYSE Index}_t = \left(\frac{\sum_{t=1}^{1720} N_{i,t} P_{i,t}}{\text{O.V.}} \right) 50.0 \qquad (7.4)$$

where:

> O.V. = original value of all shares on the NYSE as of December 31, 1965

Equation 7.4 says that the value of the NYSE index equals the current value of all shares listed on the NYSE divided by the December 1965 base value, with the result being multiplied by 50 as a simple scaling device. This gives an initial value of 50.00 for the index. By late 1974, the index stood at 32.89, was as high as 81.02 in 1980, and was about 330 in 1996.

Comparison of the Indexes

Because we will consider four futures contracts, it is important to understand the relationships among the four underlying indexes, since such knowledge is important in choosing the most appropriate contract for speculation or hedging. For hedging, the choice of an index depends on the relationship between the good being hedged and the characteristics of the index. For speculation, the volatility of the index is particularly important.

As we know from portfolio theory, the more fully diversified a portfolio is, the less unsystematic risk it should contain. With less unsystematic risk, the total risk should be lower. Based on the December 1995 futures contracts, the standard deviation of the daily percentage changes in the indexes was as follows:

MMI   .00523
Nikkei   .01621
S&P 500 .00501
NYSE   .00476

As we might expect, the more stocks in the index, the less volatile the percentage price change. Also, because big firms tend to be more stable than small firms, we would expect a value weighted index to be less volatile than an equally weighted index. Notice, however, that the Nikkei is significantly more volatile than the U.S. indexes.

In spite of differences in volatility, the correlations among the U.S. indexes are high, typically exceeding 85 percent. The correlations between the Nikkei index and the U.S. indexes is significantly lower. We might expect these results, because each index is based on a diversified portfolio. As the S&P 500 index represents about 80 percent of the value of NYSE stocks, there is an extremely high correlation between the S&P 500 and NYSE Composite indexes. The correlation between the MMI and the other two U.S. indexes is somewhat lower, reflecting the less diversified character of the MMI. Table 7.3 presents a correlation matrix of the daily percentage changes for the December 1995 futures contracts based on the four indexes. The S&P 500 and NYSE are the most closely correlated. This is due to the large number of identical stocks and the great diversification represented by these portfolios, in addition to the fact that both of these indexes are value weighted indexes. The great similarity in these indexes suggests that one index might be a good substitute for either of the other two for hedging or risk management purposes. The Nikkei is not well correlated with any U.S. index, suggesting the potential diversification benefits available from investing across the U.S. and Japanese markets.

STOCK INDEX FUTURES CONTRACTS

All four futures contracts share certain basic similarities in terms of the calculation of their value and the method by which they are settled. Table 7.4 summarizes these features. All four contracts are

Correlation of Daily Percentage Changes in Index Values			Table 7.3
	MMI	**Nikkei**	**S&P 500**	**NYSE**
MMI	1.0000	0.1185	0.8930	0.8957
Nikkei		1.0000	0.1291	0.1471
S&P 500			1.0000	0.9844
NYSE				1.0000

Table 7.4	Summary of Stock Index Futures Contracts		
Contract	**Contract Size**	**Index Composition**	**Index Weighting**
MMI	$500 × Index	20 blue-chip stocks, mostly in the DJIA	Price
Nikkei	$5 × Index	225 first section shares	Price
S&P 500	$500 × Index	500 mostly NYSE stocks	Market value
NYSE	$500 × Index	All NYSE common stocks	Market value

settled in cash, so there is no delivery in the stock index futures market, and all four contracts trade on the March, June, September, December cycle. Each futures contract has its respective index's current value multiplied by some dollar amount as the underlying contract value. For the S&P 500, the NYSE Composite, and the MMI, the multiplier is $500. For the Nikkei, the multiplier is $5. These values are set by the exchange and determine the contract size. In early 1996, the indexes and the futures contracts had the following values:

Futures	Index	Futures Contract Value
MMI	580.76	$290,380
Nikkei	20,915.44	104,577
S&P 500	650.03	325,015
NYSE	348.77	174,385

Therefore, values range widely across the four indexes and will fluctuate as market prices vary.

With the futures contracts being stated in terms of so many dollars times the value of the index, the dollar change in the futures contracts can be quite different. The relative dollar change in the different futures will depend on some factors that we have already considered, such as the different volatilities of the indexes and the correlations among the indexes. Table 7.5 presents data based on the indexes to illustrate comparative volatilities. The data in Table 7.5 are based on daily absolute changes in the December 1995 futures contract. The first line of data shows the average absolute daily change in the index values for the four indexes. To compare the dollar volatility of the futures contracts, the last two lines of Table 7.5 present the dollar changes implied for the futures. For

Table 7.5	Daily Absolute Changes in the Indexes			
	December 1995 Futures Contract			
	MMI	**Nikkei**	**S&P 500**	**NYSE**
Mean Change	1.9031	198.03	1.8115	1.0672
Standard Deviation	1.6816	190.07	1.8516	0.9398
Implied Mean Change for Futures	$951.54	$990.16	$1,055.74	$533.61
Implied Mean Standard Deviation for Futures	$840.79	$950.33	$925.80	$469.92

example, the average absolute daily change in the MMI index times the futures contract multiplier of $500 is $951.54, and the standard deviation in dollars is $840.79.

STOCK INDEX FUTURES PRICES

Figure 7.1 presents price quotations for stock index futures. The organization of the quotations is similar to those of other commodities. Like most financial futures, stock index futures essentially trade in a full carry market. Therefore, the cost-of-carry model provides a virtually complete understanding of stock index futures pricing. When the conditions of the cost-of-carry model are violated, arbitrage opportunities arise. For a cash-and-carry strategy, a trader would buy the stocks that underlie the futures contract and sell the futures. The trader would then carry these stocks until the futures

Quotations for Stock Index Futures   **Figure 7.1**

INDEX

S&P 500 INDEX (CME) $500 times index

	Open	High	Low	Settle	Chg	High	Low	Open Interest
June	652.00	655.20	650.15	655.00	+2.95	673.20	553.95	177,760
Sept	656.35	660.80	655.60	660.50	+3.00	677.80	559.70	6,070
Dec	662.70	666.00	661.40	666.00	+2.95	681.80	612.70	2,716
Mr97	668.20	671.10	667.30	671.25	+2.40	681.20	656.80	162

Est vol 65,587; vol Mn 66,748; open int 186,708, –103.
Indx prelim High 651.59; Low 647.70; Close 651.59 +3.70.

S&P MIDCAP 400 (CME) $500 times index

	Open	High	Low	Settle	Chg	High	Low	Open Interest
June	234.45	235.55	234.35	235.45	+1.00	237.90	202.45	8,538

Est vol 594; vol Mn 468; open int 8,597, +5.
The index: High 234.35; Low 232.65; Close 234.34 +1.69

NIKKEI 225 STOCK AVERAGE (CME)-$5 times index

	Open	High	Low	Settle	Chg	High	Low	Open Interest
June	22260.	22335.	22220.	22305.	+ 45	22335.	14655.	29,561
Sept	22380.	22440.	22320.	22410.	+ 50	22440.	17440.	138

Est vol 1,144; vol Mn 1,486; open int 29,724, +602.
The index: High 22216.54; Low 22104.80; Close 22119.88 –4.01

GSCI (CME)-$250 times nearby index

	Open	High	Low	Settle	Chg	High	Low	Open Interest
June	212.40	212.90	210.00	211.10	+1.40	212.90	176.40	13,690

Est vol 280; vol Mn 108; open int 13,711, +37.
The index: High 215.79; Low 212.12; Close 215.55 +3.20

CAC-40 STOCK INDEX (MATIF)-FFr 200 per index pt.

	Open	High	Low	Settle	Chg	High	Low	Open Interest
Apr	2117.0	2124.0	2109.0	2112.5	– 8.5	2124.0	1879.0	31,385
May	2107.5	2113.5	2100.0	2102.0	– 8.5	2113.5	1860.0	14,160
June	2089.0	2092.0	2079.5	2081.5	– 8.5	2092.5	1799.0	26,408
Sept	2098.0	2103.0	2098.0	2092.5	– 8.5	2103.0	1777.0	10,214
Mr97	2142.0	2142.0	2132.0	2133.5	– 9.5	2142.0	1921.0	3,035
Sept	2126.0	2126.0	2126.0	2125.5	– 9.5	2126.0	2009.5	3,435
Mr98		....	....	2184.5	– 8.5	2120.0	2115.0	700

Est vol 28,190; vol Mn 28,531; open int 89,337, +6,259.

FT-SE 100 INDEX (LIFFE)-£25 per index point

	Open	High	Low	Settle	Chg	High	Low	Open Interest
June	3851.0	3858.0	3831.0	3843.0	–21.0	3877.0	3490.0	60,076
Sept	3866.0	3866.0	3849.0	3856.0	–19.5	3876.0	3452.5	3,116

Est vol 9,927; vol Mn 8,494; open int 63,273, –1,017.

DAX-30 GERMAN STOCK INDEX (DTB)
DM 100 times index

	Open	High	Low	Settle	Chg	High	Low	Open Interest
June	2545.0	2560.0	2538.5	2552.5	+ .18	2560.0	2152.0	149,946
Sept	2563.0	2576.5	2560.0	2572.0	+ .08	2575.0	2295.5	3,988

Est vol 16,814; vol Mn 14,210; open int 154,067, –1,023.
The index: High 2555.74; Low 2538.92; Close 2549.12 –.01

ALL ORDINARIES SHARE PRICE INDEX (SFE)
A$25 times index

	Open	High	Low	Settle	Chg	High	Low	Open Interest
June	2308.0	2335.0	2303.0	2330.0	+34.0	2396.0	2068.0	78,457
Sept	2336.0	2336.0	2335.0	2358.0	+36.0	2358.0	2235.0	1,073
Dec		....	....	2370.0	+34.0	2340.0	2225.0	117
Mr97		....	....	2394.0	+34.0	2343.0	2310.0	158

Est vol 12,258; vol Mn 6,269; open int 79,805, +8,289.
The index: High na; Low na; Close na

expiration. The cash-and-carry strategy is attractive when stocks are priced too low relative to the futures. In a reverse cash-and-carry strategy, the trader would sell the stocks short and invest the proceeds, in addition to buying the futures. The reverse cash-and-carry strategy is attractive when stocks are priced too high relative to the futures. Thus, any discrepancy between the justified futures and cash market prices would lead to a profit at the expiration of the futures, simply by exploiting the appropriate strategy. From Chapter 3, the basic cost-of-carry model for a perfect market with unrestricted short selling was given by Equation 3.3:

$$F_{0,t} = S_0(1 + C) \qquad\qquad (3.3)$$

where:

$F_{0,t}$ = futures price at $t = 0$ for delivery at time t
S_0 = spot price at $t = 0$
C = the percentage cost of carrying the good from $t = 0$ to time t

The Cost-of-Carry Model for Stock Index Futures

Applying Equation 3.3 to stock index futures faces one complication – dividends. Holding the stocks gives the owner dividends; however, each of the indexes is simply a price index. The value of the index at any time depends solely on the prices of the stocks, not the dividends that the underlying stocks might pay. Because the futures prices are tied directly to the index values, the futures prices do not include dividends.

To fit stock index futures, Equation 3.3 must be adjusted to include the dividends that would be received between the present and the expiration of the futures. In essence, the chance to receive dividends lowers the cost of carrying the stocks. Carrying stocks requires that a trader finance the purchase price of the stock from the present until the futures expiration. However, the trader will receive dividends from the stock, which will reduce the value of the stocks. This contrasts directly with the cost-of-carry for holding a commodity like gold. As we have seen, gold generates no cash flows, so the cost-of-carry for gold is essentially the financing cost. For stocks, the cost-of-carry is the financing cost for the stock, less the dividends received while the stock is being carried.

As an example, assume the present is time zero and a trader decides to engage in a self-financing cash-and-carry transaction. The trader decides to buy and hold one share of Widget, Inc., currently trading for $100. Therefore, the trader borrows $100 and buys the stock. We assume that the stock will pay a $2 dividend in six months, and the trader will invest the proceeds for the remaining six months at a rate of 10 percent. Table 7.6 shows the trader's cash flows. In Table 7.6, a trader borrows funds, buys and holds a stock, receives and invests a dividend, and liquidates the portfolio after one year. At the outset, the stock costs $100, but its value in a year, P_1, is unknown. From Table 7.6, the trader's cash inflow after one year is the future value of the dividend, $2.10, plus the current value of the stock, P_1, less the repayment of the loan, $110.

From this example, we can generalize to understand the total cash inflows from a cash-and-carry strategy. First, the cash-and-carry strategy will return the future value of the stock, P_1, at the horizon of the carrying period. Second, at the end of the carrying period, the cash-and-carry strategy will return the future value of the dividends – the dividend plus interest from the time of receipt to

Cash Flows from Carrying Stock	Table 7.6

t = 0

Borrow $100 for 1 year at 10%.	+100
Buy 1 share of Widget, Inc.	−100

t = 6 months

Receive dividend of $2.	+$2
Invest $2 for 6 months at 10%.	−$2

t = 1 year

Collect proceeds of $2.10 from dividend investment	+2.10
Sell Widget, Inc., for P_1.	+P_1
Repay debt.	−110.00

Total Profit: P_1 + $2.10 − $110.00

the horizon. Against these inflows, the cash-and-carry trader must pay the financing cost for the stock purchase.

We are now in a position to determine the futures price that is consistent with the cash-and-carry strategy. From the arguments of Chapter 3, we know that Equation 3.3 holds as an equality with perfect markets and unrestricted short selling. The cash-and-carry trading opportunity requires that the futures price must be less than or equal to the cash inflows at the futures expiration. Similarly, the reverse cash-and-carry trading opportunity requires that the futures price must equal or exceed the cash inflows at the futures expiration. Therefore, the stock index futures price must equal the cost of the stocks underlying the stock index, plus the cost of carrying those stocks to expiration, $S_0(1 + C)$, minus the future value of all dividends to be received, $D_i(1 + r_i)$. The future value of dividends is measured at the time the futures contract expires. More formally:

$$F_{0,t} = S_0(1 + C) - \sum_{i=1}^{N} D_i(1 + r_i) \tag{7.5}$$

where:

$F_{0,t}$ = stock index futures price at $t = 0$ for a futures contract that expires at time t
S_0 = the value of the stocks underlying the stock index at $t = 0$
C = the percentage cost of carrying the stocks from $t = 0$ to the expiration at time t
D_i = the ith dividend
r_i = the interest earned on carrying the ith dividend from its time of receipt until the futures expiration at time t

Fair Value for Stock Index Futures

A stock index futures price has its **fair value** when the futures price fits the cost-of-carry model. In this section we consider a simplified example of determining the fair value of a stock index futures contract. We consider a futures contract on an equally weighted index, and for simplicity we assume that there are only two stocks. Table 7.7 provides the information that we will need.

Based on the data in Table 7.7, the index value is 110.56, as given by:

$$\frac{P_A + P_B}{\text{Index Divisor}} = \frac{115 + 84}{1.8} = 110.56$$

The cost of buying the stocks underlying the portfolio is simply the sum of the prices of Stocks A and B, or $199. For carrying the stocks to expiration, the interest cost will be 10 percent for 76 days or 2.11 percent. Thus, the cost of buying and carrying the stocks to expiration is $199(1.0211) = $203.20. Offsetting this cost will be the dividends received and the interest earned on the dividends. For the stocks, the future value of the dividends at expiration will be:

For Stock A: $1.50(1.0164) = $1.52
For Stock B: $1.00(1.0108) = $1.01

Therefore, the entire cost of buying the stocks and carrying them to expiration is the purchase price of the stocks plus interest, less the future value of the dividends measured at expiration:

$$\$203.20 - \$1.52 - \$1.01 = \$200.67$$

In the cost-of-carry model, we know that the futures price must equal this entire cost-of-carry. However, the futures price is expressed in index units, not the dollars of the actual stock prices. To find the fair value for the futures price, this cash value of $200.67 must be converted into index units

Table 7.7	Information for Computing Fair Value
Today's date:	July 6
Futures expiration:	September 20
Days until expiration:	76
Index:	Equally weighted index of two stocks
Index divisor:	1.80
Interest rates:	All interest rates are 10 percent
Stock A	
Today's price:	$115
Projected dividends:	$1.50 on July 23
Days dividend will be invested:	59
r_A:	.10(59/360) = .0164
Stock B	
Today's price:	$84
Projected dividends:	$1.00 on August 12
Days dividend will be invested:	39
r_B:	.10(39/360) = .0108

by dividing by the index divisor, $200.67/1.8 = 111.48$. Thus, the fair value for the futures contract is 111.48. Because it conforms to the cost-of-carry model, this fair value for the futures price is the price that precludes arbitrage profits from both the cash-and-carry and reverse cash-and-carry strategies.

INDEX ARBITRAGE AND PROGRAM TRADING

In the preceding section we saw how to derive the fair value futures price from the cost-of-carry model. From Chapter 3 we know that deviations from the theoretical price of the cost-of-carry model gives rise to arbitrage opportunities. If the futures price exceeds its fair value, traders will engage in cash-and-carry arbitrage. If the futures price falls below its fair value, traders can exploit the pricing discrepancy through a reverse cash-and-carry trading strategy. These cash-and-carry strategies in stock index futures are called **index arbitrage**. This section presents an example of index arbitrage using a simplified index with only two stocks. Because index arbitrage can require the trading of many stocks, index arbitrage is often implemented by using a computer program to automate the trading. Computer-directed index arbitrage is called **program trading**. We introduce program trading later in this section, but we reserve the fullest discussion for Chapter 8.

Index Arbitrage

Table 7.7 gave values for Stocks A and B, and we saw how to compute the fair value of a stock index futures contract based on an index composed of those two stocks. With the values in Table 7.7, the cash market index value is 110.56, and the fair value for the futures contract is 111.48, where both values are expressed in index points. If the futures price exceeds the fair value, cash-and-carry index arbitrage is possible. A futures price below its fair value creates an opportunity for reverse cash-and-carry index arbitrage.

To illustrate cash-and-carry index arbitrage, assume that the data of Table 7.7 hold, but that the futures price is 115.00. Because this price exceeds the fair value, an index arbitrageur would trade as shown in Table 7.8. At the outset on July 6, the trader borrows the money necessary to purchase the stocks in the index, buys the stocks, and sells the futures. On July 23 and August 12, the trader receives dividends from the two stocks and invests the dividends to the expiration date at 10 percent. Like all stock index futures, our simple example uses cash settlement. Therefore, at expiration on September 20, the final futures settlement price is set equal to the cash market index value. This ensures that the futures and cash prices converge and that the basis goes to zero.[3]

The profits or losses from the transactions in Table 7.8 do not depend on the prices that prevail at expiration on September 20. Instead, the profits come from a discrepancy between the futures price and its fair value. To illustrate the profits, we assume that the stock prices do not change. Therefore, the cash market index is at 110.56 at expiration. As Table 7.8 shows, these transactions give a profit of $6.32.

This will be the profit no matter what happens to stock prices between July 6 and September 20. For example, assume the prices of Stocks A and B both rose by $5, to $120 and $89, respectively. The cash market cash flows will then come from the sale of the shares, the future value of the dividends, and the debt repayment:

Table 7.8	Cash-and-Carry Index Arbitrage	
Date	**Cash Market**	**Futures Market**
July 6	Borrow $199 for 76 days at 10%. Buy Stock A and Stock B for a total outlay of $199.	Sell 1 SEP index futures contract for 115.00.
July 23	Receive dividend of $1.50 from Stock A and invest for 59 days at 10%.	
August 12	Receive dividend of $1.00 from Stock B and invest for 39 days at 10%.	
	For illustrative purposes, assume any values for stock prices at expiration. We assume that stock prices did not change. Therefore, the index value is still 110.56.	
September 20	Receive proceeds from invested dividends of $1.52 and $1.01. Sell Stock A for $115 and Stock B for $84. Total proceeds are $201.53. Repay debt of $203.20.	At expiration, the futures price is set equal to the spot index value of 110.56. This gives a profit of 4.44 index units. In dollar terms, this is 4.44 index units times the index divisor of 1.8.
	Loss: –$1.67	Profit: $7.99
	Total Profit: $7.99 – $1.67 = $6.32	

Sale of Stock A	+120.00
Sale of Stock B	+89.00
Future value of dividends on Stock A	+1.52
Future value of dividends on Stock B	+1.01
Debt repayment	−203.20
Futures profit/loss	−2.01

On the futures transaction, the index value at expiration will then equal $116.11 = (120 + 89)/1.8$. This gives a futures loss of 1.11 index points, or $2.01. Taking all of these cash flows together, the profit is still $6.32. The profit will be the same no matter what happens to stock prices.

If the futures price is too low relative to the fair value, arbitrageurs can engage in reverse cash-and-carry transactions. For example, assume that the futures price is 105.00, well below its fair value of 111.48. Now the arbitrageur will trade as shown in Table 7.9. Essentially, the transactions in Table 7.9 are just the opposite of those in Table 7.8. The most important difference is that the trader sells stock short. Having sold the stock short, the trader must pay the dividends on the stocks as they come due.

Reverse Cash-and-Carry Index Arbitrage		Table 7.9
Date	**Cash Market**	**Futures Market**
July 6	Sell Stock A and Stock B for a total of $199. Lend $199 for 76 days at 10%.	Buy 1 SEP index futures contract for 105.00.
July 23	Borrow $1.50 for 59 days at 10% and pay dividend of $1.50 on Stock A.	
August 12	Borrow $1.00 for 39 days at 10% and pay dividend of $1.00 on Stock B.	
	For illustrative purposes, assume any values for stock prices at expiration. We assume that stock prices did not change. Therefore, the index value is still 110.56.	
September 20	Receive proceeds from investment of $203.20. Repay $1.52 and $1.01 on money borrowed to pay dividends on Stocks A and B. Buy Stock A for $115 and Stock B for $84. Return stocks to repay short sale.	At expiration, the futures price is set equal to the spot index value of 110.56. This gives a profit of 5.56 index units. In dollar terms, this is 5.56 index units times the index divisor of 1.8.
	Profit: $1.67	Profit: $10.01
	Total Profit: $1.67 + $10.01 = $11.68	

The transactions give the trader a net profit of $11.68. Again, this profit does not depend upon the actual stock prices that prevail at expiration. Instead, the profit comes from the discrepancy between the actual futures price of 105.00 and the fair value of 111.48. Once the trader initiates the transactions in Table 7.9, the profit will depend only on the discrepancy between the fair value and the prevailing futures price. The profit will equal the error in the futures price times the index divisor: $(111.48 - 105.00)1.8 = \$11.68$.[4]

Program Trading

While we have illustrated the cash-and-carry and reverse cash-and-carry transactions with a hypothetical two stock index futures contract, real stock index futures trading involves many more stocks. The MMI is smallest with 20 stocks, while the S&P 500 contains (of course) 500 stocks, the NYSE index has about 1,700 underlying stocks, and the Nikkei has 225 stocks. To exploit index arbitrage opportunities with actual stock index futures requires trading the futures and simultaneously buying or selling the entire collection of stocks that underlie the index.

If we focus on the S&P 500 futures contract, we can see that the transactions of Tables 7.8 and 7.9 call for the buying or selling of 500 stocks. The success of the arbitrage depends upon identifying the misalignment between the futures price and the fair futures price. However, at a given moment the fair futures price depends upon the current price of 500 different stocks. Identifying an index arbitrage opportunity requires the ability to instantly find pricing discrepancies between the futures price and the fair futures price reflecting 500 different stocks. In addition, exploiting the arbitrage opportunity requires trading 500 stocks at the prices that created the arbitrage opportunity. Enter the computer!

Large financial institutions can communicate orders to trade stock via their computer for very rapid execution. Faced with a cash-and-carry arbitrage opportunity, one of these large traders could execute a computer order to buy each and every stock represented in the S&P 500. Simultaneously, the institution would sell the S&P 500 futures contract. The use of computers to execute large and complicated stock market orders is called **program trading**. While computers are used for other kinds of stock market transactions, index arbitrage is the main application of program trading. Often "index arbitrage" and "program trading" are used interchangeably. Program trading has been blamed for much of the recent volatility in the stock market, including the crash of October 1987. Chapter 8 presents a real-world example of program trading and analyzes the hidden risks in this kind of index arbitrage. Chapter 8 also discusses the evidence on program trading and stock market volatility.

Predicting Dividend Payments and Investment Rates

In the example of computing fair value from Table 7.7, we assumed certainty about the amount, timing, and investment rates for the dividends on Stocks A and B. In the actual market, these quantities are highly predictable, but they are not certain. Dividend amounts and payment dates can be predicted based on the past policy of the firm. However, these quantities are far from certain until the dividend announcement date when the firm announces the amount and payment date of the dividend. In practice, there is quite a bit of variability in the payment of dividends depending on the time of year. Figure 7.2 shows a typical distribution of dividend payments through the year. Notice how dividends tend to cluster at certain days in early March, June, September, and December.

In actual practice, traders follow the dividend practices of firms to project the dividends that the stocks underlying an index will pay each day. This problem varies in difficulty from one index to the next. The MMI has only 20 very large firms with relatively stable dividend policies. By contrast, the NYSE index has about 1,700 firms. Many of these firms are small and may have irregular dividend payment patterns. Therefore, it is more difficult to predict the exact dividend stream for the NYSE or the S&P 500 index. While the difficulties in predicting dividends may introduce some uncertainties into the cost-of-carry calculations, projections of dividends prove to be quite accurate in practice.

In our example of computing the fair value of a stock index futures contract and in our arbitrage examples, we also assumed that dividends could be invested at a known rate. In practice, it is difficult to know the exact rate that will be received on invested dividends. While knowing the exact rate to be received on invested dividends is difficult, good predictions are possible. For the most part, the futures expiration date is not very distant, so the current short-term interest rate can provide a good estimate of the investment rate for dividends.

Market Imperfections and Stock Index Futures Prices

In Chapter 3 we saw that four different types of market imperfections could affect the pricing of futures contracts. Those market imperfections are direct transaction costs, unequal borrowing and

| **Typical Distribution of Dividend Payments** | **Figure 7.2** |

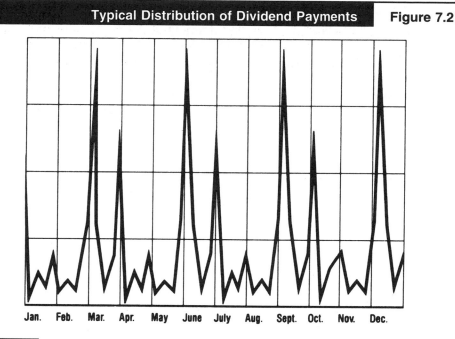

Jan. Feb. Mar. Apr. May June July Aug. Sept. Oct. Nov. Dec.

Source: From Chicago Mercantile Exchange, "Using S&P 500 Stock Index Futures and Options," 1988. Reprinted by permission of the Chicago Mercantile Exchange. S&P 500® is a trademark of The McGraw-Hill Companies, Inc. © Standard & Poor's. Reprinted by permission.

lending rates, margins and restrictions on short selling, and limitations to storage. As we also saw in Chapter 3, the effect of these market imperfections is to create a band of no-arbitrage prices within which the futures price must fall. In this section we consider these imperfections briefly in the context of stock index futures.

Direct transaction costs affect stock index futures trading to a considerable extent. Relative to many goods, transaction costs for stocks are low in percentage terms. Nonetheless, stock traders face commissions, exchange fees, and a bid-asked spread. In general, these costs may be about one-half of 1 percent for stock market transactions. Even with such modest transaction costs, we cannot expect the cost-of-carry model to hold as an exact equality. Instead, these transactions costs will lead to a no-arbitrage band of permissible stock index futures prices.

Unequal borrowing and lending costs, margins, and restrictions on short selling all play a role in stock index futures pricing. In the stock market, the restrictions on short selling are quite explicit. The Federal Reserve Board will not allow a trader to use more than 50 percent of the proceeds from a short sale. The short seller's broker may restrict that usage to an even smaller percentage. As we have seen in Chapter 3, these factors all force slight discrepancies in the cost-of-carry model. The pricing relationship of Equation 7.5 holds as an approximation, not with exactitude. Thus, these market imperfections create a no-arbitrage band of permissible futures prices. However, a highly competitive trading environment and low transaction costs keep this no-arbitrage band quite tight around the perfect markets theoretical fair value of Equation 7.5.

Because the stocks of the MMI, Nikkei, S&P 500, and NYSE indexes are so widely held by financial institutions with low transaction costs, quasi-arbitrage is a dominant feature of stock index futures trading. As an example of the importance of quasi-arbitrage, consider the differential use of short sale proceeds for a retail customer and a pension fund with a large stock portfolio. Assume that the retail customer must sell a stock short through her broker. This customer will be able to use only half of the proceeds of the short sale. By contrast, we will assume that the pension fund already owns the stocks necessary to sell short for the reverse cash-and-carry transaction. In this situation, the pension fund can simulate a short sale by selling a portion of its stock portfolio. Because the pension fund is actually selling stocks, not technically selling short, it receives the full use of its proceeds. However, selling stocks from a portfolio is a perfect substitute for an actual short sale. Thus, the pension fund faces substantially lower transaction costs than the retail customer for engaging in reverse cash-and-carry arbitrage. A similar conclusion emerges from considering program trading. A small retail trader faces enormous transaction costs in attempting to engage in index arbitrage. The quasi-arbitrage opportunities enjoyed by financial institutions ensure that no individual could ever engage in index arbitrage. In Chapter 8 we review the evidence on stock index futures pricing and show that these markets approximate full carry markets. This suggests that quasi-arbitrage is a dominant feature of stock index futures pricing.

SPECULATING WITH STOCK INDEX FUTURES

Speculating with stock index futures is exciting. Futures contracts allow the speculator to make the most straightforward speculation on the direction of the market or to enter very sophisticated spread transactions to tailor the futures position to more precise opinions about the direction of stock prices. Further, the low transactions costs in the futures market make the speculation much easier to undertake than similar speculation in the stock market itself. With four different broad market indexes from two countries, the speculative opportunities are virtually endless.

One of the simplest speculative positions arises from a belief about impending market movements. If a trader anticipates a major market rally, he could simply buy a futures contract and hope for a price rise on the futures contract when the rally actually occurs. While this course of action is very simple, it does not do full justice to the complexity of the speculative opportunity. The trader might also consider which contract maturity is desirable as a trading vehicle and which of the four contracts to trade.

In major market moves, stocks of small firms tend to move more dramatically than the stocks of large well-capitalized firms. If the trader believes that a major advance is impending, then he or she has a definite reason to prefer the NYSE index to the S&P 500 index and to prefer the S&P 500 index to the MMI. Comparing the MMI and the S&P 500 index, we would expect the MMI to be more sluggish because it is more completely dominated by large firms.

With these differential responses in mind, one conservative speculation position strategy could use a spread between two indexes. If the trader anticipates a major market increase, but wishes to closely control her risk exposure, she might use a spread between the MMI and the S&P 500 indexes. Assume that she anticipates a market rise in April. Consistent with this outlook, the transactions of Table 7.10 show how to initiate a spread to speculate on an anticipated market rally. The prescient

A Conservative Intercommodity Spread		Table 7.10
Date	**Futures Market**	
April 22	Buy 1 SEP MMI futures contract at 534.50. Sell 1 SEP S&P 500 futures contract at 333.00.	
May 6	Sell 1 SEP MMI futures contract at 556.30. Buy 1 SEP S&P 500 futures contract at 342.15.	

	MMI	**S&P 500**
Sell	556.30	333.00
Buy	534.50	342.15
Profit (points)	21.80	−9.15
× $500	$10,900.00	−$4,575.00
	Total Profit: $6,325	

speculator buys one SEP MMI futures contract at 534.50 on April 22 and sells one SEP S&P 500 futures contract at 333.00.

A few weeks later, prices have risen, with the MMI futures trading at 556.30 and the S&P 500 futures at 342.15. The wisdom in her plan is soon validated by a market rally. Not wishing to be greedy, she elects to close her position on May 6. She sells the MMI contract at 556.30 and buys the S&P 500 contract at 342.15. Her spread has worked perfectly. The MMI futures has gained 4.08 percent while the S&P 500 index contract gained only 2.75 percent. Therefore, the gain on the MMI of 21.80 index points times $500 per point is $10,900. This gain more than offsets the loss on the S&P 500 contract of $4,575, the product of 9.15 points times $500 per point. The total gain is $6,325.

Contracts farther from expiration often respond to a given market move more than the nearby contracts and the index itself. The speculator could have initiated an intracommodity spread to take advantage of this same market rally. Table 7.11 shows one possible set of transactions using the S&P contract and the same dates. The speculator believes that the more distant contracts will be more responsive to a market move than the nearby contracts. Believing that the market will rise, she buys the more distant DEC contract at 361.90 on April 22, while simultaneously selling the nearby JUN contract at 359.80. By May 6, the rally has occurred, so she reverses her position by buying the JUN contract at 367.50 and selling the DEC contract at 369.75. As the table shows, the JUN contract has moved 7.70 points and the more sensitive DEC contract has moved 7.85 points. The strategy has worked, in a certain sense, because the more distant contract was more sensitive. However, the difference in the price changes was not very large. In fact, the gross profit on the spread was only $75, hardly enough to cover the transaction costs.

In an important sense, both spreads were too conservative. In the example of Table 7.11, the trader correctly anticipated the market move. An outright long position in any contract would have worked well, but the conservative trader managed to protect herself completely out of the benefits that could have been obtained, given the major character of the market advance. For the speculator committed to spread trading, the stock index futures market presents a problem, because the different contracts tend to be so highly correlated.

Table 7.11	A Conservative Intracommodity Spread
Date	**Futures Market**
April 22	Buy 1 DEC S&P 500 contract at 361.90. Sell 1 JUN S&P 500 contract at 359.80.
May 6	Sell 1 DEC S&P 500 contract at 369.75. Buy 1 JUN S&P 500 contract at 367.50.

	June	December
Sell	359.80	369.75
Buy	367.50	361.90
Profit (points)	−7.70	7.85
× $500	−$3,850.00	$3,925.00

Total Profit: $75

To trade spreads in stock index futures, it is often desirable to use a ratio spread. In a **ratio spread**, the trader trades more contracts on one side of the spread than on the other. The example of Table 7.10 has a ratio of 1:1, because the trader used one MMI contract and one S&P 500 contract. A more aggressive trader might have used a higher ratio.

The Demise of Barings Bank

Theoretically, index arbitrage is risk free, and properly executed index arbitrage transactions involve very low levels of actual risk. The risk is limited because of the close relationship between a stock index futures contract and the underlying stock index itself. Thus, as we have seen, index arbitrage is a low risk strategy that seeks to capture small and temporary pricing discrepancies between stocks and stock index futures.

Nicholas Leeson was a trader for Barings Bank stationed in Singapore. He was originally supposed to be conducting index arbitrage between Japanese stocks and futures contracts on the Japanese index for Barings. Such trading involves taking equal and offsetting positions in stocks and futures, which were traded in both Japan and Singapore. While details remain controversial, it seems apparent that Leeson did exactly the opposite in late 1994 and early 1995. Through the futures markets, Leeson made very large one-sided bets that Japanese stocks would rise. The Kobe earthquake, however, rocked the entire Japanese economy and led to a dramatic drop in the Japanese stock market. The highly leveraged bets on a rising Japanese market turned out to be giant losers. In a short period, Leeson's trades lost about $1.5 billion. These losses completely exhausted the net worth of Barings, which declared bankruptcy and was acquired by a Dutch investment bank.

While early reports suggested that Leeson was a rogue trader who acted alone, further investigation indicates a considerable awareness of his activities on the part of senior management. Shortly after the losses became public, Leeson was arrested in Germany and held in a German jail, as Singapore pressed its extradition request. Leeson was eventually extradited to Singapore, tried, convicted, and sentenced to a six-and-one-half year jail term that he is now serving.[5]

RISK MANAGEMENT WITH STOCK INDEX FUTURES

Hedging with stock index futures applies directly to the management of stock portfolios. The usefulness of stock index futures in portfolio management stems from the fact that they directly represent the market portfolio. Before stock index futures began trading, there was no comparable way of trading an instrument that gave the price performance so directly tied to a broad market index. Further, stock index futures have great potential in portfolio management due to their very low transaction costs. In this section we consider some hedging applications of stock index futures.

A Short Hedge and Hedge Ratio Calculation

As a first case, consider the manager of a well-diversified stock portfolio with a value of $40,000,000, and assume that the portfolio has a beta of 1.22 measured relative to the S&P 500. This implies that a movement of 1 percent in the S&P 500 index would be expected to induce a change of 1.22 percent in the value of the stock portfolio. The portfolio manager fears that a bear market is imminent and wishes to hedge his portfolio's value against that possibility. One strategy would be to liquidate the portfolio and place the proceeds in short-term debt instruments and then, after the bear market, return the funds to the stock market. Such a plan is infeasible. First, the transaction costs from such a strategy are quite high. Second, if the fund is large, liquidating the portfolio could drive down stock prices. This would prevent the portfolio manager from liquidating the portfolio at the prices currently quoted for the individual stocks.

　　As an obvious alternative to liquidating the portfolio, the manager could use the S&P 500 stock index futures contract. By selling futures, the manager should be able to offset the effect of the bear market on the portfolio by generating gains in the futures market. One kind of naive strategy might involve trading one dollar of the value underlying the index futures contract for each dollar of the portfolio's value. Assuming that the S&P index futures contract stands at 212.00, the advocated number of futures contracts would be given by:

$$\frac{V_P}{V_F} = \frac{\$40,000,000}{(212)(\$500)} = 377 \text{ contracts}$$

where:

V_P = value of the portfolio
V_F = value of the futures contract

　　One problem with this approach is that it ignores the higher volatility of the stock portfolio relative to that of the S&P 500 index. As noted previously, the beta of the stock portfolio, as measured against the index, was 1.22. Table 7.12 shows the potential results of a hedge consistent with these facts. The portfolio manager initiates the hedge on March 14, selling 377 DEC futures contracts against the $40,000,000 stock portfolio. By April 16, his fears have been realized and the market has fallen. The S&P index, and the futures, have both fallen by 4.43 percent to 202.61. The stock portfolio, with its greater volatility, has fallen exactly 1.22 times as much, generating a loss of $2,161,840. This leaves a net loss on the hedge of $391,825. The failure to consider the differential volatility between the stock portfolio and the index futures contract leads to sub-optimal hedging results.

Table 7.12	A Short Hedge	
	Stock Market	**Futures Market**
March 14	Hold $40,000,000 in a stock portfolio.	Sell 377 S&P 500 December futures contracts at 212.00.
April 16	Stock portfolio falls by 5.40% to $37,838,160.	S&P futures contract falls by 4.43% to 202.61.
	Loss: –$2,161,840	Gain: $1,770,015
	Net Loss: –$391,825	

The manager might be able to avoid this result by weighting the hedge ratio by the beta of the stock portfolio. According to this scenario, the manager could use Equation 7.6 to find the number of contracts to trade:

$$\left(\frac{V_P}{V_F}\right)\beta_P = \text{number of contracts} \tag{7.6}$$

where:

β_P = beta of the portfolio that is being hedged

Using this approach for our example, the manager would trade 460 contracts:

$$\left(\frac{\$40,000,000}{(\$212)(500)}\right)1.22 = 460 \text{ contracts}$$

Had the manager traded 460 contracts, the futures gain reported in Table 7.12 would have been $2,159,700 instead of $1,770,015. This higher gain would have almost exactly offset the loss on the spot position of $2,161,840. Note, however, that these excellent results depend on two crucial assumptions. First, such results could be achieved only if the movement of the stock portfolio during the hedge period exactly corresponded to the volatility implied by its beta. Second, the technique of Equation 7.6 uses the beta of the stock portfolio as measured against the S&P 500 index itself. This assumes that the futures contracts move exactly in tandem with the spot index. This assumption is clearly violated by recent market experience, because the futures contracts for all of the indexes are more volatile than the indexes themselves. This is reflected by the fact that the futures contracts generally have betas above 1.0 when they are measured relative to the stock index itself. The methodology of Equation 7.6 does not take this into account, since it implicitly assumes the index and the futures contracts to have the same price movements, which would imply equal betas. We consider more sophisticated approaches to this type of hedging problem in Chapter 8.

A Long Hedge

As with all other futures contracts, both long and short hedges are possible in stock index futures. Imagine a pension fund manager convinced that she stands at the beginning of an extended bull market. She anticipates that $6,000,000 in new funds will become available in three months for investment. Waiting three months for the funds to invest in the stock market could mean that the bull market would be missed altogether. An alternative to missing the market move would be to use the stock index futures market. The pension manager could simply buy an amount of a stock index futures contract that would be equivalent in dollar commitments to the anticipated inflow of investable funds. On May 19, with the SEP NYSE index futures contract standing at 174.40, the futures contract represents an underlying cash value of $87,200. The pension manager can secure her position in the market by buying $6,000,000 worth of futures. Since she expects the funds in three months, the SEP contract is a natural expiration to use, so she buys 69 SEP contracts, as shown in Table 7.13. By August 15, the market has risen, so the $6,000,000 could not buy the same shares that would have been possible on May 19. To offset this fact, the pension manager has earned a futures profit of $141,450. This gain in the futures market helps offset the new higher prices that would be incurred in the stock purchase.

CONCLUSION

In this chapter we have explored the major stock indexes on which futures contracts are traded. In addition, we have considered the structure of the futures contracts based upon them and the differences among the various futures contracts. We applied familiar cash-and-carry and reverse cash-and-carry arbitrage strategies to show that stock index futures prices should conform to the cost-of-carry model. However, we noted the cost-of-carry model must be adjusted to reflect cash dividends. In the context of the cost-of-carry model, we saw that index arbitrage and program trading are applications of cash-and-carry approaches to futures pricing.

The chapter considered some speculative trading strategies that use intracommodity and inter-commodity spreads. We also considered an example of a ratio spread. In addition to speculative applications, stock index futures are useful for managing risk. We considered some examples of short and long hedges. In the short hedge example, we showed how a portfolio manager could protect against a potential bear market. With a long hedge example, we showed how a trader could capture a potential bull market by using futures as a substitute for actually buying shares.

A Long Hedge with Stock Index Futures	Table 7.13
Stock Market	**Futures Market**
May 19 — A pension fund manager anticipates having $6,000,000 to invest in three months.	Buys 69 SEP NYSE futures at 174.40.
August 15 — $6,000,000 becomes available for investment. Stock prices have risen, so the $6,000,000 will not buy the same shares that it would have on May 19.	The market has risen and the NYSE futures stands at 178.50. Futures profit: $141,450

QUESTIONS AND PROBLEMS

1. Distinguish between the MMI and the Dow Jones Industrial Average.
2. Assume that the MMI stands at 340.00 and the current divisor is 0.8. One of the stocks in the index is priced at $100.00 and it splits 2:1. Based on this information, answer the following questions:
   a. What is the sum of the prices of all the shares in the index before the stock split?
   b. What is the value of the index after the split? Explain.
   c. What is the sum of the prices of all the shares in the index after the split?
   d. What is the divisor after the split?
3. What is the main difference in the calculation of the MMI and the S&P 500 index? Explain.
4. For the S&P 500 index, assume that the company with the highest market value has a 1 percent increase in stock prices. Also, assume that the company with the smallest market value has a 1 percent decrease in the price of its shares. Does the index change? If so, in what direction?
5. Table 7.3 shows the correlations among the four indexes. Explain why the correlation between the NYSE Composite and the S&P 500 should be the highest of all correlations.
6. The S&P 500 futures is scheduled to expire in half a year, and the interest rate for carrying stocks over that period is 11 percent. The expected dividend rate on the underlying stocks for the same period is 2 percent of the value of the stocks. (The 2 percent is the half-year rate, not an annual rate.) Ignoring the interest that it might be possible to earn on the dividend payments, find the fair value for the futures if the current value of the index is 315.00.
7. Consider a very simple index like the MMI, except assume that it has only two shares, A and B. The price of A is $100.00, and B trades for $75.00. The current index value is 175.00. The futures contract based on this index expires in three months, and the cost of carrying the stocks forward is .75 percent per month. This is also the interest rate that you can earn on invested funds. You expect Stock A to pay a $3 dividend in one month and Stock B to pay a $1 dividend in two months. Find the fair value of the futures. Assume monthly compounding.
8. Using the same data as in Problem 7, now assume that the futures trades at 176.00. Explain how you would trade with this set of information. Show your transactions.
9. Using the same data as in Problem 7, now assume that the futures trades at 174.00. Explain how you would trade with this set of information. Show your transactions.
10. For a stock index and a stock index futures constructed like the MMI, assume that the dividend rate expected to be earned on the stocks in the index is the same as the cost of carrying the stocks forward. What should be the relationship between the cash and futures market prices? Explain.
11. Your portfolio is worth $100 million and has a beta of 1.08 measured against the S&P futures, which is priced at 350.00. Explain how you would hedge this portfolio, assuming that you wish to be fully hedged.
12. You have inherited $50 million, but the estate will not settle for six months and you will not actually receive the cash until that time. You find current stock values attractive and you plan to invest in the S&P 500 cash portfolio. Explain how you would hedge this anticipated investment using S&P 500 futures.

NOTES

[1] Prominent among these inactive contracts is the Value Line Contract on the Kansas City Board of Trade. Formerly, this contract was actively traded, but its construction was very complicated, being a geometric

average of 1,700 stocks. Partially for this reason, its popularity faded during the late 1980s. A change in the composition of the index did little to restore its faded luster. By 1990, daily volume had fallen to a few hundred contracts and open interest in all contracts was below 2,000. Other indexes are the S&P Mid-Cap 400 and the Russell 2000.

[2] In earlier times, the S&P 500 consisted of 400 industrial firms, 40 financial institutions, 40 utilities, and 20 transportation firms.

[3] As we will see in Chapter 8, trading for the S&P 500 and the NYSE futures contracts ends on one day, and the final settlement price is set at the next day's opening price.

[4] These calculations are sometimes off by a penny or two due to rounding.

[5] In an interesting approach to the problem of Barings, one calculation insists that Barings would have made a profit of $3 billion on its position had it simply held until the end of 1995. See Numa Financial Systems, Ltd., ''Barings Theoretical P/L 1995,'' NumaWeb home page, World Wide Web. This would have been the eventual result, although the position would also have experienced a low of −$5 billion in June 1995. For a more sober assessment, see Bank of England, ''Report of the Board of Banking Supervision Inquiry into the Circumstances of the Collapse of Barings,'' July 18, 1995. The affair has already given rise to three books: Judith Rawnsley, ''Going for Broke,'' New York: HarperCollins, 1995; Nick Leeson, ''Rogue Trader,'' Boston: Little Brown, 1996; and Stephen Fay, ''The Collapse of Barings,'' New York: Richard Cohen Books, 1996.

STOCK INDEX FUTURES: REFINEMENTS

OVERVIEW

In Chapter 7, we saw that stock index futures prices are governed by the cost-of-carry model. Because stocks often pay dividends, we saw how to tailor the cost-of-carry model to reflect the dividends on the stocks that underlie the stock index futures. In this chapter, we explore some of the empirical evidence on the relationship between theoretical and observed market prices. As in any violation of cost-of-carry principles, arbitrage opportunities should be possible if stock index futures prices do not correspond to theoretically determined prices.

Index arbitrage is the specific name given to attempts to exploit discrepancies between theoretical and actual stock index futures prices. As we also discussed in Chapter 7, index arbitrage usually proceeds through program trading. With the advent of program trading, there has been some evidence of a link between high index price variability and the style of trading used by program traders. This chapter considers some of the evidence on volatility and explores the market concern about volatility.

Because of the perception that futures trading is responsible for stock market volatility, new concern has focused on trading practices in the futures market, leading to some changes in trading rules. This chapter also considers some of the new trading practices rules recently implemented in the S&P 500 futures pit.

Chapter 7 considered some speculative and hedging applications of stock index futures. This chapter explores some more sophisticated techniques for using stock index futures that are becoming an important tool in portfolio management. By trading stock index futures in conjunction with a stock portfolio, a portfolio manager can tailor the risk characteristics of the entire portfolio. These strategies have aspects of both speculation and hedging. Two of the most notable of these are asset allocation and portfolio insurance, which we consider in some detail.

STOCK INDEX FUTURES PRICES

In this section we consider a variety of issues related to stock index futures pricing. First, we examine the empirical evidence on stock index futures efficiency. Namely, do stock index futures prices conform to the cost-of-carry model? Evidence suggests that the market was not efficient when trading began, but that it is now efficient. Second, we consider the effect of taxes on stock index futures prices. A tax-timing option available to traders of stocks, but denied to stock index futures traders, might explain the discrepancy between theoretical and actual prices for stock index futures. Third, we consider the timing relationship between stock index futures prices and the cash market index. Does the futures price lead the cash market index, or does the cash market index lead the futures? Finally, we consider seasonal impacts on stock index futures pricing. Here "seasonal" refers not only to the time of year, but also to the time of month, time of week, and even time of day.

Stock Index Futures Efficiency

In Chapter 7 we saw that cost-of-carry principles apply directly to the pricing of stock index futures. In particular, if the spot stock index price and the futures price are misaligned, cash-and-carry or reverse cash-and-carry arbitrage opportunities will become available. We considered examples of these kinds of transactions in Chapter 7. In this section, we consider whether the stock index futures market is informationally efficient. If it is efficient, then stock index futures prices should conform to the cost-of-carry model that we developed in Chapter 7. As we will see, the general conclusion suggests that the market was inefficient in the early days of trading but that it now conforms well to the cost-of-carry model.

Exploring actual market data, David Modest and Mahadevan Sundaresan apply the carrying charges model to form permissible bounds for futures prices and try to take into account the actual transaction costs that would be incurred in trading the futures and the stocks in the indexes.[1] The bounds depend critically on the assumptions of a $25 round trip transaction cost for the futures contract and $.10 per share transaction costs for the stock itself. We must also assume that the T-bill rate is the appropriate interest rate for all calculations of carrying charges.

Modest and Sundaresan's analysis makes two additional assumptions. The first concerns the assumption that we make regarding the use of proceeds from short selling stocks. If a trader does not have full use of the proceeds from short sales due to margin requirements, then the interest on the proceeds that cannot be used has a marked impact on the analysis. We have already encountered this issue in our discussion of T-bill futures efficiency. Essentially, an arbitrage opportunity might require the short sale of the stock index, which means that the individual stocks comprising the index are sold short in the stock market. In this situation, the short seller may not receive full use of the proceeds from the short sale, because the broker will hold a significant fraction of those proceeds as protection against default by the short seller. Therefore, the success of any such arbitrage depends critically upon assumptions regarding the use of short sale proceeds. Modest and Sundaresan examine alternative assumptions about the use of short sale proceeds.

A second critical assumption concerns dividends. We saw in Chapter 7 that dividends are important to the pricing of stock index futures. In addition, the extreme intertemporal variation in dividends shown in Figure 7.2 means that their effect will vary dramatically from one time period to the next. For accuracy in pricing stock index futures, taking account of dividends is very important.

We begin our discussion of this issue by focusing on a paper that examined the early history of trading, "The Relationship Between Spot and Futures Prices in Stock Index Futures Markets: Some Preliminary Evidence." This article by David Modest and Mahadevan Sundaresan addresses most of the issues that are necessary to determine the efficiency of prices in a market. For instance, we have seen that every real market has a range of permissible no-arbitrage prices. This no-arbitrage band arises because of transaction costs and restrictions on short selling. Therefore, tests of market efficiency depend critically on careful estimations of these transaction costs.

Modest and Sundaresan computed the no-arbitrage boundaries for the DEC 1982 futures contract under the assumptions outlined here and present those results in Figure 8.1. The graph tracks the futures prices from April 21 through September 15, 1982. The dotted lines on the graph show the bounds, which are adjusted for dividends and the assumption that half the proceeds from short sales are available. The solid line represents the actual futures price. Clearly, the futures price lies within the bounds except for near misses on two occasions. On the whole, these results are consistent with the rationality of futures pricing. In another part of their study, the bounds were also adjusted for dividends, but with the assumption that one has use of 100 percent of the proceeds from short sales. In this situation, arbitrage opportunities were consistently available.

In their study, Modest and Sundaresan did not attempt to include an estimate of the daily dividend payment from the S&P 500 index. Instead, they estimated the dividend rate on the index using quarterly dividend data and then interpolated that into monthly dividend data. As a result, their study does not reflect the high variability in dividends on a daily basis. The graph of Figure 8.1 applies to the DEC 1982 contract for April 21 to September 15, 1982. Over that time, dividends had very sharp quarterly peaks. Had Modest and Sundaresan been able to take these daily fluctuations into account more accurately, we would expect observed prices to lie more consistently within the no-arbitrage bounds, and their paper would be even more valuable.

Perhaps of equal importance to the exact treatment of dividends is the assumption made about the use of proceeds from short sales. In addition, we have seen that some traders face full transaction costs. By contrast, other traders face much lower transaction costs. For example, large institutions with significant portfolios can simulate short selling by selling part of their existing portfolio. In this

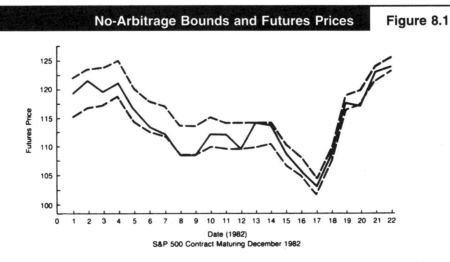

No-Arbitrage Bounds and Futures Prices   **Figure 8.1**

Source: From D. Modest and M. Sundaresan, "The Relationship Between Spot and Futures Prices in Stock Index Futures Markets: Some Preliminary Evidence," *Journal of Futures Markets* 3:2, 1983, pp. 15–41. © 1983. Reprinted by permission of John Wiley & Sons, Inc. Journals.

simulated short selling, they retain full use of the proceeds. Throughout our discussion, we have referred to arbitrage activities by these low transaction cost traders as **quasi-arbitrage**.

Modest and Sundaresan's results clearly point to quasi-arbitrage opportunities. In the early days of stock index futures trading, it appears that significant quasi-arbitrage opportunities were available. However, after the seasoning of the market, prices tended to remain within the no-arbitrage bounds. While such conclusions depend upon estimates of transaction costs, other studies substantiate the conclusion reached by Modest and Sundaresan.

Taxes and Stock Index Futures

A difference in tax treatment between futures and the stocks themselves might justify a discrepancy from the cost-of-carry model. In such a case, the market might be efficient. Comparing a long position in the stocks underlying an index and a long position in the stock index futures contract shows that there is a difference in tax treatment. The owner of a stock may have a paper gain or loss on the stock as the end of the year approaches. For example, assume that a share was purchased for $100 and that the trader pays taxes at the rate of 30 percent. If the stock sells for $90 as the end of the year approaches, the trader has the option to sell the stock for $90, realizing a $10 loss. If he or she sells the stock, taxable income will be reduced by $10. With a 30 percent tax rate, selling the stock generates a tax saving of $3. By contrast, assume that the stock price is $110 instead of $90 as the end of the year approaches. In this situation, the tax saving strategy is to wait until after the turn of the year to take the gain, thereby deferring the taxes for a full year by just waiting a few days to make the trade.

Because futures prices are marked to market at year-end for tax purposes, the futures contract possesses no tax-timing option. In the futures markets, tax rules require all paper gains or losses to be recognized as cash gains or losses each year. The tax-timing option included with the stock, but lacking with the futures contract, implies that rational pricing must reflect the value of the tax-timing option in the relationship between the cash and futures prices of the stock index.

This possibility was first noted by Bradford Cornell and Kenneth French. They showed how this tax-timing option could give extra value to the stocks relative to the futures. Cornell and French compute the value of the tax option as the difference between the observed market price and the price implied by the carrying charges model. While the tax option clearly has a value, the technique adopted by Cornell and French assumes that the stock index futures contract is priced rationally, and they compute the value of the option in accordance with that fundamental belief. For the purpose of trying to evaluate the price performance characteristics of the stock index futures contract, note that the tax-timing option would have a value, but that a trader cannot immediately assume that its value is equal to the discrepancy between the observed market price and the theoretically justified price assuming no tax-timing option. However, in an empirical study of the effect of the tax-timing option on futures prices, Cornell concludes that the tax-timing option does not appear to affect prices.[2] Cornell suggests that trading may be dominated by tax-free investors, or that other tax rules may prevent the tax-timing option from significantly affecting prices.

The Day of the Week Effect in Stock Index Futures

It has been well documented that returns on many securities vary by the day of the week. There is nothing in the financial theory to explain why returns on Thursday should be different from returns on Tuesday or Wednesday. Nonetheless, a great deal of evidence shows that returns differ depending on the day of the week. In particular, Friday returns are generally high and Monday returns (the return from Friday close to Monday close) are even negative. These return differences are substantial, and it may be possible for investors to earn a return that beats the market by timing their purchases to take advantage of these persistent differences. If so, the day of the week effect would show either that the semi-strong efficient market hypothesis (EMH) was not true or that the CAPM was not true, or both. If the CAPM is the correct pricing relationship in the market, then the EMH must be false, because it appears that prices do not adjust correctly to reflect all available information. If the EMH is true, it seems that the CAPM must be false, because there must be additional risk factors not recognized by the CAPM to explain the different returns depending on the day of the week.

The day of the week effect has also been explored in the stock index futures market. Given the strong relationship that must hold between stock index futures and the stock index itself, we would expect to find an effect in the futures market if there is one in the stock market itself. Most studies find a weekend effect – price changes from the Friday close to the Monday open are low or negative.[3]

Leads and Lags in Stock Index Prices

We have seen that arbitrage seekers force stock index cash market and futures market prices to conform to the cost-of-carry model. Thus, a movement in one price must generate a movement in the other price to keep prices in conformance with the cost-of-carry model.

At first blush, it might seem that the index should lead the futures. For example, if new information arrives in the market about a particular stock, the price of that stock will change. The index value changes to reflect the new price of the constituent stock. To keep prices in conformance with the cost-of-carry model, the index futures price must change. Under this scenario, the cash market index changes first and the futures index price changes later. Thus, the cash index leads the futures price.

However, the dominant information affecting the stock market might be more general information. If the most important information affects the general level of stock prices, rather than the price of a single firm, there may be a different transmission of stock price changes. For an example too strange to believe, assume that Iraq invades Kuwait and that this is bad news for stock prices. Traders may react to this information by trading in either the stock market or the stock index futures market. The choice of market will be affected by both the relative liquidity and the transaction costs in the two markets. If liquidity and transaction costs are most important, futures trading will be more attractive. Thus, with the invasion news, traders might first sell index futures, driving down the futures price. The cash market index must then adjust to exclude arbitrage opportunities. Under this scenario, the futures price will lead the cash market index.

These leads and lags are most likely to occur on a minute to minute basis. If the leads or lags persisted over days, for example, they could well lead to arbitrage opportunities. Whether the cash market index leads the futures, or vice versa, is essentially an empirical question. The question of leads and lags has been explored in several studies, most of which find that futures prices lead cash market prices.[4]

While stock index futures prices may lead the stock index, this differential movement does not necessarily create arbitrage opportunities. First, movements in the two prices are generally almost simultaneous. Quickly responding prices may not allow any arbitrage opportunities. Second, both prices vary constantly by small amounts as new information reaches the market. Even substantial lags would not create an arbitrage opportunity if the difference in prices is small. In other words, the futures price could always lead the cash market index. However, if the price difference is small, the difference in prices could always remain within the no-arbitrage bounds of the cost-of-carry model.

REAL WORLD PROGRAM TRADING

Chapter 7 explained the basic idea of index arbitrage through program trading. There we considered an imaginary two stock index and showed how to engage in cash-and-carry and reverse cash-and-carry strategies to exploit mispricing of the index versus the index futures. To provide a more realistic feel for real world program trade in stock index futures, this section begins with a historical example of an actual program trade. We then consider the risks inherent in program trading that make the enterprise much more perilous than our historical example would seem to indicate. Finally, we conclude with some statistics on the extent of program trading in today's markets.

Real World Program Trading: An Example

This section discusses a historical example of a cash-and-carry program trading transaction.[5] The trader buys the stocks and carries them forward while selling the futures to profit from the spot being underpriced relative to the futures. Table 8.1 shows the actual prices for the MMI stocks on February 26, 1986, when the trade began. The table also shows the MMI stock prices at the end of the trade on March 21, 1986, and the dividends that the various stocks paid between the two dates.

Faced with the prices shown for February 26, 1986, in Table 8.1, the trader bought 2,000 shares of each of 20 stocks, with a total purchase price of $2,749,000. The trader used $1,374,500 (or 50 percent) of his own funds and borrowed the same amount at 8.5 percent. At the same time, he sold 35 MAR 1986 MMI futures at 313.55. This value implies an underlying stock value of $2,743,563 (313.55 index value × $250 multiplier × 35 contracts). (In 1986, the MMI multiplier was $250. It is now $500.) Trading this number of contracts gives the spot and futures positions very similar dollar values, which is exactly the desired relationship to profit on the relative mispricing.

Risks in Index Arbitrage and Program Trading

The index arbitrage transactions on February 26 in Table 8.2 ensure a profit, subject to a few minor risks. Because the stock index contracts are settled in cash, the spot and futures values at the close of trading for the contract must converge. For the MAR 1986 MMI, trading ended on March 21. Table 8.2 shows the transactions involved in this arbitrage. All of the values in Table 8.2 are actual market prices. Notice that the purchase of shares in Table 8.2 used 50 percent debt and 50 percent investable funds. This is necessary because of Federal Reserve Board requirements that no more than 50 percent of the purchase price of stocks can be borrowed. Table 8.2 reflects the opportunity cost of those invested funds by assuming that they could have earned the 8.5 percent interest rate that was paid to borrow money.

In computing the cash flows in Table 8.2, we consider all interest, dividends, and out of pocket transaction costs. The dividends totaled $3.41 from Table 8.1. With 2,000 shares of each firm, the total dividends received were $6,820. Total transaction costs were $1,100. This is about $.014 per share to buy and the same amount to sell, including the futures contracts. Notice, however, that the analysis does not reflect the daily resettlement cash flows that may have been incurred between February 26 and March 21, nor do we consider interest that might have been earned on the dividends

	Data for Index Arbitrage		Table 8.1
Firm	**Price February 26**	**Price March 21**	**Dividends $/Share**
American Express	64.000	65.625	
AT&T	22.500	22.875	
Chevron	37.875	37.375	
Coca-Cola	92.000	100.375	.78
Dow Chemical	48.750	52.375	
DuPont	70.500	72.500	
Kodak	55.000	59.750	
Exxon	54.875	54.750	
General Electric	75.500	75.750	.58
General Motors	78.250	83.250	
IBM	158.125	148.500	
International Paper	57.000	60.000	
Johnson & Johnson	48.375	54.000	
Merck	150.750	161.250	.90
3M	97.25	104.000	
Mobil Oil	30.125	29.500	
Philip Morris	101.125	119.250	1.15
Procter & Gamble	67.000	73.500	
Sears	42.875	46.125	
U.S. Steel	22.675	22.750	
MMI Index	311.740	328.070	
MAR 86 MMI Futures	313.550	328.070	

received. In addition, the cash flow computation does not reflect the cost of searching for this opportunity.

This kind of transaction has certain elements of risk stemming from three sources. First, there is execution risk, because the trader must successfully enter and close the entire position. To establish the position, the trader must buy 2,000 shares of 20 stocks and sell 35 futures contracts. Imagine that the trader finds the opportunity and sells futures. Then the trader starts buying shares of the 20 stocks. During this time, assume that three of the stocks increase in price by $1.00 each. Because the trader has sold the futures contracts, the price of that side of the position is fixed. With three stocks increasing in price by $1.00, the long position in the stocks will cost a total of $6,000 more than anticipated. If this happens, the trader pays $6,000 more than anticipated for the stocks, and the arbitrage profit turns in to an arbitrage loss.

The second part of the execution risk exposure occurs on March 21 when the position must be closed. The profit or loss on the futures contract depends on the index value at the close of trading on March 21. However, the risk arbitrage strategy calls for the stocks to be sold at the end of trading on the same day. If the stocks are held until the next day, there will be considerable risk, because any kind of news could be received after the close of trading on March 21. Because of this risk, it

Table 8.2	Program Trading Transactions

February 26, 1986
Sell 35 MMI MAR 1986 futures at 313.55.

Use $1,374,500 of investable funds; borrow another $1,374,500 at 8.5% and use these funds to buy 2,000 shares of each of the 20 stocks comprising the MMI at a total cost of $2,749,000.

March 21, 1986
Buy 35 MMI MAR 1986 futures at 328.07.

Sell all stocks purchased on February 26, receiving $2,893,000.

Pay interest of $8,438 on borrowed $1,374,500.

Charge opportunity cost of own $1,374,500 that was invested at appropriate cost of funds of 8.5% for a total of $8,438.

Pay transaction costs: −$1,100.

Dividends received while stocks were owned: +$6,820.

Net Cash Flows:

February 26   None, because we will charge an opportunity cost for the portion of funds that were invested.

March 21		
	Futures	−$127,050
	Stocks	144,000
	Transaction Costs	−1,100
	Dividends	6,820
	Interest on Actual Loan	−8,438
	Opportunity Cost on Invested Funds	−8,438
	Arbitrage Profit	$5,794

is customary to close out such stock positions at the close of trading on the futures expiration day. To close the position, the trader enters a market on close order to sell these stocks. A **market on close order** instructs the broker to sell these shares for the market price at the close of trading. The obvious goal is to sell the shares at the settlement price of the day's trading, because that will be the share price that figures into the index, and the index value on that day determines the futures profit or loss. If the trader could be certain that the shares would be sold at the day's closing price, this element of risk would be eliminated. However, it is difficult to trade in the last 15–30 seconds to get execution at the day's final price. Therefore, there is risk involved in closing the position as well as opening the position.

In addition to execution risk, there is some risk that the dividends will not be paid as the trader anticipates. In this example, if the firms cancel their dividend payments, the trader does not receive $6,820 and the transactions will generate a loss. Such a rash of dividend cancellations is unlikely, but at least remotely possible. The final source of risk is financing risk. The trader might not be able to secure financing for the entire period at the same rate. If the stocks are financed with overnight obligations and interest rates suddenly jump, financing costs could be higher than anticipated. In summary, the index arbitrage transaction faces execution risk, dividend risk, and interest rate risk. Of these, execution risk is the most important. Nonetheless, once the transactions of February 26 are put in place, there is very little real danger of a loss.

HEDGING WITH STOCK INDEX FUTURES

In Chapter 7 we considered the basic techniques for hedging with stock index futures. We presented examples of short and long hedges and discussed a hedging strategy for hedging a portfolio with stock index futures that reflected the beta of the portfolio being hedged. The hedge position from Chapter 7 was:

$$\left(\frac{V_P}{V_F}\right)\beta_P = \text{number of contracts} \tag{7.6}$$

where:

V_P = value of the portfolio
V_F = value of the futures contract
β_P = beta of the portfolio that is being hedged

In this section we analyze stock index futures hedging. We begin by showing that the hedge Equation 7.6 gives the futures position to establish a combined stock and futures portfolio with the lowest possible risk. We illustrate this hedging technique with actual market data. It is also possible to use futures to alter the beta of an existing portfolio. For example, if a stock portfolio has a beta of 0.8 and the desired beta is 0.9, it is possible to trade stock index futures to make the combined stock and futures portfolio behave like a stock portfolio with a beta of 0.9. Finally, we consider techniques for tailing the hedge.

The Minimum Risk Hedge Ratio

In Chapter 7 we studied the problem of combining a cash market position with futures to minimize risk. There we took the cash market position as fixed and sought to find the futures hedge ratio, HR, that would minimize risk. From Equation 4.3 we saw that the risk of a combined cash and futures position equals:

$$\sigma_P^2 = \sigma_C^2 + \text{HR}^2\sigma_F^2 - 2\,\text{HR}\rho_{CF}\sigma_C\sigma_F \tag{4.3}$$

where:

σ_P^2 = variance of the portfolio
σ_C^2 = variance of asset C
σ_F^2 = variance of asset F
ρ_{CF} = correlation between assets C and F
σ_C = standard deviation of asset C
σ_F = standard deviation of asset F

From Equation 4.3, the risk-minimizing hedge ratio, HR, is:

$$HR = \frac{\rho_{CF}\sigma_C\sigma_F}{\sigma_F^2} = \frac{COV_{CF}}{\sigma_F^2}$$
(4.4)

where:

COV_{CF} = the covariance between C and F

As a practical matter, the easiest way to find the risk-minimizing hedge ratio is to estimate the following regression:

$$C_t = \alpha + \beta_{RM}F_t + \epsilon_t$$
(8.1)

where:

C_t = the returns on the cash market position in period t
F_t = the returns on the futures contract in period t[6]
α = the constant regression parameter
β_{RM} = the slope regression parameter for the risk-minimizing hedge
ϵ = an error term with zero mean and standard deviation of 1.0

The estimated beta from this regression is the risk-minimizing hedge ratio, because the estimated β_{RM} equals the sample covariance between the independent (F) and dependent (C) variables divided by the sample variance of the independent variable. The R^2 from this regression shows the percentage of risk in the cash position that is eliminated by holding the futures position.

At this point, it is important to distinguish the beta in Equation 8.1 and the beta of the portfolio in the sense of the Capital Asset Pricing Model. The CAPM beta is the beta from regressing the returns of a given asset on the returns from the "true" market portfolio. However, the returns on the true market portfolio are unobservable. Therefore, as a practical measure, proxies are used for the market portfolio and the betas of assets are estimated by regressing the returns of a particular asset on the returns from the proxy of the market portfolio. The potential confusion becomes more dangerous because the S&P 500 spot index is one of the best-known proxies for the true market portfolio.

In Equation 7.6 we computed a hedge ratio using the beta for the portfolio. This beta is the estimated CAPM beta, because it is estimated by regressing the returns from a portfolio on the proxy for the market portfolio. By contrast, the beta in Equation 8.1 is the beta for a risk-minimizing hedge ratio and is not the same as the estimated CAPM beta. The beta in Equation 8.1 is found by regressing the returns of the portfolio on the returns from the futures contract. The estimated CAPM beta is found by regressing the returns of the portfolio on the returns of the spot market index being used as a proxy for the unobservable true market portfolio. Thus, the hedging position in Equation 7.6 is not a risk-minimizing hedge. Nonetheless, such hedges can be very useful. We might think of the hedge ratio in Equation 7.6 as a rough-and-ready approximation to risk-minimizing hedging.

Having found the risk-minimizing hedge ratio, β_{RM}, we need to compute the number of contracts to trade. The solution to this problem almost exactly matches the hedging position in Equation 7.6, but we use the risk-minimizing hedge ratio, β_{RM}, instead of the CAPM beta for the portfolio, β_P. Thus, the risk-minimizing futures position is:

$$\left(\frac{V_P}{V_F}\right)\beta_{RM} = \text{number of contracts}$$

A Minimum Risk Hedging Example

In this section we consider an example of a minimum risk hedge in stock index futures using actual market data. Let us assume a trader has a portfolio worth $10 million on November 28. The portfolio is invested in the 20 stocks in the MMI. The portfolio manager will hedge this cash market portfolio using the S&P 500 JUN futures contract. We consider each step that the portfolio manager follows to compute the hedge ratio and to implement the hedge.

Organize Data and Compute Returns. The manager plans to hedge according to Equation 7.6. Therefore, she needs to find the beta for the hedge ratio. Accordingly, she collects data for her portfolio value for 101 days from July 6 through yesterday, November 27. She also finds the price of the S&P 500 JUN futures for each day. There is nothing magic about using 101 days, but these data are available and she believes that this procedure will provide a sufficient sample to estimate the hedging beta. From the 101 days of prices, she computes the daily percentage change in the value of the cash market portfolio and the futures price. This gives 100 paired observations of daily returns data.

Estimate Hedging Beta. With the data in place, the portfolio manager regresses the cash market returns on the returns from the futures contract as shown in Equation 8.1. From this regression the estimated beta is .8801, so $\beta_{RM} = .8801$. This indicates that each dollar of the cash market position should be hedged with $.8801 dollars in the futures position. The R^2 from the regression is .9263, and this high R^2 encourages the belief that the hedge is likely to perform well. Again, for emphasis, the estimated beta from regressing the portfolio's returns on the stock index futures returns is not the same as the portfolio's CAPM beta; β_P does not equal β_{RM}.

Compute Futures Position. The portfolio manager wants to hedge a $10 million cash portfolio with the S&P JUN futures contract. Having found the risk-minimizing hedge ratio, she needs to translate the hedge ratio into the correct futures position that takes account of the size of the futures contract. On November 27, the S&P futures closed at 354.75. The futures contract value is for the index times $500. Therefore, applying Equation 7.6, she computes the number of contracts as:

$$\left(\frac{V_P}{V_F}\right)\beta_{RM} = \left(\frac{\$10,000,000}{(354.75)(\$500)}\right).8801 = 49.6180$$

The estimated risk-minimizing futures position is 49.62 contracts, so the portfolio manager decides to sell 50 contracts.

Evaluate Hedging Results. Figure 8.2 shows the value of the unhedged and hedged portfolio for the next 60 days until February 22 of next year, when our trader decides to terminate the hedge. The unhedged portfolio's ending value is $9,656,090. The settlement price for the futures on February 22

Figure 8.2   Hedged and Unhedged Portfolio Values

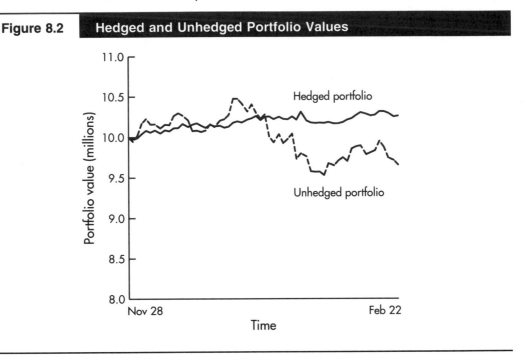

is 330.60. Therefore, the futures profit is 50($500)(354.75 - 330.60) = $603,750. The futures profit results from trading 50 contracts with each index point being worth $500 and the index having fallen 24.15 points. The value of the hedged portfolio consists of the cash market portfolio plus the futures profit, so the hedged portfolio's terminal value is $10,259,840. In this example, the hedge protected the portfolio against a substantial loss.

Ex-Ante versus Ex-Post Hedge Ratios

In our risk-minimizing hedging example, we computed β_{RM} = .8801 using historical data and applied the hedge ratio to a future period. It is highly unlikely that the estimated hedge ratio would equal the hedge ratio that we would have used if we had perfect foresight about the behavior of the cash market position and the futures price. This is the difference between an ex-ante and an ex-post hedge ratio. **Ex-ante**, or **before the fact**, the best hedge ratio we could find was .8801. **Ex-post**, or **after the fact**, some other hedge ratio would likely perform better than the ex-ante hedge ratio of .8801. In this section we consider the difference between ex-ante and ex-post hedge ratios in the context of our example.

The portfolio manager used historical returns from July 7 to November 27 to estimate the hedge ratio of .8801. She applied this hedge ratio on November 28, and maintained the hedged position until February 22 of the next year. The ex-post risk-minimizing hedge ratio was not available to her when she made her hedging decision on November 28. What would have been the ideal risk-minimizing hedge ratio, if she had complete knowledge about how prices would move from November 28 to February 22? To find this ex-post hedge ratio, we estimated Equation 8.1 using data from

November to February and found an ex-post hedge ratio of .9154. This implies a futures position of 51.61 contracts. We round this to 52 contracts. Figure 8.3 shows the results from hedging with the ex-ante and ex-post hedge ratios.

In a world with perfect foresight, the ex-post hedge ratio is the risk-minimizing hedge ratio we would like to use. However, the ex-ante hedge ratio is the best estimate we can make at the time the decision must be implemented. As Figure 8.3 shows, the ex-ante hedge ratio performs quite well. The terminal value of the hedge with the ex-ante hedge ratio is $10,259,840. With the ex-post hedge ratio, the terminal value is $10,283,990. While the ex-ante hedge ratio performed well, the ex-post hedge ratio would have been even better. This is exactly the result that we would expect.

Altering the Beta of a Portfolio

Portfolio managers often adjust the CAPM betas of their portfolios in anticipation of bull and bear markets. If a manager expects a bull market, she might increase the beta of the portfolio to take advantage of the expected rise in stock prices. Similarly, if a bear market seems imminent, the manager might reduce the beta of a stock portfolio as a defensive maneuver. If the manager trades only in the stock market itself, changing the beta of the portfolio involves selling some stocks and buying others. For example, to reduce the beta of the portfolio, the manager would sell high beta stocks and use the funds to buy low beta stocks. With transaction costs in the stock market being relatively high, this procedure can be expensive.

The portfolio manager has an alternative. She can use stock index futures to create a combined stock/futures portfolio with the desired response to market condition. In this section we consider techniques for changing the risk of a portfolio using stock index futures.

Ex-Ante versus Ex-Post Hedging Results   **Figure 8.3**

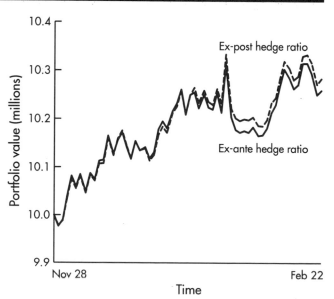

In the CAPM all risk is either systematic or unsystematic. **Systematic risk** is associated with general movements in the market and affects all investments. By contrast, **unsystematic risk** is particular to a certain investment or a certain range of investments. Diversification can almost completely eliminate unsystematic risk from a portfolio. The remaining systematic risk is unavoidable. Studies show that a random selection of 20 stocks will create a portfolio with very little unsystematic risk. Therefore, in this section we restrict our attention to portfolios that are well diversified and consequently have no unsystematic risk.

Starting with a stock portfolio that has systematic risk only and combining it with a risk-minimizing short position in stock index futures creates a combined stock/futures portfolio with zero systematic risk. According to the CAPM, a portfolio with zero systematic risk should earn the risk-free rate of interest. Instead of eliminating all systematic risk by hedging, it is possible to hedge only a portion of the systematic risk to reduce, but not eliminate, the systematic risk inherent in the portfolio. Similarly, a portfolio manager can use stock index futures to increase the systematic risk of a portfolio.

A risk-minimizing hedge matches a long position in stock with a short position in stock index futures in an attempt to create a portfolio whose value will not change with fluctuations in the stock market. To reduce, but not eliminate the systematic risk, a portfolio manager could sell some futures, but fewer than the risk-minimizing amount. For example, to eliminate half of the systematic risk, the portfolio manager could sell half of the number of contracts stipulated by the risk-minimizing hedge. The combined stock/futures position would then have a level of systematic risk equal to half of the stock portfolio's systematic risk.

It is also possible to trade stock index futures to increase the systematic risk of a stock portfolio. If a trader buys stock index futures, he increases his systematic risk. Therefore, if a portfolio manager holds a stock portfolio and buys stock index futures, the resulting stock/futures position has more systematic risk than the stock portfolio alone. For example, assume a portfolio manager buys, instead of sells, the risk-minimizing number of stock index futures. Instead of eliminating the systematic risk, the resulting stock/long futures position should have twice the systematic risk of the original portfolio.

We can illustrate this principle by considering the same data we used to illustrate the risk-minimizing hedge. In that example, the risk-minimizing futures position was to sell 50 contracts. Selling 50 contracts created a stock/futures position with zero systematic risk. By selling just 25 contracts, the portfolio manager could cut the systematic risk of the original portfolio in half. Similarly, by buying 50 contracts, the resulting stock/futures position would have twice the systematic risk of the original futures position.

Figure 8.4 shows the price paths of two portfolios over the 60-day hedging period from November 28 to February 22. First, the graph shows the unhedged portfolio. Its value begins at $10 million and terminates at $9,656,090, as we have seen. Over this period, the unhedged portfolio lost about $350,000. The graph also shows the portfolio created by holding the stocks and buying 50 futures contracts. In our analysis of the risk-minimizing hedge, we found that the trader could minimize risk by selling 50 futures contracts. Buying 50 contracts doubles the systematic risk. The new portfolio of stock plus a long position of 50 contracts increases the sensitivity of the portfolio to swings in the stock market. In effect, holding the stock portfolio and buying stock index futures simulates more than 100 percent investment in the stock index. Stock prices in general fell during this 60-day period. For example, the all-stock portfolio lost 3.44 percent of its value over this period.

Price Paths for Hedged and Unhedged Portfolios   Figure 8.4

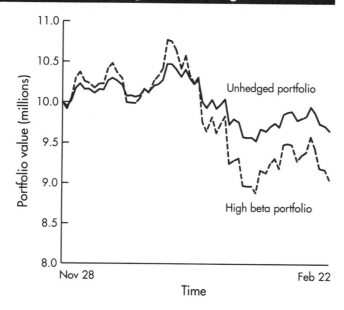

By buying stock index futures, the portfolio manager would increase the overall sensitivity of the portfolio to changes in the stock market. Not surprisingly, then, the stock/long futures portfolio lost more than the pure stock portfolio, As Figure 8.4 shows, every move of the stock/long futures portfolio exaggerates the movement of the all stock portfolio. For the portfolio of stock plus a long position of 50 index futures, the terminal value is $9,052,340. This portfolio lost 9.48 percent of its value. However, as Figure 8.4 also shows, for periods when the stock prices advanced from their initial level, the stock/long futures position rose even more. This is just what we expect, because buying futures increases the systematic risk of the existing stock portfolio.

ASSET ALLOCATION

In **asset allocation**, an investor decides how to divide funds among broad asset classes. For example, the decision to invest 60 percent in equities and 40 percent in T-bills is an asset allocation decision. The choice between investing in General Motors and Ford Motors is not an asset allocation decision. Thus, asset allocation focuses on the macro level commitment of funds to various asset classes and the shifting of funds among these major asset classes. In this section, we use the basic cost-of-carry model to show how a trader can radically adjust an initial portfolio to move from equities to T-bills or from T-bills to equities by using stock index futures. Because these portfolio maneuvers radically change the type of asset the trader holds, the maneuvers implement asset allocation decisions.

The basic cost-of-carry model we have used since Chapter 3 asserts that the futures price equals the spot price times one plus the cost-of-carry under suitable market conditions:

$$F_0 = S_0(1 + C) \tag{3.3}$$

where:

F_0 = the futures price at $t = 0$
S_0 = the spot price at $t = 0$
C = the percentage cost of carrying the spot good from $t = 0$ to the futures expiration

The cost-of-carry includes the financing cost of purchasing the asset, plus storage, insurance, and transportation. As we have seen in Chapter 3, for financial futures the cost-of-carry essentially equals the financing cost, because storage, insurance, and transportation are negligible. Therefore, in a full carry market, a cash-and-carry strategy of selling a futures and buying and holding the spot good until the futures expires should earn the financing rate, which essentially equals the risk-free rate of interest. We can express this relationship as:

$$\text{Short-Term Riskless Debt} = \text{Stock} - \text{Stock Index Futures} \qquad (8.2)$$

Creating a Synthetic T-Bill

From the analysis in the preceding section, we see that the basic cash-and-carry strategy of holding the stock and selling futures gives a resulting stock/futures portfolio that mimics a T-bill. Of course, it does not create a real T-bill. Instead, the stock/futures portfolio behaves like a T-bill. We might say that the trader creates a synthetic T-bill by holding stock and selling futures.

$$\text{Synthetic T-bill} = \text{Stock} - \text{Stock Index Futures}$$

This synthetic T-bill is related to risk-minimizing hedging. In a minimum risk hedge, a trader sells futures against a stock portfolio to create a combined stock/futures portfolio that has no systematic risk. A portfolio with no systematic risk has an expected return that equals the risk-free rate. Thus, the position created by risk-minimizing hedging is essentially the creation of a synthetic T-bill.

Consider the asset allocation decision of a trader with a stock portfolio. Assume the trader believes that a bear market is imminent and that the proper asset allocation decision is to hold no equities and to invest all funds in T-bills. The trader can sell all of the equities and invest the funds in T-bills. However, selling an entire portfolio can incur substantial transaction costs. Instead, the manager can implement the asset allocation decision by selling stock index futures against the portfolio. By implementing a risk-minimizing hedge, the manager creates a synthetic T-bill.

Creating a Synthetic Equity Position

It is also possible to use stock index futures to create a synthetic stock market position. Consider now a trader who holds all assets in T-bills. We assume that this trader expects a stock market surge, and she would like to take advantage of the rising stock prices. However, she is reluctant to incur all of the transaction costs associated with buying stocks. She too can implement her asset allocation decision by using stock index futures. Rearranging Equation 8.2 shows how to create the risky stock position:

$$\text{Synthetic Stock Portfolio} = \text{T-bills} + \text{Stock Index Futures}$$

The trader can buy stock index futures and hold the futures in conjunction with T-bills to mimic a stock portfolio. Thus, she implements her asset allocation decision by trading stock index futures.

In our discussion of asset allocation, we have considered examples of using stock index futures to change from 100 percent stock investment to 100 percent T-bill investment, and vice versa. Of course, the change in the portfolio need not be so radical. When we considered hedging, we saw that a trader can implement a risk-minimizing hedge or a transaction that shapes the risk of the portfolio. For example, by trading half of the risk-minimizing futures position, a trader could cut the systematic risk of the stock position in half. Similarly, by holding stock and buying stock index futures, the trader could increase the systematic risk of the position. The same principles apply to asset allocation decisions. For the trader with an initial stock position, selling half of the risk-minimizing number of futures results in a portfolio that behaves like a portfolio that is invested half in stock and half in T-bills. Similarly, a trader with a long position in stock who buys stock index futures creates a combined stock/futures portfolio that behaves like a leveraged stock portfolio.

PORTFOLIO INSURANCE

As we have seen, traders can tailor the risk of a stock portfolio by trading stock index futures. For a given well-diversified portfolio, selling stock index futures can create a combined stock/futures portfolio with reduced risk. Holding a stock portfolio and buying stock index futures results in a portfolio with greater risk and expected return than the initial portfolio.

Portfolio insurance refers to a collection of techniques for managing the risk of an underlying portfolio. With most portfolio insurance strategies, the goal is to manage the risk of a portfolio to ensure that the value of the portfolio does not drop below a specified level, while at the same time allowing for the portfolio's value to increase. Portfolio insurance strategies are often implemented using options, as we will discuss in Chapter 11. However, stock index futures are equally important tools for portfolio insurance. Implementing portfolio insurance strategies using futures is called **dynamic hedging**. Although the mathematics of dynamic hedging are too complex for full treatment here, we can understand the basic idea behind portfolio insurance with stock index futures.

A Portfolio Insurance Example

Consider a fully diversified stock portfolio worth $100 million. The value of this portfolio can range from zero to infinity. Many investors would like to put a floor beneath the value of the portfolio. For example, it would be very desirable to ensure that the portfolio's value never falls below $90 million. Portfolio insurance offers a way to control the downside risk of a portfolio. However, in a financial market there is no free lunch, so it is only possible to limit the risk of a large price fall by sacrificing some of the potential for a gain. Portfolio insurance, like life insurance, is not free, but it may be desirable for some traders.

We have seen that a risk-minimizing hedge converts a stock portfolio to a synthetic T-bill. By fully hedging our example stock portfolio, we can keep the portfolio's value above $100 million. A fully hedged portfolio will increase in value at the risk-free rate, although full hedging eliminates all of the potential gain in the portfolio beyond the risk-free rate. In dynamic hedging, however, the trader holds the stock portfolio and sells some futures contracts. The more insurance the trader wants, the more futures he or she will sell.

Let us assume that a stock index futures contract has an underlying value of $100 million and a trader sells futures contracts to cover $50 million of the value of the portfolio. Thus, in the initial position, the trader is long $100 million in stock and short $50 million in futures, so 50 percent of the portfolio is hedged. Table 8.3 shows this initial position in the time zero row. At $t = 0$, there has been no gain or loss on either the stock or futures. In the first period, we assume that the value of the stock portfolio falls by $2 million. The 50 futures contracts cover half of that loss with a gain of $1 million. Therefore, at t = 1, the combined stock/futures portfolio is worth $99 million. Now the manager increases the coverage in the futures market by selling five more contracts. This gives a total of 55 short positions and coverage for 56 percent (55/99) of the total portfolio. In the second period, the stock portfolio loses another $2 million, but with 55 futures contracts, the futures gain is (55/99)$2 million = $1.11 million. This gives a total portfolio value of $98.11 million.

By $t = 4$, the stock portfolio has fallen $10 million, but the futures profits have been $6.21 million. This gives a total portfolio value of $96.21 million. Also, the manager has increased the futures position in response to each drop in stock prices. At $t = 4$, the trader is short 80 contracts, hedging 83 percent of the stock market portfolio. At $t = 5$, the stock price drops dramatically, losing $35.86 million. The futures profit covers $30.65 million. This leaves a total portfolio value of $90 million. However, this is the floor amount of the portfolio, so the trader must now move to a fully hedged position. If the stock portfolio is only partially hedged, the next drop in prices can take the value of the entire portfolio below the floor amount of $90 million. At $t = 6$, the price of the stocks drops $10 million, but the futures position fully covers the loss. Therefore, the combined portfolio maintains its floor value of $90 million.

Table 8.3 shows the basic strategy of portfolio insurance with dynamic hedging. Initially, the portfolio is partially hedged. If stock prices fall, the trader increases the portion of the portfolio that is insured. Had the stock portfolio risen in value, the futures position would have lost money. However, the loss on the futures position would have been less than the gain on the stocks, because the portfolio was only partially hedged. As the stock prices rose, the manager would have bought futures, thereby hedging less and less of the portfolio. Less hedging would be needed if the stock price rose, because there would be little chance of the portfolio's total value falling below $90 million.

Implementing Portfolio Insurance

By design, Table 8.3 is highly simplistic. First, it does not show how the starting futures position was determined. Second, it does not show how the adjustments in the futures position were determined.

Table 8.3	Portfolio Insurance Transactions and Results				
	Gain/Loss $ millions		Total	Futures	Portion
Time	Stocks	Futures	Value	Position	Hedged
0	0.00	0.00	100.00	−50	.50
1	−2.00	1.00	99.00	−55	.56
2	−2.00	1.11	98.11	−60	.61
3	−2.00	1.22	97.33	−70	.72
4	−4.00	2.88	96.21	−80	.83
5	−36.86	30.65	90.00	−90	1.00
6	−10.00	10.00	90.00	−90	1.00

Third, it considers only large changes in the value of the stock portfolio. For instance, the smallest change in the table is 2 percent of the stock portfolio's value. The exact answer to these questions is highly mathematical; however, we can explore these issues in an intuitive way.

Choosing the initial futures position depends on several factors. First, it depends on the floor that is chosen relative to the initial value of the portfolio. For example, if the lowest acceptable value of the portfolio is $100 million, then the manager must hedge 100 percent at $t = 0$. Thus, the lower the floor relative to the portfolio value, the lower the percentage of the portfolio the manager will need to hedge. Second, the purpose of the insurance strategy is to guarantee a minimum terminal portfolio value while allowing for more favorable results. As a consequence, the futures position must take into account the volatility of the stock portfolio. The higher the estimated volatility of the stock portfolio, the greater the chance of a large drop in value that will send the total portfolio value below the floor. Therefore, the portion of the portfolio that is to be hedged depends critically on the estimated volatility of the stock portfolio. Of course, this will differ both across time and for portfolios of different risk.

Adjustments in the futures position depend upon the same kinds of considerations that determine the initial position. First, the value of the portfolio relative to the floor is critical. Second, new information about the volatility of the stock portfolio also affects the futures position. In Table 8.3, the volatility of the stock portfolio accelerates. Each percentage drop is larger than the previous. Therefore, this increasing volatility will lead to a larger short futures position than would otherwise be necessary.

In Table 8.3, the drops in the stock portfolio's values are large. In actual practice, dynamic hedging works by continually monitoring the value of the portfolio. Small changes in the portfolio can trigger small adjustments in the futures position. For many portfolios, monitoring and updating can occur many times a month. This is the reason it is called dynamic hedging – the hedge is monitored and updated continuously, often with computerized trading programs. Table 8.3 does not show that continual monitoring. Instead, we might take the different rows in the table as snapshots of the portfolio's value at different times.

Table 8.3 abstracts from some of the cash flow issues that dynamic hedging will raise. For example, it does not explicitly consider the cash flows that come from daily settlement of the futures position. There are a host of technical issues such as these that actual dynamic hedging must face.

INDEX FUTURES AND STOCK MARKET VOLATILITY

The link between stock market volatility and stock index futures trading has become important in public policy debates. Some critics of index futures have already sought limitations of index trading on the principal grounds that index trading contributes to increased stock market volatility. As we will see, the evidence supporting this proposition is far from conclusive. However, even if it were proven that stock index futures trading did increase stock market volatility, is that bad? To most economists, price volatility results from the arrival of new information in the market. Traders receive new information that causes them to reassess the true value of the good being traded. In an efficient market, the price quickly adjusts to reflect this new information. One result of this process is volatility. Thus, economists often interpret volatile prices as evidence of a properly functioning and informationally efficient market. Under this view, volatility is good, not bad. Nonetheless, if stock index futures trading contributed to volatility in a way that was not tied to information or a properly functioning market, the futures trading could be deleterious to the market.

In this section we consider the links between stock index trading and stock market volatility. Even before the Crash of October 1987, critics of index futures trading claimed that the stock index futures market was responsible for an increase in the volatility of the stock market. In essence, the argument asserts that strategies such as program trading and portfolio insurance disrupt the stock market and cause stock prices to swing wildly as they are forced into alignment with stock index futures prices. We begin by considering the evidence on stock market volatility itself. While there may be a general perception of greater stock market volatility, the evidence on this issue is mixed. Next, we consider possible links between stock market volatility and stock index futures trading, particularly index arbitrage and portfolio insurance. Finally, we analyze the Crash of 1987 and the mini-crash of October 1989 to consider the impact of stock index futures on the stock market itself.

Has Stock Market Volatility Increased?

Here we consider whether there has been an increase in stock market volatility. While this may seem to be a fairly straightforward question, the evidence is mixed. These diverse conclusions stem in part from differences in the time periods examined. For instance, some studies compare volatility across the decades, while others focus on changes in volatility within the 1980s. Also, some studies consider volatility from month to month, others focus on day to day volatility, while still other articles examine volatility within a single day and ask whether this intraday volatility is increasing.

Stock Volatility: The Long View. Several studies have examined stock market volatility for periods of many decades, some even going into the last century. For the most part, these studies focus on monthly stock portfolio returns. The general conclusion is clear: There has been no tendency for stock market volatility to increase from decade to decade. The 1930s had the highest volatility in this century, but there is weak evidence that the 1980s was the most volatile decade since World War II. Figure 8.5 depicts this long-run pattern of volatility.

Stock Volatility in the 1980s. Even if the 1980s were not more volatile than other decades, it is still possible that volatility increased within the decade. With the 1980s, we consider conclusions using daily data and intraday data. Within the 1980s, October-December 1987 show high volatility. (The Crash occurred on October 19, 1987.) However, there appears to be no general tendency for volatility to have increased over the 1980s.

Becketti and Sellon suggest that we distinguish normal volatility and jump volatility. The ordinary variability of stock returns, perhaps measured best by the standard deviation, is **normal volatility**. By contrast, **jump volatility** is the occasional extreme jump in prices. Figure 8.6 shows the frequency of large jumps in stock returns from 1962–1988.[7] Sellon and Becketti conclude that 1986–1988 exhibit high jump volatility, but they are quick to point out that this evidence does not suggest a permanent shift to a market with higher jump volatility. More data are needed to answer that question. Further, even in terms of jump volatility, the 1980s were not high compared to other decades before the 1960s. For example, only four of the 34 largest daily drops in 105 years occurred in the 1980s.[8] This is approximately the number of observations one would expect to find by chance.

Schwert also considered intraday data in his analysis of stock market volatility. He examined returns over 15-minute intervals for February 1, 1983 through October 19, 1989. He found that October 19–31, 1987, and October 13, 1989, stood out. (Friday, October 13, 1989, was the date of the ''mini-crash.'') However, volatility quickly returned to normal levels after these episodes of high volatility. From this review of a century of stock prices, we can conclude that there has been no

Index of Stock Market Volatility: 1927–1987   **Figure 8.5**

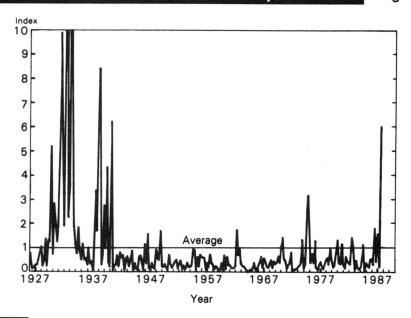

Source: From P. Fortune, "An Assessment of Financial Market Volatility: Bills, Bonds, and Stocks," *New England Economic Review,* November/December 1989, p. 16. Reprinted by permission.

increase in long-term volatility. Jump volatility seems to have been high in 1986–1988 compared to the 1960–1988 period. However, jump volatility for the 1980s appears to be about normal compared to the rest of the century.

Do Stock Index Futures Cause Market Volatility?

There are two main practices in stock index futures trading that are alleged to cause stock market volatility. These are index arbitrage (particularly program trading) and portfolio insurance. Both practices contribute to volatility, critics say, because they quickly dump large orders on the market at critical times. These large orders can reinforce existing trends in prices, thereby contributing to stock market volatility. We consider each in turn.

Index Arbitrage and Stock Market Volatility. In index arbitrage, traders search for discrepancies between stock prices and futures prices. When the two prices differ from the cost-of-carry model enough to cover transaction costs, index arbitrageurs sell the overpriced side of the pair and buy the underpriced. Typically, the arbitrageur holds the combined stock/futures position until expiration. At expiration, the cash settlement procedures for index futures guarantee that the stock and futures prices will converge. This convergence is guaranteed to hold at the open of trading on the expiration day, because the last futures settlement price is set equal to the opening cash market index value on that day. Some stock index futures also use the closing price as the final settlement price. In that case,

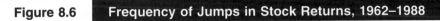

Figure 8.6 | **Frequency of Jumps in Stock Returns, 1962–1988**

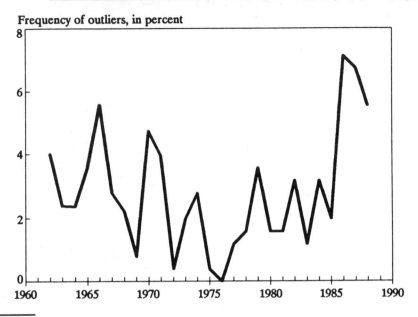

Source: From S. Becketti and G. Sellon, "Has Financial Market Volatility Increased?" Federal Reserve Bank of Kansas City *Economic Review,* June 1989, p. 22. Reprinted by permission.

to take advantage of convergence, index arbitrageurs often unwind their positions by entering market-on-close orders for the last trading day of the futures. A market-on-close order sells or buys a stock at the market price prevailing at the close of trading.

Consider now an index arbitrageur who is long stock and short futures. We assume that the futures settles based on the closing price and that the trader enters a market-on-close order to sell the stocks. Assume also that other arbitrageurs are also long stock and short futures and seek to unwind their positions in a similar manner. All of these stocks will come to market at the same time, so there could be an extremely large number of stocks to be sold all at once at the close of trading. Critics fear that this practice can lead to dramatic volatility in the market in a way that disrupts trading. Particularly, they fear that such high jump volatility might scare away some investors.

Notice that this effect occurs only if there is a substantial order imbalance among index arbitrageurs. There may be a very high level of index arbitrage with no serious order imbalance. Assume for a moment that, over the life of the futures, the stock and futures prices vary in being high or low relative to the cost-of-carry model. Some traders will initiate their index arbitrage transactions by buying stocks, while others will arbitrage by selling stocks. At the expiration of the futures, the unwinding could result in roughly equal numbers of buy and sell orders for stocks. In such a situation, we would not expect index arbitrage to have any effect on prices, and it could not contribute to volatility.

Portfolio Insurance and Stock Market Volatility. Portfolio insurance can also contribute to potential order imbalances that might affect stock prices. From our example of a portfolio insurance trade in Table 8.3, we see that a drop in stock prices requires the portfolio insurer to sell additional stock index futures. Similarly, when prices rise, the insurer buys stock index futures. A potential problem for market volatility arises because portfolio insurance generates trading in the same direction that the market happens to be moving. Thus, portfolio insurance can contribute to the existing momentum of the market.

To see the potential effects of portfolio insurance in exacerbating an existing trend, assume that the stock and futures prices are tightly linked by the cost-of-carry model. Due to this linkage, a drop in stock prices will quickly stimulate a drop in futures. The same transmission will occur from a drop in futures to a drop in stock prices. Now assume that there is a large drop in stock prices.

In response to the drop in stock prices, the futures price will have to fall. The cost-of-carry model requires this adjustment. However, the drop in stock prices also stimulates a large number of orders from portfolio insurers to sell index futures. This is clear from our example in Table 8.3. Critics fear that the sell orders from portfolio insurers might temporarily depress the futures price below the price justified by the cost-of-carry model. Assuming this happens, stock prices must again fall to match the depressed futures price. Now, with this next drop in stock prices, the portfolio insurers must again sell futures. Critics of portfolio insurance fear that this selling-price fall-selling scenario could create a spiral of falling prices and more sell orders, putting the entire market into a tailspin that could be disastrous.

Summary. According to critics, unrestricted stock index futures trading can contribute to stock market volatility, or even panics, by creating order imbalances that force stock prices below the prices justified by economic fundamentals. For index arbitrage, the feared order imbalance is most likely to occur at the expiration of the futures. Critics fear that portfolio insurers will respond to a sudden drop in stock prices by dumping sell orders onto the stock index futures market, thereby depressing prices. These depressed prices will feed into the stock market causing another drop in prices. The portfolio insurer will again sell stock index futures, and perhaps help create a downward price spiral. (On the other hand, if prices fall too much, the stocks will be cheap, and value-oriented investors will be attracted to buy. This buying would help restore prices to their rational levels.)

Volatility and Stock Index Futures Before the Crash

Long before the Crash of October 1987 and the mini-crash of October 1989, critics charged that stock index futures increased volatility. Here we consider the empirical evidence on this issue that is not related to the Crash or mini-crash. The Crash and crashlet we discuss later. We begin by considering the pre- and post-futures trading periods in general. Later, we consider the expiration days for the futures.

Volatility and the Introduction of Stock Index Futures. To determine whether stock index futures increase stock market volatility, some studies have compared the volatility of the stock market before and after the introduction of stock index futures in 1982. Santoni computed the means and standard deviations of percentage changes in the S&P 500 index before and after the introduction of S&P 500 futures in April 1982. Table 8.4 presents his key results. Focusing on the standard deviations, we see that weekly and daily standard deviations changed little. The weekly standard deviations rose slightly, while the daily standard deviations fell just a little. Neither difference is statistically significant. Santoni

Table 8.4	S&P 500 Index Statistics: Before and After Futures Trading			
	Before April 1982		After April 1982	
	Mean	**Std. Dev.**	**Mean**	**Std. Dev.**
Weekly	.130	1.68	.306	1.74
Daily	.004	0.95	.069	0.88

Source: From G. Santoni, "Has Programmed Trading Made Stock Prices More Volatile?" *Federal Reserve Bank of St. Louis Review,* May 1987, pp. 18–29. Reprinted by permission of the Federal Reserve Bank of St. Louis.

also considered intraday variability and concluded that it fell slightly, but statistically significantly, after the introduction of the S&P 500 futures. Other studies have examined the issue using a similar approach. Most of these studies find no increase in overall volatility after the introduction of futures trading. However, some do find increases in volatility for intraday data.

While comparing pre- and post-index futures trading may shed some light on the volatility effect of futures trading, the technique has some dangers. For example, if volatility increases, might there be some other factor that explains the increase, such as inflation or deficits? Also, even if volatility does not change, it is still possible that stock index futures stimulated volatility and some other factors offset the increase in volatility caused by futures.

Stock Volatility on Expiration Days. Even if index futures trading cannot be charged with a general increase in stock market volatility, it might still be associated with episodic increases in volatility – the jump volatility that Santoni considered. In particular, the unwinding of index arbitrage programs at the futures expiration might cause an order imbalance that could increase volatility. Accordingly, this section focuses on stock index futures and expiration day volatility.

In 1985–86, stock index futures, options on the stock index, and options on the stock index futures had common expiration dates four times per year and generally settled based on closing prices. (Now some instruments settle based on opening prices.) The convergence of these three expirations gave them the name of the **triple witching hour** – witching because of the fear of high volatility. For these expiration days, most studies find higher volatility than on other days. For the most part, the higher volatility is concentrated in the last hour of trading. (Recall that this study covered a period when the final settlement price was determined at the close of trading. Now there is a trend for the opening price to be used as the final settlement price for the futures.)

Table 8.5 summarizes some key results from the Stoll and Whaley 1986 study of expiration day volatility. The table shows the mean and standard deviation of returns computed from minute by minute price data. As the table shows, the standard deviation was higher when the futures expired than when nothing expired. However, when the Chicago Board Options Exchange (CBOE) S&P 100 option expired, but the futures did not, the volatility was not significantly higher than days on which nothing expired. Also, stock prices tend to fall on expiration days. If we compare the behavior of the S&P 500 index on expiration days with its behavior on nonexpiration days, the price effect and the volatility effect are both statistically significant.

Figure 8.7, also drawn from the Stoll and Whaley study, illustrates the dramatic price movements that can occur as the futures expires. Figure 8.7 traces the minute by minute level of the S&P 500 index for the last 30 minutes of trading on December 20, 1985, and for the first 30 minutes on the

Expiration Day Stock Price Volatility (Final Hour of Trading)			Table 8.5
S&P 500	**Expiring Instrument**		
	Futures	**CBOE S&P Options**	**Nothing**
Mean	−.352	.026	.061
Std. Dev.	.641	.261	.211
Observ.	10	16	97

Source: From H. Stoll and R. Whaley, "Expiration Day Effects of Index Options and Futures," New York University: Monograph Series in Finance and Economics, 1986. Reprinted by permission.

Minute-By-Minute S&P 500 Index Values
(December 1985 Expiration)   Figure 8.7

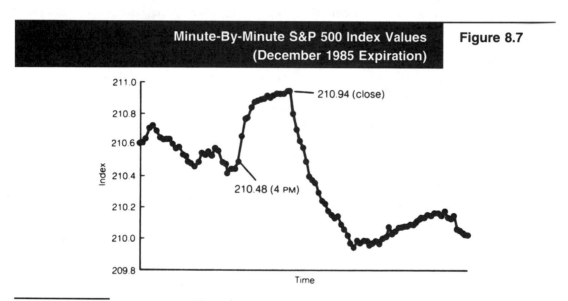

Source: From H. Stoll and R. Whaley, "Expiration Day Effects of Index Options and Futures," New York University: Monograph Series in Finance and Economics, 1986. Reprinted by permission.

next trading day. This figure gives a visual impression of the kinds of swings the index can take in a very short period of trading time. Stoll and Whaley found also that stock prices tend to rise in the first 30 minutes of trading on the first trading day after expiration. In summary, higher volatility does appear to be associated with futures expirations, particularly in the final hour of trading when many index arbitrage positions are being closed.

INDEX FUTURES AND STOCK MARKET CRASHES

Even if futures expirations cause higher volatility for an hour once per quarter, the effect cannot be very serious. However, if futures are somehow responsible for market crashes, the matter has a completely different and more ominous character. In October 1987, the Crash led some to believe that the entire financial system was threatened. The events of October 19, 1987, touched off a series of debates and policy discussions that still continues. This section analyzes the relationship between stock index futures and stock prices during October 1987. Later we consider the mini-crash of October 13, 1989.

The Crash of October 19, 1987, is as controversial as it is dramatic. The Dow Jones Industrial Average lost 22.61 percent of its value that day. Trading volume was so heavy that it brought the trade processing divisions of brokerage houses to a virtual halt. During the day, it was often impossible to trade or even obtain accurate price quotations. In many respects, there was no stock market on that Black Monday. No sooner did trading cease than finger pointing started. Some fingers pointed at the trade deficit, while others pointed at the budget deficit. Still others pointed to the futures market as the cause of the crash. Here are a few choice quotations. Anis C. Wallace: ''Investors knew that stocks were overpriced by any traditional valuation measure such as price/earnings ratios and price to book value. They also knew that the combination of program trading and portfolio insurance could send prices plummeting.'' David E. Sanger: ''On Monday, October 19, Wall Street's legendary herd instinct, now embedded in digital code and amplified by hundreds of computers, helped turn a sell-off into a panic.'' Donald Regan: ''In my mind, we should start by banning index option arbitrage and then proceed with other reforms which will restore public confidence in the financial markets.'' Marshall Front: ''Futures and options are like barnacles on a ship. They take their life from the pricing of stocks and bonds. When the barnacles start steering the ship, you get into trouble, as we saw last week.''[9]

In the aftermath of the crash, the government formed a presidential task force under Nicholas Brady, who later became Secretary of the Treasury, to study the crash and its causes. The report of the task force is widely known as the Brady Report. While most observers agree that the inability of cash markets to handle the incredible order flow contributed to the market turmoil, the Brady Report attributed the fall in prices to index arbitrage and portfolio insurance. This view of the Crash has become known as the **cascade theory**. According to the Brady Report, portfolio insurers sought to liquidate their equity exposure by selling stock index futures. This selling action drove futures prices below their equilibrium price. In terms of the cost-of-carry model, the selling by portfolio insurers created a reverse cash-and-carry arbitrage. Seeing a profit opportunity, index arbitrageurs implemented reverse cash-and-carry strategies by buying futures and selling stocks. This action depressed prices further, and with new lower equity prices, portfolio insurers dumped more stock index futures, depressing prices still further. The vicious cycle was started. The repeated action of index arbitrageurs and portfolio insurers caused a downward ''cascade'' in prices. Thus, the Brady Report maintained that ''mechanical, price-insensitive selling'' by institutions was a key cause of the crash.[10]

The Stock/Futures Basis on October 19

The cascade theory, and thus the conclusions of the Brady Report, rest on the view that the stock/futures basis on October 19 was disrupted by the actions of ''mechanical, price-insensitive'' trading systems. Specifically, the Brady Report alleged that futures prices that day were too low relative to stock values. Therefore, the stock/futures basis became a critical empirical issue. The price relationships between stocks and stock index futures have been studied on a minute-to-minute basis for both the S&P 500 and the MMI.[11] Both markets reveal a similar story. At first glance, the usually tight relationship of the cost-of-carry model apparently failed completely. However, in large part, this appearance was due to the inability to trade or even to know the current value of individual shares.

For instance, even though the market opened at 9:30 New York time, some stocks did not trade for more than an hour. Among the MMI stocks, Exxon was the last one to start trading at 11:23 A.M. With stocks failing to trade in New York, traders were forced to use Friday prices as guides to Monday values. Such an estimate was, to say the least, imprecise.

Figure 8.8 shows the spread between the cash and futures using Chicago time. The extremely large difference at the open was due largely to the late opening of the individual stocks in New York. Until the stocks began to trade, there was no cash market for the traders in Chicago to use as a guide to proper values for the futures. However, it appears that the futures and stock did track each other with some accuracy during the middle of the day when prices were somewhat more available. The situation in the S&P 500 was similar. Lawrence Harris summarizes: ''Nonsynchronous trading explains part of the large absolute futures-cash basis observed during the crash. The remainder may be due to disintegration of the two markets.''[12] Thus, even in the madness, the cost-of-carry model was functioning with the available information. There was simply very little information flow. However, the stock/futures basis did seem to respond to the information that was available.

Order Imbalance, Index Arbitrage, and Portfolio Insurance on October 19

Even if the basis held to the cost-of-carry model as well as one could expect given the dramatic events on October 19, there is still a residual concern about the role of index arbitrage and portfolio

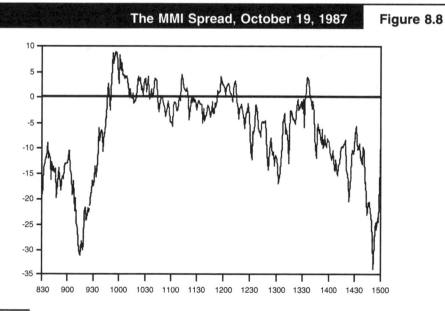

The MMI Spread, October 19, 1987   **Figure 8.8**

Source: From G. Bassett, V. France, and S. Pliska, "The MMI Cash-Futures Spread on October 19, 1987," *Review of Futures Markets* 8:1, 1989, p. 119. Reprinted by permission of The Chicago Board of Trade.

insurance. That day, 16 firms accounted for almost all stock index arbitrage and portfolio insurance trading. Twelve firms concentrated on index arbitrage, while four focused on portfolio insurance. About 9 percent of NYSE volume was generated by index arbitrage trading. For stock index futures, 12–24 percent of selling originated through portfolio insurance activity.[13] As a percentage of activity, these numbers suggest the possibility that futures-related activity was large enough to significantly affect the day's trading.

One interesting piece of evidence comes from comparing S&P 500 stocks with non-S&P 500 stocks. Blume, MacKinlay, and Terker found that S&P stocks fell about seven percentage points farther than non-S&P 500 stocks on October 19. By mid-morning during the recovery on October 20, the difference had been almost eliminated. In other words, stocks in the S&P 500 fell more during the crash, but bounced back to parity with other stocks very quickly.[14] Also, Blume, MacKinlay, and Terker found that the fall in S&P 500 stock prices was positively correlated with order imbalances on October 19. With heavy sell orders awaiting execution, stock prices fell more than at other times. If this order imbalance was related to futures trading, then the futures market could share some responsibility for the drop in the market.

Some evidence appears to show that futures trading is not necessary to start a panic in a given market, but this theory does not really absolve futures of all responsibility. The Crash was a worldwide phenomenon, as Richard Roll points out.[15] Of 23 markets worldwide, 19 fell by more than 20 percent. Further, the Crash seems to have begun in non-Japanese Asian markets, spread to European markets, then North American, then Japanese. This progression took place around the clock as trading developed on October 19 and 20. Comparing market performance and the presence of computer-directed trading in isolation, Roll found that, if computer trading had any impact at all, it actually helped reduce the market decline.

The fact that the Crash started in markets with limited futures trading does appear to show that other factors were at work besides futures trading. This opens the possibility of a **contagion theory** of the Crash. A crash develops in one country's market for some unknown reason. News arrives in other markets carrying the disease of the crash, which helps a crash develop in the second market. This kind of contagion theory was developed by King and Wadhwani.[16]

Assume that the U.S. market is infected and a Crash starts to develop. The U.S. Crash is then intensified by order imbalance resulting from futures trading. Now other countries could catch the crash disease from the United States in its more heightened and virulent form. Yet this does not seem to fit the facts for October 1987. First, the United States lost less than most other markets, both those that had crashed before and those that crashed later. Based on the version of the contagion theory just explained, we would expect the U.S. Crash to be deeper than that of countries that crashed earlier.

Summarizing the portion of evidence related to futures, the Crash did not start in the United States, so the futures markets could not have been the original source of the problem. The Crash in the United States was not relatively more severe, even though futures markets are more developed in the United States than elsewhere. There was no tendency for the crashes in markets trading after the U.S. Crash to be more severe than crashes in markets trading before the U.S. Nonetheless, if futures contributed to the U.S. Crash and if the contagion theory has merit, then the U.S. Crash could have contributed to crashes that occurred later.

Thus, residual suspicion about the role of futures remains, even though there is no compelling evidence to show that futures trading, whether index arbitrage or portfolio insurance, caused the Crash.[17] Study continues and the issue remains controversial. However, there does seem to be fairly widespread rejection of the Brady Report's main conclusion that the Crash was caused by index arbitrage and portfolio insurance leading to a cascade in stock prices.[18]

Policy Recommendations and Changing Trading Rules

In proposals for reform, the Brady Report recommended that the regulatory system be modified to have a single agency, that there be a unified clearing system for all financial markets, that margins be consistent between cash and futures markets, and that information systems across markets be improved. The report also recommended that exchanges implement **circuit breakers** – systems of planned trading halts – in times of volatility. There is continuing action on all of these fronts and much has already been implemented.

Since the Crash, circuit breakers have been put in place and refinements to the system continue. In essence, a circuit breaker is a planned decoupling of the stock index futures market and the stock market through price limits and trading halts. The system also permits delaying program trades. The idea is to halt trading when prices fall below their fundamental values. During the pause in trading, the effect of mob psychology will dissipate, and when trading resumes, prices will return to rational levels. These circuit breakers are controversial and their value is unknown.

However, even if trading is halted, prices can continue to fall and traders will be stuck with additional losses. According to market lore, the worst fear of many traders is to be stuck in a position. Some scholars believe that trading halts may create more panic than calm and consequently assert that trading halts are unwise. Nonetheless, futures markets already embody something like circuit breakers in the form of daily price limits. Also, defenders of circuit breakers believed they performed well in the mini-crash of October 13, 1989.

Probably the most controversial recommendation of the Brady Report is that there be "consistent margins" between stock and futures markets. This has been interpreted as calling for a large increase in futures margins. Such a policy would destroy the futures market as it now exists. According to defenders of futures, this policy recommendation shows a complete lack of understanding of futures margins.[19] Futures margins are not a partial payment for a good as they are in the stock market. Instead, futures margins serve as a security bond for the changes in the futures price that day. The bond is payable daily and renewable daily. In the ensuing debate, margin levels have become a political football in the struggle between the CFTC and the SEC. Also, stock index margins have been raised by the futures exchanges in an apparent effort to deter any move for even higher margins. In defense of the futures margining system, it is important to realize that no customer funds were lost due to failure to meet margin calls and no clearinghouse failed because of the Crash.

The Mini-Crash of October 13, 1989

Almost exactly two years after the Crash, it seemed that history would repeat itself. On October 13, 1989, a Friday the thirteenth, stock prices began a sickening slide. That day, the Dow dropped 190 points, with a 135 point drop in the final hour of trading. This mini-crash provided an opportunity to test some of the procedures instituted after the Crash.

Falling prices triggered a circuit breaker at 2:15 P.M. for the MMI futures and at 3:07 P.M. for the S&P 500 futures. For both contracts, trading could resume only at prices above the price that triggered the circuit breaker. Trading resumed and the circuit breaker was hit again for the S&P 500. In assessing the performance of the circuit breakers, both the CFTC and the exchanges seem to feel that they performed well.[20] Further efforts to refine the system continue and the market awaits further, perhaps more severe, tests of the system.

CONCLUSION

This chapter reviewed a wide range of issues related to stock index futures. We began by examining stock index futures pricing. We considered the efficiency of the stock index futures markets, the effect of taxes on stock index futures prices, the influence of seasonal factors on prices, and leads and lags between the futures market and the stock market. Next, we considered a real-world example of program trading, focusing on an index arbitrage example. This example showed the hidden risks in the apparently riskless strategy of index arbitrage. We also reviewed the level of program trading in recent years.

To extend the introduction to hedging in Chapter 7, we worked through an example of minimum risk hedging in detail, and we considered the difference between ex-ante and ex-post hedge ratios. We also saw how to use a hedging approach to adjust the beta of a portfolio. Adjusting the beta by a small amount may be a hedging activity, but we also explored asset allocation using stock index futures. Using stock index futures, traders holding riskless bonds can simulate full investment in equities. Similarly, a trader fully invested in equities can use stock index futures to make the combined stock/futures portfolio behave like a riskless bond.

This chapter also focused on the connection between stock index futures and stock market volatility. As we saw, the main arguments for a connection rely on order imbalances that might be caused by index arbitrage or portfolio insurance. We saw some evidence of these order imbalances and increased volatilities on expiration days. Finally, we considered the Crash of 1987 and the mini-crash of 1989. Although futures do not appear to be responsible for the price changes observed on these days, the events have been important in changing the institutional arrangements in the futures market.

QUESTIONS AND PROBLEMS

1. Explain the market conditions that cause deviations from a computed fair value price and that give rise to no-arbitrage bounds.
2. The No-Dividend Index consists only of stocks that pay no dividends. Assume that the two stocks in the index are priced at $100 and $48, and assume that the corresponding cash index value is 74.00. The cost of carrying stocks is 1 percent per month. What is the fair value of a futures contract on the index that expires in one year?
3. Using the same facts as in Problem 2, assume that the round-trip transaction cost on a futures is $30. The contract size, we now assume, is for 1,000 shares of each stock. Trading stocks costs $.05 per share to buy and the same amount to sell. Based on this additional information, compute the no-arbitrage bounds for the futures price.
4. Using the facts in Problems 2 and 3, we now consider differential borrowing and lending costs. Assume that the 1 percent per month is the lending rate and assume that the borrowing rate is 1.5 percent per month. What are the no-arbitrage bounds on the futures price now?
5. Using the facts in Problems 2–4, assume now that the short seller receives the use of only half of the funds in the short sale. Find the no-arbitrage bounds.

6. Consider the trading of stocks in an index and trading futures based on the index. Explain how different transaction costs in the two markets might cause one market to reflect information more rapidly than the other.

7. For index arbitrage, explain how implementing the arbitrage through program trading helps to reduce execution risk.

8. Index arbitrageurs must consider the dividends that will be paid between the present and the futures expiration. Explain how overestimating the dividends that will be received could affect a cash-and-carry arbitrage strategy.

9. Explain the difference between the beta in the CAPM and the beta one finds by regressing stock returns against returns on a stock index.

10. Explain the difference between an ex-ante and an ex-post minimum risk hedge ratio.

11. Assume you hold a well-diversified portfolio with a beta of 0.85. How would you trade futures to raise the beta of the portfolio?

12. An index fund is a mutual fund that attempts to replicate the returns on a stock index, such as the S&P 500. Assume you are the manager of such a fund and that you are fully invested in stocks. Measured against the S&P 500 index, your portfolio has a beta of 1.0. How could you transform this portfolio into one with a zero beta without trading stocks?

13. You hold a portfolio consisting of only T-bills. Explain how to trade futures to create a portfolio that behaves like the S&P 500 stock index.

14. In portfolio insurance using stock index futures, we noted that a trader sells additional futures as the value of the stocks falls. Explain why traders follow this practice.

NOTES

[1] D. Modest and M. Sundaresan, ''The Relationship Between Spot and Futures Prices in Stock Index Futures Markets: Some Preliminary Evidence,'' *Journal of Futures Markets*, 3:1, Spring 1983, pp. 15–41.

[2] B. Cornell and K. French, ''Taxes and the Pricing of Stock Index Futures,'' *Journal of Finance*, 38:3, June 1983, pp. 675–94; and B. Cornell, ''Taxes and the Pricing of Stock Index Futures: Empirical Results,'' *Journal of Futures Markets*, 5:1, 1985, pp. 89–101.

[3] See, for example, E. Dyl and E. Maberly, ''The Weekly Pattern in Stock Index Futures: A Further Note,'' *Journal of Finance*, 41:5, December 1986, pp. 1149–52.

[4] For a more extended survey of these studies, see R. Kolb, *Understanding Futures Markets*, 5e, Malden, MA: Blackwell Publishing, 1997.

[5] This example was the focus of a *Business Week* article, ''A Real Life Strategy for Making 14% Risk-Free,'' April 7, 1986.

[6] Strictly speaking, there is no return on a futures contract because a position in a futures contract requires no investment. By the futures return we mean the percentage change in the futures price.

[7] The definition used for large jumps is somewhat complex, but essentially a large jump is a daily return that is substantially larger than the typical change in prices.

[8] C. Jones and J. Wilson, ''Is Stock Price Volatility Increasing?'' *Financial Analysts Journal*, 45:6, November-December 1989, pp. 20–26.

[9] All quoted in G. Santoni, ''The October Crash: Some Evidence on the Cascade Theory,'' *Review*, Federal Reserve Bank of St. Louis, May/June 1988, pp. 18–33.

[10] *Report of the Presidential Task Force on Market Mechanisms*, 1988, p. v. See also G. Santoni, "The October Crash: Some Evidence on the Cascade Theory," *Review*, Federal Reserve Bank of St. Louis, May/June 1988, pp. 18–33, for a thoughtful critique of the Brady Report. P. Tosini, "Stock Index Futures and Stock Market Activity in October 1987," *Financial Analysts Journal*, 44:1, January/February 1988, pp. 28–37 also discusses the cascade theory.

[11] See L. Harris, "The October 1987 S&P 500 Stock-Futures Basis," *Journal of Finance*, 44:1, March 1989, pp. 77–99; G. Bassett, V. France, and S. Pliska, "The MMI Cash-Futures Spread on October 19, 1987," *Review of Futures Markets*, 8:1, 1989, pp. 118–38; G. Wang, E. Moriarty, R. Michalski, and J. Jordan, "Empirical Analysis of the Liquidity of the S&P 500 Index Futures Market During the October 1987 Market Break," Commodity Futures Trading Commission Staff Working Paper #88-6, February 1989; G. Santoni, "The October Crash: Some Evidence on the Cascade Theory," *Review*, Federal Reserve Bank of St. Louis, May/June 1988, pp. 18–33.

[12] L. Harris, "The October 1987 S&P 500 Stock-Futures Basis," *Journal of Finance*, 44:1, March 1989, p. 77. This view is supported by A. Kleidon and R. Whaley, "One Market? Stocks, Futures, and Options During October 1987," *Journal of Finance*, 47:3, July 1992, pp. 851–77. Kleidon and Whaley find that the market conformed well to cost-of-carry relationships in early October, but very poorly during the crash.

[13] These values are drawn from P. Tosini, "Stock Index Futures and Stock Market Activity in October 1987," *Financial Analysts Journal*, 44:1, January-February 1988, pp. 28–37.

[14] M. Blume, A. MacKinlay, and B. Terker, "Order Imbalances and Stock Price Movements on October 19 and 20, 1987," *Journal of Finance*, 44:4, September 1989, pp. 827–48.

[15] R. Roll, "The International Crash of October 1987," *Financial Analysts Journal*, 44:5, September-October 1988, pp. 19–35.

[16] M. King and S. Wadhwani, "Transmission of Volatility Between Stock Markets," *Review of Financial Studies*, 3:1, 1990, pp. 5–33.

[17] The Office of Technology Assessment, U.S. Congress, studied the Crash and reported on it in its study, "Electron Bulls & Bears: U.S. Securities Markets & Information Technology," September 1990. The study concluded that the responsibility of futures for the Crash could not be resolved by statistical analysis.

[18] Among those who reject the Brady Report conclusions of a futures induced cascade are: G. Santoni, "The October Crash: Some Evidence on the Cascade Theory," *Review*, Federal Reserve Bank of St. Louis, May/June 1988, pp. 18–33; J. Hill, "Program Trading, Portfolio Insurance, and the Stock Market Crash: Concepts, Applications and an Assessment," Kidder Peabody, January 1988; R. Roll, "The International Crash of October 1987," *Financial Analysts Journal*, 44:5, September-October 1988, pp. 19–35; D. Harrington, F. Fabozzi, and H. Fogler, *The New Stock Market*, Chicago: Probus Publishing Co., 1990; M. Miller, B. Malkiel, M. Scholes and J. Hawke, "Stock Index Futures and the Crash of '87," *Journal of Applied Corporate Finance*, 1:4, Winter 1989, pp. 6–17.

[19] See, for example, M. Miller, B. Malkiel, M. Scholes, and J. Hawke, "Stock Index Futures and the Crash of '87," *Journal of Applied Corporate Finance*, 1:4, Winter 1989, pp. 6–17.

[20] See "CFTC Reviews Friday the 13th," *Futures Industry Association Review*, November/December 1989, pp. 10–11.

CHAPTER	FOREIGN EXCHANGE FUTURES
9	

OVERVIEW

Foreign currencies are traded in both a highly active forward market and a futures market. The foreign exchange market is the only one in which a successful futures market has grown up in the face of a robust forward market. The forward market for foreign exchange has existed for a long time, but the foreign exchange futures market developed only in the early 1970s, with trading beginning on May 16, 1972, on the International Monetary Market (IMM) of the Chicago Mercantile Exchange (CME). Without doubt, the presence of such a strong and successful forward market retarded the development of a futures market for foreign exchange. This dual market system means that the futures market cannot be understood in isolation from the forward market. The conceptual bond arises both from the similarity of the two markets and from the fact that the forward market continues to be much larger than the futures market. Because many traders are active in both markets, familiar cash-and-carry and reverse cash-and-carry strategies ensure that the proper price relationships between the two markets are maintained.

As discussed in Chapter 3, forward and futures markets for a given commodity are similar in many respects. Because of this similarity, specific price relationships must hold between the two markets to prevent arbitrage opportunities. While any observer might be more impressed by the similarities in the two markets, the forward and futures markets differ in several key respects. Particularly important are the differences in the cash flow patterns (due to daily resettlement in the futures market) and the different structures of the contracts with respect to their maturities.

To understand foreign exchange futures trading, this chapter begins with a brief discussion of the markets for foreign exchange: the spot, forward, and futures markets. Next, we review the most important factors in determining exchange rates between two currencies, including the exchange rate regimes of fixed versus floating rates, the question of devaluation, and the influence of balance-of-payments. Against this institutional background, we analyze no-arbitrage pricing relationships, such as the Interest Rate Parity Theorem (IRP) and the Purchasing Power Parity Theorem (PPP). These theorems essentially express the pricing relationship of the cost-of-carry model. We also examine the

279

relationship between forward and futures prices and the accuracy of foreign exchange forecasting. As always in the futures market, the twin issues of speculation and hedging play an important role, and we consider them in detail.

PRICE QUOTATIONS

In the foreign exchange market, every price, or exchange rate, is a relative price. To say that one dollar is worth 2.5 Deutsche marks (DM 2.5) also implies that DM 2.5 will buy $1.00, or that DM 1 is worth $.40. All foreign exchange rates are related to each other as reciprocals, a relationship that is quite apparent in Figure 9.1, which shows the foreign exchange quotations as they appear daily in *The Wall Street Journal.* The quotations consist of two double columns of rates, one for the U.S.

Figure 9.1 | **Foreign Exchange Quotations**

CURRENCY TRADING

EXCHANGE RATES

Tuesday, April 23, 1996

The New York foreign exchange selling rates below apply to trading among banks in amounts of $1 million and more, as quoted at 3 p.m. Eastern time by Dow Jones Telerate Inc. and other sources. Retail transactions provide fewer units of foreign currency per dollar.

Country	U.S. $ equiv. Tue	U.S. $ equiv. Mon	Currency per U.S. $ Tue	Currency per U.S. $ Mon
Argentina (Peso)	1.0012	1.0012	.9988	.9988
Australia (Dollar)	.7900	.7868	1.2658	1.2710
Austria (Schilling)	.09371	.09374	10.671	10.668
Bahrain (Dinar)	2.6525	2.6525	.3770	.3770
Belgium (Franc)	.03204	.03210	31.210	31.150
Brazil (Real)	1.0152	1.0152	.9850	.9850
Britain (Pound)	1.5170	1.5123	.6592	.6612
30-Day Forward	1.5162	1.5116	.6595	.6616
90-Day Forward	1.5150	1.5103	.6601	.6621
180-Day Forward	1.5131	1.5085	.6609	.6629
Canada (Dollar)	.7339	.7338	1.3625	1.3628
30-Day Forward	.7343	.7342	1.3618	1.3621
90-Day Forward	.7350	.7349	1.3606	1.3608
180-Day Forward	.7524	.7528	1.3290	1.3283
Chile (Peso)	.002455	.002453	407.25	407.65
China (Renminbi)	.1198	.1198	8.3502	8.3500
Colombia (Peso)	.0009671	.0009671	1034.00	1034.00
Czech. Rep. (Koruna)	....	....	....	....
Commercial rate	.03610	.03610	27.697	27.702
Denmark (Krone)	.1708	.1710	5.8536	5.8469
Ecuador (Sucre)	....			
Floating rate	.0003277	.0003282	3052.00	3047.00
Finland (Markka)	.2081	.2095	4.8059	4.7740
France (Franc)	.1946	.1948	5.1380	5.1335
30-Day Forward	.1949	.1950	5.1306	5.1269
90-Day Forward	.1954	.1956	5.1168	5.1127
180-Day Forward	.1962	.1964	5.0961	5.0923
Germany (Mark)	.6572	.6592	1.5215	1.5170
30-Day Forward	.6585	.6604	1.5187	1.5143
90-Day Forward	.6608	.6627	1.5134	1.5089
180-Day Forward	.6648	.6666	1.5043	1.5001
Greece (Drachma)	.004134	.004134	241.91	241.91
Hong Kong (Dollar)	.1293	.1293	7.7362	7.7356
Hungary (Forint)	.006685	.006686	149.59	149.57
India (Rupee)	.02923	.02921	34.215	34.230
Indonesia (Rupiah)	.0004298	.0004297	2326.50	2327.00
Ireland (Punt)	1.5657	1.5613	.6387	.6405
Israel (Shekel)	.3153	.3147	3.1720	3.1775
Italy (Lira)	.0006436	.0006436	1553.75	1553.70
Japan (Yen)	.009375	.009378	106.67	106.63
30-Day Forward	.009415	.009420	106.21	106.16
90-Day Forward	.009489	.009493	105.38	105.34
180-Day Forward	.009604	.009605	104.13	104.12
Jordan (Dinar)	1.4124	1.4124	.7080	.7080
Kuwait (Dinar)	3.3333	3.3322	.3000	.3001
Lebanon (Pound)	.0006327	.0006327	1580.50	1580.50
Malaysia (Ringgit)	.4003	.4014	2.4980	2.4915
Malta (Lira)	2.7435	2.7435	.3645	.3645
Mexico (Peso)	....			
Floating rate	.1350	.1353	7.4100	7.3900
Netherlands (Guilder)	.5874	.5894	1.7023	1.6967
New Zealand (Dollar)	.6838	.6870	1.4624	1.4556
Norway (Krone)	.1532	.1534	6.5257	6.5210
Pakistan (Rupee)	.02915	.02915	34.310	34.310
Peru (new Sol)	.4241	.4241	2.3582	2.3582
Philippines (Peso)	.03820	.03818	26.180	26.190
Poland (Zloty)	.3790	.3793	2.6388	2.6365
Portugal (Escudo)	.006429	.006431	155.54	155.50
Russia (Ruble) (a)	.0002023	.0002032	4942.00	4922.00
Saudi Arabia (Riyal)	.2667	.2667	3.7501	3.7498
Singapore (Dollar)	.7097	.7098	1.4090	1.4088
Slovak Rep. (Koruna)	.03285	.03285	30.446	30.446
South Africa (Rand)	.2361	.2352	4.2350	4.2525
South Korea (Won)	.001284	.001284	779.05	778.75
Spain (Peseta)	.007919	.007938	126.28	125.98
Sweden (Krona)	.1489	.1491	6.7174	6.7078
Switzerland (Franc)	.8107	.8137	1.2335	1.2290
30-Day Forward	.8133	.8161	1.2296	1.2254
90-Day Forward	.8179	.8210	1.2226	1.2181
180-Day Forward	.8252	.8285	1.2118	1.2070
Taiwan (Dollar)	.03681	.03683	27.170	27.155
Thailand (Baht)	.03956	.03964	25.280	25.228
Turkey (Lira)	.00001351	.00001351	74001.50	74001.50
United Arab (Dirham)	.2757	.2723	3.6270	3.6725
Uruguay (New Peso)	....			
Financial	.1314	.1314	7.6100	7.6100
Venezuela (Bolivar)b	.002058	.002024	486.00	494.00
Brady Rate	.002062	.002020	485.00	495.00
SDR	1.4468	1.4484	.6912	.6904
ECU	1.2381	1.2375	....	....

Special Drawing Rights (SDR) are based on exchange rates for the U.S., German, British, French and Japanese currencies. Source: International Monetary Fund.

European Currency Unit (ECU) is based on a basket of community currencies.

a-fixing, Moscow Interbank Currency Exchange. b-Changed to market rate effective Apr. 22.

Dollar Equivalent of the foreign currency and one set of two columns for the amount of foreign currency per U.S. dollar. Each set of quotations shows the rates for the current and the preceding business day We focus only on the two columns of current quotations. The rate in one column has its reciprocal in the other column. (Sometimes these are not exact due to transaction costs.) The value of $/DM($ per DM) is just the reciprocal of the value of DM/$(DM per $). For some countries, such as Australia, the quotations show only the spot rate, the rate at which Australian and U.S. dollars may be exchanged at the moment.

For many major currencies, such as those of Germany, England, Japan, and Canada, the quotations show forward rates for periods of 30, 90, and 180 days into the future. The 30-day forward rate, for example, indicates the rate at which a trader can contract today for the delivery of some foreign currency 30 days hence. If the trader buys the foreign currency, then he or she agrees to pay the 30-day forward rate in 30 days for the currency in question, with the actual transaction taking place in 30 days. This kind of transaction exactly fits the description of forward markets in Chapter 1.

The quotations shown in Figure 9.1 are provided by Bankers' Trust Company, a major participant in the foreign exchange market. The market from which these quotations are drawn is made up of large banks in the U.S. and abroad. This market is known as the **interbank market**. As Figure 9.1 notes, the quotations pertain to transactions in amounts of $1 million or more. As is typical of forward markets, there is no physical location where trading takes place. Instead, banks around the world are linked electronically with each other. The large banks in the market have trading rooms elaborately equipped with electronic communications devices. A trader in such a room may have access to 60 telephone lines and five or more video quotation screens.[1] The market has no regular trading hours and is open somewhere in the world 24 hours per day. In addition to banks, some large corporations have access to the market through their own trading rooms.

Regional banks are unlikely to have their own trading rooms. Instead, they clear their foreign exchange transactions through correspondent banks with whom they have the appropriate arrangements. Corporations that are too small to have their own trading room, as well as individuals, make foreign exchange transactions through their own banks. As Figure 9.1 notes, the rates quoted are not available to small retail traders. Instead, retail transactions will be subject to a larger bid-asked spread that allows the bank providing the foreign exchange service to make a profit.

GEOGRAPHICAL AND CROSS-RATE ARBITRAGE

A number of pricing relationships exist in the foreign exchange market, the violation of which would imply the existence of arbitrage opportunities. The first two to be considered involve **geographical arbitrage** and **cross-rate arbitrage**. One of the best ways to learn about the relationships that must exist among currency prices is to explore the potential arbitrage opportunities that arise if the pricing relationships were violated.

Geographical arbitrage occurs when one currency sells for two prices in two different markets. Such pricing would be a simple violation of the law of one price. As an example, consider the following exchange rates between German marks and U.S. dollars as quoted in New York and Frankfurt. These are 90-day forward rates.

New York	$/DM	.42
Frankfurt	DM/$	2.35

The New York price, quoted as $ per DM, implies a DM/$ price equal to the inverse of the $/DM price:

$$\frac{1}{.42} = DM/\$ = 2.381$$

In New York, the DM/$ rate is 2.381, but in Frankfurt, it is 2.35. Since these are not equal, an arbitrage opportunity exists. To test for a geographical arbitrage opportunity, simply take the inverse of the price prevailing in one market and compare it with the price quoted in another market.

To conduct the arbitrage, the trader purchases the currency where it is cheap and sells it where it is expensive. In New York, a trader receives 2.381 DM per dollar, but only 2.35 DM per dollar in Frankfurt. Therefore, the DM is cheaper in New York. To exploit this pricing discrepancy, the trader transacts as shown in Table 9.1. These transactions represent the exploitation of an arbitrage opportunity since they ensure a profit with no investment. At the outset, there is no cash flow. The only cash flow involved in the transactions occurs simultaneously when the commitments initiated at $t = 0$ are completed at $t = 90$. The profit, however, was certain from the time of the initial transactions.

Arbitrage is also possible to exploit misalignments in cross-rates. To understand a cross-rate, consider the following example. In New York, an exchange rate is quoted for the dollar versus the German mark. There is also a rate quoted for the dollar versus the British pound. Together, these two rates imply an equilibrium exchange rate between the German mark and the British pound. This implied exchange rate is a **cross-rate**. Therefore, the exchange rates in New York involving the dollar imply an exchange rate between the mark and pound that do not involve the dollar. Figure 9.2 shows quotations for cross-rates from *The Wall Street Journal.*

If the direct rate quoted elsewhere for the mark versus the pound does not match the cross-rate in New York, an arbitrage opportunity exists. As an example, assume that the following rates are observed, where SF indicates the Swiss franc, and all of the rates are 90-day forward rates:

Table 9.1	Geographical Arbitrage

This is an arbitrage transaction since it has a certain profit with no investment. Notice that the arbitrage is not complete until the transactions at $t = 90$ are completed.

$t = 0$ (the present)
        Buy DM 1 in New York 90 days forward for $.42.
        Sell DM 1 in Frankfurt 90 days forward for $.4255.

$t = 90$
        Deliver DM 1 in Frankfurt; collect $.4255.
        Pay $.42; collect DM 1.

                               Profit: $.4255
                                    −.4200
                                 $.0055

Cross-Rates **Figure 9.2**

Key Currency Cross Rates Late New York Trading Apr 23, 1996

	Dollar	Pound	SFranc	Guilder	Peso	Yen	Lira	D-Mark	FFranc	CdnDlr
Canada	1.3625	2.0669	1.1046	.80039	.18387	.01277	.00088	.89550	.26518	....
France	5.1380	7.7943	4.1654	3.0183	.69339	.04817	.00331	3.3769	....	3.7710
Germany	1.5215	2.3081	1.2335	.89379	.20533	.01426	.00098	....	.29613	1.1167
Italy...........	1553.8	2357.0	1259.6	912.74	209.68	14.566	....	1021.2	302.4	1140.4
Japan	106.67	161.82	86.478	62.662	14.395	....	.06865	70.108	20.761	78.29
Mexico........	7.4100	11.241	6.0073	4.3529	....	.06947	.00477	4.8702	1.4422	5.4385
Netherlands..	1.7023	2.5824	1.3801	....	.22973	.01596	.00110	1.1188	.33132	1.2494
Switzerland..	1.2335	1.8712	....	.72461	.16646	.01156	.00079	.81071	.24007	.90532
U.K.............	.65920	....	.53441	.38724	.08896	.00618	.00042	.43325	.12830	.48381
U.S.............	....	1.5170	.81070	.58744	.13495	.00937	.00064	.65725	.19463	.73394

Source: Dow Jones Telerate Inc.

Source: From *The Wall Street Journal*, April 24, 1996, p. C22. Reprinted by permission of *The Wall Street Journal*, © 1996 Dow Jones & Company, Inc. All rights reserved worldwide.

New York	$/DM	.42
	$/SF	.49
Frankfurt	DM/SF	1.2

The exchange rates quoted in New York imply the following cross-rate in New York for the DM/SF:

$$DM/SF = \left(\frac{1}{\$/DM}\right)\$/SF = \left(\frac{1}{.42}\right).49 = 1.167$$

Because the rate for the directly quoted DM/SF in Frankfurt differs from the cross-rate quoted in New York, an arbitrage opportunity exists. To exploit the arbitrage opportunity, one can trade only the exchange rates actually shown. For example, in New York there may not be a market for DM in terms of the Swiss franc.[2] To exchange DM for SF in the New York market involves two transactions. First, a trader sells DM for $ and then buys SF with $.

To know how to trade, one must know which currency is relatively cheaper in a given market. In New York one receives DM 1.167 per SF, but in Frankfurt SF 1 is worth DM 1.2. The DM, therefore, is cheaper in Frankfurt than in New York. Table 9.2 shows the transactions required to conduct the arbitrage.

FORWARD AND FUTURES MARKET CHARACTERISTICS

The institutional structure of the foreign exchange futures market resembles that of the forward market, with a number of notable exceptions. While the forward market is a worldwide market with no particular geographical location, the principal futures market is the International Monetary Market (IMM) of the Chicago Mercantile Exchange (CME). In the futures market, contracts trade on the

Table 9.2	Cross-Rate Arbitrage Transactions

$t = 0$ (the present)

        Sell SF 1 90 days forward in Frankfurt for DM 1.2.

        Sell DM 1.2 90 days forward in New York for $.504.

        Sell $.504 90 days forward in New York for SF 1.0286.

$t = 90$ (delivery)

        Deliver SF 1 in Frankfurt; collect DM 1.2.

        Deliver DM 1.2 in New York; collect $.504.

        Deliver $.504 in New York; collect SF 1.0286.

Profit: SF 1.0286

−1.0000

SF .0286

most important currencies, such as the German mark, the British pound, the Canadian dollar, the Swiss franc, and the Japanese yen. All of the contracts trade on the MAR, JUN, SEP, DEC cycle with expiration on the third Wednesday of the expiration month. By contrast, forward market quotations are stated for a given number of days into the future.[3] In the futures market, the exchange determines the maturity date of each contract. With each passing day, the futures expiration comes one day closer. In the forward market, contracts for expiration 30, 90, and 180 days into the future are available each trading day. In the futures market, contracts mature on only four days of the year; in the forward market, contracts mature every day. In the forward market, contract size is negotiated. In the futures market, the rules of the exchange determine the contract size. Table 9.3 summarizes the differences between forward and futures markets for foreign exchange. The most important differences are the standardized contract, the standardized delivery dates, the differences in daily cash flows, and the differences in the ways contracts are closed. It is particularly interesting to note that less than 1 percent of all foreign exchange futures are completed by delivery, but delivery occurs on more than 90 percent of all forward contracts.

The forward market for foreign exchange dates back to beyond the reaches of history, while the futures market began only in the 1970s. The major center for the forward market continues to be London, but New York has been gaining in importance as the market for foreign exchange in the U.S. has grown rapidly. While foreign currency futures trading has grown dramatically, the forward market still dwarfs the futures market by a factor of about 20 to one, as measured by the U.S. dollar volume of trading. Since banks are the major participants in the forward market, it is not too surprising that their level of activity in the futures market is rather limited.

Figure 9.3 shows foreign exchange futures price quotations. The columns of quotations follow the pattern set for other types of contracts, showing the open, high, low, and settlement prices, and the change in the settlement price since the preceding day. The next two columns present the high and low lifetime prices for each contract, while the final column shows the open interest in each contract. The final line of data for each contract shows the estimated volume of the current day, the actual volume of the preceding day, the current open interest across all contract maturities for each contract, and the change in the open interest since the preceding day.

	Futures vs. Forward Markets	Table 9.3
	Forward	**Futures**
Size of Contract	Tailored to individual needs.	Standardized.
Delivery Date	Tailored to individual needs.	Standardized.
Method of Transaction	Established by the bank or broker via telephone contract with limited number of buyers and sellers.	Determined by open auction among many buyers and sellers on the exchange floor.
Participants	Banks, brokers, and multinational companies. Public speculation not encouraged.	Banks, brokers and multinational companies. Qualified public speculation encouraged.
Commissions	Set by "spread" between bank's buy and sell price. Not easily determined by customer.	Published small brokerage fee and negotiated rates on block trades.
Security Deposit	None as such, but compensating bank balances required.	Published small security deposit required.
Clearing Operation (Financial Integrity)	Varies across individual banks and brokers. No separate clearinghouse function.	Handled by exchange clearinghouse. Daily settlements to the market.
Marketplace	Over the telephone worldwide.	Central exchange floor with worldwide communications.
Economic Justification	Facilitate world trade by providing hedge mechanism.	Same as forward market. In addition, it provides a broader market and an alternative hedging mechanism via public participation.
Accessibility	Limited to very large customers who deal in foreign trade.	Open to anyone who needs hedge facilities, or has risk capital with which to speculate.
Regulation	Self-regulating.	April 1975 – Regulated under the Commodity Futures Trading Commission.
Frequency of Delivery	More than 90% settled by actual delivery.	Less than 1% settled by actual delivery.
Price Fluctuations	No daily limit.	No daily limit.
Market Liquidity	Offsetting with other banks.	Public offset. Arbitrage offset.

Source: Reprinted by permission of the Chicago Mercantile Exchange. S&P 500® is a trademark of The McGraw-Hill Companies, Inc. © Standard & Poor's. Reprinted by permission.

| Figure 9.3 | Foreign Exchange Futures Quotations |

CURRENCY

	Open	High	Low	Settle	Change	Lifetime High	Lifetime Low	Open Interest
JAPAN YEN (CME)-12.5 million yen; $ per yen (.00)								
June	.9450	.9479	.9422	.9446	– .0002	1.3130	.9259	68,687
Sept	.9564	.9588	.9555	.9558	– .0002	1.2085	.9390	2,034
Dec	.9695	.9700	.9680	.9669	– .0002	1.0500	.9520	1,180
Est vol 16,261; vol Mn 14,971; open int 71,998, –3.								
DEUTSCHEMARK (CME)-125,000 marks; $ per mark								
June	.6613	.6620	.6592	.6596	– .0017	.7315	.6592	81,550
Sept	.6652	.6655	.6633	.6635	– .0017	.7312	.6633	3,285
Dec	....	....	....	.6676	– .0017	.7070	.6698	388
Est vol 20,262; vol Mn 21,455; open int 85,244, +1,777.								
CANADIAN DOLLAR (CME)-100,000 dlrs.; $ per Can $								
June	.7341	.7353	.7341	.7346	+ .0001	.7500	.6930	34,723
Sept	.7360	.7361	.7355	.7353	+ .0001	.7490	.7170	1,834
Dec	.7367	.7367	.7362	.7359	+ .0001	.7460	.7130	1,676
Mr97	....	....	....	.7364	+ .0001	.7395	.7117	439
June	....	....	....	.7365	+ .0001	.7395	.7185	197
Est vol 2,765; vol Mn 2,857; open int 38,871, –173.								
BRITISH POUND (CME)-62,500 pds.; $ per pound								
June	1.5100	1.5170	1.5090	1.5164	+ .0054	1.5870	1.4910	59,363
Sept	1.5080	1.5160	1.5080	1.5148	+ .0054	1.5840	1.4910	146
Est vol 10,234; vol Mn 5,200; open int 59,547, –1,748.								
SWISS FRANC (CME)-125,000 francs; $ per franc								
June	.8180	.8208	.8156	.8157	– .0025	.9120	.8140	40,170
Sept	.8262	.8270	.8229	.8231	– .0025	.9188	.8212	1,521
Dec	....	....	....	.8306	– .0025	.8999	.8290	670
Est vol 13,480; vol Mn 12,233; open int 42,364, –853.								
AUSTRALIAN DOLLAR (CME)-100,000 dlrs.; $ per A.$								
June	.7845	.7890	.7845	.7870	+ .0025	.7904	.7260	11,697
Est vol 840; vol Mn 1,398; open int 11,725, –85.								
MEXICAN PESO (CME)-500,000 new Mex. peso, $ per MP								
June	.12950	.12960	.12880	.12930	– .0005	.13400	.09020	10,522
Sept	.12135	.12160	.12050	.12100	– .0025	.12700	.08600	3,994
Dec	.11310	.11410	.11310	.11370	– .0035	.11500	.09900	1,322
Mr97	.10650	.10750	.10600	.10700	– .0045	.10800	.10070	408
Est vol 2,863; vol Mn 3,276; open int 16,246, –152.								

While the price quotations for each currency are similar, there are some differences. First, different contracts trade a different number of units of the foreign currency. For instance, one contract is for 12.5 million yen but only 125,000 marks. The difference in quantity reflects the vast difference in the value between a single mark and a single yen. In 1996, one U.S. dollar was worth slightly more than 100 yen but less than two marks. Notice also that the quotations for the yen have two zeroes suppressed.

The foreign exchange futures market grew rapidly until 1992, with total volume falling from that high in recent years, as depicted by Figure 9.4. From a level of only 199,920 contracts in 1975, the total trading volume on foreign exchange futures climbed to just over 38 million by 1992. By 1995, volume was down to 24.3 million. Figure 9.5 shows the share of volume for key currencies in 1995.

In 1993, the CME introduced a new foreign exchange concept called the ''rolling spot.'' As we have seen, the forward market in foreign exchange dominates the futures market, yet futures markets have some advantages over the forward market in terms of default risk control and financial integrity. In essence, a rolling spot contract trades like a regular cash market transaction with a five-day horizon, but any fluctuations in the foreign exchange rate must be realized in cash through the customary futures market resettlement and margining process. In essence, the rolling spot contract performs like a typical spot agreement in the foreign exchange market with the financial backing of the CME

Growth in Trading in Foreign Exchange Futures   Figure 9.4

clearinghouse. Further, the contracts have a standard size and expiration date, like a futures, and all transactions are publicly reported like any futures. British pound rolling spot contracts began trading on June 15, 1993, with contracts scheduled to follow in the Canadian dollar, the German mark, the Japanese yen, and the Swiss franc. These have not been as successful as the CME had hoped.

DETERMINANTS OF FOREIGN EXCHANGE RATES

As with almost any good, fundamental factors shape the exchange rate that prevails between the currencies of two countries. These factors are numerous and quite complex, with entire books being written on the subject. Consequently, the brief discussion that follows merely indicates some of the most important influences on exchange rates. One way of thinking about currencies is to regard them as essentially similar to other assets, subject to the same basic laws of supply and demand. When a particular currency is unusually plentiful, its price might be expected to fall. Of course, the price of a given currency, in terms of some other currency, is merely the exchange rate between the two currencies. In foreign exchange, the flow of payments between residents of one country and the rest of the world gives rise to the concept of a balance of payments. The balance of payments is generally calculated on a yearly basis. If expenditures by a particular country exceed receipts, then that country has a deficit in its balance of payments; if receipts exceed expenditures, then the country has a surplus. The balance of payments encompasses all kinds of flows of goods and services among nations, including the movement of real goods, services, international investment, and all types of financial flows.

   To illustrate how the balance of payments influences exchange rates, consider the following example. A country, Importeria, trades with other countries and always imports more goods than it

Figure 9.5   Market Share for Foreign Currencies Futures in 1995

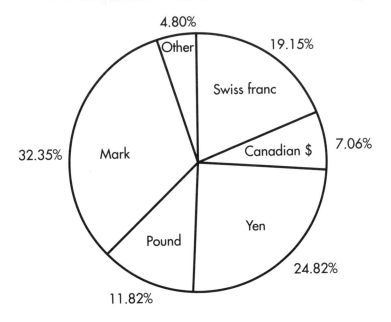

Source: From Commodity Futures Trading Commission, Annual Report, 1995.

exports. This means that there is always a net flow of real goods into Importeria. Importeria must pay for these goods in some way, so we assume that the government of Importeria simply prints additional currency to pay for the excess goods that it imports. Such a practice must eventually cause a change in the exchange rates between Importeria and its trading partners. As the trading partners continue to send more and more goods to Importeria, they collectively have fewer and fewer real goods themselves, but a growing supply of the currency of Importeria.

As the world's supply of Importeria's currency swells, it becomes apparent that it has only a few uses. It can be used to acquire other currencies, or it can be used to purchase goods from Importeria. However, the accumulation of Importeria's currency continues until there is an excess supply at the prevailing exchange rate, so the value of Importeria's currency must fall. Just as Importeria cannot continually import more than it exports without causing the value of its currency to fall, no country can continually consume more than it creates without eventually causing a fall in the value of its currency.

Fixed Exchange Rates

The currency adjustment that Importeria might have to suffer depends on the international exchange rate system. For most of the history of the United States, there has been a system of **fixed exchange rates**. A fixed exchange rate is a stated exchange rate between two currencies at which anyone may transact. A country, such as Importeria, might import more than it exports for quite some time without causing a change in the fixed exchange rate. However, even fixed exchange rates are only fixed in the short run, and they are subject to periodic adjustments. For Importeria, the continual excess of imports over exports puts pressure on the value of Importeria's currency as the world supply of Importeria's currency continues to grow. Eventually, the fixed exchange rate between Importeria's currency and that of other nations will be adjusted. For Importeria, the value of the currency will have to fall or be **devalued**. The value of other currencies will increase relative to Importeria's, so these currencies are said to have been **revalued**. Devaluations and revaluations, when they occur, are usually large in size. It is not uncommon for the value to change by 25 to 50 percent, or even more.

It may seem perplexing that the value of the currencies would not adjust smoothly over time, as Importeria continued its program of excess imports. A fixed exchange rate system, however, prevents gradual adjustment. Rates are fixed through the intervention of the central banks of Importeria and other countries. As excess supplies of Importeria's currency accumulate, central banks may use their reserves of other currencies to buy Importeria's, thereby easing the imbalance between supply and demand that would arise at the fixed level of rates. In effect, central banks would be absorbing the excess supply of Importeria's currency which would otherwise exist at the fixed level of exchange rates. If the pressures against the currency of Importeria are not too severe, purchases by central banks may succeed in maintaining the fixed level of exchange rates. Often, however, the excess supply of a currency may become excessive. Then central banks become unable, or unwilling, to purchase all of the currency that is supplied. When this happens, a country like Importeria would be forced to devalue its currency and set a new rate of exchange as the official rate. If the value of the Importeria unit of currency was one-tenth of a U.S. dollar before the devaluation, it might be reset at one-twelfth of a dollar after the devaluation. After the devaluation, Importeria would try to maintain the new exchange rate. If Importeria continues to import much more than it exports, it would soon face another devaluation.

One obvious and apparently disadvantageous feature of a fixed exchange rate system is that changes in the exchange rates occur infrequently, but when they do, the changes are rather large. There are, however, considerable advantages to a fixed exchange rate system. First, fixed exchange rates make planning exchange transactions considerably easier. If businesses can depend on a fixed exchange rate for the next year, they would not face **exchange risk** – the risk that the value of a currency will change relative to other currencies. Freedom from exchange risk facilitates business planning and promotes international trade. Second, for firms engaged in international commerce, fixed exchange rates mean that accounting income is not sensitive to exchange rate fluctuations. Third, a fixed exchange rate may provide a form of discipline for economic policies by the participating countries. According to this argument, governments would realize that pursuing certain policies would be likely to lead to devaluation.

Perhaps for these reasons, and also as a signal of financial probity, the industrialized West pursued a fixed exchange rate policy from the end of World War II until 1971. During this period, the dollar was even convertible into gold at a rate of $35 per ounce, according to the Bretton Woods Agreement. Other major currencies fixed their value in terms of the U.S. dollar. In August 1971, faced with a weakening dollar and a soaring balance of payments deficit, the United States abandoned the gold standard. In spite of attempts to re-establish some semblance of a fixed rate system, notably the Smithsonian Agreement of 1971, March 1973 witnessed a new era in international foreign exchange. The fixed rate system was abandoned, with daily fluctuations in exchange rates becoming the norm.

Other Exchange Rate Systems

This free market system of exchange rates prevails today, but there are a number of important exceptions and variations that the foreign exchange trader must consider. With the breakdown of the Bretton Woods system and the failure of the Smithsonian Agreement, countries were free to adopt a variety of strategies where their exchange rates were concerned. This freedom has led to such strategies as free floats, managed or dirty floats, pegs, and joint floats. A currency is **freely floating** if it has no system of fixed exchange rates and if the country's central bank does not attempt to influence the value of the currency by trading in the foreign exchange market. Few countries have truly freely floating exchange rates, because central banks seem unable to resist the temptation to intervene. When the central bank of a country engages in market transactions to influence the exchange value of its currency, but the rate is basically a floating rate, the country is following a policy of a **managed float** or a **dirty float**. Opposed to this floating system, a number of countries use a **pegged** exchange rate system. The value of one currency might be pegged to the value of another currency, that itself floats. For example, Importeria might try to maintain a fixed exchange rate with the dollar, but the dollar itself floats against most of the world's currencies. In such a situation, the currency of Importeria is pegged to the dollar. Pegged currencies may be pegged to a single currency, while others could be pegged to a basket, or portfolio, of currencies.

One other policy for exchange rate management is particularly important for the foreign exchange futures market – the policy of a joint float. In a **joint float**, currencies participating in the joint float have fixed exchange values relative to other currencies in the joint float, but the *group* of currencies floats relative to other currencies that do not participate in the joint float. The prime example of the joint float technique comes from the European Economic Community (EEC), or the Common Market. The member nations formed the European Monetary System (EMS) in 1979 and created the European Currency Unit (ECU). The basic strategy of the EMS agreement is to maintain very narrowly fluctuating exchange rates among the currencies of the participating countries.

In theory, a joint float system means that the values of the currencies of the participating countries will be fixed relative to one another but will float relative to external countries. This has important implications for speculation and hedging in all of these currencies, particularly where the futures market is concerned. Recent experience has shown that some countries may be forced to devalue their currencies relative to those of the group. Italy has faced the problem several times since the inception of the EMS. More recently, France has devalued several times. In such cases, it is apparent that a trader may have difficulty using the German mark as a cross-hedge against the Italian lira or the French franc.

FORWARD AND FUTURES PRICES FOR FOREIGN EXCHANGE

As we discussed in Chapter 3, a distinction between forward and futures prices emerges from the daily resettlement feature of futures contracts. Consider forward and futures contracts on foreign exchange that have the same expiration. Both the futures and the forward will have the same profit in the end, exclusive of interest earned on the resettlement payments. If the futures position is likely to have more favorable interim cash flows due to its positive correlation with interest rates, the futures price should exceed the forward price. By the same token, if the futures price is negatively correlated with interest rates, then the futures price should be lower than the forward price. This conclusion follows, because the futures trader will then tend to experience losses just as interest rates rise. Finally, if the price of a commodity is uncorrelated with interest rates, then the forward and futures prices should be equal. Notice that all these conclusions arise strictly from economic reasoning and hold if investors are risk-neutral.

While futures and forward prices differ in theory, the magnitude and practical significance of that difference is an empirical question. Generally, studies of this issue find very little difference between foreign exchange forward and futures prices. As one study concluded, "The foreign exchange data reveal that mean differences between forward and futures prices are insignificantly different from zero, both in a statistical and economic sense."[4] In view of these findings, we will regard the results based on research in the forward market as holding for the futures market as well.

MORE FUTURES PRICE PARITY RELATIONSHIPS

Earlier in this chapter, we noted the geographical or cross-rate arbitrage opportunities that occur when foreign exchange rates are improperly aligned among single contracts. The arbitrage examples of Tables 9.1 and 9.2 arose from a pricing discrepancy in the foreign exchange rates for a single maturity of 90 days forward. Other price relationships are equally important and determine the permissible price differences that may exist between foreign exchange rates for delivery at different times. These relationships are expressed as the **Interest Rate Parity Theorem** (IRP) and the **Purchasing Power Parity Theorem** (PPP). As we will see, the IRP is simply the cost-of-carry model in a very thin disguise.

Interest Rate Parity Theorem

The interest rate parity theorem asserts that interest rates and exchange rates form one system. According to IRP, foreign exchange rates will adjust to ensure that a trader earns the same return by investing in risk-free instruments of any currency, assuming that the proceeds from investment are repatriated into the home currency by a forward contract initiated at the outset of the holding period. We can use the rates of Table 9.4 to illustrate interest rate parity. Faced with the rates in Table 9.4 and assuming interest rate parity holds, a trader must earn the same return by following either of two strategies:

Interest Rates and Exchange Rates to Illustrate Interest Rate Parity			Table 9.4
	Interest Rates		
Exchange Rates	**$/DM**	**U.S.**	**Germany**
Spot	.42	–	–
30-day	.41	.18	.576
90-day	.405	.19	.33
180-day	.40	.20	.323

Strategy 1: Invest in the U.S. for 180 days.

Strategy 2: (a) Sell $ for DM at the spot rate.
            (b) Invest DM proceeds for 180 days in Germany.
            (c) Sell the proceeds of the German investment for dollars through a forward contract
                initiated at the outset of the investment horizon.

With our sample data, the following equation expresses the same equivalence:

$$\$1(1.20)^{.5} = [(\$1/.42)(1.323)^{.5}](.40)$$

In the equation, Strategy 1 is on the left-hand side. There one dollar is invested at the 20 percent
U.S. rate for one-half year. For Strategy 2 on the right-hand side, the dollar is first converted into
marks at the spot rate of $.42 per DM. The trader invests these proceeds at the German mark rate
for one-half year. This 180-day rate is 32.3 percent. Investment of the German funds will pay DM
2.7386 in 180 days. The investment proceeds are sold for dollars using the 180-day forward rate of
.40. For this 180-day horizon, the equivalence between the two strategies holds, so no arbitrage
opportunity is available. In this example, the interest rate parity theorem holds.

Interest Rate Parity and the Cost-of-Carry Model

In essence, the interest rate parity theorem is simply the exchange rate equivalent of the cost-of-carry
model. To see this equivalence, consider the cash-and-carry strategy for the interest rate market. In
a cash-and-carry transaction a trader follows these steps: Borrow funds and buy a bond, carry the
bond to the futures/forward expiration, and sell the good through a futures/forward contract arranged
at the initial date. The cost-of-carry is the difference between the rate paid on the borrowed funds
and the rate earned by holding the bond. Our familiar cash-and-carry strategy is known as **covered
interest arbitrage** in the foreign exchange market. In covered interest arbitrage, a trader borrows
domestic funds and buys foreign funds at the spot rate. The trader then invests these funds at the
foreign interest rate until expiration of the forward/futures contract. The trader also initiates a futures/
forward contract to convert the proceeds from the foreign investment back into the domestic currency.
The cost-of-carry is the difference between the interest rate paid to borrow funds and the interest
earned on the investment in foreign funds.

Thus, a trader borrows the domestic currency, DC, at the domestic rate of interest, r_{DC}, and
exchanges these funds for foreign currency, FC, at the spot exchange rate. The trader receives DC/
FC units of the foreign currency and invests at the foreign interest rate, r_{FC}. This rate, r_{FC}, is the
interest rate applicable to the time from the present to the expiration of the forward or futures. At
the outset of these transactions, $t = 0$, the trader also sells the forward or futures contract at price $F_{0,t}$
for the amount of funds $(DC/FC)(1 + r_{FC})$. With these transactions, the trader has no net cash flow
at $t = 0$. At expiration the trader receives $(DC/FC)(1 + r_{FC})$ units of the foreign currency from the
investment of foreign funds. The trader delivers this foreign currency against the forward or futures
contract and receives $F_{0,t}$ in the domestic currency. The trader then must pay the debt on the original
borrowing, which is $DC(1 + r_{DC})$. If IRP, or equivalently, the cost-of-carry model, holds, the trader
must be left with zero funds. Otherwise an arbitrage opportunity exists.

Applying this notation to our previous example of the cost-of-carry transactions for the 180-day horizon, we can generalize this example to write an equation for IRP or the cost-of-carry model as it applies to foreign exchange. For convenience, we begin with $1 as the amount of the domestic currency, DC. Before, for our example, we wrote:

$$\$1(1.20)^5 = [(\$1/.42)(1.323)^5](.40)$$

In the new notation this translates as:

$$DC(1 + r_{DC}) = (DC/FC)(1 + r_{FC})F_{0,t}$$

Remember that r_{DC} and r_{FC} are the interest rates for the specific period between the present, $t = 0$, and the expiration of the futures at time t.

Isolating the futures price on the left-hand side gives:

$$F_{0,t} = \frac{DC(1 + r_{DC})}{\left(\dfrac{DC}{FC}\right)(1 + r_{FC})} = FC\left(\frac{1 + r_{DC}}{1 + r_{FC}}\right) \qquad (9.1)$$

Equation 9.1 says that, for a unit of foreign currency, the futures price equals the spot price of the foreign currency times the quantity:

$$\left(\frac{1 + r_{DC}}{1 + r_{FC}}\right) \qquad (9.2)$$

This quantity is the ratio of the interest factor for the domestic currency to the interest factor for the foreign currency. We can compare this to our familiar Equation 3.3 for the cost-of-carry model in perfect markets with unrestricted short selling:

$$F_{0,t} = S_0(1 + C) \qquad (3.3)$$

where:

$F_{0,t}$ = the futures or forward price at $t = 0$ for a foreign exchange contract to expire at time t
S_0 = the spot price of the good at $t = 0$
C = the percentage cost of carrying the good from $t = 0$ to time t

Equations 3.3 and 9.1 have the same form. Therefore, the quantity in Equation 9.2 equals one plus the cost of carry, $(1 + C)$. The cash-and-carry strategy requires borrowing at the domestic rate, r_{DC}, so this is an element of the carrying cost. However, the borrowed domestic funds are converted to foreign currency and earn at the foreign interest rate r_{FC}. Therefore, the foreign earnings offset the cost being incurred through the domestic interest rate. The net result is that the quantity of Equation 9.2 gives the value for one plus the carrying cost. As a simpler approximation, we note that:

$$1 + \text{Cost-of-Carry} = \left(\frac{1 + r_{DC}}{1 + r_{FC}}\right) \approx 1 + (r_{DC} - r_{FC}) \qquad (9.3)$$

Therefore, the cost-of-carry approximately equals the difference between the domestic and foreign interest rates for the period from $t = 0$ to the futures expiration. To complete this discussion, let us apply this equation for the 180-day horizon using the rates in Table 9.4. We have already seen that there is no arbitrage possible for this horizon. For this example data we have:

$F_{0,t} = .40$
$S_0 = .42$
$r_{DC} = .095445$ for the half-year
$r_{FC} = .150217$ for the half-year

Applying Equation 9.1 to this data, we have:

$$.40 = .42\left(\frac{1.095445}{1.150217}\right)$$

This equation holds exactly. The cost-of-carry is -0.047619. For this example, the approximate cost-of-carry for the half-year is:

$$r_{DC} - r_{FC} = .095445 - .150217 = -0.054772$$

Thus, the cost-of-carry for the half-year is approximately $-.05$. The cost-of-carry is negative because the cash-and-carry trader pays at the domestic rate but earns interest at the higher foreign rate. For the same reason, the futures price of the foreign currency must exceed the spot price. If the foreign rate of interest had been lower, the futures price of the foreign currency would have to be lower than the spot price to avoid arbitrage.

Exploiting Deviations from Interest Rate Parity

The analysis of the values in Table 9.4 shows that there is not an arbitrage opportunity in the 180-day contract. If the interest rate parity theorem is to hold in general, there cannot be an arbitrage opportunity for any investment horizon. In Table 9.4, the rates allow an arbitrage opportunity in the 90-day contract. This is apparent when one realizes that the strategy of holding the U.S. dollar and DM investment does not yield the same 90-day terminal wealth in U.S. dollars when the marks are converted into dollars by issuing a forward contract. The following computation illustrates the different terminal dollar values earned by the two strategies:

Strategy 1: (hold in U.S.)
$$\$1(1.19)^{.25} = \$1.0444$$

Strategy 2: (convert to DM, invest, and use forward contract)
$$(\$1/.42)(1.33)^{.25}(.405) = \$1.0355$$

Strategy 1, investing in the U.S., gives a higher payoff than converting dollars to marks and investing in Germany. This difference implies that an arbitrage opportunity exists.

This is also evident by applying the cost-of-carry model for foreign exchange to the 90-day values in Table 9.4. For this horizon, the values in Table 9.4 imply:

$F_{0,t} = .405$
$S_0 = .42$
$r_{DC} = .044448$ for the quarter-year
$r_{FC} = .073898$ for the quarter-year

With these values, the futures price should be 0.408482:

$$FC\left(\frac{1 + r_{DC}}{1 + r_{FC}}\right) = .42\left(\frac{1.044448}{1.073898}\right) = .408482$$

Because the futures price is less than this amount, an arbitrage opportunity exists. With our example data, it is clearly better to invest funds in the U.S. rather than Germany. Table 9.5 shows the transactions that will exploit this discrepancy, assuming that the transactions begin with $1.00.

This kind of arbitrage in foreign exchange is covered interest arbitrage. With these transactions, the trader uses a forward contract to cover the proceeds from the DM investment. The proceeds are covered, because the trader arranges through the forward contract to convert the DM proceeds into dollars as soon as the proceeds are received. The IRP theorem asserts that such opportunities should not exist. The section on market efficiency explores whether the IRP theorem actually holds.

Purchasing Power Parity Theorem

The purchasing power parity theorem (PPP) asserts that the exchange rates between two currencies must be proportional to the price level of traded goods in the two currencies. Purchasing power parity is intimately tied to interest rate parity, as we discuss later. Violations of PPP can lead to arbitrage opportunities, such as the following example of "Croissant Arbitrage."

Covered Interest Arbitrage	Table 9.5

$t = 0$ (present)
        Borrow DM 2.3810 in Germany for 90 days at 33%.
        Sell DM 2.3810 spot for $1.00.
        Invest $1.00 in the U.S. for 90 days at 19%.
        Sell $1.0355 90 days forward for DM 2.5570.

$t = 90$ (delivery)
        Collect $1.0444 on investment in U.S.
        Deliver $1.0355 on forward contract; collect DM 2.5570.
        Pay DM 2.5570 on DM 2.3810 that was borrowed.

Profit: $1.0444
        −1.0355
         .0089

For croissant arbitrage we assume that transportation and transaction costs are zero and that there are no trade barriers, such as quotas or tariffs. These assumptions are essentially equivalent to our usual assumptions of perfect markets. The spot value of the French franc is $.10 and the cost of a croissant in Paris is FF 1, as Table 9.6 shows. In New York a croissant sells for $.15, so this price creates an arbitrage opportunity. A trader can exploit this opportunity by transacting as shown in the bottom portion of Table 9.6. Given the other values, the price of a croissant in New York must be $.10 to exclude arbitrage.

Over time, exchange rates must also conform to PPP. The left column of Table 9.7 presents prices and exchange rates consistent with PPP at $t = 0$. The right column shows values one year later at $t = 1$, after a year of inflation in France and the United States. During this year, French inflation was 20 percent, so a croissant now sells for FF 1.2. In the U.S. inflation was 10 percent, so a croissant is now $.11. To be consistent with PPP, the exchange rates must also have adjusted to keep the relative value of the franc and dollar consistent with the relative purchasing power of the two currencies. As a consequence, the dollar must now be worth FF 10.91. Any other exchange rate would create an arbitrage opportunity. The requirement that PPP holds at all times means that the exchange rate must change proportionately to the relative price levels in the two currencies.

Table 9.6   Croissant Arbitrage

	FF/$	Cost of One Croissant
Paris	10	FF 1
New York	10	$.15

Arbitrage Transactions:
Sell $1 for FF 10 in the spot market.
Buy 10 croissants in Paris.
Ship the croissants to New York.
Sell 10 croissants in New York at .15 for $1.50.

Profit: $1.50
−1.00
.50

Table 9.7   Purchasing Power Parity Over Time

Expected Inflation Rates from $t = 0$ to $t = 1$:	$	.10
	FF	.20

	$t = 0$	$t = 1$
Exchange Rates FF/$	10.00	10.91
Croissant Prices		
Paris	FF 1.00	FF 1.20
New York	$ .10	$ .11

Purchasing Power and Interest Rate Parity

The intimate relationship that exists between the purchasing power parity theorem and the interest rate parity theorem originates from the link between interest rates and inflation rates. According to the analysis of Irving Fisher, the nominal, or market, rate of interest consists of two elements, the **real** rate of interest and the **expected** inflation rate. This relationship can be expressed mathematically as follows:

$$(1 + r_n) = (1 + r^*)[1 + E(I)] \qquad (9.4)$$

where r_n is the nominal interest rate, r^* is the real rate of interest, and $E(I)$ is the expected inflation rate over the period in question. Since the expected inflation is the expected change in purchasing power, the purchasing power parity theorem expresses the linkage between exchange rates and relative inflation rates. A difference in nominal interest rates between two countries is most likely due to differences in expected inflation. This means that interest rates, exchange rates, price levels, and foreign exchange rates form an integrated system.

Foreign Exchange Futures Prices and Expected Future Exchange Rates

Throughout this book, and particularly in Chapter 3, we have stressed the relationship between futures prices and expected future spot prices. If risk-neutral speculators are available in sufficient quantity, their profit-seeking activity will drive the futures price toward equality with the expected future spot price. The same process occurs in the foreign exchange market. The linkages among interest rates, price levels, expected inflation, and exchange rates merely emphasize the fundamental relationship that exists between forward and futures foreign exchange prices, on the one hand, and the expected future value of the currencies, on the other.

To investigate these relationships, consider the exchange rates and price levels of Table 9.8. In the left panel, a set of consistent exchange rates, interest rates, expected inflation rates, and croissant prices are presented for March 20, 1998. The right panel presents the expected spot exchange rate for March 20, 1999, along with expected croissant prices, consistent with the expected levels of inflation in France and the United States.

Assume that all of these values hold and that the expected spot exchange rate in one year is FF 11 per dollar. With the MAR 1999 futures price of 10.45 FF/$, a speculative opportunity exists as follows. A speculator might buy a futures contract for the delivery of dollars in one year for FF 10.45 per dollar. If the expectation that the dollar will be worth FF 11 in one year is correct, the speculator will earn a profit that results from acquiring a dollar via the futures market for FF 10.45 and selling it for the price of FF 11. If we assume that avaricious risk-neutral speculators are present in the foreign exchange market, the discrepancy between the futures price of 10.45 FF/$ and an expected spot exchange rate of 11 FF/$ (at the time the futures contract matures) cannot exist. In fact, given a profusion of risk-neutral speculators, the only expected spot exchange rate to prevail on March 20, 1999, which would eliminate the incentive to speculate, would be 10.45 FF/$. Of course, different market participants have different expectations regarding inflation rates and expected future spot exchange rates, and this difference in expectations is the necessary requirement for speculation.

Table 9.8	Price Levels, Interest Rates, Expected Inflation and Exchange Rates	

March 20, 1998		March 20, 1999	
Exchange Rates FF/$		Expected Spot Exchange Rate	
Spot	10.00	10.45	
MAR 1999 Futures	10.45		
Interest Rates (1-year maturities)			
U.S.	.12		
France	.17		
Expected Inflation Rates (for the next year)			
U.S.	.10		
France	.15		
Croissant Prices		Expected Croissant Prices	
U.S.	$ .10	U.S.	$ .11
France	FF 1.00	France	FF 1.15

FOREIGN EXCHANGE FORECASTING ACCURACY

In this section we examine the accuracy of foreign exchange futures and forward prices as forecasts of future spot exchange rates. As we have just argued, the presence of risk-neutral speculators should drive the futures and forward prices into equality with the expected future spot rate of exchange. If today's expectation of future exchange rates is unbiased, and if the forward and futures prices equal that expectation, we would find that today's forward or futures exchange rate should, on average and in the long run, equal the subsequently observed spot exchange rate. Thus, there are two parts to this equivalence. First, does the forward or futures price equal the market's expectation of the future spot exchange rate? Second, is today's expectation of the future spot exchange rate unbiased? That is, does today's expectation of the future spot exchange rate, on average and in the long run, equal the actual subsequently observed spot rate?

Methodology for Tests of Forecasting Accuracy

Unfortunately, there is no truly accurate way to observe today's market expectation of future exchange rates. Therefore, most tests assume that the market expectation is an unbiased estimate of the future spot exchange rate. Under this assumption, scholars test the relationship between the forward and futures price today and the subsequently observed spot rate. In our notation, they test the following equivalence:

$$F_{0,t} = S_t \tag{9.5}$$

where:

$F_{0,t}$ = the forward or futures price at $t = 0$ for a contract expiring at time t
S_t = the spot exchange rate observed at time t

Testing the equivalence in Equation 9.5 determines whether the forward or futures price is a good estimate of the future spot rate of exchange. Even if there are large deviations between the two prices in Equation 9.5, it is still possible that the forward or futures price could provide an unbiased prediction of the future spot rate. An **unbiased predictor** is a predictor whose expected value equals the variable being predicted. In other words, if the quantity $F_{0,t} - S_t$ equals zero, on average, the forward or futures price would provide an unbiased estimate of the future spot rate of exchange.

No predictor is perfect. Therefore, it is possible that the forward or futures price may seem to be error ridden. However, the most relevant test of any predictor comes from testing the accuracy of the predictor against alternative predictors. As we will see, forward and futures prices do not provide very good predictions of future spot rates – unless we compare them to alternative forecasting schemes.

Earlier in this chapter, we reviewed the evidence on the relationship between futures and forward prices of foreign exchange. There we saw that the evidence strongly suggests that the two are equal. We rely on that equivalence in this section. In the discussion that follows, we speak of futures and forward prices in general, without distinguishing the two.

Tests of Market-Based Forecasts

A **market-based forecast** is a forecast of a future economic value derived from an examination of current market prices. In the context of foreign exchange, we ask whether the current futures price provides a good market-based forecast of the future foreign exchange rate. As we have seen, this essentially amounts to testing the equivalence of futures prices and subsequently observed spot exchange rates.

While earlier studies generally found that futures prices were unbiased predictors of future spot rates, later studies clearly find bias and large errors in the futures forecasts of subsequent spot prices. However, most studies do not find biases that are sufficiently large or consistent enough to allow profitable trading strategies. In summary, the errors in forecasts of future exchange rates appear to be large, and biases do seem to exist in these forecasts, although the biases appear to be too small to allow profitable exploitation.[5]

Competitors of Market-Based Forecasts

If we consider the futures price as a forecast of the future spot rate of exchange, we must conclude that the forecast is likely to have large errors, and we must acknowledge that the forecast may be biased. These two features do not appear to recommend market-based forecasts of future spot exchange rates. Perhaps some other type of forecast is better. The usefulness of market-based forecasts of future exchange rates depends, however, on a whole range of factors, including availability, cost, extent of bias, size of the forecast error, and performance of the forecast relative to other methods. In this section, we compare market-based forecasts with the performance of commercial forecasting firms. As will become apparent, in spite of their limitations, the futures forecasts have important advantages.

Clearly, the futures forecast has an advantage in availability and cost. Both are readily available every day for the price of *The Wall Street Journal*. If forward and futures prices provide the best forecast of the future spot rate that is available, the biases in the forecasts are probably not too serious. Even if the biases are substantial, the futures forecast may still be the best forecast available. Perhaps the most severe challenge to the market-based forecasts comes from the forecasting services that prepare and disseminate forecasts of exchange rates. However, market-based forecasts appear to have smaller errors than forecasts from commercial firms.[6]

THE EFFICIENCY OF FOREIGN EXCHANGE FUTURES MARKETS

The efficiency of the foreign exchange market has been explored by numerous researchers over an extended time. In spite of this attention, the efficiency of the market remains an open question. This situation is not unusual when a complex empirical issue in finance is at stake. If arbitrage opportunities such as geographical, cross-rate, or covered interest arbitrage exist, then the foreign exchange market is inefficient. Reflection on the structure of the market helps support the case for efficiency. With a worldwide network of active traders, all linked by sophisticated information systems and all aware of the profits implied by arbitrage opportunities, we might expect any incipient arbitrage opportunities to be detected very early. As quasi-arbitrage opportunities appear, we would expect traders to adjust their trading patterns to exploit even the slightest opportunity. This activity, we expect, should eliminate any observable arbitrage opportunities.

On the other hand, the foreign exchange market is unique in attracting central bank intervention from a variety of countries. If central banks cannot leave their hands off the market and insist on managing floating rates, the character of the market could be affected. If the market is subject to the actions of well-capitalized governmental agencies with agendas that are not profit-determined, then we might expect profit opportunities to arise from betting against central banks. In this section, we explore the evidence on market efficiency, beginning with an example of interest rate parity.

We have seen that deviations from interest rate parity create opportunities for cash-and-carry and reverse cash-and-carry trading strategies. With transaction costs, slight deviations from interest rate parity are possible, because transaction costs make it unprofitable for traders to exploit minor discrepancies. The arbitrage opportunity depends upon finding deviations from interest rate parity large enough to cover all transaction costs and still leave a profit. As a result, one way of searching for the existence of violations of the interest rate parity theorem is to look for the occurrence of large deviations from interest rate parity. Table 9.9 shows deviations from interest rate parity for some major currencies on which futures contracts trade. Richard M. Levich selected .25 percent as a permissible deviation from interest rate parity, which would still be consistent with the absence of arbitrage opportunities. He believed that this fourth of one percent would be a reasonable bound for

Table 9.9	Percentage of Deviations from Interest Parity Within +/−.25% (All assets are for 3-month maturities)	
	Country	**Percentage within Bounds**
	Canada	93.43
	United Kingdom	96.68
	Germany	98.82
	Switzerland	78.59

Source: From Richard M. Levich, "The Efficiency of Markets for Foreign Exchange: A Review and Extension." Reprinted in Kolb and Gay, *International Finance: Concepts and Issues,* Richmond, VA: Robert F. Dame, Inc., 1982.

transaction costs to form a no-arbitrage band around the price exactly consistent with IRP. As Table 9.9 shows, a high percentage of Levich's observations fall within that band. From this, Levich concludes, "Therefore, the Eurocurrency market is efficient in that there are few unexploited opportunities for risk-free profit through covered interest arbitrage."[7]

To what extent do deviations outside the band of .25 percent represent arbitrage opportunities? If we find only a few opportunities, it may still be worthwhile to look for them. Based on Table 9.9, it seems potentially worthwhile to follow the Swiss franc, since over 20 percent of the observations appear to lie outside the stated boundaries. The critical question here is the selection of the no-arbitrage boundaries. If transactions costs exceed .25 percent, then the bounds are too narrow. By the same token, perhaps transactions costs are really less than .25 percent, and the no-arbitrage boundaries are too lax. These questions are not easy to answer, since it is virtually impossible to know what measure of transaction costs to use. The most striking feature of Table 9.9, however, appears to be the prevalent tendency for so many opportunities to fall within .25 percent of exact interest rate parity. While it may not be possible to say that no arbitrage opportunities are to be found in the foreign exchange market, it is much more impressive to note how closely the observations tended to correspond to interest rate parity.[8]

Levich's study characterizes the earlier evidence on the efficiency of foreign exchange markets. Nonetheless, more recent evidence on forward and futures markets for foreign exchange suggests that the markets are not efficient. Most studies of foreign exchange market efficiency find significant departures from theoretical pricing relationships. Further, some studies find that speculative strategies can earn significant profits. Part of the findings seem to be due to intervention in the foreign exchange markets by central banks. As a tentative explanation, it seems possible that central banks intervene to stabilize currencies. In the process, they provide profits to savvy speculators. However, most of these opportunities appear to be quite small.[9]

SPECULATION IN FOREIGN EXCHANGE FUTURES

We have seen that the market for foreign exchange has some significant inefficiencies. This inefficiency appears to open the door to speculative strategies. Nonetheless, we should not expect gross inefficiencies in the market. For example, it still appears that market-based forecasts outperform professional forecasts. This suggests that attempts to "beat the market" may still be hazardous. In this section, we illustrate strategies to speculate with foreign exchange. These strategies presume that the trader has well-developed expectations about the value of foreign exchange rates.

Speculating with an Outright Position

In speculation, the most important single point to remember is that the trader opposes his or her wisdom to the opinion of the entire market, since prices available in the market reflect the consensus opinion of all participating parties. The dependence of speculative profits on superior estimation of future exchange rates is demonstrated in Tables 9.10 and 9.11. Imagine a speculator who confronts the exchange rates of Table 9.10 between the U.S. dollar and the German mark on April 7. As an expression of the market's beliefs, these exchange rates imply that the mark will rise relative to the dollar. The speculator, however, strongly disagrees. She believes that the price of the mark, in terms of dollars, will actually fall over the rest of the year. Table 9.11 shows the speculative transactions she enters to take advantage of her belief.

Table 9.10	Foreign Exchange Prices – Spot and Futures, April 7

	$/DM
Spot	.4140
JUN Futures	.4183
SEP Futures	.4211
DEC Futures	.4286

Table 9.11	Speculation in Foreign Exchange

	Cash Market	Futures Market
April 7	Anticipates a fall in the value of the DM over the next eight months.	Sell 1 DEC DM futures contract at .4286.
December 10	Spot Price $/DM = .4211	Buy 1 DEC DM futures contract at .4218.
Profit:	$ .4286	
	−.4218	
Profit per DM	$ .0068	
Times DM per contract	× 125,000	
Total Profit	$ 850	

Since the speculator expects the mark to fall, she sells the DEC futures contract for .4286. If the subsequent spot price is less, she makes a profit. The speculator does not actually need to be correct in the stated belief that the spot exchange value of the mark will fall over the next eight months. A profit is assured if the mark is worth less than the DEC futures price. On December 10, as Table 9.11 shows, the DEC futures is .4218 and the spot exchange rate is 0.4211. Notice that the belief that the mark would fall in value was incorrect. The December 10 spot price still exceeds the original spot price, as does the price of the DEC futures contract. Nonetheless, the drop in the futures price from .4286 to .4218 generates a profit of $.0068 per mark. Since the DM contract calls for delivery of 125,000 marks, the total profit is $850.

Speculating with Spreads

In addition to outright positions, such as the position in the previous example, various spread strategies are also possible. These include intracommodity and intercommodity spreads. Some intercommodity spreads are important, because they allow positions that might not be easily attainable in other markets. The only U.S. futures market for individual foreign exchange contracts is the IMM. In the IMM all prices are stated in terms of dollars. A speculator might believe that the Swiss franc will gain in value relative to the German mark but might also be uncertain about the future value of the dollar relative to either of these currencies. It is possible to speculate on the SF/DM exchange rate by trading on the IMM futures market.

Table 9.12 presents market prices on the IMM for June 24 for the $/DM and $/SF spot and future exchange rates. The futures prices imply cross-rates between the mark and franc as well, as shown in the right column. The rate structure is peculiar, with the DM/SF rate dipping first and then rising. In particular, a speculator finds the implied cross-rate for December to be too low. The speculator believes that the Swiss franc will tend to appreciate against the mark over the coming year. Even though it is impossible to trade the mark against the Swiss franc directly on the IMM, given the available rate quotations, the speculator can use a spread to achieve the desired speculative position.

Since the speculator believes that the value of the mark will fall relative to the Swiss franc, he must also believe that the value of the mark relative to the dollar will perform worse than the value of the Swiss franc relative to the dollar. In other words, even if the mark appreciates against the dollar, his belief about the relative value of the Swiss franc implies that the Swiss franc would appreciate even more against the dollar. Likewise, if the mark falls against the dollar, the speculator would believe that the Swiss franc would either gain or not fall as much as the mark. It is important to realize that the speculator need not have any belief regarding the performance of the dollar relative to either of the European currencies. He is merely going to trade through the dollar to establish a position in the DM/SF exchange rate.

Table 9.13 shows the transactions necessary to exploit the belief that the December cross-rate is too low. If the speculator is correct, the mark will fall relative to the Swiss franc. Therefore, he sells 1 DEC mark contract at .4115 and buys 1 DEC Swiss franc contract at .4635. This spread is equivalent to speculating that the implied cross-rate of 1.1264 is too low, or that it will require more than 1.1264 DM to buy 1 SF by December. By December 11, the two contracts are approaching expiration, and the speculator offsets both contracts. He buys the DEC DM contract at .3907 and sells the SF contract at .4475. This generates a profit of $.0208 per DM and a loss of $.0160 per SF. Both contracts are written for 125,000 units of the foreign currency, so the net profit on the spread transaction is $600.

As a final example of currency speculation, consider the spot and futures prices for the British pound in Table 9.14. A speculator observes these relatively constant prices, but believes that the British economy is even worse than generally appreciated. Specifically, she anticipates that the British inflation rate will exceed the U.S. rate. Therefore, the trader expects the pound to fall relative to the dollar. One easy way to act on this belief is to sell a distant futures contract, but this position trader is very risk averse, and she decides to trade a spread instead of an outright position. She believes that the equal prices for the DEC and MAR contracts will not be sustained, so she trades as shown in Table 9.15, selling what she believes to be the relatively overpriced MAR contract and buying the

	Spot and Futures Exchange Rates, June 24		Table 9.12
	$/DM	$/SF	Implied DM/SF Cross-Rate
Spot	.3853	.4580	1.1887
SEP	.3915	.4616	1.1791
DEC	.4115	.4635	1.1264
MAR	.4163	.4815	1.1566
JUN	.4180	.5100	1.2201

Table 9.13	A Speculative Cross-Rate Futures Spread
Date	Futures Market
June 24	Sell 1 DEC DM futures contract at .4115.
	Buy 1 DEC SF futures contract at .4635.
December 11	Buy 1 DEC DM futures contract at .3907.
	Sell 1 DEC SF futures contract at .4475.

Futures Trading Results:

	DM	SF
Sold	.4115	.4475
Bought	−.3907	−.4635
	$.0208	−$.0160
× 125,000	= $2,600	−$2,000

Total Profit: $600

Table 9.14	Spot and Futures Prices, August 12

	$/British Pound
Spot	1.4485
SEP	1.4480
DEC	1.4460
MAR	1.4460
JUN	1.4470

relatively underpriced DEC contract. By December, the speculator's expectations have been realized and the pound has fallen relative to the dollar, with the more distant futures contract falling even more. The speculator then closes her position on December 5 and realizes a total profit of $150, as Table 9.15 shows. As a result of her conservatism, the profit is only $150. Had the trader taken an outright position by selling the MAR contract, the profit would have been $517.50. In these examples of successful speculations it must be recognized that the speculator pits his or her knowledge against the collective opinion of the entire market, as that opinion is expressed in market prices.

Hedging with Foreign Exchange Futures

Many firms, and some individuals, find themselves exposed to foreign exchange risk. Importers and exporters, for example, often need to make commitments to buy or sell goods for delivery at some future time, with the payment to be made in a foreign currency. Likewise, multinational firms operating foreign subsidiaries receive payments from their subsidiaries that may be denominated in a foreign currency. A wealthy individual may plan an extended trip abroad and may be concerned about the chance that the price of a particular foreign currency might rise unexpectedly. All of these different

Time Spread Speculation in the British Pound	Table 9.15
Date	**Futures Market**

Date	Futures Market
August 12	Buy 1 DEC BP futures contract at 1.4460. Sell 1 MAR BP futures contract at 1.4460.
December 5	Sell 1 DEC BP futures contract at 1.4313. Buy 1 MAR BP futures contract at 1.4253.

	December	March
Sold	1.4313	1.4460
Bought	−1.4460	−1.4253
	−$.0147	$.0207
× 25,000	= −$367.50	+ $517.50

Total Profit: $150

parties are potential candidates for hedging unwanted currency risk by using the foreign exchange futures market.

If a trader faces the actual exchange of one currency for another, the risk is called **transaction exposure**, because the trader will transact in the market to exchange one currency for another. Firms often face **translation exposure**, the need to restate one currency in terms of another currency. For example, a firm may have a foreign subsidiary that earns profits in a foreign currency. However, the parent company prepares its accounting statements in the domestic currency. For accounting purposes, the firm must translate the foreign earnings into the domestic currency. While this procedure does not involve an actual transaction in the foreign exchange market, the reported earnings of the firm expressed in the domestic currency can be volatile due to the uncertain exchange rate at which the subsidiary's foreign earnings will be translated into the domestic currency. In the examples that follow, we consider hedges of both transaction and translation exposure.

Hedging Transaction Exposure

The simplest kind of example arises in the case of someone like Moncrief Snobbody, who is planning a six-month trip to Switzerland. Moncrief plans to spend a considerable sum during this trip, enough to make it worthwhile to attend to exchange rates, as shown in Table 9.16. With the more distant

Swiss Exchange Rates, January 12	Table 9.16

Spot	.4935
MAR	.5034
JUN	.5134
SEP	.5237
DEC	.5342

rates lying above nearby rates, Moncrief fears that spot rates may rise even higher, so he decides to lock-in the existing rates by buying Swiss franc futures. Because he plans to depart for Switzerland in June, he buys 2 JUN SF futures contracts at the current price of .5134. He anticipates that SF 250,000 will be enough to cover his six-month stay, as Table 9.17 shows. By June 6, Moncrief's fears have been realized, and the spot rate for the SF is .5211. Moncrief, consequently, delivers $128,350 and collects SF 250,000. Had he waited and transacted in the spot market on June 6, the SF 250,000 would have cost $130,275. Hedging his foreign exchange risk, Moncrief has saved $1,925, which is enough to finance a few extra days in Switzerland.

In this example, Moncrief had a preexisting risk in the foreign exchange market, since it was already determined that he would acquire the Swiss francs. By trading futures, he guaranteed a price of $.5134 per franc. Of course, the futures market can be used for purposes even more serious than reducing the risk surrounding Moncrief Snobbody's Swiss vacation.

Hedging Import/Export Transactions

Consider a small import/export firm that is negotiating a large purchase of Japanese watches from a firm in Japan. The Japanese firm, being a very tough negotiator, has demanded that payment be made in yen upon delivery of the watches. (If the contract had called for payment in dollars, rather than yen, the Japanese firm would bear the exchange risk.) Delivery will take place in seven months, but the price of the watches is agreed today to be ¥2850 per watch for 15,000 watches. This means that the purchaser will have to pay ¥42,750,000 in about seven months. Table 9.18 shows the current exchange rates on April 11. With the current spot rate of .004173 dollars per yen, the purchase price for the 15,000 watches would be $178,396. If the futures prices on April 11 are treated as a forecast

Table 9.17	Moncrief Snobbody's Swiss Franc Hedge	
	Cash Market	**Futures Market**
January 12	Moncrief plans to take a six-month vacation in Switzerland, to begin in June; the trip will cost about SF 250,000.	Moncrief buys 2 JUN SF futures contracts at .5134 for a total cost of $128,350.
June 16	The $/SF spot rate is now .5211, giving a dollar cost of $130,275 for SF 250,000.	Moncrief delivers $128,350 and collects SF 250,000.
	Savings on the Hedge = $130,275 − 128,350 = $1,925	

Table 9.18	$/Yen Foreign Exchange Rates, April 11	
	Spot	.004173
	JUN Futures	.004200
	SEP Futures	.004237
	DEC Futures	.004265

of future exchange rates, it seems that the dollar is expected to lose ground against the yen. With the DEC futures trading at .004265, the actual dollar cost might be closer to $182,329. If delivery and payment are to occur in December, the importer might reasonably estimate the actual dollar outlay to be about $182,000 instead of $178,000.

To avoid any worsening of his exchange position, the importer decides to hedge the transaction by trading foreign exchange futures. Delivery is expected in November, so the importer decides to trade the DEC futures. By selecting this expiration, the hedger avoids having to roll over a nearby contract, thereby reducing transaction costs. Also, the DEC contract has the advantage of being the first contract to mature after the hedge horizon, so the DEC futures exchange rate should be close to the spot exchange rate prevailing in November when the yen are needed.

The importer's next difficulty stems from the fact that the futures contract is written for Yen 12.5 million. If he trades three contracts, his transaction will be for 37.5 million. If he trades four contracts, however, he would be trading 50 million, when he really only needs coverage for 42.75 million. No matter which way he trades, the importer will be left with some unhedged exchange risk. Finally, he decides to trade three contracts. Table 9.19 shows his transactions. On April 11 he anticipates that he will need ¥42.75 million, with a current dollar value of $178,396 and an expected future value of $182,329, where the expected future worth of the yen is measured by the DEC futures price. This expected future price is the most relevant price for measuring the success of the hedge. In the futures market, the importer buys three DEC yen contracts at .004265 dollars per yen.

On November 18, the watches arrive, and the importer purchases the yen on the spot market at .004273. Relative to his anticipated cost of yen, he pays $342 more than expected. Having acquired the yen, the importer offsets his futures position. Since the futures has moved only .000005, the futures profit is only $187. This gives a total loss on the entire transaction of $155. Had there been no hedge, the loss would have been the full change of the price in the cash market, or $342. This

		The Importer's Hedge	Table 9.19
	Cash Market	**Futures Market**	
April 11	The importer anticipates a need for ¥42,750,000 in November, the current value of which is $178,396, and which have an expected value in November of $182,329.	The importer buys ¥3 DEC futures contracts at .004265 for a total commitment of $159,938.	
November 18	Receives watches; buys ¥42,750,000 at the spot market rate of .004273 for a total of $182,671.	Sells ¥3 DEC futures contracts at .004270 for a total value of $160,125.	
	Spot Market Results:	Futures Market Results:	
	Anticipated Cost $182,329 – Actual Cost −182,671 −$342	Profit = $187	
	Net Loss: −$155		

hedge was only partially effective for two reasons. First, the futures price did not move as much as the cash price. The cash price changed by .000008 dollars per yen, but the futures price changed by only .000005 dollars per yen. Second, the importer was not able to fully hedge his position, due to the fact that his needs fell between two contract amounts. Since he needed ¥42.75 million and only traded futures for ¥37.5 million, he was left with an unhedged exposure of ¥5.25 million.

Hedging Translation Exposure

Many corporations in international business have subsidiaries that earn revenue in foreign currencies and remit their profits to a U.S. parent company. The U.S. parent reports its income in dollars, so the parent's reported earnings fluctuate with the exchange rate between the dollar and the currency of the foreign country in which the subsidiary operates. This necessity to restate foreign currency earnings in the domestic currency is **translation exposure**. For many firms, fluctuating earnings are an anathema. To avoid variability in earnings stemming from exchange rate fluctuations, firms can hedge with foreign exchange futures.

Table 9.20 shows DM exchange rates for January 2 and December 15. Faced with these exchange rates is the Schropp Trading Company of Neckarsulm, a subsidiary of an American firm. Schropp Trading expects to earn DM 4.3 million this year and plans to remit those funds to its American parent. With the DEC futures trading at .4211 dollars per DM on January 2, the expected dollar value of those earnings is $1,810,730. If the mark falls, however, the actual dollar contribution to the earnings of the parent will be lower.

The firm can either hedge or leave unhedged the value of the earnings in marks, as Table 9.21 shows. With the rates in Table 9.20, the 4.3 million marks will be worth only $1,727,310 on December 15. This shortfall could have been avoided by selling the expected earnings in marks in the futures

Table 9.20	Exchange Rates for the German Mark		
		January 2	December 15
	Spot	.4233	.4017
	DEC Futures	.4211	.4017

Table 9.21	Schropp Trading Company of Neckarsulm		

January 2

Expected earnings in Germany for the year		DM 4.3 million
Anticipated value in U.S. dollars (computed @ .4211 $/DM)		$1,810,730

Schropp Trading Company's Contribution to Its Parent's Income:

	Unhedged	Hedged
Contribution to parent's income in U.S. dollars from DM 4.3 million earnings (assumes spot rate of .4017)	$1,727,310	$1,727,310
Futures profit or loss (closed at the spot rate of .4017)	0	$ 84,875
Total	$1,727,310	$1,812,185

market in January at the DEC futures price of .4211. Table 9.21 shows this possibility. With a contract size of DM 125,000, the firm could have sold 35 contracts at the January 2 price. This strategy would have generated a futures profit of $84,875 (35 contracts × 125,000 marks × $.0194 profit per mark). This futures profit would have almost exactly offset the loss in the value of the mark, and Schropp Trading could successfully make its needed contribution to the American parent by remitting $1,812,185.

CONCLUSION

This chapter began by exploring the foreign exchange spot and forward markets. Of all goods with futures markets, the foreign exchange market is unique in the strength of the forward market. In fact, the forward market is much larger than the futures market. Nonetheless, as we discussed, forward prices and futures prices for foreign exchange are virtually identical.

Because foreign exchange rates represent the price of one unit of money in terms of another unit of money, every foreign exchange rate is clearly a relative price. Because of this unique character of foreign exchange markets, we considered the determinants of foreign exchange rates, such as the balance of payments. With modern money being a creation of governments, government intervention in the foreign exchange market is more dominant than in most other markets. Governments attempt to establish exchange rate systems that either fix the value of a currency in terms of another currency, or allow the value of currencies to float. Even when the value of a currency is allowed to float, governments often intervene to manage the value of their currency.

As we have seen for all markets, no-arbitrage conditions constrain foreign exchange rates. One of the most famous of these relationships is the interest rate parity theorem. As we discuss in detail, the IRP theorem is just the cost-of-carry model for foreign exchange. Thus, foreign exchange pricing principles match the concepts we have developed for other markets.

Compared to many other markets, there have been a number of studies of the forecasting accuracy of futures and forward exchange rates. These studies ask whether the futures price is a good forecast of the spot price that will prevail at the futures expiration. In general, most of these studies find significant errors or biases in the futures-based forecast. However, compared with most professional forecasting services, the futures price still provides a superior forecast of future spot prices.

The evidence on the efficiency of the foreign exchange market is probably more negative than the evidence for any of the other markets we have considered. Most studies seem to agree in finding significant departures from efficiency. These range from violations of parity conditions to finding successful speculative strategies. The reason for this apparent inefficiency is unclear, but several studies point to central bank intervention as a possible explanation: Central banks enter the market to pursue policy objectives, thereby providing speculators with profit opportunities. Whether this tentative explanation can be sustained is not totally clear.

As with all futures markets, the foreign currency futures market has numerous hedging applications. We showed how to use foreign currency futures to hedge risk for importers and exporters. Also, we considered the problems of transaction and translation exposure. In transaction exposure, a trader actually faces the exchange of one currency for another and wishes to hedge the future commitment of funds. In translation exposure, funds received in one currency will be restated for accounting purposes in another currency. Because it concerns only accounting, translation exposure need not require the actual exchange of one currency for another. Nonetheless, firms can hedge translation exposure to avoid the volatility of reported earnings in the home currency.

QUESTIONS AND PROBLEMS

1. The current spot exchange rate for the dollar against the Japanese yen is 146 yen per dollar. What is the corresponding U.S. dollar value of one yen?
2. You hold the current editions of *The Wall Street Journal* and *The Financial Times,* the British answer to the WSJ. In the WSJ, you see that the dollar/pound 90-day forward exchange rate is $2.00 per pound. In *The Financial Times,* the pound 90-day dollar/pound rate is £.45 per U.S. dollar. Explain how you would trade to take advantage of these rates, assuming perfect markets.
3. In Problem 2, we assumed that markets are perfect. What are some practical impediments that might frustrate your arbitrage transactions in Problem 2?
4. In the WSJ, you see that the spot value of the German mark is $.63 and the Swiss franc is worth $.72. What rate of exchange do these values imply for the Swiss franc and German mark? Express the value in terms of marks per franc.
5. Explain the difference between a pegged exchange rate system and a managed float.
6. Explain why covered interest arbitrage is just like our familiar cash-and-carry transactions from Chapter 3.
7. For covered interest arbitrage, what is the cost-of-carry? Explain carefully.
8. The spot value of the German mark is $.65, and the 90-day forward rate is $.64. If the U.S. dollar interest factor to cover this period is 2 percent, what is the German rate? What is the cost of carrying a German mark forward for this period?
9. The French franc is worth $.21 in the spot market. The French franc futures that expires in one year trades for $.22. The U.S. dollar interest rate for this period is 10 percent. What should the French franc interest rate be?
10. Using the data in Problem 9, explain which country is expected to experience the higher inflation over the next year. If the expected inflation rate in the U.S. is 7 percent, what inflation rate for the French franc does this imply?
11. Using the data of Problem 9, assume that the French franc interest rate for the year is also 10 percent. Explain how you might transact faced with these values.
12. Many travelers say that shoes in Italy are a big bargain. How can this be, given the purchasing power parity theorem?
13. For the most part, the price of oil is denominated in dollars. Assume that you are a French firm that expects to import 420,000 barrels of crude oil in six months. What risks do you face in this transaction? Explain how you could transact to hedge the currency portion of those risks.
14. A financial comptroller for a U.S. firm is reviewing the earnings from a German subsidiary. This sub earns DM 1 million every year with exactitude, and it reinvests those earnings in its own German operations. This plan will continue. The earnings, however, are translated into U.S. dollars to prepare the U.S. parent's financial statements. Explain the nature of the foreign exchange risk from the point of view of the U.S. parent. Explain what steps you think the parent should take to hedge the risk that you have identified.

NOTES

[1] One such trading room was featured in the film, *Rollover,* starring Kris Kristofferson and Jane Fonda. In this story of international financial intrigue and panic, Kristofferson played the brilliant hard-nosed manager of the trading room, who saves the world from financial collapse.

[2] Actually, in major foreign exchange centers such as New York, some traders will make markets in the major cross-rates. For many currencies in many markets, however, a separate quotation for cross-rates is not available.

[3] Although maturities of 30, 90, and 180 days are normally listed, forward market transactions may be arranged with different maturities to suit the needs of the customer.

[4] See B. Cornell and M. Reinganum, ''Forward and Futures Prices: Evidence from the Forward Exchange Markets,'' *Journal of Finance,* 36:5, December 1981, pp. 1035–45. For a more detailed summary of tests in this area, see R. Kolb, *Understanding Futures Markets,* 5e, Malden, MA: Blackwell Publishing, 1997, Chapter 11.

[5] For representative studies in this area, see the following articles: L. Hansen and R. Hodrick, ''Forward Exchange Rates as Optimal Predictors of Future Spot Rates: An Econometric Analysis,'' *Journal of Political Economy,* 88:5, 1980, pp. 829–53; R. Hodrick and S. Srivastava, ''Foreign Currency Futures,'' *Journal of International Economics,* 22:1/2, 1987, pp. 1–24; L. Kodres, ''Tests of Unbiasedness in Foreign Exchange Futures Markets: The Effects of Price Limits,'' *Review of Futures Markets,* 7:1, 1988, pp. 139–66; S. Kohlhagen, ''The Forward Rate as an Unbiased Predictor of the Future Spot Rate,'' *Columbia Journal of World Business,* 14:4, Winter 1979, pp. 77–85.

[6] See, for example, R. Levich, ''Evaluating the Performance of the Forecasters,'' in R. Ensor (ed.), *The Management of Foreign Exchange Risk,* 2e, Euromoney Publications, 1982, pp. 121–34.

[7] See R. Levich, ''The Efficiency of Markets for Foreign Exchange: A Review and Extension,'' in G. Gay and R. Kolb, *International Finance: Concepts and Issues,* Richmond, VA: Robert F. Dame, 1982, p. 406.

[8] Many other empirical tests tend to confirm the conclusion of efficiency reached by Levich, and a number of these are included in the bibliography to his article.

[9] For studies of foreign exchange market efficiency, see K. Cavanaugh, ''Price Dynamics in Foreign Currency Futures Markets,'' *Journal of International Money and Finance,* 6:3, 1987, pp. 295–314, and D. Glassman, ''The Efficiency of Foreign Exchange Futures Markets in Turbulent and Non-Turbulent Periods,'' *Journal of Futures Markets,* 7:3, 1987, pp. 245–67.

THE OPTIONS MARKET

OVERVIEW

As we discussed in Chapter 1, options can be either call options or put options. A **call option** is a financial instrument that gives its owner the right to purchase an underlying good at a specified price for a specified time. A **put option** is a financial instrument that gives its owner the right to sell the underlying good at a specified price for a specified time. This chapter considers the options exchanges and the well-defined options contracts that trade on these exchanges.

In modern options trading, an individual can contact a broker and trade an option on an exchange in a matter of moments. This chapter explains how orders flow from an individual to the exchange, and it shows how the order is executed and confirmed for the trader. At first, the options exchanges only traded options on stocks. Now exchanges trade options on a wide variety of underlying goods, such as bonds, futures contracts, and foreign currencies. The chapter concludes with a brief consideration of these diverse types of options.

The importance of options goes well beyond the profit-motivated trading that is most visible to the public. Today, sophisticated institutional traders use options to execute extremely complex strategies. For instance, large pension funds and investment banking firms trade options in conjunction with stock and bond portfolios to control risk and capture additional profits. Corporations use options to execute their financing strategies and to hedge unwanted risks that they could not avoid in any other way. Option research has advanced in step with the exploding option market. Scholars have found that there is an option way of thinking that allows many financial decisions to be analyzed using an option framework. Together, these developments constitute an options revolution.

AN OPTION EXAMPLE

Consider an option with a share of XYZ stock as the underlying good. Assume that today is March 1 and that XYZ shares trade at $110. The market, we assume, trades a call option to buy a share of XYZ at $100 with this right lasting until August 15 and the price of this option being $15. In this example, the owner of a call must pay $100 to acquire the stock. This $100 price is called the **exercise**

price or the **striking price**. The price of the option, or the **option premium**, is $15. The option expires in 5.5 months, which gives 168 days until expiration.

If a trader buys the call option, he pays $15 and receives the right to purchase a share of XYZ stock by paying an additional $100, if he so chooses, by August 15. The seller of the option receives $15, and she promises to sell a share of XYZ for $100 if the owner of the call chooses to buy before August 15. Notice that the price of the option, the option premium, is paid when the option trades. The premium the seller receives is hers to keep whether or not the owner of the call decides to exercise the option. If the owner of the call exercises his option, he will pay $100 no matter what the current price of XYZ stock may be. If the owner of the option exercises his option, the seller of the option will receive the $100 exercise price when she delivers the stock as she promised.

At the same time, puts will trade on XYZ. Consider a put with a striking price of $100 trading on March 1 that also expires on August 15. Assume that the price of the put is $5. If a trader purchases a put, he pays $5. In exchange, he receives the right to sell a share of XYZ for $100 at any time until August 15. The seller of the put receives $5, and she promises to buy the share of XYZ for $100 if the owner of the put option chooses to sell before August 15.

In both the put and call example, the payment by the purchaser is gone forever at the time the option trades. The seller of the option receives the payment and keeps it, whatever the owner of the option decides to do. If the owner of the call exercises his option, then he pays the exercise price as an additional amount and receives a share. Likewise, if the owner of the put exercises his option, then he surrenders the share and receives the exercise price as an additional amount. The owner of the option may choose never to exercise. In that case, the option will expire on August 15. The payment the seller receives is hers to keep whether or not the owner exercises. If the owner chooses not to exercise, the seller has a profit equal to the premium received and does not have to perform under the terms of the option contract. Table 10.1 shows the disposition of stock options. It gives a good guide to the frequency with which options are disposed of by exercise, by sale, or by expiring worthless. Most are sold, while many others expire worthless. A relatively small percentage of options are exercised.

MONEYNESS

''Moneyness'' is an option concept that is as important as the word is awkward. It refers to the potential profit or loss from the immediate exercise of an option. An option may be **in-the-money**, **out-of-the-money**, or **at-the-money**.

Table 10.1	Disposition of Equity Options, 1995		
		Percentage Disposition	
	Disposition	Calls	Puts
	Exercise	10.6	11.7
	Sale	60.4	49.5
	Long expired worthless	29.0	38.8

Source: From Chicago Board Options Exchange, *Market Statistics,* 1995. Reprinted by permission of the Chicago Board Options Exchange.

A call option is in-the-money if the stock price exceeds the exercise price. For example, a call option with an exercise price of $100 on a stock trading at $110 is $10 in-the-money. A call option is out-of-the-money if the stock price is less than the exercise price. For example, if the stock is at $110 and the exercise price on a call is $115, the call is $5 out-of-the-money. A call option is at-the-money if the stock price equals (or is very near to) the exercise price.

A put option is in-the-money if the stock price is below the exercise price. As an example, consider a put option with an exercise price of $70 on a stock that is worth $60. The put is $10 in-the-money, because the immediate exercise of the put would give a $10 cash inflow. Similarly, if the put on the same stock had an exercise price of $55, the put would be $5 out-of-the-money. If the put had an exercise price equal to the stock price, the put would be at-the-money. Puts and calls can also be **deep-in-the-money** or **deep-out-of-the-money**, if the cash flows from an immediate exercise would be judged to be large.

AMERICAN AND EUROPEAN OPTIONS

There are two fundamental kinds of options: the American option and the European option. An **American option** permits the owner to exercise at any time before or at expiration. The owner of a **European option** can exercise only at expiration. Thus, the two kinds of options differ because the American option permits early exercise. To this point, we have considered option values only at expiration. If the option is at expiration, American and European options will have the same value. Both can be exercised immediately or be allowed to expire worthless. Prior to expiration, we will see that the two options are conceptually distinct. Further, they may have different values under certain circumstances. In this chapter, and through the remainder of this section on options, we will need to distinguish the principles that apply to each kind of option.

Consider any two options that are exactly alike, except one is an American option and the other is a European option. By saying that the two options are exactly alike, we mean that they have the same underlying stock, the same exercise price, and the same time remaining until expiration. The American option gives its owner all the rights and privileges that the owner of the European option possesses. However, the owner of the American option also has the right to exercise the option before expiration if he desires. From these considerations, we can see that the American option must be worth at least as much as the European option.

The owner of an American option can treat the option as a European option just by deciding not to exercise until expiration. Therefore, the American option cannot be worth less than the European option. However, the American option can be worth more. The American option will be worth more if it is desirable to exercise earlier. Under certain circumstances, which we explore later, the right to exercise before expiration can be valuable. In this case, the American option will be worth more than the otherwise identical European option.

In some cases, the right to exercise before expiration will be worthless. For these situations, the American option will have the same value as the European option. In general, the European option is simpler and easier to analyze. However, in actual markets, most options are American options. This is true both in the United States and throughout the world. We should not associate the names ''American'' and ''European'' with geographic locations. In the present context, the names simply refer to the time at which holders can exercise these options.

WHY TRADE OPTIONS?

Options trading today is more popular than ever before. For the investor, options serve a number of important roles. First, many investors trade options to speculate on the price movements of the underlying stock. However, investors could merely trade the stock itself. As we will see, trading the option instead of the underlying stock can offer a number of advantages. Call options are always cheaper than the underlying stock, so it takes less money to trade calls. Generally, but not universally, put options are also cheaper than the underlying goods. In relative terms, the option price is more volatile than the price of the underlying stock, so investors can get more price action per dollar of investment by investing in options instead of investing in the stock itself.

Options are extremely popular among sophisticated investors who hold large stock portfolios. Accordingly, institutional investors, such as mutual funds and pension funds, are prime users of the options market. By trading options in conjunction with their stock portfolios, investors can carefully adjust the risk and return characteristics of their entire investment. As we will see, a sophisticated trader can use options to increase or decrease the risk of an existing stock portfolio. For example, it is possible to combine a risky stock and a risky option to form a riskless combined position that performs like a risk-free bond.[1]

Many investors prefer to trade options rather than stocks in order to save transaction costs, to avoid tax exposure, and to avoid stock market restrictions.[2] We already mentioned that some investors trade options to achieve the same risk exposure with less capital. In many instances, traders can use options to take a particular risk position and pay lower transaction costs than stocks would require. Likewise, specific provisions of the tax code may favor option trading over trading the underlying stock. If different traders face different tax schedules, one may find advantage in buying options and another may find advantage in selling options, relative to trading stocks. Finally, the stock and option markets have their own institutional rules. Differences in these rules may stimulate option trading. For example, selling stock short is highly restricted.[3] By trading in the option market, it is possible to replicate a short sale of stock and to avoid some stock market restrictions.[4]

THE OPTION CONTRACT

One of the major reasons for the success of options exchanges is that they offer standardized contracts. In a financial market, traders want to be able to trade a good quickly and at a fair price. They can do this if the market is **liquid**. A liquid market provides an efficient and cost-effective trading mechanism with a high volume of trading. Standardizing the options contract has helped promote liquidity. The standardized contract has a specific size and expiration date. Trading on the exchange occurs at certain well-publicized times, so traders know when they will be able to find other traders in the marketplace. The exchange standardizes the exercise prices at which options will trade. With fewer exercise prices, there will be more trading available at a given exercise price. This too promotes liquidity.

Each option contract is for 100 shares of the underlying stock. Exercise prices are specified at intervals of $10, $5, or $2.50, depending on the share price. For example, XYZ trades in the $100 range, and XYZ options have exercise prices spaced at $5 intervals. Every option has a specified expiration month. The option expires on the Saturday after the third Friday in the exercise month. Trading in the option ceases on the third Friday, but the owner may exercise the option on the final Saturday.

THE OPTIONS MARKET

In this section, we consider the most important facets of the options market in the United States. We begin by considering the exchanges where options trade. We then consider an extended example to see how to read option prices as they appear in *The Wall Street Journal*. We conclude this section by analyzing the market activity in the different types of options that are traded on the various exchanges.

Reading Option Prices

Table 10.2 shows typical price quotations for options on a common stock from a U.S. newspaper. Prices are for January 26 for trading options on the stock of XYZ corporation. On that day, XYZ closed at 96 7/8 per share. The table shows listings for XYZ options with striking prices of $90, 95, 100, and 105. It would not be unusual for other striking prices to be represented as well. Options expire in February, March, and April of the same year, and the table shows option prices for both puts and calls. An "r" indicates that the option was not traded on the day for which prices are reported, while an "s" shows that the specific option is not listed for trading.[5]

As an example, consider the call option with a striking price of $100 that expires in March. This option has a price of $1 7/8 or $1.875. This is the price of the call for a single share. However, each option contract is written for 100 shares. Therefore, to purchase this option, the buyer would pay $187.50 for one contract. Owning this call option would give the buyer the right to purchase 100 shares of XYZ at $100 per share until the option expires in March.

We can learn much from a careful consideration of the price relationships revealed in the table. First, notice that option prices are generally higher the longer the time until the option expires. This is true for both calls and puts. Other things being equal, the longer one has the option to buy or sell, the better. Thus, we expect options with longer terms to expiration to be worth more. Second, for a call, the lower the striking price, the more the call option is worth. For a call, the striking price is the amount the call holder must pay to secure the stock. The lower the amount one must pay, the better; therefore, the lower the exercise price, the more the call is worth. Third, for a put option, the higher the striking price, the more the put is worth. For a put, the striking price is the value the put holder receives when he exercises his option to sell the put. Therefore, the more the put entitles its owner to receive, the greater the value of the put. A moment's reflection shows that these simple relationships make sense. Following chapters in this section explore these and similar relationships in detail.

XYZ	Strike Price	Calls			Puts		
		FEB	MAR	APR	FEB	MAR	APR
96 7/8							
	$ 90	6 5/8	s	9 1/8	5/8	s	1 3/8
	95	2 7/8	4 3/8	5 1/2	1 5/8	2 5/8	3 1/8
	100	7/8	1 7/8	3 1/8	4 5/8	r	6 1/4
	105	1/4	13/16	1 5/8	9 1/2	r	11

Option Price Quotations — Table 10.2

Option Exchanges

Trading options undoubtedly grew up with the development of financial markets. In the nineteenth century, investors traded options in an informal market; however, the market was subject to considerable corruption. For example, some sellers of options would refuse to perform as obligated. In the twentieth century, the United States developed a more orderly market called the Put and Call Broker and Dealers Association. Member firms acted to bring buyers and sellers of options together. However, this was an over-the-counter market – the market had no central exchange floor, and standardization of option contract terms was not complete. The lack of an exchange and imperfect standardization of the contracts kept this option market from flourishing.

In 1973, the Chicago Board of Trade, a large futures exchange, created the Chicago Board Options Exchange (CBOE). The CBOE is an organized options exchange that trades highly standardized option contracts. It opened to trade calls on April 26, 1973; put trading began in 1977. Since 1973, other exchanges have begun to trade options, with annual trading of about 300,000,000 options.

Options trading on organized exchanges in the United States embraces a number of different underlying instruments. First among these is the stock option – an option on an individual share of common stock issued by a corporation. While we focus most closely on this type of option for the majority of our discussion of options, there are other important classes of options with very different underlying instruments. Options trade on various financial indexes. These indexes can be indexes to measure the performance of groups of stocks, or precious metals, or any other good for which an index can be constructed as a measure of value. Options also trade on foreign currencies. For these foreign currency options, the underlying good is a unit of a foreign currency, such as a Japanese yen, and traders buy and sell call and put options on the yen, as well as other currencies. Another major type of underlying good is a futures contract. For an option on futures, also known as futures options, the underlying good is a position in a futures contract. As we will see, this is an important class of options. Futures contracts are written on a wide variety of goods, such as agricultural products, precious metals, petroleum products, stock indexes, foreign currency, and debt instruments. Therefore, futures options by themselves embrace a tremendous diversity of goods.

Table 10.3 lists the principal option exchanges in the United States, and it shows the kinds of options traded on each exchange. The exchanges in Table 10.3 may be classified into three groups depending upon whether the primary business of the exchange is the trading of options, stocks, or futures. The Chicago Board Options Exchange (CBOE) deals exclusively in options, although as the leading option exchange in the United States, it trades a wide variety of different kinds of options. The Philadelphia Stock Exchange (PHLX), the American Stock Exchange (AMEX), the Pacific Stock Exchange (PSE), and the New York Stock Exchange (NYSE) are principally stock markets that also trade options. The underlying instruments for the options at these exchanges go far beyond stocks, as we will see. The third group consists of futures exchanges, such as the Chicago Board of Trade (CBOT), the Chicago Mercantile Exchange (CME), the Coffee, Sugar and Cocoa Exchange (CSCE), the Kansas City Board of Trade (KCBT), the MidAmerica Exchange (MIDAM), the New York Cotton Exchange (NYCE), the New York Futures Exchange (NYFE), and the New York Mercantile Exchange (NYME). These futures exchanges trade options on futures exclusively, and they tend to trade options on the futures contracts in which they specialize.

Exchange Diversity and Market Statistics

In this section, we consider the options market in more detail. Table 10.4 shows the volume of all exchange-traded options in the United States by the type of option – stock option, index option,

Principal Option Exchanges in the United States	Table 10.3
Chicago Board Options Exchange (CBOE)	Options on individual stocks, options on stock indexes, and options on Treasury securities
Philadelphia Stock Exchange (PHLX)	Stocks, futures, and options on individual stocks, currencies, and stock indexes
American Stock Exchange (AMEX)	Stocks, options on individual stocks, and options on stock indexes
Pacific Stock Exchange (PSE)	Options on individual stocks and a stock index
New York Stock Exchange (NYSE)	Stocks and options on individual stocks and a stock index
Chicago Board of Trade (CBOT)	Futures, options on futures for agricultural goods, precious metals, stock indexes, and debt instruments
Chicago Mercantile Exchange (CME)	Futures, options on futures for agricultural goods, stock indexes, debt instruments, and currencies
Coffee, Sugar and Cocoa Exchange (CSCE)	Futures and options on agricultural futures
Kansas City Board of Trade (KCBT)	Futures and options on agricultural futures
MidAmerica Commodity Exchange (MIDAM)	Futures and options on futures for agricultural goods and precious metals
Minneapolis Grain Exchange (MGE)	Futures and options on agricultural futures
New York Cotton Exchange (NYCE)	Futures and options on agricultural, currency, and debt instrument futures
New York Futures Exchange (NYFE)	Futures and options on stock indexes
New York Mercantile Exchange (NYME)	Futures and options on energy futures

foreign currency option, and options on futures. Stock options continue to lead in terms of volume, but they are closely followed by index options. Options on futures are also widely traded, but foreign currency options account for only about 4 percent of all options traded.[6]

Stock Options. Options on individual stocks trade on the Chicago Board Options Exchange and four exchanges that principally trade stocks themselves. These same five exchanges trade all options in the United States, except options on futures, which trade on futures exchanges.

Table 10.4	Option Volume in the United States by Type of Option	

	1995 Volume	
Type of Option	Contracts	Percentage
Stock Options	174,380,271	45.58
Index Options	107,810,490	28.18
Foreign Currency Options	4,978,519	1.30
Options on Futures	95,406,042	24.94
Total	382,575,322	100.00

Source: From Chicago Board Options Exchange, *Market Statistics,* 1992; Commodity Futures Trading Commission, *Annual Report,* 1995; Philadelphia Stock Exchange. Data for options on futures are for the fiscal year ending September 30, 1995.

Table 10.5 shows the relative importance of these five exchanges (CBOE, AMEX, PHLX, PSE, and NYSE) in options trading. The CBOE clearly dominates the trading volume, with options on stocks as the most prevalent. Table 10.6 shows the distribution of trading volume in stock options among the five exchanges. Again, the CBOE dominates, but the American Stock Exchange (AMEX) is also a strong contender.

Figure 10.1 shows a sample of the price quotations for options on individual stocks that appears each day in *The Wall Street Journal.* The first column lists the identifier for the stock and shows the closing stock price for the shares immediately beneath the identifier. The next two columns of data show the exercise price and the month the option expires. The option will expire on a specific date in the expiration month. For the call and the put separately, the quotations show the volume and the final price for the option. Options trade on hundreds of individual stocks.

Index Options. Table 10.7 shows the distribution of trading in index options by exchange. The lead of the CBOE is overwhelming. Most index options are based on various stock indexes. The most successful single index contract is based on the S&P 100 and trades at the CBOE. While the S&P

Table 10.5	Total Option Volume by Exchange, 1995	
Exchange	**Contract Volume**	**Percentage**
Chicago Board Options Exchange	178,533,465	62.27
American Stock Exchange	52,391,899	18.27
Philadelphia Stock Exchange	22,000,030	7.67
Pacific Stock Exchange	30,905,131	10.78
New York Stock Exchange	2,885,698	1.01
Total	286,716,223	100.00

Source: From Chicago Board Options Exchange, *Market Statistics,* 1995. Reprinted by permission of the Chicago Board Options Exchange.

Equity Option Volume by Exchange, 1995		Table 10.6
Exchange	**1995 Volume**	**Percentage**
Chicago Board Options Exchange	77,040,466	44.18
American Stock Exchange	48,886,858	28.03
Philadelphia Stock Exchange	14,739,706	8.45
Pacific Stock Exchange	30,852,968	17.69
New York Stock Exchange	2,860,273	1.65
Total	174,380,271	100.00

Source: From Chicago Board Options Exchange, *Market Statistics,* 1995. Reprinted by permission of the Chicago Board Options Exchange.

100 index captures the price movements of the largest stocks in the market, many index options are based on more narrow stock market indexes. For example, the AMEX trades index options based on biotech stocks. Figure 10.2 shows a sample of the quotations for index options from *The Wall Street Journal.* It also indicates the wide variety of indexes that underlie various options. Notice that these include stock indexes for foreign stock markets. The quotations show the expiration month, the exercise price, whether the option is a call or a put, the volume, the closing price, the change since the previous day's close, and the open interest.

Foreign Currency Options. Option trading on individual foreign currencies is concentrated at the Philadelphia Stock Exchange (PHLX).[7] Each option contract is written for a specific number of units of the foreign currency. For example, a contract is for 62,500 German marks, 31,250 British pounds, or 6,250,000 Japanese yen. These different amounts of the foreign currencies place the U.S. dollar value of each contract in the range of $25,000 to $75,000. Prices for the options are quoted in U.S. dollars and the exercise prices are stated in U.S. dollars as well. The dominant currency is the German mark, with the Japanese yen being a distant second.[8]

Figure 10.3 shows price quotations for these options from *The Wall Street Journal,* and the quotations are organized in the same fashion as the others we have already considered. The PHLX trades American and European style options, and it also trades some options with expirations at the end of selected months. However, the American style options continue to be the dominant market.

Options on Futures. In the United States, options on futures trade only on futures exchanges, and futures exchanges trade only options on futures. In general, each futures exchange trades options on its own active futures contracts. Therefore, the variety of options on futures is almost as diverse as futures contracts themselves.

Because the futures market is dominated by two large exchanges, the Chicago Board of Trade (CBOT) and the Chicago Mercantile Exchange (CME), these two exchanges have the largest share of trading of options on futures. Table 10.8 shows the relative volume of trading in options on futures by exchange. Together the CBOT and CME have about 85 percent of all volume. Both of these exchanges trade options on agricultural commodities and financial instruments. The New York Mercantile Exchange (NYME) is the third largest exchange for trading options on futures, largely because of its successful oil-related products. The other exchanges have only minor volume.

Figure 10.1   Price Quotations for Stock Options

MOST ACTIVE CONTRACTS

Option/Strike			Vol	Exch	Last	Net Chg	a-Close	Open Int
Dig Eq	May	60	12,517	XC	3 1/4	+ 1 3/4	60 5/8	5,469
Cisco	Jul	50	6,486	XC	2 7/8	+ 1/8	48 5/8	13,451
Wlwrth	Jun	20	6,148	PB	1 3/16	+ 9/16	19 3/4	86
Compaq	May	45	5,943	PC	1 11/16	+ 11/16	43 7/8	10,639
Motrla	May	60	5,789	AM	2 15/16	+ 1 3/16	61 3/4	8,313
TelMex	May	35 p	5,487	XC	3/4	+ 1/8	36	11,636
BnkNwk	May	35	4,845	XC	1 3/16	+ 3/16	32 5/8	7,305
Iomega	May	45	4,354	XC	9 7/8	+ 7 1/8	51 7/8	1,572
Dig Eq	May	50	4,167	XC	10 1/2	+ 4	60 5/8	8,042
IntgDv	May	12 1/2	4,047	XC	2 1/4	+ 1 7/16	14 1/4	5,649
Iomega	May	40 p	3,674	XC	1 11/16	-1 13/16	51 7/8	1,279
MicrTc	May	35	3,650	XC	1 1/16	+ 1/8	33 1/4	11,056
TelMex	May	35	3,633	XC	1 15/16	- 7/8	36	28,369
SunMic	May	55	3,586	PC	2 3/8	+1 11/16	54 3/4	3,149
Iomega	May	40	3,508	XC	13 1/2	+ 8 1/2	51 7/8	6,755
BayNwk	May	25	3,332	XC	7 3/4	+ 1 1/2	32 5/8	3,992
Seagte	May	50 p	3,267	XC	1 1/16	- 5/16	54	647
SunMic	May	50	3,081	PC	5 1/2	+ 3 1/2	54 3/4	5,609
SunMic	Jul	40 p	3,022	PC	5/8	- 3/8	54 3/4	4,137
Dig Eq	May	50 p	2,980	XC	5/16	- 13/16	60 5/8	1,929
Cisco	Jun	50	2,965	XC	2 7/16	+ 7/16	48 5/8	8,634
Dig Eq	May	55	2,958	XC	6 3/8	+ 2 7/16	60 5/8	3,088
Cisco	May	50	2,952	XC	1 1/2	+ 3/8	48 5/8	6,824
Cisco	Jul	40 p	2,855	XC	1 7/16	- 1/2	48 5/8	8,299
Cisco	Jun	40 p	2,512	XC	15/16	- 7/16	48 5/8	3,836
StrlCh	Jul	12 1/2	2,511	XC	13/16	- 1/4	12 5/8	2,339
Seagte	May	55 p	2,460	XC	2 3/4	...	54	2,691
MicrTc	May	37 1/2	2,415	XC	7/16	+ 1/16	33 1/4	3,201
Iomega	May	45 p	2,373	XC	3 3/8	- 3 3/8	51 7/8	546
Intel	Jul	70	2,347	AM	3 3/8	+ 1/4	68 7/64	11,653
Intel	May	70	2,342	AM	1 1/4	+ 3/8	68 7/64	4,409
I B M	May	115	2,259	CB	1 1/4	- 5/16	107	18,339
L S I	Jul	40	2,194	CB	1 1/2	+ 1/4	34 3/4	2,415
Chase o	May	70	2,182	AM	1 1/2	...		250
AmerOn	May	65	2,181	XC	4 1/8	+ 1 7/16	65 1/8	2,882
I B M	May	110	2,153	CB	2 5/8	- 1/2	107	12,446
Seagte	May	60	2,136	XC	1 5/8	+ 1/16	54	2,806
CmpAsc	Oct	80	2,100	CB	6	+ 1	74 1/2	104
Dig Eq	May	65	2,093	XC	1 5/8	+ 13/16	60 5/8	2,237
K mart	May	10	2,081	CB	1/2	+ 1/16	10 1/8	5,383

Option/Strike		Exp.	Call Vol.	Call Last	Put Vol.	Put Last
ABR Inf	55	May	55	6 1/2	...	...
60 1/4	60	Jun	75	4 3/8	...	...
ADC Tel	40	May	143	2 3/4	...	...
41 1/2	40	Nov	65	6 5/8	...	...
ADT	17 1/2	Sep	100	1 1/4	...	...
AGCO	25	May	130	1 1/4	...	...
AMR	80	May	15	9 1/8	125	1/4
90	85	May	20	5	161	7/8
90	90	May	116	2 3/4	122	2 1/2
90	90	Nov	100	9 1/8	...	...
90	95	May	97	1 1/8	2	5 1/2
APACT	75	May	52	9 1/4	4	2 7/8
ASA	42 1/2	May	...	...	80	7/16
45	45	May	126	1 3/16	66	1 3/8
45	45	Aug	255	2 7/8	260	2 3/4
AT&T	60	May	172	1 7/8	591	3/4
60 5/8	60	Jun	...	...	125	1 1/4
60 5/8	65	May	440	3/16	5	4 1/4
60 5/8	65	Jun	293	9/16	...	...
60 5/8	65	Jul	236	13/16	...	...
60 5/8	65	Oct	91	1 11/16	...	...
AVX Cp	22 1/2	Nov	85	3 3/4	...	...
23 3/4	25	Jun	120	1	...	...
23 3/4	25	Aug	135	2 1/8	...	...
23 3/4	25	Nov	52	3	...	...
Aames	45	Jun	80	3 1/2	...	...
44 1/8	45	Sep	210	6	...	...
Abbt L	40	Jun	3	2 7/16	100	7/8
41 3/4	45	May	202	1/4	...	...
41 3/4	45	Aug	79	15/16	...	...
Aclaim	10	Jul	75	1 3/16	...	...
AccuStff	23 3/4	Jul	403	8 1/8	...	...
30	25	May	61	5 1/2	8	3/4
30	27 1/2	May	10	5	71	1 7/8
30	30	May	193	2 5/8	68	2 15/16
30	30	Jun	52	3 3/4	...	...
30	30	Jul	56	4 1/2	...	...
30	35	Oct	127	4 5/8	4	9
Actel	15	May	70	3 5/8	...	...
Adaptc	50	May	151	6 1/4	60	1 3/16
55	55	May	256	3 3/8	102	3 1/8
AdobeS	30	May	132	8 1/4	...	...
38 1/8	35	May	61	4	52	7/8
38 1/8	35	Jul	125	5 5/8	17	2 1/2
38 1/8	40	May	345	1 3/16	3	3 5/8
38 1/8	40	Jun	56	2 1/8	10	3 7/8
38 1/8	45	May	90	5/8	...	...
Adtran	45	Aug	...	...	70	2 7/8
59 3/4	60	May	100	4 1/8	...	...
A M D	15	Jul	...	...	158	5/8
17 3/8	17 1/2	May	248	5/8	38	3/4
17 3/8	17 1/2	Jul	328	1 7/16	172	1 3/8
17 3/8	20	Jul	266	1/2	2	3 1/2
17 3/8	20	Oct	70	1 1/4	...	...
Baan	65	May	182	1 15/16	...	...
BabySst	40	May	10	6 3/8	95	1
BakrHu	25	May	525	5 3/8	...	...
BallyEnt	15	Jul	111	6 5/8	...	...
21 7/8	17 1/2	Jul	...	...	425	13/16
21 7/8	20	May	1480	2 9/16	196	7/8
21 7/8	20	Jun	240	3	290	1 1/4
21 7/8	22 1/2	May	1001	1	27	1 7/8
21 7/8	22 1/2	Jun	546	1 7/8	300	2 9/16
21 7/8	22 1/2	Jul	55	2	...	...
21 7/8	25	May	1041	7/16	...	...
BancOne	35	May	158	7/8	2	1 1/16
BncoFrn	30	May	148	7/8	...	...
27 1/2	30	Jul	128	1 3/8	...	...
BkBost	42 1/2	Jun	1000	4 3/4	...	...
47 3/4	45	May	75	3 1/8	...	...
47 3/4	47 1/2	May	68	7/8	...	...
47 3/4	47 1/2	Jun	1000	1 5/16	...	...
BankNY	45	May	230	2 3/4	...	...
47 1/2	50	Jul	53	1 1/2	...	...
47 1/2	50	Oct	79	7/8	...	...
BankAm	75	May	170	1 3/8	...	...
BarNbl	40	Jun	102	13/16	...	...
BarickG	30	May	468	1 1/8	70	7/8
30 1/4	30	Jun	122	1 5/8	5	1 7/16
30 1/4	30	Jul	640	2	10	1 11/16
30 1/4	35	May	757	1/2	...	...
30 1/4	35	Jun	220	1 1/8	...	...
30 1/4	35	Oct	220	1 1/8	...	...
BattlM	10	Jul	104	7/16	...	...
8 7/8	10	Oct	1511	13/16	...	...
BausLm	40	May	10	5/8	70	13/16
BayNwk	25	May	3332	7 3/4	149	3/4
32 5/8	25	Jun	235	8 1/8	139	11/16
32 5/8	25	Sep	86	9 3/4	55	1 11/16
32 5/8	27 1/2	Jun	...	...	90	1 1/16
32 5/8	30	May	1088	3 1/2	335	7/8
32 5/8	35	May	4845	1 3/16	125	3 1/4
32 5/8	40	May	463	1/4	...	...
32 5/8	45	Jun	765	5/16	...	...
32 5/8	50	Sep	1660	7/8	...	...
BearSt	25	May	121	1 1/8	...	...
BedBth	45	May	94	8 1/8	...	...
52 1/4	50	May	67	4 3/4	20	3 1/8
52 1/4	55	May	85	2 1/8	...	...
BellAtl	60	Oct	2	8 3/4	60	1 5/16
66 1/4	65	May	60	2 3/4	170	7/8
66 1/4	70	Jun	82	1	...	...
BellSo	40	May	198	15/16	30	7/8
39 7/8	45	Jun	54	1 9/16	...	...
39 7/8	40	Jul	36	2	101	1 3/4
BestBuy	15	Jun	203	4 3/4	38	1 3/4
19 3/8	17 1/2	May	55	1 7/8	25	5/16
19 3/8	17 1/2	Jun	97	2 1/8	...	...
19 3/8	20	May	518	7/16	43	1 1/4
19 3/8	20	Jun	454	1	40	1 5/8
81	75	Jun	1	7 1/4	55	1 1/8
81	75	Aug	5	8 1/2	106	2
81	80	May	92	2 5/8	168	1 1/2
81	80	Jun	124	4	2	2 3/4
81	80	Aug	70	5 5/8	11	3 5/8
81	85	May	1064	1/2	2	5
81	85	Jun	74	1 1/2	...	...
81	85	Aug	180	3 1/2	...	...
CCFems	30	May	1000	5/16	...	...
Cognos	55	May	72	8 1/4	...	...
Cohrnt	45	May	211	7 1/4	...	...
52 5/16	50	May	103	3 1/8	...	...
ColgPl	85	May	...	...	150	8 1/8
ColData	20	May	...	...	150	3/4
21 3/8	25	Jun	120	1	...	...
ColHsp	55	May	188	3/4	...	...
52 3/8	55	Aug	113	2 5/8	...	...
ColLb	10	Jun	81	2	...	...
Comeric	40	May	305	4 1/8	...	...
43 3/4	45	Jul	63	1 11/16	...	...
CmpUSA	25	May	32	7 1/2	224	1/8
32 1/2	27 1/2	May	564	5	60	3/8
32 1/2	27 1/2	Aug	266	6 7/8	5	1 7/16
32 1/2	30	May	964	3 1/4	1145	5/8
32 1/2	30	Jun	285	4 1/8	20	1 3/16
32 1/2	30	Aug	63	5 1/8	200	2 3/8
32 1/2	32 1/2	May	145	1 11/16	228	1 5/8
32 1/2	32 1/2	Aug	142	3 3/4	190	3 1/4
ChileT	90	May	80	4	...	...
93 7/8	95	May	184	1 1/2	15	4 1/4
Compaq	32 1/2	May	20	12	100	1/16
43 7/8	35	May	58	9	221	7/16
43 7/8	37 1/2	May	63	6 3/4	53	5/16
43 7/8	37 1/2	Jul	76	7 3/4	46	7/8
43 7/8	40	May	835	5	1954	5/8
43 7/8	40	Jul	272	6 1/8	291	1 5/8
43 7/8	40	Oct	56	8	70	2 7/16
43 7/8	42 1/2	May	1159	3 1/2	644	1 1/4
43 7/8	42 1/2	Jun	31	3 7/8	185	2
43 7/8	42 1/2	Jul	80	4 1/2	13	4
43 7/8	45	May	5943	1 11/16	1439	2 3/8
43 7/8	45	Jun	552	2 1/2	15	3
43 7/8	45	Jul	831	3 1/4	42	3 1/2
43 7/8	45	Oct	979	5	10	4 3/4
43 7/8	47 1/2	May	422	15/16	...	...
43 7/8	47 1/2	Jun	288	1 1/2	...	...
43 7/8	47 1/2	Jul	299	2 3/8	10	5 5/8
43 7/8	50	May	472	7/16	...	...
43 7/8	50	Jun	169	7/8	...	...
43 7/8	50	Jul	1085	1 1/2	...	...
43 7/8	50	Oct	246	3	...	...
43 7/8	55	Jul	57	9/16	...	...
43 7/8	55	Oct	68	1 5/8	...	...
43 7/8	60	Oct	120	1	...	...

Index Option Contract Volume by Exchange, 1995		Table 10.7
Exchange	**Total Volume**	**Percentage**
Chicago Board Options Exchange	101,427,897	94.08
American Stock Exchange	3,505,041	3.25
Philadelphia Stock Exchange	2,799,964	2.60
Pacific Stock Exchange	52,163	0.05
New York Stock Exchange	25,425	0.02
Total	107,810,490	100.00

Source: From Chicago Board Options Exchange, *Market Statistics,* 1995. Reprinted by permission of the Chicago Board Options Exchange.

Table 10.9 shows the volume of trading in futures options by the type of the underlying futures. Financial instruments account for the majority of futures options and include options on stock index futures and interest rate futures. Options on foreign exchange futures, traded principally at the CME, come next. Options on energy and wood product futures constitute the third largest category, and this volume stems mainly from options on oil-related futures traded primarily at the NYME. Options on traditional agricultural futures are much less important than options on financial instruments, currencies, and energy products. Figure 10.4 shows a sample of the quotations for options on futures.

OPTION TRADING PROCEDURES

Every options trader needs to be familiar with the basic features of the market. This section explores the action that takes place on the market floor and the ways in which traders away from the exchange can have their orders executed on the exchange. From its image in the popular press and television, one gets the impression that the exchange floor is the scene of wild and chaotic action. While the action may become wild, it is never chaotic. Understanding the role of the different participants on the floor helps dispel the illusion of chaos. Essentially, there are three types of people on the exchange floor: traders, clerical personnel associated with the traders, and exchange officials. First we describe the system that the CBOE uses. Later, we note some differences among exchanges.

Types of Traders

There are three different kinds of traders on the floor of the exchange: market makers, floor brokers, and order book officials. A trader who trades for his own account is a market maker. A trader who executes orders for another is a floor broker. The order book official is an employee of the exchange who makes certain kinds of option trades and keeps the book of orders awaiting execution at specified prices.

The Market Maker. The typical market maker owns or leases a seat on the options exchange and trades for his or her own account to make a profit. However, as the name implies, the market maker has an obligation to make a market for the public by standing ready to buy or sell options. Typically, a market maker will concentrate on the options of just a few stocks. Focusing on a few issues allows

Figure 10.2 | Price Quotations for Index Options

INDEX OPTIONS TRADING

Tuesday, April 23, 1996.

Volume, last, net change and open interest for all contracts. Volume figures are unofficial. Open interest reflects previous trading day.
p-Put c-Call

CHICAGO

Strike		Vol.	Last	Net Chg.	Open Int.
CB MEXICO INDEX (MEX)					
Jun	70 c	10	$19^5/_8$	+ 2	20
May	80 p	25	$^{13}/_{16}$	+ $^1/_{16}$	65
Jun	80 c	20	$10^3/_4$	– $^5/_8$	248
Jun	85 c	30	$8^1/_8$	– 1	144
Dec	85 p	20	$8^3/_4$	– $2^5/_8$	20
May	90 c	132	$3^1/_8$	– $^5/_8$	101
May	90 p	10	4	+ $^1/_8$	110
Jun	95 c	10	3	– 2	190
Sep	95 c	10	$6^7/_8$	– $^3/_4$	40
Dec	95 p	10	$13^1/_2$	+ $1^3/_8$	30
Call Vol.		**212**	**Open Int.**		**2,364**
Put Vol.		**65**	**Open Int.**		**2,685**
CB TECHNOLOGY (TXX)					
Jun	155 c	22	$2^3/_4$	– $4^1/_2$	20
May	160 p	2	$2^{11}/_{16}$	– $1^3/_{16}$	95
Jun	160 c	19	$12^1/_2$	+ 3	56
Jun	160 p	10	$4^1/_2$	– $1^3/_8$	77
May	170 c	2	$3^7/_8$	+ $1^1/_2$	17
Jun	170 c	55	6	+ 1	120
May	175 p	10	$10^1/_2$	...	...
Jun	175 c	15	$4^3/_8$	+ $2^3/_4$	102
Jun	190 c	20	$1^1/_4$	+ $^3/_8$	12
Call Vol.		**113**	**Open Int.**		**1,952**
Put Vol.		**46**	**Open Int.**		**3,278**
NASDAQ-100 (NDX)					
May	565 p	5	$^1/_2$	– $5^3/_4$	5
May	575 p	12,200	1	– $^1/_8$	14,301
Jun	580 c	22	$3^1/_4$	– $5^1/_4$	40
Jun	590 p	2	$4^1/_4$	– $12^1/_8$	239
Jul	590 p	10	$7^1/_2$	...	...
May	600 p	7,866	2	– $^3/_4$	270
Jun	600 p	13	$6^1/_8$	– $1^3/_4$	250
Jun	600 c	33	6	– $1^5/_8$	126
Jun	605 c	6	53	+ $9^1/_8$	38
May	605 p	5,006	2	– $1^1/_4$	584
Jun	610 p	33	3	– 1	512
Jun	610 c	10	50	+ 10	15
Jun	610 p	600	8	...	1
May	615 p	1,220	$3^1/_2$	– $1^3/_4$	1,092
May	620 c	5	$39^3/_4$	+ $8^7/_8$	564
May	620 p	26	$3^3/_4$	– $2^1/_4$	251
Jun	620 p	18	$10^1/_8$	– $1^7/_8$	58
May	625 p	28	$4^3/_4$	– 3	86
May	630 p	2,221	$6^1/_4$	– $2^3/_4$	367
Jun	630 p	5	12	– $2^7/_8$	4
Jul	630 p	20	$16^1/_8$	...	...
May	635 p	43	$7^3/_4$	– $4^1/_4$	28
May	640 c	46	24	+ $7^3/_4$	340
May	640 p	1,427	9	– $3^1/_4$	351
Jun	640 p	5	$16^5/_8$	– $2^1/_4$	2
May	645 c	52	10	– $4^3/_8$	22
May	645 p	42	$18^1/_4$	– $1^7/_8$	5
May	650 c	4	$15^1/_4$	+ 4	150
May	650 p	55	12	– $5^1/_8$	...
May	650 p	138	$18^7/_8$	– $5^1/_8$	10
Jun	650 p	36	$18^7/_8$	...	3
Jul	650 p	10	$27^1/_2$	...	...
May	655 c	2	$8^3/_4$	– $^1/_4$	2,310
May	655 p	20	$13^3/_4$	...	...
May	660 c	21	$8^3/_4$	+ 2	398
Jun	660 c	51	$17^3/_4$	...	...
Jun	660 c	25	$17^3/_4$	+ 3	85
Jun	660 p	22	$23^3/_4$	– $4^3/_4$	...
Jun	660 p	20	$24^3/_4$	...	2
May	665 c	6,095	$8^3/_4$	+ $3^1/_2$	6,010
Jun	665 c	2	14	+ $3^7/_8$	10

RANGES FOR UNDERLYING INDEXES

Tuesday, April 23, 1996

	High	Low	Close	Net Chg.	From Dec. 31	% Chg.
S&P 100 (OEX)	628.77	624.97	628.62	+ 3.30	+ 42.70	+ 7.3
S&P 500 A.M.(SPX) ..	651.59	647.70	651.58	+ 3.69	+ 35.65	+ 5.8
S&P Banks (BIX) ...	358.11	355.92	356.94	+ 0.39	+ 26.44	+ 8.0
CB-Tech (TXX)	167.74	163.50	167.66	+ 4.15	+ 11.13	+ 7.1
CB-Mexico (MEX) ..	90.17	88.12	88.95	– 1.22	+ 17.21	+ 24.0
CB-Lps Mex (VEX) .	9.02	8.81	8.89	– 0.13	+ 1.72	+ 24.0
Nasdaq 100 (NDX) ...	654.63	643.02	654.49	+ 10.20	+ 78.26	+ 13.6
Russell 2000 (RUT) .	343.53	340.99	343.52	+ 2.53	+ 27.55	+ 8.7
Lps S&P 100 (OEX) .	62.88	62.50	62.86	+ 0.33	+ 4.27	+ 7.3
Lps S&P 500 (SPX) .	65.16	64.77	65.16	+ 0.37	+, 3.57	+ 5.8
S&P Midcap (MID) .	234.55	232.65	234.34	+ 1.69	+ 16.50	+ 7.6
Major Mkt (XMI) ...	578.35	575.49	578.10	+ 1.69	+ 42.50	+ 7.9
Leaps MMkt (XLT) .	57.84	57.55	57.81	+ 0.17	+ 4.25	+ 7.9
Hong Kong (HKO) ..			220.62	– 0.43	+ 17.71	+ 8.7
Leaps HK (HKL)			22.06	– 0.05	+ 1.77	+ 8.7
IW Internet (IIX) ...	243.77	234.84	243.73	+ 8.89	+ 10.53	+ 4.5
AM-Mexico (MXY) ..	103.86	101.20	102.06	– 1.80	+ 18.44	+ 22.1
Institutl A.M.(XII) ..	674.55	671.08	674.50	+ 2.86	+ 37.78	+ 5.9
Japan (JPN)			224.88	+ 0.04	+ 23.04	+ 11.4
MS Cyclical (CYC) ..	388.12	385.44	387.84	+ 2.30	+ 47.62	+ 14.0
MS Consumr (CMR)	291.45	289.87	290.88	– 0.21	+ 6.13	+ 2.2
MS Hi Tech (MSH) .	339.39	331.82	339.29	+ 7.24	+ 23.52	+ 7.5
Pharma (DRG)	298.89	295.91	296.93	– 0.86	+ 0.98	+ 0.3
Biotech (BTK)	146.78	144.01	144.69	– 0.67	+ 10.92	+ 8.2
Comp Tech (XCI) ...	262.12	256.73	261.99	+ 4.84	+ 33.37	+ 14.6
NYSE (NYA)	349.60	347.74	349.60	+ 1.78	+ 20.09	+ 6.1
Gold/Silver (XAU) ..	141.47	139.81	141.47	+ 2.00	+ 21.05	+ 17.5
OTC (XOC)	472.97	465.23	472.97	+ 6.47	+ 48.27	+ 11.4
Utility (UTY)	247.54	246.26	247.16	– 0.02	– 30.44	– 11.0
Value Line (VLE) ...	618.51	614.52	618.47	+ 3.95	+ 48.57	+ 8.5
Bank (BKX)	425.86	423.12	424.35	+ 0.40	+ 30.50	+ 7.7
Semicond (SOX)	202.37	195.41	202.37	+ 6.38	+ 1.17	+ 0.9
Top 100 (TPX)	583.12	580.18	583.09	+ 2.45	+ 30.07	+ 5.4

Strike		Vol.	Last	Net Chg.	Open Int.
Jun	650 c	79	$5^5/_8$	+ $^3/_4$	2,213
Jun	650 p	16	$25^3/_4$	– $^7/_8$	262
Jul	650 c	100	$8^1/_2$	+ $^1/_4$	203
Jul	650 p	6	27	– $4^3/_4$	367
May	655 c	1,461	$^3/_4$	+ $^3/_{16}$	10,205
Jun	655 c	78	$4^1/_8$	+ $^1/_4$	895
May	660 p	1,127	$^3/_8$	...	9,785
May	660 p	1	35	– $16^5/_8$	61
Jun	660 p	241	$2^7/_8$	+ $^3/_4$	4,111
Jun	660 p	1	$34^3/_4$	– $4^3/_4$	15
Jul	660 c	53	$5^1/_2$	– $^1/_8$	577
Aug	660 c	102	$7^3/_4$	...	...
May	665 c	2,762	$^1/_4$	+ $^1/_8$	8,778
Jun	665 c	1,421	$1^{11}/_{16}$	+ $^1/_{16}$	2,349
May	670 c	218	$^1/_8$	– $^1/_{16}$	4,577
Jun	670 c	385	$1^1/_4$	...	4,427
Jul	670 c	1,855	$3^1/_4$	+ $^3/_8$	1,276
Call Vol.		**42,608**	**Open Int.**		**217,802**
Put Vol.		**44,657**	**Open Int.**		**201,543**

Strike		Vol.	Last	Net Chg.	Open Int.
May	100 c	10	$4^7/_8$	...	...
Jun	100 p	10	$5^1/_8$	+ $^7/_8$	10
Call Vol.		**21**	**Open Int.**		**738**
Put Vol.		**10**	**Open Int.**		**717**
COMP TECH(XCI)					
May	225 p	5	$^7/_{16}$	– $1^1/_{16}$	44
Jun	240 p	5	$4^3/_8$	– $^3/_4$	5
Jul	240 c	2	$26^5/_8$	+ $2^7/_8$	2
May	245 p	5	$2^1/_4$	– 1	168
May	250 c	30	$13^1/_8$	+ $1^3/_4$	133
May	250 p	50	$3^1/_2$	– $1^3/_8$	160
May	255 c	25	$11^3/_4$	+ $3^1/_4$	98
May	255 p	42	5	– $1^3/_8$	51
May	260 c	36	$7^1/_2$	+ $2^1/_8$	70
Jun	260 c	35	$10^1/_4$	...	...
Jun	270 c	5	$6^1/_8$	+ $^5/_8$	10
May	275 c	3	$1^7/_8$	– $^{11}/_{16}$	150
Jul	275 c	6	$7^3/_4$	...	...

Source: From *The Wall Street Journal,* April 24, 1996, p. C14. Reprinted by permission of *The Wall Street Journal,* © 1996 Dow Jones & Company, Inc. All rights reserved worldwide.

Price Quotations for Foreign Currency Options — Figure 10.3

OPTIONS
PHILADELPHIA EXCHANGE

		Calls Vol.	Calls Last	Puts Vol.	Puts Last
JYen					**93.74**
6,250,000 Japanese Yen-100ths of a cent per unit.					
91	Jun	...	...	200	0.28
93	May	27	1.43	6	0.37
93	Jun	...	...	200	0.74
94	May	30	0.69	...	...
95	May	20	0.41	...	...
96	May	50	0.21	...	...
98	Jun	5	0.29	...	...
99	Jun	10	0.23	...	...
Australian Dollar					**79.03**
50,000 Australian Dollars-cents per unit.					
79	Jun	...	...	17	1.02
British Pound					**151.58**
31,250 British Pounds-European Style.					
150	Jun	...	...	3	0.67
British Pound-GMark					**230.51**
31,250 British Pound-German Mark cross.					
230	Sep	42	2.12	...	...
31,250 British Pound-German Mark EOM.					
228	Apr	10	1.94	...	...
Canadian Dollar					**73.40**
50,000 Canadian Dollars-cents per unit.					
77½	Jun	...	...	10	0.12
77	Jun	...	...	64	3.62
French Franc					**194.80**
250,000 French Francs-10ths of a cent per unit.					
19¾	May	50	0.34	...	...
GMark-JYen					**70.15**
62,500 German Mark-Japanese Yen cross EOM.					
70	Apr	...	...	32	0.19

		Calls Vol.	Calls Last	Puts Vol.	Puts Last
62,500 German Mark-Japanese Yen cross.					
71½	Jun	5	0.32	...	...
German Mark					**65.76**
62,500 German Marks EOM-cents per unit.					
60	May	...	...	10	0.39
64	May	...	...	10	0.16
65½	Apr	...	...	1550	0.11
66	Apr	350	0.21	...	...
66½	Apr	930	0.06	...	...
67	Apr	...	...	200	1.06
62,500 German Marks-European Style.					
66	Jun	200	0.94	...	...
66½	May	25	0.21	...	...
67½	Jun	16	0.36	...	...
62,500 German Marks-cents per unit.					
62	Jun	...	...	4	0.07
64	Sep	...	...	10	0.74
65	May	80	0.97	495	0.15
65	Jun	...	...	6	0.51
65½	May	...	...	25	0.35
66	May	...	...	350	0.47
66	Jun	5	0.95	147	0.88
66½	May	366	0.27	...	...
66½	Jun	325	0.73	...	...
67	Sep	...	...	33	1.98
67½	Jun	650	0.39	...	...
68	Jun	...	...	5	2.22
68	Sep	110	1.04	...	...
69	Sep	50	0.72	...	...

		Calls Vol.	Calls Last	Puts Vol.	Puts Last
70	Jun	...	...	600	4.18
71	Jun	...	...	310	5.19
73	Jun	...	...	960	7.19
Japanese Yen					**93.74**
92½	Apr	7	1.21	...	...
92½	May	...	...	8	0.17
93½	May	56	1.03	...	...
6,250,000 Japanese Yen EOM-100ths of a cent per unit.					
93	Apr	...	...	20	0.07
94	Apr	50	0.42	...	...
95	May	30	0.76	...	...
6,250,000 Japanese Yen-European Style.					
97	Jun	70	0.53	...	...
Swiss Franc					**81.24**
62,500 Swiss Franc EOM-cents per unit.					
82	Apr	40	0.09	...	...
62,500 Swiss Francs-European Style.					
78	Jun	10	4.00	...	...
81	May	...	...	20	0.40
82	Jun	10	1.18	...	...
85	May	...	...	5	3.43
88	Sep	10	0.59	...	...
62,500 Swiss Francs-cents per unit.					
75	Sep	...	...	164	0.26
80	Sep	...	...	8	1.24
81½	May	70	0.61	...	...
82	May	...	...	5	1.00
82	Sep	...	...	13	2.10
83½	May	18	0.15	...	...
85	Jun	80	0.28	...	...
Call Vol.	7,873	Open Int.	153,290		
Put Vol.	8,386	Open Int.	163,609		

Source: From *The Wall Street Journal,* April 24, 1996, p. C2. Reprinted by permission of *The Wall Street Journal,* © 1996 Dow Jones & Company, Inc. All rights reserved worldwide.

Futures Option Volume, by Exchange, 1995 — Table 10.8

	Contracts Traded (millions)	
Exchange	**Contracts**	**Percentage**
Chicago Board of Trade	42.90	44.93
Chicago Mercantile Exchange	38.33	40.14
New York Mercantile Exchange	6.50	6.81
Commodity Exchange	3.25	3.40
Coffee, Sugar & Cocoa Exchange	2.62	2.74
New York Cotton Exchange & Association	1.62	1.70
Kansas City Board of Trade	0.09	0.09*
New York Futures Exchange	0.09	0.09*
MidAmerica Commodity Exchange	0.03	0.03*
Minneapolis Grain Exchange	0.05	0.05*
Total	95.48	

Source: From Annual Report, Commodity Futures Trading Commission, 1995. Data are for the fiscal year of the CFTC ending September 30, 1995. *Negligible.

Table 10.9	Futures Option Open Interest and Volume, 1995			
	Average Open Interest		Contracts Traded	
Type of Underlying Good	Contracts	Percentage	Contracts	Percentage
Financial Instruments	3,287	60.45	65.5	68.73
Currencies	430	7.91	7.7	8.08
Energy/Wood Products	429	7.89	6.4	6.72
Grains	350	6.44	4.3	4.51
Other Agricultural	374	6.88	4.2	4.41
Metals	312	5.74	3.3	3.46
Oilseeds	183	3.37	3.1	3.25
Livestock	73	1.34	0.8	0.84
Total	5,438		95.3	

Source: From Annual Report, Commodity Futures Trading Commission, 1995. Data are for the fiscal year of the CFTC ending September 30, 1995.

the market maker to become quite knowledgeable about the other traders who deal in options on those stocks.

Market makers follow different trading strategies, and they switch freely from one strategy to another. Some market makers are scalpers. The scalper follows the psychology of the trading crowd and tries to anticipate the direction of the market in the next few minutes. The scalper tries to buy if the price is about to rise and tries to sell just before it falls. Generally, the scalper holds a position for just a few minutes, trying to make a profit on moment to moment fluctuations in the option's price. By contrast, a position trader buys or sells options and holds a position for a longer period. This commitment typically rests on views about the underlying worth of the stock or movements in the economy. Both scalpers and position traders often trade option combinations. For example, they might buy a call at a striking price of 90 and sell a call with a striking price of 95. Such a combination is called a **spread**. A spread is any option position in two or more related options. In all such combination trades, the trader seeks to profit from a change in the price of one option relative to another.

The Floor Broker. Many option traders are located away from the trading floor. When an off-the-floor trader enters an order to buy or sell an option, the floor broker has the job of executing the order. Floor brokers typically represent brokerage firms, such as Merrill Lynch or Prudential Bache. They work for a salary or receive commissions, and their job is to obtain the best price on an order while executing it rapidly. Almost all brokers have support personnel that assist in completing trades. For example, major brokerage firms will have clerical staff that receive orders from beyond the trading floor. These individuals deal with all of the record keeping necessary to execute an order and assist in transmitting information to and from the floor brokers. In addition, many brokerage firms engage in proprietary trading – trading for their own account. Therefore, they have a number of trained people on the floor of the exchange to seek trading opportunities and to execute transactions through a floor broker.

Price Quotations for Options on Futures   **Figure 10.4**

FUTURES OPTIONS PRICES

Tuesday, April 23, 1996.

AGRICULTURAL

CORN (CBT)
5,000 bu.; cents per bu.

Strike	Calls-Settle			Puts-Settle		
Price	Jly	Sep	Dec	Jly	Sep	Dec
440	36	17	10	16	....	....
450	31	....	....	21	....	....
460	26¹/₂	13	8¹/₂	25¹/₂	....	....
470	22	....	....	31	....	....
480	19¹/₄	11	....	....	....	....
490	16¹/₂	....	....	....	....	....

Est vol 30,000 Mn 14,064 calls 16,898 puts
Op int Mon 210,467 calls 220,267 puts

SOYBEANS (CBT)
5,000 bu.; cents per bu.

Strike	Calls-Settle			Puts-Settle		
Price	Jly	Aug	Sep	Jly	Aug	Sep
775	61	69¹/₂	66	14	25	37¹/₂
800	47¹/₄	58³/₄	57	25¹/₂	39	53¹/₈
825	37	49	49	40	53⁷/₈	....
850	29¹/₄	41³/₈	42³/₈	56³/₄	71	88
875	23¹/₂	35	37¹/₂	75³/₄	....	107
900	19¹/₂	30	32	96³/₄	108¹/₂	....

Est vol 25,000 Mn 15,112 calls 9,366 puts
Op int Mon 134,896 calls 110,667 puts

SOYBEAN MEAL (CBT)
100 tons; $ per ton

Strike	Calls-Settle			Puts-Settle		
Price	Jly	Aug	Sep	Jly	Aug	Sep
240	24.10	27.50	27.50	3.75	6.75	9.75
250	18.00	22.00	22.75	7.50	11.00	15.00
260	13.50	18.00	19.00	12.75	17.00	....
270	10.50	14.50	16.50	....	....	....
280	8.00	12.00	14.00	....	....	....
290	6.50	10.50	12.25	....	....	....

Est vol 2,800 Mn 2,532 calls 1,252 puts
Op int Mon 24,818 calls 17,537 puts

SOYBEAN OIL (CBT)
60,000 lbs.; cents per lb.

Strike	Calls-Settle			Puts-Settle		
Price	Jly	Aug	Sep	Jly	Aug	Sep
2600	1.500	1.850	2.060	.450	.650	....
2650	1.230	1.620	1.770	.650	.880	....
2700	1.000	1.400	1.590	.920	....	....
2750	.800	1.250	1.400	....	....	....
2800	.680	....	1.250	....	....	....
2850	.550	....	1.100	....	....	....

Est vol 2,000 Mn 668 calls 146 puts
Op int Mon 13,758 calls 10,455 puts

WHEAT (CBT)
5,000 bu.; cents per bu.

Strike	Calls-Settle			Puts-Settle		
Price	Jly	Sep	Dec	Jly	Sep	Dec
590	49¹/₂	58	24³/₄	....	....	....
600	46¹/₂	56	64³/₄	31¹/₂	45	48
610	40	50¹/₂	57	35	....	....
620	34¹/₂	47	50	39¹/₂	....	....
630	32	43¹/₂	47¹/₂	....	....	....
640	29	42	43¹/₂	....	....	....

Est vol 20,000 Mn 13,673 calls 15,627 puts
Op int Mon 77,329 calls 62,412 puts

COTTON (CTN)
50,000 lbs.; cents per lb.

Strike	Calls-Settle			Puts-Settle		
Price	Jly	Oct	Dec	Jly	Oct	Dec
81	4.78	5.53	4.84	1.28	3.10	3.98
82	4.13	5.00	4.37	1.62	3.54	....
83	3.53	4.50	4.03	2.01	4.02	....
84	3.00	4.05	3.53	2.46	4.53	5.56
85	2.52	3.65	3.16	2.98	....	....
86	2.10	3.30	2.82	3.54	....	6.78

220	.151	.171	.181	.058	.072	.088
225	.120	.144	.157	.077	.094	....
230	.090	.120	.134	.097	.120	....
235	.070	.099	.115	.127	.149	....
240	.055	.082	.100	.161	....	....

Est vol 4,024 Mn 1,117 calls 795 puts
Op int Mon 49,154 calls 39,444 puts

BRENT CRUDE (IPE)
1,000 net bbls.; $ per bbl.

Strike	Calls-Settle			Puts-Settle		
Price	June	July	Aug	June	July	Aug
19.50	1.26	.80	.70	.53	1.08	1.61
20.00	.98	.61	.54	.75	1.39	1.95
20.50	.77	.46	.42	1.04	1.74	2.33
21.00	.59	.34	.32	1.36	2.12	2.73
21.50	.44	.25	.24	1.71	2.53	3.15
22.00	.32	.18	.18	2.09	2.96	3.59

Est vol 1,756 Mn 200 calls 1,760 puts
Op int Mon 13,230 calls 18,200 puts

GAS OIL (IPE)
100 metric tons; $ per ton

Strike	Calls-Settle			Puts-Settle		
Price	May	Jun	Jly	May	Jun	Jly
165	9.25	7.15	9.55	1.25	4.65	6.85
170	5.80	5.25	6.85	2.80	7.75	9.60
175	3.00	3.50	4.60	5.00	11.00	11.00
180	1.90	2.20	3.15	8.90	14.70	17.00
185	0.50	1.35	2.00	12.50	18.85	21.25
190	0.15	0.75	1.25	17.15	23.25	25.75

Est vol 495 Mn 100 calls 20 puts
Op int Mon 5,838 calls 4,144 puts

LIVESTOCK

CATTLE-FEEDER (CME)
50,000 lbs.; cents per lb.

Strike	Calls-Settle			Puts-Settle		
Price	Apr	May	Aug	Apr	May	Aug
50	....	1.25	....	0.10	1.50	1.82
51	0.05	....	....	0.50	....	....
52	0.00	0.47	....	1.42	2.65	2.65
53	0.00	....	....	2.45	....	....
54	0.00	....	1.95	3.45	4.40	3.75

Est vol 1,451 Mn 550 calls 693 puts
Op int Mon 12,167 calls 9,397 puts

CATTLE-LIVE (CME)
40,000 lbs.; cents per lb.

Strike	Calls-Settle			Puts-Settle		
Price	May	June	Aug	May	June	Aug
55	....	....	....	....	....	1.07
56	....	2.77	....	....	1.40	1.25
57	....	....	....	....	1.82	1.52
58	....	1.70	3.60	1.80	2.32	1.85
59	....	1.27	....	....	2.90	2.25
60	....	0.92	2.52	3.30	3.52	2.75

Est vol 4,538 Mn 1,881 calls 1,806 puts
Op int Mon 17,382 calls 20,149 puts

HOGS-LIVE (CME)
40,000 lbs.; cents per lb.

Strike	Calls-Settle			Puts-Settle		
Price	June	July	Aug	June	July	Aug
55	4.45	3.40	....	0.50	1.45	....
56	3.65	2.82	1.45	0.70	1.85	....
57	2.95	2.32	....	1.00	2.35	....
58	2.37	1.90	0.90	1.40	....	....
59	1.82	1.55	....	1.85	....	....
60	1.37	1.17	0.52	2.40	4.20	....

Est vol 612 Mn 416 calls 192 puts
Op int Mon 8,021 calls 16,245 puts

METALS

COPPER (CMX)
25,000 lbs.; cents per lb.

Strike	Calls-Settle	Puts-Settle

15500	0.02	0.20	....	....	3.54	....

Est vol 8,447 Mn 519 calls 841 puts
Op int Mon 57,801 calls 55,901 puts

SWISS FRANC (CME)
125,000 francs; cents per franc

Strike	Calls-Settle			Puts-Settle		
Price	May	June	July	May	June	July
8050	....	1.76	....	0.17	0.70	....
8100	....	1.46	....	0.29	0.89	0.97
8150	0.55	1.17	....	0.48	1.10	....
8200	0.32	0.94	....	0.75	1.37	....
8250	0.18	0.75	....	1.11	1.67	....
8300	0.11	0.58	....	1.54	2.00	1.92

Est vol 1,564 Mn 882 calls 893 puts
Op int Mon 17,558 calls 18,547 puts

INTEREST RATE

T-BONDS (CBT)
$100,000; points and 64ths of 100%

Strike	Calls-Settle			Puts-Settle		
Price	Jun	Sep	Dec	Jun	Sep	Dec
108	2-44	3-30	3-50	0-28	1-48	2-40
109	1-61	....	....	0-45	....	....
110	1-21	2-23	2-50	1-05	2-40	3-35
111	0-55	....	....	1-39	....	....
112	0-33	1-33	1-61	2-17	3-50	4-43
113	0-17	....	....	3-01	....	....

Est. vol. 75,000;
Mn vol. 39,361 calls; 66,549 puts
Op. int. Mon 440,897 calls; 278,074 puts

T-NOTES (CBT)
$100,000; points and 64ths of 100%

Strike	Calls-Settle			Puts-Settle		
Price	Jun	Sep	Dec	Jun	Sep	Dec
106	2-22	2-51	2-52	0-12	0-61	1-36
107	1-35	2-10	2-17	0-25	1-19	1-63
108	0-58	1-39	....	0-47	1-47	....
109	0-29	1-12	1-25	1-19	2-19	3-04
110	0-13	0-53	1-03	2-03	2-59	....
111	0-05	0-36	0-50	2-58	3-41	....

Est vol 30,000 Mn 24,662 calls 15,993 puts
Op int Mon 318,806 calls 245,463 puts

5 YR TREAS NOTES (CBT)
$100,000; points and 64ths of 100%

Strike	Calls-Settle			Puts-Settle		
Price	Jun	Sep	Dec	Jun	Sep	Dec
10500	1-36	1-53	....	0-10	0-46	....
10550	1-11	1-33	....	0-16	0-57	....
10600	0-51	1-15	....	0-25	1-06	....
10650	0-33	0-63	....	0-39	1-22	....
10700	0-19	0-50	....	0-57	1-40	....
10750	0-10	0-38	....	1-16	1-60	....

Est vol 5,000 Mn 1,583 calls 2,384 puts
Op int Mon 103,915 calls 88,711 puts

EURODOLLAR (CME)
$ million; pts. of 100%

Strike	Calls-Settle			Puts-Settle		
Price	May	Jun	Jly	May	Jun	Jly
9400	....	0.55	....	....	0.00	0.03
9425	....	0.31	0.21	0.00	0.01	0.08
9450	0.07	0.09	0.08	0.02	0.04	0.20
9475	0.01	0.01	0.02	0.21	0.21	0.39
9500	0.00	0.01	0.01	0.45	0.45	....
9525	0.00	0.00	....	....	0.70	....

Est. vol. 52,469;
Mn vol. 12,328 calls; 20,482 puts
Op. int. Mon 790,506 calls; 954,622 puts

2 YR. MID-CURVE EURODLR (CME)
$1,000,000 contract units; pts. of 100%

Strike	Calls-Settle		Puts-Settle	
Price	Jun	Sep	Jun	Sep
9300	0.48	....	0.08	....
9325	0.31	0.38	0.16	0.30

The Order Book Official. The order book official is an employee of the exchange who can also trade. However, the official cannot trade for his or her own account. Instead, the order book official primarily facilitates the flow of orders. The order book is the listing of orders that are awaiting execution at a specific price. The order book official discloses the best limit orders (highest bid and lowest ask) awaiting execution. In essence, the order book official performs many of the functions of a specialist on a stock exchange. However, the order book official cannot trade for his own account. The order book official also has support personnel to help keep track of the order book and to log new orders into the book as they come in.

Exchange Officials. Exchange officials comprise the third group of floor participants. We have already noted that the order book official and assistants are exchange employees serving the special functions just described. However, there are other exchange employees on the floor, such as price reporting officials and surveillance officials. After every trade, price reporting officials enter the order into the exchange's price reporting system. The details of the trade immediately go out over a financial reporting system so that traders all over the world can obtain the information reflected in the trade. This process takes just a few seconds. Then traders and other interested parties around the world will know the price and quantity of a particular option that just traded. In addition to personnel involved with price reporting, the exchange has personnel on the floor to monitor floor activity. The exchange has the responsibility of providing an honest marketplace, so it strives to maintain an orderly market and to ensure that brokers and market makers follow exchange rules.

Other Trading Systems

The alignment of personnel described here follows the practice at the CBOE and the Pacific Stock Exchange. Other exchanges, such as the American and Philadelphia Stock Exchanges, use a specialist instead of an order book official. In this system, the specialist keeps the limit order book but does not disclose the outstanding orders. Also, the specialist alone bears the responsibility of making a market, rather than relying on a group of market makers. In place of market makers, these exchanges have registered option traders who buy and sell for their own account or act as brokers for others.

One of the most important differences between the two systems is the role of the market makers and registered option traders. At the CBOE and the Pacific Stock Exchange, a market maker cannot act as a broker and trade for his account on the same day. The same individual can play different roles on different days, however. Restricting individuals from simultaneously acting as market makers and brokers helps avoid a conflict of interest between the role of market maker and broker. The system of allowing an individual simultaneously to trade for himself (as a market maker) and to execute orders for the public (as a broker) is called **dual trading**. Many observers believe that dual trading involves inherent conflicts of interest between the role of broker and market maker. For example, consider a dual trader who holds an order to execute as a broker. If this dual trader suddenly confronts a very attractive trading opportunity, he may well decide to take it for his own profit, rather than execute the order for his customer.

Types of Orders

Every option trade falls into one of four categories. It can be an order to:

1. open a position with a purchase;
2. open a position with a sale;
3. close a position with a purchase; or
4. close a position with a sale.

For example, a trader could open a position by buying a call and later close that position by selling the call. Alternatively, one could open a position by selling a put and close the position by buying a put. An order that closes an existing position is an **offsetting order**.

As in the stock market, there are numerous types of orders in the options market. The simplest order is a market order. A market order instructs the floor broker to transact at whatever price is currently available in the marketplace. For example, one might place an order to buy one call contract for a stock on the market. The floor broker will fill this order immediately at the best price currently available. As in the stock market, the alternative to a market order is a limit order. In a limit order, the trader instructs the broker to fill the order only if certain conditions are met. For example, assume an option trades for $5 1/8. In this situation, one might place a limit order to buy an option only if the price is $5 or less. In a limit order, the trader tells the broker how long to try to fill the order. If the limit order is a day order, the broker is to fill the order that day if it can be filled within the specified limit. If the order cannot be filled that day, the order expires. Alternatively, a trader can specify a limit order as being good-until-canceled. In this case, the order stays on the limit order book indefinitely.

Order Routing and Execution

To get a better idea of how an order is executed, let's trace an order from an individual trader. A college professor in Miami decides that today is the day to buy an option on XYZ. He calls his local broker and places a market order to buy a call. The broker takes the order and makes sure she has recorded the order correctly. The broker then transmits the order to the brokerage firm's representatives at the exchange. Usually this is done over a computerized system operated by the brokerage firm.

The brokerage firm's clerical staff on the floor of the exchange receives the order and gives it to a runner. The runner quickly moves to the trading area and finds the firm's floor broker who deals in XYZ options. The floor broker executes the order by trading with another floor broker, a market maker, or an order book official. Then the floor broker records the price obtained and information about the opposite trader. The runner takes this information from the floor broker back to the clerical staff on the exchange floor. The brokerage firm clerks confirm the order to the Miami broker, who tells the professor the result of the transaction. In the normal event, the entire process takes about two minutes and the professor can reasonably expect to receive confirmation of his order in the same phone call used to place the order.

THE CLEARINGHOUSE

In executing the trade just described, the buyer of a call has the right to purchase 100 shares of XYZ at the exercise price. However, it might seem that the buyer of the call is in a somewhat dangerous position, because the seller of the call may not want to fulfill his part of the bargain if the price of XYZ rises. For example, if XYZ sells for $120, the seller of the call may be unwilling to part with the share for $100. The purchaser of the call needs a mechanism to secure his position without having to force the seller to perform.

The clearinghouse, the Options Clearing Corporation (OCC), performs this role. After the day's trading, the OCC first attempts to match all trades. For the college professor's transaction, there is an opposite trading party. When the broker recorded the purchase for the professor, she traded with someone else who also recorded the trade. The clearinghouse must match the paperwork from both sides of the transaction. If the two records agree, the trade is a matched trade. This process of matching trades and tracking payments is called **clearing**. Every options trade must be cleared. If records by the two sides of the trade disagree, the trade is an **outtrade** and the exchange works to resolve the disagreement.

Assuming the trade matches, the OCC guarantees both sides of the transaction. The OCC becomes the seller to every buyer and the buyer to every seller. In essence, the OCC interposes its own credibility for that of the individual traders. This has great advantages. The college professor did not even know the name of the seller of the option. Instead of being worried about the credibility of the seller, the professor needs only to be satisfied with the credibility of the OCC. But the OCC is well capitalized and anxious to keep a smoothly functioning market. Therefore, the college professor can be assured that the other side of his option transaction will be honored. If an option trader fails to perform as promised, the OCC absorbs the loss and proceeds against the defaulting trader. Because the OCC is a buyer to every seller and a seller to every buyer, it has a zero net position in the market. It holds the same number of short and long positions. Therefore, the OCC has very little risk exposure from fluctuating prices.

MARGINS

Besides having a net zero position, the clearinghouse further limits its risk by requiring margin payments from its clearing members. A clearing member is a securities firm having an account with the clearinghouse. All option trades must be channeled through a clearing member to the clearinghouse. Most major brokerage firms are clearing members. However, individual market makers are not clearing members, and they must clear their trades through a clearing member. In effect, the clearing member represents all of the parties that it clears to the clearinghouse. By demanding margin payments from its clearing members, the clearinghouse further ensures its own financial integrity. Each clearing member in turn demands margin payments from the traders it clears. The margin payments are immediate cash payments that show the financial integrity of the traders and help limit the risk of the clearing member and the clearinghouse.

To understand margins, we recall that there are four basic positions: long a call or long a put and short a call or short a put. The margin rules differ with the type of position. First, options cannot be bought on credit. The buyer of an option pays the full price of the option by the morning of the next business day. For example, the college professor in Miami who buys a call or put must pay his broker in full for the purchase. We may think of long option positions as requiring 100 percent margin in all cases.

For option sellers, margin rules become very important. The Federal Reserve Board sets minimum margin requirements for option traders. However, each exchange may impose additional margin requirements. Also, each broker may require margin payments beyond those required by the Federal Reserve Board and the exchanges. A single broker may also impose different margin requirements on different customers. Further, options on different underlying instruments are subject to different margin requirements. Because these option requirements may differ so radically and because they are subject to frequent adjustment, this section illustrates the underlying principles of margin rules for options on stocks.[9]

The seller of a call option may be required to deliver the stock if the owner of a call exercises his option. Therefore, the maximum amount the seller can lose is the value of the share. If the seller keeps money on deposit with the broker equal to the share price, then the broker, clearing member, and clearinghouse are completely protected. This sets an upper bound on the reasonable amount of margin that could be required. Sometimes the seller of a call has the share itself on deposit with the broker. In this case, the seller has sold a **covered call** – the call is covered by the deposit of the shares with the broker. If the call is exercised against the seller of a covered call, the stock is immediately available to deliver. Therefore, there is no risk to the system in a covered call. Accordingly, the margin on a covered call is zero.

If the seller of a call does not have the underlying share on deposit with the broker, the seller has sold an **uncovered call** or a **naked call**. We have just seen that the maximum possible loss is the value of the share. For the writer of a put, the worst result is being forced to buy a worthless stock at the exercise price. This worst case gives a loss equal to the exercise price. Therefore, if the margin equaled the exercise price, the broker, clearing member, and clearinghouse would be fully protected. Instead of demanding complete protection, the seller of a call or put must deposit only a fraction of the potential loss as an **initial margin**.

For a seller of an option, the margin requirement depends on whether the option is in-the-money or out-of-the-money. If the option is in-the-money, the initial margin equals 100 percent of the proceeds from selling the option plus an amount equal to 20 percent of the value of the underlying stock. For example, assume a stock currently sells for $105 and a trader sells a call contract for 100 shares with a striking price of $100 on this stock for $6 per share. Ignoring brokerage fees, the proceeds from selling the call would be $600. To this we add 20 percent of the value of the underlying stock, or $2,100 for the 100 shares. Therefore, the initial margin requirement is $2,700.

If the option is out-of-the-money, the rule is slightly different. The initial margin equals the margin sale proceeds plus 20 percent of the value of the underlying stock minus the amount the option is out-of-the-money. However, this margin rule could result in a negative margin, so the initial margin must also equal 100 percent of the option proceeds plus 10 percent of the value of the underlying security. Consider a call that is out-of-the-money, with the stock trading at $15 per share and the option having an exercise price of $20 and trading for $1. Based on a 100-share contract and ignoring any brokerage commissions, the margin must be the proceeds from selling the option ($100), plus 20 percent of the value of the underlying stock (.20 × $15 × 100 = $300), less the amount the option is out-of-the-money ([$20 − $15] × 100 = $500). This gives a margin requirement that is negative ($100 + $300 − $500 = −$100). Therefore, the second part of the rule comes into play. The minimum margin must equal the sale proceeds from the option ($100) plus 10 percent of the value of the underlying stock (.10 × $15 × 100 = $150). Therefore, the margin for this trade will be $250.

The margins we have been discussing are initial margin requirements. The trader must make these margin deposits when he or she first trades. If prices move against the trader, he or she will be required to make additional margin payments. As the stock price starts to rise and cause losses for the short trader, the broker requires additional margin payments, called maintenance margin. By requiring maintenance margin payments, the margin system protects the broker, clearing member, and clearinghouse from default by traders. This system also benefits traders, because they can be confident that payments due to them will be protected from default as well.

Many option traders trade option combinations. Margin rules apply to these transactions as well, but the margin requirements reflect the special risk characteristics of these positions. For many option combinations, the risk may be less than the risk of a single long or short position in a put or call.[10]

COMMISSIONS

As we have seen, the same brokerage system that trades stocks can execute option transactions. In stocks, commission charges depend on the number of shares and the dollar value of the transaction.

A similar system applies for call option contracts. The following schedule shows a representative commission schedule from a discount broker. Full-service brokerage fees can be substantially higher.[11] In addition to these fees, each transaction can be subject to certain minimum and maximum fees. For instance, a broker might have a maximum fee per contract of $40.

Representative Discount Brokerage Commissions

Dollar Value of Transaction	Commission
$0–2,500	$29 + 1.6% of principal amount
$2,500–10,000	$49 + 0.8% of principal amount
$10,000 +	$99 + 0.3% of principal amount

As an example of commissions with this fee schedule, assume that you buy five contracts with a quoted price of $6.50. The cost of the option would be $650 per contract, for a total cost of $3,250. The commission would be: $49 + (.008 × $3,250) = $75. For the same dollar value of a transaction in stocks, the commission tends to be lower. However, once the dollar amount of the transaction approaches $10,000, commissions on stocks and options tend to be similar.

Even though the commission per dollar of options traded may be higher than for stocks, there can be significant commission savings in trading options. In our example, the option price is $6.50 per share of stock. The share price might well be $100 or more. If it were $100, trading 500 shares would involve a transaction value of $50,000. Commissions on a stock transaction of $50,000 would be much higher than commissions on our option transaction. Trading the option on a stock and trading the stock itself can give positions with very similar price actions. Therefore, option trading can provide commission savings over stock trading. This principle holds, even though option commissions tend to be higher than stock commissions for a given dollar transaction.

Another way to see this principle is to realize that options inherently have more leverage than a share of stock. As an example, assume the stock price is $100 and the option on the stock trades for $6.50. If the stock price rises 3 percent to $103, the option price could easily rise 30 percent to $8.45. On a percentage basis, the option price moves more than the stock price. Unfortunately for option traders, this happens for price increases and decreases. With this greater leverage, the same dollar investment in an option will give a greater dollar price movement than investment in the stock.

TAXATION

Taxation of option transactions is no simple matter. We cannot hope to cover all of the nuances of the tax laws in this brief section. Therefore, this section attempts merely to illustrate the basic principles.

Disposition of an option, either through sale, exercise, or expiration, gives rise to a profit or loss. Profits and losses on options trading are treated as capital gains and losses. Therefore, option profits and losses are subject to all the regular rules that pertain to all capital gains and losses. Capital gains may be classified as long-term or short-term capital gains. A capital gain is a long-term gain if the instrument generating the gain has been held longer than one year, otherwise the gain or loss is short-term. In general, long-term capital gains qualify for favorable tax treatment.

Capital losses offset capital gains and thereby reduce taxable income. However, capital losses are deductible only up to the amount of capital gains plus $3,000. Any excess capital loss cannot be deducted, but must be carried forward to offset capital gains in subsequent years. For example, assume that a trader has capital gains of $17,500 from securities trading. Unfortunately for the trader, he also has $25,000 in capital losses. Therefore, $17,500 of the losses completely offset the capital gains, freeing the trader from any taxes on those gains. This leaves $7,500 of capital losses to consider. The trader can then use $3,000 of this excess loss to offset other income, such as wages. In effect, this protects $3,000 of wages from taxation. The remaining $4,500 of losses must be carried forward to the next tax year, where it can be used to offset capital gains realized in that tax year.

Option transactions give rise to capital gains and losses, and the tax treatment differs for buyers and sellers of options. Further, the tax treatment becomes very complicated for combinations of options. Therefore, we consider only the four simplest stock option positions: long a call, short a call, long a put, or short a put.

Long a Call. If a call is exercised, the price of the option, the exercise price, and the brokerage commissions associated with purchasing and exercising the option are treated as the cost of the stock for tax purposes. The holding period for the stock begins on the day after the call is exercised, so the stock must be held for a year to qualify for treatment as a long-term capital gain. If the call expires worthless, it gives rise to a short-term or long-term capital loss equal to the purchase price of the option plus any associated brokerage fees incurred in purchasing the option. If the option is sold before expiration, the capital gain or loss is the sale price of the option minus the purchase price of the option minus any brokerage fees incurred.

Short a Call. When a trader sells a call, the premium that is received is not treated as immediate income. Instead, the treatment of this premium depends upon the disposition of the short call. If the call expires without being exercised, the gain on the transaction equals the prices of the option less any brokerage fees, and this gain is always treated as a short-term gain, no matter how long the position was held. If the trader offsets the position before expiration, the capital gain or loss equals the sale price minus the purchase price minus any commissions, and this gain or loss is considered a short-term gain or loss without regard to how long the position is held. If the call is exercised against the trader, the strike price plus the premium received minus any commissions becomes the sale price of the stock for determining the capital gain or loss. The gain or loss will be short-term or long-term depending upon how the stock that is delivered was acquired. For example, if the trader delivers stock that had been held for more than one year, the gain or loss would be a long-term gain or loss.

Long a Put. If a put is purchased and sold before expiration, the gain or loss equals the sale price minus the purchase price minus any brokerage commissions, and the gain or loss will be short-term or long-term depending on how long the put was held. If the put expires worthless, the loss equals the purchase price plus the brokerage commissions, and the loss can be either short-term or long-term. If the trader exercises the put, the cost of the put plus commission reduces the amount realized upon the sale of the stock delivered to satisfy the exercise. The resulting gain or loss can be either short-term or long-term depending upon how long the delivered stock was held.

Short a Put. The premium received for selling a put is not classified as income until the obligation from the sale of the put is completed. If the trader offsets the short put before expiration, the capital gain or loss equals the sale price minus the purchase price minus the brokerage commissions, and the resulting gain or loss is always a short-term gain or loss. If the put expires worthless, the capital gain equals the sale price less the brokerage commissions, and the capital gain is a short-term gain. If the put is exercised against the trader, the basis of the stock acquired in the exercise equals the strike price plus the commission minus the premium received when the put was sold. The holding period for determining a capital gain or loss begins for the stock on the day following the exercise.

There are other special and more complicated rules for taxing option transactions, so the account here is not definitive. Additional complications arise for some options on stock indexes, for example. Also, there are special tax rules designed to prevent option trading merely to manipulate taxes.

CONCLUSION

This chapter has introduced the options market. In the short time since they started trading on the Chicago Board Options Exchange, options have helped revolutionize finance. They permeate the world of speculative investing and portfolio management. Corporations use them in their financing decisions to control risk. Beyond their uses as trading vehicles, options provide a new way to analyze many financial transactions.

QUESTIONS AND PROBLEMS

1. State the difference between a call and a put option.
2. How does a trader initiate a long call position, and what rights and obligations does such a position involve?
3. Can buying an option, whether a put or a call, result in any obligations for the option owner? Explain.
4. Describe all of the benefits that are associated with taking a short position in an option.
5. What is the difference between a short call and a long put position? Which has rights associated with it, and which involves obligations? Explain.
6. Consider the following information. A trader buys a call option for $5 that gives the right to purchase a share of stock for $100. In this situation, identify: the exercise price, the premium, and the striking price.
7. Explain what happens to a short trader when the option he or she has sold expires worthless. What benefits and costs has the trader incurred?
8. Explain why an organized options exchange needs a clearinghouse.
9. What is the difference between an American and a European option?
10. Assume a trader does not want to continue holding an option position. Explain how this trader can fulfill his or her obligations, yet close out the option position.

NOTES

[1] Christopher K. Ma and Ramesh P. Rao, ''Information Asymmetry and Options Trading,'' *Financial Review,* 23:1, February 1988, pp. 39–51, discuss the different roles that options can play for informed and uninformed traders. The informed trader is one with special knowledge about the underlying stock; the uninformed trader has no special knowledge. In their analysis, the informed trader tends to take an outright position in the option, while the uninformed trader is likely to use options to reduce the risk of an existing stock position. While these factors may benefit market participants, the same authors analyze the effect of a new

listing of options on stock prices in, "The Effect of Call-Option-Listing Announcement on Shareholder Wealth," *Journal of Business Research,* 15:5, October 1987, pp. 449–65. Ma and Rao show that the listing of an option on a stock that never had options before leads to stock price declines and thus to a loss of shareholder wealth. Apparently, this drop in stock prices reflects the market's view that new option trading is likely to make the stock more volatile. However, Ma and Rao also find that stock prices rebound when the option actually begins to trade.

[2] Consider an option position and a stock position designed to give the same profits and losses for a given movement in the stock price. If we consider a short-term investment horizon, the option strategy will almost always be cheaper and incur lower transaction costs. This is not necessarily true for a long-term investment horizon. All exchange-traded options are dated; that is, they expire within the next few months. Therefore, maintaining an option position in the long-term involves trading to replace expiring options. By contrast, taking the stock position requires only one transaction, and the stock can be held indefinitely. Therefore, the repeated transaction costs incurred with the option strategy can involve greater transaction costs in the long-term than the stock strategy.

[3] Selling stock short involves borrowing a share, selling it, repurchasing the share later, and returning it to its owner. The short seller hopes to profit from a price decline by selling before the decline and repurchasing after the price falls. Rules on the stock exchange restrict the timing of short selling and the use of short sale proceeds.

[4] Stephen A. Ross, "Options and Efficiency," *Quarterly Journal of Economics, 90,* February 1976, pp. 75–89, shows that options serve a useful economic role by completing markets. In a complete market, a trader can trade for any pattern of payoffs that he or she desires. The more nearly complete a market is, the greater is its likely efficiency. Thus, because options help complete markets, they contribute to economic efficiency and thereby raise the welfare level of society as a whole.

[5] The "r" and "s" have no specific meaning. However, this is the convention used by *The Wall Street Journal* for its option price reports.

[6] However, some futures options are options on foreign currency futures, and these are traded on the CME.

[7] The CME trades foreign currency futures and options on those futures in a robust market. However, the CME trades no options on the foreign currencies themselves.

[8] Figure 10.3 does not show statistics on very small market currencies, such as the European Currency Unit (ECU).

[9] George Sofianos, "Margin Requirements on Equity Instruments," *Federal Reserve Bank of New York Quarterly Review,* 13:2, Summer 1988, pp. 47–60, explains margin rules in more detail. Stephen Figlewski, "Margins and Market Integrity: Margin Setting for Stock Index Futures and Options," *Journal of Futures Markets,* 4:3, Fall 1984, pp. 385–416, argues that margins on stocks are set too high relative to margins on options and futures. According to his analysis, the margin requirements give different levels of protection for different instruments.

[10] Margins can be devilishly complicated. Andrew Rudd and Mark Schroeder, "The Calculation of Minimum Margin," *Management Science, 28,* December 1982, pp. 1368–79, present a linear program to compute minimum margin under a variety of scenarios.

[11] A discount broker executes unsolicited orders for its customers. It provides little or no research information but seeks to offer fully competitive order execution at reduced prices. Charles Schwab and Quick and Reilly are two leading discount brokerage firms. By contrast, full discount brokers typically have account executives that actively solicit orders from their customer base. The full discount broker also maintains a research department.

OPTION PAYOFFS AND OPTION STRATEGIES

OVERVIEW

This chapter considers the factors that determine the value of an option at expiration and introduces the principal strategies used in options trading. When an option is about to expire, it is relatively easy to determine its value. Thus, we begin our analysis by considering option values at expiration. When we say that an option is at expiration, we mean that the owner has a simple choice: exercise the option immediately or allow it to expire as worthless. As we will see, the value of an option at expiration depends only on the stock price and the exercise price. We also give rules for whether an owner should exercise an option or allow it to expire.

With all assets, we consider either the value of the asset or the profit or loss incurred from trading the asset. The value of an asset equals its market price. As such, the value of an asset does not depend on the purchase price. However, the profit or loss on the purchase and sale of an asset depends critically on the purchase price. In considering options, we keep these two related ideas strictly distinct. We present graphs for both the value of options and the profits from trading options, but we want to be sure not to confuse the two. By graphing the value of options and the profits or losses from options at expiration, we develop our grasp of option pricing principles. To focus on the principles of pricing, we ignore commissions and other transaction costs in this chapter.

Option traders often trade options with other options and with other assets, particularly stocks and bonds. This chapter analyzes the payoffs from combining different options and from combining options with the underlying stock. Many of these combinations have colorful names such as spreads, straddles, and strangles. Beyond the terminology, these combinations interest us because they offer special profit and loss characteristics. We also explore the particular payoff patterns that traders can create by trading options in conjunction with stocks and bonds.

We can use **OPTION!**, the software that accompanies this book, to explore the concepts we develop in this chapter. The first module of **OPTION!** analyzes values, profits, and losses of options and option combinations at expiration. **OPTION!** can prepare reports of outcomes, and it can graph profit and losses of all the combinations we explore in this chapter. Detailed instructions for using **OPTION!** appear at the end of this book.

STOCKS AND BONDS

We begin our analysis with the two most familiar securities – common stock and a default-free bond. Figure 11.1 presents the graph of the value of a share of stock and the value of a bond at a certain date. At any time, the value of a risk-free pure discount bond is just the present value of the par value. The graph expresses the value of a share of stock and the value of a bond as functions of stock price. In other words, we graph the stock price, or stock value, against the stock price. In the graph, a line runs from the bottom left to the upper right corner. Also, the graph has a horizontal line that intersects the y-axis at $100.

    The diagonal line shows the value of a single share of the stock. When the stock price on the x-axis is $100, the value of the stock is $100. The horizontal line reflects the value of a $100 face value default-free bond at maturity. The value of the bond does not depend on the price of the stock. Because it is default-free, the bond pays $100 when it matures, no matter what happens to the stock price. For convenience, we assume that the bond matures in one year, and we graph the value of the stock and bond on that future date. Notice that the value of these instruments does not depend in any way on the purchase price of the instruments.

    We now consider possible profits and losses from the share of stock and the risk-free bond. Let us assume that the stock was purchased for $100 at time t and that the pure discount (zero coupon) risk-free bond was purchased one year before maturity at $90.91. This implies an interest rate of 10 percent on the bond. Figure 11.2 graphs the profit and losses from a long and short position in the stock. The solid line running from the bottom left to the top right of Figure 11.2 shows the profits and losses for a long position of one share in the stock, assuming a purchase price of $100. When

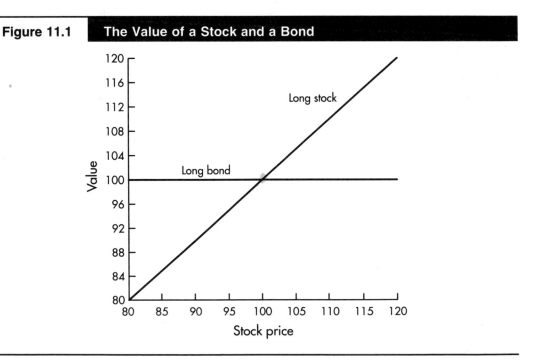

Figure 11.1   **The Value of a Stock and a Bond**

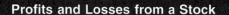

Profits and Losses from a Stock   **Figure 11.2**

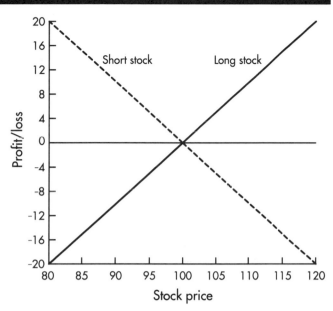

the stock price is $100, our graph shows a zero profit. If the stock price is $105, there is a $5 profit, which equals the stock price of $105 minus the purchase price of $100.

The dotted line in Figure 11.2 runs from the upper left corner to the bottom right corner and shows the profits or losses from a short position of one share, assuming that the stock was sold at $100. Throughout our discussion of options, we used dotted lines to indicate short positions in value and profit and loss graphs. If the stock is worth $105, the short position shows a loss of $5. The short trader loses $5 because he sold the stock for $100. Now with the higher stock price, the short trader must pay $105 to buy the stock and close the short trade. As Figure 11.2 shows, the short trader bets that the stock price will fall. For example, if the trader sells the stock short at a price of $100 and the stock price falls to $93, the short trader can buy the stock and repay the person from whom he borrowed the share, earning a $7 profit (+$100 − $93).

As a final point on stock values and profits, consider the profit and loss profile for a combination of a position that is long one share and short one share. If the stock trades at $105, the long position has a profit of $5 and the short position has a loss of $5. Similarly, if the stock trades at $95, the long position has a loss of $5 and the short position has a profit of $5. No matter what stock price we consider, the profits and losses from the long and short positions cancel each other. The profit or loss is always zero. Thus, taking a long and short position in exactly the same good is a foolish exercise.

Figure 11.3 graphs the profits from the bond that we considered. The purchase price of the bond is $90.91, and it matures in one year paying $100 with certainty. The profit equals the payoff of $100 minus the cost of $90.91. Thus, the owner of the bond has a sure profit of $9.09 at expiration. Figure 11.3 shows this profit with the solid line in the upper portion of the graph. Similarly, the issuer of

Figure 11.3   **Profits from a Bond**

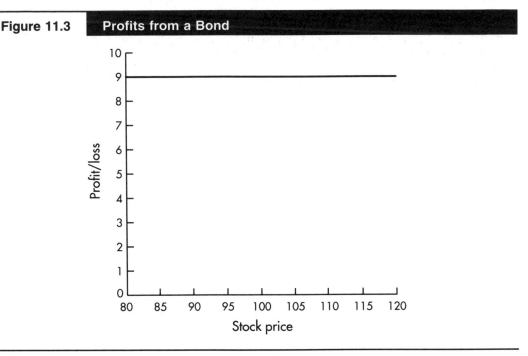

the bond will lose $9.09. The issuer receives $90.91, but pays $100. Presumably, the issuer has some productive use for the bond proceeds during the year that will yield more than $9.09.

OPTION NOTATION

We now introduce some notation for referring to options. As we will see, in analyzing options we are often interested in the option price as a function of the stock price, the time until expiration, and the exercise price. The options may be either calls or puts, and the options may be either European or American. Therefore, we adopt the following notation:

S_t = price of the underlying stock at time t
X = the exercise price for the option
T = the expiration date of the option
c_t = the price of a European call at time t
C_t = the price of an American call at time t
p_t = the price of a European put at time t
P_t = the price of an American put at time t

We will often write the value of an option in the following form:

$$c_t(S_t, X, T - t)$$

which means the price of a European call at time t given a stock price at t of S_t, for a call with an exercise price of X, that expires at time T, which is an amount of time $T - t$ from now (time t). For convenience, we sometimes omit the "t" subscript, as in:

$$p(S, X, T)$$

In such a case, the reader may assume that the current time is time $t = 0$, and that the option expires T periods from now. In this chapter, we focus principally on the value of options at expiration, so we will mainly be concerned with values such as:

$$C_T(S_T, X, T)$$

indicating the price of an American call option at expiration, when the stock price is S_T, the exercise price is X, and the option expires at time T, which happens to be immediately.

EUROPEAN AND AMERICAN OPTION VALUES AT EXPIRATION

In general, the difference between an American and a European option concerns only the exercise privileges associated with the option. An American option can be exercised at any time, while a European option can be exercised only at expiration. At expiration, both European and American options have exactly the same exercise rights. Therefore, European and American options at expiration have identical values, assuming the same underlying good and the same exercise price:

$$C_T(S_T, X, T) = c_T(S_T, X, T) \text{ and } P_T(S_T, X, T) = p_T(S_T, X, T)$$

Throughout this chapter, we focus on option values and profits at expiration. Therefore, we use the notation for an American option throughout, but the results hold perfectly well for European options as well.

BUY OR SELL A CALL OPTION

We now consider the value of call options at expiration, along with the profits or losses that come from trading call options. At expiration, the owner of an option has an immediate choice: exercise the option or allow it to expire worthless. Therefore, the value of the option will either be zero or it will be the **exercise value** or the **intrinsic value** – the value of the option if it is exercised immediately. The value of a call at expiration (whether European or American) equals zero, or the stock price minus the exercise price, whichever is greater. At expiration, there is no question of early exercise, so the principles we explore pertain equally to both American and European calls. For our discussion of option values and profits at expiration, we use the notation for American options (C_T or P_T), but the principles apply identically to European options as well.

$$C_T = \text{MAX}\{0, S_T - X\} \tag{11.1}$$

To understand this principle, consider a call option with an exercise price of $100 and assume that the underlying stock trades at $95. At expiration, the call owner may either exercise the option or allow it to expire worthless. With the prices we just specified, the call owner must allow the option to expire. If the owner of the call exercises the option, he pays $100 and receives a stock that is worth $95. This gives a loss of $5 on the exercise, so it is foolish to exercise. Instead of exercising, the owner of the call can merely allow the option to expire. If the option expires, there is no additional loss involved with the exercise, because the owner of the call avoids exercising. In our example:

$$S_T - X = \$95 - \$100 = -\$5$$

The call owner need not exercise. By allowing the option to expire, the option owner acknowledges the call is worthless. With our example numbers at expiration:

$$C_T = \text{MAX}\{0, S_T - X\} = \text{MAX}\{0, \$95 - \$100\} = \text{MAX}\{0, -\$5\} = 0$$

We can extend this example to any ending stock price we wish to consider. For any stock price less than the exercise price, the value of $S_T - X$ will be negative. Therefore, for any stock price less than the exercise price, the call will be worthless. If the stock price equals the exercise price, the value of $S_T - X$ equals zero, so the call will still be worthless. Thus, for any stock price equal to or less than the exercise price at expiration, the call is worth zero.

If the stock price exceeds the exercise price, the call is worth the difference between the stock price and the exercise price. For example, assume that the stock price is $103 at expiration. The call option with an exercise price of $100 now allows the holder to exercise the option by paying the exercise price. Therefore, the owner of the call can acquire the stock worth $103 by paying $100. This gives an immediate payoff of $3 from exercising. Notice that this example conforms to our principle. Using these numbers we find:

$$C_T = \text{MAX}\{0, S_T - X\} = \text{MAX}\{0, \$103 - \$100\} = \text{MAX}\{0, \$3\} = \$3$$

Figure 11.4 graphs the value of our example call at expiration. Here the value of the call equals the maximum of zero or the stock price minus the exercise price. As the graph shows, the value of the call is unlimited, at least in principle. If the stock price were $1,000 at expiration, the call would be worth $\text{MAX}\{0, S_T - X\} = \$900$. This graph shows the characteristic shape for a long position in a call option.

Figure 11.4 also shows the value of a short position in the same call option. The dotted line graphs the short position. (For stock prices between 0 and $100, both graphs lie on the same line.) Notice that the short position has a zero value for all stock prices equal to or less than the exercise price. If the stock price exceeds the exercise price, the short position is costly. Using our notation, the value of a short call position at expiration is:

$$-C_T = -\text{MAX}\{0, S_T - X\}$$

Assume that the stock price is $107 at expiration. In this case, the call owner will exercise the option. The seller of the call must then deliver a stock worth $107 and receive the exercise price of $100. This means that holding a short position in the call is worth −$7. The short position never has a value greater than zero, and when the stock price exceeds the exercise price, the short position is worse than worthless. From this consideration, it appears that no one would ever willingly take a short

| | The Value of a Call at Expiration | Figure 11.4 |

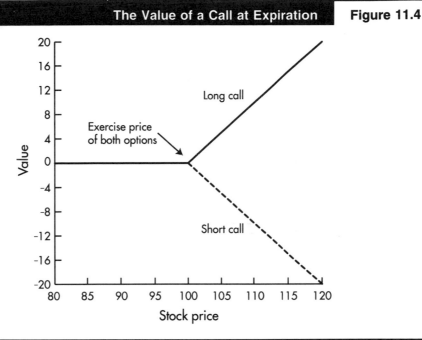

position in a call option. However, this leaves out the payments made from the buyer to the seller when the option first trades.

Continuing with our same example of a call option at expiration with a striking price of $100, we consider profit and loss results. We assume that the call option was purchased for $5. To profit, the holder of a long position in the call needs a stock price that will cover the exercise price and the cost of acquiring the option. For a long position in a call acquired at time $t < T$, the cost of the call is C_t. The profit or loss on the long call position held until expiration is:

$$C_T - C_t = \text{MAX}\{0, S_T - X\} - C_t$$

The seller of a call receives payment when the option first trades. The seller continues to hope for a stock price at expiration that does not exceed the exercise price. However, even if the stock price exceeds the exercise price, there may still be some profit left for the seller. The profit or loss on the sale of a call, with the position being held until expiration, is:

$$C_t - C_T = C_t - \text{MAX}\{0, S_T - X\}$$

Figure 11.5 graphs the profit and losses for the call option positions under the assumptions we have been considering. Graphically, bringing profits and losses into consideration shifts the long call graph down by the $5 purchase price and shifts the short call graph up by the $5 purchase price.

We can understand Figure 11.5 for both the long and short positions by considering a few key stock values. We begin with the long position. To acquire a long position in the call option, the trader

Figure 11.5   Profits and Losses from a Call at Expiration

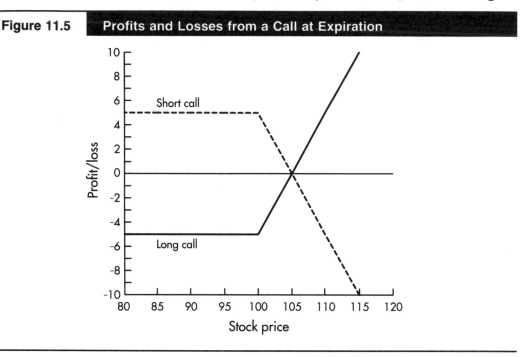

paid $5. If the stock price is $100 or less, the value of the option is zero at expiration and the owner of the call lets it expire. Therefore, for any stock price equal to or less than the $100 exercise price, the call owner simply loses the entire purchase price of the option. If the stock price at expiration is above $100 but less than $105, the graph shows that the holder of the long call still loses, but loses less than the total $5 purchase price. For example, if the stock price at expiration is $103, the long call holder loses $2 in total. The call owner exercises, buying the $103 stock for $100, and makes $3 on the exercise. This $3 exercise value, coupled with the $5 paid for the option, gives a net loss of $2. As another example, if the stock price is $105 at expiration, the holder of the call makes $5 by exercising, a profit that exactly offsets the purchase price of the option, so there is no profit or loss. From this example, we see that the holder of a call makes a zero profit if the stock price equals the exercise price plus the price paid for the call. To profit, the call holder needs a stock price that exceeds the exercise price plus the price paid for the call.

Figure 11.5 shows several important points. First, for the call buyer, the worst that can happen is losing the entire purchase price of the option. Comparing Figure 11.5 with Figure 11.2, we can see that the potential dollar loss is much greater if we hold the stock rather than the call. However, a small drop in the stock price can cause a complete loss of the option price. Second, potential profits from a long position in a call option are theoretically unlimited. The profits depend only on the price of the stock at expiration. Third, our discussion and graph show that the holder of a call option will exercise any time the stock price at expiration exceeds the exercise price. The call holder will exercise to reduce a loss or to capture a profit.

We now consider profit and loss on a short position in a call option. When the long trader bought a call, he paid $5 to the seller. As we noted in Chapter 10, the premium paid by the purchaser at the time of the initial trade belongs to the seller no matter what happens from that point forward. As Figure 11.5 shows, the greatest profit the seller of the call can achieve is $5. The seller attains this maximum profit when the holder of the call cannot exercise. In our example, the seller's profit is $5 for any stock price of $100 or less, because the call owner will allow the option to expire worthless for any stock price at expiration at or below the exercise price.

If the call owner can exercise, the seller's profits will be lower and the seller may incur a loss. For example, if the stock price is $105, the owner of the call will exercise. In this event, the seller will be forced to surrender a share worth $105 in exchange for the $100 exercise price. This represents a loss for the seller in the exercise of $5, which exactly offsets the price the seller received for the option. So with a stock price of $105, the seller makes a zero profit, as does the call owner. If the stock price exceeds $105, the seller will incur a loss. For example, with a stock price of $115, the call owner will exercise. At the exercise, the seller of the call delivers a share worth $115 and receives the $100 exercise price. The seller thereby loses $15 on the exercise. Coupled with the $5 the seller received when the option traded, the seller now has a net loss of $10.

In summary, we can note two key points about the profits and losses from selling a call. First, the best thing that can happen to the seller of a call is never to hear any more about the transaction after collecting the initial premium. As Figure 11.5 shows, the best profit for the seller of the call is to keep the initial purchase price. Second, potential losses from selling a call are theoretically unlimited. As the stock price rises, the losses for the seller of a call continue to mount. For example, if the stock price went to $1,000 at expiration, the seller of the call would lose $895.

Figure 11.5 also provides a dramatic illustration of one of the most important and sobering points about options trading. The profits from the buyer and seller of the call together are always zero. The buyer's gains are the seller's losses, and vice versa.

$$\text{Long call profits} + \text{Short call profits} =$$
$$(C_T - C_t) + (C_t - C_T) = (\text{MAX}\{0, S_T - X\} - C_t) + (C_t - \text{MAX}\{0, S_T - X\}) = 0$$

Therefore, the options market is a **zero-sum game**; there are no net profits or losses in the market.[1] The trader who hopes to speculate successfully must be planning for someone else's losses to provide his profits. In other words, the options market is a very competitive arena, with profits coming only at the expense of another trader.

CALL OPTIONS AT EXPIRATION AND ARBITRAGE

What happens if option values stray from the relationships we analyzed in the preceding section? In this section, we use the no-arbitrage pricing principle to show that call option prices must obey the rules we just developed.[2] If prices stray from these relationships, arbitrage opportunities arise. In the preceding section, we considered an example of a call option with an exercise price of $100. At expiration, with the stock trading at $103, the price of a call option must be $3. In this section, we show that any other price for the call option will create an arbitrage opportunity. If the price is too high, say $4, there is one arbitrage opportunity. If the call is too cheap, say $2, there is another arbitrage opportunity. To see why the call must trade for at least $3, consider the arbitrage opportunity that arises if the call is only $2. In this case, the money hungry arbitrageur would transact as follows.

Transaction	*Cash Flow*
Buy 1 call	−2
Exercise the call	−100
Sell the share	+103
Net Cash Flow	+$1

These transactions meet the conditions for arbitrage. First, there is no investment because all the transactions occur simultaneously. The only cash flow is a $1 cash inflow. Second, the profit is certain once the trader enters the transaction. Therefore, these transactions meet our conditions for arbitrage: they offer a riskless profit without investment. If the call were priced at $2, traders would follow our strategy mercilessly. They would madly buy options, exercise, and sell the share. These transactions would cause tremendous demand for the call and a tremendous supply of the share. These supply and demand forces would subside only after the call and share price adjusted to prevent the arbitrage.

We now consider why the call cannot trade for more than $3 at expiration. If the call price exceeds $3, a different arbitrage opportunity arises. If the call were priced at $4, for example, arbitrageurs would simply sell the overpriced call. Then they would wait to see whether the purchaser of the call exercises. We consider transactions for both possibilities – the purchaser exercises or does not exercise.

If the purchaser exercises, the arbitrageur has already sold the call and received $4. Now to fulfill his exercise commitment, the seller acquires a share for $103 in the market and delivers the share. Upon delivery, the seller of the call receives the exercise price of $100. These three transactions yield a profit of $1. If the purchaser foolishly neglects to exercise, the situation is even better for the arbitrageur. The arbitrageur already sold the call and received $4. If the purchaser fails to exercise, the option expires and the arbitrageur makes a full $4 profit. The worst case scenario still provides the arbitrageur with a profit of $1. Therefore, these transactions represent an arbitrage transaction. First, there is no investment. Second, the transactions ensure a profit.

With a $4 call price, an exercise price of $100 and a stock price at expiration of $103, traders would madly sell call options. The excess supply of options at the $4 price would drive down the price of the option. The process would stop only when the price relationships offer no more arbitrage opportunities. This happens when the prices of the call and stock conform to the relationships we developed in the preceding section. In other words, prices in financial markets must conform to our no-arbitrage principle by adjusting to eliminate any arbitrage opportunity.

The Purchaser Exercises

Transaction	*Cash Flow*
Sell 1 call	+4
Buy 1 share	−103
Deliver share and collect exercise price	+100
Net Cash Flow	+$1

The Purchaser Does Not Exercise

Transaction	*Cash Flow*
Sell 1 call	+4
Net Cash Flow	+$4

BUY OR SELL A PUT OPTION

This section deals with the value of put options and the profits and losses from buying and selling puts when the put is at expiration. Again, we use the notation for an American put (P_T), but all of the conclusions hold identically for European puts. In most respects, we can analyze put options in the same way we analyzed call options. At expiration, the holder of a put has two choices – exercise or allow the option to expire worthless. If the holder exercises, he surrenders the stock and receives the exercise price. Therefore, the holder of a put will exercise only if the exercise price exceeds the stock price. The value of a put option at expiration equals zero, or the exercise price minus the stock price, whichever is higher:

$$P_T = MAX\{0, X - S_T\} \tag{11.2}$$

We can illustrate this principle with an example. Consider a put option with an exercise price of $100 and assume that the underlying stock trades at $102. At expiration, the holder of the put can either exercise or allow the put to expire worthless. With an exercise price of $100 and a stock price of $102, the holder cannot exercise profitably. To exercise the put, the trader would surrender the stock worth $102 and receive the exercise price of $100, thereby losing $2 on the exercise. Consequently, if the stock price is above the exercise price at expiration, the put is worthless. With our example numbers we have:

$$P_T = MAX\{0, X - S_T\} = MAX\{0, \$100 - \$102\} = MAX\{0, -\$2\} = 0$$

Now consider the same put option with the stock trading at $100. Exercising the put requires surrendering the stock worth $100 and receiving the exercise price of $100. There is no profit in exercising and the put is at expiration, so the put is still worthless. In general, if the stock price equals or exceeds the exercise price at expiration, the put is worthless.

When the stock price at expiration falls below the exercise price, the put has value. In this situation, the value of the put equals the exercise price minus the stock price. For example, assume the stock trades at $94 and consider the same put with an exercise price of $100. Now the put is worth $6 because it gives its owner the right to receive the $100 exercise price by surrendering a stock worth only $94. Using these numbers we find:

$$P_T = MAX\{0, X - S_T\} = MAX\{0, \$100 - \$94\} = MAX\{0, \$6\} = \$6$$

Figure 11.6 graphs the value of our example put option at expiration. The graph shows the value of a long position as the solid line and the value of a short position as the dotted line. For stock values equaling or exceeding the $100 exercise price, the put has a zero value. If the stock price is below the exercise price, however, the put is worth the exercise price minus the stock price. As our example showed, if the stock trades for $94, the put is worth $6. The graph reflects this valuation.

Figure 11.6 also shows the value of a short position in the put. For stock prices equaling or exceeding the exercise price, the put has a zero value. This zero value results from the fact that the holder of the long put will not exercise. However, when the stock price at expiration is less than the exercise price, a short position in the put has a negative value, which results from the opportunity that the long put holder has to exercise. For example, if the stock price is $94, the holder of a short

Figure 11.6   The Value of a Put at Expiration

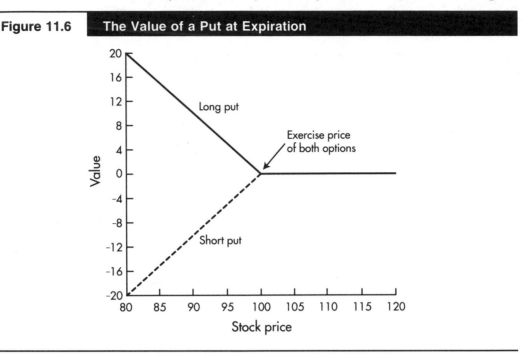

position in the put must pay $100 for a stock worth only $94 when the long put holder exercises. In this situation, the short position in the put will be worth −$6.

Our analysis of put values parallels our results for call options in several ways. First, as we saw with the values of call options at expiration, the value of long and short positions in puts always sums to zero for any stock price. We noted in our discussion of call options that the option market is a zero-sum game. The same principle extends to put options with equal force. Second, we see for put options, as we noted for call options, that a short position can never have a positive value at expiration. The seller of a call or put hopes that nothing happens after the initial transaction when he collects the option price. The best outcome for the seller of either a put or a call is that there will be no exercise and that the option will expire worthless. Third, noting that a short put position has a zero value at best, we might wonder why anyone would accept a short position. As we saw with a call option, the rationality of selling a put requires us to consider the sale price. This leads to a consideration of put option profits and losses.

We continue with our example of a put option with an exercise price of $100. Now we assume that this option was purchased for a price of $4. We consider how profits and losses on long and short put positions depend on the stock price at expiration. As we did for calls, we consider a few key stock prices.

First, we analyze the profits and losses for a long position in the put, where the purchase price is $4 and the exercise price is $100. If the stock price at expiration exceeds $100, the holder of the put cannot exercise profitably and the option expires worthless. In this case, the put holder loses $4, the purchase price of the option. Likewise, if the stock price at expiration equals $100, there is no profitable exercise. Exercising in this situation would only involve surrendering a stock worth $100 and receiving the $100 exercise price. Again, the buyer of the put option loses the purchase price of $4. Therefore, if the stock price at expiration equals or exceeds the exercise price, the buyer of a put loses the full purchase price. Figure 11.7 shows the profits and losses for long and short positions in the put.

If the stock price at expiration is less than the exercise price, there will be a benefit to exercising. For example, assume the stock price is $99 at expiration. Then, the owner of the put will exercise, surrendering the $99 stock and receiving the $100 exercise price. In this case, the exercise value of the put is $1. With the $99 stock price, the holder of the put makes $1 on the exercise but has already paid $4 to acquire the put. Therefore, the total loss is $3. If the stock price is $96 at expiration, the buyer of the put makes a zero profit. The $4 exercise value exactly offsets the price of the put. When the stock price is less than $96, the put buyer makes a profit. For example, if the stock price is $90 at expiration, the owner of a put exercises. In exercising, he surrenders a stock worth $90 and receives the $100 exercise price. This gives a $6 profit after considering the $4 purchase price of the option.

MONEYNESS

In the preceding sections, we have explored the value of calls and puts at expiration. We noted that calls have a positive value at expiration if the stock price exceeds the exercise price, and puts have a positive value at expiration if the exercise price exceeds the stock price. We now introduce important terminology, called **moneyness**, that applies to options both before and at expiration. Both calls and puts can be **in-the-money**, **at-the-money**, or **out-of-the-money**. The following table shows the conditions for puts and calls to meet these moneyness conditions for any time *t*.

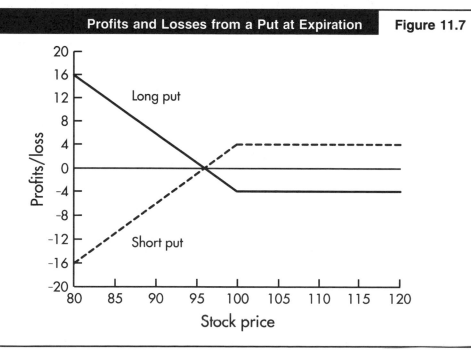

Profits and Losses from a Put at Expiration   **Figure 11.7**

	Calls	Puts
In-the-money	$S_t > X$	$S_t < X$
At-the-money	$S_t = X$	$S_t = X$
Out-of-the-money	$S_t < X$	$S_t > X$

In addition, options can be **near-the-money** if the stock price is close to the exercise price. Further, a call is **deep-in-the-money** if the stock price is considerably above the exercise price, and a put is deep-in-the-money if the stock price is considerably smaller than the exercise price.

OPTION COMBINATIONS

This section discusses some of the most important ways that traders can combine options. By trading option combinations, traders can shape the risk and return characteristics of their option positions, which allows more precise speculative strategies. For example, we will see how to use option combinations to profit when stock prices move a great deal or when they stagnate.

The Straddle

A **straddle** consists of a call and a put with the same exercise price and the same expiration. The buyer of a straddle buys the call and put, while the seller of a straddle sells the same two options.[3] Consider a call and put, both with $100 exercise prices. We assume the call costs $5 and the put trades for $4. Figure 11.8 shows the profits and losses from purchasing each of these options. The profit and losses for buying the straddle are just the combined profits and losses from buying both options. If we designate T as the expiration date of the option and let t be the present, then C_t is the current price of the option and C_T is the price of the option at expiration. Similarly, P_t is the present price of the put and P_T is the price of the put at expiration. Using this notation, the cost of the long straddle is:

$$C_t + P_t$$

and the value of the straddle at expiration will be:

$$C_T + P_T = \text{MAX}\{0, S_T - X\} + \text{MAX}\{0, X - S_T\} \tag{11.3}$$

Similarly, the short straddle position costs:

$$-C_t - P_t$$

so the short trader receives a payment for accepting the short straddle position. The value of the short straddle at expiration will be:

$$-C_T - P_T = -\text{MAX}\{0, S_T - X\} - \text{MAX}\{0, X - S_T\}$$

Because the options market is always a zero-sum game, the short trader's profits and losses mirror those of the long position. Figure 11.9 shows the profits and losses from buying and selling

Profits and Losses at Expiration from the Options in a Straddle   **Figure 11.8**

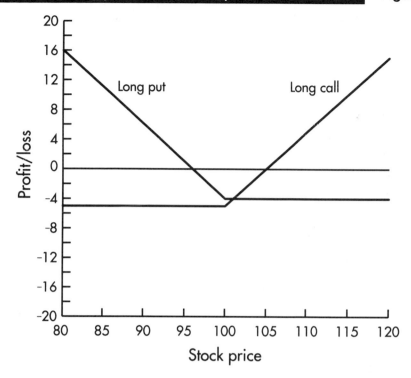

the straddle. As the graph shows, the maximum loss for the straddle buyer is the cost of the two options. Potential profits are almost unlimited for the buyer if the stock price rises or falls enough. As Figure 11.9 also shows, the maximum profit for the short straddle trader occurs when the stock price at expiration equals the exercise price. If the stock price equals the exercise price, the straddle owner cannot exercise either the call or the put profitably. Therefore, both options expire worthless and the short straddle trader keeps both option premiums for a total profit of $9. However, if the stock price diverges from the exercise price, the long straddle holder will exercise either the call or the put. Any exercise decreases the short trader's profits and may even generate a loss. If the stock price exceeds the exercise price, the call owner will exercise, while if the stock price is less than the exercise price, the straddle owner will exercise the put.

Figure 11.9 shows that the short trader essentially bets that the stock price will not diverge too far from the exercise price, so the seller is betting that the stock price will not be too volatile. In making this bet, the straddle seller risks theoretically unlimited losses if the stock price goes too high. Likewise, the short trader's losses are almost unlimited if the stock price goes too low.[4] The short trader's cash inflows equal the sum of the two option prices. At expiration, the short trader's cash outflow equals the exercise result for the call and for the put. If the call is exercised against him at expiration, the short trader loses the difference between the stock price and the exercise price. If the

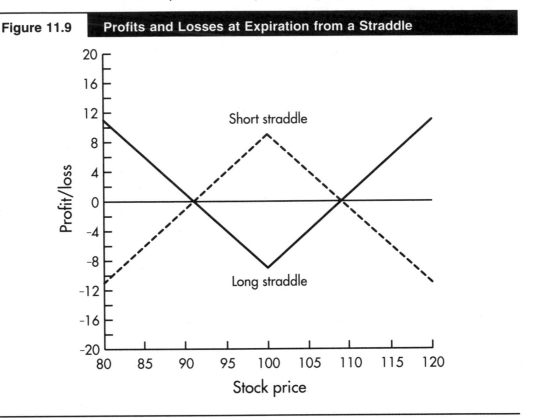

Figure 11.9   Profits and Losses at Expiration from a Straddle

put is exercised against him, the short trader loses the difference between the exercise price and the stock price.

The Strangle

Like a straddle, a **strangle** consists of a put and a call with the same expiration date and the same underlying good. In a strangle the call has an exercise price above the stock price and the put has an exercise price below the stock price. Let X_1 and X_2 be the two exercise prices, such that $X_1 > X_2$. Therefore, a strangle is similar to a straddle, but the put and call have different exercise prices. Let $C_{t,1}$ denote the cost of the call with exercise price X_1 at time t, and let $P_{t,2}$ indicate the cost of the put with exercise price X_2. The long strangle trader buys the put and call, while the short trader sells the two options. The cost of the long strangle is:

$$C_t(S_t, X_1, T) + P_t(S_t, X_2, T)$$

Then the value of the strangle at expiration will be:

$$C_T(S_T, X_1, T) + P_T(S_T, X_2, T) = \text{MAX}\{0, S_T - X_1\} + \text{MAX}\{0, X_2 - S_T\} \tag{11.4}$$

The cost of the short strangle is:

$$-C_t(S_t, X_1, T) - P_t(S_t, X_2, T)$$

The value of the short strangle at expiration will be:

$$-C_T(S_T, X_1, T) - P_T(S_T, X_2, T) = -MAX\{0, S_T - X_1\} - MAX\{0, X_2 - S_T\}$$

To illustrate the strangle, we use a call with an exercise price of $85 and a put with an exercise price of $80. The call price is $3 and the put price is $4. Figure 11.10 graphs the profits and losses for long positions in these two options. The call has a profit for any stock price above $88, and the put has a profit for any stock price below $76. However, for the owner of a strangle to profit, the price of the stock must fall below $76 or rise above $88. Figure 11.11 shows the profits and losses from buying and selling the strangle based on these two options. The total outlay for the two options is $7. To break even, either the call or the put must give an exercise profit of $7. The call makes an exercise profit of $7 when the stock price is $7 above the exercise price of the call. This price is $92. Similarly, the put has an exercise profit of $7 when the stock price is $73. Any stock price between $73 and $92 results in a loss on the strangle, while any stock price outside the $73–$92 range gives a profit on the strangle.

Figure 11.11 shows that buying a strangle is betting that the stock price will move significantly below the exercise price on the put or above the exercise price on the call. The buyer of the strangle has the chance for very large profits if the stock price moves dramatically away from the exercise

Profits and Losses at Expiration from the Options in a Strangle   **Figure 11.10**

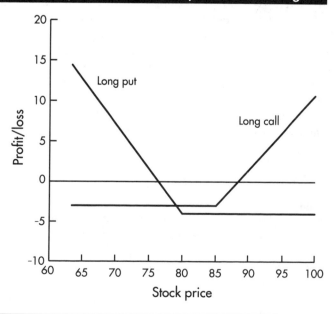

Figure 11.11   Profits and Losses at Expiration from a Strangle

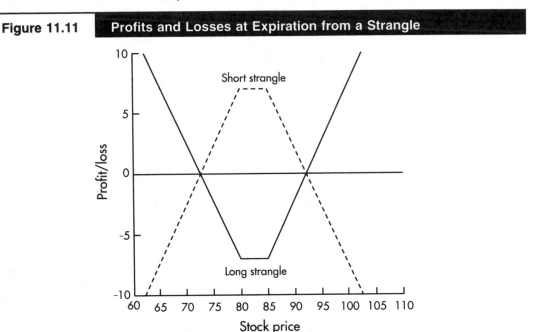

prices. Theoretically, the profit on a strangle is boundless. A stock price at expiration of $200, for example, gives a profit on the strangle of $108.

The profits on the short position are just the negative values of the profits for the long position. Figure 11.11 shows the profits and losses for the short strangle position as dotted lines. At any stock price from $80–$85, the short strangle has a $7 profit. Between these two prices, the long trader cannot profit by exercising either the put or the call, so the short trader keeps the full price of both options. For stock prices below $80, the straddle buyer exercises the put, and for stock prices above $85, the straddle buyer exercises the call. Any exercise costs the short trader, who still has some profit if the stock price stays within the $73–$92 range. However, for very low stock prices, the short strangle position gives large losses, as it does for very high stock prices. Therefore, the short strangle trader is betting that stock prices stay within a fairly wide band. In essence, the short strangle trader has a high probability of a small profit, but accepts the risk of a very large loss.

Bull and Bear Spreads with Call Options

A **bull spread** in the options market is a combination of options designed to profit if the price of the underlying good rises.[5] A bull spread utilizing call options requires two calls with the same underlying stock and the same expiration date, but with different exercise prices. The buyer of a bull spread buys a call with an exercise price below the stock price and sells a call option with an exercise price above the stock price. The spread is a ''bull'' spread, because the trader hopes to profit from a price rise in the stock. The trade is a ''spread,'' because it involves buying one option and selling a related option. Compared to buying the stock itself, the bull spread with call options limits the trader's risk, but the bull spread also limits the profit potential.

The cost of the bull spread is the cost of the option that is purchased, less the cost of the option that the trader sells. Letting $C_{t,1}$ be the cost of the first option that is purchased at time t with exercise price X_1, and letting $C_{t,2}$ be the cost of the second option with exercise price X_2, such that $X_1 < X_2$, the cost of the bull spread is:

$$C_t(S_t, X_1, T) - C_t(S_t, X_2, T)$$

At expiration, the value of the bull spread will be:

$$C_T(S_T, X_1, T) - C_T(S_T, X_2, T) = \mathrm{MAX}\{0, S_T - X_1\} - \mathrm{MAX}\{0, S_T - X_2\} \qquad (11.5)$$

To illustrate the bull spread, assume that the stock trades at $100. One call option has an exercise price of $95 and costs $7. The other call has an exercise price of $105 and costs $3. To buy the bull spread, the trader buys the call with the lower exercise price, and sells the call with the higher exercise price. In our example, the total outlay for the bull spread is $4. Figure 11.12 graphs the profits and losses for the two call positions individually. The long position profits if the stock price moves above $102. The short position profits if the stock price does not exceed $108. As the graph shows, low

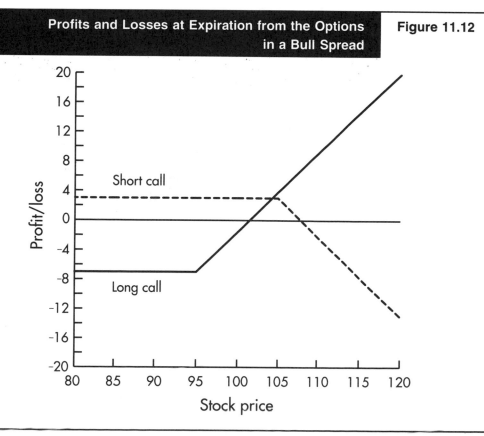

Profits and Losses at Expiration from the Options in a Bull Spread   **Figure 11.12**

stock prices result in an overall loss for the bull spread, because the cost of buying the call with the lower exercise price exceeds the proceeds from selling the call with the higher exercise price. It is also interesting to consider prices at $105 and above. For every dollar by which the stock price exceeds $105, the long call portion of the spread generates an extra dollar of profit, but the short call component starts to lose money. Thus, for stock prices above $105, the additional gains on the long call exactly offset the losses on the short call. Therefore, no matter how high the stock price goes, the bull spread can never give a greater profit than it does for a stock price of $105.

Figure 11.13 graphs the bull spread as the solid line. For any stock price at expiration of $95 or below, the bull spread loses $4. This $4 is the difference between the cash inflow for selling one call and buying the other. The bull spread breaks even for a stock price of $99. The highest possible profit on the bull spread comes when the stock sells for $105. Then the bull spread gives a $6 profit. For any stock price above $105, the profit on the bull spread remains at $6. Therefore, the trader of a bull spread bets that the stock price goes up, but he hedges his bet. We can see that the bull spread protects the trader from losing any more than $4. However, the trader cannot make more than a $6 profit. We can compare the bull spread with a position in the stock itself in Figure 11.2. Comparing the bull spread and the stock, we find that the stock offers the chance for bigger profits, but it also has greater risk of a serious loss.

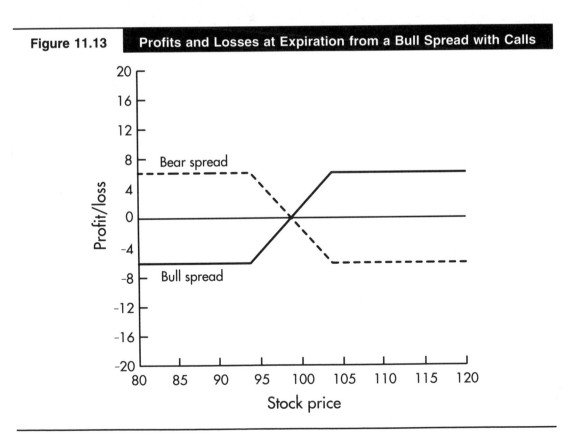

Figure 11.13   **Profits and Losses at Expiration from a Bull Spread with Calls**

A **bear spread** in the options market is an option combination designed to profit from falling stock prices. To execute a bear spread with call options requires two call options with the same underlying stock and the same expiration date. The two calls, however, have different exercise prices. To execute a bear spread with calls, a trader would sell the call with the lower exercise price and buy the call with the higher exercise price. In other words, the bear spread with calls is just the short position to the bull spread with calls.

The cost of a bear spread is:

$$-C_t(S_t, X_1, T) + C_t(S_t, X_2, T)$$

At expiration, the value of the bear spread will be:

$$-C_T(S_T, X_1, T) + C_T(S_T, X_2, T) = -\text{MAX}\{0, S_T - X_1\} + \text{MAX}\{0, S_T - X_2\} \qquad (11.6)$$

Figure 11.13 shows the profit and loss profile for a bear spread with the same options we have been considering. The dotted line shows how profit and losses vary if a trader sells the call with the $95 strike price and buys the call with the $105 strike price. In a bear spread, the trader bets that the stock price will fall. However, the bear spread also limits the profit opportunity and the risk of loss compared to a short position in the stock itself. We can compare the profit and loss profiles of the bear spread in Figure 11.13 with the short position in the stock shown as the dotted line in Figure 11.2.[6]

Bull and Bear Spreads with Put Options

It is also possible to execute bull and bear spreads with put options in a manner similar to the bull and bear spread with call options. The bull spread consists of buying a put with a lower exercise price and selling a put with a higher exercise price. The bear spread trader sells a put with a lower exercise price and buys a put with a higher exercise price. Consistent with our notation for call options, the cost of the bull spread with puts is:

$$P_t(S_t, X_1, T) - P_t(S_t, X_2, T)$$

with exercises prices X_1 and X_2, respectively, such that $X_1 < X_2$. The value of the bull spread at expiration will be:

$$P_T(S_T, X_1, T) - P_T(S_T, X_2, T) = \text{MAX}\{0, X_1 - S_T\} - \text{MAX}\{0, X_2 - S_T\} \qquad (11.7)$$

It is also possible to initiate a bear spread with puts. The bear spread is just the opposite of a bull spread. For a put bear spread, the trader uses two options on the same underlying good that have the same time until expiration. The trader sells the put with the lower exercise price and buys the put with the higher exercise price. The bear spread with puts is simply the complementary position to the bull spread, and costs:

$$-P_t(S_t, X_1, T) + P_t(S_t, X_2, T)$$

The value of the bear spread with puts at expiration is:

$$-P_T(S_T, X_1, T) + P_T(S_T, X_2, T) = -\text{MAX}\{0, X_1 - S_T\} + \text{MAX}\{0, X_2 - S_T\}$$

To illustrate bull and bear spreads with put options, consider two puts with the same expiration date and the same underlying stock. Assume that one put has an exercise price of $90 and the other has an exercise price of $110. The put with an exercise price of $90 trades at $3, while the put with an exercise price of $110 trades at $9.

The bull trader would buy the put with $X = \$90$ and sell the put with $X = \$110$, for a total cash inflow of $6. Assume the stock price at expiration is $90. The bull trader cannot exercise the put option with $X = \$90$. However, the put option with $X = \$110$ that the trader sold will be exercised, giving our trader an exercise loss of $20. Thus, the total loss for the bull trader will be $14, the initial cash inflow of $6, minus the $20 exercise loss. For any terminal stock price lower than $90, the bull trader will lose an additional dollar on the short put position. However, if the stock price falls below $90, the bull trader can exercise the long put with a striking price of $90. Thus, the gain on the long put will offset any further losses on the short put for stock prices lower than $90. Therefore, the maximum loss on the bull spread of $14 occurs with a stock price of $90 or lower.

If the stock price at expiration is $110 or higher, the short put cannot be exercised against the bull trader of our example. Also, the long put cannot be exercised, because it cannot be exercised at any price of $90 or higher. With no exercises occurring, the bull trader merely keeps the initial cash inflow that occurred when the position was assumed, and the bull trader nets a profit of $6.

For prices between $90 and $110, the short put will be exercised against the bull trader and will reduce the trader's profits or generate a loss. For example, if the stock price is $100 at expiration, the bull trader will lose $10 on the exercise of the put with $X = \$110$. This loss, coupled with the initial cash inflow of $6, gives a total loss on the trade of $4. Figure 11.14 shows the profits and losses from this bull trade with puts as the solid line, and it shows the bear spread with puts as a dotted line. As Figure 11.14 shows, the bear trader takes the opposite position from the bull trader.

In terms of our example, the bear trader would buy the put with $X = \$110$ and sell the put with $X = \$90$, for a total outlay of $6. For any terminal stock price less than $110, the bear trader can exercise the put with $X = \$110$, and will break even for a terminal stock price of $104. For any stock price below $90, the bear trader's short call will be exercised against her as well, giving an exercise loss on that option. This exercise loss will offset any further profits on the long put with $X = \$110$. As a result, the bear trader cannot make more than $14. This $14 profit occurs for any stock price of $90 or less. For example, if the terminal stock price is $85, the bear trader has an exercise profit of $25 on the long put with $X = \$110$ and an exercise loss of -$5 on the short put with $X = \$90$. This total exercise profit of $20 must be reduced by the $6 outlay required to assume the bear spread, for a net gain of $14. This gain of $14 when the stock price is $85 exactly equals the loss of $14 that the bull spread holder would incur.

The Box Spread

A **box spread** consists of a bull spread with calls plus a bear spread with puts, with the two spreads having the same pair of exercise prices. In terms of our notation, the box spread costs:

$$C_t(S_t, X_1, T) - C_t(S_t, X_2, T) + P_t(S_t, X_1, T) - P_t(S_t, X_2, T)$$

Profits and Losses at Expiration from a Bull Spread with Puts   **Figure 11.14**

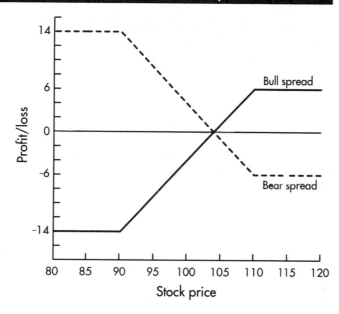

The value of the box spread at expiration is:

$$C_T(S_T, X_1, T) - C_T(S_T, X_2, T) - P_T(S_T, X_1, T) + P_T(S_T, X_2, T) \qquad (11.8)$$
$$= \text{MAX}\{0, S_T - X_1\} - \text{MAX}\{0, S_T - X_2\} - \text{MAX}\{0, X_1 - S_T\} + \text{MAX}\{0, X_2 - S_T\}$$

As an example, consider the following four transactions:

Transaction	Exercise Price
Long 1 Call	$95
Short 1 Call	$105
Long 1 Put	$105
Short 1 Put	$95

The value of the box spread at expiration will be:

$$\text{MAX}\{0, S_T - \$95\} - \text{MAX}\{0, S_T - \$105\} + \text{MAX}\{0, \$105 - S_T\} - \text{MAX}\{0, \$95 - S_T\}$$

For a stock price of $102 at expiration, the payoff will be:

$$\$7 - \$0 + \$3 - \$0 = \$10$$

For a stock price of $80, the payoff at expiration will be:

$$\$0 - \$0 + \$25 - \$15 = \$10$$

In fact, for any terminal stock price, the box spread will pay the difference between the high and low exercise prices, $X_2 - X_1$, which is $10 in this example. Thus, the box spread is a riskless investment strategy. To avoid potential arbitrage opportunities, the price of the box spread must be the present value of the certain payoff. Therefore, the cost of the box spread purchased at time t must be:

$$\frac{X_2 - X_1}{(1 + r)^{(T-t)}}$$

Continuing with this example, let us assume that the options expire in one year and that the risk-free interest rate is 10 percent. Under these assumptions, the box spread must cost $9.09. Any other price would lead to arbitrage.

The Butterfly Spread with Calls

A **butterfly spread** can be executed by using three calls with the same expiration date on the same underlying stock. The long trader buys one call with a low exercise price, buys one call with a high exercise price, and sells two calls with an intermediate exercise price. Continuing to let X_i represent exercise prices such that $X_1 < X_2 < X_3$, the cost of the long butterfly spread is:

$$C_t(S_t, X_1, T) - 2C_t(S_t, X_2, T) + C_t(S_t, X_3, T)$$

The value of the butterfly spread at expiration is:

$$\begin{aligned} &C_T(S_T, X_1, T) - 2C_T(S_T, X_2, T) + C_T(S_T, X_3, T) \\ &= \text{MAX}\{0, S_T - X_1\} - 2\text{MAX}\{0, S_T - X_2\} + \text{MAX}\{0, S_T - X_3\} \end{aligned} \qquad (11.9)$$

The short trader takes exactly the opposite position, selling one call with a low exercise price, selling one call with a high exercise price, and buying two calls with an intermediate exercise price. The cost of the short position is:

$$-C_t(S_t, X_1, T) + 2C_t(S_t, X_2, T) - C_t(S_t, X_3, T)$$

The value of the short butterfly spread at expiration is:

$$\begin{aligned} &-C_T(S_T, X_1, T) + 2C_T(S_T, X_2, T) - C_T(S_T, X_3, T) \\ &= -\text{MAX}\{0, S_T - X_1\} + 2\text{MAX}\{0, S_T - X_2\} - \text{MAX}\{0, S_T - X_3\} \end{aligned}$$

For the long trader, the spread profits most when the stock price at expiration is at the intermediate exercise price. In essence, the butterfly spread gives a payoff pattern similar to a straddle. Compared to a straddle, however, a butterfly spread offers lower risk at the expense of reduced profit potential.

As an example of a butterfly spread, assume that a stock trades at $100 and a trader buys a butterfly spread by trading options with the prices shown in the following table. As the table shows, the buyer of a butterfly spread sells two calls with a striking price near the stock price and buys one each of the calls above and below the stock price.

	Exercise Price	Option Premium
Long 1 Call	$105	$3
Short 2 Calls	100	4
Long 1 Call	95	7

Figure 11.15 graphs the profits and losses from each of these three option positions. To understand the profits and losses from the butterfly spread, we need to combine these profits and losses, remembering that the spread involves selling two options and buying two, a total of four options with three different exercise prices.

Let us consider a few critical stock prices to see how the butterfly spread profits respond. The critical stock prices always include the exercise prices for the options. First, if the stock price is $95, the call with an exercise price of $95 is worth zero and a long position in this call loses $7. The long call with the $105 exercise price also cannot be exercised, so it is worthless, giving a loss of the $3 purchase price. The short call position gives a profit of $4 per option and the spread sold two of these options, for an $8 profit. Adding these values gives a net loss on the spread of $2, if the stock price is $95. Second, if the stock price is $100, the long call with a striking price of $95 loses $2 (the $5 stock profit minus the $7 purchase price). The long call with an exercise price of $105 loses its full purchase price of $3. Together, the long calls lose $5. The short call still shows a profit of

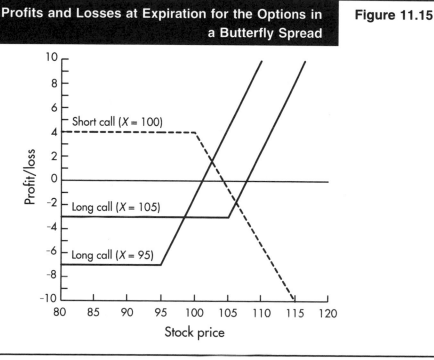

Profits and Losses at Expiration for the Options in a Butterfly Spread

Figure 11.15

$4 per option, for a profit of $8 on the two options. This gives a net profit of $3 if the stock price is $100. Third, if the stock price is $105 at expiration, the long call with an exercise price of $95 has a profit of $3. The long call with an exercise price of $105 loses $3. Also, the short call position loses $1 per option for a loss on two positions of $2. This gives a net loss on the butterfly spread of $2. In summary, we have a $2 loss for a $95 stock price, a $3 profit for a $100 stock price, and a $2 loss for a $105 stock price.

    Figure 11.16 shows the entire profit and loss graph for the butterfly spread. At a stock price of $100, we noted a profit of $3. This is the highest profit available from the spread. At stock prices of $95 and $105, the spread loses $2. For stock prices below $95 or above $105, the loss is still $2. As the graph shows, the butterfly spread has a zero profit for stock prices of $97 and $103. The buyer of the butterfly spread essentially bets that stock prices will hover near $100. Any large move away from $100 gives a loss on the butterfly spread. However, the loss can never exceed $2. Comparing the butterfly spread with the straddle in Figure 11.9, we see that the butterfly spread resembles a short position in the straddle. Compared to the straddle, the butterfly spread reduces the risk of a very large loss. However, the reduction in risk necessarily comes at the expense of a chance for a big profit.

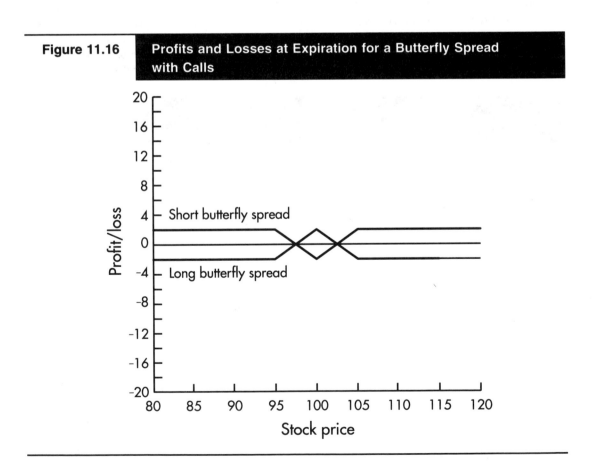

Figure 11.16   **Profits and Losses at Expiration for a Butterfly Spread with Calls**

The Butterfly Spread with Puts

The butterfly spread can also be initiated with a combination of put options. For a long position in a butterfly spread, the trader buys a put with a low exercise price, buys a put with a high exercise price, and sells two puts with an intermediate exercise price. The short trader sells a put with a low exercise price, sells a put with a high exercise price, and buys two puts with an intermediate exercise price.

For the long position in the butterfly spread with puts, the cost is:

$$P_t(S_t, X_1, T) - 2P_t(S_t, X_2, T) + P_t(S_t, X_3, T)$$

The value at expiration is:

$$
\begin{aligned}
&P_T(S_T, X_1, T) - 2P_T(S_T, X_2, T) + P_T(S_T, X_3, T) \\
&= \text{MAX}\{0, X_1 - S_T\} - 2\text{MAX}\{0, X_2 - S_T\} + \text{MAX}\{0, X_3 - S_T\}
\end{aligned}
\tag{11.10}
$$

For the short trader, the cost of the short position is:

$$-P_t(S_t, X_1, T) + 2P_t(S_t, X_2, T) - P_t(S_t, X_3, T)$$

The value at expiration for the short butterfly spread with puts is:

$$
\begin{aligned}
&-P_T(S_T, X_1, T) + 2P_T(S_T, X_2, T) - P_T(S_T, X_3, T) \\
&= -\text{MAX}\{0, X_1 - S_T\} + 2\text{MAX}\{0, X_2 - S_T\} - \text{MAX}\{0, X_3 - S_T\}
\end{aligned}
$$

The long and short butterfly trades with puts give a profit pattern just like the butterfly trade with calls, as illustrated in Figure 11.16.

To explore these transactions more fully, consider the following transactions for a long butterfly spread with puts.

	Exercise Price	Option Premium
Long 1 Put	$ 95	$ 5
Short 2 Puts	100	7
Long 1 Put	105	10

The total cost of this position is $1. If the stock price at expiration is exactly $95, the put with $X = \$95$ cannot be exercised. However, both puts with $X = \$100$ will be exercised against the long trader, for an exercise loss of $10. The long trader will be able to exercise the put with $X = \$105$, for an exercise profit of $10, so the long butterfly trader will experience no net gain or loss on the exercise. The same is true for any stock price lower than $95. Lower stock prices will generate larger losses on the exercise of the puts with $X = \$100$, but these will be exactly offset by higher exercise gains on the two long puts that constitute the long butterfly spread. Thus, for any stock price of $95 or lower, there is no exercise gain or loss, and the trader loses the $1 cost of the butterfly spread. At a terminal stock price of $105 or higher, no put can be exercised, so there is no exercise gain or loss, and the purchase of the butterfly spread loses the $1 cost of the position. Figure 11.17 shows these profits and losses as a solid line.

For a stock price at expiration between $95 and $105, the long trader has an exercise gain that will offset the $1 cost of the position and may even make the entire transaction profitable. For example, if the terminal stock price is $100, the puts with $X = \$95$ and $X = \$100$ cannot be exercised. In this situation, the trader can exercise the put with $X = \$105$ for a $5 exercise profit. This exercise profit, offset by the $1 cost of the position, gives a total gain on the trade of $4, and this is the maximum profit from the trade. For terminal stock prices between $95 and $100 or between $100 and $105, the gain will be less and may even be a loss. For a terminal stock price of $96, for example, the trader will exercise the put with $X = \$105$ for a $9 exercise profit. However, the two short puts with $X = \$100$ will be exercised against her, for an exercise loss of −$8. The net exercise gain will be $1, which exactly offsets the $1 cost of the position. Thus, the trade has a zero gain/loss at a terminal stock price of $96. The same occurs if the terminal stock price is $104. For a terminal stock price between $96 and $104, there is some profit, with the maximum profit of $4 occurring when the stock price is $100.

As we noted at the beginning of this section, it is also possible to initiate a short butterfly position with puts. With the options of this example, the short butterfly transaction would require selling a put with $X = \$95$, selling a put with $X = \$105$, and buying two puts with $X = \$100$, for a total cash inflow of $1. This short butterfly position would have profits and losses that exactly mirror those of the long position. Figure 11.17 shows the profits and losses for this short butterfly position with puts as a dotted line.

Figure 11.17	Profits and Losses at Expiration for a Butterfly Spread with Puts

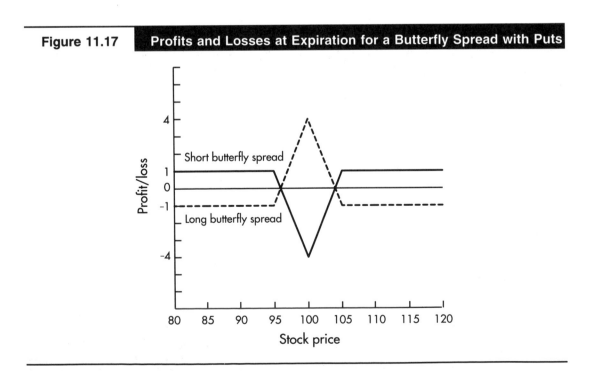

The Condor with Call Options

A **condor** is a specialized position that involves four options on the same underlying good and the same expiration date. The four options have different exercise prices. For a long condor entered with call options, a trader buys a call with a low exercise price, sells a call with a somewhat higher exercise price, sells a call with a yet higher exercise price, and buys a call with the highest exercise price. Notice that this is like a butterfly, in that the long trader buys two calls with extreme exercise prices, and sells two calls with intermediate exercise prices. In a butterfly, the intermediate exercise price is the same for the two calls, while a condor uses two different intermediate exercise prices. Thus, the cost of a long condor is:

$$C_t(S_t, X_1, T) - C_t(S_t, X_2, T) - C_t(S_t, X_3, T) + C_t(S_t, X_4, T)$$

The value of the long condor at expiration is:

$$C_T(S_T, X_1, T) - C_T(S_T, X_2, T) - C_T(S_T, X_3, T) + C_T(S_T, X_4, T) \tag{11.11}$$
$$= MAX\{0, S_T - X_1\} - MAX\{0, S_T - X_2\} - MAX\{0, S_T - X_3\} + MAX\{0, S_T - X_4\}$$

For the short condor position executed with calls, the cost of the position is:

$$-C_t(S_t, X_1, T) + C_t(S_t, X_2, T) + C_t(S_t, X_3, T) - C_t(S_t, X_4, T)$$

For the short condor, the value at expiration is:

$$-C_T(S_T, X_1, T) + C_T(S_T, X_2, T) + C_T(S_T, X_3, T) - C_T(S_T, X_4, T) =$$
$$-MAX\{0, S_T - X_1\} + MAX\{0, S_T - X_2\} + MAX\{0, S_T - X_3\} - MAX\{0, S_T - X_4\}$$

The following transactions illustrate a long condor position entered with call options.

	Exercise Price	Option Premium
Long 1 Call	$ 90	$10
Short 1 Call	95	7
Short 1 Call	100	4
Long 1 Call	105	2

The total cost of the condor is $1. If the terminal stock price is $90 or less, no call can be exercised and the position expires worthless for a total loss of $1. If the stock price at expiration is $95, for example, the long trader can exercise the call with $X = \$90$ for an exercise profit of $5. This gives a total profit on the position of $4. For any stock price above $95, the short call with $X = \$95$ will be exercised against the purchase of the condor, and for any stock price above $100, the short call with $X = \$100$ will also be exercised. For example, if the terminal stock price is $102, the transactions give the following result. The long call with $X = \$90$ will have a $12 exercise profit, the short call with $X = \$95$ will generate an exercise loss of $7, and the short call with $X = \$100$ will generate an exercise loss of $2. These exercise results, coupled with the $1 initial cost of the position, give a final profit of $4.

For higher terminal stock prices, those of $105 or higher, the exercise gains and losses are exactly offsetting. For example, if the terminal stock price is $107, the exercise gains and losses are $17 for the call with $X = \$90$, $-\$12$ for the call with $X = \$95$, $-\$7$ for the call with $X = \$100$, and $2 for the call with $X = \$105$, for a net exercise result of zero. This leaves a loss of $1, which was the original cost to enter the position. Figure 11.18 shows the short condor position with the dotted line. As usual, the results for the short position are a mirror image of those for the long position. In a zero-sum game, the winner's gains exactly match the loser's losses.

The Condor with Puts

As with the other strategies we have considered, it is also possible to initiate a condor with puts as well as with calls. Again, all options have the same underlying stock and the same expiration date. For a long condor with puts, the trader buys a put with the lowest exercise price, sells a put with a higher exercise price, sells a put with a yet higher exercise price, and buys a put with the highest exercise price. The short condor trader takes the opposite side of the long position, selling a put with the lowest exercise price, buying a put with a higher exercise price, buying a put with a yet higher exercise price, and selling a put with the highest exercise price.

The cost of a long condor with puts is:

$$P_t(S_t, X_1, T) - P_t(S_t, X_2, T) - P_t(S_t, X_3, T) + P_t(S_t, X_4, T)$$

The value of the long condor with puts at expiration is given by:

Figure 11.18	**Profits and Losses at Expiration for a Condor with Calls**

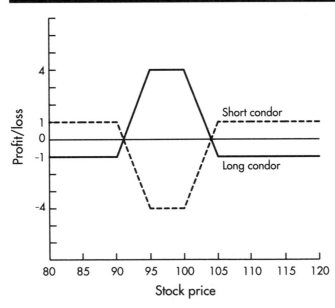

$$P_T(S_T, X_1, T) - P_T(S_T, X_2, T) - P_T(S_T, X_3, T) + P_T(S_T, X_4, T) = \quad (11.12)$$
$$\text{MAX}\{0, X_1 - S_T\} - \text{MAX}\{0, X_2 - S_T\} - \text{MAX}\{0, X_3 - S_T\} + \text{MAX}\{0, X_4 - S_T\}$$

The following transactions illustrate a long condor initiated with puts.

	Exercise Price	Option Premium
Long 1 Put	$ 90	$ 2
Short 1 Put	95	5
Short 1 Put	100	9
Long 1 Put	105	13

With these prices, the long condor position costs $1. For a terminal stock price of $105 or higher, none of these puts can be exercised, so the total loss on the position is $1. For a stock price of $90, three puts will be exercised, but there will be no net gain or loss on the exercise. The long trader will exercise the put with $X = \$105$ for an exercise gain of $15, but two puts will be exercised against the trader for an exercise loss of $5 on the put with $X = \$95$ and a loss of $10 on the put with $X = \$100$. This gives a zero result from the exercise, and the long trader loses the $1 cost of the position. For any stock price less than $90, the long condor trader can exercise the put with $X = \$90$, so the exercise result is zero for any stock price of $90 or less.

As with the long condor executed with calls, the long condor with puts pays best when the terminal stock price is between the two intermediate exercise prices. In our example, this range extends from $95 to $100. For a terminal stock price of $100, for example, the long trader can exercise the put with $X = \$105$ for an exercise gain of $5. Given the $1 cost of the position, the total profit on the transaction would then be $4. This is the same for any terminal stock price in the range of $95 to $100 as Figure 11.19 shows.

The short condor trader could use puts as well, again taking the mirror position of the long trader. Specifically, the short condor with puts requires selling the put with the lowest exercise price, buying a put with a higher exercise price, buying a put with a yet higher exercise price, and selling a put with the highest exercise price. Thus, the short condor executed with puts costs:

$$-P_t(S_t, X_1, T) + P_t(S_t, X_2, T) + P_t(S_t, X_3, T) - P_t(S_t, X_4, T)$$

The value of the short condor with puts at expiration is given by:

$$- P_T(S_T, X_1, T) + P_T(S_T, X_2, T) + P_T(S_T, X_3, T) - P_T(S_T, X_4, T) =$$
$$-\text{MAX}\{0, X_1 - S_T\} + \text{MAX}\{0, X_2 - S_T\} + \text{MAX}\{0, X_3 - S_T\} - \text{MAX}\{0, X_4 - S_T\}$$

With our example prices, that would involve selling a put with $X = \$90$, buying a put with $X = \$95$, buying a put with $X = \$100$, and selling a put with $X = \$105$. Figure 11.19 shows the profits and losses for the short condor position as a dotted line.

Ratio Spreads

A **ratio spread** is a spread transaction in which two or more related options are traded in a specified proportion. For example, a trader might buy a call with a lower exercise price and sell three calls

Figure 11.19   **Profits and Losses at Expiration for a Condor with Puts**

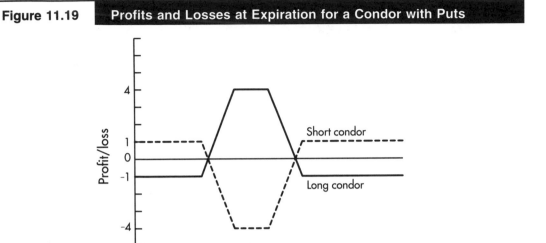

with a higher exercise price. As the ratio of one instrument to the other can be varied without limit, there are infinitely many different ratio spreads that are possible. Consequently, we will consider just one fairly simple ratio spread as a guide to the variety of ratio spreads available.

In a ratio spread, the number of contracts bought differs from the number of contracts sold to form the spread. For example, buying two options and selling one gives a 2:1 ratio spread. The spread can be varied infinitely by changing the ratio between the options that are bought and sold. Thus, it is impossible to provide a complete catalog of ratio spreads. Consequently, we illustrate the idea behind ratio spreads by considering a 2:1 ratio spread.

Earlier we considered a bull spread using call options and illustrated this trade by considering two call options, one with an exercise price of $95 and costing $7, the other with an exercise price of $105 and costing $3. Figure 11.13 presented the profits and losses from that position. For comparison, consider a ratio spread in which a trader buys two calls with $X = \$95$ and sells one call with $X = \$105$. (In this case, the trader has utilized a 2:1 ratio.) The total cost of the position is $11. For any terminal stock price of $95 or less, neither call can be exercised, and the trader loses $11. If the stock price exceeds $95, the trader can exercise both of the purchased calls. For example, with a stock price of $105, the trader exercises both calls for an exercise profit of $20, giving a total gain on the trade of $9. For any stock price above $105, the trader will exercise the two calls purchased with $X = \$95$, but the call sold with $X = \$105$ will be exercised against her as well. This partially offsets the benefits derived from exercising the two calls with $X = \$95$. For example, a stock price of $110 gives an exercise profit on the two options with $X = \$95$ of $30. This gain is partially offset by the exercise against our trader of the option with $X = \$105$, for an exercise loss of $5. The net gain at exercise is $25, which more than compensates for the $11 cost of the position and gives a net profit of $14 on the trade.

Figure 11.20 shows the profits and losses for the bull spread with call options, repeating the information of Figure 11.13, and it shows profits and losses from the ratio spread we are considering. In comparing these two profit and loss patterns, we see that the ratio spread costs more to undertake, but that it also offers higher profits if the stock price rises sufficiently.

As we observed, the profit on the ratio spread is $9 for a terminal stock price of $105. For higher stock prices, the ratio call profits increase dramatically. By contrast, the bull spread we have been considering reaches its maximum profitability of $4.00 at a terminal stock price of $105. By varying the ratio between the options in a spread, it is possible to create a wide variety of payoff patterns.

Summary

In this section, we have considered the wide variety of option combinations available when all of the options have a common expiration date. As the variety of combinations shows, it is possible to construct a wide range of profit and loss profiles by choosing the correct combination of options. Table 11.1 summarizes the variety of positions we have considered and tabulates the cost to undertake

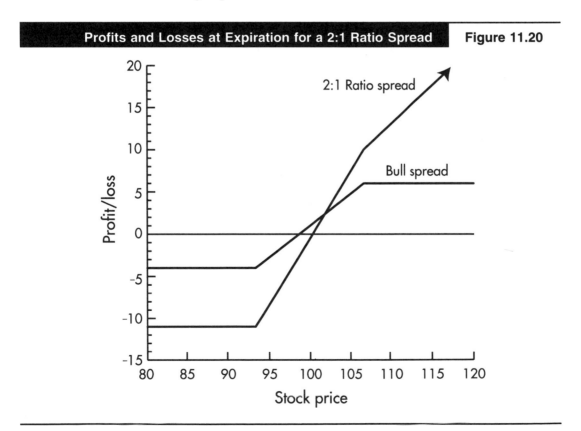

Profits and Losses at Expiration for a 2:1 Ratio Spread   **Figure 11.20**

Table 11.1	Option Combinations and Their Profits		
Position	**Cost**	**Value at Expiration**	**Trader Expects**
Long call	C_t	$\text{MAX}\{0, S_T - X\}$	Rising stock price
Short call	$-C_t$	$-\text{MAX}\{0, S_T - X\}$	Stock price stable or falling
Long put	P_t	$\text{MAX}\{0, X - S_T\}$	Falling stock price
Short put	$-P_t$	$-\text{MAX}\{0, X - S_T\}$	Stock price stable or rising
Long straddle	$C_t + P_t$	$C_T + P_T$	Stock price volatile, rising or falling
Short straddle	$-C_t - P_t$	$-C_T - P_T$	Stock price stable
Long strangle	$C_t(S_t, X_1, T)$ $+P_t(S_t, X_2, T)$	$C_T(S_T, X_1, T)$ $+P_T(S_T, X_2, T)$	Stock price very volatile, rising or falling
Short strangle	$-C_t(S_t, X_1, T)$ $-P_t(S_t, X_2, T)$	$-C_T(S_T, X_1, T)$ $-P_T(S_T, X_2, T)$	Stock price generally stable
Bull spread with calls	$C_t(S_t, X_1, T)$ $-C_t(S_t, X_2, T)$	$C_T(S_T, X_1, T)$ $-C_T(S_T, X_2, T)$	Stock price rising
Bear spread with calls	$-C_t(S_t, X_1, T)$ $+C_t(S_t, X_2, T)$	$-C_T(S_T, X_1, T)$ $+C_T(S_T, X_2, T)$	Stock price falling
Bull spread with puts	$P_t(S_t, X_1, T)$ $-P_t(S_t, X_2, T)$	$P_T(S_T, X_1, T)$ $-P_T(S_T, X_2, T)$	Stock price rising
Bear spread with puts	$-P_t(S_t, X_1, T)$ $+P_t(S_t, X_2, T)$	$-P_T(S_T, X_1, T)$ $+P_T(S_T, X_2, T)$	Stock price falling
Box spread	$C_t(S_t, X_1, T)$ $-C_t(S_t, X_2, T)$ $-P_t(S_t, X_1, T)$ $+P_t(S_t, X_2, T)$	$X_2 - X_1$	Riskless strategy
Long butterfly spread with calls	$C_t(S_t, X_1, T)$ $-2C_t(S_t, X_2, T)$ $+C_t(S_t, X_3, T)$	$C_T(S_T, X_1, T)$ $-2C_T(S_T, X_2, T)$ $+C_T(S_T, X_3, T)$	Stock price stable
Short butterfly spread with calls	$-C_t(S_t, X_1, T)$ $+2C_t(S_t, X_2, T)$ $-C_t(S_t, X_3, T)$	$-C_T(S_T, X_1, T)$ $+2C_T(S_T, X_2, T)$ $-C_T(S_T, X_3, T)$	Stock price volatile, rising or falling
Long butterfly spread with puts	$P_t(S_t, X_1, T)$ $-2P_t(S_t, X_2, T)$ $+P_t(S_t, X_3, T)$	$P_T(S_T, X_1, T)$ $-2P_T(S_T, X_2, T)$ $+ P_T(S_T, X_3, T)$	Stock price stable
Short butterfly spread with puts	$-P_t(S_t, X_1, T)$ $+2P_t(S_t, X_2, T)$ $-P_t(S_t, X_3, T)$	$-P_T(S_T, X_1, T)$ $+2P_T(S_T, X_2, T)$ $-P_T(S_T, X_3, T)$	Stock price volatile, rising or falling

	Option Combinations and Their Profits (continued)		Table 11.1
Position	**Cost**	**Value at Expiration**	**Trader Expects**
Long condor with calls	$C_t(S_t, X_1, T)$ $-C_t(S_t, X_2, T)$ $-C_t(S_t, X_3, T)$ $+C_t(S_t, X_4, T)$	$C_T(S_T, X_1, T)$ $-C_T(S_T, X_2, T)$ $-C_T(S_T, X_3, T)$ $+C_T(S_T, X_4, T)$	Stock price stable
Short condor with calls	$-C_t(S_t, X_1, T)$ $+C_t(S_t, X_2, T)$ $+C_t(S_t, X_3, T)$ $-C_t(S_t, X_4, T)$	$-C_T(S_T, X_1, T)$ $+C_T(S_T, X_2, T)$ $+C_T(S_T, X_3, T)$ $-C_T(S_T, X_4, T)$	Stock price volatile
Long condor with puts	$P_t(S_t, X_1, T)$ $-P_t(S_t, X_2, T)$ $-P_t(S_t, X_3, T)$ $+P_t(S_t, X_4, T)$	$P_T(S_T, X_1, T)$ $-P_T(S_T, X_2, T)$ $-P_T(S_T, X_3, T)$ $+P_T(S_T, X_4, T)$	Stock price stable
Short condor with puts	$-P_t(S_t, X_1, T)$ $+P_t(S_t, X_2, T)$ $+P_t(S_t, X_3, T)$ $-P_t(S_t, X_4, T)$	$-P_T(S_T, X_1, T)$ $+P_T(S_T, X_2, T)$ $+P_T(S_T, X_3, T)$ $-P_T(S_T, X_4, T)$	Stock price volatile
Ratio spreads		Too various to catalog	

Note: $X_1 < X_2 < X_3 < X_4$

the position, along with the value of the position at expiration. In addition, the table shows the condition that would make such a trade reasonable.

It is also possible to create an option combination with options that have different expiration dates. When an option combination has more than one expiration date represented in the options that constitute the spread, the combination is called a **calendar spread**. The absence of a uniform expiration date adds greater complication and requires that we consider calendar spreads in Chapter 14 after we introduce the pricing principles for options before expiration.

In this section, we have studied options combined with other options. However, it is also possible to combine options with other instruments to form additional profit and loss profiles. Most interestingly, options can be combined with the underlying stock and with the risk-free asset. We now turn to a consideration of combinations of options with bonds and stocks.

COMBINING OPTIONS WITH BONDS AND STOCKS

Thus far we have considered some of the most important combinations of options. We now show how to combine options with stocks and bonds to adjust payoff patterns to fit virtually any taste for risk and return combinations. These combinations show us the relationships among the different classes of securities. By combining two types of securities, we can generally imitate the payoff patterns of a third. In addition, this section extends the concepts we have developed earlier in this chapter. Specifically, we learn more about shaping the risk and return characteristics of portfolios by using options.

In this section we consider five combinations of options with bonds or stocks. First, we consider the popular strategy of the **covered call** – a long position in the underlying stock and a short position in a call option. Second, we explore portfolio insurance. During the 1980s, portfolio insurance became one of the most discussed techniques for managing the risk of a stock portfolio. We illustrate some of the basic ideas of portfolio insurance by showing how to insure a stock portfolio. Third, we show how to use options to mimic the profit and loss patterns of the stock itself. For investors who do not want to invest the full purchase price of the stock, it is possible to create an option position that gives a profit and loss pattern much like the stock itself. Fourth, by combining options with the risk-free bond, we can synthesize the underlying stock. In this situation, the option and bond position gives the same profit and loss pattern as the stock and it has the same value as the stock as well. Finally, we show how to combine a call, a bond, and a share of stock to create a synthetic put option.

The Covered Call: Stock Plus a Short Call

In a covered call transaction, a trader is generally assumed to already own a stock and writes a call option on the underlying stock. (The strategy is "covered" because the trader owns the underlying stock, and this stock covers the obligation inherent in writing the call.) This strategy is generally undertaken as an income enhancement technique. For example, assume a trader owns a share currently priced at $100. She might write a call option on this share with an exercise price of $110 and an assumed price of $4. The option premium will be hers to keep. In exchange for accepting the $4 premium, our trader realizes that the underlying stock might be called away from her if the stock price exceeds $110. If the stock price fails to increase by $10, the option she has written will expire worthless, and she will be able to keep the income from selling the option without any further obligation. As this example indicates, the strategy turns on selling an option with a striking price far removed from the current value of the stock, because the intention is to keep the premium without surrendering the stock through exercise.

While writing covered calls can often serve the purpose of enhancing income, it must be remembered that there is no free lunch in the options market. The writer of the covered call is actually exchanging the chance of large gains on the stock position in favor of income from selling the option. For example, if the stock price were to rise to $120, the trader would not receive this benefit, because the stock would be called away from her.

Figure 11.21 graphs the profits and losses at expiration for the example we have been considering. The solid line shows the profits and losses for the stock itself, while the dotted line shows the profits and losses for the covered call (the stock plus short call). For any stock price less than or equal to $110, the written call cannot be exercised against our trader, and she receives whatever profits or losses the stock earns plus the $4 option premium. Thus, she is $4 better off with the covered call than she would be with the stock alone for any stock price of $110 or less. If the stock price exceeds $110, the option will be exercised against her, and she must surrender the stock. This potential exercise places an upper limit on her profit at $14. If the stock price had risen to $120 and the trader had not written the call, her profit would have been $20 on the stock investment alone. In the covered call position, she would have made only $14, because the stock would have been called away from her. The desirability of writing a covered call to enhance income depends upon the chance that the stock price will exceed the exercise price at which the trader writes the call.

Profits and Losses at Expiration for a Covered Call Figure 11.21

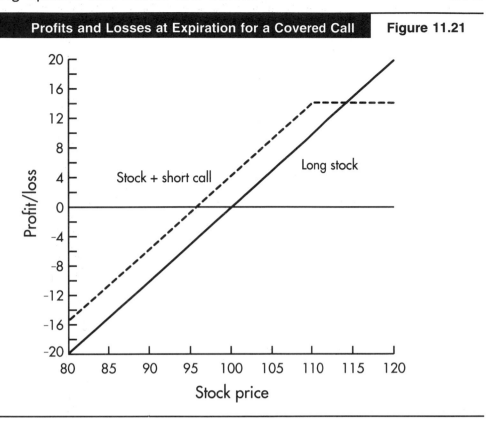

Portfolio Insurance: Stock Plus a Long Put

Along with program trading, portfolio insurance was a dominant investing technique developed in the 1980s. **Portfolio insurance** is an investment management technique designed to protect a stock portfolio from severe drops in value. Investment managers can implement portfolio insurance strategies in various ways. Some use options, while others use futures, and still others use combinations of other instruments. We analyze a simple strategy for implementing portfolio insurance with options. Portfolio insurance applies only to portfolios, not individual stocks. Therefore, for our discussion we assume that the underlying good is a well-diversified portfolio of common stocks. We may think of the portfolio as consisting of the Standard & Poor's 100. This is convenient because a popular stock index option is based on the S&P 100. Therefore, the portfolio insurance problem we consider is protecting the value of this stock portfolio from large drops in value.[7]

In essence, portfolio insurance with options involves holding a stock portfolio and buying a put option on the portfolio.[8] If we have a long position in the stock portfolio, the profits and losses from holding the portfolio consist of the profits and losses from the individual stocks. Therefore, the profits and losses for the portfolio resemble the typical stock's profits and losses.

Let S_t be the cost of the stock portfolio at time t, and let P_t be a put option on the portfolio. The cost of an insured portfolio is, therefore:

$$S_t + P_t$$

Because the price of a put is always positive, it is clear that an insured portfolio costs more than the uninsured stock portfolio alone. At expiration, the value of the insured portfolio is:

$$S_T + P_T = S_T + MAX\{0, X - S_T\} \qquad (11.13)$$

As the profit on an uninsured portfolio is $S_T - S_t$, the insured portfolio has a superior performance when $MAX\{0, X - S_T\} - P_t - S_t > 0$.

As an example of an insured portfolio, consider an investment in the stock index at a value of 100.00. Figure 11.22 shows the profit and loss profiles for an investment in the index at 100 and for a put option on the index. The figure assumes that the put has a striking price of 100.00 and costs 4.00 (we are expressing all values in terms of the index). Figure 11.23 shows the effects of combining an investment in the index stocks and buying a put on the index. For comparison, Figure 11.23 also shows the profits and losses from a long position in the index itself.

The insured portfolio, the index plus a long put, offers protection against large drops in value. If the stock index suddenly falls to 90.00, the insured portfolio loses only 4.00. No matter how low the index goes, the insured portfolio can lose only 4.00 points. However, this insurance has a cost. Investment in the index itself shows a profit for any index value over 100.00. By contrast, the insured portfolio has a profit only if the index climbs above 104.00. In the insured portfolio, the index must climb high enough to offset the price of buying the insuring put option. Because the put option will expire, keeping the portfolio insured requires that the investor buy a series of put options to keep the

Figure 11.22	Profits and Losses at Expiration for a Stock Index and a Put

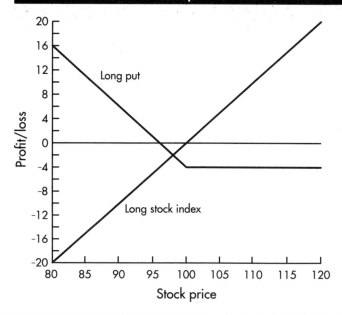

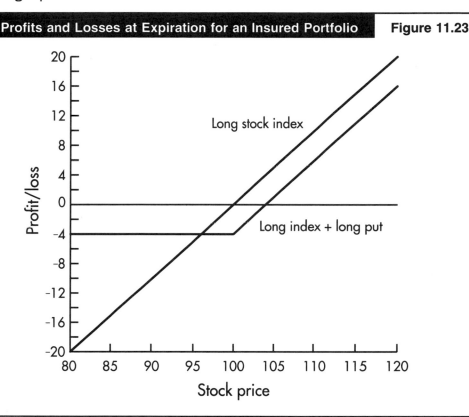

Profits and Losses at Expiration for an Insured Portfolio   **Figure 11.23**

insurance in force. In Figure 11.23, notice that the combined position of a long index and a long put gives a payoff shape that matches a long position in a call. Like a call, the insured portfolio protects against extremely unfavorable outcomes as the stock price falls. This similarity between the insured portfolio and a call position suggests that a trader might buy a call and invest the extra proceeds in a bond in order to replicate a position in an insured portfolio.

As a further comparison, we consider the likely profits from holding the stock portfolio and the insured portfolio. Let us assume that the option expires in one year. The stock portfolio is expected to appreciate about 10 percent and have a standard deviation of 15 percent. We also assume that the returns on the stock portfolio are normally distributed. Thus, a $100 investment in the stock portfolio would have an expected terminal value of $110 in one year. Under these assumptions, Figure 11.24 shows the probability distribution of the stock portfolio's terminal value. With a standard deviation of 15 percent there is approximately a two-thirds chance that the terminal value of the portfolio will lie between $95 and $125 dollars. This conclusion results from a feature of the normal distribution. About 67 percent of all observations from a normal distribution lie within one standard deviation of the mean.

With the insured portfolio, we have already seen that the maximum loss is $4. Therefore, the terminal value of the insured portfolio must be at least $96. However, Figures 11.23 and 11.24 imply that there is a good chance that the insured portfolio's terminal value will be $96. For the stock

Figure 11.24   **Probability Distribution for a Stock Index's Terminal Value**

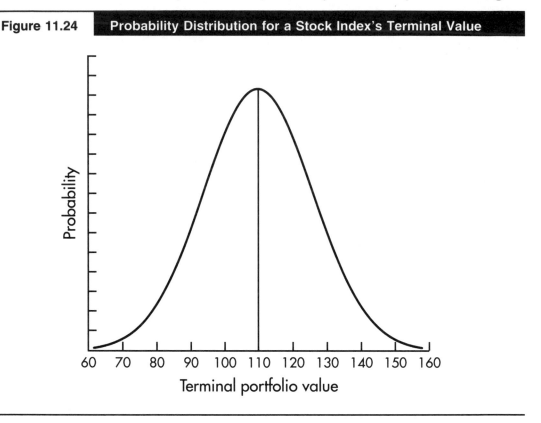

portfolio, any terminal value of $100 or less gives a $96 terminal value for the insured portfolio. While the insured portfolio protects against large losses, it has a lower chance of a really large payoff. For the insured portfolio to have a terminal value of $136, for example, the stock portfolio must be worth $140. This is two standard deviations above the expected return on the stock portfolio, however, and there is little chance of such a favorable outcome.

Figure 11.25 compares the distribution of returns for the stock and for the insured portfolios. The figure presents the cumulative probability distribution for each portfolio. For the stock portfolio, the line in Figure 11.25 merely presents the cumulative probability consistent with Figure 11.24. The kinked line in Figure 11.25 corresponds to the insured portfolio. The probability of a terminal value below $96 for the insured portfolio is zero, because that is exactly what the insurance guarantees. However, there is a very good chance that the terminal value for the insured portfolio will be $96. The probability of a $96 terminal value for the insured portfolio equals the probability that the stock portfolio will be worth $100 or less. As the graph shows, this probability is 25 percent. Notice also that the probability of a $96 or lower terminal value for the stock portfolio is 18 percent. This means that there is an 82 percent chance that the stock portfolio will outperform the insured portfolio, because there is an 82 percent chance that the stock portfolio will be worth more than $96.

As we consider terminal stock portfolio values above $96, we see that the line for the insured portfolio lies above the line for the stock portfolio in Figure 11.25. Consider a $110 terminal value

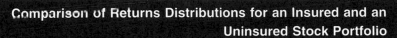

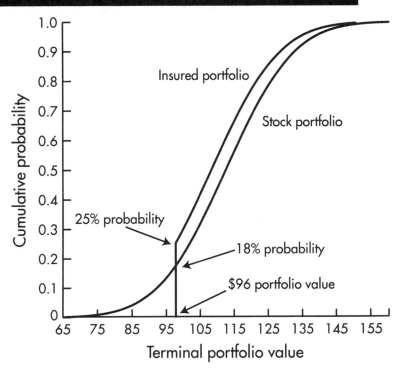

Comparison of Returns Distributions for an Insured and an Uninsured Stock Portfolio   **Figure 11.25**

for the stock portfolio. Because the distribution is normal and the expected return is 10 percent, there is a 50 percent chance that the terminal value of the stock portfolio will be $110 or less. Because the line for the insured portfolio lies above the line for the stock portfolio, there is a higher probability that the insured portfolio's value will be $110 or less. The probability of a terminal value for the insured portfolio of $110 or less is 61 percent. Correlatively, there is a 50 percent chance of a terminal stock portfolio value above $110 and only a 39 percent chance of a terminal value above $110 for the insured portfolio. Thus, because the insured portfolio's cumulative probability line lies above that for the stock portfolio at higher terminal prices, the stock portfolio has a better chance of higher returns. Figure 11.25 shows that the insured portfolio sacrifices chances of a large gain to avoid the chance of a large loss. Which investment is better depends on the risk preferences of the investor. The important point to recognize is the role of options in adjusting the returns distribution for the underlying investment. With options, we can adjust the distribution to fit our tastes – subject to the risk and return trade-off governing the entire market.[9]

Finally, we also observe that the insured portfolio has the same profits and losses as a call option. In fact, the profit and loss graph for the insured portfolio matches that of a call option with a striking price of 100.00 and a price of 4.00. This does not mean, however, that the insured portfolio and such a call option would have the same value. At expiration, the call will have no residual value beyond its profit and loss at that moment. By contrast, the insured portfolio will still include the underlying value of the investment in the stock index. Therefore, for a particular time horizon, two different investments can have the same profit and loss patterns without having the same value.

Mimicking and Synthetic Portfolios

We now study how European options can be combined with other instruments (notably the underlying stock and the risk-free bond) to create specialized payoff patterns at expiration. As we will see, it is possible to create portfolios of European options, the underlying stock, and the risk-free bond that simulate another instrument in key respects. We define two basic types of relationships, mimicking portfolios and synthetic instruments.[10]

A **mimicking portfolio** has the same profits and losses as the instrument or portfolio that it mimics, but it does not necessarily have the same value. A **synthetic instrument** has the same profits and losses, as well as the same value, as the instrument it synthetically replicates. For example, we will see that it is possible to create a portfolio of instruments that has the same value and the same profits and losses as a put. In this case, the portfolio would be known as a synthetic put.

Mimicking Stock: Long Call plus a Short Put. By combining a long position in a European call and a short position in a European put, we can create an option position that has the same profit and loss pattern at expiration as does the underlying stock. This long call/short put position costs:

$$c_t - p_t$$

At expiration, the payoff on this option combination is:

$$c_T - p_T = MAX\{0, S_T - X\} - MAX\{0, X - S_T\} \tag{11.14}$$

Assume for the moment that the call and put are chosen so that the exercise price equals the stock price at the time the put is purchased. That is, assume $X = S_t$. Under this special condition, the payoff on the long call/short put position is:

$$MAX\{0, S_T - S_t\} - MAX\{0, S_t - S_T\}$$

If the stock price rises, $S_T > S_t$, so the call is worth $S_T - S_t$ and the put is worth nothing. Notice that $S_T - S_t$ is just the profit on the stock portfolio alone. If the stock price falls, $S_t > S_T$. In this case, the call is worth zero, and the put is worth $S_t - S_T$. As the option combination includes a short position in the put, the payoff to the portfolio is $S_T - S_t$, which is the same as the stock portfolio. Thus, the long call/short put portfolio has a value that equals the profit or loss from investing in the underlying stock. Notice again that this special condition arises when the exercise price on the options equals the stock price at the time the option combination is purchased.

To illustrate this idea, consider a stock priced at $100 and call and put options with exercise prices of $100. Assume that the call costs $7 and the put costs $3. We want to compare two investments. The first investment is buying one share of stock for $100. The second investment is buying one call for $7 and selling one put for $3.

When the options expire, the two investments have parallel profits and losses. However, the profit on the stock will always be $4 greater than the profit on the option position. For example, assume the stock price is $110 at expiration. The stock has a profit of $10 and the option investment has a profit of $6. For the option position, the put expires worthless and the call has an exercise value of $10. From this exercise value we subtract the $4 net investment required to purchase the option position. Figure 11.26 graphs the profits and losses for both options, the stock, and the combined option position.

Investing in the stock costs $100, while the option position costs only $4. Yet the option position profits mimic those of the stock fairly closely. In a sense, the options give very high leverage by simulating the stock's profits and losses with a low investment. Many option traders view this high leverage of options as one of their prime advantages. Thus, a very small investment in the option position gives a position that mimics the profits and losses of a much more costly investment in the stock. In other words, the option position is much more elastic than the similar stock position.

The profit on the stock is always $4 greater than the profit on the option position. However, the stock investment costs $100, while the option position costs only $4. Therefore, the stock costs $96 more than the option position to guarantee a certain $4 extra profit over the option position. While the long call plus short put option position mimics the profits and losses on the stock, it does not

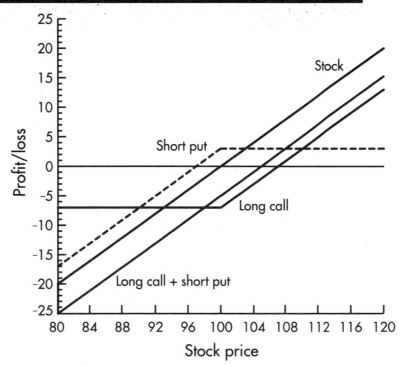

Profits and Losses at Expiration for the Elements of a Mimicking Portfolio   **Figure 11.26**

synthetically replicate the stock. As we will see, we can create a synthetic stock by adding investment in the risk-free bond to the option.

Synthetic Stock: Long Call, plus a Short Put, plus Bonds. As we have just seen, a long call combined with a short put can mimic the profit and loss pattern at the expiration date for the underlying stock. By adding an investment in the risk-free bond, we can create a portfolio that synthesizes the stock. In this case the synthetic stock will have the same value as well as an identical profit and loss pattern as the stock being synthesized. Therefore, this section shows that a long call, plus a short put, plus the right investment in the risk-free bond, can synthesize a stock investment. (Again, we are focusing on European options throughout this discussion, which we denote as c_t and p_t for the values of European calls and puts at time t.) As we will demonstrate, the investment in the risk-free bond should be the present value of the exercise price on the call and the put. Therefore, this formula for a synthetic stock is:

$$S_t = c_t - p_t + Xe^{-r(T-t)} \tag{11.15}$$

where:

r = risk-free rate of interest

At expiration, the value of this portfolio (for both American and European options) will be:

$$c_T - p_T + X = \text{MAX}\{0, S_T - X\} - \text{MAX}\{0, X - S_T\} + X$$

We know that the stock price can be above, equal to, or below the exercise price. If the stock price at expiration exceeds the exercise price, the call is worth $S_T - X$, and the put is worthless. The value of the portfolio consists of the value of the call, plus the maturing bond, or $S_T - X + X = S_T$. This is exactly the same value as the stock at the expiration date. If the stock price is below the exercise price on the expiration date of the options, then the call is worthless and the put has a value equal to $X - S_T$. Because the portfolio consists of a short position in the put, the value of the portfolio, including the maturing bond, is $S_T - X + X = S_T$. Again, the value of the long call/short put/long bond is the same as that of the underlying stock. If the terminal value of the stock equals the exercise price, X, then both the call and put are worthless and the value of the synthetic stock portfolio is just X, the value of the maturing risk-free investment. But in this situation, it remains true that the value of the synthetic stock is equal to that of the stock itself, because $S_T = X$.

We can illustrate this synthetic stock by considering the same stock selling for $100 and the same options we considered in the previous section. Comparing just the value of the stock position versus the value of the option position at expiration, the stock position will always be worth $100 more than the option position. For example, assume the stock price is $120 at expiration. Then, the stock investment is worth $120. The option position will be worth $20, because the call can be exercised for $20 and the put will be worthless. To synthesize the stock, we need to buy a risk-free bond that pays $100 at expiration. We can think of this investment as buying a one-year Treasury bill with a face value of $100. Notice that the payoff on the Treasury bill equals the exercise price for the options. We now have two portfolios that will have identical values at the expiration date:

Investment	Cash Flow
Portfolio A	
Long position in the stock	$100
Portfolio B	
Long position in the call	–$7
Short position in the put	+3
A bond paying the exercise price of $100 at expiration	?

Thus far in the example, we have not said how much the bond should cost. However, we can employ our no-arbitrage principle for guidance. We know that both portfolios will have the same value in one year when the option expires. To avoid arbitrage, the two portfolios must have the same value now as well. This condition implies that the bond must cost $96 and that the interest rate must be 4.17 percent.

To see why the bond must cost $96, we consider the arbitrage opportunity that results with any other bond price. For example, assume that the bond costs $93. With this low bond price, Portfolio A is too expensive relative to Portfolio B. To exploit the arbitrage opportunity, we sell the overpriced Portfolio A and buy the underpriced Portfolio B, transacting as follows:

Transaction	Cash Flow
Sell the stock	$100
Buy the call	–7
Sell the put	+3
Buy the bond	–93
Net Cash Flow	+$3

When the options expire in one year, we can close out all the positions without any additional investment. To close the position, we buy back the stock and honor any obligation we have from selling the put. Fortunately, we will have $100 in cash from the maturing bond we bought. For example, if the stock price at expiration is $90, our call is worthless and the put is exercised against us. Therefore, we use the proceeds from the maturing T-bill to pay the $100 exercise price for the put that is exercised against us. We now have the stock and in return use it to close our short position in the stock. The total result at expiration is that we can honor all obligations with zero cash flow. This is true no matter what the stock price is. Therefore, the cheap price on the bond gave us an arbitrage profit of $3 when we made the initial transaction. The transactions are an arbitrage because they require no investment and offer a riskless profit. With an initial cash inflow of $3, there is clearly no investment. Also, we make a riskless profit immediately when we transact. Any bond price below $96 will permit the arbitrage transactions we have just described.

If the bond is priced higher than $96, Portfolio B is overpriced relative to Portfolio A. We then sell Portfolio B and buy Portfolio A. Again, we have an arbitrage profit. To see how to make an arbitrage profit from a bond price that is too high, assume the bond price is $98. We then transact as follows:

Transaction	Cash Flow
Buy the stock	−$100
Sell the call	+7
Buy the put	−3
Sell the bond	+98
Net Cash Flow	+$2

In one year, the options will expire and the bond will mature. Selling the bond means that we borrow $98 and promise to repay $100, so we will owe $100 on the bond at expiration. However, no matter what the stock price is at expiration, we can dispose of the stock and close the option positions for a cash inflow of $100. This gives exactly what we need to pay our debt on the bond. For example, assume the stock price is $93. The call we sold expires worthless, but we can exercise the put. When we exercise the put, we deliver the stock and receive the $100 exercise price. This amount repays the bond debt. Any bond price greater than $96 will permit this same kind of arbitrage transaction.

The Synthetic Put: The Put-Call Parity Relationship. We have just seen that we can buy a call, short a put, and invest in a risk-free bond to create a synthetic stock. In fact, with any three of these four instruments, we can synthesize the fourth. This section illustrates **put-call parity** – the relationship between put, call, stock, and bond prices. Specifically, put-call parity shows how to synthesize a put option by selling the stock, buying a call, and investing in a risk-free bond. Put-call parity asserts that a put is worth the same as a long call, short stock, and a risk-free investment that pays the exercise price on the common expiration date of the put and call. The put-call parity relationship is:

$$p_t = c_t - S_t + Xe^{-r(T-t)} \qquad (11.16)$$

To create a put from the other instruments, we use our previous example of a stock selling at $100, a call option worth $7 with a strike price of $100, and a bond costing $96 that will pay $100 in one year. From these securities, we can synthesize the put option costing $3 with an exercise price of $100. To create a synthetic put, we transact as follows:

Investment	Cash Flow
Portfolio C	
Buy the call	−$7
Sell the stock	+100
Buy a bond that pays the exercise price at maturity	−$96
Net Cash Flow	−$3

In buying Portfolio C, we have the same cash outflow of $3 that buying the put requires. To show that Portfolio C is equivalent to a put with a $3 price and a $100 exercise price, we consider the value of Portfolio C when the stock price equals, exceeds, or is less than $100.

If the stock price is $100 at expiration, the call in Portfolio C is worthless, but we receive $100 from the maturing bond, with which we buy the stock. This disposes of the entire portfolio. The entire portfolio is worth zero, just as the put is worth zero. For any stock price above $100, Portfolio C, like the put itself, is worthless. We can then exercise the call and use the proceeds from the bond to pay the exercise price on the call. This gives us the stock, which we owe to cover our earlier sale of the stock. Thus, we have met all obligations arising from owning Portfolio C. To illustrate this outcome, consider a terminal stock price of $105. In this case, the put would be worthless. Therefore, Portfolio C should be worthless as well. With a stock price of $105, we would exercise the call, paying for the exercise with the proceeds of our maturing bond. We receive a stock worth $105. However, we must repay our short sale of the stock by returning this share. Therefore, there is no net cash flow at the exercise date. Finally, for a stock price less than $100, Portfolio C is worth the difference between the exercise price and the stock price. If the stock price is $95, the call option expires worthless. We receive $100 on the bond investment and use $95 of this to repurchase the stock that we owe. Thus Portfolio C is worth $5, just as the put itself would be.

Considering our profits on Portfolio C, we lose $3 for any stock price of $100 or more, because Portfolio C is then worthless at expiration and it costs $3. For any stock price at expiration less than $100, Portfolio C is worth the exercise price of $100 minus the stock price. Notice that this is an exact description of the profit and losses on the put. Therefore, Portfolio C synthetically replicates the put option with an exercise price of $100 that costs $3.

Put-call parity has another important implication. Assume that $S_t = X$. In this situation, the call will be worth more than the put. To prove this principle, consider the following rearrangement of the put-call parity formula:

$$c_t - p_t = S_t - Xe^{-r(T-t)}$$

If $S_t = X$, the right-hand side of this equation must be positive, because the exercise price X is being discounted. Therefore, the quantity $c_t - p_t$ must also be positive, and this implies that the call price must exceed the put price in this special circumstance.

CONCLUSION

This chapter has explored the value and profits from option positions at expiration. The concept of arbitrage provided a general framework for understanding option values and profits. We began by studying the characteristic payoffs for positions in single options, noting that there are four basic possibilities of being long or short a call or a put.

We then considered how to combine options to create special positions with unique risk and return characteristics. These option combinations included straddles, strangles, bull and bear spreads, butterfly spreads, condors, and a box spread. As we observed, a trader can either buy or sell each of these option combinations and most can be created using either puts or calls. Each gives its own risk and return profile, which differs from the position in a single option.

We also considered combinations among options, stocks, and bonds. We considered the advantages and disadvantages of covered call writing, and explored how to insure a portfolio by using a put option. We also showed that a combination of options could mimic the profit and loss profile of a stock. To create a synthetic stock we used a call, a put, and investment in a risk-free bond. The mimicking portfolio has the same profit and loss patterns, while a synthetic instrument has the identical profit and loss characteristics and the same value as the instrument being synthesized. We also showed how to create a synthetic put by trading a call, a stock, and the risk-free bond to illustrate the put-call parity relationship. In general, we conclude that put, call, bond, and stock prices are all related and that any one can be synthesized by a combination of the other three.

QUESTIONS AND PROBLEMS

1. Consider a call option with an exercise price of $80 and a cost of $5. Graph the profits and losses at expiration for various stock prices.

2. Consider a put option with an exercise price of $80 and a cost of $4. Graph the profits and losses at expiration for various stock prices.

3. For the call and put in Questions 1 and 2, graph the profits and losses at expiration for a straddle comprising these two options. If the stock price is $80 at expiration, what will be the profit or loss? At what stock price (or prices) will the straddle have a zero profit?

4. A call option has an exercise price of $70 and is at expiration. The option costs $4 and the underlying stock trades for $75. Assuming a perfect market, how would you respond if the call is an American option? State exactly how you might transact. How does your answer differ if the option is European?

5. A stock trades for $120. A put on this stock has an exercise price of $140 and is about to expire. The put trades for $22. How would you respond to this set of prices? Explain.

6. If the stock trades for $120 and the expiring put with an exercise price of $140 trades for $18, how would you trade?

7. Consider a call and a put on the same underlying stock. The call has an exercise price of $100 and costs $20. The put has an exercise price of $90 and costs $12. Graph a short position in a strangle based on these two options. What is the worst outcome from selling the strangle? At what stock price or prices does the strangle have a zero profit?

8. Assume that you buy a call with an exercise price of $100 and a cost of $9. At the same time, you sell a call with an exercise price of $110 and a cost of $5. The two calls have the same underlying stock and the same expiration. What is this position called? Graph the profits and losses at expiration from this position. At what stock price or prices will the position show a zero profit? What is the worst loss that the position can incur? For what range of stock prices does this worst outcome occur? What is the best outcome and for what range of stock prices does it occur?

9. Consider three call options with the same underlying stock and the same expiration. Assume that you take a long position in a call with an exercise price of $40 and a long position in a call with an exercise price of $30. At the same time, you sell two calls with an exercise price of $35. What position have you created? Graph the value of this position at expiration. What is the value of this position at expiration if the stock price is $90? What is the position's value for a stock price of $15? What is the lowest value the position can have at expiration? For what range of stock prices does this worst value occur?

10. Assume that you buy a portfolio of stocks with a portfolio price of $100. A put option on this portfolio has a striking price of $95 and costs $3. Graph the combined portfolio of the stock plus a long position in the put. What is the worst outcome that can occur at expiration? For what range of portfolio prices will this worst outcome occur? What is this position called?

11. Consider a stock that sells for $95. A call on this stock has an exercise price of $95 and costs $5. A put on this stock also has an exercise price of $95 and costs $4. The call and the put have the same expiration. Graph the profit and losses at expiration from holding the long call and short put. How do these profits and losses compare with the value of the stock at expiration? If the stock price is $80 at expiration, what is the portfolio of options worth? If the stock price is

$105, what is the portfolio of options worth? Explain why the stock and option portfolio differ as they do.

12. Assume a stock trades for $120. A call on this stock has a striking price of $120 and costs $11. A put also has a striking price of $120 and costs $8. A risk-free bond promises to pay $120 at the expiration of the options in one year. What should the price of this bond be? Explain.

13. In the preceding question, if we combine the two options and the bond, what will the value of this portfolio be relative to the stock price at expiration? Explain. What principle does this illustrate?

14. Consider a stock that is worth $50. A put and call on this stock have an exercise price of $50 and expire in one year. The call costs $5 and the put costs $4. A risk-free bond will pay $50 in one year and costs $45. How will you respond to these prices? State your transactions exactly. What principle do these prices violate?

15. A stock sells for $80 and the risk-free rate of interest is 11 percent. A call and a put on this stock expire in one year and both options have an exercise price of $75. How would you trade to create a synthetic call option? If the put sells for $2, how much is the call option worth? (Assume annual compounding.)

16. A stock costs $100 and a risk-free bond paying $110 in one year costs $100 as well. What can you say about the cost of a put and a call on this stock that both expire in one year and that both have an exercise price of $110? Explain.

17. Assume that you buy a strangle with exercise prices on the constituent options of $75 and $80. You also sell a strangle with exercise prices of $70 and $85. Describe the payoffs on the position you have created. Does this portfolio of options have a payoff pattern similar to that of any of the combinations explored in this chapter?

18. If a stock sells for $75 and a call and put together cost $9 and the two options expire in one year and have an exercise price of $70, what is the current rate of interest?

19. Assume you buy a bull spread with puts that have exercise prices of $40 and $45. You also buy a bear spread with puts that have exercise prices of $45 and $50. What will this total position be worth if the stock price at expiration is $53? Does this position have any special name? Explain.

20. Explain the difference between a box spread and a synthetic risk-free bond.

21. Within the context of the put-call parity relationship, consider the value of a call and a put option. What will the value of the put option be if the exercise price is zero? What will the value of the call option be in the same circumstance? What can you say about potential bounds on the value of the call and put option?

22. Using the put-call parity relationship, write the value of a call option as a function of the stock price, the risk-free bond, and the put option. Now consider a stock price that is dramatically in excess of the exercise price. What happens to the value of the put as the stock price becomes extremely large relative to the exercise price? What happens to the value of the call option?

NOTES

[1] Recall that we are ignoring transaction costs. In the options market, both buyers and sellers incur transaction costs. Therefore, the options market is a negative sum game if we include transaction costs in our analysis.

[2] The arbitrage arguments used in this chapter stem from a famous paper by R. C. Merton, "Theory of Rational Option Pricing," *Bell Journal of Economics and Management Science,* 4, Spring 1973, pp. 141–83.

[3] The buyer of a straddle need not be matched with a trader who specifically sells a straddle. Opposite the buyer of a straddle could be two individuals, one of whom sells a call and the other of whom sells a put.

[4] The theoretically maximum loss for the short straddle trader occurs when the stock price goes to zero. In this case, the call cannot be exercised against the short trader, but the put will be exercised. Thus, the trader will lose $X - S = X - 0 = X$ on the exercise. This loss will be partially offset by the funds received from selling the straddle $(C_t + P_t)$, so the total loss will be: $X - C_t - P_t$.

[5] It is also possible to execute similar strategies with combinations of options and the underlying instrument.

[6] The reader should note that the use of terms such as bear spread and bull spread is not standardized. While this book uses these terms in familiar ways, other traders may use them differently.

[7] Three introductory studies of portfolio insurance are: P. A. Abken, "An Introduction to Portfolio Insurance," *Federal Reserve Bank of Atlanta, Economic Review,* 72:6, November/December 1987, pp. 2–25; and T. J. O'Brien, "The Mechanics of Portfolio Insurance," *Journal of Portfolio Management,* 14:3, Spring 1988, pp. 40–47. In his paper, "Simplifying Portfolio Insurance," *Journal of Portfolio Management,* 14:1, Fall 1987, pp. 48–51, Fischer Black shows how to insure a portfolio without using option pricing theory, and he shows how to establish an insured portfolio without a definite horizon date.

[8] It is possible to create an insured portfolio without using options. These alternative strategies employ stock index futures with continuous rebalancing of the futures position. Because of this continuous rebalancing, these strategies are called "dynamic hedging" strategies. Hayne E. Leland, "Option Pricing and Replication with Transaction Costs," *Journal of Finance,* 40, December 1985, pp. 1283–1301, discusses these dynamic strategies. With a dynamic strategy, the insurer must rebalance the portfolio very frequently, leading to a trade-off between having an exactly insured portfolio and high transaction costs. J. Clay Singleton and Robin Grieves discuss this trade-off in their paper, "Synthetic Puts and Portfolio Insurance Strategies," *Journal of Portfolio Management,* 10:3, Spring 1984, pp. 63–69. Richard Bookstaber, "Portfolio Insurance Trading Rules," *Journal of Futures Markets,* 8:1, February 1988, pp. 15–31, discusses some recent technological innovations in portfolio insurance strategies and foresees increasing complexity and sophistication in the implementation of insurance techniques.

[9] Several studies have explored the cost of portfolio insurance. Richard J. Rendleman, Jr., and Richard W. McEnally, "Assessing the Cost of Portfolio Insurance," *Financial Analysts Journal,* 43, May/June 1987, pp. 27–37, compare the desirability of an insured portfolio relative to a utility-maximizing strategy. They conclude that only extremely risk-averse investors will be willing to incur the costs of insuring a portfolio. Richard Bookstaber found similar results in his paper, "The Use of Options in Performance Structuring: Modeling Returns to Meet Investment Objectives," in *Controlling Interest Rate Risk: New Techniques and Applications for Money Management,* Robert B. Platt (ed.), New York: Wiley, 1986. According to Bookstaber, completely insuring a portfolio costs about 25 percent of the portfolio's total return. C. B. Garcia and F. J. Gould, "An Empirical Study of Portfolio Insurance," *Financial Analysts Journal,* July/ August 1987, pp. 44–54, find that fully insuring a portfolio causes a loss of returns of about 100 basis points. They conclude that an insured portfolio is not likely to outperform a static portfolio of stocks and T-bills. Roger G. Clarke and Robert D. Arnott study the costs of portfolio insurance directly in their paper, "The Cost of Portfolio Insurance: Tradeoffs and Choices," *Financial Analysts Journal,* 43:6, November/ December 1987, pp. 35–47. Clarke and Arnott explore the desirability of only insuring part of the portfolio, increasing the risk of the portfolio, and attempting to insure a portfolio for a longer horizon. As they conclude, transaction costs are an important factor in choosing the optimal strategy.

[10] These synthetic relationships hold exactly only for European options. In Chapter 15, we explore the reasons for this restriction within the context of our discussion of American options.

CHAPTER 12

BOUNDS ON OPTION PRICES

OVERVIEW

This chapter continues to use no-arbitrage conditions to explore option pricing principles. In the last chapter, we considered the prices options could have at expiration, consistent with no-arbitrage conditions. In this chapter, we consider option prices before expiration. Extending our analysis to options with time remaining until expiration brings new factors into consideration.

The value of an option before expiration depends on five factors: the price of the underlying stock, the exercise price of the option, the time remaining until expiration, the risk-free rate of interest, and the possible price movements on the underlying stock.[1] For stocks with dividends, the potential dividend payments during an option's life can also influence the value of the option. In this chapter, we focus on the intuition underlying the relationship between put and call prices and these factors. The next chapter builds on these intuitions to specify these relationships more formally.

We first consider how option prices respond to changes in the stock price, the time remaining until expiration, and the exercise price of the option. These factors set general boundaries for possible option prices. Later in the chapter, we discuss the influence of interest rates on option prices, and we consider how the riskiness of the stock affects the price of the option.

THE BOUNDARY SPACE FOR CALL AND PUT OPTIONS

In Chapter 11, we saw that the value of a call (either European or American) at expiration must be:

$$C_T = \text{MAX}\{0, S_T - X\} \tag{12.1}$$

Similarly, the value of a put (either European or American) at expiration is:

$$P_T = \text{MAX}\{0, X - S_T\} \tag{12.2}$$

where:

C_t = the call price at time t
P_t = the put price at time t
S_t = the stock price at time t
X = the exercise price at time t
T = the expiration date of the option

Corresponding to Equations 12.1 and 12.2, we saw that call and put options had distinctive graphs that specified their values at expiration. Figure 11.4 for a call and Figure 11.6 for a put gave the value of the options at expiration. These two figures simply graph Equations 12.1 and 12.2, respectively. Now we want to consider the range of possible values for call and put options more generally. Specifically, we want to analyze the values that options can have before expiration.[2]

Said another way, we want to explore the values of options as a function of the stock price, S, the exercise price, X, and the time remaining until expiration, $T - t$. In Chapter 11, we only considered options that were at expiration, with $t = T$. Thus, we were considering option values for various ranges of stock price and exercise prices, but with zero time to expiration. Now, we want to consider option prices when the stock price, the exercise price, and the time to expiration all vary.

Before expiration, call and put values need not conform to Equations 12.1 and 12.2. Therefore, our first task is to determine the entire possible range of prices that calls and puts may have before expiration. We call this range of possibilities the **boundary space** for an option. Once we specify the largest range of possible prices, we consider no-arbitrage principles that will help us specify the price of an option more precisely.

The Boundary Space for a Call Option

To define the boundary space for a call option, we consider extreme values for the variables that affect call prices. Because we first focus on the stock price, exercise price, and the time remaining until expiration, we consider extremely high and low values for each of these variables. First, the value of a call option will depend on the stock price. We have already seen that a call option at expiration is worth more the greater the price of the stock. Second, the value of a call option depends on the exercise price of the option. Third, the value of a call can depend on the time remaining until the option expires.

The owner of a call option receives the stock upon exercise. The stock price represents the potential benefit that will come to the holder of a call, so the higher the stock price, the greater the value of a call option. We have already observed this to be true at expiration, as Equation 12.1 shows. Also, the exercise price is a cash outflow if the call owner exercises. As such, the exercise price represents a potential liability to the call owner. The lower the liability associated with a call, the better for the call owner. Therefore, the lower the exercise price, the greater the value of a call. Finally, consider the time remaining until expiration. For clarity we focus on two American options that differ only because one has a longer time remaining until expiration. Comparing these two options, we see that the one with the longer time until expiration gives every benefit that the one with the shorter time until expiration does. At a given moment, if the shorter term option permits expiration, so does the option with a longer term until expiration. In addition, the longer term option allows the privilege of waiting longer to decide whether to exercise. Generally, this privilege of waiting is quite valuable, so the option with the longer life tends to have a higher value. However, no matter what happens, the option with the longer life must have a price at least as great as the option with the shorter life. We will see that the same holds true for European options. The longer the time until expiration, the greater the value of the option, holding other factors constant.

We have seen that lower exercise prices and longer lives generally increase the value of an option. Therefore, the value of an option will be highest for an option with a zero exercise price and an infinite time until expiration. Similarly, the value will be lowest for an option with a higher exercise price and the shortest time until expiration. A call that is about to expire, with $t = T$, will be the call with the lowest price for a given stock price and a given exercise price. We already know the possible values that such an expiring option can have. This value is simply the call option's price at expiration, which is given by Equation 12.1. At the other extreme, the call with the highest possible value for a given stock price will be the call with a zero exercise price and an infinite time until expiration.

This call option with a zero exercise price and an infinite time until it expires allows us to exercise the option with zero cost and acquire the stock. In short, we can transform this option into the stock any time we wish without paying anything. Therefore, the value of this call must equal the price of the underlying stock. If we can get the stock for zero any time we wish, the price of the call cannot be more than the stock price. Also, the price of the call cannot exceed the stock price, because the call can only be used to acquire the stock. Therefore, we know that a call on a given stock, with a zero exercise price, and an infinite time to expiration, must have a value equal to the stock price. In this special limiting case, $C_t = S_t$.

From this analysis, we have now determined the upper and lower bounds for the price of a call option before expiration. Figure 12.1 depicts the boundaries for the price of a call option as the

The Boundary Space for a Call Option   **Figure 12.1**

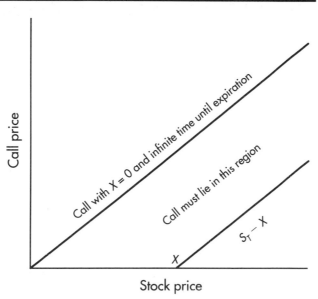

interior area between the upper and lower bounds. The upper bound for any call option is the stock price. The figure shows this boundary as the 45 degree line from the origin. Along this line, the call option is worth the same as the stock. The lower bound is the value of the call option at expiration. At expiration, if the stock price is at or below the exercise price, the call is worth zero. For any stock price above the exercise price, the expiring call is worth the stock price minus the exercise price. Therefore, the value of a call option must always fall somewhere on or within the bounds given by these lines. Later in this chapter, we develop principles that help us to specify much more precisely where within these bounds the actual option price must lie.

The Boundary Space for a Put Option

We now consider the range of possible put prices. We have already considered prices for puts at expiration, and we found the value of a put at expiration to conform to Equation 12.2. Equation 12.2 gives the lower bound for the value of a put option. To find the upper bounds for a put option, we need to consider the best possible circumstances for the owner of a put option.

Upon exercise, the owner of a put surrenders the stock and receives the exercise price. The most the put holder can receive is the exercise price, and he can obtain this only by surrendering the stock. Therefore, the lower the stock price, the more valuable the put must be. This is true before expiration and at expiration, as we have already seen. The owner of an American put can exercise the option at any time. Therefore, the maximum value for an American put is the exercise price. The price of an American put equals the exercise price if the stock is worthless and is sure to remain worthless until the option expires. If the put is a European put, it cannot be exercised immediately, but only at expiration. For a European put before expiration, the maximum possible price equals the present value of the exercise price. The European put price cannot exceed the present value of the exercise price, because the owner of a European put must wait until expiration to exercise.

Figure 12.2 shows the bounds for American and European puts. The price of a put can never fall below the maximum of zero or $X - S_T$. This is the put's value at expiration, which Equation 12.2 specifies. For an American put, the price can never exceed X. For a European put, the price can never exceed the present value of the exercise price, $Xe^{-r(T-t)}$. Therefore, the interior of Figure 12.2 defines the range of possible put prices. By developing more exact no-arbitrage conditions, we can say where in this interior area the price of a put can be found.[3]

RELATIONSHIPS BETWEEN CALL OPTION PRICES

In this section we focus on price relationships between call options. These price differences arise from differences in exercise price and time until expiration. We have already seen in an informal way that the exercise price is a potential liability associated with call ownership. The greater the value of this potential liability, the lower the value of the call option. In this section, we illustrate this principle more formally by appealing to our familiar no-arbitrage arguments. We use similar no-arbitrage arguments to explicate other pricing relationships. Unless explicitly stated otherwise, all of these relationships hold for both American and European calls.

The Lower the Exercise Price, the More Valuable the Call. Let us consider a single underlying stock on which there are two call options. The two call options have the same expiration date, but one option has a lower exercise price than the other. In this section, we want to show why the option

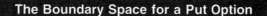

The Boundary Space for a Put Option   **Figure 12.2**

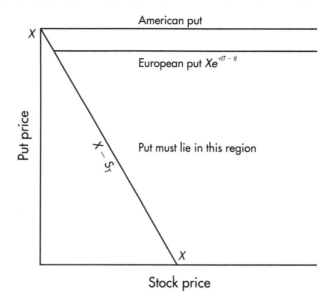

with the lower exercise price must be worth as much or more than the option with the higher exercise price. For example, assume that two calls exist that violate this principle:

	Time Until Expiration	Exercise Price	Call Price
Call A	6 months	$100	$20
Call B	6 months	95	15

These two calls violate our principle because Call A has a higher exercise price and a higher call price. These prices give rise to an arbitrage opportunity, as we now show. Faced with these prices, the trader can transact as follows:

Transaction	Cash Flow
Sell Call A	+$20
Buy Call B	−$15
Net Cash Flow	+$5

Once we sell Call A and buy Call B, we have a sure profit of at least $5. To see this, we consider profits and losses for various stock prices, such as $95 and below and $100 and above. If the stock price is $95, neither option can be exercised. If the stock price stays at $95 or below, both options expire worthless, and we keep our $5 from the initial transactions. If the stock price is greater than $100, say $105, Call A will be exercised against us. When that happens, we surrender the stock worth $105 and receive $100, losing $5 on the exercise against us. However, we ourselves exercise Call

B, receiving the stock worth $105 and paying the exercise price of $95. So, we can summarize our profits and losses from the exercises that occur when the stock trades at $105.

Surrender stock	−$105
Receive $100 exercise price	+100
Pay $95 exercise price	−95
Receive stock	+105
Net Cash Flow	+$5

As the calculation shows, if Call A is exercised against us, we exercise Call B and make $5 on the double exercise. Therefore, we make a total of $10, $5 from the initial transaction and $5 on the exercises.

Next, we consider what happens if the stock price lies between $95 and $100, say at $97. This outcome is also beneficial for us, because the option we sold with a $100 strike price cannot be exercised against us. However, we can exercise our option. When we exercise, we pay the $95 exercise price and receive a stock worth $97. We add the $2 profit on this exercise to the $5 we made initially, for a total profit of $7. Figure 12.3 graphs the total profit on the position for all stock prices. With a stock price at or below $95, we make $5 because neither option can be exercised. With a stock price of $100 or above, we make $10–$5 from our initial transaction and $5 from the difference between the two exercise prices. If the stock price is between $95 and $100, we make $5 from our initial transaction plus the difference between the stock price and the $95 exercise price we face.

Figure 12.3   Arbitrage with Calls A and B

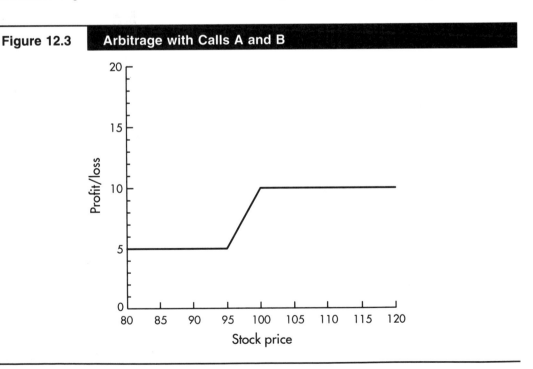

These transactions guarantee an arbitrage profit of at least $5, and perhaps as much as $10. Figure 12.3 reflects the arbitrage profit because it shows there is at least a $5 profit for any stock price. If the profit and loss graph shows profits for all possible stock prices with no investment, then there is an arbitrage opportunity. In the real world, an investment strategy that requires no initial investment may show profits for some stock price outcomes, but it must also show losses for other stock prices. Otherwise, there is an arbitrage opportunity.

In stating our principle, we said that the call with the lower exercise price must cost at least as much as the call with the higher exercise price. Why doesn't the call with the lower exercise price have to cost more than the call with the higher exercise price? In most real market situations, the call with the lower exercise price will, in fact, cost more. However, we cannot be sure that will happen as a general rule. To see why, assume the stock underlying Calls A and B trades for $5 and there is virtually no chance that the stock price could reach $90 before the two options expire. When the underlying stock is extremely far out-of-the-money, the calls might have the same, or nearly the same, price. In such a situation, both calls would have a very low price. If it is certain that the stock price can never rise to the lower exercise price, both calls would be worthless.

The Difference in Call Prices Cannot Exceed the Difference in Exercise Prices. Consider two call options that are similar in all respects except that they have exercise prices that differ by $5. We have already seen that the price of the call with the lower exercise price must equal or exceed the price of the call with the higher exercise price. Now we show that the difference in call prices cannot exceed the difference in exercise prices. We illustrate this principle by considering two call options with the same underlying stock:

	Time Until Expiration	**Exercise Price**	**Call Price**
Call C	6 months	$ 95	$10
Call D	6 months	100	4

The prices of Calls C and D do not meet our condition, and we want to show that these prices give rise to an arbitrage opportunity. To profit from this mispricing, we trade as follows:

Transaction	**Cash Flow**
Sell Call C	+$10
Buy Call D	−4
Net Cash Flow	+$6

Selling Call C and buying Call D gives a net cash inflow of $6. Because we sold a call, however, we also have the risk that the call will be exercised against us. We now show that no matter what stock price occurs, we still make a profit.

If the stock price is $95 or below, both options expire worthless, and we keep our initial cash inflow of $6. If the stock price exceeds $100, Call C is exercised against us and we exercise Call D. For example, assume the stock price is $102. We exercise, pay the $100 exercise price, and receive the stock. Call C is exercised against us, so we surrender the stock and receive the $95 exercise price. Therefore, we lose $5 on the exercise. This loss partially offsets our initial cash inflow of $6. Thus, for any stock price of $100 or more, we make $1. We now consider stock prices between $95 and $100. If the stock price is $98, Call C will be exercised against us. We surrender the stock worth

$98 and receive $95, for a $3 loss. The option we own cannot be exercised, because the exercise price of $100 exceeds the current stock price of $98. Therefore, we lose $3 on the exercise, which partially offsets our initial cash inflow of $6. This gives a $3 net profit.

Figure 12.4 shows the profits and losses on this trade for a range of stock prices. As the figure shows, we make at least $1, and we may make as much as $6. Because all outcomes show a profit with no investment, these transactions constitute an arbitrage. The chance to make this arbitrage profit stems from the fact that the call option prices differed by more than the difference between the exercise prices. In real markets, the difference between two call prices will usually be less than the difference in exercise prices. However, the difference in call prices cannot exceed the difference in exercise prices without creating an arbitrage opportunity.[4]

A Call Must Be Worth at Least the Stock Price Less the Present Value of the Exercise Price. We have already noted that a call at expiration is worth the maximum of zero or the stock price less the exercise price. Before expiration, the call must be worth at least the stock price less the present value of the exercise price. That is:

$$C_t \geq S_t - Xe^{-r(T-t)} \tag{12.3}$$

To see why prices must observe this principle, we consider the following situation. Assume the stock trades for $103 and the current risk-free interest rate is 6 percent. A call with an exercise price of $100 expires in six months and trades for $2. These prices violate our rule, because the call option price is too low: $2 is less than the stock price less the present value of $100. These prices give rise to an arbitrage opportunity. To take advantage, we trade as follows:

Figure 12.4   **Arbitrage with Calls C and D**

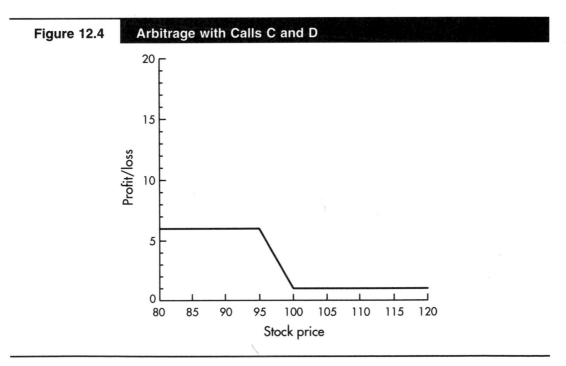

Sell the stock	+$103
Buy the call option	−2
Buy a bond with remaining funds	−101
Net Cash Flow	0

With these transactions, we owe one share of stock. However, with our call option and the money we have left from selling the stock, we can honor our obligations at any time and still have a profit. For example, at the beginning of the transactions, we can exercise our option, pay the $100 exercise price, return the stock, and keep $1.

Alternatively, we can wait until our option reaches expiration in six months. Then the bond we purchased with be worth $101e^{(.06)(.5)} = $104.08. Whatever the stock is worth at expiration, we can repay with profit. For example, if the stock price is higher than the exercise price, we exercise the option and pay $100 to get the stock. This gives a profit at expiration of $4.08. If the stock price is below the exercise price, we allow our option to expire. We then buy the stock in the open market and repay our debt of one share. For example, if the stock price is $95 at expiration, our option expires, and we pay $95 for the share to repay our obligation. Our profit then is $104.08 − $95 = $9.08. Figure 12.5 graphs the profits from this transaction.

From this analysis, we can see that our option must cost at least $103 −$100e^{-(.06)(.5)} = $103 − $97.04 = $5.96. Any lower price allows an arbitrage profit. If the call is priced at $5.96, we have $97.04 to invest in bonds after selling the stock at $103 and buying the option at $5.96. At expiration, our bond investment pays $100, which is the exercise price. If the option sold at $5.96, the profit line in Figure 12.5 would shift down to show a zero profit for any stock price of $100 or more. This

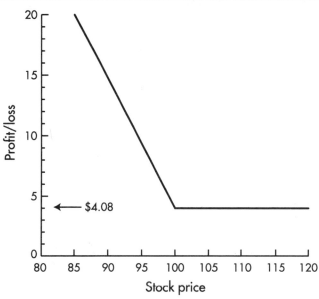

Arbitrage of a Call Against a Stock and Bond   **Figure 12.5**

would eliminate the arbitrage because there would be some stock prices that would give zero profits. However, in real markets the price of this call would generally be higher than $5.96. A price of $5.96 ensures against any loss and gives profits for any stock price below $100. If there is any chance that the stock price might be below $100 at expiration, then the call of our example should be worth more than $5.96.

The More Time Until Expiration, the Greater the Call Price. If we consider two call options with the same exercise price on the same underlying good, then the price of the call with more time remaining until expiration must equal or exceed the price of the call that expires sooner. Violating this principle leads to arbitrage, as the following example shows.

Consider two options on the same underlying good.

	Time Until Expiration	**Exercise Price**	**Call Price**
Call E	3 months	$100	$6
Call F	6 months	100	5

These prices violate our principle, which implies that Call F must cost at least as much as Call E. To capture the arbitrage profits, we trade as follows:

Transaction	**Cash Flow**
Sell Call E	+$6
Buy Call F	−5
Net Cash Flow	+$1

With a net cash inflow at the time of contracting, the transactions clearly require no investment. Therefore, they meet the first condition for an arbitrage. Next, we need to show that the strategy produces a profit for all stock price outcomes.

First, we show how to protect the arbitrage profit if the options are American options. Any time that Call E is exercised against us, we can exercise Call F to secure the stock to give to the holder of Call E. For example, assume that Call E is about to expire and is exercised against us with the stock price at $105. In that case, we simply exercise Call F and surrender the stock to the holder of Call E, as the following transactions show.

Assuming Call E and Call F Are American Options

Transaction	**Cash Flow**
Call E is exercised against us	
Receive $100 exercise price	+$100
Surrender stock worth $105	−105
Exercise Call F	
Receive stock worth $105	+105
Pay $100 exercise price	−100
Net Cash Flow	0

As these transactions show, if the call we sold is exercised against us, we can fulfill all our obligations by exercising our call. There will be no net cash flow on the exercise, and we keep the $1 profit from our original transaction.

Notice that our concluding transactions assumed that both Call E and Call F were American options. This allowed us to exercise our Call F before expiration. Had the options been European options, we could not exercise Call F when Call E was exercised against us. However, the principle still holds for European options – the European option with more time until expiration must be worth at least as much as the option with a shorter life. We can illustrate this principle for European options with the following transactions.

Assuming Call E and Call F Are European Options

Transaction	Cash Flow
Call E is exercised against us	
Receive $100 exercise price	+$100
Surrender stock worth $105	−105
Sell Call F	
Receive $S - Xe^{-r(T-t)} \geq \$5$	at least +5
Net Cash Flow	at least 0

As these transactions show, we will receive at least $5 for selling Call F. Earlier we used no-arbitrage arguments to show that an in-the-money call must be worth at least the stock price minus the present value of the exercise price. The worst situation for these transactions occurs at very low interest rates. However, the arbitrage still works for a zero interest rate. Then, Call F must still be worth at least $S - X = \$105 - \$100 = \$5$. If we get $5 from selling Call F, we still have a net zero cash flow when Call E is exercised against us. If we get more, any additional net cash flow at the time of exercise is just added to the $1 cash inflow we had at the time we initially transacted.

Do Not Exercise Call Options on No-Dividend Stocks Before Expiration. In this section, we show that a call option on a nondividend paying stock is always worth more than its mere exercise value. Therefore, such an option should never be exercised. If the trader wants to dispose of the option, it will always be better to sell the option than to exercise it.

For a call option, the **intrinsic value** or the **exercise value** of the option equals $S_t - X$. This is the value of the option when it is exercised, because the holder of the call pays X and receives S_t. We have seen that, prior to expiration, a call option must be worth at least $S_t - Xe^{-r(T-t)}$. Therefore, exercising a call before expiration discards at least the difference between X and $Xe^{-r(T-t)}$. The difference between the call price and the exercise value is the **time value** of the option. For example, consider the following values:

$$S_t = \$105$$
$$X = \$100$$
$$r = .10$$
$$T - t = 6 \text{ months}$$

The intrinsic value of this call option is $5, or $S_t - X$. However, we know that the market price of the call option must meet the following condition:

$$C_t \geq S_t - Xe^{-r(T-t)}$$
$$\geq \$105 - \$100e^{-(.1)(.5)}$$
$$\geq \$9.88$$

Therefore, exercising the call throws away at least $X - Xe^{-r(T-t)} = \$100 - \$95.12 = \$4.88$. Alternatively it discards the difference between the lower bound on the call price and the exercise value of the call, $\$9.88 - \$5.00 = \$4.88$. For a nondividend paying stock, early exercise can never be optimal. This means that the call will not be exercised until expiration. However, this makes an American option on a nondividend paying stock equivalent to a European option. For a stock that pays no dividends, the American option will not be exercised until expiration and a European option cannot be exercised until expiration. Therefore, the two have the same price. Notice that this rule holds only for a call option on a stock that does not pay dividends. In some circumstances, it can make sense to exercise a call option on a dividend paying stock before the option expires. The motivation for the early exercise is to capture the dividend immediately and to earn interest on those funds. We explore these possibilities in Chapter 15.

RELATIONSHIPS BETWEEN PUT OPTION PRICES

In Chapter 11, we saw that the value of either an American put or a European put at expiration is given by:

$$P_T = \text{MAX}\{0, X - S_T\}$$

Essentially, the put holder anticipates receiving the value of the exercise price and paying the stock price at expiration. Now we want to consider put values before expiration and the relationship between pairs of puts. As we did for calls, we illustrate these pricing relationships by invoking no-arbitrage conditions. Further, the relationships hold for both American and European puts unless explicitly stated otherwise.

Before Expiration, an American Put Must Be Worth at Least the Exercise Price Less the Stock Price. The holder of an American put option can exercise any time. Upon exercising, the put holder surrenders the put and the stock and receives the exercise price. Therefore, the American put must be worth at least the difference between the exercise price and the stock price.

$$P_t \geq \text{MAX}\{0, X - S_t\}$$

where P_t is the price of an American put at time t.

We illustrate this principle by showing how to reap an arbitrage profit if the principle does not hold. Consider the following data:

$S_t = \$95$
$X = \$100$
$P_t = \$3$

With these prices, the put is too cheap. The put's price does not equal or exceed the $5 difference between the exercise price and the stock price. To take advantage of the mispricing, we transact as shown below With these transactions, we capture an immediate cash inflow of $2. Also, we have no further obligations, so our arbitrage is complete. Notice that these transactions involve the immediate exercise of the put option. Therefore, this kind of arbitrage is possible only for an American put option. To prevent this kind of arbitrage, the price of the American put option must be at least $5. In actual markets, the price of a put will generally exceed the difference between the exercise price and the stock price.

Transaction	Cash Flow
Buy put	−$3
Buy stock	−95
Exercise option	+100
Net Cash Flow	+$2

Before Expiration, a European Put Must Be Worth at Least the Present Value of the Exercise Price Minus the Stock Price. We have just seen that an American put must be worth at least the difference between the exercise price and the stock price, $X - S_t$. The same rule does not hold for a European put, because we cannot exercise the European put before expiration to take advantage of the mispricing. However, a similar rule holds for a European put. Specifically, the value of a European put must equal or exceed the present value of the exercise price minus the stock price:

$$p_t \geq Xe^{-r(T-t)} - S_t$$

We can illustrate this price restriction for a European put by using our same stock and option, except we treat the put as a European put. Also, the risk-free interest rate is 6 percent and we assume that the option expires in three months.

$$S_t = \$95$$
$$X = \$100$$
$$p_t = \$3$$
$$T - t = 3 \text{ months}$$
$$r = .06$$

where p_t is the price of a European put at time t. With these values, our principle states:

$$p_t \geq Xe^{-r(T-t)} - S_t = \$100e^{-(.06)(.25)} - \$95 = \$98.51 - \$95 = \$3.51$$

Because the put must be worth at least $3.51 but the actual price is only $3, we can reap an arbitrage profit by trading as follows:

Transaction	Cash Flow
Borrow $98 at 6 percent for 3 months	+$98
Buy put	−3
Buy stock	−95
Net Cash Flow	0

After making these initial transactions, we wait until the option is about to expire and we transact as follows:

Transaction	Cash Flow
Exercise option, deliver stock, and collect exercise price	+$100.00
Repay debt = $98e^{(.06)(.25)}$	−99.48
Net Cash Flow	+$.52

These transactions give an arbitrage profit of $.52 at expiration. Notice that there was a zero net cash flow when we first transacted, so there was no investment. These initial transactions guaranteed the $.52 profit at expiration. Therefore, we have an arbitrage – a riskless profit with no investment.

From these two examples, we can see that an American put must be worth at least as much as a European put. The lower bound for the price of an American put is $X - S_t$, but the lower bound for the European put is $Xe^{-r(T-t)} - S_t$. Also, we know that the American put gives all the rights of the European put, plus the chance to exercise early. Therefore, the American put must be worth at least as much as the European put.

The Longer Until Expiration, the More Valuable an American Put. Consider two American put options that are just alike except that one has a longer time until expiration. The put with the longer time until expiration must be worth at least as much as the other. Informally, the put with the longer time until expiration offers every advantage of the shorter term put. In addition, the longer term put offers the chance for greater price increases on the put after the shorter term put expires. Without this condition, arbitrage opportunities exist.

To illustrate the arbitrage opportunity, assume the underlying stock trades for $95 and we have two American puts with exercise prices of $100 as follows:

	Time Until Expiration	Put Price
Put A	3 months	$7
Put B	6 months	6

These prices permit arbitrage, because the put with the longer life is cheaper. Therefore, we sell Put A and buy Put B for an arbitrage profit, as shown below.

Transaction	Cash Flow
Sell Put A	+$7
Buy Put B	−6
Net Cash Flow	+$1

After making these transactions, we must consider what happens if Put A is exercised against us. Assume that Put A is exercised against us when the stock price is $90. In this situation, the following events occur.

Transaction	Cash Flow
On the exercise of Put A	
Receive stock worth $90	$90
Pay exercise price of $100	−100
We exercise Put B	
Deliver stock worth $90	−90
Receive exercise price of $100	+100
Net Cash Flow	0

When the holder of Put A exercises against us, we immediately exercise Put B. No matter what the stock price may be, these transactions give a zero net cash flow. Therefore, the original transaction gave us $1, which represents an arbitrage profit of at least $1. The profit could be greater if Put A expires worthless. Then we have our $1 profit to keep, plus we still hold Put B, which may have additional value. Therefore, the longer term American put must be worth at least as much as the shorter term American put. Notice that this rule holds only for American puts. Our arbitrage transactions require that we exercise Put B when the holder of Put A exercises against us. This we could only do with an American option.

For European put options, it is not always true that the longer term put has greater value. A European put pays off the exercise price only at expiration. If expiration is very distant, the payoff will be diminished in value because of the time value of money. However, the longer the life of a put option, the greater its advantage in allowing something beneficial to happen to the stock price. Thus, the longer the life of the put, the better for this reason. Whether having a longer life is beneficial to the price of a European put depends on which of these two factors dominates. We will be able to evaluate these more completely in the next chapter.

The fact that a European put with a shorter life can be more valuable than a European put with a longer life shows two important principles. First, early exercise of a put can be desirable even when the underlying stock pays no dividends. This follows from the fact that a short-term European put can be worth more than a long-term European put. Second, American and European put prices may not be identical, even when the underlying stock pays no dividends. If early exercise is desirable, the American put allows it and the European put does not. Therefore, the American put can be more valuable than a European put, even when the underlying stock pays no dividend.

The Higher the Exercise Price, the More Valuable the Put. For both American and European put options, a higher exercise price is associated with a higher price. A put option with a higher exercise price must be worth at least as much as a put with a lower exercise price. Violations of this principle lead to arbitrage.

To illustrate the arbitrage, consider a stock trading at $90 with the following two put options having the same time until expiration:

	Exercise Price	Put Price
Put C	$100	$11
Put D	95	12

These prices violate the rule, because the price of Put D is higher, even though Put C has the higher exercise price. To reap the arbitrage profit, we transact as follows:

Transaction	Cash Flow
Sell Put D	+$12
Buy Put C	−11
Net Cash Flow	+$1

If the holder of Put D exercises against us, we immediately exercise Put C. Assuming the stock price is $90 at the time of exercise, we consider the appropriate transactions when we face the exercise of Put D:

Transaction	Cash Flow
Exercise of Put D against us:	
Receive stock worth $90	+$90
Pay exercise price	−95
Our exercise of Put C:	
Deliver stock worth $90	−90
Receive exercise price	+100
Net Cash Flow	+$5

No matter what the stock price is at the time of exercise, we have a cash inflow of $5 if we both exercise. Further, Put D can be exercised only when it is profitable for us to exercise Put C. Notice that this principle holds for both American and European puts. Put C and Put D can be exercised either before expiration (for an American option) or at expiration only (for a European option). Figure 12.6 shows the profits for alternative stock prices. For any stock price of $100 or above, both puts expire worthless and we keep our initial $1 inflow. For a stock price between $95 and $100, we can exercise our option, but Put D cannot be exercised. For example, if the stock is at $97, we exercise and receive $100 for a $97 stock. This $3 exercise profit gives us a total profit of $4. If the stock price is below $95, both puts will be exercised. For example, with the stock price at $90, the exercise profit on Put D is $5, as we have seen. However, our exercise profit on Put C is $10. Thus, we lose $5 on the exercise of Put D against us, but we make $10 by exercising Put C, and we still have our $1 initial inflow, for a net arbitrage profit of $6.

The Price Difference Between Two American Puts Cannot Exceed the Difference in Exercise Prices. The prices of two American puts cannot differ by more than the difference in exercise prices, assuming other features are the same. If prices violate this condition, there will be an arbitrage opportunity. To illustrate this arbitrage opportunity, consider the following puts on the same underlying stock:

	Exercise Price	Put Price
Put E	$100	$ 4
Put F	105	10

These prices violate our condition, because the price difference between the puts is $6, while the difference in exercise prices is only $5. To exploit this mispricing, we transact as follows:

Arbitrage with Puts C and D **Figure 12.6**

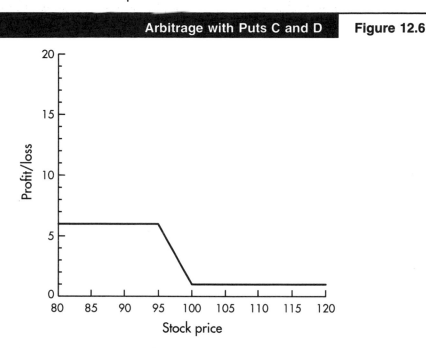

Transaction	Cash Flow
Sell Put F	+$10
Buy Put E	−$4
Net Cash Flow	+$6

With this initial cash inflow of $6, we have enough to pay any loss we might sustain when the holder of Put F exercises against us. For example, assume the stock trades at $95 and the holder of Put F exercises:

The exercise of Put F against us:	
Receive stock worth $95	+$95
Pay exercise price	−$105
Our exercise of Put E:	
Receive exercise price	+$100
Deliver stock worth $95	−$95
Net Cash Flow	−$5

On the exercise, we lose $5. However, we already received $6 with the initial transactions. This leaves an arbitrage profit of at least $1. As Figure 12.7 shows, we could have larger profits, depending on the stock price. If the stock price equals or exceeds $105, no exercise is possible and we keep the entire $6 of our initial transaction. For stock prices between $100 and $105, the holder of Put F can exercise against us, but we cannot exercise. For example, if the stock price is $103, we must pay

Figure 12.7   **Arbitrage with Puts E and F**

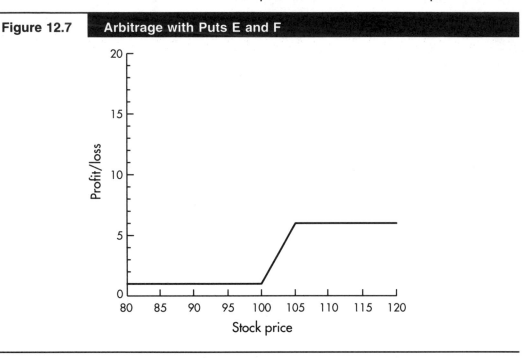

$105 and receive a stock worth only $103, for a $2 exercise loss. However, with our initial cash inflow of $6, we still have a net profit of $4. For stock prices below $100, we can both exercise, as in the transactions we showed for a stock price of $95. In this case, we lose $5 on the exercise, but we still make a net profit of $1.

For Two European Puts, the Price Difference Cannot Exceed the Difference in the Present Value of the Exercise Prices. A similar principle holds for European puts, except the difference in put prices cannot exceed the difference in the present values of the exercise prices. If Puts E and F are European puts, the interest rate is 10 percent, and the options expire in six months, then the present values of the exercise prices are:

	Exercise Price	Present Value of Exercise Price
Put E	$100	$95.12
Put F	105	99.88

According to this principle, the price of Put F cannot exceed the price of Put E by more than $4.76 ($99.88 − $95.12). With prices of $4 and $10 for Puts E and F, there should be an arbitrage profit.

To capture the profit, we sell Put F and buy Put E, as we did with the American puts. This gives a cash inflow of $6, which we invest for six months at 10 percent. The European puts cannot be exercised until expiration, at which time our investment is worth (6e^{(.1)(.5)}$) = $6.31. The most we can lose on the exercise is $5, the difference in the exercise prices. As we saw for the American puts, this happens when the stock price is $100 or less. However, we have $6.31 at expiration, so we can easily sustain this loss. If the stock price exceeds $105, neither option can be exercised, and we keep our entire $6.31. For the European puts, the graph of the arbitrage profit is exactly like Figure 12.7, except we add $.31 to every point. If the options had been priced $4.76 apart, our investment would have yielded $5 at expiration ($4.76$e^{(.1)(.5)}$). This $5 would protect us against any loss at expiration, but it would guarantee no arbitrage profit.

Summary

To this point, we have considered how call and put prices respond to stock and exercise prices and the time remaining until expiration. We have expressed all of these relationships as an outgrowth of our basic no-arbitrage condition: Prevailing option prices must exclude arbitrage profits. For call options, the story is very clear. The higher the stock price, the higher the call price. The higher the exercise price, the lower the call price. The longer the time until expiration, the higher the call price. For put options, the higher the stock price, the lower the put price. The higher the exercise price, the higher the put price. For time until expiration, the effects are slightly more complicated. For an American put, the longer time until expiration, the more valuable the put. For a European put, a longer time until expiration can give rise to either a lower or higher put price.

We have also seen that no-arbitrage conditions restrict how call and put prices for different exercise prices can vary. For two call options or two American put options that are alike except for their exercise prices, the two option prices cannot differ by more than the difference in the exercise prices. For two European put options with different exercise prices, the option prices cannot differ by more than the present value of the difference in the exercise prices.

Throughout this discussion, we have been trying to tighten the bounds we can place on option prices. For example, Figure 12.1 gave the most generous bounds for call options. There we noted that the call price could never exceed the stock price as an upper bound. As a lower bound, the call price must always be at least zero or the stock price minus the exercise price, whichever is higher. The price relationships we considered in this section tighten these bounds by placing further restrictions on put and call prices. Figure 12.8 illustrates how we have tightened these bounds for call options. First, we showed that the call price must be at least zero or the stock price minus the present value of the exercise price. Figure 12.8 reflects this restriction by pulling in the right boundary. Now we know that the call price must lie in this slightly smaller area. Also, if we consider a call with a lower exercise price, we know that the call price must be at least as high for the call with the lower exercise price.

Further, we have considered price relationships between pairs of options that differ in some respects. For example, assume that Option X in Figure 12.8 is priced correctly. We want to consider Option Y, which is another call like X, except it has a longer time until expiration. With its longer time until expiration, the price of Y must equal or exceed the price of X. For example, Y in Figure 12.8 would have to lie on or above the horizontal line *abc* that runs through X. Based on our information, Y in Figure 12.8 has a permissible location.

Consider another option, Z, which is just like X except Z has an exercise price that is $5 higher than X's. The price of Z can never fall below the stock price minus the present value of Z's exercise price. Therefore, the right boundary for the stock price minus the present value of Z's exercise price gives a floor for the price of Z. The price of Z must lie above the line *eb*. With a higher exercise price, the price of Option Z cannot exceed the price of X. Therefore, the price of Z must lie on or below the line *abc*. Combining these two restrictions, we know that the price of Z must lie in the area given by *abed*.

Figure 12.8   **Call Price Relationships**

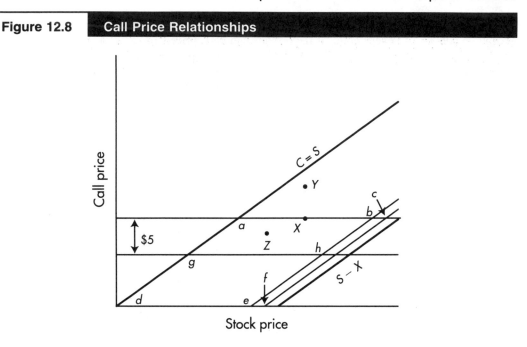

However, we can locate the price of Z more exactly. We know from our discussion that two calls that differ only in their exercise prices must have prices that differ no more than their exercise prices. In our example, the exercise price of Z is $5 more than the exercise price of X. In Figure 12.8, line *gh* is $5 below line *abc*. Therefore, continuing to assume that the price of X is correct, Z must have a price that lies on or above *gh*. If it did not, the price of Z would be too low relative to X. Putting these principles together, we know that the price of Z must lie within the area defined by *abhg*. Z in Figure 12.8 conforms to these rules.

We cannot specify exactly where Z must lie within area *abhg*. Option prices also depend on two additional factors that we must now consider: interest rates and the way in which the stock price moves. After considering these additional factors in this chapter and in Chapter 13, we will be able to pinpoint the price that an option must have.

OPTION PRICES AND THE INTEREST RATE

We now apply our no-arbitrage approach to examine the effect of interest rates on option prices. For a call option, the exercise price represents a potential liability the owner of a call option faces at expiration. Before expiration, the lower the present value of the liability associated with owning a call, the better for the call owner. Therefore, as we show in the following section, call option prices increase with higher interest rates. The result may seem counterintuitive because we generally associate higher asset prices with lower interest rates. This is not so for call options, as our no-arbitrage argument shows. The owner of a put option may exercise and receive the exercise price in exchange for surrendering the stock, so the exercise price represents a potential asset for a put owner. The lower the interest rate, the higher the present value of that potential asset. Therefore, the lower the interest rate, the higher the price of a put. This section presents a no-arbitrage argument to show why the price of a put must fall as interest rates rise.

Call Prices and Interest Rates

We have already observed that the price of either an American or a European call must equal or exceed the larger of zero or the stock price minus the present value of the exercise price:

$$C_t \geq \text{MAX}\{0, S_t - Xe^{-r(T-t)}\} \tag{12.4}$$

In Equation 12.3, $Xe^{-r(T-t)}$ is the present value of the exercise price. The larger the interest rate, r, the smaller that present value, and thus a higher interest rate gives a larger value for $S_t - Xe^{-r(T-t)}$. This makes sense because the exercise price is a liability the call owner incurs upon exercise.

We can also show that the call price must rise if interest rates rise by the following no-arbitrage example. Consider a call option on a stock trading at $100. The exercise price of the call is $100. The option expires in six months and the current interest rate is 10 percent. From Equation 12.3, the price of this call must equal or exceed $4.88:

$$C_t \geq \text{MAX}\{0, \$100 - \$100e^{-(.1)(.5)}\} \geq \$4.88$$

For convenience, we assume that the option is correctly priced at $4.88.[5]

Suddenly, interest rates jump from 10 to 12 percent, but the option price remains at $4.88. Now the option price does not meet the condition in Equation 12.3. The option price is too low, so we want to transact to guarantee an arbitrage profit. Accordingly, we trade as follows:

Transaction	Cash Flow
Sell stock	+$100.00
Buy call	−4.88
Buy bond maturing in 6 months and yielding 12 percent	−95.12
Net Cash Flow	0

In six months, the option is at expiration and our bond matures. The bond will pay $101.

How we deal with the call and stock depends on the stock price relative to the option price. If the stock trades for $100, the call option is worthless. In this case, we buy the stock for $100 and return it, leaving a profit of $1. If the stock price is less than $100, our profit increases. For example, with a $95 stock price, the option is worthless and we buy the stock for $95. These transactions leave a total profit of $6. If the stock price exceeds $100, we exercise our call and pay the exercise price of $100. After exercising and returning the stock, we still have $1. Therefore, we have a profit at expiration with no investment. This arbitrage opportunity arose because the option price did not increase as the interest rate rose. With our example, the price of the call should have risen to at least $5.82 to exclude arbitrage:

$$C_t \geq \text{MAX}\{0, S_t - Xe^{-r(T-t)}\} \geq \text{MAX}\{0, \$100 - \$100e^{-(.12)(.5)}\} \geq \$5.82$$

Because the price did not respond, we were able to reap an arbitrage profit. To exclude arbitrage, the price of a call must be higher the higher the interest rate. Otherwise, a riskless profit without investment will be possible.

Put Prices and Interest Rates

Interest rates also affect put prices. When exercising, the holder of a put receives the exercise price. Therefore, for a put owner, the exercise price is a potential cash inflow. The greater the present value of that potential inflow, the higher will be the value of the put. As a consequence, the put price should be higher the lower the interest rate. If a put price fails to adjust to changing interest rates, there will be an arbitrage opportunity. This rule holds for both American and European puts.

   To show how put prices depend on interest rates, consider a stock trading at $90. A European put option on this stock expires in six months and has an exercise price of $100. Interest rates are at 10 percent. We know that the European put price must meet the following condition:

$$p_t \geq \text{MAX}\{0, \, Xe^{-r(T-t)} - S_t\} \geq \text{MAX}\{0, \, \$100e^{-(.1)(.5)} - \$90\} \geq \$5.12$$

For convenience, we assume that the put is priced at $5.12.

   Let us now assume that interest rates suddenly fall to 8 percent, but that the put price does not change. Our principle asserts that the put should be worth at least $6.08 now. With the put price staying at $5.12, when it should be $6.08, we trade as follows:

Transaction	Cash Flow
Borrow $95.12 at 8 percent	+$95.12
Buy stock	−90.00
Buy put	−5.12
Net Cash Flow	0

With these transactions in place, we wait until expiration in six months to reap our arbitrage profit. At expiration, we owe $99.00 on our borrowings. From the stock and the put, we must realize enough to cover that payment. Any remaining money will be profit. If the stock price at expiration is $100, we allow our put to expire and we sell the stock. We receive $100, from which we pay $99.00. This leaves a $1 profit. If the stock price at expiration is below $100, we exercise our put. For example, with a stock price of $95, we exercise our put, deliver the stock, and collect $100. This gives a $1 profit. We make exactly $1 at expiration for any stock price of $100 or less. For any stock price above $100, our put is worthless and our profit equals the difference between the stock price and our $99 debt. From these transactions, we see that we will make at least $1 at expiration. This we achieve with zero investment. Therefore, the failure of the put option price to adjust to changing interest rates generates an arbitrage opportunity. The put price must rise as interest rates fall.

OPTION PRICES AND STOCK PRICE MOVEMENTS

Up to this point, we have studied the way in which four factors constrain call and put prices. These factors are the stock price, the exercise price, the time remaining until expiration, and the interest rate. Even with these four factors, we cannot say exactly what the option price must be before expiration. There is a fifth factor to consider – stock price movements before expiration. If we consider a stock with options on it that expire in six months, we know that the stock price can change thousands of times before the option expires. Further, for two stocks, the pattern of changes and the volatility of the stock price changes can differ dramatically. However, if we can develop a model for understanding stock price movements, we can use that model to specify what the price of an option must be.

We now make a drastic, but temporary, simplifying assumption. Between the current moment and the expiration of an option, we assume that the stock price will rise by 10 percent or fall by 10 percent. With this assumption about the stock's price movement, we can use our no-arbitrage approach to determine the exact value of a European call or put. Therefore, knowing the potential pattern of stock price movements gives us the final key to understanding option prices. This chapter illustrates how to determine option prices based on this simplifying model of stock price movements. The next chapter shows how to apply more realistic models of stock price movements to compute accurate option prices.

Let us assume that a stock trades for $100. In the next year, the price can rise or fall exactly 10 percent. Therefore, the stock price next year will be either $90 or $110. Both a put and a call option have exercise prices of $100 and expire in one year. The current interest rate is 6 percent. We want to know how much the put and call will be worth. With these data, the call price is $7.55, and the put is worth $1.89. Other prices create arbitrage opportunities. This section shows that the options must have these prices. Chapter 13 explains why these no-arbitrage relationships must hold. (As we consider a single period in this section, we employ discrete compounding.)

The Call Price

We have asserted that the call price must be $7.55 given our other data, if the call price is to exclude an arbitrage opportunity. If the option price is lower, we will enter arbitrage transactions that include buying the option. Similarly, if the option price is higher, our arbitrage transactions will include selling the call. We illustrate each case in turn. Let us begin by assuming that the call price is $7.00, which is below our no-arbitrage price of $7.55. If the call price is too low, we transact as follows:

Transaction		Cash Flow
Sell 1 share of stock		+$100.00
Buy 2 calls		−14.00
Buy bond		−86.00
	Net Cash Flow	0

At expiration, the stock price will be either $110 or $90. If the stock price is $110, the calls will be worth $10 each – the stock price minus the exercise price. If the stock price is $90, the calls are worthless. In either case, the bond will pay $91.16. If the stock price is $90, we repurchase a share with our bond proceeds for $90. This leaves a profit of $1.16. If the stock price is $110, we sell our two options for $20. Adding this $20 to our bond proceeds, we have $111.16. From this amount, we buy a share for $110 to repay the borrowing of a share. This leaves a profit of $1.16. Therefore, we make $1.16 whether the stock price rises or falls. We made this certain profit with zero investment, so we have an arbitrage profit.

Now assume the call price is $8.00, exceeding $7.55. In this case, the call price is too high, so we sell the call as part of the following transactions.

Transaction	Cash Flow
Buy 1 share of stock	−$100.00
Sell 2 calls	+16.00
Sell a bond (borrow funds)	+84.00
Net Cash Flow	0

At expiration, we know we must repay $89.04. If the stock price at expiration is $90, the calls cannot be exercised against us. So we sell our stock for $90 and repay our debt of $89.04. This leaves a profit of $.96.

If the stock price goes to $110, the calls we sold will be exercised against us. To fulfill one obligation, we deliver our share of stock and receive the exercise price of $100. We then buy back the other call that is still outstanding. It costs $10, the difference between the stock price and the exercise price. This leaves $90, from which we repay our debt of $89.04. Now we have completed all of our obligations and we still have $.96. Therefore, with a call priced at $8.00, we will have a profit of $.96 from these transactions no matter whether the stock price goes up or down. We captured this sure profit with zero investment, so we have an arbitrage profit.

To eliminate arbitrage, the call must trade for $7.55. If that call price prevails, both transaction strategies fail. For example, we might try to transact as follows if the call price is $7.55.

Transaction	Cash Flow
Buy 1 share of stock	−$100.00
Sell 2 calls	+15.10
Sell a bond (borrow funds)	+84.90
Net Cash Flow	0

At expiration, we owe $90.00. If the stock price is $90, our calls are worthless. However, we can sell our share for $90 and repay our debt. Our net cash flow at expiration is zero. If the stock price is $110, the calls will be exercised against us. We deliver our one share and receive $100. From this $100 we repay our debt of $90. This leaves $10, the exact difference between the stock and exercise price. Therefore, we can use our last $10 to close our option position. Our net cash flow is zero. With a call price of $7.55, our transactions cost us zero and they yield zero. This is exactly the result we expect in a market that is free from arbitrage opportunities.[6]

The Put Price

Based on the same data we have just considered for the call option, the put price must be $1.89 to avoid arbitrage. We can see that this must be the case in two ways. First, we show that put-call parity requires a price of $1.89. Second, we show how any other price leads to arbitrage opportunities similar to those that occurred when the call was priced incorrectly.

From Chapter 11 we know that put-call parity expresses the value of a European put as a function of a similar call, the stock, and investment in the risk-free bond.

$$p_t = c_t - S_t + Xe^{-r(T-t)}$$

where $Xe^{-r(T-t)}$ is the present value of the exercise price. For our example, we know that the correct call price is $7.55 and that the stock trades for $100. With one year remaining until expiration, the present value of the exercise price is $94.34. According to put-call parity for our example:

$$p_t = \$7.55 - \$100.00 + \$94.34 = \$1.89$$

If the put is not worth $1.89, arbitrage opportunities arise. This makes sense because the put-call parity relationship is itself a no-arbitrage condition.[7]

We now show how to reap arbitrage profits if the put does not trade for $1.89. We consider the transactions if the put price is above or below its correct price of $1.89. First, let us assume that the put price is $1.50. In this case, the put is too cheap relative to other assets. The other assets that replicate the put are too expensive, taken together. These are the call, stock, bond combination on the right-hand side of the put-call parity formula. The put-call parity relationship suggests that we should buy the relatively underpriced put and sell the relatively overpriced portfolio that replicates the put. To initiate this strategy, we transact as follows:

Transaction	Cash Flow
Buy put	−$1.50
Sell call	+7.55
Buy stock	−100.00
Borrow $93.95 and invest at 6 percent for one year	+93.95
Net Cash Flow	0

In one year, our debt is $99.59 and the put and call are at expiration. The stock price will be either $90 or $110. We consider the value of our position for both possible stock prices. If the stock price is $90, we exercise our put and deliver our share of stock. This gives a cash flow of $100, from which we repay our debt of $99.59. We have no further obligations, yet $.41 remains. Thus, we make a profit with no initial investment.

If the stock price is $110, our put is worthless and the stock will be called away from us. When the call is exercised against us, we receive $100. From this $100, we repay our debt of $99.59. Again, this leaves us with $.41. No matter whether the stock goes to $90 or to $110, we make $.41. We achieved this profit with no initial investment. Consequently, we have a certain profit with zero investment, a sure sign of an arbitrage profit.

We now consider how to transact if the put price is higher than $1.89. Let us assume that the put trades for $2.00. With the put being too expensive, we sell the relatively overpriced put and purchase the relatively underpriced portfolio that replicates the put. In this case, our transactions are just the reverse of those we made when the put price was too low. We transact as follows:

Transaction	Cash Flow
Sell put	+$2.00
Buy call	−7.55
Sell stock	+100.00
Lend $94.45 at 6 percent for one year	−94.45
Net Cash Flow	0

In one year, our loan matures, so we collect $100.12. If the stock price is $90, our call is worthless and the put will be exercised against us. We must accept the $90 stock and pay the $100 exercise price. This leaves one share of stock and $.12. We use the share to cover our original sale of stock, and we have $.12 after meeting all obligations.

If the stock price goes to $110.00, the put we sold will expire worthless. We exercise our call, paying the $100 exercise price to acquire the stock. We now have $.12 and one share, so we cover our original share sale by returning the stock. Again, we have completed all transactions and $.12 remains. Therefore, no matter whether the stock goes to $90 or $110 over the one-year investment horizon, we make $.12. We did this with zero investment, so we have an arbitrage profit.

These transactions illustrate why the put must trade for $1.89 in our example. Any other price allows arbitrage. If the put price is $1.89, both of the transactions we have just considered will cost zero to execute, but they will be sure to return zero when the options expire. In a market free of arbitrage opportunities, this is just what we expect.

OPTION PRICES AND THE RISKINESS OF STOCKS

As we have seen, option prices depend on several factors, including stock prices. In this section, we explore how stock price changes affect option prices. Specifically, we consider how the riskiness of the stock affects the price of the put or call. We use a simple model of the way a stock price changes to illustrate a very important result: The riskier the underlying stock, the greater the value of an option. This principle holds for both put and call options. While it may seem odd for an option price to be higher if the underlying good is riskier, we can use no-arbitrage arguments to show why this must be true.

Essentially, a call option gives its owner most of the benefits of rising stock prices and protects the owner from suffering the full cost of a drop in stock prices. Thus, a call option offers insurance against falling stock prices and holds out the promise of high profits from surging stock prices. The riskier the underlying stock, the greater the chance of an extreme stock price movement. If the stock price falls dramatically, the insurance feature of the call option comes into play. This limits the call holder's loss. However, if the stock price increases dramatically, the call owner participates fully in the price increase. The protection against large losses, coupled with participation in large gains, makes call options more valuable when the underlying stock is risky.

For put options, risk has a parallel effect. Put owners benefit from large stock price drops and suffer from price increases. However, a put protects the owner from the full force of a stock price rise. In effect, a put embodies insurance against large price rises. At the same time, the put allows its owner to benefit fully from a stock price drop. Because the put incorporates protection against rising prices and allows its owner to capture virtually all profits from falling prices, a put is more valuable the riskier the underlying stock.

In the preceding section, we used a very simple model of stock price movement to show how to price put and call options. In this section, we extend the same model and example to evaluate the effect of riskiness on stock prices. Earlier, we assumed a stock traded for $100 and that its price would go to either $90 or $110 in one year. We assumed that the risk-free rate of interest was 6 percent and that a call and put option both had exercise prices of $100 and expired in one year. Under these circumstances, the call was worth $7.55 and the put was worth $1.89. Any other price for the put or call led to arbitrage opportunities. To explore the effect of risk, we consider two other possible outcomes for the stock price. First, we assume that the stock is not risky. In this case, the stock price increases by the risk-free rate of 6 percent with certainty. Second, we consider stock price movements in which the stock price goes to either $80 or $120.

Option Prices for Riskless Stock

If the stock is risk free, its value grows at the risk-free rate. Otherwise, there would be an arbitrage opportunity between the stock and the risk-free bond.[8] Consequently, we consider prices of our example options assuming that the stock price in one year will be $106 with certainty. Under these circumstances, the call option will be worth $5.66 and the put will be worth zero.

The put will be worth zero one year before expiration because it is sure to be worth zero at expiration. If the stock price is sure to be $106 at expiration, the put only gives the right to force someone to accept a stock worth $106 for $100. Thus, the put is worthless, because there is no chance the stock price will be below the exercise price of the put.

The call has a certain payoff at expiration, because the stock price is certain. At expiration, the call is worth $MAX\{0, S_T - X\} = \$6$. With a riskless stock, the call is also riskless. Investment in the call pays a certain return of $6 in one year, so the call must be worth the present value of $6, or $5.66. Any other price for the call creates an arbitrage opportunity. For example, if the option trades at $5.80, we sell the call and invest the $5.80 at 6 percent. In one year, our investment is worth $6.15 and the exercise of the call against us costs us $6. This yields a $.15 arbitrage profit. For any other price of either the put or the call, our familiar transactions guarantee an arbitrage profit.

Earlier, we placed the following bound on the European call price before expiration:

$$c_t \geq MAX\{0, S_t - Xe^{-r(T-t)}\}$$

Now we see that this relationship holds exactly if the stock is risk free. In other words, the European call price is on the lower boundary if the stock has no risk. Therefore, holding the other factors constant, any excess value of the call above the boundary is due solely to the riskiness of the stock.

Comparing our two examples of stock price movements, we saw that the risk-free stock implied a call price of $5.66. If the stock price was risky, moving up or down 10 percent in the next year, the call price was $7.55. This call price difference is due to the difference in the riskiness of the stock. As we now show, higher risk implies higher option prices.

Riskier Stocks Result in Higher Option Prices

In our model of stock price movements, we assumed that stock prices change over a year in a very specific way. When we assumed that stock prices could increase or decrease 10 percent, we found certain option prices. We now consider the same circumstances but allow for more radical stock price movements of 20 percent up or down. All other factors remain the same. In summary, a stock trades today at $100. In one year, its price will be either $80 or $120. The risk-free interest rate is 6 percent. A call and put each have an exercise price of $100 and expire in one year. Under these circumstances, the call price must be $12.26, and the put price must be $6.60. Any other prices create arbitrage opportunities. Therefore, we have observed the price effects of the following three stock price movements on option prices.

Stock Price Movement	Call Price	Put Price
Stock price increases by a certain 6 percent	$ 5.66	$0.00
Stock price rises or falls by 10 percent	7.55	1.89
Stock price rises or falls by 20 percent	12.26	6.60

In these examples, we held other factors constant. Each example used options with the same exercise price and time to expiration. Also, each example employed the same risk-free rate. As these examples illustrate, greater risk in the stock increases both put and call prices.

CONCLUSION

In this chapter, we discussed the relationships that govern option prices. We began by considering general boundary spaces for calls and puts. By linking relationships between option features, such as time to expiration and exercise prices, we specified price relationships between options. For example, we saw that the price of a call with a lower exercise price must equal or exceed the price of a similar call with a higher exercise price. We discussed the five factors on which option prices depend: the exercise price, the stock price, the risk-free interest rate, the time to expiration, and the riskiness of the stock. We found that option prices have a definitive relationship to these factors, as Table 12.1 summarizes. We explore these price reactions in detail in Chapter 14.

Understanding these factors helps us place bounds on call and put prices. However, to determine an exact price, we must specify how the stock price can move. To illustrate the important influence of stock price movements on option prices, we considered a very simple model of stock price movements. For example, we assumed that the stock prices can change 10 percent in the next year. With this assumption, we were able to find exact option prices. However, this assumption about the movement of stock prices is very unrealistic. A year from now, a stock may have a virtually infinite number of prices, not just two. With unrealistic assumptions about stock price movements, the option prices we compute are likely to be unrealistic as well. In the next chapter, we work toward more realistic assumptions about stock price movements, and we develop a more exact option pricing model.

Table 12.1	**Option Price Response to Changes in Underlying Variables**	
For an Increase in the:	**The Call Price**	**The Put Price**
Stock Price	Rises	Falls
Exercise Price	Falls	Rises
Time Until Expiration	Rises	May Rise or Fall
Interest Rate	Rises	Falls
Stock Risk	Rises	Rises

QUESTIONS AND PROBLEMS

1. What is the maximum theoretical value for a call? Under what conditions does a call reach this maximum value? Explain.

2. What is the maximum theoretical value for an American put? When does it reach this maximum? Explain.

3. Answer Question 2 for a European put.

4. Explain the difference in the theoretical maximum values for an American and a European put.

5. How does the exercise price affect the price of a call? Explain.

6. Consider two calls with the same time to expiration that are written on the same underlying stock. Call 1 trades for $7 and has an exercise price of $100. Call 2 has an exercise price of $95. What is the maximum price that Call 2 can have? Explain.

7. Six months remain until a call option expires. The stock price is $70 and the exercise price is $65. The option price is $5. What does this imply about the interest rate?

8. Assume the interest rate is 12 percent and four months remain until an option expires. The exercise price of the option is $70 and the stock that underlies the option is worth $80. What is the minimum value the option can have based on the no-arbitrage conditions studied in this chapter? Explain.

9. Two call options are written on the same stock that trades for $70 and both calls have an exercise price of $85. Call 1 expires in six months and Call 2 expires in three months. Assume that Call 1 trades for $6 and that Call 2 trades for $7. Do these prices allow arbitrage? Explain. If they do permit arbitrage, explain the arbitrage transactions.

10. Explain the circumstances that make early exercise of a call rational. Under what circumstances is early exercise of a call irrational?

11. Consider a European and an American call with the same expiration and the same exercise price that are written on the same stock. What relationship must hold between their prices? Explain.

12. Before exercise, what is the minimum value of an American put?

13. Before exercise, what is the minimum value of a European put?

14. Explain the differences in the minimum values of American and European puts before expiration.

15. How does the price of an American put vary with time until expiration? Explain.

16. What relationship holds between time until expiration and the price of a European put?

17. Consider two puts with the same term to expiration (six months). One put has an exercise price of $110, the other has an exercise price of $100. Assume the interest rate is 12 percent. What is the maximum price difference between the two puts if they are European? If they are American? Explain the difference, if any.

18. How does the price of a call vary with interest rates? Explain.

19. Explain how a put price varies with interest rates. Does the relationship vary for European and American puts? Explain.

20. What is the relationship between the risk of the underlying stock and the call price? Explain in intuitive terms.

21. A stock is priced at $50 and the risk-free rate of interest is 10 percent. A European call and a European put on this stock both have exercise prices of $40 and expire in six months. What is the difference between the call and put prices? (Assume continuous compounding.) From the information supplied in this question, can you say what the call and put prices must be? If not, explain what information is lacking.

22. A stock is priced at $50 and the risk-free rate of interest is 10 percent. A European call and a European put on this stock both have exercise prices of $40 and expire in six months. Assume that the call price exceeds the put price by $7. Does this represent an arbitrage opportunity? If

so, explain why and state the transactions you would make to take advantage of the pricing discrepancy.

NOTES

[1] The price of an option depends on these five factors when the underlying stock pays no dividends. As we will discuss in Chapter 14, if the underlying stock pays a dividend, the dividend is a sixth factor that we must consider.

[2] Like Chapter 11, the discussion of these rational bounds for option prices relies on a paper by Robert C. Merton, "Theory of Rational Option Pricing," *Bell Journal of Economics and Management Science*, 4, 1973, pp. 141–83.

[3] Scholars have tested market data to determine how well puts and calls meet these boundary conditions. Dan Galai was the first to test these relationships in his paper, "Empirical Tests of Boundary Conditions for CBOE Options," *Journal of Financial Economics*, 6, June/September 1978, pp. 182–211. Galai found some violations of the no-arbitrage conditions in the reported prices. However, these apparent arbitrage opportunities disappeared if a trader faced a 1 percent transaction cost. Mihir Bhattacharya conducted similar, but more extensive, tests in his paper, "Transaction Data Tests on the Efficiency of the Chicago Board Options Exchange," *Journal of Financial Economics*, 1983, pp. 161–85. Like Galai, Bhattacharya found that a trader facing transaction costs could not exploit apparent arbitrage opportunities. However, both studies found that a very low cost trader, such as a market maker, could have a chance for some arbitrage returns.

[4] As we discuss in Chapter 14, differences between European and American call options require some slight revisions of these rules. In this section, we have said that the difference in the price of two calls cannot exceed the difference in exercise prices. Our arbitrage arguments for this principle assumed immediate exercise before expiration, thus implicitly assuming that the option is American. For a similar pair of European options, the price differential cannot exceed the present value of the difference between the two exercise prices. The arbitrage profit equals the excess difference between the exercise prices. With European options, this excess differential is not available until expiration, when traders can exercise. Therefore, for European options, the arbitrage profit will be the excess difference in the exercise prices discounted to the present.

[5] Assuming that the option is correctly priced at the lower bound implicitly assumes that the stock price has no risk. In other words, we implicitly assume that the stock price will not change before expiration. Making this assumption does not affect the validity of our example, because we are focusing on the single effect of a change in interest rates.

[6] The next chapter explains why we need to buy one share of stock and sell two calls in this example. In brief, by combining a bond, a stock, and the right number of calls, we can form a riskless portfolio.

[7] The put-call parity relationship was first addressed by Hans Stoll, "The Relationship Between Put and Call Option Prices," *Journal of Finance*, 24, May 1969, pp. 801–24. Robert C. Merton extended the concept in his paper, "The Relationship Between Put and Call Option Prices: Comment," *Journal of Finance*, 28, pp. 183–84. Robert C. Klemkosky and Bruce G. Resnick tested the put-call parity relationship empirically with market data. Their two papers are: "An Ex-Ante Analysis of Put-Call Parity," *Journal of Financial Economics*, 8, 1980, pp. 363–72 and "Put-Call Parity and Market Efficiency," *Journal of Finance*, 34, 1979, pp. 1141–55. While they find that market prices do not agree perfectly with the put-call parity relationship, the differences are not sufficiently large to generate trading profits after considering all transaction costs.

[8] If the stock earned a riskless rate above the risk-free rate, we would borrow at the risk-free rate and invest in the stock. Later, we could sell the stock, repay our debt, and have a certain return from the difference in the two riskless rates. If the stock earned a riskless rate below the risk-free rate, we would sell the stock and invest the proceeds in the higher rate of the risk-free bond. Therefore, for a given horizon, there is only one risk-free rate.

EUROPEAN OPTION PRICING

OVERVIEW

In Chapter 12 we showed how to compute call and put prices assuming that stock prices behave in a highly simplified manner. Specifically, we assumed that stock prices could rise by a certain percentage or fall by a certain percentage for a single period. After that single period, we assumed that the option expired. Under these unrealistic and highly restrictive assumptions, we found that calls and puts must each have a unique price; any other price leads to arbitrage. In this chapter, we develop similar option pricing models, but we use more realistic models of stock price movement.

To develop a more realistic option pricing model, this chapter first analyzes option pricing under the simple percentage change model of stock price movements. Now, however, we show how to find the unique prices that the no-arbitrage conditions imply. This framework is the **single-period binomial model**. Analyzing the single-period model leads to more realistic models of stock price movements. One of these more realistic models is the **multi-period binomial model**. By considering several successive models of stock price changes, we eventually come to one of the most elegant models in all of finance – the **Black-Scholes option pricing model**.

Throughout this chapter, we focus on European options. Later, in Chapter 15, we consider American option pricing and the complications arising from the potential for early exercise. At the beginning of this chapter, we focus on stocks with no dividends. Later in this chapter, we consider the complications that dividends bring in evaluating the prices of European options.

OPTION! provides support for the diverse models that we study in this chapter. With **OPTION!**, we can make virtually all of the computations discussed in this chapter, including the single-period and multi-period binomial model call and put values and Black-Scholes model prices. In each case, using the software can save considerable computational labor.

THE SINGLE-PERIOD BINOMIAL MODEL

In Chapter 12, we considered a stock priced at $100 and assumed that its price would be $90 or $110 in one year. In this example, the risk-free interest rate was 6 percent. We then considered a call and put on this stock, with both options having an exercise price of $100 and expiring in one year. The call was worth $7.55, and the put was worth $1.89. As we showed in Chapter 12, any other option price creates arbitrage opportunities.

Now we want to create a synthetic European call option – a portfolio that has the same value and profits and losses as the call being synthesized. Consider a portfolio comprised of one-half share of stock plus a short position in a risk-free bond that matures in one year and has an initial purchase price of $42.45. In one year, the portfolio's value depends on whether the stock price is $110 or $90. Depending on the stock price, the half-share will be worth $55 or $45. In either event, we will owe $45.00 to repay our bond. If the stock price rises, the portfolio will be worth $10. If the stock price falls, the portfolio will be worth zero. These are exactly the payoffs for the call option. Therefore, the value of the portfolio must be the same as the value of the call option. Figure 13.1 shows values for the stock, the call, the risk-free bond, and the portfolio value at the outset and one year later. The stock price moves to $110 or $90, and the call moves accordingly to $10 or zero. The risk-free bond increases at a 6 percent rate no matter what the stock does, so borrowing $42.45 generates a debt of $45 due in one year. Likewise, our portfolio of one-half share and a $42.45 borrowing will be worth $10 or zero in one year, depending on the stock price. The diagrams appearing in Figure 13.1 are known as binomial "trees" or "lattices."

Because our portfolio and the call option have exactly the same payoffs in all circumstances, they must have the same initial value. Otherwise, there would be an arbitrage opportunity. This means that an investment of one-half share of stock, S_t, and a bond, B_t, of $42.45 must equal the value of the call.

$$c_t = .5S_t - \$42.45 = \$50 - 42.45 = \$7.55$$

Therefore, the call must be worth $7.55. This is the same conclusion we reached in Chapter 12. This result shows that a combined position in the stock and the risk-free bond can replicate a call option for a one-period horizon.

Figure 13.1   One-Period Payoffs

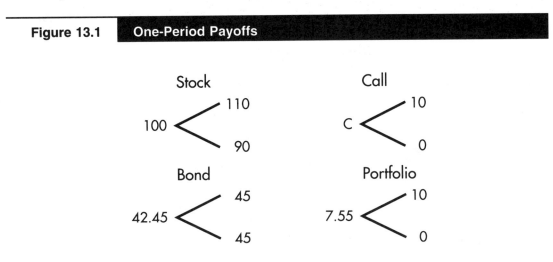

We now show how to find the replicating portfolio made of the stock and the risk-free investment. At the outset, $T - t = 1$, the value of the portfolio, $PORT_t$, depends on the stock price, the number of shares, N, and the price of the bond, B_t.

$$PORT = NS_t - B_t$$

At the end of the horizon, $T - t = 0$, the debt equals the amount borrowed, B_t, plus interest, $B_T = RB_t$. The portfolio's value also depends on the stock price. If the stock price rises, the value of the portfolio will be:

$$PORT_{U,T} = NUS_T - RB_t$$

where:

> $PORT_{U,T}$ = value of the replicating portfolio at time T if the stock price goes up
> $U = 1 +$ percentage of stock price increase
> $R = 1 + r$

Likewise, if the stock price falls, the value of the portfolio will be:

$$PORT_{D,T} = NDS_T - RB_t$$

where:

> $PORT_{D,T}$ = value of the replicating portfolio at time T if the stock price goes down
> $D = 1 -$ percentage of stock price decrease

At expiration, $T - t = 0$, the value of the call also depends on whether the stock price rises or falls. For each circumstance, we represent the call's price as c_U and c_D.

As our example showed, we can choose the number of shares to trade, N, and the amount of funds to borrow, B_t, to replicate the call. Replicating the call means that the portfolio will have the same payoff. Therefore, if the stock price rises:

$$PORT_{U,T} = NUS_T - RB_t = c_U$$

If the stock price falls:

$$PORT_{D,T} = NDS_T - RB_t = c_D$$

After these algebraic manipulations, we have two equations with two unknowns, N and B_t. Solving for the values of the unknowns that satisfy the equations, N^* and B_t^*, we find:

$$N^* = \frac{c_U - c_D}{(U - D)S_t}$$

$$B_t^* = \frac{c_U D - c_D U}{(U - D)R}$$

Therefore,

$$c_t = N^*S_t - B_t^*$$ (13.1)

This is the single-period binomial call pricing model. It holds for a call option expiring in one period when the stock price will rise by a known percentage or fall by a known percentage. The model shows that the value of a call option equals a long position in the stock, plus some borrowing at the risk-free rate. Applying our new notation to our example, we have:

$$c_U = \$10$$

$$c_D = \$0$$

$$U = 1.1$$

$$D = .9$$

$$R = 1.06$$

$$B_t^* = \frac{c_U D - c_D U}{(U - D)R}$$

$$= \frac{10(0.9) - 0(1.1)}{(1.1 - 0.9)(1.06)} = \$42.45$$

$$N^* = \frac{c_U - c_D}{(U - D)S_t} = \frac{10 - 0}{(1.1 - 0.9)100} = 0.5$$

The Role of Probabilities

In discussing the single-period binomial model, we have not used the concept of probability. For example, we have not considered the likelihood that the stock price will rise or fall. While we have not explicitly used probabilistic concepts, the array of prices does imply a certain probability that the stock price will rise, if we are willing to assume that investors are risk neutral.[1] We assume a risk neutral economy in this section to show the role of probabilities. The option prices that we compute under the assumption of risk neutrality are the same as those we found from strict no-arbitrage conditions without any reference to probabilities.

Assuming risk neutrality and given the risk-free interest rate and the up and down percentage movements, we can compute the probability of a stock price increase. Using our definitions of N^* and B_t^*, the call is worth:

$$c_t = \left(\frac{c_U - c_D}{(U - D)S_t}\right)S_t - \frac{c_U D - c_D U}{(U - D)R}$$

Simplifying, we have:

$$c_t = \frac{c_U - c_D}{U - D} - \frac{c_U D - c_D U}{(U - D)R}$$

Isolating the c_U and c_D terms gives:

$$c_t = \frac{\left(\dfrac{R-D}{U-D}\right)c_U + \left(\dfrac{U-R}{U-D}\right)c_D}{R}$$

In this equation, the call value equals the present value of the future payoffs from owning the call. If the stock price goes up, the call pays C_U at expiration. If the stock goes down, the call pays C_D. The numerator of this equation gives the expected value of the call's payoffs at expiration. Therefore, the probability of a stock price increase is also the probability that the call is worth c_U. The probability of a stock price increase is $(R-D)/(U-D)$, and the probability of a stock price decrease is $(U-R)/(U-D)$.

For our continuing example, we have the following values: $c_U = \$10$, $c_D = \$0$, $U = 1.1$, $D = 0.9$, $R = 1.06$. Therefore, the probability of an increase in the stock price (π_U) is 0.8 and the probability of a decrease (π_D) is 0.2. The value of the call in our single period model is:

$$c_t = \frac{\pi_U c_U + \pi_D c_D}{R} = \frac{.8 \times 10 + .2 \times 0}{1.06} = \$7.55$$

This result shows that the value of a call equals the expected payoff from the call at expiration, discounted to the present at the risk-free rate, assuming a risk-neutral economy.

Summary

Our single-period model is a useful tool. We have seen how to replicate an option by combining a long position in stock with a short position in the risk-free asset. Also, we used the single-period model to show that the value of a call equals the present value of the call's expected payoffs at expiration. Nonetheless, our single-period model suffers from two defects. First, it holds only for a single period. We need to be able to value options that expire after many periods. Second, our assumption about stock price changes is still unrealistic. Obviously we do not really know how stock prices can change in one period. In fact, if we define one year as a period, we know that stock prices can take almost an infinite number of values by the end of the period. We now proceed to refine our model to consider these objections.

THE MULTI-PERIOD BINOMIAL MODEL

The principles that we developed for the single-period binomial model also apply to a multi-period framework.[2] Here we illustrate the underlying principles by considering a two-period horizon. Over two periods, the stock price must follow one of four patterns. For the two periods, the stock can go: up-up, up-down, down-up, or down-down. Assuming fixed down and up percentages, the up-down and down-up sequences result in the same terminal stock price. For each terminal stock price, a call option has a specific value. Figure 13.2 shows the binomial trees for the stock and call. To clarify the notation, S_{UU} indicates the terminal stock price if the stock price goes up in both periods. C_{UU} is the resulting call price at expiration when the stock price rises in both periods. For the two-period case, the notation π_{UU} indicates the probability of an up-up sequence of price movements, and π_{DD} indicates the probability of a down-down sequence of price movements. We define other patterns accordingly.

Figure 13.2   **Two-Period Payoffs**

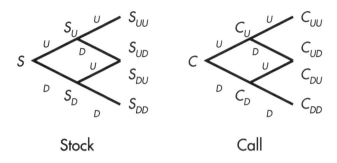

We can express the value of a call option two periods before expiration as:

$$c_t = \frac{\pi_{UU}C_{UU} + \pi_{UD}C_{UD} + \pi_{DU}C_{DU} + \pi_{DD}C_{DD}}{R^2}$$

In this equation, the call value equals the expected value of the payoffs at expiration discounted at the risk-free rate.

   We continue to use our example of a $100 stock that can rise or fall by 10 percent. The probability that the stock price will increase is .8, so this gives a .2 probability of a price drop. Also, the probability of an increase in one period is independent from the probability of an increase in any other period. We now assume that the call is two periods from expiration and that the stock trades for $100. In the first period, the stock can go up or down, giving $US_t = \$110$, $DS_t = \$90$. After the second period, there are four possible patterns with three actually different stock prices: $UUS_t = \$121$, $DDS_t = \$81$, and $UDS_t = DUS_t = \$99$. The probabilities of these different terminal stock prices are: $\pi_{UU} = (.8)(.8) = .64$, $\pi_{UD} = (.8)(.2) = .16$, $\pi_{DU} = (.2)(.8) = .16$, and $\pi_{DD} = (.2)(.2) = .04$. The call price at expiration equals the terminal stock price minus the exercise price of $100, or zero, whichever is larger. Therefore, we have $C_{UU} = \$21$, $C_{DD} = 0$, $C_{DU} = C_{UD} = 0$.

   To determine the call price two periods before expiration, we apply our formula for a call option two periods before expiration. In doing so, we compute the expected value of the call at expiration and discount for two periods:

$$c = \frac{.64(\$21) + .16(0) + .16(0) + .04(0)}{1.06^2} = \frac{\$13.44}{1.06^2} = \$11.96$$

If the call expires in two periods and the stock trades for $100, the call will be worth $11.96. Notice that our sample call pays off at expiration only if the stock price rises twice. Any other pattern of stock price movement in our example gives a call that is worthless at expiration. With one period until expiration and the stock trading at $100, we saw that the call was worth $7.55. With the same initial stock price and two periods until expiration, the call is worth $11.96. This price difference reflects the difference in the present value of the expected payoffs from the call.

In the single-period binomial model, there are two possible stock price outcomes. With two periods until expiration, there are four possible stock price patterns. In general, there are 2^n possible stock price patterns, where n is the number of periods until expiration. Thus, the number of stock and call outcomes increases very rapidly. For example, if the option is just 20 periods from expiration, there are more than 1 million stock price outcomes and the same number of call outcomes to consider.[3] It quickly becomes apparent that we need a more general formula for the multi-period binomial pricing model. Also, for options with many periods until expiration, we need a computer. **OPTION!** can compute binomial model call and put values.

We have explored the single-period and two-period binomial model in detail, and we have analyzed examples for each. The principles we have developed remain true no matter how many periods we consider. However, the computations become more numerous and cumbersome, as we just saw. Therefore, we now make a mathematical jump to present the formula, which we discuss in intuitive terms.

The Multi-Period Binomial Call Pricing Model

In this section, we begin by introducing the multi-period binomial call pricing model. As Equation 13.2 shows, it is undeniably complex. However, a little study will show that the equation is not really so intimidating.

$$c_t = \frac{\sum_{j=0}^{n} \left(\frac{n!}{j!(n-j)!} \right) [\pi_U^j \pi_D^{n-j}] \text{MAX}[0, U^j D^{n-j} S_t - X]}{R^n} \qquad (13.2)$$

To understand this formula, we need to break it into simpler elements. From our previous discussion, we know that the formula gives the present value of the expected payoffs from the call at expiration. The denominator R^n is the discount factor raised to n, the number of periods until expiration. The numerator gives the expected payoff on the call option. Thus, we need to focus on the numerator.

With the multi-period model, we are analyzing an option that expires in n periods. As a feature of the binomial model, we know that the stock price either goes up or down each period. Let us say that it goes up j of the n periods. Then the stock price must fall $n - j$ periods. Our summation runs from $j = 0$ to $j = n$, which includes every possibility. When $j = 0$, we evaluate the possibility that the stock price never rises. When $j = n$, we evaluate the possibility that the stock price rises every period. The summation considers these extreme possibilities and every intermediate possibility.

For any random number of stock price increases, j, the numerator expresses three things about the call for the j stock price increases among the n periods. First, starting from the right, the numerator gives the payoff on the option if the stock price rises j times. This is our familiar expression beginning with MAX. The value of the call at expiration is either zero, or the stock price minus the exercise price, whichever is greater. The expression $U^j D^{n-j} S_t$ gives the stock price at expiration if the stock price rises j periods and falls the other $n - j$ periods. Second, the numerator expresses the probability of exactly j stock price increases and $n - j$ stock price decreases. Earlier, we saw how to find the probability of up and down movements. Therefore, $\pi_U^j \pi_D^{n-j}$ gives the probability of observing j up movements and $n - j$ down movements. Third, more than one sequence of stock price movements can result in the same terminal stock price. For instance, in the two-period model we saw that UDS_t gave the same terminal stock price as DUS_t. The numerator also computes the number of different combinations of stock price movements that result in the same terminal stock price. The expression:

$$\frac{n!}{j!(n-j)!}$$

computes the number of possible combinations of j rises from n periods. In essence, the combination weights the possibility of exactly n rises and $n - j$ falls by the number of different patterns that result in exactly j rises and $n - j$ falls. For example, only one pattern results in n rises – the stock must rise in every period. By contrast, if $j = n - j$, there will usually be many patterns that can give j rises and $n - j$ falls.

In the expression for the combination, $n!$ is call n-factorial. Its value equals n multiplied by $n - 1$ times $n - 2$ and so on down to 1:

$$n! = n(n - 1)(n - 2)(n - 3) \ldots \quad (1)$$

To illustrate, if $n = 5$, then $5! = 5(4)(3)(2)(1) = 120$. For example, with the two-period model we could have the pattern up-down or down-up resulting in the same stock price. Thus, there are two combinations of one increase over two periods. The increase could be first or second. For any j value, the numerator in Equation 13.2 computes the number of combinations of j increases from n periods, times the probability of having exactly j increases times the payoff on the call if there are j increases. The summation ensures that the numerator reflects all possible j values.

In our two-period example, the option pays off at expiration only if the stock price rises both times. In general, many stock price patterns leave the option out-of-the-money at expiration. For valuing the option, stock price patterns that leave the option out-of-the-money are a dead end, because they result in a zero option price. As a consequence, we do not need to fully evaluate stock price patterns that leave the option out-of-the-money at expiration. Instead, we only need to evaluate those values of j for which the option expires in-the-money. In our two-period example, we do not need to compute the entire formula for $j = 0$ and $j = 1$. If the stock price never goes up or goes up only once, the option expires out-of-the-money. For our two-period example, we only need to consider what happens to the option when the stock price rises twice, that is, when $j = 2$. Only then does the option finish in-the-money. Let us define m as the number of times the stock price must rise for the option to finish in-the-money. Thus, when the stock price rises exactly m times, it must fall $n - m$ times. However, this pattern still leaves the option in-the-money, because the stock price rose the needed m times. Then we need only consider values of $j = m$ to $j = n$. In our two-period example, $m = 2$ because the stock price must rise in both periods for the option to finish in-the-money. Therefore, the following formula gives an alternative expression for the value of an option:

$$c_t = \frac{\sum_{j=m}^{n} \left(\frac{n!}{j!(n-j)!}\right)(\pi_U{}^j \pi_D{}^{n-j})[U^j D^{n-j} S_t - X]}{R^n} \quad (13.3)$$

Notice that the summation begins with m, the minimum number of stock price increases needed to bring the option into-the-money. Because we consider only the events that put the option in-the-money, we no longer need to worry about the call being worth the maximum of zero or the stock price less the exercise price at expiration. With at least m stock price rises, the option will be worth more than zero because it necessarily finishes in-the-money. Now we divide the formula into two parts – one associated with the stock price and the other associated with the exercise price.

$$c_t = S_t \left[\sum_{j=m}^{n} \left(\frac{n!}{j!(n-j)!} \right) (\pi_U^j \pi_D^{n-j}) \frac{U^j D^{n-j}}{R^n} \right] - XR^{-n} \left[\sum_{j=m}^{n} \left(\frac{n!}{j!(n-j)!} \right) \pi_U^j \pi_D^{n-j} \right] \qquad (13.4)$$

This version of the binomial formula starts to resemble our familiar expression for the value of the call as the stock price minus the present value of the exercise price. If the option is in-the-money and the stock price is certain to remain unchanged until expiration, the call price equals the stock price minus the present value of the exercise price. Our formula has exactly that structure except for the two complicated expressions in brackets. These two expressions reflect the riskiness of the stock. This uncertainty or riskiness about the stock gives the added value to the call above the stock price minus the present value of the exercise price.

The multi-period binomial model can reflect numerous stock price outcomes, if there are numerous periods. Just 20 periods gives more than 1 million stock price movement patterns. In our examples, we kept the period length the same and added more periods. This lengthened the total time until expiration. As an alternative, we could keep the same time to expiration and consider more periods of shorter duration. For example, we originally treated a year as a single period. For that year, we could regard each trading day as a period, giving about 250 periods per year. We could evaluate an option with the multi-period model by assuming that the stock price could change once a day.

The binomial model requires that the price move up a given percentage or down a given percentage. Therefore, if we shorten the period, we need to adjust the stock price movements to correspond to the shorter period. While up or down 10 percent might be reasonable for a period of one year, it certainly would not be reasonable for a period of one day. Similarly, a risk-free rate of 6 percent makes sense for a period of one year, but not for a period of one day.

By adjusting the period length, the stock price movement, and the interest rate, we can refine the binomial model as much as we wish. For example, we could assume that the stock price could move one-hundredth of a percent every minute of the year if we wished. Under this assumption, the model would have finer partitions than exist in the market for most stock. However, with the price changing every minute and a time to expiration of one year, we would have trillions of possible stock price outcomes to consider. While having so many periods would be computationally expensive, we could apply the model if we wished. Conceptually, we could make each period so short that the stock price would change continuously. However, if the stock price truly changed continuously, there would be an infinite number of periods to consider. While we cannot compute binomial model values for an infinite number of periods, mathematical techniques do exist to compute option prices when stock prices change continuously.

Binomial Put Option Pricing

In discussing binomial option pricing, we have used call options as an example. However, the model also applies to put options. To value put options, we follow the same reasoning process that we have

428 Chapter 13 European Option Pricing

considered in detail for call options. Rather than detail all of the reasoning leading to the formula, we begin with the formula for the price of a European put option.

$$p_t = \frac{\sum_{j=0}^{n} \left(\frac{n!}{j!(n-j)!}\right)(\pi_U{}^j \pi_D{}^{n-j}) \text{MAX}[0, X - U^j D^{n-j} S_t]}{R^n} \tag{13.5}$$

This formula matches our binomial call formula, except we substitute the expression for the value of a put at expiration, $X - U^j D^{n-j} S_t$, in place of the value of a call at expiration.

In pricing the call option, we only considered stock price patterns that left the call in-the-money at expiration. The same is true for the put. The put finishes in-the-money if the stock price does not increase often enough to make the stock price exceed the exercise price. We defined m as the number of price increases needed to bring the call into the money. If the price increases $m - 1$ or fewer times, the put finishes in-the-money. Therefore, we can also write the formula for the put as follows:

$$p_t = \frac{\sum_{j=0}^{m-1} \left(\frac{n!}{j!(n-j)!}\right)(\pi_U{}^j \pi_D{}^{n-j})[X - U^j D^{n-j} S_t]}{R^n} \tag{13.6}$$

Rearranging terms gives:

$$P_t = XR^{-n}\left(\sum_{j=0}^{m-1} \left(\frac{n!}{j!(n-j)!}\right)(\pi_U{}^j \pi_D{}^{n-j})\right) - S_t\left(\sum_{j=0}^{m-1} \left(\frac{n!}{j!(n-j)!}\right)(\pi_U{}^j \pi_D{}^{n-j})\frac{U^j D^{n-j}}{R^n}\right) \tag{13.7}$$

This formula for the put parallels our familiar expression for the put as equaling the present value of the exercise price minus the stock price. As with the call, the two bracketed expressions account for the risky movement of the stock price.

We can also value the put through put-call parity. We have the value of the call under the binomial model as given in Equation 13.7. Put-call parity tells us that:

$$p_t = c_t - S_t + Xe^{-r(T-t)}$$

Both approaches must necessarily give the same answer.

STOCK PRICE MOVEMENTS

In actual markets, stock prices change to reflect new information. During a single day, a stock price may change many times. From the ticker, we can observe stock prices when transactions occur. When trading ceases overnight, however, we cannot observe the stock price for hours at a time. Where the price wanders during the night, no one can know. Our observations are also limited, because stock prices are quoted in eighths of a dollar. The true stock price need not jump from one eighth to the next, but the observed stock price does. Sometimes the observed price remains the same from one transaction to another. But just because we observe the same price twice in succession does not mean it remained at that price between the two observations. From these reflections, we see that we can never know exactly how stock prices change because we cannot observe the true stock price at every instant. Therefore, any model of stock price behavior deviates from an exact description of how stock prices move. Nonetheless, it is possible to develop a realistic model of stock price movements. In this section, we review a particular model that has been very successful in a wide range of finance applications.

Let us consider the random information that affects the price of a stock. We assume that the information arrives continuously and that each bit of information is small in importance. Under this scenario, we consider a stock price that rises or falls a small proportion in response to each bit of information. We know that finance depends conceptually on the twin ideas of expected return and risk. Thus, we might also think of a stock as having a positive expected rate of return. In the absence of special events, we expect the stock price to grow along the path of its expected rate of return. However, the world is risky. Information about the stock is sometimes favorable and sometimes unfavorable. As this random information becomes known, it pushes the stock away from its expected growth path. When the information is better than expected, the stock price jumps above its growth path. Negative information has the opposite effect; it pushes the stock price below its expected growth path. Thus, we might imagine the stock price growing along its expected growth path just as a drunk walks across a field. We expect the drunk to reach the other side of the field, but we also think he will wander and stumble in unpredictable short-term deviations from the straight path. Similarly, we expect a stock price to rise, because it has a positive expected return, but we also expect it to wander above and below its growth path, due to new information.

Finance uses a standard mathematical model that is consistent with the story of the preceding paragraph. It assumes that the stock grows at an expected rate μ with a standard deviation σ over some period of time Δt:

$$\Delta S = S_{t+1} - S_t = S_t \mu \Delta t + S_t N(0,1) \sigma \sqrt{\Delta t} \tag{13.8}$$

where:

S_t = the stock price at the beginning of the interval
ΔS = the stock price change during time Δt
$S_t \mu \Delta t$ = expected value of the stock price change during time Δt
$N(0,1)$ = normally distributed random variable with $\mu = 0$, $\sigma = 1$
σ = standard deviation of the stock price

Equation 13.8 says that the stock price change during Δt depends on two factors: the expected growth rate in the price and the variability of the growth. First, the expected growth in the stock price over a given interval depends on the mean growth rate, μ, and the amount of time, Δt. Therefore, if the stock price starts at S_t, the expected stock price increase after an interval of Δt equals $S_t \mu \Delta t$. However, this is only the expected stock price increase after the interval. Due to risk, the actual price change can be greater or lower. Deviations from the expected stock price depend on chance and on the volatility of the stock. The equation captures risk by using the normal distribution. For convenience, the model uses the standard normal distribution, which has a zero mean and a standard deviation of 1. The standard deviation represents the variability of a particular stock. We multiply the standard deviation of the stock by a random drawing from the normal distribution to capture the riskiness of the stock. Also, the equation says that the variability increases with the square root of the interval Δt. In other words, the farther into the future we project the stock price with our model, the less certain we can be about what the stock price will be.

Dividing both sides of Equation 13.8 by the original stock price, S_t, gives the percentage change in the stock price during Δt:

$$\frac{\Delta S}{S_t} = \mu \Delta t + N(0,1)\sigma\sqrt{\Delta t}$$

From this equation, it is possible to show that the percentage change in the stock price is normally distributed:

$$\frac{\Delta S}{S_t} \sim N[\mu \Delta t,\ \sigma\sqrt{\Delta t}] \qquad\qquad (13.9)$$

Figure 13.3 shows two stock price paths over the course of a year, with both stock prices starting at $100. The straight line graphs a stock that grows at 10 percent per year with no risk. The jagged line shows a stock price path with an expected growth rate of 10 percent and a standard deviation of .2 per year. We generated the second price path by taking repeated random samples from a normal distribution to create price changes according to Equation 13.8. As the jagged line in Figure 13.3

Figure 13.3   Two Stock Price Paths

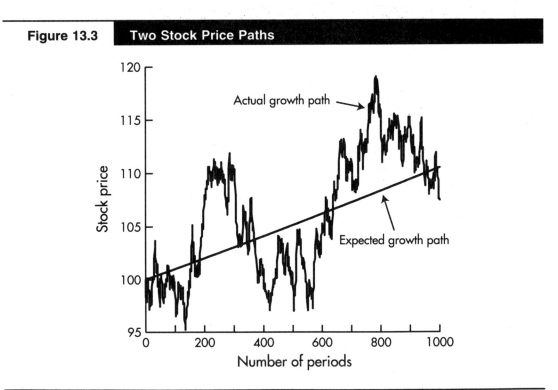

shows, a stock might easily wander away from its growth path due to the riskiness represented by its standard deviation.

To construct Figure 13.3, we used 1,000 periods per year and a growth rate of 10 percent. To construct the straight line, we assumed that the stock price increased by .1/1000 each period. However, this gives an ending stock price of $110.51, not the $110 we expect if the stock price grows at 10 percent per year. This difference results from using 1,000 compounding intervals during the year.

However, we hypothesize that information arrives continuously, so that the stock price could always change. To avoid worrying about the compounding interval, we now employ continuous compounding. Therefore, we focus on logarithmic stock returns. For example, consider a beginning stock price of $100 and an ending price of $110 a year later. The logarithmic stock return over the year is $\ln(S_t/S_0) = \ln(\$110/\$100) = \ln(1.1) = .0953$. The logarithmic stock return is just the continuous growth rate that takes the stock price from its original value to its ending value. Thus, $\$100e^{ut} = \$100e^{.0953(1)} = \$110$. We now need a continuous growth model of stock prices that is consistent with our model for the percentage change stock price model of Equation 13.9. With some difficult math, it is possible to prove the following result:

$$\ln\left(\frac{S_{t+\Delta t}}{S_t}\right) \sim N[(\mu - .5\sigma^2)(\Delta t), \sigma\sqrt{\Delta t}] \tag{13.10}$$

This expression asserts that logarithmic stock returns are distributed normally with the given mean and standard deviation. For a later time, $t + \Delta t$, the expected stock price and the variance of the stock price are:

$$E(S_{t+\Delta t}) = S_t e^{\mu\Delta t}$$

$$VAR(S_{t+\Delta t}) = S_t^2 e^{2\mu\Delta t}(e^{\sigma^2\Delta t}-1)$$

Thus, the expected stock price at $t + \Delta t$ depends on the original stock price, S_t, the expected growth rate, μ, and the amount of time that elapses, Δt. Similarly, the variance of the stock price depends on the original stock price, the expected growth rate, and the elapsed time as well. The longer the time horizon, the larger will be the variance. The increasing variance reflects our greater uncertainty about stock prices far in the future.

As an example, consider a stock with an initial price of $100 and an expected growth rate of 10 percent. If the stock has a standard deviation of .2 per year, we can compute the expected stock price and variance for six months into the future. For this example, we have the following values:

$$S_t = \$100$$
$$\mu = .1$$
$$\sigma = .2$$
$$\Delta t = .5$$
$$E(S_{t+\Delta t}) = \$100e^{.1(.5)} = \$105.13$$
$$VAR(S_{t+\Delta t}) = (\$100)(\$100)(e^{2(.1)(.5)})(e^{(.2)(.2)(.5)} - 1) = \$223.26$$

The standard deviation of the price over period Δt is $14.94. Figure 13.4 shows stock price realizations that are consistent with this example. We found these prices by drawing random values from a normal

Figure 13.4   **Possible Stock Prices**

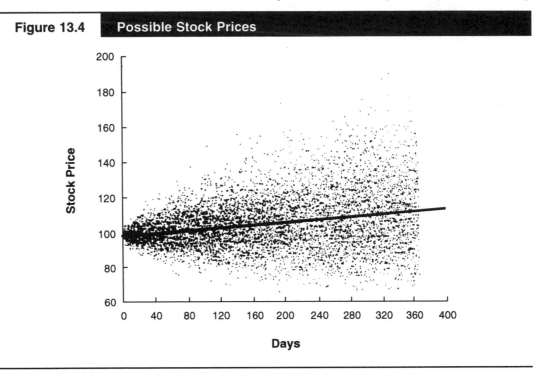

distribution and using our example growth rate and standard deviation. Each dot in the figure represents a possible stock price realization. Notice that the price tends to drift higher over time, consistent with a rising expected value. This is shown by the regression line that is fitted through the points. However, there is considerable uncertainty about what the price will be at any future date. The farther we go into the future, the greater that uncertainty becomes.

Research on actual stock price behavior shows that logarithmic stock returns are approximately normally distributed. So we say that, as an approximation, stock returns follow a **log-normal distribution**. Stock returns themselves are not normally distributed. As an example, Figure 13.5 shows a distribution of stock returns with a mean of 1.2 and a standard deviation of .6. It is easy to see that this distribution is not normal because it is skewed to the right. There is a greater chance of larger returns than one would expect with a normal distribution. Figure 13.6 shows the log-normal distribution that corresponds to the values in Figure 13.5. The values graphed in Figure 13.6 are the logarithms of the values used to construct Figure 13.5. The graph in Figure 13.6 shows a normal distribution. We will assume that stock returns are distributed as Figure 13.6 shows, except the mean and standard deviation differ from stock to stock.

While the log-normal distribution only approximates stock returns, it has two great virtues. First, it is mathematically tractable, so we can obtain solutions for the value of call options if stock returns are log-normally distributed. Second, the resulting call option prices that we compute are very good approximations of actual market prices. In the remainder of this chapter, we treat stock returns as log-normally distributed with a specified mean and variance.

A Log-Normal Distribution **Figure 13.5**

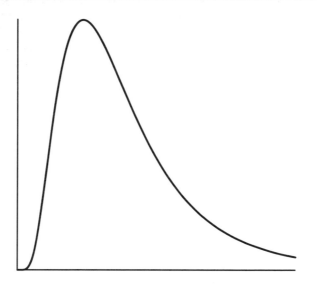

The Normal Distribution **Figure 13.6**

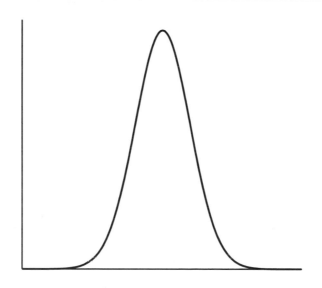

THE BINOMIAL APPROACH TO THE BLACK-SCHOLES MODEL

We have seen how to generalize the binomial model to any number of periods. Increasing the number of periods allows for many possible stock price outcomes at expiration, thereby increasing the realism of the results. However, three problems remain. First, as the number of periods increases, computational difficulties begin to arise. Second, increasing the number of periods while holding the time until expiration constant means that the period length becomes shorter. We must adjust the up and down movement factors, U and D, and the risk-free rate to fit the time horizon. Obviously, we cannot use factors with a scale appropriate to a year when the period length is, say, one day. Third, we have worked with more or less arbitrarily selected up and down factors. The price that the model gives can only be as good as its inputs. The example inputs we have been considering serve well as illustrations, but they are not appropriate for analyzing real options. Therefore, we need a better way to determine the up and down factors.

Modeling stock returns by a log-normal process solves these three problems simultaneously. If stock returns are log-normally distributed with the mean return given by μ and a standard deviation of σ for some unit of calendar time Δt, then we define the following binomial inputs as:

$$U = e^{\sigma\sqrt{\Delta t}}$$

$$D = \frac{1}{U} \qquad\qquad (13.11)$$

$$\pi_u = \frac{e^{\mu \Delta t} - D}{U - D}$$

As the entire analysis takes place within a risk-neutral framework μ, the expected return on the stock must equal the risk-free rate. Therefore, the probability of an upward stock price movement becomes:

$$\pi_u = \frac{e^{r \Delta t} - D}{U - D} \qquad\qquad (13.12)$$

Notice that the values of R, U, and D adjust automatically as the tree is adjusted to include more and more periods during the fixed calendar interval $T - t$. The absolute value of each becomes smaller, exactly as we would expect for a shorter time period. The values for U and D depend on the riskiness of the stock returns. The probability of a stock price increase depends upon the mean return on the stock. Thus, if we can estimate the standard deviation of stock returns, we have reasonable inputs to the binomial model. These can replace the arbitrary example values that we have been using.[4]

To illustrate how the binomial model gives increasingly refined estimates as the number of periods increases, consider a European call option that has one year until expiration and an exercise price of $100. Assume that the underlying stock trades for $100, with a standard deviation of 0.10. The risk-free rate of interest is 6 percent. Figure 13.7 shows how the binomial prices converge to the true option price of $7.46 as the number of periods increases. The binomial prices oscillate around the true price: for a single-period binomial model, the price is $7.76. With two periods, the binomial model gives a price of $6.96. With 20 periods, the binomial price is $7.40, and with 100 periods, the binomial price is $7.45. In general, the greater the number of periods in the lattice, the more

Convergence of Binomial Prices as the Number of Periods Increases

Figure 13.7

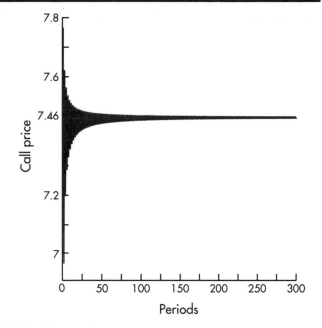

accurate is the computed binomial price. **OPTION!** can compute call and put prices for the single-period and multi-period binomial models.

As we show in the next section, using the model of stock returns discussed in this section allows us to compute the value of an option with an infinite number of periods until expiration. With the strict binomial model, we could never employ an infinite number of periods because it would take forever to add all the individual results.

THE BLACK-SCHOLES OPTION PRICING MODEL

To this point, we have developed the binomial option pricing model. We have discussed the log-normal distribution of stock returns and have presented up and down factors for the binomial model that are consistent with the log-normal distribution of stock returns. Also, we have seen how to adjust the precision of the binomial model by dividing a given unit of calendar time into more and more periods. As we deal with more periods, however, the calculations in the binomial model become cumbersome. As the number of periods in the binomial model becomes very large, the binomial model converges to the famous Black-Scholes option pricing model.

Fischer Black and Myron Scholes developed their option pricing model under the assumptions that asset prices adjust to prevent arbitrage, that stock prices change continuously, and that stock returns follow a log-normal distribution.[5] Also, their model holds for European call options on stocks with no dividends. Further, they assume that the interest rate and the volatility of the stock remain constant over the life of the option. The mathematics they used to derive their result include stochastic calculus, which is beyond the scope of this text. In this section, we present their model and illustrate the basic intuition that underlies it. We show that the form of the Black-Scholes model parallels the bounds on option pricing that we have already observed. In fact, the form of the Black-Scholes model is very close to the binomial model we have just been considering.

The Black-Scholes Call Option Pricing Model

The following expression gives the Black-Scholes option pricing model for a call option:

$$c_t = S_t N(d_1) - Xe^{-r(T-t)}N(d_2) \tag{13.13}$$

where:

$$N(\cdot) = \text{cumulative normal distribution function}$$

$$d_1 = \frac{\ln\left(\frac{S_t}{X}\right) + (r + .5\sigma^2)(T - t)}{\sigma\sqrt{T - t}} \tag{13.14}$$

$$d_2 = d_1 - \sigma\sqrt{T - t}$$

This model has the general form we have long considered – the value of a call must equal or exceed the stock price minus the present value of the exercise price:

$$c_t \geq S_t - Xe^{-r(T-t)}$$

To adapt this formula to account for risk, as in the Black-Scholes model, we multiply the stock price and the exercise price by some factors to account for risk, giving the general form:

$$c_t = S_t \times \text{Risk Factor 1} - Xe^{-r(T-t)} \times \text{Risk Factor 2}$$

The binomial model shares this general form with the Black-Scholes model. With the binomial model, the risk adjustment factors were the large bracketed expressions of Equation 13.2. With the Black-Scholes model, the risk factors are $N(d_1)$ and $N(d_2)$. In the Black-Scholes model, these risk adjustment factors are the continuous time equivalent of the bracketed expressions in the binomial model.

Computing Black-Scholes Option Prices

In this section, we show how to compute Black-Scholes option prices. Assume that a stock trades at $100 and the risk-free interest rate is 6 percent. A call option on the stock has an exercise price of $100 and expires in one year. The standard deviation of the stock's returns is .10 per year. We compute the values of d_1 and d_2 as follows:

$$d_1 = \frac{\ln\left(\frac{100}{100}\right) + (.06 + .5(.01))1}{.1\sqrt{1}} = .65$$

$$d_2 = .65 - .1 \times 1 = .55$$

Next, we find the cumulative normal values associated with d_1 and d_2. These values are the probability that a normally distributed variable with a zero mean and a standard deviation of 1.0 will have a value equal to or less than the d_1 or d_2 term we are considering. Figure 13.8 shows a graph of a normally distributed variable with a zero mean and a standard deviation of 1.0. It shows the values of d_1 and d_2 for our example. For illustration, we focus on d_1, which equals .65. In finding $N(d_1)$, we want to know which portion of the area under the curve lies to the left of .65. This is the value of $N(d_1)$. Clearly, the value we seek is larger than .5, because d_1 is above the mean of zero. We can find the exact value by consulting a table of the cumulative normal distribution for this variable. We present this table as Appendix A. Also, we can use **OPTION!** to find these values. For a value of .65 drawn from the border of the table, we find our probability in the interior: $N(.65) =$ .7422. Similarly, $N(d_2) = N(.55) = .7088$. We now have:

$$c_t = \$100 \times .7422 - \$100 \times .9418 \times .7088 = \$7.46$$

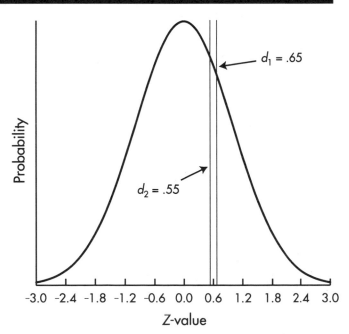

The Standardized Normal Distribution | **Figure 13.8**

Probability

$d_1 = .65$

$d_2 = .55$

-3.0 -2.4 -1.8 -1.2 -0.6 0.0 0.6 1.2 1.8 2.4 3.0

Z-value

We chose these values for our example because they parallel the values from our original binomial example. There we also assumed that the stock traded for $100 and that the risk-free rate was 6 percent. We assumed an up factor of 10 percent and a down factor of −10 percent. With a single-period binomial model and these values, we found that a call must be priced at $7.55. The two results are close. However, if we use more periods in the binomial model and use up and down factors that are consistent with a log-normal distribution of stock returns, the binomial model will converge to the Black-Scholes model price. The reader can explore this possibility by using **OPTION!**.

The Black-Scholes Put Option Pricing Model

Black and Scholes developed their option pricing model for calls only. However, we can find the Black-Scholes model for European puts by applying put-call parity:

$$p_t = c_t - S_t + Xe^{-r(T-t)}$$

Substituting the Black-Scholes call formula in the put-call parity equation gives:

$$p_t = S_t N(d_1) - Xe^{-r(T-t)}N(d_2) - S_t + Xe^{-r(T-t)}$$

Collecting like terms simplifies the equation to:

$$p_t = S_t[N(d_1) - 1] + Xe^{-r(T-t)}[1 - N(d_2)]$$

If we consider the cumulative distribution of all values from −∞ to +∞, the maximum value is 1.0. For any value of d_1 we consider, part of the whole must lie at or below the value and the remainder must lie above it. For example, if $N(d_1)$ is .7422, for $d_1 = .65$, then .2578 of the total area under the curve must lie at values greater than .65. Now we apply a principle of normal distributions. The normal distribution is symmetrical, so the same percentage of the area under the curve that lies above d_1 must lie below $-d_1$. Therefore, for any symmetrical distribution and any arbitrary value, w:

$$N(w) + N(-w) = 1$$

Following this pattern and substituting for $N(d_1)$ and $N(d_2)$ gives the equivalent Black-Scholes value for a put option.

$$p_t = Xe^{-r(T-t)}N(-d_2) - S_t N(-d_1) \tag{13.15}$$

This equation has the familiar form that we have been exploring since Chapter 11. We emphasize that the Black-Scholes model for puts holds only for European puts.

INPUTS FOR THE BLACK-SCHOLES MODEL

We have seen that the Black-Scholes model for the price of an option depends on five variables: the stock price, the exercise price, the time until expiration, the risk-free rate, and the standard deviation of the stock. Of these, the stock price is observable in the financial press or on a trading terminal.

The exercise price and the time until expiration can be known with certainty. We want to consider how to obtain estimates of the other two parameters: the risk-free interest rate and the standard deviation of the stock.

Estimating the Risk-Free Rate of Interest

Estimates of the risk-free interest rate are widely available and are usually quite reliable.[6] There are still a few points to consider, however. First, we need to select the correct rate. Because the Black-Scholes model uses a risk-free rate, we can use the Treasury bill rate as a good estimate. Quoted interest rates for T-bills are expressed as discount rates. We need to convert these to regular interest rates and express them as continuously compounded rates. As a second consideration, we should select the maturity of the T-bill carefully. If the yield curve has a steep slope, yields for different maturities can differ significantly. With T-bills maturing each week, we choose the bill that matures closest to the option expiration.

We illustrate the computation with the following example. Consider a T-bill with 84 days until maturity. Its bid yield is 8.83 and its asking yield is 8.77. Letting BID and ASK be the bid and asked yields, the following formula gives the price of a T-bill as a percentage of its face value:

$$P_{TB} = 1 - .01\left(\frac{BID + ASK}{2}\right)\left(\frac{Days\ Until\ Maturity}{360}\right)$$

$$= 1 - .01\left(\frac{8.83 + 8.77}{2}\right)\left(\frac{84}{360}\right)$$

$$= .97947$$

In this formula, we average the bid and asked yields to estimate the unobservable true yield which lies between the observable bid and asked yields. For our example, the price of the T-bill is 97.947 percent of its face value. To find the corresponding continuously compounded rate, we solve the following equation for r:

$$e^{r(T-t)} = \frac{1}{P_{TB}}$$

$$e^{r(.23)} = 1/.97947$$

$$.23r = \ln(1.02096) = .0207$$

$$r = .0902$$

In the equation, $T - t = .23$ because 84 days is 23 percent of a year. Thus, the appropriate interest rate in this example is 9.02 percent. Securing good estimates of the risk-free interest rate is fairly easy. However, having an exact estimate is not critical, as option prices are not very sensitive to the interest rate.

Estimating the Stock's Standard Deviation

Estimating the standard deviation of the stock's returns is more difficult and more important than estimating the risk-free rate. The Black-Scholes model takes as its input the current, instantaneous standard deviation of the stock. In other words, the immediate volatility of the stock is the riskiness of the stock that affects the option price. The Black-Scholes model also assumes that the volatility is constant over the life of the option.[7] There are two basic ways to estimate the volatility. The first method uses historical data, while the second technique employs fresh data from the options market itself. This second method uses option prices to find the option market's estimate of the stock's standard deviation. An estimate of the stock's standard deviation that is drawn from the options market is called an **implied volatility**. We consider each method in turn.[8]

Historical Data.   To estimate volatility using historical data, we compute the price relatives, logarithmic price relatives, and the mean and standard deviation of the logarithmic price relatives. Letting PR_t indicate the price relative for day t so that $PR_t = P_t/P_{t-1}$, we give the formulas for the mean and variance of the logarithmic price relatives as follows:

$$\overline{PR} = \frac{1}{T}\sum_{t=1}^{T}\ln PR_t$$

$$VAR(PR) = \frac{1}{T-1}\sum_{t=1}^{T}(\ln PR_t - \overline{PR})^2$$

As an example, we apply these formulas to data in the following table, which gives 11 days of price information for a stock. With 11 price observations, we compute ten daily returns. The first column tracks the day, while the second column records the stock's closing price for the day. The third column computes the price relative from the prices in column 2. The fourth column gives the log of the price relative in column 3. The last column contains the result of subtracting the mean of the logarithmic price relatives from each observation and squaring the result.

The mean, variance, and standard deviation that we have calculated are all based on our sample of daily data. We use the sample standard deviation as an input to the Black-Scholes model.

Three inputs to the Black-Scholes model depend on the unit of time. These inputs are the interest rate, the time until expiration, and the standard deviation. We can use any single measure we wish, but we need to express all three variables in the same time units. For example, we can use days as our time unit and express the time until expiration as the number of days remaining. Then we must also use a daily estimation of the standard deviation and the interest rate for a single day. Generally, one year is the most convenient common unit of time. Therefore, we need to convert our daily standard deviation into a comparable yearly estimate. We have estimated our daily standard deviation of ten days. However, these are ten trading days, not calendar days. Accordingly, we recognize that we are working in trading time, not calendar time. Deleting weekend days and holidays, each year has about 250–252 trading days. We use 250 trading days per year.

We have already seen that stock prices are distributed with a standard deviation that increases as the square root of time. Accordingly, we can adjust the time dimension of our volatility estimate by multiplying it by the square root of time. For example, we convert from our daily standard deviation estimate to an equivalent yearly value by multiplying the daily estimate times the square root of 250.[9]

$$\text{Annualized } \sigma = \text{Daily } \sigma \times \sqrt{250} \tag{13.16}$$

For our daily estimate of .021843, the estimated standard deviation in annual terms is .3454.

In our example, we have used ten days of data. In actual practice, we face a trade-off between using the most recent possible data and using more data. In statistics, we almost always get more reliable estimates by using more data. However, the Black-Scholes model takes the instantaneous standard deviation as an input. This gives great importance to using current data. If we use the last year of historical data, then we have a rich data set for estimating the old volatility. Using just ten days, as we did in our example, emphasizes current data, but it is really not very much data for getting a reliable estimate.

To emphasize the importance of using current data, consider the Crash of 1987. On Bloody Monday, October 19, 1987, the market lost about 22 percent of its value. If we used a full year of daily data to estimate a stock's historical volatility the next day, our estimate would be too low. In the light of the Crash, the instantaneous volatility had surely increased.

Implied Volatility. To overcome the limitations inherent in using historical data to estimate standard deviations, some scholars have turned to techniques of implied volatility. In this section, we show how to use market data and the Black-Scholes model to estimate a stock's volatility. There are five inputs to the Black-Scholes model, which the model relates to a sixth variable, the call price. With a total of six variables, any five imply a unique value for the sixth. The technique of implied volatility uses known values of five variables to estimate the standard deviation. The estimated standard deviation is an implied volatility because it is the value implied by the other five variables in the model.[10]

To find implied volatilities, we begin with established values for the stock price, exercise price, interest rate, time until expiration, and the call price. We use these to find the implied standard deviation. However, the standard deviation enters the Black-Scholes model through the values for d_1 and d_2, which are used to determine the values of the cumulative normal distribution. As a result, we cannot solve for the standard deviation directly. Instead, we must search for the volatility that makes the Black-Scholes equation hold. To do this, we need a computer. Otherwise, we would have to try an estimate of the standard deviation, make all of the Black-Scholes computations by hand, and adjust the standard deviation for the next try. This would be cumbersome and time-consuming. Therefore, implied volatilities are almost always found using a computer. **OPTION!** has a module for finding implied volatilities.

For most stocks with options, several options with different expirations trade at once. Some researchers have argued that all of these options should be used to find the volatility implied by each. The resulting estimates are then given weights and averaged to find a single volatility estimate. The single estimate is known as a **weighted implied standard deviation**. In principle, this is a good idea because it uses more information. Other things being equal, estimates based on more information should dominate estimates based on less information. However, some options trade infrequently, which makes their prices less reliable for computing implied volatilities. In addition, options way out-of-the-money give somewhat spurious volatility estimates. Virtually all weighting schemes give the highest weight to options closest to-the-money. At-the-money options tend to give the least biased volatility estimates, and many option traders derive implied volatilities by focusing on at-the-money options.[11]

Consider the following example of an implied standard deviation based on a call option. We assume that $X = \$100$ and the option is at-the-money, so $S = \$100$. We also assume that the option has 90 days remaining until expiration and that the risk-free interest rate is 10 percent, so we have $T - t = 90$ days and $r = .10$. The call price is $5.00. To find the implied standard deviation, we need to find the standard deviation that is consistent with these other values. To do this, we can compute the Black-Scholes model price for alternative standard deviations. We adjust the standard deviation to make the option price converge to its actual price of $5.00. The sequence of standard deviations and corresponding call prices below shows this relationship. In our example, we first try $\sigma = .1$, which gives a call price of $3.41. This price is too low. Thus, we know the correct standard deviation must be larger, because the call price varies directly with the standard deviation. Next, $\sigma = .5$ results in a call price of $11.03, which is too high. Now we know that the standard deviation must be greater than .1, but less than .5. The task is to find the standard deviation that gives a call value equal to the specified $5.00. This happens with $\sigma = .187$. Using the implied volatility module of **OPTION!**, we find that the exact standard deviation is .186800.[12]

Standard Deviation	Corresponding Call Price	
.1	$ 3.41	too low
.5	11.03	too high
.3	7.16	too high
.2	5.24	too high
.15	4.31	too low
.175	4.78	too low
.18	4.87	too low
.185	4.97	too low
.19	5.06	too high
.188	5.02	too high
.187	5.00	success

EUROPEAN OPTIONS AND DIVIDENDS

Most of the stocks that underlie stock options pay dividends. Yet the Black-Scholes model assumes that the underlying stock pays no dividends. While the Black-Scholes model might be elegant and provide a great deal of insight into option pricing, successful real-world application of the model depends upon resolving the dividend problem. In this section, we consider the impact of dividends on option values and we show how slight adjustments in the Black-Scholes model allow it to apply to options on dividend-paying stocks. We continue to focus on European options.

The Effect of Dividends on Option Prices

As we have seen, the value of a call option at expiration equals the maximum of zero or the stock price minus the exercise price, and a put option at expiration is worth the maximum of zero or the exercise price minus the stock price. In our familiar notation:

$$c_T = \text{MAX}\{0, S_T - X\}$$
$$p_T = \text{MAX}\{0, X - S_T\}$$

For both the call and the put, anything that affects the stock price at expiration will affect the price of the option. Dividends that might be paid during the life of the option can obviously affect the stock price. We may regard a dividend as a repayment of a portion of the share's value to the shareholder. As such, we would expect the stock price to fall by the amount of the dividend payment.[13]

As a metaphor, we might think of the dividend on a stock as a leakage of value from the stock. As the value of the stock drops due to the leakage of dividends, the changing stock price will affect the value of options on the stock.

A drop in the stock price due to a dividend will have an adverse effect on the price of a call and a beneficial effect on the price of a put. For a call, the stock price at expiration will be lower than it would have been had there been no dividend. Thus, the dividend will reduce the quantity $S_T - X$, thus reducing the value of the call at expiration. For the put, the dividend will reduce the stock price at expiration, and it will therefore increase the quantity $X - S_T$.

We can illustrate the effect of dividends with an example of a call and put that have a common exercise price of $100. Assume the options are moments from expiration, and that the stock price is $102. Without bringing dividends into consideration, the value of the options would be:

$$c_T = \text{MAX}\{0, S_T - X\} = \text{MAX}\{0, \$102 - \$100\} = \$2$$
$$p_T = \text{MAX}\{0, X - S_T\} = \text{MAX}\{0, \$100 - \$102\} = \$0$$

Just before expiration, the stock pays a dividend of $3, causing the stock price to drop from $102 to $99. With a stock price of $99 at expiration, the call option will be worth zero, and the put will be worth $1. Failing to take into account the looming dividend payment could cause large pricing errors from a blind application of the Black-Scholes model. We now turn to adjustments in the Black-Scholes model that reflect dividends.

Adjustments for Known Dividends

For most stocks, the dividend payments likely to occur during the life of an option can be forecast with considerable precision. If we are looking ahead to a dividend forecasted to occur in three months, we expect the stock price to drop by the amount of the dividend when the stock goes ex-dividend. At the present moment, three months before the ex-dividend date, we can build that looming dividend into our analysis. To do so, we subtract the present value of the dividend from the current stock price. We then apply the Black-Scholes model as usual, except we use the adjusted stock price as an input to the model instead of the current stock price.

As an example, consider call and put options with a common exercise price of $100 and 150 days until expiration. Assume that the underlying stock trades for $102, and that you expect the stock to pay a $3 dividend in 90 days. The risk-free rate is 9 percent, and the standard deviation for the stock is 0.30. The present value of the $3 dividend is:

$$\$3e^{-r(90/365)} = \$2.93$$

According to this technique, we reduce the stock price now by the present value of the dividend, giving an adjusted stock price of $99.07. We then apply the Black-Scholes model in the usual way, except we use the adjusted stock price of $99.07 instead of the current price of $102. The following table shows the results of applying the adjusted and unadjusted models to the call and the put.

Black-Scholes Model Price	Call	Put
Adjusted for known dividends	8.91	6.21
Unadjusted	10.74	5.11

Applying the Black-Scholes model, with the adjustment for known dividends that we have just discussed, gives a call value of $8.91 and a put value of $6.21. With no adjustment for dividends, the Black-Scholes prices are $10.74 for the call option and $5.11 for the put option. The difference in prices is substantial, amounting to almost 20 percent. Also, as we hypothesized, subtracting the present value of the dividends from the stock price reduces the value of the call and increases the value of the put.

The same technique applies in situations when there are several dividends. The stock price should be adjusted by subtracting the present value of all dividends that are expected to occur before the expiration date of the option. Dividends expected after the option expires can be ignored, because the option will already have been exercised or allowed to expire before those dividends affect the value of the stock. **OPTION!** can compute the prices of call and put options under the Black-Scholes model adjusted for known dividends.

Adjustments for Continuous Dividends – Merton's Model

Robert Merton has shown how to adjust the Black-Scholes model to account for dividends when the dividend is paid at a continuous rate. Instead of focusing on the quarterly dividends that characterize individual stocks, Merton's model applies when the dividend is paid continuously. Essentially, the adjustment for continuous dividends treats the dividend rate as a negative interest rate. We have already seen that dividends reduce the value of a call option, because they reduce the value of the stock that underlies the option. In effect, we have a continuous leakage of value from the stock that equals the dividend rate. We let the Greek letter delta, δ, represent this rate of leakage.[14]

Merton's model applies particularly well to options on goods such as foreign currency. In such an option, the foreign currency is treated as paying a continuous dividend equal to the foreign interest rate. (We explore options on foreign currency in Chapter 16.) Merton's model also applies fairly well to options on individual stocks, if we treat the quarterly dividends as being earned at a continuous rate. Merton's adjustment to the Black-Scholes model for continuous dividends is:

$$c_t^M = e^{-\delta(T-t)}S_t N(d_1^M) - Xe^{-r(T-t)}N(d_2^M)$$

$$d_1^M = \frac{\ln\left(\dfrac{S_t}{X}\right) + (r - \delta + .5\sigma^2)(T - t)}{\sigma\sqrt{T - t}}$$

$$(13.17)$$

$$d_2^M = d_1^M - \sigma\sqrt{T - t}$$

where:

δ = the continuous dividend rate on the stock

To adjust the regular Black-Scholes model, we replace the current stock price with the stock price adjusted for the continuous dividend. That is, we replace S_t with:

$$e^{-\delta(T-t)}S_t$$

Substituting this expression into the formulas for d_1 and d_2 gives d_1^M and d_2^M as shown earlier. Merton's adjusted put value is:

$$p_t^M = Xe^{-r(T-t)}N(-d_2^M) - Se^{-\delta(T-t)}N(-d_1^M) \tag{13.18}$$

When $\delta = 0$, Merton's model reduces immediately to the Black-Scholes model. Thus, the Merton model is a more general model than the original Black-Scholes and it will appear repeatedly in the remainder of the text. As an example of how to apply the continuous dividend adjustment, consider the following data:

$$S_t = \$60$$
$$X = \$60$$
$$r = .09$$
$$\sigma = .2$$
$$T - t = 180 \text{ days}$$

The stock will pay a quarterly dividend of $2 in 90 days, implying a continuous dividend rate, δ, of 13.75 percent. We compute the call price, c_t^M, as follows:

$$d_1^M = \frac{\ln\left(\frac{60}{60}\right) + [.09 - .1375 + .5(.2)(.2)]\left(\frac{180}{365}\right)}{.2\sqrt{\frac{180}{365}}}$$

$$= \frac{0 - 0.01356}{0.14045} = -0.09656$$

$$d_2^M = -0.09656 - .2\sqrt{\frac{180}{365}} = -0.23701$$

$N(d_1^M) = N(-0.09656) = 0.4615$, and $N(d_2^M) = N(-0.23701) = 0.4063$. Therefore, $N(-d_1^M) = 0.5385$, and $N(-d_2^M) = 0.5937$. The call and put values adjusted for continuous dividends are:

$$c_t^M = 60e^{-.1375(180/365)}(0.4615) - 60e^{-.09(180/365)}(0.4063) = \$2.55$$

$$p_t^M = 60e^{-.09(180/365)}(0.5937) - 60e^{-.1375(180/365)}(0.5385) = \$3.88$$

OPTION! allows the direct estimation of European call and put values according to Merton's model.

The Binomial Model and Dividends

The binomial model can evaluate European option prices for options on dividend paying stocks. There are three alternative dividend treatments within the context of the binomial model, and all involve adjusting the lattice to reflect the impact of dividends on the stock price. The first considers options on stocks paying a continuous dividend. This binomial approach is the analog to the Merton model that we considered earlier. The second binomial approach applies to options on a stock that will pay a known dividend yield at a certain time. For example, a stock might pay a dividend equal to some fraction of its value on a certain date, such as a dividend of 3 percent of the stock's value 120 days from now. The third approach applies to a known dollar dividend that will occur at a certain time. For example, 90 days from now a stock might pay a $1 dividend. The binomial model can accommodate any number of dividend payments between the present and the expiration of the option.

Continuous Dividends. To apply the binomial model to options on a stock paying a continuous dividend, we need to adjust the binomial parameters to reflect the continuous leakage of value from the stock that the dividend represents. For Merton's model for European options on a stock paying a continuous dividend, we saw that the adjustment largely involved subtracting the continuous dividend rate, δ, from the risk-free rate, r. This is exactly the adjustment required for the binomial model. For options on a stock paying a continuous dividend δ, the U, D, and π_U factors are:

$$U = e^{\sigma\sqrt{\Delta t}}$$

$$D = \frac{1}{U} \qquad\qquad (13.19)$$

$$\pi_U = \frac{e^{(r-\delta)\Delta t} - D}{U - D}$$

We illustrated Merton's model by considering a call option on a stock with a price of $60, a standard deviation of .2, and a continuous dividend rate of 13.75 percent. The call had an exercise price of $60 and expired in 180 days. The risk-free rate was 9 percent. We saw that the price of this option according to Merton's model was $2.5557. According to the binomial model, with 200 periods, the price would be $2.5516, which is almost identical. For the same data, the European put according to Merton's model was worth $3.8845. The binomial model with 200 periods gives a put price of $3.8805.

Known Dividend Yield. Consider a stock that will pay w percent of its value as a dividend in 55 days. An option on the stock expires in 120 days, and we model the price of the option using a three-period binomial model. In this situation, the dividend will occur in the second period. The binomial tree for the stock will appear as shown in Figure 13.9. At the second period in the binomial tree, the stock price will be reduced to $(1 - w)$ percent of its value. If the stock price rose in each of the first two periods, the stock price at period 2 would be $S_t UU(1 - w)$. Because of the known dividend yield occurring at day 55, the value of the stock is reduced by the w percent dividend. Given that the stock price went up the first two periods, the value of the stock in the third period could be either $S_t UUU(1 - w)$ if the stock price goes up again, or it could be $S_t UUD(1 - w)$ if the stock price falls in the final period. To value either a call or a put in the context of the binomial model with a known dividend yield, we apply the usual technique to work from the terminal stock prices back to the current stock price and current options price. **OPTION!** can compute call and put prices under the binomial model adjusted for known dividend yields.

Extending this example, let us assume that the initial stock price is $80, that the exercise price for a call and a put is $75, that the standard deviation of the stock is 0.3, and the risk-free rate of interest is 7 percent. The percentage dividend that will be paid is 3 percent, so $w = 0.03$. With 120 days until expiration and a three-period binomial model, $\Delta t = 40/365 = 0.1096$. Therefore:

The Binomial Tree for a Stock with a Known Dividend Yield | **Figure 13.9**

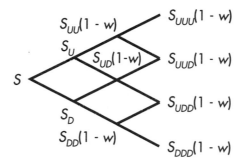

$$U = e^{.3\sqrt{.1096}} = 1.1044$$

$$D = \frac{1}{1.1044} = .9055$$

$$\pi_U = \frac{1.0077 - .9055}{1.1044 - .9055} = .5138$$

The discounting factor for a single period is $e^{-r\Delta t} = e^{-.07(40/365)} = .9924$. Figure 13.10 shows the binomial tree for the stock of our example. In the top panel, the stock price without dividends appears, while the bottom tree shows the effect of the 3 percent dividend on the stock price. For example, in the bottom tree reflecting dividends, the stock price pattern generated by a rise, a rise, and a fall is:

$$S_tUUD(1 - w) = \$80(1.1044)(1.1044)(.9055)(1.0 - .03) = \$85.70$$

Figure 13.11 shows two binomial trees for the call option. The top tree in Figure 13.11 does not reflect the dividends and shows that the option's value would be $9.37. The bottom tree, which does reflect the 3 percent dividend yield, shows that the call is worth $7.94. The difference in the two prices is due entirely to taking account of the dividend.

Figure 13.12 parallels Figure 13.11, except it shows trees for the put option. The top tree ignores the dividend and shows that the put's value would be $2.67 if there were no dividend. Taking account of the dividend in the bottom tree gives a put price of $3.64. The effect of the dividend increases the put's value by 36 percent, from $2.67 to $3.64, and decreases the call's value by 15 percent, from $9.37 to $7.94. Clearly dividends can have a profound effect on option prices.

Known Dollar Dividend. Most stocks that underlie stock options pay a fixed dollar dividend, rather than pay a dividend that equals some percentage of their value. This presents a complication, because the tree may develop a tremendous number of branches. For example, assume that the stock price is initially $80 and that $U = 1.1$. Therefore, $D = .9091$. After one period, the stock price is either $88

Figure 13.10   **Example Stock Price Lattices With and Without a Known Dividend Yield**

Without dividends

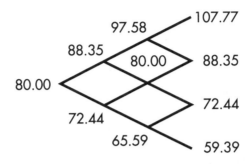

With dividends

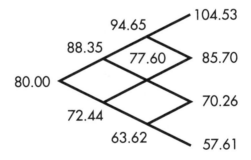

or $72.73, as Figure 13.13 shows. Assume that a $2 dividend is paid just before the first period. Taking the dividend payment into account, the stock price will be either $86 or $70.73 at the first period. In the next period the stock price will either rise or fall. If it was $86, it will then be $94.60 if the price rises again or $78.18 if the price falls. If the stock price fell in the first period, so that it was $70.73 after the dividend payment, in the second period it will either rise to $77.80 or fall to $64.30. Figure 13.13 shows that there are four possible prices after two periods: $94.60, $78.18, $77.80, or $64.30. In the normal tree, there would only be three prices to consider, because $S_tUD = S_tDU$. That is not the case with known dollar dividends. Letting DIV$ indicate a given dollar dividend, $(S_tU - DIV\$)D$ does not equal $(S_tD - DIV\$)U$. For many periods and multiple dividend payments, the number of nodes to evaluate can explode, making this model very difficult to apply.

Example Call Price Lattices With and Without a Known Dividend Yield   **Figure 13.11**

Without dividends

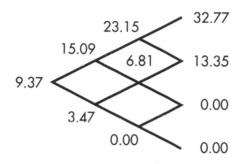

With dividends

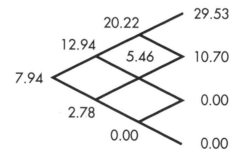

We can avoid these difficulties by making a simplifying assumption. We assume that the stock price reflects the dividend, which is known with certainty, and all other factors that might affect the stock price, which are uncertain. We then adjust the uncertain component of the stock price for the impending dividends and model the uncertain component of the stock price with the binomial tree, adding back the present value of all future dividends at each node. Specifically, we follow these steps:

1. Compute the present value of all dividends to be paid during the life of the option as of the present time = t.
2. Subtract this present value from the current stock price to form $S_t' = S_t - PV$ of all dividends.

Figure 13.12   **Example Put Price Lattices With and Without a Known Dividend Yield**

Without dividends

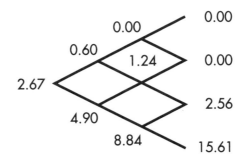

With dividends

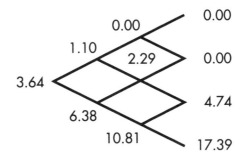

3. Create the binomial tree by applying the up and down factors in the usual way to the initial stock price S_t'.
4. After generating the tree, add to the stock price at each node the present value of all future dividends to be paid during the life of the option.
5. Compute the option values in the usual way by working through the binomial tree.

    To make this discussion more concrete, consider again the tree that failed to recombine in Figure 13.13. The initial stock price was $80, $U = 1.1$, $D = .9091$, and a dividend was to be paid just before the time of the first period. We now additionally assume that one period is .25 years and the interest rate is 10 percent. Therefore, the one-period discount factor is:

Stock Price Lattice Unadjusted for a Known Dollar Dividend   **Figure 13.13**

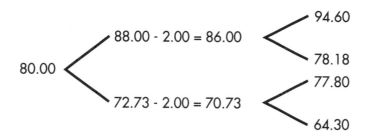

$$e^{-r(\Delta t)} = e^{-.1(.25)} = .9753$$

At the outset, the present value of the dividend is $1.95 = .9753($2). To form S_t' we subtract this present value from S_t:

$$S_t' = S_t - \text{PV of all dividends} = \$80 - \$1.95 = \$78.05$$

Figure 13.14 shows the binomial tree generated from a starting price of $78.05. Notice that the present value of the dividends ($1.95) has been added to the first node only, because only the first node represents a time before the payment of the dividend. Notice also that the tree recombines at the second period, in contrast to Figure 13.13. **OPTION!** can compute call and put prices under the binomial model adjusted for known dollar dividends.

Stock Price Lattice Adjusted for a Known Dollar Dividend   **Figure 13.14**

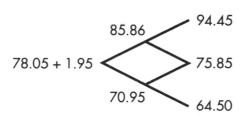

Summary

In this section, we have considered the effect of dividends on European options. In general, a dividend on a stock reduces the value of the stock by the amount of the dividend. Dividends reduce the value of call options because they reduce the stock price. Dividends increase the value of put options because the dividend reduces the price of the stock. The Black-Scholes model as originally developed pertained only to options on nondividend paying stocks. However, the stocks that underlie most stock options do pay dividends, so the limitation of the Black-Scholes model is potentially serious.

There are several adjustments to the Black-Scholes model to account for dividends. The first one adjusts for known dividends by subtracting the present value of the dividends from the stock price and then applying the Black-Scholes model in the usual way. When the underlying stock pays a continuous dividend, Merton showed how to adjust the Black-Scholes model to account for the dividend.

We also considered adjustments to the binomial model to account for dividends. When the stock pays a known dividend yield at a given date, the binomial model can reflect the impact of this dividend on the stock price and the option quite easily. When the dividend is a given dollar amount, the binomial model requires a more elaborate adjustment, but it too can adjust the stock price and compute option values that reflect the impact of the dividend.

TESTS OF THE OPTION PRICING MODEL

If the Black-Scholes option pricing model correctly captures the factors that affect option prices, the price computed according to the model should correspond closely to the price observed in the market. Otherwise, either the model is inadequate or prices in the market are irrational. Therefore, each of the tests that we will consider in this section test a joint hypothesis – adequacy of the option pricing model and market rationality. If we find a discrepancy between the two, we can account for this divergence by claiming that the model is inadequate or by allowing that market participants are foolish. Note, however, that the Black-Scholes model was derived under the assumption that prices should not permit arbitrage. Accordingly, any major discrepancy between the model price and the market price would be serious indeed.

The Black-Scholes Study

The first empirical study of option pricing was conducted by Black and Scholes.[15] In this 1972 test, they examined over-the-counter option prices, because listed options did not yet trade. Black and Scholes computed a theoretical option price based on their model. If the market price exceeded their theoretical price, they assumed that they sold the option. Similarly, if the market price was below the price they computed, they assumed that they bought the option. In both cases, they assumed that they held a stock position in conjunction with the option that gave a riskless position. (In other words, if they were long the call option, they would hold $-N(d_1)$ shares of stock as well.) This risk-free position should earn the risk-free rate if option prices in the market and their model are identical. They maintained this position until expiration, adjusting the portfolio as needed to maintain its riskless character. Their results showed significant profit opportunities. In other words, actual market prices differed significantly from the theoretical price given by the model. However, this difference was statistically significant, but not economically important. When Black and Scholes considered trans-action costs, they found that the costs of trading would erode any potential profit. Therefore, option traders could not follow their strategy and make a profit. This result helped show the strong correspondence between market prices and option prices computed from theoretical models, such as the Black-Scholes model.

The Galai Studies

As in the Black-Scholes study, Dan Galai created hedged portfolios of options and stock and used these portfolios to study the correspondence between the Black-Scholes model price and actual market prices for options.[16] In contrast to the Black-Scholes study, Galai used listed option data from the Chicago Board Options Exchange. With options trading on an exchange, Galai had access to daily price quotations. Therefore, he was able to compute the rate of return on the hedged option-stock portfolio for each option for each day. He also adjusted the hedge ratio each day to maintain the neutral hedge – neutral in the sense that a change in the stock price would not change the overall value of the combined option-stock position. Comparing market prices to Black-Scholes model prices, Galai assumed that he sold overpriced options and bought underpriced options each day.

Galai's results showed that this strategy could earn excess returns. In other words, his initial results seemed to be inconsistent with an efficient market. However, this apparent result disappeared when Galai considered transaction costs. If transaction costs were only 1 percent, the apparent excess returns disappeared. Most traders outside the market face transaction costs of 1 percent or higher. However, market makers can transact for less than 1 percent transaction costs. This suggests that market makers could have followed Galai's strategy to earn excess returns. Yet even market makers face some additional transaction costs implied by their career choice. For instance, the market maker must buy or lease a seat on the exchange and the market maker must forego alternative employment. When Galai brought these additional implicit transaction costs into the analysis, the market maker's apparent excess returns diminished or disappeared. At any rate, Galai's results showed that Black-Scholes model prices closely match actual market prices for options.

The Bhattacharya Study

Mihir Bhattacharya used an approach like the Black-Scholes and Galai studies to analyze the correspondence between actual market prices and theoretical prices.[17] Bhattacharya discussed the adherence of market prices to theoretical boundaries implied by no-arbitrage conditions. We focus on one of his three boundaries. As we discussed in Chapter 12, a call option should be worth more than its exercise value if time remains until expiration. Bhattacharya compiled a sample of 86,000 transactions and examined them to determine if immediate exercise was profitable. He found 1,100 such exercise opportunities, meaning that the stock price exceeded the exercise price plus the call price. As we argued in Chapter 12, such a price relationship should not exist. However, these exercise opportunities assumed that the exercise could be conducted without transaction costs. When Bhattacharya considered transaction costs, these apparently profitable exercise opportunities disappeared. The apparent violation of the boundary condition was observed only because transaction costs were not considered. This means that traders could not exploit the deviation from the boundary condition to make a profit.

The MacBeth-Merville Study

James MacBeth and Larry Merville used the Black-Scholes model to compute implied standard deviations for the underlying stocks.[18] They assumed that the Black-Scholes model correctly priced at-the-money options with at least 90 days until expiration. Based on these assumptions and the estimated standard deviation, they evaluated how well the Black-Scholes model priced options that were in-the-money or out-of-the-money and how well the model priced options that had fewer than 90 days until expiration. They found some systematic discrepancies between market prices and Black-Scholes model prices. First, the Black-Scholes prices tended to be less than market prices for in-the-money options, and the Black-Scholes prices tended to be higher than market prices for out-of-the-money options. Second, this first effect was larger the farther the options were from the money. However, it was smaller the shorter the time until expiration. Therefore, we expect to find the greatest discrepancy between market prices and the Black-Scholes model price for options with a long time until expiration and options that are far in- or far out-of-the-money.

The Rubinstein Study

Mark Rubinstein compared market prices with theoretical option prices from the Black-Scholes model and other models of option prices.[19] Some other models out-performed the Black-Scholes model in some respects, yet none did so consistently. Further, Rubinstein confirmed some of the biases noted by MacBeth and Merville for the Black-Scholes model. However, none of the other models was consistently free of bias either. In general, Rubinstein was unable to conclude that there was a single model superior to the others.

Summary

Testing of the option pricing model is far from complete. Recently, attention has turned to the information inherent in option prices that might not be reflected in stock prices or that might be reflected first in option prices and later in stock prices. For example, Joseph Anthony finds that trading volume in call options leads trading volume in the underlying stock by one day.[20] While this lead-lag relationship does not necessarily imply any inefficiency in either market, it does seem to suggest that information that reaches the market affects options first.[21] In recent years the proliferation of many new kinds of options has attracted attention away from options on individual stocks. The kinds of studies on options on individual stocks that were conducted by Black and Scholes and Galai, Bhattacharya, and Rubinstein have recently been conducted for these new kinds of options. In large part, these new results corroborate the earlier results that were found for options on individual stocks. In this section, it has been possible to discuss only some of the most famous studies. There are many other worthwhile studies that have been conducted and many more still that remain to be conducted.

CONCLUSION

We began this chapter by developing the binomial model. We showed that the single-period binomial model emerges directly from no-arbitrage conditions that govern all asset prices. We extended the single-period model to the multi-period binomial model. With this model, we found that we could apply our no-arbitrage principles to value options with numerous periods remaining until expiration. Throughout this development, we considered price movements that were somewhat arbitrary.

Researchers have studied the actual price movements of stocks in great detail. We found that logarithmic stock returns are distributed approximately normally and that this model of stock price movements has proven to be very useful as a working approximation of stock price behavior. Using this model of stock price behavior, a binomial model with many periods until expiration approaches the Black-Scholes model. The Black-Scholes model gives an elegant equation for pricing a call option as a function of five variables: the stock price, the exercise price, the risk-free rate, the time until expiration, and the standard deviation of the stock. Only two of these variables, the interest rate and the standard deviation, are not immediately observable. We showed how to estimate these two parameters.

OPTION! is a useful tool for analyzing the concepts we developed in this chapter. A module for the binomial model allows the user to specify one or many periods for analysis. In this module, the user specifies the up and down percentage factors. A separate module uses up and down factors that are consistent with the Black-Scholes model. With this module, we can study the convergence of the binomial price to the Black-Scholes price. Another module of **OPTION!** allows us to compute Black-Scholes call and put values. A separate module finds the implied volatility of the stock based on the Black-Scholes model. Yet another module computes values of the cumulative normal distribution for input values of d_1 or d_2. Finally, **OPTION!** also includes a module to generate random price paths consistent with initial values that the user specifies.

QUESTIONS AND PROBLEMS

1. What is binomial about the binomial model? In other words, how does the model get its name?
2. If a stock price moves in a manner consistent with the binomial model, what is the chance that the stock price will be the same for two periods in a row? Explain.
3. Assume a stock price is $120 and in the next year it will either rise by 10 percent or fall by 20 percent. The risk-free interest rate is 6 percent. A call option on this stock has an exercise price of $130. What is the price of a call option that expires in one year? What is the chance that the stock price will rise?
4. Based on the data in Question 3, what would you hold to form a risk-free portfolio?
5. Based on the data in Question 3, what will the price of the call option be if the option expires in two years and the stock price can move up 10 percent or down 20 percent in each year?
6. Based on the data in Question 3, what would the price of a call with one year to expiration be if the call has an exercise price of $135? Can you answer this question without making the full calculations? Explain.
7. A stock is worth $60 dollars today. In a year, the stock price can rise or fall by 15 percent. If the interest rate is 6 percent, what is the price of a call option that expires in three years and has an exercise price of $70? What is the price of a put option that expires in three years and has an exercise price of $65? (Use **OPTION!** to solve this problem.)
8. Consider our model of stock price movements given in Equation 13.8. A stock has an initial price of $55 and an expected growth rate of .15 per year. The annualized standard deviation of the stock's return is .4. What is the expected stock price after 175 days?
9. A stock sells for $110. A call option on the stock has an exercise price of $105 and expires in 43 days. If the interest rate is .11 and the standard deviation of the stock's returns is .25, what

is the price of the call according to the Black-Scholes model? What would be the price of a put with an exercise price of $140 and the same time until expiration?

10. Consider a stock that trades for $75. A put and a call on this stock both have an exercise price of $70 and they expire in 150 days. If the risk-free rate is 9 percent and the standard deviation for the stock is .35, compute the price of the options according to the Black-Scholes model.

11. For the options in Question 10, now assume that the stock pays a continuous dividend of 4 percent. What are the options worth according to Merton's model?

12. Consider a Treasury bill with 173 days until maturity. The bid and asked yields on the bill are 9.43 and 9.37. What is the price of the T-bill? What is the continuously compounded rate on the bill?

13. Consider the following sequence of daily stock prices: $47, $49, $46, $45, $51. Compute the mean daily logarithmic return for this share. What is the daily standard deviation of returns? What is the annualized standard deviation?

14. A stock sells for $85. A call option with an exercise price of $80 expires in 53 days and sells for $8. The risk-free interest rate is 11 percent. What is the implied standard deviation for the stock? (Use **OPTION!** to solve this problem.)

15. For a particular application of the binomial model, assume that $U = 1.09$, $D = .91$, and that the two are equally probable. Do these assumptions lead to any particular difficulty? Explain. (*Note:* These are specified up and down movements and are not intended to be consistent with the Black-Scholes model.)

16. For a stock that trades at $120 and has a standard deviation of returns of .4, use the Black-Scholes model to price a call and a put that expire in 180 days and that have an exercise price of $100. The risk-free rate is 8 percent. Now assume that the stock will pay a dividend of $3 on day 75. Apply the known dividend adjustment to the Black-Scholes model and compute new call and put prices.

17. A call and a put expire in 150 days and have an exercise price of $100. The underlying stock is worth $95 and has a standard deviation of .25. The risk-free rate is 11 percent. Use a three-period binomial model and stock price movements consistent with the Black-Scholes model to compute the value of these options. Specify U, D, and π_u, as well as the values for the call and put.

18. For the situation in Problem 17, assume that the stock will pay 2 percent of its value as a dividend on day 80. Compute the value of the call and the put under this circumstance.

19. For the situation in Problem 17, assume that the stock will pay a dividend of $2 on day 80. Compute the value of the call and the put under this circumstance.

20. Consider the first tree in Figures 13.10 and 13.12. If the stock price falls in both of the first two periods, the price is $65.59. For the first tree in Figure 13.12, the put value is $8.84 in this case. Given that the exercise price on the put is $75, does this present a contradiction? Explain.

21. Consider the second tree in Figures 13.10 and 13.11. If the stock price increases in the first period, the price is $88.35. For the second tree in Figure 13.11, the call price is $12.94 in this case. Given that the exercise price on the put is $75, does this present a contradiction? Explain.

NOTES

[1] A risk-neutral investor considers only the expected payoffs from an investment. For such an investor, the risk associated with the investment is not important. Thus, a risk-neutral investor would be indifferent

between an investment with a certain payoff of $50 or an investment with a 50 percent probability of paying $100 and a 50 percent probability of paying zero.

[2] The development of the binomial model stems from two seminal articles: R. Rendleman and B. Bartter, "Two-State Option Pricing," *Journal of Finance,* 34, December 1979, pp. 1093–1110, and J. Cox, S. Ross, and M. Rubinstein, "Option Pricing: A Simplified Approach," *Journal of Financial Economics,* 7, September 1979, pp. 229–63. J. Cox and M. Rubinstein develop and discuss the binomial model in their book *Option Pricing,* Prentice Hall, 1973, and their paper "A Survey of Alternative Option Pricing Models," which appears in *Option Pricing,* M. Brenner (ed.), Lexington: D. C. Heath, 1983, pp. 3–33.

[3] Not every one of these stock price outcomes will be unique. Even in the two-period model we saw that *UDS = DUS.* Strictly speaking, with 20 periods, there are more than one million stock price paths.

[4] To this point, we have considered the binomial model in some detail, and we have considered the log-normal model of stock prices. In essence, each different assumption about stock price movements leads to a different class of option pricing models. For instance, we have already observed that assuming stock prices can either rise or fall by a given amount in a period leads to the binomial model. The log-normal assumption that we have just been considering assumes that the stock price path is continuous. In other words, for the stock price to go from $100 to $110, the price must pass through every value between the two. Another entire class of assumptions about stock price movements assumes that the stock price follows a jump process – that the stock price jumps from one price to another without taking on each of the intervening values. A quick way to distinguish these two models is to determine whether the stock price path can be drawn without lifting pen from paper. If so, then the stock price path is continuous. The following papers analyze option pricing under alternative assumptions about stock price movements: J. Cox and S. Ross, "The Valuation of Options for Alternative Stochastic Processes," *Journal of Financial Economics,* 3, January-March 1976, pp. 145–66; R. Merton, "Option Pricing when Underlying Stock Returns Are Discontinuous," *Journal of Financial Economics,* 3, January-March 1976, pp. 125–44; F. Page and A. Saunders, "A General Derivation of the Jump Process Option Pricing Formula," *Journal of Financial and Quantitative Analysis,* 21:4, December 1986, pp. 437–46; C. Ball and W. Torous, "On Jumps in Common Stock Prices and Their Impact on Call Option Pricing," *Journal of Finance,* 40:1, March 1985, pp. 155–73; and E. Omberg, "Efficient Discrete Time Jump Process Models in Option Pricing," *Journal of Financial and Quantitative Analysis,* 23:2, June 1988, pp. 161–74.

[5] F. Black and M. Scholes, "The Pricing of Options and Corporate Liabilities," *Journal of Political Economy,* May 1973, pp. 637–59, provides the classic statement of the model. In his paper, "Fact and Fantasy in the Use of Options," *Financial Analysts Journal,* 1975, May/June, 31:4, pp. 36–41 and 61–72, Fischer Black developed many of the same ideas in a more intuitive manner. Fischer Black told the story of how Myron Scholes and he discovered the option pricing formula. See F. Black, "How We Came Up With the Option Formula," *Journal of Portfolio Management,* Winter 1989, pp. 4–8.

[6] In imperfect markets, there may not be a single interest rate, but traders may face a borrowing rate and a lending rate. J. Gilster and W. Lee consider this possibility in their paper, "The Effects of Transaction Costs and Different Borrowing and Lending Rates on the Option Pricing Model: A Note," *Journal of Finance,* 39:4, September 1984, pp. 1215–21. They also consider transaction costs and show that considering both imperfections in the debt market and transaction costs results in two offsetting influences. As such, they conclude, neither has a strong effect on the estimation of the option price, and Black-Scholes option prices conform well to actual prices observed in the market. Thus, neither market imperfection is too important because the two imperfections tend to cancel each other.

[7] Of course, it is possible that the stock volatility could change over the life of the option. But shifting volatilities present difficulties in finding an option pricing model. J. Hull and A. White, "The Pricing of Options on Assets with Stochastic Volatilities," *Journal of Finance,* 42:2, June 1987, pp. 281–300, address

this issue. While Hull and White acknowledge that no formula for an option price assuming changing volatility has been found, they develop techniques for approximating the value of an option with changing volatility. In doing so, they assume that changes in volatility are correlated with changes in the stock price. This problem has also been studied by L. Scott, "Option Pricing when the Variance Changes Randomly: Theory, Estimation, and an Application," *Journal of Financial and Quantitative Analysis,* 22:4, December 1987, pp. 419–38. Scott uses simulation techniques to approximate option prices, but concedes that no formula for an option price under shifting volatilities has been found. Finally, James Wiggins explores this problem as well in his paper, "Option Values Under Stochastic Volatility: Theory and Empirical Estimates," *Journal of Financial Economics,* 19:2, December 1987, pp. 351–72. He also acknowledges that an actual formula for the price of an option under shifting volatilities is lacking. Wiggins applies a numerical estimation technique to develop estimates of option prices assuming that volatility follows a continuous process. Under this assumption, Wiggins is able to compute estimated option prices.

[8] There is a third potentially useful method that we do not consider in this book. M. Parkinson, "The Random Walk Problem: Extreme Value Method for Estimating the Variance of the Displacement," *Journal of Business,* 53, January 1980, pp. 61–65, showed that focusing on high and low prices for a few days could give as good an estimate as using historical data for five times as many days. His model assumes that stock prices are distributed log-normally. Compared with the use of historical data on the closing price for a given day, Parkinson's method uses both the high and low prices for the day. This method would allow a good estimate from more recent historical data than simply focusing on the history of closing prices. M. Garman and M. Klass, "On the Estimation of Security Price Volatilities from Historical Data," *Journal of Business,* 53:1, 1980, pp. 67–78 pointed out some difficulties with Parkinson's approach. First, his method is very sensitive to any errors in the reported high and low prices. Further, if trading during the day is sporadic, Parkinson's method will generate biased estimates of volatility. In particular, with discontinuities in the trading, the reported high will almost certainly be lower than the high that would have been observed with continuous trading. Similarly, the reported low will be higher than the value that would have been achieved under continuous trading. Garman and Klass also show how to improve Parkinson's type of estimate.

[9] Similarly, assume that we estimate the standard deviation with weekly data. We would convert this raw data to annualized data by multiplying the weekly standard deviation times the square root of 52. Similarly, if we begin with monthly data, we annualize our monthly standard deviation by multiplying it times the square root of 12.

[10] In principle, we can take any five of the values as given and solve for the sixth. For example, Menachem Brenner and Dan Galai, "Implied Interest Rates," *Journal of Business,* 59, July 1986, pp. 493–507, find that interest rates implied in the options market correspond to other short-term rates of interest. These implied rates are nearer to the borrowing rate than to the lending rate. Further, in situations where early exercise is imminent, the interest rates implied in the option markets can differ widely from short-term rates on other instruments. Steve Swidler takes this approach a step further in his paper, "Simultaneous Option Prices and an Implied Risk-Free Rate of Interest: A Test of the Black-Scholes Model," *Journal of Economics and Business,* 38:2, May 1986, pp. 155–64. Swidler uses two options, which allow him to estimate two parameters simultaneously – two equations in two unknowns. Swidler estimates the implied interest and the implied standard deviation. While the standard deviation can differ from stock to stock, there should be a common interest rate for all options on a given date. For most of the stocks he examines, Swidler finds that a single interest rate can be found. Accordingly, he regards his evidence as supporting the reasonableness of the Black-Scholes model.

[11] For a discussion of these weighting techniques, see H. A. Latane and R. J. Rendleman, Jr., "Standard Deviations of Stock Price Ratios Implied in Option Prices," *Journal of Finance,* 31, 1976, pp. 369–82; D. P. Chiras and S. Manaster, "The Information Content of Option Prices and a Test of Market Efficiency,"

Journal of Financial Economics, 6, 1978, pp. 213–34; and R. E. Whaley, "Valuation of American Call Options on Dividend Paying Stocks: Empirical Tests," *Journal of Financial Economics,* 10, 1982, pp. 29–58. In his paper, Stan Beckers, "Standard Deviations Implied in Option Prices as Predictors of Future Stock Price Variability," *Journal of Banking and Finance,* 5, 1981, pp. 363–82, concludes that using the option with the highest sensitivity to the standard deviation provides the best estimate of future volatility. For a review of the literature on implied volatility, see Stewart Mayhew, "Implied Volatility," *Financial Analysts Journal,* 51:4, July/August 1995, pp. 8–20.

[12] **OPTION!** searches for the correct standard deviation in a way similar to the sequence of standard deviations and prices shown here. However, it uses a somewhat more sophisticated procedure for choosing the next standard deviation to try.

[13] In fact, considerable research shows that the stock price falls when a stock goes ex-dividend, but the drop in the stock price does not equal the full amount of the dividend. In this text, we make the simplifying assumption that the stock price falls by the amount of the dividend. Alternatively, the reader may regard the dividend as being equal to the amount of the fall in the stock price occasioned by the dividend payment.

[14] This is not the same as capital delta, Δ, which stands for the sensitivity of the call option price to a change in the stock price.

[15] F. Black and M. Scholes, "The Valuation of Option Contracts and a Test of Market Efficiency," *Journal of Finance,* 27:2, 1972, pp. 399–417.

[16] D. Galai, "Tests of Market Efficiency of the Chicago Board Options Exchange," *Journal of Business,* 50:2, April 1977, pp. 167–97, and "Empirical Tests of Boundary Conditions for CBOE Options," *Journal of Financial Economics,* 6:2/3, June-September 1978, pp. 182–211.

[17] M. Bhattacharya, "Transaction Data Tests on the Efficiency of the Chicago Board Options Exchange," *Journal of Financial Economics,* 12:2, 1983, pp. 161–85.

[18] J. D. MacBeth and L. J. Merville, "An Empirical Examination of the Black-Scholes Call Option Pricing Model," *Journal of Finance,* 34:5, 1979, pp. 1173–86.

[19] M. Rubinstein, "Nonparametric Tests of Alternative Option Pricing Models Using All Reported Trades and Quotes on the 30 Most Active CBOE Option Classes from August 23, 1976 Through August 31, 1978," *Journal of Finance,* 40:2, 1985, pp. 455–80. The other models tested were extensions of the Black-Scholes model based on changing assumptions about how stock prices move. For instance, they included option models based on the assumption that stock prices jump from one price to another, rather than moving continuously through all intervening prices as the stock price moves from one price to another. Rubinstein tested the following models: the Black-Scholes model, the jump model, the mixed diffusion jump model, the constant elasticity of variance model, and the displaced diffusion model.

[20] J. H. Anthony, "The Interrelation of Stock and Options Market Trading-Volume Data," *Journal of Finance,* 43:4, September 1988, pp. 949–64.

[21] Option prices may react before stock prices due to the trading preferences of informed traders. We have already seen that option markets often offer lower transaction costs than the market for the underlying good. For traders with good information, the options market may be the preferred market to exploit their information. On this scenario, we would expect to see option prices and volume change before stock prices and volume. The trading of the informed traders would move option prices, and the arbitrage linkages between options and stocks would lead to an adjustment of the corresponding stock prices.

CHAPTER 14 | OPTION SENSITIVITIES AND OPTION HEDGING

OVERVIEW

Chapter 13 developed the principles of pricing for European options. There we analyzed option pricing within the framework of the binomial model and extended the discussion to encompass the Black-Scholes model, which gives a closed-form solution for the price of a European option on a non-dividend stock. We also considered the Merton model, which provides a solution for the price of a European option on a stock paying a continuous dividend.

In this chapter, we continue our exploration of these models by focusing on the response of option prices to the factors that determine the price. Specifically, we noted in Chapter 13 that the price of a European option depends on the price of the underlying stock, the exercise price, the interest rate, the volatility of the underlying stock, and the time until expiration. This chapter analyzes the sensitivity of option prices to these factors and shows how a knowledge of these relationships can direct trading strategies and can improve option hedging techniques.

With **OPTION!**, we can compute all of the sensitivity measures that we consider in this chapter. Also, **OPTION!** can graph the response of the option price to the different factors.

OPTION SENSITIVITIES IN THE MERTON AND BLACK-SCHOLES MODELS

Throughout this chapter, we focus on the Merton model (given in Equations 13.17 and 13.18) and the sensitivity of option prices in this model to the underlying factors. This approach embraces the Black-Scholes model (presented in Equations 13.13–13.15), as we may regard the Merton model simply as the Black-Scholes model extended to account for stocks that pay continuous dividends. As we saw in Chapter 13, the Merton model simplifies to the Black-Scholes model if we assume that the underlying stock pays no dividends. Similarly, the sensitivities of option prices in the Merton model reduce to those for the Black-Scholes model if we assume that the underlying stock pays no dividends.

The option price sensitivities that we consider in this chapter all derive from calculus. For example, the sensitivity of the option price with respect to the stock price is simply the first derivative of the option pricing formula with respect to the stock price. For readers unfamiliar with calculus, we illustrate this basic idea in two ways. The first derivative of the call price with respect to the stock price is just the change in the call price for a change in the stock price:

$$\frac{\Delta c}{\Delta S}$$

This change in the call price is measured for an extremely small change in the stock price. In fact, in terms of calculus, the change in the call price is measured for an infinitesimal change in the stock price. As a second illustration, consider a European call option on a stock priced at $100 with a standard deviation of .3. The option expires in 180 days, has a striking price of $100, and the current risk-free rate of interest is 8 percent. Table 14.1 shows the value of this call for stock prices in the neighborhood of $100. It also shows the value of $N(d_1)$ computed at each price as well. Consider a change in the stock price from $100.00 to $102.00. For this change of $2.00 in the stock price, the call price changes from $10.3044 to $11.5702. Therefore:

$$\frac{\Delta c}{\Delta S} = \frac{1.2658}{2.00} = .6329$$

Next consider a change in the stock price from $100.00 to $100.10. In this case the call price would change from $10.3044 to $10.3660, giving:

$$\frac{\Delta c}{\Delta S} = \frac{0.0616}{0.10} = .6160$$

Table 14.1	Call Prices for Various Stock Prices		
	Call Price	Stock Price	$N(d_1)$
	$9.1111	$98.00	.5780
	$9.4024	$98.50	.5874
	$9.6984	$99.00	.5967
	$9.9991	$99.50	.6060
	$10.1512	$99.75	.6105
	$10.3044	$100.00	.6151
	$10.3660	$100.10	.6169
	$10.4587	$100.25	.6196
	$10.6142	$100.50	.6241
	$10.9284	$101.00	.6330
	$11.2472	$101.50	.6418
	$11.5702	$102.00	.6505

For these two cases, we now compare the relative change in call prices to $N(d_1)$. For a stock price of \$100.00, $N(d_1)$ = .6151, and our $\Delta c/\Delta S$ term has a value in that neighborhood. We also note that for a \$2.00 stock price change, $\Delta c/\Delta S$ is .6329, but for a \$.10 change, $\Delta c/\Delta S$ = .6160. As the change becomes smaller, the value for $\Delta c/\Delta S$ approaches the value of $N(d_1)$ for a stock price of \$100.00, which is .6151. For an infinitesimally small change in the stock price, the change in the value of the call option will exactly equal $N(d_1)$. In fact, $N(d_1)$ is the first derivative of the call price with respect to the stock price for a nondividend stock. The line for the call in Figure 14.1 shows how the value of our example option changes as a function of the stock price. The straight line tangent to the option price curve in the top graph of Figure 14.1 shows the instantaneous rate of change in the call price for a change in the stock price. The slope of this straight line is the first derivative of the call price with respect to the stock price. As the figure shows, the straight line indicates the slope of the call price curve at a stock price of \$100.00, which is .6151.

All of the sensitivity measures we consider in this chapter are similarly conceived and derived. They all derive from calculus, and they all express the sensitivity of an option price to a change in one of the underlying parameters. In the common calculus notation for our example, the first derivative of the call price with respect to the stock price is denoted as $\partial c/\partial S$. Table 14.2 presents the standard sensitivities used in option analysis for the Merton model as it applies to calls, while Table 14.3 gives the same equations for puts. (See Chapter 13 for the equations for the two models and other terms.)

As we saw in Chapter 13, the Black-Scholes model is the same as the Merton model in the special case of there being no dividends on the stock. Similarly, we can derive the sensitivities for the Black-Scholes model from those of the Merton model if we assume that the stock pays no dividends. Tables 14.4 and 14.5 parallel Tables 14.2 and 14.3 and give the sensitivities for the Black-Scholes model.

Earlier we considered a call option on a stock priced at \$100 with a standard deviation of .3 and no dividend. The call had 180 days until expiration, and we assumed a risk-free rate of 8 percent. Table 14.6 shows all of the sensitivities for calls and puts for both the Black-Scholes model (assuming no dividend) and for the Merton model (assuming a continuous dividend of 3 percent). **OPTION!** computes all of these sensitivity measures. We now consider each of the measures in turn.

DELTA

DELTA is the first derivative of an option's price with respect to a change in the price of the stock. As such, DELTA measures the sensitivity of the option's price to changing stock prices. $DELTA_c$ is always positive, while $DELTA_p$ is always negative. Thus, the value of a call increases with a stock price increase, while the value of a put decreases if the stock price increases. In Table 14.6 for the options on a nondividend stock, $DELTA_c$ = .6151 and $DELTA_p$ = −.3849. These sensitivities can be interpreted as follows. If the stock price rises by \$1, the price of the call will rise by approximately \$.6151, while the price of the put will fall by about \$.3849.

These estimations of the change in the option price are only approximate. If the change in the stock price were infinitesimal, the DELTAs would give us an exact price change for the options. Because a \$1 change in the stock price is discrete, our computed prices remain estimates. If the stock price is \$101, we have c = \$10.9284, and p = \$6.0601. Thus, the call price increases by \$.6240 (compared to the predicted \$.6151), and the put price falls by \$.3759 (compared to the predicted fall of \$.3849).

Figure 14.1   **Call and Put Prices as a Function of the Stock Price**

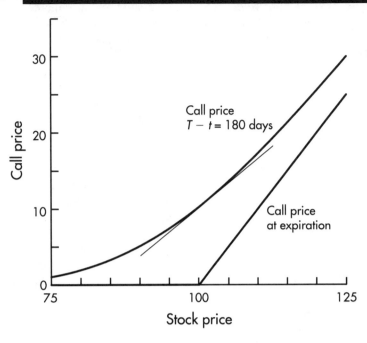

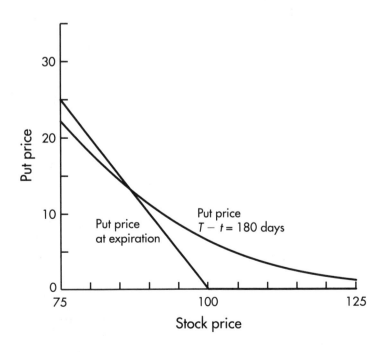

$X = \$100$; $\sigma = .3$; $r = .08$; $T - t = 180$ days

| Call Sensitivities for the Merton Model | Table 14.2 |

Name	Sensitivity
DELTA$_c$	$\dfrac{\partial c}{\partial S} = e^{-\delta(T-t)}N(d_1^M)$
THETA$_c$	$-\dfrac{\partial c}{\partial(T-t)} = -\dfrac{SN'(d_1^M)\sigma e^{-\delta(T-t)}}{2\sqrt{T-t}}$ $+ \delta SN'(d_1^M)e^{-\delta(T-t)} - rXe^{-r(T-t)}N(d_2^M)$
VEGA$_c$	$\dfrac{\partial c}{\partial \sigma} = S\sqrt{T-t}N'(d_1^M)e^{-\delta(T-t)}$
RHO$_c$	$\dfrac{\partial c}{\partial r} = X(T-t)e^{-r(T-t)}N(d_2^M)$
GAMMA$_c$	$\dfrac{\partial \text{DELTA}_c}{\partial S} = \dfrac{\partial^2 c}{\partial S^2} = \dfrac{N'(d_1^M)e^{-\delta(T-t)}}{S\sigma\sqrt{T-t}}$
Note:	$N'(d_1^M) = \dfrac{1}{\sqrt{2\pi}}e^{-.5(d_1^M)^2}$

| Put Sensitivities for the Merton Model | Table 14.3 |

Name	Sensitivity
DELTA$_p$	$\dfrac{\partial p}{\partial S} = e^{-\delta(T-t)}[N(d_1^M) - 1]$
THETA$_p$	$-\dfrac{\partial p}{\partial(T-t)} = -\dfrac{SN'(d_1^M)\sigma e^{-\delta(T-t)}}{2\sqrt{T-t}}$ $- \delta SN'(d_1^M)e^{-\delta(T-t)} + rXe^{-r(T-t)}N(-d_2^M)$
VEGA$_p$	$\dfrac{\partial p}{\partial \sigma} = S\sqrt{T-t}N'(d_1^M)e^{-\delta(T-t)}$
RHO$_p$	$\dfrac{\partial p}{\partial r} = X(T-t)e^{-r(T-t)}N(-d_2^M)$
GAMMA$_p$	$\dfrac{\partial \text{DELTA}_p}{\partial S} = \dfrac{\partial^2 p}{\partial S^2} = \dfrac{N'(d_1^M)e^{-\delta(T-t)}}{S\sigma\sqrt{T-t}}$
Note:	$N'(d_1^M) = \dfrac{1}{\sqrt{2\pi}}e^{-.5(d_1^M)^2}$

Table 14.4	Call Sensitivities for the Black-Scholes Model	
Name	**Sensitivity**	
DELTA$_c$	$\dfrac{\partial c}{\partial S} = N(d_1)$	
THETA$_c$	$-\dfrac{\partial c}{\partial(T-t)} = -\dfrac{SN'(d_1)\sigma}{2\sqrt{T-t}}$ $- rXe^{-r(T-t)}N(d_2)$	
VEGA$_c$	$\dfrac{\partial c}{\partial\sigma} = S\sqrt{T-t}N'(d_1)$	
RHO$_c$	$\dfrac{\partial c}{\partial r} = -X(T-t)e^{-r(T-t)}N(d_2)$	
GAMMA$_c$	$\dfrac{\partial \text{DELTA}_c}{\partial S} = \dfrac{\partial^2 c}{\partial S^2} = \dfrac{N'(d_1)}{S\sigma\sqrt{T-t}}$	
Note:	$N'(d_1^M) = \dfrac{1}{\sqrt{2\pi}}e^{-.5(d_1^M)^2}$	

Table 14.5	Put Sensitivities for the Black-Scholes Model	
Name	**Sensitivity**	
DELTA$_p$	$\dfrac{\partial p}{\partial S} = N(d_1) - 1$	
THETA$_p$	$-\dfrac{\partial p}{\partial(T-t)} = -\dfrac{SN'(d_1)\sigma}{2\sqrt{T-t}}$ $+ rXe^{-r(T-t)}N(-d_2)$	
VEGA$_p$	$\dfrac{\partial p}{\partial\sigma} = S\sqrt{T-t}N'(d_1)$	
RHO$_p$	$\dfrac{\partial p}{\partial r} = -X(T-t)e^{-r(T-t)}N(-d_2)$	
GAMMA$_p$	$\dfrac{\partial \text{DELTA}_p}{\partial S} = \dfrac{\partial^2 p}{\partial S^2} = \dfrac{N'(d_1)}{S\sigma\sqrt{T-t}}$	
Note:	$N'(d_1^M) = \dfrac{1}{\sqrt{2\pi}}e^{-.5(d_1^M)^2}$	

	Option Sensitivities		Table 14.6	
	Black-Scholes Model δ = 0.0		Merton Model δ = 0.03	
	Call	Put	Call	Put
Option prices	$10.3044	$6.4360	$9.4209	$7.0210
DELTA	.6151	−.3849	.5794	−.4060
THETA	−12.2607	−4.5701	−10.3343	−5.5997
VEGA	26.8416	26.8416	26.9300	26.9300
RHO	25.2515	−22.1559	23.9250	−23.4823
GAMMA	.0181	.0181	.0182	.0182

$S = \$100; X = \$100; r = .08; \sigma = .3; T - t = 180$ days

The lower graph of Figure 14.1 shows how the put price of our example varies with the stock price. Notice that the price of a European put can be less than its intrinsic value, as we discussed in Chapter 13. As the two panels of Figure 14.1 indicate, option prices are extremely dependent upon stock prices, and the price of the underlying stock is the key determinant of an option price. Therefore, DELTA is the most important of all of the sensitivity measures that we consider in this chapter.

Delta-Neutral Positions

Consider a portfolio, P, of a short position of one European call on a nondividend stock combined with a long position of DELTA units of the stock. The portfolio would have the value:

$$P = -c + N(d_1)S \qquad (14.1)$$

Continuing to use our sample options of Table 14.6, the cost of the portfolio, assuming a current stock price of $100.00, would be:

$$P = -c + N(d_1)S = -\$10.3044 + .6151(\$100.00) = \$51.2056$$

If the stock price were to suddenly change to $100.10, the portfolio's value would be:

$$P = -c + N(d_1)S = -\$10.3660 + .6151(\$100.10) = \$51.2055$$

Thus, the value of the portfolio would change by only $.0001 for a $.10 change in the stock price. If the change in the stock price were infinitesimal, the price of the portfolio would not change at all. If the change in the stock price were larger, the change in the value of the portfolio would be larger, but it would still be quite small relative to the change in the stock price. For example, if the stock price rose from $100 to $110, the portfolio's value would be:

$$P = -c + N(d_1)S = -\$17.2821 + .6151(\$110.00) = \$50.3789$$

In this case, a change of $10 in the stock price caused a change of $.8267 in the value of the portfolio. Figure 14.2 shows how the value of this portfolio changes for changes in the stock price.

A portfolio like the one we are considering, and described by Equation 14.1, is known as a **delta-neutral portfolio**. It is delta-neutral because an infinitesimal change in the price of the stock does not affect the price of the portfolio. Put another way, we could say that the DELTA of this portfolio is zero; the value of the portfolio is insensitive to the value of the stock.

As we saw in Chapter 13, the Black-Scholes model assumes that the stock price changes continuously. Imagine now that we can trade shares and options continuously as the stock price changes. We see from the equation for DELTA in Table 14.2 that DELTA changes when the stock price changes. (DELTA also changes when other factors change as well, such as the standard deviation and the time remaining until the option expires.) Assume now that we trade continuously to rebalance our portfolio as the stock price changes. In rebalancing, we seek to maintain the condition of Equation 14.1. In particular, we trade continuously to maintain our portfolio as a delta-neutral portfolio. By trading continuously, the portfolio is delta-neutral at every instant and never loses or gains value in response to changes in the stock price. By following this strategy of continuously rebalancing our portfolio, we know that it has zero price risk as a function of changing stock prices. In effect, by

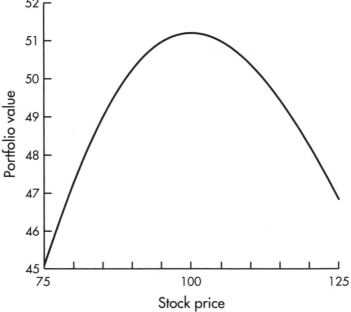

| Figure 14.2 | Value of a Delta-Neutral Portfolio as a Function of the Stock Price (Portfolio includes –1 call and .6151 shares) |

X = $100; σ = .3; r = .08; $T - t$ = 180 days

continuously rebalancing we have created a risk-free portfolio. Further, if the portfolio is risk-free, it must earn the risk-free rate of return.

This is the key intuition of the Black-Scholes model. Black and Scholes realized that continuous trading could maintain a delta-neutral portfolio as a risk-free portfolio earning the risk-free rate. This was an important step that enabled them to find a solution for their option pricing model.

As a practical matter, creating a delta-neutral portfolio in the manner described appears to be a difficult way of buying a risk-free security. Why not just buy a Treasury bill? Later in this chapter, we explore the extremely valuable practical consequences of using DELTA-oriented hedging technologies. However, at the present we can easily see how the idea of a delta-neutral portfolio can be very useful in adjusting the riskiness of a stock trading strategy.

For the call option and the stock that we have been considering, assume that an outright investment in the stock is too risky. An investor in this position could use the idea of delta-neutrality to shape the risk characteristics of the investment to her particular needs. For example, assume that a trader holds a portfolio as follows:

$$-.5c + N(d_1)S = -.5(\$10.3044) + .6151(\$100.00) = \$56.3578$$

This portfolio is similar to the delta-neutral portfolio that we considered earlier, except instead of selling a call, the investor sells only one-half of a call. In considering the delta-neutral portfolio, we saw that selling the call in conjunction with investing in the stock gave a risk-free portfolio. Now, by selling one-half of a call, the investor diminishes the risk, but does not totally eliminate it. Figure 14.3 shows how the value of the delta-neutral portfolio and this new portfolio will vary as the stock price changes. This new portfolio has some risk exposure to changing stock prices, but it is much less risky than the stock itself. Later in this chapter, we consider a variety of strategies for using options to accept, avoid, or transform various investment risks.

As we noted earlier, DELTA changes as the stock price and other parameters of the option pricing model change. For our continuing example, Figure 14.4 shows how the DELTAs of the call and put vary with changing stock prices. $DELTA_c$ tends to approach 1.0 when the call option is deep-in-the-money. Similarly, when the call is deep-out-of-the-money, $DELTA_c$ approaches zero. When the stock price is near the exercise price, $DELTA_c$ is most sensitive to a change in the stock price. For $DELTA_p$, similar principles apply. $DELTA_c$ is always greater than zero, while $DELTA_p$ is always less than zero. The DELTA of a deep-in-the-money put approaches -1, while the DELTA of a deep-out-of- the-money put approaches zero. **OPTION!** can make graphs similar to those of Figure 14.4.

THETA

If the stock price and all other parameters of the option pricing model remain constant, the price of options will still change with the passage of time. THETA is the negative of the first derivative of the option price with respect to the time remaining until expiration. $THETA_c$ and $THETA_p$ can be greater or less than zero depending upon circumstances. However, $THETA_c$ and $THETA_p$ are generally less than zero.[1]

The tendency for option prices to change due merely to the passage of time is known as **time decay**. To see how the passage of time affects option prices, consider our continuing example of call and put options with $S = \$100$, $X = \$100$, $\sigma = .3$, $r = .08$, and $T - t = 180$ days. For these values, we noted earlier that $c = \$10.30$, and $p = \$6.44$. For these values, $THETA_c = -12.2607$, and $THETA_p =$

Figure 14.3 | Value of a Delta-Neutral Portfolio as a Function of the Stock Price (One portfolio includes –1 call and .6151 shares, and one portfolio includes –.5 calls and .6151 shares)

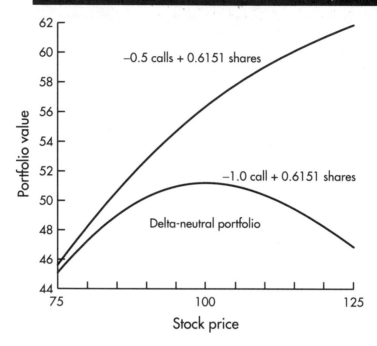

$X = \$100$; $\sigma = .3$; $r = .08$; $T - t = 180$ days

−4.5701. These values of THETA are expressed in terms of years. Suppose that the time to expiration changes by .1 years (37 days) from 180 days until expiration to 143 days. Recalling that THETA is the negative of the first derivative of the option price with respect to time until expiration, we would expect the call and put prices to be $c = \$10.30 + .1(-12.2607) = \$9.07$, and $p = \$6.44 + .1(-4.5701) = \$5.98$. Recalling that all of these computed prices are approximations, the actual prices would be $c = \$9.01$, and $p = \$5.92$.

If all parameters remain constant, except the expiration date draws nearer, both options will have to fall in value. Both the call and the put will be worthless at expiration, because $S = X = \$100$. Therefore, the call and put options will lose their entire value through time decay. Figure 14.5 illustrates time decay for our sample options.

THETA$_c$ and THETA$_p$ both vary with changing stock prices and with the passage of time. For the options of our continuing example, Figure 14.6 shows how the call and put THETAs vary with the stock price. (Notice that the graph shows how a put that is deep-in-the-money can have a positive THETA.) THETA$_c$ and THETA$_p$ also both change with the passage of time. If the stock price is near the exercise price, THETA$_c$ and THETA$_p$ will become quite negative as expiration nears, as Figure

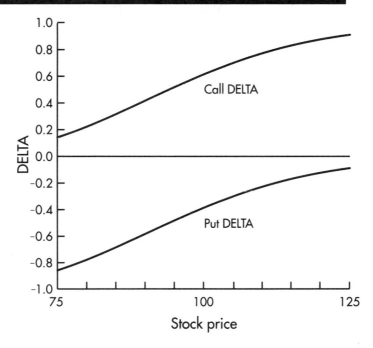

Call and Put DELTAs as a Function of the Stock Price   **Figure 14.4**

$X = \$100; \sigma = .3; r = .08; T - t = 180$ days

14.7 shows. However, this is not true for options that are deep-in-the-money or deep-out-of-the-money. Figure 14.7 shows how THETA$_c$ and THETA$_p$ change in very different manners depending upon whether the options are in-the-money or out-of-the-money. For example, a European put that is in-the-money will have a positive THETA as expiration nears.

VEGA

VEGA is the first derivative of an option's price with respect to the volatility of the underlying stock. VEGA$_c$ and VEGA$_p$ are identical and always positive. (VEGA is sometimes known as *kappa, lambda,* or *sigma* as well. We use the term VEGA throughout.)

The VEGA is an important determinant of option prices. A sudden substantive change in the standard deviation of the underlying stock can cause a dramatic change in option values. As we noted for our example options, $c = \$10.30$ and $p = \$6.44$ when $\sigma = .3$. If volatility were to suddenly increase by .2 so that $\sigma = .5$, we would expect new prices of $c = \$10.30 + .2(26.8416) = \$15.67$ and $p = \$6.44 + .2(26.8416) = \$11.81$.

The actual call and put prices with $\sigma = .5$ would be $c = \$15.69$ and $p = \$11.82$, causing a price increase of 52 percent for the call and 84 percent for the put. During and immediately following the Crash of 1987 (when the stock market lost 20–25 percent of its value in one day), the perceived

Figure 14.5   Call and Put Prices as a Function of the Time Until Expiration

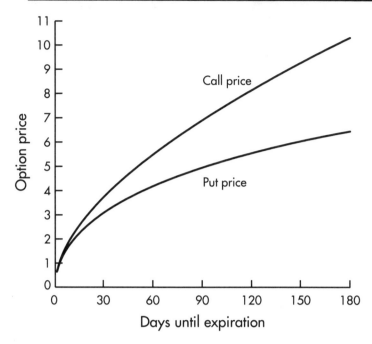

$S = \$100; X = \$100; \sigma = .3; r = .08$

volatility for stocks increased tremendously causing an increase in option values. (Of course, calls generally lost value due to falling prices, and puts increased in value for the same reason.) Figure 14.8 shows how call and put prices vary with the standard deviation for our example options.

VEGA tends to be greatest for an option near-the-money. When an option is deep-in-the-money or deep-out-of-the-money, the VEGA is low and can approach zero. Figure 14.9 shows how VEGA varies with respect to the stock price for the call and put of our continuing example. Because the two example options are at-the-money, VEGA is at its maximum. For calls or puts in-the-money or out-of-the-money, the VEGA will be lower.

RHO

RHO is the first derivative of an option's price with respect to the interest rate. RHO_c is always positive, while RHO_p is always negative. In general, option prices are not very sensitive to RHO. In Table 14.6, $RHO_c = 25.2515$, and $RHO_p = -22.1559$. If the interest rate were to increase by 1 percent, then the call price should increase by $.01(25.2515) = \$.2525$, while the price of the put should fall by $.01(-22.1559) = \$-.2216$. Figure 14.10 shows how the prices of our example options would change given varying interest rates. Large changes in the interest rate have relatively little effect on the option prices.

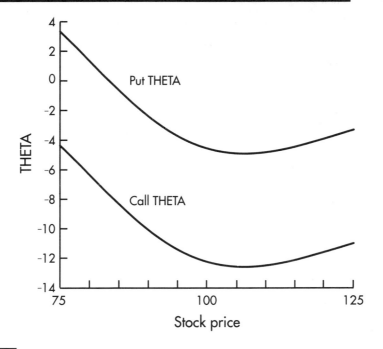

Call and Put THETAs as a Function of the Stock Price   **Figure 14.6**

$X = \$100$; $\sigma = .3$; $r = .08$; $T - t = 180$ days

RHO changes as a function of both the stock price and the time until expiration. RHO_c tends to be low for an option that is deep-out-of-the-money and high for a deep-in-the-money call. RHO_c tends to be sensitive to the stock price when a call is near-the-money. For a deep-in-the-money put, RHO_p is generally low, and RHO_p is generally large for a deep-out-of-the-money put. When the put is near-the-money, RHO_p tends to be more sensitive to the stock price. Figure 14.11 illustrates the sensitivity of RHO_c and RHO_p to the stock price for the options in our continuing example.

RHO$_c$ and RHO$_p$ change as time passes, with both tending toward zero as expiration approaches. The interest rate affects the price of an option in conjunction with the time remaining until expiration mainly through the time value of money. If little time remains until expiration, the interest rate is relatively unimportant, and the price of an option becomes less sensitive to the interest rate. For our example options, Figure 14.12 shows how RHO_c and RHO_p tend to zero as expiration approaches.

GAMMA

Unlike the other sensitivity measures we have considered thus far, GAMMA does not measure the sensitivity of the price of an option to one of the parameters. Instead, GAMMA measures how DELTA changes with changes in the stock price. The GAMMA of a put and a call are always identical, and GAMMA can be either positive or negative. (In terms of calculus, GAMMA is the second derivative

Figure 14.7   **Call and Put THETAs as a Function of the Time Until Expiration**

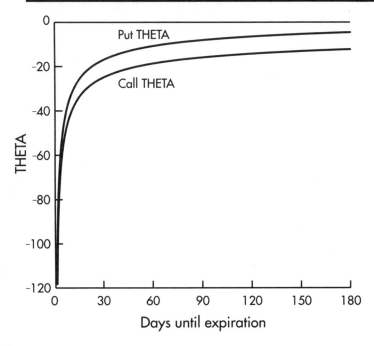

$X = \$100; \sigma = .3; r = .08$

of the option price with respect to the stock price.) GAMMA is the only second-order effect that we consider, but it is an important one.

From our example computations in Table 14.6, we see that $\text{GAMMA}_c = \text{GAMMA}_p = .0181$. The table also shows $\text{DELTA}_c = .6151$, and $\text{DELTA}_p = -.3849$. If the stock price were to increase by $1 from $100 to $101, we would expect the two DELTAs to change. The new expected $\text{DELTA}_c = .6151 + 1(.0181) = .6332$, and the new expected $\text{DELTA}_p = -.3849 + 1(.0181) = -.3668$. With a stock price of $101, the actual values are: $\text{DELTA}_c = .6330$, and $\text{DELTA}_p = -.3670$.

GAMMA tends to be large when an option is near-the-money. A large GAMMA for a given stock price simply means that the DELTA is highly sensitive to changes in the stock price around its current level. For our sample options, Figure 14.4 shows that DELTA_c and DELTA_p are sensitive to the stock price when the price is near the exercise price of $100. When an option is deep-in-the-money, the DELTA is near 1.0 and is not very sensitive to changing stock prices. Because of DELTA's low sensitivity to stock prices, the GAMMA for a call or a put that is deep-in-the-money must be low. A similar principle applies for a call or a put that is deep-out-of-the-money. In such a situation, the DELTA of either a call or a put will be quite low, and it will be insensitive to changing stock prices. Due to this low sensitivity, the GAMMA will be small for either a call or a put that is deep-out-of-the-money.

Call and Put Prices as a Function of the Standard Deviation Figure 14.8

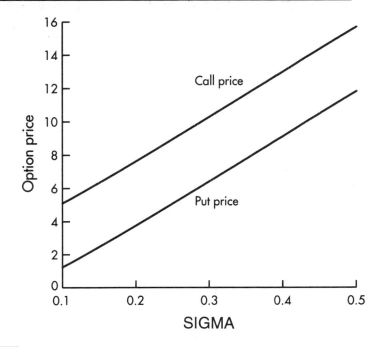

$S = \$100$; $X = \$100$; $r = .08$; $T - t = 180$ days

Figure 14.4 shows how DELTA$_c$ and DELTA$_p$ vary with the stock price for our sample options. GAMMA essentially measures the slope of the graphs in Figure 14.4. Because the slopes of the graphs in Figure 14.4 are near zero for calls or puts that are deep-in-the-money or deep-out-of-the-money, GAMMA must be low as well. When the calls or puts are near-the-money, the rate of change in the DELTA as a function of the stock price is high – that is, the slope of the graph in Figure 14.4 is high. Therefore, for near-the-money options, GAMMA must be large.

Figure 14.13 shows how GAMMA varies with the stock price for our sample options. The figure applies to both the put and the call, because the GAMMAs are the same for a put and call with the same underlying instrument, time to expiration, and strike price. As the figure shows, GAMMA is large when the option is near-the-money and small when the option is deep-in-the-money or when it is deep-out-of-the-money.

GAMMA also varies with the time remaining until expiration. For an option that is near-the-money, GAMMA increases as expiration approaches. This large GAMMA reflects the heightened sensitivity of the DELTA to the stock price when the option is near-the-money and expiration is near. For an option that is deep-out-of-the-money or deep-in-the-money, GAMMA will fall dramatically as expiration becomes very close. For in-the-money or out-of-the-money options, with expiration distant, the GAMMA will tend to rise as time passes. However, it is difficult to make solid generalizations about how GAMMA will change without actually calculating the effects of the passage of time.

Figure 14.9   Call and Put VEGA as a Function of the Stock Price

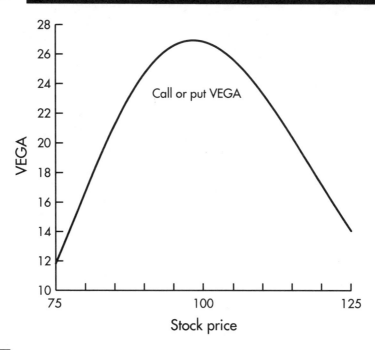

$X = \$100$; $r = .08$; $T - t = 180$ days

Both our example options are at-the-money, so the GAMMAs of the call and put will rise as expiration nears. Figure 14.14 shows how GAMMA varies with time remaining until expiration for options at-the-money, in-the-money, and out-of-the-money.

Positive and Negative GAMMA Portfolios

Earlier in this chapter, we created an example of a DELTA-neutral portfolio. For our sample call option, we saw that we could create a DELTA-neutral portfolio consisting of a long position of .6151 shares of the underlying stock and a short position of one call. Figure 14.2 shows how the value of this portfolio changes as the stock price changes. As the price of the stock moves away from $100, the value of the portfolio decreases.

The underlying stock has a DELTA of 1.0, which never changes. The change in the value of the stock is always 1:1 for changes in the value of the stock. Because the DELTA of the stock never changes, its GAMMA must be zero; the DELTA of the stock is completely insensitive to changes in the stock price. For our example call, the GAMMA is .0181. Because we have sold one call with a GAMMA of .0181 and .6151 shares with a GAMMA of zero, the GAMMA of this portfolio must be −.0181. Because the portfolio has a negative GAMMA, the DELTA of the portfolio must decrease if the stock price changes.

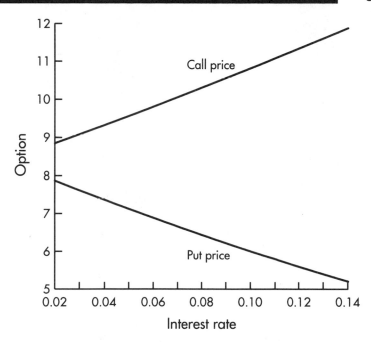

Call and Put Prices as a Function of the Interest Rate   **Figure 14.10**

$S = \$100; \; X = \$100; \; \sigma = .3; \; T - t = 180$ days

For small changes in the stock price, we know that the price of the portfolio of −1 call and .6151 shares will not change, because the portfolio was constructed to be DELTA-neutral. For large changes in the stock price, however, the value of this portfolio will fall. The following data show the value of the elements of the portfolio and the total portfolio for stock prices of $90, $100, and $110.

Stock Price	Call Price	.6151 Shares	Portfolio Value (−1 Call + .6151 Shares)
$90	$5.12	$55.36	$50.24
$100	$10.30	$61.51	$51.21
$110	$17.28	$67.66	$50.38

The negative GAMMA of this portfolio ensures that large changes in the stock price will make the portfolio lose value. This is true whether the stock price rises or falls.

By contrast, consider a DELTA-neutral portfolio with a positive GAMMA. We can construct such a portfolio by combining our example put with the underlying stock to form a new portfolio. From Table 14.6, $p = \$6.4360$, $\text{DELTA}_p = -.3849$, and $\text{GAMMA}_p = .0181$. A portfolio of one put and .3849 shares of stock will be DELTA-neutral, will be worth $44.926, and will have a GAMMA

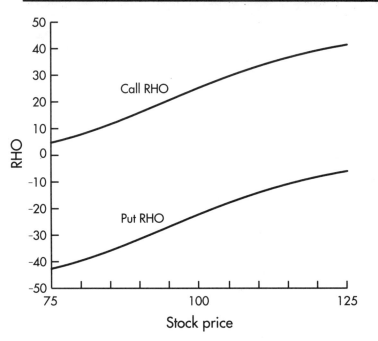

Figure 14.11   **Call and Put RHOs as a Function of the Stock Price**

$X = \$100; \, \sigma = .3; \, r = .08; \, T - t = 180$ days

of .0181. The following table shows how the value of this positive GAMMA portfolio will vary with large changes in the stock price.

Stock Price	Put Price	.3849 Shares	Portfolio Value (1 Put + .3849 Shares)
$90	$11.25	$34.64	$45.89
$100	$6.44	$38.49	$44.93
$110	$3.41	$42.34	$45.75

These examples of a negative GAMMA portfolio and a positive GAMMA portfolio show the desirability of positive GAMMAs. If a trader holds a position with a positive GAMMA, large changes in the stock price will cause the portfolio value to increase. We have explored this within the context of a DELTA-neutral portfolio, but the principle holds for all portfolios.

CREATING NEUTRAL PORTFOLIOS

We have seen that a trader can create a DELTA-neutral portfolio from a stock and a call or from a stock and a put. In some situations, a trader might like to create a position that is neutral with respect

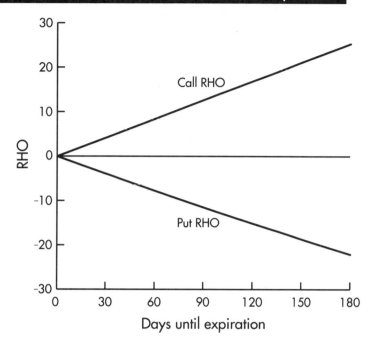

Call and Put RHOs as a Function of the Time Until Expiration — Figure 14.12

$S = \$100$; $X = \$100$; $\sigma = .3$; $r = .08$

to some other parameter, such as the THETA or VEGA of a portfolio. We now focus on stock plus option portfolios, and show how to ensure various types of neutrality for these portfolios.

We saw that a stock plus call or a stock plus put portfolio could be created as a DELTA-neutral portfolio. In general, a stock plus a single option portfolio can be made neutral with respect to just one parameter. For example, when we created the DELTA-neutral portfolios analyzed earlier, we found that the resulting portfolios were not GAMMA-neutral. A portfolio comprising a stock and a single option can never be DELTA-neutral and GAMMA-neutral unless the GAMMA of the option happens to be zero. However, we can control both the DELTA and the GAMMA of a stock plus option portfolio by creating a portfolio of a stock and two different options.

To illustrate this idea, we introduce another call option on the same underlying stock that we have been considering throughout this chapter. This call option has the same time to expiration, but its exercise price is $X = \$110$. For this call, we have $c = \$6.06$, $DELTA_c = .4365$, and $GAMMA_c = .0187$. To create a portfolio that is DELTA-neutral and GAMMA-neutral using our stock and these two calls, we create a portfolio that meets the two following conditions:

$$N_s DELTA_s + N_1 DELTA_1 + N_2 DELTA_2 = 0$$
$$N_s GAMMA_s + N_1 GAMMA_1 + N_2 GAMMA_2 = 0$$

Figure 14.13   **GAMMA as a Function of the Stock Price**

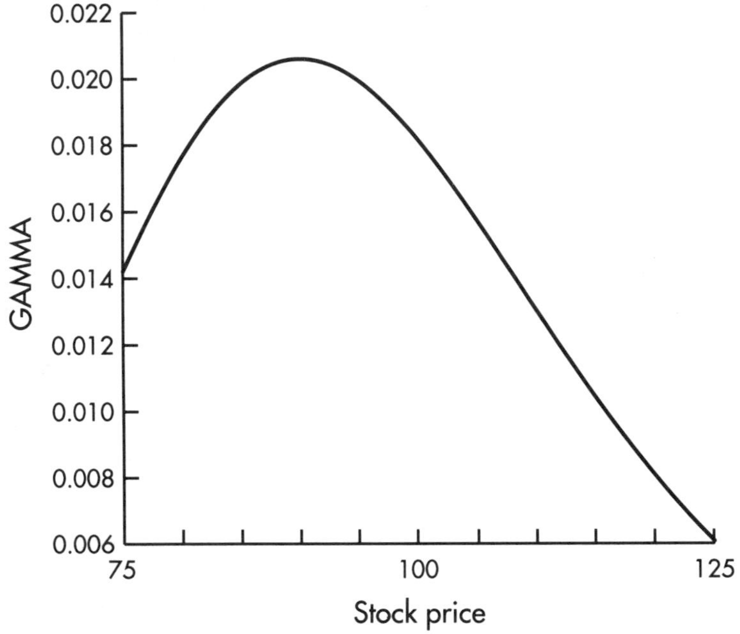

$X = \$100$; $\sigma = .3$; $r = .08$; $T - t = 180$ days

where: N_s, N_1, and N_2 are the number of shares, the number of the first call (with $X = \$100$), and the number of the second call (with $X = \$110$) to be held in the portfolio. We choose to create the portfolio with one share of stock, so $N_s = 1$. This leaves two equations with two unknowns, N_1 and N_2. We must choose these values to meet the two neutrality conditions.

For our example stock and options, we have:

$$1(1) + N_1(.6151) + N_2(.4365) = 0$$
$$1(0) + N_1(.0181) + N_2(.0187) = 0$$

If $N_1 = -5.1917$ and $N_2 = 5.0251$, the conditions will be met. Therefore, we create a DELTA-neutral and GAMMA-neutral portfolio by buying one share, selling 5.1917 calls with $X = \$100$, and buying 5.0251 calls with $X = \$110$. The resulting portfolio will be both DELTA-neutral and GAMMA-neutral.

This portfolio may be DELTA-neutral and GAMMA-neutral, but its value will still be sensitive to other parameters, such as the standard deviation of the underlying stock or the time until expiration. If we wanted to make the portfolio neutral with respect to DELTA, GAMMA, and VEGA, for example, we would need to add a third option to the portfolio. In general, we need to use one option for each sensitivity parameter that we want to control.

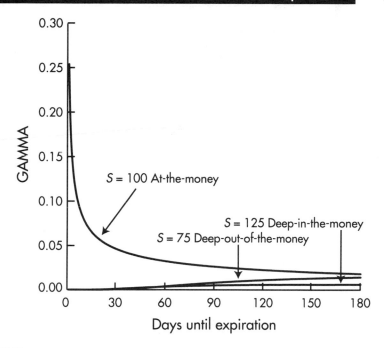

GAMMA as a Function of the Time Until Expiration   **Figure 14.14**

$X = \$100; \sigma = .3; r = .08; T - t = 180$ days

OPTION SENSITIVITIES AND OPTION TRADING STRATEGIES

Thus far in this chapter, we have seen that a trader can use a knowledge of option sensitivities to control risk. By the same token, this knowledge can be used to guide speculative trading strategies as well. By knowing the sensitivities of the various positions, a trader can create strategies to exploit certain expectations efficiently. Further, a trader should be aware of the various sensitivities of a position so she does not suffer unpleasant surprises.

In Chapter 11, we considered a wide variety of strategies, such as straddles, strangles, butterfly spreads, and condors, and we evaluated the profitability of these trades at expiration. Now, armed with the Black-Scholes model and the Merton model, we can understand how the value of these positions will behave prior to expiration. Further, given a knowledge of the sensitivities, we can analyze how a given trading strategy is likely to behave when the stock price changes, when volatility changes, or when the option approaches expiration. To explore the characteristics of option strategies, we consider the sample options shown in Table 14.7, which we use to illustrate some of the typical strategies.

The Straddle

Consider a long straddle consisting of call $C2$ and put $P2$ from Table 14.7. The cost of this position is $16.74. If the stock price at expiration is $100, which is the common exercise price for the two

Table 14.7	Sample Options			

Calls

	C1 X = $90 T − t = 180 days	C2 X = $100; T − t = 180 days	C3 X = $110; T − t = 180 days	C4 X = $100; T − t = 90 days
Price	16.33	10.30	6.06	6.91
DELTA	.7860	.6151	.4365	.5820
GAMMA	.0138	.0181	.0187	.0262
THETA	−11.2054	−12.2607	−11.4208	−15.8989
VEGA	20.4619	26.8416	27.6602	19.3905
RHO	30.7085	25.2515	18.5394	12.6464

Puts

	P1 X = $90 T − t = 180 days	P2 X = $100; T − t = 180 days	P3 X = $110; T − t = 180 days	P4 X = $100; T − t = 90 days
Price	2.85	6.44	11.80	4.95
DELTA	−.2140	−.3849	−.5635	−.4180
GAMMA	.0138	.0181	.0187	.0262
THETA	−4.2839	−4.5701	−2.9612	−8.0552
VEGA	20.4619	26.8416	27.6602	19.3905
RHO	−11.9582	−22.1559	−33.6087	−11.5295

$S = \$100; r = .08; \sigma = .3; \delta = 0$

options, the position will expire worthless. At expiration, the value of the straddle will equal the intrinsic value of the call if the stock price exceeds $100, or it will equal the intrinsic value of the put if the stock price is below $100.

At the present, 180 days before expiration, the straddle has a DELTA of .2302, so the value of the straddle will vary directly with the stock price, but at a much reduced rate. The GAMMA of the straddle is .0362, so large shifts in the stock price will be beneficial. The VEGA of the straddle is 53.6832, indicating that any increase in volatility will increase the value of the position. The THETA of the straddle is −16.8308, emphasizing that the passage of time will reduce the value of the position. In fact, if the stock price remains at $100 for the 180 days that remain until expiration, the value of the straddle will decay from $16.74 to zero over this period. A single day is .00273973 years. Therefore, with a THETA of −16.8303, we would expect a loss in the value of the straddle from day 180 to day 179 of −$.046, assuming the stock price remains steady at $100. While the straddle might lose only about $.05 of its value per day due to time decay, it will decay to just $11.86 in 90 days. Figure 14.15 shows how the profit and loss from this straddle varies for 180, 90, and zero days to expiration as a function of the stock price.

Time decay works to the benefit of the seller of this straddle, reducing the potential liability each day. By the same token, the seller is exposed to volatility risk. If the volatility of the underlying

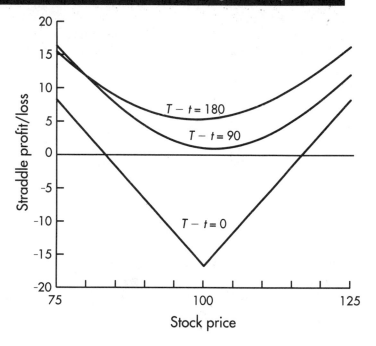

The Profit/Loss of a Straddle as a Function of the Stock Price with Various Times Remaining Until Expiration   Figure 14.15

$X = \$100$; $\sigma = .3$; $r = .08$

stock increases, both option values will rise and the short straddle position will lose. Finally, the positive GAMMA on the straddle is unfortunate from the point of view of the seller.

The Strangle

As we saw in Chapter 11, a strangle is similar to a straddle because it involves the purchase of a put and a call. Unlike a straddle, however, the striking prices of the put and call are not identical. To purchase a strangle, the trader buys a call with a lower exercise price and purchases a put with a higher exercise price. Here we consider two different strangle purchases using the example options detailed in Table 14.7.

The first strangle covers the exercise price range from $90 to $110. To purchase the strangle, the trader buys $C1$ with an exercise price of $90 and buys $P3$ with an exercise price of $110. For $C1$ we have $c = \$16.33$, DELTA $= .7860$, GAMMA $= .0138$, THETA $= -11.2054$, VEGA $= 20.4619$, and RHO $= 30.7085$. For $P3$, $p = 11.80$, DELTA $= -.5635$, GAMMA $= .0187$, THETA $= -2.9612$, VEGA $= 27.6602$, and RHO $= -33.6087$. Because both options are $10 into-the-money, they are fairly expensive, and the total cost of this strangle is $28.13. $C1$ has a large DELTA, due to its being well into-the-money. For $C1$ RHO is positive, but RHO is negative for $P3$. As a result, the strangle is not very sensitive to interest rates.

As a second strangle, we focus on an exercise price range from $100 to $110. This strangle requires the purchase of $C2$ and $P3$. For $C2$, $c = 10.30$, DELTA = .6151, GAMMA = .0181, THETA = -12.2607, VEGA = 26.8416, and RHO = 25.2515. $P3$ is the same put we considered in the preceding paragraph, as it is used in both strangles that we consider. This second strangle costs $22.10. The DELTA of the call (.6151) and put ($-.5635$) almost offset each other, so this strangle is almost DELTA-neutral. However, the strangle has a positive GAMMA, and a high positive sensitivity to volatility. The RHOs of $C2$ (25.2515) and $P3$ (-33.6087) have different signs and largely offset each other. Therefore, the strangle has a low sensitivity to interest rates.

Figure 14.16 shows the profit and loss profiles for both strangles as a function of the current stock price. At the current stock price of $100, the profit or loss on the two positions is equal. For any stock price below $100, the first strangle has a greater profit (or a smaller loss). If the stock price moves above $100, the second strangle has a greater profit.

Notice that the two strangles have quite different risk profiles. As we noted earlier, the first strangle (with $X_1 = \$90$ and $X_2 = \$110$) is almost DELTA-neutral. The second strangle (with $X_1 = \$100$ and $X_2 = \$110$) is much more sensitive to changes in the stock price around $S = \$100$. The

Figure 14.16   **The Profit/Loss of Two Strangles as a Function of the Stock Price**

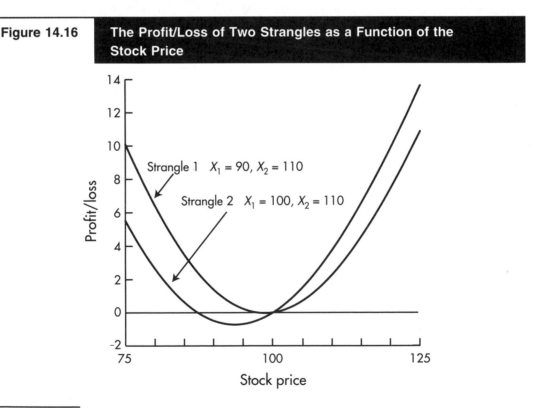

$\sigma = .3$; $r = .08$; $T - t = 180$ days

VEGA for the first strangle is 48.1221, while the VEGA for the second strangle is 54.5018. As both strangles employ the same put ($P3$), this difference in VEGA is due to the difference in VEGA between $C1$ and $C2$, and demonstrates the greater sensitivity to risk of the first strangle.

The Butterfly Spread with Calls

In a butterfly spread, a purchaser employs calls with three different exercise prices with the same underlying good and the same expiration. To illustrate the investment characteristics of this position, we use calls $C1$–$C3$ from Table 14.7. To purchase a butterfly spread, the trader would buy $C1$ (with $X = \$90$), buy $C3$ (with $X = \$110$), and sell two C_2 (with $X = \$100$). Thus, the position is long $C1$, long $C3$, and short two $C2$. This position costs $1.79:

$$16.33 - 2(10.30) + 6.06 = \$1.79$$

At a price of $1.79, we might expect future payoffs to be unlikely and small, and we should be aware of potential risks. From Chapter 11, we know that a butterfly spread with calls has the greatest payoff at expiration if the stock price equals the exercise price of the calls that were sold. For our example, that price would be $100. If the stock price at expiration were $100, $C1$ (with $X = \$90$) would be worth $10, and all other options in the spread would expire worthless.

The DELTA of this butterfly spread is:

$$.7860 - 2(.6151) + .4365 = -.0077$$

Thus, the DELTA of the spread is almost zero, but just slightly negative. Any change in the stock price will cause a slight fall in the value of the position. Further, the GAMMA is near zero, but also slightly negative:

$$.0138 - 2(.0181) + .0187 = -.0037$$

There is also little to hope for from a change in volatility, because the VEGA for the spread is negative:

$$20.4619 - 2(26.8416) + 27.6602 = -5.5611$$

Therefore, the position is not very sensitive to volatility, but an increase in volatility would cause some loss in value.

The butterfly spread has a RHO of −1.2551:

$$30.7085 - 2(25.2515) + 18.5394 = -1.2551$$

The value of the butterfly spread will vary inversely with interest rates, but the position is not very sensitive to interest rates.

The THETA for the butterfly spread is:

$$-11.2054 - 2(-12.2607) - 11.4208 = 1.8952$$

The positive THETA indicates that time decay will increase the value of the position.

These relationships are clear from Figure 14.17. As we noted, DELTA for the spread is slightly negative. In Figure 14.17, this leads to a shallow curve for the figure, but with a downward slope for stock prices greater or less than $100. The negative GAMMA is shown in the figure as the increasing downward curvature of the line. Figure 14.17 also shows the profit and loss on the butterfly spread as a function of the stock price at expiration. If the stock price remains at $100, time decay will cause the value of the butterfly spread to rise to $10 at expiration. Thus, time decay increases the value of this position, consistent with the positive THETA noted earlier.

The Bull Spread with Calls

To create a bull spread with calls, a trader purchases a call with a lower exercise price and sells a call with a higher exercise price. The two calls have the same underlying good and same term to expiration. We illustrate the bull spread with calls by considering options $C1$ and $C2$ from Table 14.7. These calls have exercise prices of $90 and $100, respectively. Option $C1$ costs $16.33, and Option $C2$ costs $10.30. Therefore, the spread will cost $6.03.

Figure 14.17	The Profit/Loss of a Butterfly Spread as a Function of the Stock Price

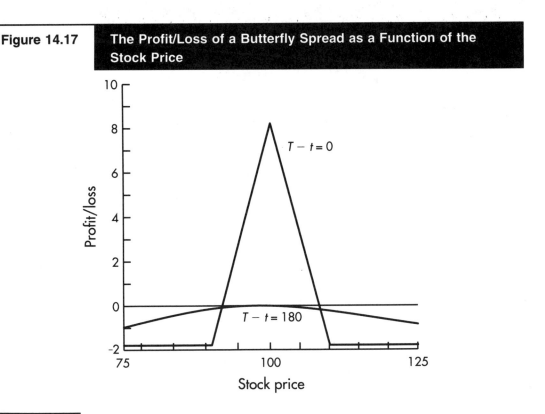

$\sigma = .3$; $r = .08$; $T - t = 180$ days; $X_1 = \$90$; $X_2 = \$100$; $X_3 = \$110$

The sensitivities for the spread are: DELTA = .7860 − .6151 = .1709; GAMMA = .0138 − .0181 = −.0043; THETA = −11.2054 + 12.2607 = 1.0553; VEGA = 20.4619 − 26.8416 = −6.3797; and RHO = 30.7085 − 25.2515 = 5.4570. Therefore, we see that a stock price increase will cause an increase in the value of the spread, which will be partially offset for large stock price changes by the negative GAMMA. Time decay will cause an increase in the value of the spread, as shown by the positive THETA. The spread has a negative VEGA, indicating that an increase in the stock's volatility will cause a decrease in the value of the spread. Finally, the RHO is positive, so an increase in interest rates will cause the spread to increase in value.

Figure 14.18 shows the profit and loss profile for the spread as a function of the price of the underlying stock. The graph shows that the value of the spread is positively related to the stock price. Further, Figure 14.18 illustrates that time decay will cause an increase in profits on the position. If no other parameters change, the profit and loss profile for the spread will collapse to its value at expiration as shown in the graph.

The VEGA of the option with the higher exercise price ($C2$ with $X = \$100$) is larger than that of $C1$ (with $X = \$90$). Because the position is long $C1$ and short $C2$, the spread's VEGA is negative. Therefore, an increase in volatility will cause the price of the spread to fall. Figure 14.19 shows the profitability of the spread as a function of the standard deviation.

The Profit/Loss of a Bull Spread with Calls as a Function of the Stock Price　　**Figure 14.18**

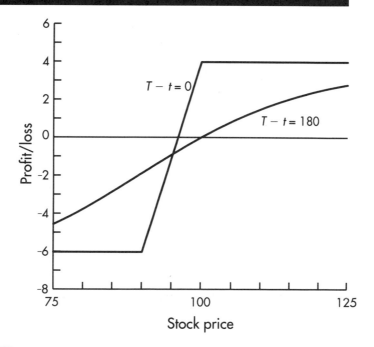

$\sigma = .3$; $r = .08$; $T - t = 180$ days; $X_1 = \$90$; $X_2 = \$100$

Figure 14.19	**The Profit/Loss of a Bull Spread with Calls as a Function of the Standard Deviation**

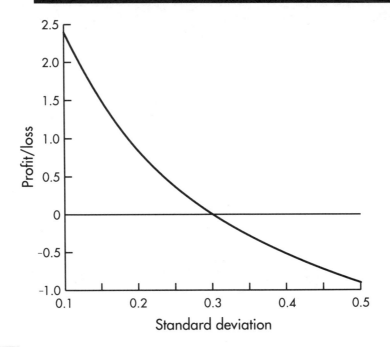

$S = \$100; \; r = .08; \; T - t = 180 \text{ days}; \; X_1 = \$90; \; X_2 = \$100$

A Ratio Spread with Calls

As discussed in Chapter 11, there are infinitely many possible ratio spreads, because a new position can be created merely by changing the ratio between the options that comprise the spread. Therefore, we illustrate the general technique of ratio spreads with a fairly simple ratio spread using just two options.

Earlier we considered the straddle composed of call $C2$ and put $P2$ from Table 14.7. We noted that the straddle costs $16.74 and has a DELTA $= .6151 - .3849 = .2302$. The straddle had a VEGA $= 26.8416 + 26.8416 = 53.6832$. Thus, the straddle is essentially a volatility strategy with a relatively low DELTA and a high VEGA.

Consider now a trader's desire to create a position with most of the characteristics of a straddle, but to make it more purely a volatility strategy. In other words, the trader anticipates a volatility increase for the underlying stock, but does not wish to take a position on whether stock prices might rise or fall. Therefore, this trader would like to create a DELTA-neutral position with a high VEGA. The trader can create such a position by using a ratio spread that is similar to the straddle. However, instead of buying one $C2$ and one $P2$, the trader decides to buy one $C2$ and to buy enough puts ($P2$) to create a DELTA-neutral position. Therefore, the trader buys one $C2$ and 1.5981 $P2$, which costs:

$10.30 + 1.5981(6.44) = $20.59. This position is DELTA-neutral because the DELTA of the spread is:

$$DELTA = .6151 + 1.5981(-.3849) = 0.0$$

The other sensitivities for the ratio spread are: GAMMA = .0181 + 1.5981(.0181) = .0470; THETA = −12.2607 + 1.5981(−4.5701) = −19.5642; VEGA = 26.8416 + 1.5981(26.8416) = 69.7372; and RHO = 25.2515 + (1.5981)(−22.1559)= −10.1558. Therefore, this ratio spread has zero DELTA, and a high VEGA. The value of the spread will suffer from time decay and will fall if interest rates rise.

Figure 14.20 shows the profitability of the straddle and the ratio spread as a function of the stock price. The ratio spread is much less sensitive to changing stock prices. This is consistent with its creation as a DELTA-neutral position. Both the straddle and the spread are essentially a bet on increasing volatility. However, the ratio spread is a purer bet on volatility because it is insensitive to stock price changes. Figure 14.21 shows how the profitability of the straddle and the ratio spread change with changing volatility. Clearly, the ratio spread is more sensitive to changing volatility, as is shown by its greater slope in Figure 14.21.

One of the advantages of ratio spreads is the ability to avoid risk exposure to one parameter and to accept risk exposure to another. For example, one could use a ratio spread of the form we have

The Profit/Loss of a Straddle and a Ratio Spread as a Function of the Stock Price　　　**Figure 14.20**

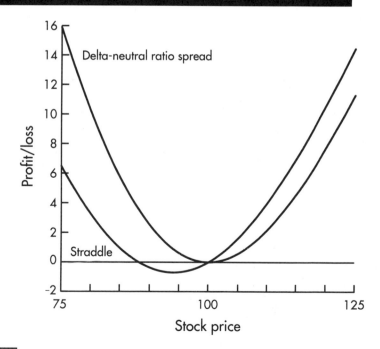

$\sigma = .3$; $r = .08$; $T - t = 180$ days; $X = \$100$

Figure 14.21	The Profit/Loss of a Straddle and a Ratio Spread as a Function of the Standard Deviation

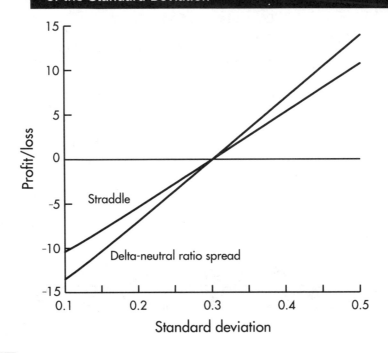

$S = \$100; \ r = .08; \ T - t = 180 \text{ days}; \ X = \$100$

considered to create a position that is VEGA-neutral but with a large DELTA, indicating a high sensitivity to changes in the stock price. This VEGA-neutral position could be created by buying $C2$ and selling $P2$ in a ratio of 1:1. The resulting spread would have a DELTA = 1.0. Thus, with a ratio spread of two options, one can maintain neutrality with respect to one parameter and accept sensitivity with respect to a second parameter.

The Calendar Spread

All of the option strategies we have considered thus far have employed options with the same expiration date. A **calendar spread** or a **time spread** is an option combination that employs options with different expiration dates but a common underlying stock. These spreads all have a horizon that terminates by the time the near-expiration option expires.

By using calendar spreads, a trader can adopt speculative strategies designed to exploit beliefs about future stock prices. Bullish and bearish calendar spreads are both possible. The trader can also exploit differential sensitivities to create positions that are neutral with respect to some option parameter, while selecting exposure to others. For example, a trader might create a DELTA-neutral calendar spread that will profit with time decay.

A Calendar Spread with Calls. As a first example of a calendar spread, consider calls C2 and C4 in Table 14.7. These calls are identical, except call C2 expires in 180 days, while C4 expires in 90 days. Assume that a trader creates a calendar spread by buying C2 and selling C4. The cost of this position is: $10.30 − $6.91 = $3.39. The sensitivities for the spread are: DELTA = .6151 − .5820 = .0331; GAMMA = .0181 − .0262 = −.0081; THETA = −12.2607 − (−15.8989) = 3.6382; VEGA = 26.8416 − 19.3905 = 7.4511; and RHO = 25.2515 − 12.6464 = 12.6051. In purchasing this position, the trader has obtained a position that will gain value for an increase in the stock price, volatility, and interest rate. Further, the position will increase in value with time decay.

Figure 14.22 shows the profitability of the calendar spread at the time it is initiated (with 180 days until C2 expires and 90 days until C4 expires). It also shows the value of the spread in 90 days (when C4 expires and C2 has 90 days remaining until expiration). We first consider the value profile of the spread at the time it is initiated. At S = $100, the spread is worth $3.39, the price the trader paid. As we have seen, it is essentially DELTA-neutral and GAMMA-neutral, with a relatively low sensitivity to the standard deviation and the interest rate. The spread does have a positive THETA, however, indicating that time decay will increase the value of the position.

This positive time decay is also shown in Figure 14.22, because the figure shows the profitability of the position in 90 days, when C4 expires. If the stock price is at $100, C4 will expire worthless,

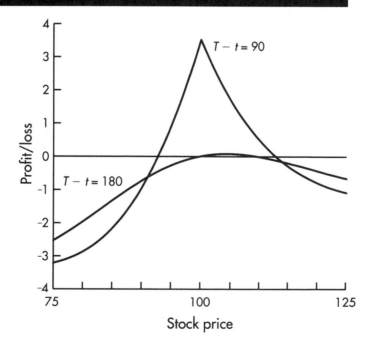

The Value of a Calendar Spread with Calls as a Function of the Stock Price

Figure 14.22

$r = .08$; $T_1 - t = 180$ days; $T_2 - t = 90$ days; $X_1 = X_2 = \$100$

but C2 will be worth $6.91. Therefore, the price of the spread will rise from $3.39 to $6.91 over 90 days if the stock price does not change. This increase in profits is due strictly to time decay. Therefore, this type of calendar spread with calls is essentially an attempt to take advantage of time decay.

A Calendar Spread with Puts. Consider the spread in which a trader buys a put with a distant expiration and sells a put with a nearby expiration. We illustrate this spread by considering puts P2 and P4 from Table 14.7. The trader buys P2 for $6.44 and sells put P4 for $4.95, for a total cost of $1.49.

The sensitivities for the spread are: DELTA = −.3849 − (−.4180) = .0331; GAMMA = .0181 − .0262 = −.0081; THETA = −4.5701 − (−8.0552) = 3.4851; VEGA = 26.8416 − 19.3905 = 7.4511; and RHO = −22.1559 − (−11.5295) = −10.6264. The most important features of this spread are its low DELTA and its significantly positive THETA. The position is not very sensitive to changes in stock prices, but it should appreciate with time decay. Figure 14.23 shows the profitability of this spread as a function of the stock price at the time it is initiated (when P2 has 180 days until expiration and P4 has 90 days until expiration). The figure also shows the profitability of the spread at the expiration date of the nearby put. Notice that this graph is almost (but not quite) identical to Figure 14.22. Implementing a calendar spread with puts or calls gives virtually the same profit and loss profile. If the stock price remains constant at S = $100, the value of the spread will rise from $1.49

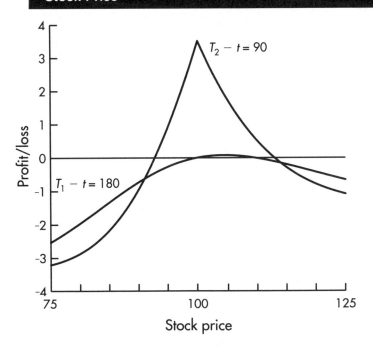

Figure 14.23   **The Value of a Calendar Spread with Puts as a Function of the Stock Price**

$r = .08$; $T_1 - t = 180$ days; $T_2 - t = 90$ days; $X_1 = X_2 = \$100$

to $4.95 over the 90 days until *P*4 expires. Thus, this calendar spread with puts is essentially an attempt to exploit time decay.

CONCLUSION

This chapter has explored the sensitivity of option prices to the key parameters that determine the price of an option – the stock price, the standard deviation of the stock's returns, the interest rate, and the time remaining until expiration. We explored these measures within the context of the Merton model, and showed that the Merton model embraces the Black-Scholes model. Given a knowledge of these sensitivities, a trader can use options more effectively, both for hedging and for speculating.

We have seen that DELTA measures the sensitivity of the price of an option to the price of the underlying stock. GAMMA measures the tendency for DELTA to change as the stock price changes, providing a measure of a second order for the key sensitivity DELTA. VEGA gauges the sensitivity of an option's price to the volatility of the underlying stock, while RHO measures the sensitivity of the option price to the interest rate. Finally, THETA measures the sensitivity of the option price to the time to expiration of the option.

By combining options with the underlying stock, or by combining options into portfolios, the trader can create positions with exactly the desired risk exposures. For example, we saw that a trader could use a stock and a call to create a portfolio that is DELTA-neutral. A DELTA-neutral portfolio does not change in value as the stock price changes infinitesimally. We also saw how to use two options in conjunction with a stock to make a portfolio both DELTA-neutral and GAMMA-neutral.

In many instances, a trader will seek exposure to one or more of the option parameters as a speculative technique. For example, we saw how traders can use straddles to accept exposure to volatility while minimizing exposure to changes in the stock price. Such a strategy is essentially a bet on increasing volatility, if the trader buys a straddle. We also observed that strangles created with different pairs of exercise prices could have substantially different DELTAs, even when all other factors are equal. A speculator interested in making money is well advised to master these relationships. A hedger needs to know how a given position responds to changing parameters to understand a hedge completely and to create more effective hedges. Given a knowledge of these sensitivities, a speculator or a hedger can understand the full spectrum of risk entailed by a position.

QUESTIONS AND PROBLEMS

1. Consider Call A, with: $X = \$70$; $r = .06$; $T - t = 90$ days; $\sigma = .4$; and $S = \$60$. Compute the price, DELTA, GAMMA, THETA, VEGA, and RHO for this call.
2. Consider Put A, with: $X = \$70$; $r = .06$; $T - t = 90$ days; $\sigma = .4$; and $S = \$60$. Compute the price, DELTA, GAMMA, THETA, VEGA, and RHO for this put.
3. Consider a straddle comprised of Call A and Put A. Compute the price, DELTA, GAMMA, THETA, VEGA, and RHO for this straddle.
4. Consider Call A. Assuming the current stock price is $60, create a DELTA-neutral portfolio consisting of a short position of one call and the necessary number of shares. What is the value of this portfolio for a sudden change in the stock price to $55 or $65?
5. Consider Call A and Put A from above. Assume that you create a portfolio that is short one call and long one put. What is the DELTA of this portfolio? Can you find the DELTA without

computing? Explain. Assume that a share of stock is added to the short call/long put portfolio. What is the DELTA of the entire position?

6. What is the GAMMA of a share of stock if the stock price is $55 and a call on the stock with $X = \$50$ has a price $c = \$7$ while a put with $X = \$50$ has a price $p = \$4$? Explain.

7. Consider Call B written on the same stock as Call A with: $X = \$50$; $r = .06$; $T - t = 90$ days; $\sigma = .4$; and $S = \$60$. Form a bull spread with calls from these two instruments. What is the price of the spread? What is its DELTA? What will the price of the spread be at expiration if the terminal stock price is $60? From this information, can you tell whether THETA is positive or negative for the spread? Explain.

8. Consider again the sample options, C2 and P2, of the chapter discussion as given in Table 14.7. Assume now that the stock pays a continuous dividend of 3 percent per annum. See if you can tell how the sensitivities will differ for the call and a put without computing. Now compute the DELTA, GAMMA, VEGA, THETA, and RHO of the two options if the stock has a dividend.

9. Consider three calls, Call C, Call D, and Call E, all written on the same underlying stock. $S = \$80$; $r = .07$; $\sigma = .2$. For Call C, $X = \$70$, and $T - t = 90$ days. For Call D, $X = \$75$, and $T - t = 90$ days. For Call E, $X = \$80$, and $T - t = 120$ days. Compute the price, DELTA, and GAMMA for each of these calls. Using Calls C and D, create a DELTA-neutral portfolio assuming that the position is long one Call C. Now use calls C, D, and E to form a portfolio that is DELTA-neutral and GAMMA-neutral, again assuming that the portfolio is long one Call C.

NOTE

[1] THETA$_p$ could be positive for a put that is deep-in-the-money. For example, if $S = \$50$, $X = \$100$, $r = .08$, $\sigma = .3$, and $T - t = 180$ days, then $p = \$46.1354$, and THETA$_p = 7.6377$. Notice that the put is worth less than $X - S$, because the put is European and the owner cannot exercise. However, if none of the parameters change over the life of the option, the put price must rise to $50 at the expiration date.

CHAPTER 15

AMERICAN OPTION PRICING

OVERVIEW

Chapter 13 considered the principles of pricing for European options – those options that can be exercised only at the expiration of the option. There we considered the binomial model and saw how it could be extended logically to the Black-Scholes model. Strictly speaking, the Black-Scholes model holds only for European options on nondividend paying stocks. However, we saw that it was possible to extend the Black-Scholes model to account for dividends by several adjustment procedures, such as the known dividend adjustment and Merton's model, which accounts for continuous dividends. In addition, we saw that the binomial model can price options on stocks that pay dividends, either in the form of a proportional dividend or an actual dollar dividend. Therefore, the tools for pricing European options are quite robust. However, all of the models considered in Chapter 13 pertain strictly to European options.

This chapter focuses on American options – those that can be exercised at any time during the option's life. Most publicly traded options are American options, so it is important to develop techniques for pricing these instruments. However, the early exercise feature of American options brings with it substantial complexity. As we will see, there are no general closed-form pricing models for American options that would parallel the Black-Scholes model for European options.

This chapter begins by analyzing the differences between American and European options. It then turns to consider some attempts to estimate the value of American options. Also, we consider a special case in which there is an exact option pricing formula. Later in the chapter, we return to the binomial model and show how it can be used to price American options with a high degree of accuracy. **OPTION!** can compute prices for all of the option models considered in this chapter.

AMERICAN VERSUS EUROPEAN OPTIONS

Consider two calls or two puts that are just alike in terms of having the same underlying good, the same exercise price, and the same time to expiration, but one option is American and the other is

European. In this context, American options are just like European options, except the American option allows the privilege of early exercise. Because of this parallel between the two kinds of options, we analyze American options by contrasting them with the simpler European options that we have already considered, under the assumption that the options are parallel – have the same underlying good, the same exercise price, and the same time until expiration. The difference in price between parallel American and European options must stem from the early exercise feature of the American option. Thus, if we know the price of a European option, we can price the parallel American option by determining the impact of the early exercise privilege. The value of the right to exercise before expiration is the **early exercise premium**. Much of our analysis of American options will concentrate on valuing the early exercise premium.

Because an American option affords every benefit of a parallel European option, plus the potentially valuable benefit of early exercise, we know that, for parallel options:

$$C_t \geq c_t \text{ and } P_t \geq p_t$$

where American options are denoted by capital C or P, and European options are indicated by lower case c or p. While the American option must be worth at least as much as the parallel European option, it may not actually be worth more; the early exercise premium may have no value in some circumstances. In some situations, however, the early exercise premium may be extremely valuable, and the American option can be worth much more than the parallel European option.

American versus European Puts

In Chapter 12 we considered various boundary conditions that limited the arbitrage-free range of option prices. Due to its early exercise feature, an American put can always be converted into its exercise value $X - S_t$. Therefore:

$$P_t \geq X - S_t$$

For a European put we saw in Chapter 12 that:

$$p_t \geq Xe^{-r(T-t)} - S_t$$

The difference in prices of parallel American and European options depends largely on the extent to which the option is in-the-money, the interest rate, and the amount of time remaining until expiration. The early exercise of an American put discards the value of waiting to see how stock prices evolve. On the other hand, by exercising immediately, the owner of an American put captures the exercise value, $X - S_t$, and can invest those proceeds from the time of exercise until the expiration date of the option. The greater this amount of time, and the higher the interest rate, the greater the incentive for early exercise.

To illustrate this idea consider a European put option with an exercise price of $100 and 180 days until expiration. The underlying stock has a standard deviation of .1 and the risk-free rate is 10 percent. If the stock price is $100, the European put is worth $.9749, well above its immediate exercise value of zero. However, if the stock price is $85, the European put is worth $10.33, well below $X - S_t = \$15$. With a stock price of $85, we know that the parallel American put would be worth at least $15. Figure 15.1 graphs the value of this European put and the quantity $X - S_t$ for various stock prices. As the graph shows, for stock prices near $85, the value of the European put approaches its lower bound of $Xe^{-r(T-t)} - S_t$ and changes almost 1:1 for changes in the stock price. Figure 15.1 suggests why American puts can be worth considerably more than their parallel European puts – the American put gives its owner the right to capture the exercise value immediately. With lower interest rates or a shorter time to expiration, the difference between $X - S_t$ would be lower relative to the value of the European put. For example, for this option with a stock price of $85 and only 20 days until expiration, the European put would be worth $14.45, much closer to the exercise value of $15.

Notice that this substantial difference in the value of American and European puts arises without any consideration of dividends, because the stock considered in our previous example had no dividends. As Figure 15.1 shows, the difference between $X - S_t$ and the value of a European put is larger when the put is deep-in-the-money. For a put, large dividends reduce the value of the underlying stock substantially and tend to push a put deeper into-the-money. Thus, dividends can also increase the difference in value between European and American puts.

For an American put on a dividend paying stock, the optimal time to exercise is generally immediately after a dividend payment. Certainly, exercising just before a dividend payment would not make sense; it would be much better to wait for the dividend payment to reduce the stock price and push the put further into-the-money.

In this discussion of early exercise of American puts, the critical point to realize is that a substantial difference between European and American puts can arise even when there are no dividends. Further, it can be quite rational to exercise an American put before expiration on a nondividend

The Boundary Space for European and American Puts   Figure 15.1

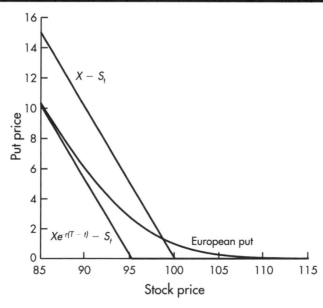

paying stock. Later in this chapter, we will see exactly when it is rational to exercise an American put before expiration.

American versus European Calls

In understanding the differences between American and European calls, we begin with the simpler situation in which the underlying stock pays no dividends. For calls on a nondividend paying stock, early exercise is never rational, and the price of an American and European call will be the same.

In Chapter 12 we explored boundary conditions for European call options and showed that before expiration the call must be worth at least as much as the stock price minus the present value of the exercise price. That is:

$$c_t \geq S_t - Xe^{-r(T-t)}$$

The immediate exercise value of a call is only $S_t - X$. As long as there is some time remaining until expiration and the interest rate is not zero, the European call will be worth more than the immediate exercise value.

Relative to its parallel European call, an American call gives benefits from the right to exercise early. However, the boundary condition on the call shows that early exercise is never desirable if the underlying stock pays no dividend. Therefore, the right to exercise early that is inherent in the American call can have no value, and for calls on a nondividend paying stock, the price of an American call is the same as the price of a parallel European call.

We now consider the importance of dividends on call values. If the underlying stock pays a dividend, it can be rational to exercise early, and an American call can be worth more than its parallel European call. We emphasize this point by considering a radical situation. Assume that a stock trades for $80 and the firm has announced that it will pay a liquidating dividend of $80 one minute before the options on this stock expire. Assume that American and European calls on this share have an exercise price of $60 and the present time is two minutes before expiration. (The time is just before expiration in this example so that we can ignore the time value of money.) What would be the value of the American and European calls?

For the owner of the American call, the strategy is clear. The owner should exercise the option immediately, paying the exercise price of $60 and receiving the liquidating dividend of $80. This gives a cash flow of +$20, so the value of the American call must be $20. The European call cannot be exercised until expiration. But, under the terms of this example, the stock will be worth zero at the expiration of the option due to the payment of the liquidating dividend one minute before expiration. Therefore, the European call must be worth zero. Another way to see that the European call is worth zero is from the adjustment for known dividends, discussed in Chapter 13. There we saw that one could adjust the stock price by subtracting from the stock price the present value of all dividends to be paid during the life of the option. The Black-Scholes model could then be applied as usual if we substituted this dividend-adjusted stock price for the current stock price as an input to the model. In our present example, we would subtract the $80 dividend from the $80 stock price, giving an adjusted stock price of zero. Because the call is at expiration, it will be worth the maximum of zero or the adjusted stock price minus the exercise price. Therefore, the European call will be worth zero in the extreme circumstance we are considering.

In less extreme circumstances – when the dividend is smaller relative to the value of the stock and when there is more time remaining until expiration – it can still be rational to exercise before expiration. The decision to exercise early depends mainly on the amount of the dividend, the interest rate, and the time remaining until expiration. Our extreme example shows a general principle about early exercise. If there is to be early exercise of a call, it should occur immediately before a dividend payment. Later in this chapter, we will explore more fully the conditions that lead to the early exercise of calls. We now turn to models for pricing American options.

PSEUDO-AMERICAN CALL OPTION PRICING

The **pseudo-American call option pricing model** was created by Fischer Black.[1] It does not provide an exact pricing technique for American calls, but it does provide an estimated call price that draws on the intuitions of the Black-Scholes model. Later we explore more exact methods for pricing American calls, but the pseudo-American model is important because it clearly shows the factors that lead to early exercise, and it highlights the differences between European and American calls. Essentially, the valuation technique requires four steps.

1. From the current stock price, subtract the present value of all dividends that will be paid before the option expires. So far, this is the same procedure we followed for the known dividend adjustment for European calls.
2. For each dividend date, reduce the exercise price by the present value of all dividends yet to be paid, including the dividend that is about to go ex-dividend.
3. Taking each dividend date and the actual expiration date of the option as potential expiration dates, compute the value of a European call using the adjusted stock and exercise prices.
4. Select the highest of these European call values as the estimate of the value of the American call.

Each step has a clear rationale. In the first step, we adjust the stock price to reflect its approximate value after it pays the dividends. In the second step, we effectively add back the value of dividends to be received from the stock if we exercise. This is accomplished by reducing the liability of the exercise price by the present value of the dividends we will capture if we exercise. In the third step, we evaluate different exercise decisions. If we exercise, we will do so just before a dividend payment to capture the dividend from the stock. Thus, in the third step we consider the payoffs from each potential exercise date. Finally, in the fourth step, we compare the different payoffs associated with each exercise strategy that we computed in the third step. Assuming that we plan to follow the best exercise strategy, we approximate the current American call price as the highest of these computed European call prices.

As an example, consider the following data.

$$S_t = \$60$$
$$X = \$60$$
$$T - t = 180 \text{ days}$$
$$r = .09$$
$$\sigma = .2$$
$$D_1 = \$2, \text{ to be paid in } 60 \text{ days}$$
$$D_2 = \$2, \text{ to be paid in } 150 \text{ days}$$

What is the pseudo-American call worth? The present value of the dividends is:

$$D_1 e^{-rt} + D_2 e^{-rt} = \$2e^{-(.09)(60/365)} + \$2e^{-(.09)(150/365)} = \$3.90$$

We subtract this present value from the stock price, so we use \$56.10 as our stock price in all subsequent calculations. We will use this adjusted stock price to compute call values, assuming the option expires at three different times: the actual expiration date, the date of the last dividend, and the date of the first dividend. Three inputs remain constant for each computation: $S = \$56.10$, $r = .09$, and $\sigma = .2$. The time until expiration will vary, and we must adjust the exercise price for different dividend amounts.

We begin with the actual expiration date. Applying the Black-Scholes model with $T - t = 180$ days and $X = \$60$ gives a call value of \$2.57. (This is the same as the known dividend adjustment for European calls discussed in Chapter 13.) Next, we deal with each dividend date, starting with the final dividend. The dividend is just about to be paid, so we adjust the exercise price by subtracting \$2. Thus, for $X = \$58$ and $T - t = 150$ days, the call value is \$2.97. Next, we consider the date of the first dividend. The present value of the dividends at that time consists of the dividend that is just about to be paid, \$2, plus the present value of the second dividend that will be paid in 90 days, $\$2e^{-(.09)(90/365)} = \$1.96$. Together, these dividends have a present value of \$3.96, so we adjust the exercise price to \$56.04. Therefore, for $X = \$56.04$ and $T - t = 60$ days, the call price is \$2.28.

Now we have three estimated call prices corresponding to two dividend dates and the actual expiration date of the option. The estimates are \$2.28 for the first dividend date, \$2.97 for the second date, and \$2.57 for the actual expiration date. Therefore, we take the largest value, \$2.97, as the estimate of the pseudo-American call value. According to Whaley, the average error for this pseudo-American model is about 1.5 percent.[2]

The strategy behind the pseudo-American option technique is to realize that an American call on a dividend paying stock can be analyzed as consisting of a series of options. Given that early exercise is only optimal just prior to a dividend payment, we may think of the American call as consisting of a portfolio of European options that expire just before each dividend and at the actual exercise date. In the pseudo-American technique, we evaluate each of those European options, and treat the American option as being worth the maximum of all of the European options.

EXACT AMERICAN CALL OPTION PRICING

In general, there is no closed-form solution to the value of an American call option on a dividend paying stock. However, an exact pricing formula is possible in one special case. It is possible to compute the exact price for an option on a stock that pays a single dividend during the life of the option.[3] The model is also known as the **compound option model**.

As discussed in the previous section on the pseudo-American model, an American call option really consists of a series of options that expire just before the various dividend dates and at the actual expiration of the option. We now focus on the situation when there is just one dividend between the present and the expiration date of the option, time T. We assume that the dividend occurs at time t_1. The time line in Figure 15.2 shows the decision points that we must consider. As t_1 approaches, the owner of the call must decide whether to exercise. If she exercises, she does so the instant before t_1 and receives the stock with dividends and pays the exercise price. If she does not exercise, the stock pays the dividend and she continues to hold a call on the stock, now without the dividend. The

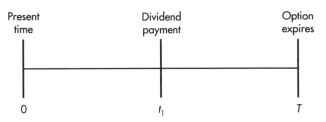

Decision Points for Options on a Dividend Paying Stock   **Figure 15.2**

instant after the dividend payment occurs, the call is effectively a European call, because there are no more dividend payments and early exercise on a European call is never rational. Letting S_1 be the stock price just after the dividend, D_1, is paid, and letting C_1 be the call price just after the dividend is paid, her choice is:

Exercise: Receive stock with dividend; pay the exercise price.
                     $S_1 + D_1 - X$

Don't Exercise: Own call on the stock with the stock's value reduced by the dividend amount.
                     C_1

Considering the American call before the dividend date, we can see that it is really a compound option, or an option on an option. It is an option on an option because she has the option to refrain from exercising and to own a European option.

The exercise decision as t_1 approaches depends principally on the stock price. If the stock reaches some critical level, the owner should exercise. If it is below that level, the call owner will be better off not exercising and owning the resulting (effectively European) call. The critical stock price, S^*, is the stock price at which the owner is indifferent about the exercise decision, and the owner will be indifferent if the exercise decision leaves her wealth unchanged. The critical stock price is the stock price that makes the two outcomes equal:

$$S^* + D_1 - X = C_1 \tag{15.1}$$

For example, assume that the dividend date t_1 is at hand and that 90 days remain until the option expires. The exercise price is $100, the standard deviation of the stock is .2, the risk-free rate is 10 percent, and the dividend that is to be paid is $5. If the stock price immediately after the dividend is paid is $100.67, the call option is worth $5.67. For these data, $S^* = \$100.67$, because:

$$\$100.67 + \$5.00 - \$100.00 = \$5.67$$

If the stock price is higher than $100.67 the instant before t_1, the call owner should exercise. If the stock price is less than $100.67, she should not exercise.

We now turn to the valuation of the American call before the dividend date. In this case, the value of the call is:

$$C_t = (S - D_1 e^{-r(t_1-t)})N(b_1) - (X - D_1)e^{-r(t_1-t)}N(b_2) \tag{15.2}$$

$$+ (S - D_1 e^{-r(t_1-t)})N_2\left(a_1; -b_1; -\sqrt{\frac{t_1-t}{T-t}}\right) - Xe^{-r(T-t)}N_2\left(a_2; -b_2; -\sqrt{\frac{t_1-t}{T-t}}\right)$$

where:

$$a_1 = \frac{\ln\left(\dfrac{S - D_1 e^{-r(t_1-t)}}{X}\right) + (r + .5\sigma^2)(T - t)}{\sigma\sqrt{T - t}}$$

$$a_2 = a_1 - \sigma\sqrt{T - t}$$

$$b_1 = \frac{\ln\left(\dfrac{S - D_1 e^{-r(t_1-t)}}{S*}\right) + (r + .5\sigma^2)(t_1 - t)}{\sigma\sqrt{t_1 - t}}$$

$$b_2 = b_1 - \sigma\sqrt{t_1 - t}$$

The function $N_2(a; b; \rho)$ is the standardized cumulative bivariate normal distribution. For two variables, x and y, that are distributed according to the standardized bivariate normal function, and have a correlation of ρ, $N_2(a; b; \rho)$ is the probability that $x \leq a$ and that $y \leq b$. N_2 is like the standard normal function used in the Black-Scholes model, except it takes into account two variables that are correlated. Considered singly, variables x and y are distributed normally with a mean of zero and a standard deviation of 1.0. Assume for the moment that $a = 0$, $b = 0$, and the correlation between x and y is zero, so $\rho = 0$. In that case, N_2 would give the probability of both x and y being less than or equal to zero. Considered alone, the chance that $x \leq 0$ is 50 percent, and the same is true of y considered by itself. Because we assume that the correlation between the two is zero, the joint probability of both x and y being less that 0 is just the product of the two individual probabilities, or 25 percent. **OPTION!** can compute these bivariate probabilities.

We now turn to a close examination of the formula, which bears close similarities to the Black-Scholes model. At time t, the value of the call must equal the present value of the expected payoffs on the option. We have already seen that these are somewhat complex. First, at the dividend date, if the stock price exceeds the critical stock price, the call owner will exercise. In that case the payoff is the stock with dividend minus the exercise price, and this payoff occurs at t_1. If the stock price is less than the critical price at t_1, she will not exercise. The payoffs from the option then become either zero, if the exercise price equals or exceeds the stock price at expiration, or the stock price less the exercise price, if the stock price exceeds the exercise price at expiration. In the exact American call pricing formula, the cumulative normal (N) and bivariate cumulative normal (N_2) express various probabilities of certain stock price outcomes. These probabilities give different weights to possible outcomes from the option investment. For example, the term:

$$N_2\left(a_2; -b_2; -\sqrt{\frac{t_1-t}{T-t}}\right) \tag{15.3}$$

measures the probability that $S^* + D_1 \leq S_t$ and that $S_T \leq X$. This probability would be associated with the payoff that arises when the owner does not exercise the option at the dividend date, but the option is in-the-money at expiration. Thus, without exploring all of the mathematics, we see that the call price is a function of the payoffs that arise in the various possible circumstances, such as not exercising and having the call finish in the money, coupled with the probability of those circumstances arising.

We now show how to compute the exact value of an American call on a stock with one dividend according to this model. Continuing with our example, we have an American call with an exercise price of $100 on a stock with a standard deviation of .2. The risk-free rate is 10 percent. The stock will pay a $5 dividend when the option has 90 days remaining until expiration. We will find the price of the call when it has 180 days remaining until expiration and the stock price is $110.

The first step is to compute the value of the stock less the present value of the dividend:

$$S - D_1 e^{-r(t_1 - t)} = \$110 - \$5 e^{-.1(90/365)} = \$105.12$$

Other terms are:

$$a_1 = \frac{\ln\left(\dfrac{110.00 - 4.88}{100.00}\right) + [.1 + .5(.2)(.2)](180/365)}{.2\sqrt{180/365}}$$

$$= \frac{.0499 + .0592}{.1404} = .7771$$

$$a_2 = .7771 - .2\sqrt{180/365} = .6367$$

$$b_1 = \frac{\ln\left(\dfrac{110.00 - 4.88}{100.67}\right) + [.1 + .5(.2)(.2)](90/365)}{.2\sqrt{90/365}}$$

$$= \frac{.0433 + .0296}{.0993} = .7341$$

$$b_2 = .7341 - .2\sqrt{90/365} = .6348$$

$$\sqrt{\frac{t_1 - t}{T - t}} = \sqrt{\frac{90}{180}} = .7071$$

Given these values, we now compute the cumulative normal and cumulative bivariate normal terms.

$$N(b_1) = N(.7341) = .768556$$
$$N(b_2) = N(.6348) = .737221$$

$$N_2\left(a_1; -b_1; -\sqrt{\frac{t_1 - t}{T - t}}\right) = N_2(.7771; -.7341; -.7071) = .099098$$

$$N_2\left(a_2; -b_2; -\sqrt{\frac{t_1 - t}{T - t}}\right) = N_2(.6367; -.6348; -.7071) = .101320$$

We now compute the value of the American call as:

$$C_t = (105.12)(.768556) + (105.12)(.099098)$$
$$- 100e^{-.1(180/365)}(.101320) - (100.00 - 5.00)e^{-.1(90/365)}(.737221)$$
$$= 80.79 + 10.42 - 9.64 - 68.33$$
$$= \$13.24$$

Thus, with 180 days until expiration, this American call should be worth $13.24. This compares with a pseudo-American value in the same circumstances of $12.91. **OPTION!** can compute the value of a call under the exact American call option pricing model.

Strictly speaking, this model holds only for an American call on a stock paying a single dividend before the option's expiration date. However, when there is more than one dividend, exercise is normally rational only for the final dividend. Therefore, we can use the exact pricing model if we subtract the present value of all dividends other than the final one from the stock price and then use the adjusted stock price in all computations. (Notice that this parallels the logic of the known dividend adjustment to the Black-Scholes model.)

As we have just noted, it is only for this special case of a call with one dividend that we can compute an exact American option price. For all other circumstances, we must use a variety of approximation techniques. Fortunately, these techniques work very well, and we turn now to a consideration of them.

ANALYTICAL APPROXIMATIONS OF AMERICAN OPTION PRICES

In Chapter 13, we considered the Merton model which extended the Black-Scholes model to European options on stocks that pay a continuous dividend at a constant rate. The analytical approximations that we now consider apply to American options on an underlying instrument that pays a continuous dividend at a constant rate. The Merton model provides a closed-form solution to the problem of European options on stocks with continuous dividends. For American options, no closed-form solutions are available. The analytical approximations for American options considered in this section are extremely accurate and computationally inexpensive. **OPTION!** can compute both call and put values according to the analytical approximation presented in this section.

To understand the incentive for early exercise of an option on a stock with a continuous dividend, consider again the Merton model developed in Chapter 13.

$$c_t^M = Se^{-\delta(T-t)}N(d_1^M) - Xe^{-r(T-t)}N(d_2^M)$$

The difference in value between this European option and a parallel American option arises from the potential benefits of early exercise. Thus, we focus on an option that is deep in-the-money. In such a situation, d_1^M will be large, and d_2^M will be large as well. Consequently, $N(d_1^M)$ and $N(d_2^M)$ will approach 1.0. In the limit then, for an option that is extremely deep-in-the-money, Merton's model approaches:

$$c_t = S_t e^{-\delta(T-t)} - Xe^{-r(T-t)}$$

By contrast, an American option would have to be worth at least its immediately available exercisable proceeds:

$$C_t \geq S_t - X$$

If a trader owns the American option, she has a choice between these two quantities. Which is preferable depends upon how deep-in-the-money the option is, the dividend rate on the stock, δ, the interest rate, r, and the time remaining until the option expires, $T - t$. If the stock price reaches a critical level, S^*, such that:

$$S_t^* - X = c(S^*, X, T - t) + \text{Early exercise premium} \qquad (15.4)$$

the owner of an American option is indifferent about exercising. If the stock price exceeds S^* she will exercise immediately to capture the exercise proceeds $S_t - X$. If the stock price is below S^* she will not exercise. Figure 15.3 presents a graph of these relationships. Notice that the European call in Figure 15.3 can be worth less than $S_t - X$ because of the dividend. (As we noted earlier, a deep-in-the-money European call will tend to its lower bound of $S_t e^{-\delta(T-t)} - Xe^{-r(T-t)}$.) At the critical stock price, S^*, the European call is worth exactly $S^* - X$. For any stock price greater than S^*, the European call will be worth less than the exercisable proceeds for the American call. This explains why the owner of the American call is indifferent about exercise at a stock price of S^*; at that stock price the American and European calls are worth the same: $S^* - X$. For higher stock prices, the value of the European call falls below that of the American, and the value of the American call becomes equal to its exercisable proceeds. Thus, the owner of the American call should exercise to capture the quantity $S_t - X$. Those funds can then be invested from the exercise date to the expiration date to earn a return that will be lost if the option is not exercised.

American Calls and the Incentive for Early Exercise   **Figure 15.3**

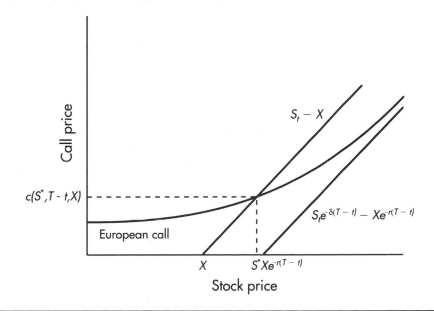

A similar argument applies to American put options. As the stock price falls well below the exercise price, there comes a point at which:

$$X - S^{**} = p(S^{**}, X, T - t) + \text{Early exercise premium} \qquad (15.5)$$

S^{**} is the critical stock price for an American put. If the stock price falls below S^{**}, the American put should be exercised to capture the exercised proceeds of $X - S_t$. Figure 15.4 presents a graph of this relationship for the European and American put. As the graph shows, for any stock price less than S^{**}, the American put should be exercised immediately.

While a complete discussion of the mathematics is beyond the scope of this text, we present the formulas for an analytic approximation of the American call and put options, and we discuss the computation of call and put values under the terms of the model.

The analytic approximation for an American call is:

$$
\begin{aligned}
C_t &= c_t + A_2\left(\frac{S_t}{S^*}\right)^{q_2} &&\text{if } S_t < S^* \\
&= S_t - X &&\text{if } S_t \geq S^*
\end{aligned}
\qquad (15.6)
$$

where:

$$A_2 = \frac{S^*[1 - e^{-\delta(T-t)}N(d_1)]}{q_2}$$

Figure 15.4   American Puts and the Incentive for Early Exercise

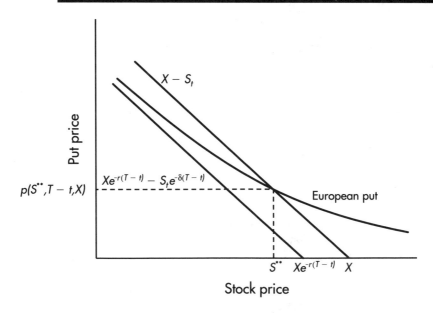

and $S*$ is the solution to:

$$S* - X = c_t(S*, X, T - t) + \{1 - e^{-\delta(T-t)}N(d_1)\}(S*/q_2) \qquad (15.7)$$

$N(d_1)$ and $p(S*, X, T - t)$ are evaluated at $S*$. To find $S*$ requires an iterative search for the value that makes the equation balance. Other terms are:

$$q_2 = \frac{1 - n + \sqrt{(n-1)^2 + 4k}}{2}, \qquad n = \frac{2(r - \delta)}{\sigma^2}, \qquad k = \frac{2r}{\sigma^2(1 - e^{-r(T-t)})}$$

For an American put, the analytic approximation is:

$$P_t = p_t + A_1 \left(\frac{S_t}{S**}\right)^{q_1} \qquad \text{if } S_t > S** \qquad (15.8)$$

$$= X - S_t \qquad \text{if } S_t \leq S**$$

where:

$$A_1 = \frac{S**[1 - e^{-\delta(T-t)}N(-d_1)]}{q_1}$$

$$q_1 = \frac{1 - n - \sqrt{(n-1)^2 + 4k}}{2}$$

$S**$ is found by an iterative search to make the following equation hold:

$$X - S** = p_t(S**, X, T - t) - [1 - e^{-\delta(T-t)}N(-d_1)](S**/q_1) \qquad (15.9)$$

$N(-d_1)$ and $p_t(S**, X, T - t)$ are evaluated at the critical stock price $S**$.

To illustrate the application of this model, consider an American call option on an underlying stock that is currently priced at \$60, has a standard deviation of .2, and pays a continuous dividend of 13.75 percent. The call has a striking price of \$60 and 180 days until expiration. The risk-free rate is 9 percent. In Chapter 13 we illustrated the Merton model with a European call having the same terms and found that the price of the European call was \$2.5557.

The first step in computing the value of this American call is to find the value of the intermediate terms n, k, and q_2. They are:

$$n = \frac{2(.09 - .1375)}{(.2)(.2)} = -2.375$$

$$k = \frac{2(.09)}{(.2)(.2)\left[1 - e^{-.09\left(\frac{180}{365}\right)}\right]} = 103.6555$$

$$q_2 = \frac{1 - (-2.375) + \sqrt{(-2.375 - 1)^2 + 4(103.6555)}}{2} = 12.0007537$$

We next search for the critical stock price, S^*, and find that $S^* = 70.2336$. (This search must be done by trial and error until the correct one is discovered.) If the actual stock price equaled the critical price, the European call would be worth \$9.0152. Then, d_1 and $N(d_1)$, computed at that critical stock price of \$70.2336, would be 1.024716 and .847251, respectively. Based on these values, we calculate A_2 as:

$$A_2 = \frac{70.2336\left[1 - e^{-.1375\left(\frac{180}{365}\right)}(.847251)\right]}{12.007537} = 1.218344$$

We can now compute the American call price. Because the current stock price of \$60 lies below the critical price of \$70.2336, the value of the American call is:

$$C_t = 2.5557 + 1.218344\left(\frac{60}{70.2336}\right)^{12.007537} = 2.5557 + .183878 = 2.7396$$

Thus, the early exercise premium is \$.18. Because this computation involves an iterative search for S^*, it is quite tedious to perform without a computer. **OPTION!** solves for the critical stock price and the price of American calls and puts directly using this analytic approximation.

THE BINOMIAL MODEL AND AMERICAN OPTION PRICES

Thus far in this chapter, we have considered various option pricing models for finding the value of American options on dividend paying stocks. As we have seen, there is no general exact solution for this problem. In fact, only for the case of an American call on a stock paying a single dividend during the option's life is it possible to compute an exact price. In all other circumstances, we must rely on estimation techniques. The analytic approximation method we have studied in this chapter applies only to continuous dividends. With stocks typically paying discrete dividends, the need for other estimation techniques is particularly important.

The binomial model is particularly important for American options because it applies to both American calls and puts on stocks with all kinds of dividend payments. These include the case of no dividends, continuous dividends, known dividend yields, and known dollar dividends. There is a common strategy for applying the binomial model that applies to all types of dividend patterns, and we begin our discussion by analyzing the underlying strategy for the binomial model for American options. We then consider each of the different dividend strategies in turn.

No Dividends

In Chapter 12 we explored the boundary conditions on the pricing of European options on stocks paying no dividends. For nondividend stocks we saw that it can never be optimal to exercise a call before expiration. This means that the American call and the European call on a nondividend stock must have the same value. Therefore, for the case of a call on a nondividend stock we can price the American call as if it were a European call. It can often be advantageous to exercise puts on nondividend stocks, so the value of European and American puts can differ substantially. We illustrate this point for an American put and explicate the basic strategy for applying the binomial model to American options.

The Basic Strategy

In Chapter 13 we explored the binomial model for European options on stocks with and without dividends. For European options on nondividend stocks, we derived the possible stock prices at expiration and determined the value of the option (call or put) at expiration from our no arbitrage condition. We then computed the value of an option one period before expiration as the expected value of the option at expiration discounted for one period. We continued this strategy, working through the binomial lattice, until we found the value of the option at the current time.

For options on stocks with dividends, we applied the binomial model by creating a lattice for the stock that reflected the timing and amount of dividend payments that the stock would make. These adjustments affected the distribution of possible stock values at the expiration date. We then computed the option values in the usual way by working from the exercise date back to the present.

To apply the binomial model for American options, we follow the same basic valuation strategy as for European options. There is, however, one important difference. For the option lattice for an American option, the option value is set equal to the maximum of:

1. The expected option value in one period discounted for one period at the risk-free rate.
2. The immediate exercise value of the option, $S_t - X$ for a call, or $X - S_t$ for a put.

Except for this treatment of each node in the lattice for an American option, the binomial model for an American option is applied in exactly the same way as it is for a European option.

We illustrate this technique by considering an American put on a stock that pays no dividend. We assume the following data:

$S_t = \$80$
$X = \$75$
$r = .07$
$\sigma = .3$
$T = 120$ days

Assuming a three-period binomial model, a single period is 40 days or .1096 years. This gives a discount factor of .9924 per period, and the following parameter values:

$U = 1.1044$
$D = .9055$
$\pi_u = .5138$

Figure 15.5 shows the stock price tree consistent with these data. (The careful reader may recall the same example from Figure 13.10.) The upper tree of Figure 15.6 repeats the upper tree from Figure

Figure 15.5   Three-Period Stock Price Lattice

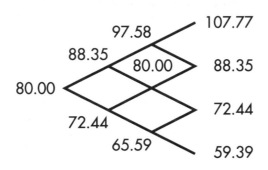

13.12, which is the binomial tree for a European put option on this stock. As the tree shows, the value of the European put is $2.67 at node *c*. The lower tree in Figure 15.6 is the binomial tree for an American put. Aside from the upper tree's being for a European put and the lower tree's pertaining to an American put, all other circumstances are the same. An examination of the two trees shows that they are identical except for the prices at nodes *a*, *b*, and *c*.

Before turning to the differences at nodes *a*, *b*, and *c*, we first consider why the other nodes are identical. First, consider the nodes at expiration. At expiration, European and American options are identical. Both can be exercised and both have the same payoffs from the exercise decision. Therefore, European and American options at expiration must have the same value. Second, consider a node one period before expiration, such as the middle node of the tree at which the stock price is $80 and both the European and American put prices are $1.24. If the stock price one period prior to expiration is $80, the American put cannot be exercised because the put is out-of-the-money. Therefore, it offers no advantage over the parallel European put. Consequently, the value must be the same.

These reflections lead us to see a condition for an American and a European option to have identical prices at a given node: If the option cannot be exercised at the given node, and if all nodes that can be reached subsequent to the node under consideration have identical prices for American and European options, then the price of the American and European options must be identical at the node in question. We can illustrate this point from the same tree by considering the node two periods before expiration in which the stock price is $88.35 and the value of the put (either European or American) is $.60. The American put cannot be exercised at that node, because it is out-of-the-money with a stock price of $88.35. Further, all subsequent nodes have identical prices for the American and European puts. Therefore, the price of the European and American puts must be the same at that node.

We now turn to consider those nodes at which prices differ for the European and American put. At node *a*, the stock price is $65.59, the European put price is $8.84, and the American put price is $9.41. The European put price is just the expected value of the put's expiration values contingent upon the stock's rising or falling. The value at node *a* for the American put is:

Three-Period Price Lattices for a European and an American Put — **Figure 15.6**

European put

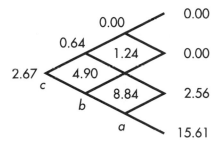

American put

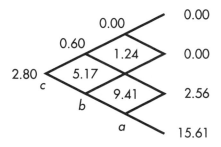

$$P = MAX(X - S, p) = MAX(\$75 - \$65.59, \$8.84) = \$9.41$$

If the stock price reaches node a, the holder of an American put should exercise and capture the exercise value of $9.41. This is higher than the present value of the expected payoff at expiration, which is the price of the European put – $8.84. As this example shows, the American put derives its higher value from its right to exercise early when conditions warrant.

At node b, the stock price is $72.44, and the European put is worth $4.90. The owner of the American put could exercise immediately for an exercise value of $75.00 – $72.44 = $2.56, but this would be foolish. One period later, the put will be worth $1.24 if the stock price rises or $9.41 if the stock price falls. Given that the probability of a stock price rise is .5138, the present value of the put's expected value in one period is:

$$[.5138(\$1.24) + .4862(\$9.41)]e^{-.07\left(\frac{40}{365}\right)} = \$5.21(.9924) = \$5.17$$

The value of the put at node b is therefore:

$$MAX\{\$2.56, \$5.17\} = \$5.17$$

Therefore, at node b, the put should not be exercised, and it is worth $5.17 – the present value of the expected put value in one period.

At node c, the present time at which we want to value the option, the same rule applies. The American put cannot be exercised rationally, because it is out-of-the-money with $75 – $80 = –$5. The present value of the expected value of the put in one period is:

$$[.5138(\$.60) + .4862(\$5.17)]e^{-.07\left(\frac{40}{365}\right)} = \$2.80$$

The value of the American put at node c, which represents the present time, is:

$$MAX\{-\$5.00, \$2.80\} = \$2.80$$

Because the exercise value (–$5.00) is negative, the value of the American put equals the present value of the expected value in one period ($2.80), and the American put should not be exercised.

This example illustrates the basic principle of applying the binomial model to American options. As we work back through the tree, discounting the next period's expected option values, we must ask at every node whether the immediate exercise value or the computed present value is greater. The value at the node is the maximum of those two quantities. Further, we may note that the stock tree is unaffected by whether the option we are analyzing is an American or a European option. We now consider how to apply the binomial model to American options on dividend paying stocks.

Continuous Dividends

In Chapter 13 we explored Merton's model, which adjusts the Black-Scholes model to price European options on stocks that pay a continuous dividend. We also showed how to use the binomial model to price European options on stocks that pay continuous dividends. There we saw that the parameters for the binomial model for a stock paying a continuous dividend were:

$$U = e^{\sigma\sqrt{\Delta t}}$$

$$D = \frac{1}{U}$$

(15.10)

$$\pi_U = \frac{e^{(r-\delta)\Delta t} - D}{U - D}$$

As we have discussed in this chapter, the stock price tree is identical whether we are pricing European or American options. Therefore, these parameters apply to generating the binomial tree of stock prices for American options on stocks paying a continuous dividend. As an examination of these parameters shows, the stock price tree will be identical in both cases. However, the probability of a stock price increase varies inversely with the level of the continuous dividend rate, δ.

To illustrate the binomial model for pricing options on stocks with continuous dividends, consider the following data:

$S_t = \$60$
$X = \$60$
$T = 180$ days
$\sigma = .2$
$r = .09$

Based on these data, consider a European and an American call option on this stock in the context of a two-period binomial model.

$$U = e^{\sigma\sqrt{\Delta t}} = e^{.2\sqrt{\frac{90}{365}}} = 1.104412$$

$$D = \frac{1}{U} = .905460$$

$$\pi_U = \frac{e^{(r-\delta)\Delta t} - D}{U - D} = \frac{e^{(.09-.1375)\left(\frac{90}{365}\right)} - .905460}{1.104412 - .905460} = .416663$$

The single-period discount factor is $e^{-.09(90/365)} = .978053$. Figure 15.7 gives the two-period stock price tree for these data, while Figure 15.8 shows the trees for a European and an American call. At expiration, the call will be in-the-money only if the stock price rises twice to a terminal price of $73.18. In this case, both the European and American calls are worth $13.18. One period before expiration, the present value of the expected terminal call value is:

$$\$13.18(.416663)(.978053) = \$5.37$$

This is the value of the European call at the node with a stock price of $66.26. For the American call, the same expected value prevails, but the owner of the American call could exercise. The exercise value of the American call is $66.26 − $60.00 = $6.26. Therefore, the value of the American call is:

Two-Period Stock Price Lattice   **Figure 15.7**

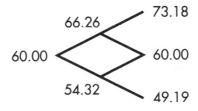

| **Figure 15.8** | **Two-Period Price Lattices for a European and an American Call** |

European call

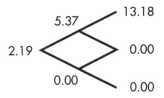

American call

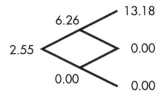

$$C = \text{MAX}\{S - X, c\} = \text{MAX}\{\$6.26, \$5.37\} = \$6.26$$

If the stock price reaches $66.26 in one period, then the holder of the American call should exercise. In terms of the binomial tree for the American call, the value at this node becomes $6.26. At the present time, the present values of the expected call values one period hence are $2.19 for the European call and $2.55 for the American call. Thus, the current price of the European call is $2.19. At the present, the stock price and exercise price are both $60, so the American option cannot be exercised rationally. This means that the current American call price is $2.55, based on a two-period tree. With 200 periods, the European call value is $2.55 and the American call price is $2.73. Table 15.1 shows how the two call prices converge to their true value as the number of periods in the binomial tree ranges from one to 200. For comparison, the Merton model price for the European option is $2.5557 and the American analytic approximation is $2.7395. Thus, the binomial method provides estimates that are extremely close to other model prices that we have explored.

Known Dividend Yields

In Chapter 13 we considered options on a stock that pays a known dividend yield at a certain date. For example, a stock might pay a dividend equal to 1 percent of its value in 90 days. The dividend

The Convergence of European and American Call Prices		Table 15.1
Number of Periods	**European Call**	**American Call**
1	3.3129	3.3129
2	2.1894	2.5530
3	2.8139	2.9399
4	2.3625	2.6380
5	2.7099	2.8517
10	2.4763	2.6909
25	2.5861	2.7554
50	2.5396	2.7216
100	2.5476	2.7256
200	2.5516	2.7275

payment obviously affects the stock price tree for the binomial model, and the loss of value from the stock will affect the value of calls and puts. This is true for both European and American options. While the existence of dividends will affect the value of European calls and puts, they do not call for European option owners to make any special decisions, as they cannot exercise even if they wished. For the holder of an American call or put, there is an exercise decision, because the American option owner can exercise immediately before the dividend payment (in the case of a call), exercise immediately after the dividend payment (in the case of a put), or not exercise. While the dividend will affect the stock price tree, we note again that the stock price tree will be identical whether we are considering a European or an American option.

To apply the binomial model for an American call or put, we begin with the terminal stock price and the value of the option at expiration and work from expiration back to the present in the normal way. However, at each node, we must take account of the potential for early exercise. As we have seen, we take early exercise into account by finding the value of a European option at each node and compare this value with the exercise value of the American option. If the exercise value exceeds the European value, the option price at the node should be the exercise value. Otherwise, the price at the node should be the European option price.

To see how to apply the binomial model to compute American option prices on a stock with a known dividend yield, consider the following data. A stock is currently priced at $80, and it will pay a dividend equal to 3 percent of its value in 55 days. The standard deviation of the stock is .3, and the risk-free rate is 7 percent. A call option on this stock has 120 days until expiration and an exercise price of $75. Based on these data, and with a three-period binomial model, $\Delta t = 40/365 = 0.1096$. Therefore:

$$U = e^{.3\sqrt{.1096}} = 1.1044$$

$$D = \frac{1}{1.1044} = .9055$$

$$\pi_U = \frac{1.0077 - .9055}{1.1044 - .9055} = .5138$$

The discounting factor for a single period is $e^{-r\Delta t} = e^{-.07(40/365)} = .9924$. Figure 15.9 shows the stock price tree for this example. (This same example was considered in Chapter 13 for European calls.) In terms of Figure 15.9, the dividend occurs between time 1 (day 40) and time 2 (day 80). The call owner might exercise at time 1 before the dividend is paid, but if she waits until time 2, the dividend will already be paid, and the dividend's value will be lost from the stock.

Figure 15.10 shows option price trees for European and American calls consistent with the stock price tree of Figure 15.9. At expiration and the period prior to expiration, the European and American call option trees are identical. This is because the exercise value for the American option never exceeds the value of the European call. In the first period, if the stock price rises from $80 to $88.35, the owner of an American call should exercise. We can see the desirability of exercise in this case as follows. At the node with a stock price of $88.35, the present value of the expected value of the call in the next period is $12.94, the value of the European call. With a stock price of $88.35 and an exercise price of $75.00, the American call can (and should) be exercised for an exercise value of $13.35. Thus, in the tree for the American call, the value at this node is the exercise value of $13.35. This difference in the two trees affects the current value of the European and American calls, which are $7.94 and $8.15, respectively. With 200 periods, the European and American calls are worth $7.61 and $8.04, respectively. The binomial model applies to options on stocks with any number of dividend yields during the life of the option.

For these options, none of the other models we have considered apply. From the valuation date, the dividend amount is uncertain, as it will be 3 percent of whatever stock price prevails in 55 days. Therefore, the exact American option pricing model does not apply. Further, the analytic approximation method for American options does not apply because the dividend is not continuous. For European options, we cannot apply the known dividend adjustment, because the dollar amount of the dividend is unknown. Similarly, we cannot apply the Merton model because the dividend is not continuous. Of all the methods we have studied, only the binomial model can deal with the known dividend yield for an American option. **OPTION!** can compute prices for American call and put options on stocks with as many as three known dividend yields by using the binomial model.

Known Dollar Dividends

For options on stocks with known dollar dividends, the binomial model can be applied in a manner almost identical to that appropriate for known dividend yields. The first step is to generate the tree

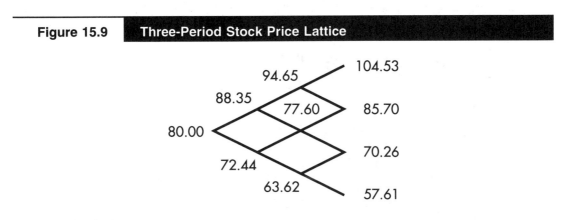

Figure 15.9   **Three-Period Stock Price Lattice**

Three-Period Price Lattices for a European and an American Call	Figure 15.10

European call

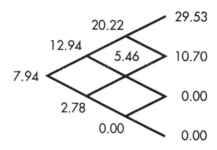

American call

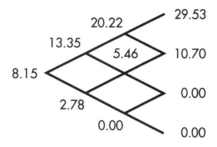

describing the potential stock price movements. As we saw in Chapter 13 when we considered the pricing of European options on stocks with known dollar dividends, there can be a problem with the tree failing to recombine after the dividend has been paid. In this situation, the number of nodes can increase dramatically, particularly when there are many periods and several dividends. (For details on why the tree fails to recombine, see Chapter 13.)

We can solve this problem as we did in Chapter 13 by making a simplifying assumption. We assume that the stock price reflects the dividend, which is known with certainty, and all other factors that might affect the stock price, which are uncertain. We then adjust the uncertain component of the stock price for the impending dividends and model the uncertain component of the stock price with the binomial tree, adding back the present value of all future dividends at each node. Specifically, we follow these steps:

1. Compute the present value of all dividends to be paid during the life of the option as of the present time = t.
2. Subtract this present value from the current stock price to form $S_t' = S_t - $ PV of all dividends.

3. Create the binomial tree by applying the up and down factors in the usual way to the initial stock price S'_t.
4. After generating the tree, add to the stock price at each node the present value of all future dividends to be paid during the life of the option.
5. Compute the option values in the usual way by working through the binomial tree.

These were exactly the steps we used in Chapter 13 to resolve this difficulty.

The application of this procedure to American options is exactly the same as with European options, with one exception. In working through the tree to generate the option price tree, we must compare the present value of the next period's expected option value with the exercise value of the option. The option price at the node is the higher of the present value or the exercise value. The computation of the value at a node is exactly the same as in other cases we have already considered, such as the application of the binomial model to options on stocks with known dividend yields.

We illustrate the application of the binomial model to options on stocks with a known dollar dividend by considering a comprehensive example. A stock now trades for $50, has a standard deviation of .4, and will pay a dividend of $2 in 90 days. An American call and put on this stock expire in 120 days, and both have an exercise price of $50. The risk-free rate of interest is 9 percent, and we will model the price of the options with a five-period binomial model.

According to the five steps outlined earlier, we begin by subtracting the present value of the dividends to be paid during the life of the option from the current stock price. The present value of the dividend is $1.96, so the adjusted stock price, S', is $48.04. A single period is 24 days, and the discount factor for one period is .9941. The parameters for the binomial model with five periods are:

$$\Delta t = \frac{24}{365} = .065753 \text{ years}$$

$$U = e^{\sigma\sqrt{\Delta t}} = e^{.4\sqrt{.065753}} = 1.108015$$

$$D = \frac{1}{U} = .902515$$

$$\pi_U = \frac{e^{r\Delta t} - D}{U - D} = \frac{e^{.09(.065753)} - .902515}{1.108015 - .902515} = .503262$$

The top panel of Figure 15.11 shows the stock price lattice generated with a starting price of $48.04 and the up and down factors shown above. This upper lattice does not reflect the dividend. Having generated this lattice, we account for dividends by adding the present value of all future dividends to be paid during the life of the option to each node. The bottom lattice of Figure 15.11 shows the adjusted stock prices. As the dividend will be paid in 90 days, the dividend falls between the third and fourth periods. This means that for periods four and five, there are no dividends to consider, and the two lattices have identical stock prices in periods four and five. For all periods before the dividend, the stock price at each node is adjusted by adding the present value of the dividend. For example, the node for the second period represents a time that is 48 days from now. At that time, the dividend will be 42 days away, and the present value of the dividend at that point is $1.98. Therefore, if we compare the stock prices in the two lattices for period 2, the prices in the bottom lattice will exceed their counterparts in the upper lattice by $1.98. All other stock prices in

Five-Period Stock Price Lattices Unadjusted and Adjusted for a Known Dollar Dividend

Figure 15.11

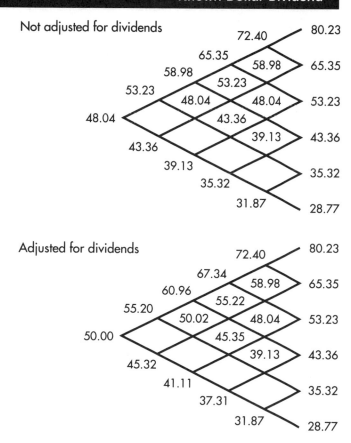

Not adjusted for dividends

Adjusted for dividends

periods 1–3 are adjusted similarly. The bottom stock price lattice in Figure 15.11 is the lattice that we will use to compute the option prices.

In Figure 15.12, the upper lattice pertains to the American call, while the lower lattice prices the American put. Some prices are preceded by an asterisk, indicating that the price represents the exercise value of the option at that node. For example, the call lattice has a price of $17.34 in period 4. The present value of the two option values in period 4 is $15.93. However, the stock price at that node is $67.34, implying an exercise value of $17.34. Because the exercise value exceeds $15.93, the call value at that node is $17.34. Working back through the lattice to the present shows an American call value of $4.48 and an American put value of $4.90. With the five-period lattice, the European call and put are worth $4.31 and $4.81, respectively. For the same data, except using a lattice with 200 periods, the American call is worth $4.59, and the American put is $4.78. With a 200-period lattice, the European call and put are $4.17 and $4.66, respectively. We also note that

Figure 15.12	Five-Period Price Lattices for an American Call and Put on a Stock with a Known Dollar Dividend

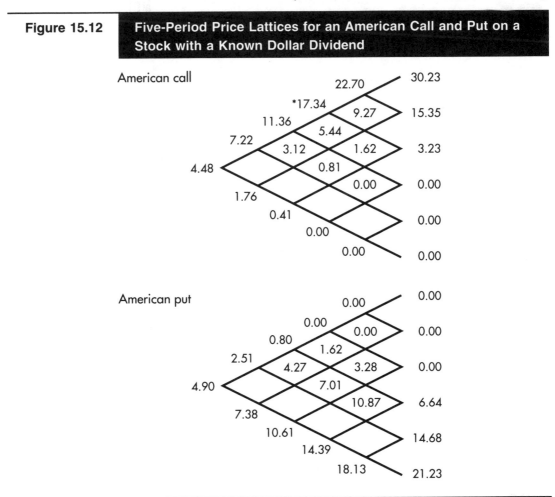

American call

American put

this example can be solved using the exact American call option pricing model, which gives a call price of $4.59, the same as the binomial model with 200 periods.

CONCLUSION

This chapter explored the pricing of American options. We began by reviewing the differences between American and European options. For nondividend stocks, the American and European calls have the same value, as early exercise is never desirable. For puts, however, we showed that there are incentives to early exercise even when there are no dividends. Therefore, the price of an American put can exceed that of a European put even in the absence of dividends. When the underlying stock pays dividends, circumstances can arise in which it would be desirable to exercise a call and a put before expiration, and the prices of American and European options diverge.

The discussion then turned to models for pricing American options, beginning with Black's pseudo-American option pricing model. We then considered the exact pricing model for an American call with a single dividend before the option's expiration. We noted that this is the only situation in which an exact pricing formula exists for American options. In all other pricing situations, we must use approximation techniques.

When the underlying stock pays a continuous dividend, an approximation for American options applies. This analytical approximation is analogous to the Merton model for European options, and it accurately estimates the prices of American calls and puts when the underlying instrument pays a continuous dividend.

Most stocks pay discrete dividends, so the analytical approximation does not apply. Accordingly, we turned to the binomial model and showed how it can apply to American options when the underlying good pays dividends in a variety of different ways. We considered the binomial model for American options when the underlying good pays a continuous dividend, when it pays a known dividend yield, and when it pays a known dollar dividend. In the last two cases, the binomial model can accommodate any number of dividends.

Many of the calculations of this chapter are quite tedious and time-consuming. (Imagine, for instance, the tedium of computing the binomial model price for a lattice of 100 periods.) **OPTION!** computes option prices for all of the models considered in this chapter.

QUESTIONS AND PROBLEMS

1. Explain why American and European calls on a nondividend stock always have the same value.
2. Explain why American and European puts on a nondividend stock can have different values.
3. Explain the circumstances that might make the early exercise of an American put on a nondividend stock desirable.
4. What factors might make an owner exercise an American call?
5. Do dividends on the underlying stock make the early exercise of an American put more or less likely? Explain.
6. Do dividends on the underlying stock make the early exercise of an American call more or less likely? Explain.
7. Explain the strategy behind the pseudo-American call pricing strategy.
8. Consider a stock with a price of $140 and a standard deviation of .4. The stock will pay a dividend of $2 in 40 days and a second dividend of $2 in 130 days. The current risk-free rate of interest is 10 percent. An American call on this stock has an exercise price of $150 and expires in 100 days. What is the price of the call according to the pseudo-American approach?
9. Could the exact American call pricing model be used to price the option in Question 8? Explain.
10. Explain why the exact American call pricing model treats the call as an "option on an option."
11. Explain the idea of a bivariate cumulative standardized normal distribution. What would be the cumulative probability of observing two variables both with a value of zero, assuming that the correlation between them was zero? Explain.
12. In the exact American call pricing model, explain why the model can compute the call price with only one dividend.
13. What is the critical stock price in the exact American call pricing model?
14. Explain how the analytical approximation for American option values is analogous to the Merton model.

15. Explain the role of the critical stock price in the analytic approximation for an American call.

16. Why should an American call owner exercise if the stock price exceeds the critical price?

17. Consider the binomial model for an American call and put on a stock that pays no dividends. The current stock price is $120, and the exercise price for both the put and the call is $110. The standard deviation of the stock returns is .4, and the risk-free rate is 10 percent. The options expire in 120 days. Model the price of these options using a four-period tree. Draw the stock tree and the corresponding trees for the call and the put. Explain when, if ever, each option should be exercised. What is the value of a European call in this situation? Can you find the value of the European call without making a separate computation? Explain.

18. Consider the binomial model for an American call and put on a stock whose price is $120. The exercise price for both the put and the call is $110. The standard deviation of the stock returns is .4, and the risk-free rate is 10 percent. The options expire in 120 days. The stock will pay a dividend equal to 3 percent of its value in 50 days. Model and compute the price of these options using a four-period tree. Draw the stock tree and the corresponding trees for the call and the put. Explain when, if ever, each option should be exercised.

19. Consider the binomial model for an American call and put on a stock whose price is $120. The exercise price for both the put and the call is $110. The standard deviation of the stock returns is .4, and the risk-free rate is 10 percent. The options expire in 120 days. The stock will pay a $3 dividend in 50 days. Model and compute the price of these options using a four-period tree. Draw the stock tree and the corresponding trees for the call and the put. Explain when, if ever, each option should be exercised.

20. Consider the analytic approximation for American options. A stock sells for $130, has a standard deviation of .3, and pays a continuous dividend of 3 percent. An American call and put on this stock both have an exercise price of $130, and they both expire in 180 days. The risk-free rate is 12 percent. Find the value of the call and put according to this model. Demonstrate that you have found the correct critical stock price for both options.

21. An American call and put both have an exercise price of $100. An acquaintance asserts that the critical stock price for both options is $90 under the analytic approximation technique. Comment on this claim and explain your reasoning.

NOTES

[1] Fischer Black first proposed this idea in his paper "Fact and Fantasy in the Use of Options," *Financial Analysts Journal,* July/August 1975, pp. 36–72.

[2] R. E. Whaley, "Valuation of American Call Options on Dividend Paying Stocks: Empirical Tests," *Journal of Financial Economics,* 10, March 1982, pp. 29–58.

[3] This model was developed in a series of papers. R. Roll, "An Analytical Formula for Unprotected American Call Options on Stocks with Known Dividends," *Journal of Financial Economics,* 5, 1977, pp. 251–58; R. Geske, "A Note on an Analytic Valuation Formula for Unprotected American Call Options on Stocks with Known Dividends," *Journal of Financial Economics,* 7, 1979, pp. 375–80; R. Whaley, "On the Valuation of American Call Options on Stocks with Known Dividends," *Journal of Financial Economics,* 9, 1981, pp. 207–11; R. Geske, "Comments on Whaley's Note," *Journal of Financial Economics,* 9, 1981, pp. 213–15.

OPTIONS ON STOCK INDEXES, FOREIGN CURRENCY, AND FUTURES

OVERVIEW

This chapter considers three different kinds of options: options on stock indexes, options on foreign currency, and options on futures. We consider these different types of options together because the principles that determine the pricing of these options are almost identical. In essence, the three types of options considered in this chapter are united by the fact that the good underlying each option can be treated as paying a continuous dividend. The pricing of these options is further unified by the conceptual connections among the different options. For example, we will consider options on stock index futures as well as options on stock indexes themselves, and we analyze options on foreign currency futures as well as options on foreign currencies alone.

While there may be common principles for the pricing of these three types of options, the markets for each of these options (which were explored in Chapter 10) are quite large and have their own features. Consequently, this chapter begins by analyzing the pricing principles for these options. As noted above, the underlying instruments may all be treated as paying a continuous dividend – particularly when we think of a dividend as a leakage of value from the instrument paying the dividend. For a stock index, the continuous dividend really is a dividend – the aggregate dividends on the stocks represented in the index. For a foreign currency, we may treat the foreign interest rate as a continuous dividend. For a futures, the cost of financing and storing the underlying good (a bond, 5,000 bushels of wheat, or the proverbial pork bellies) is a leakage of value from the commodity.

Because the underlying good pays a continuous dividend, we know that the Merton model, which was discussed in Chapter 13, pertains directly to pricing these three types of European options. Also, the binomial model directly applies as well. For American options, discussed in Chapter 15, two approaches are clearly applicable. First, the analytic approximation technique works extremely well in pricing the types of options discussed in this chapter. Second, we can also apply the binomial model under the assumption of continuous dividends.

EUROPEAN OPTION PRICING

In Chapter 13 we considered the Merton model, which extends the Black-Scholes model, to provide an exact pricing model for European options on stocks that pay dividends at a continuous rate. We also discussed the binomial model and saw that it can apply to European option pricing on stocks that pay a continuous dividend. In this section, we extend both of these models to the pricing of European options on stock indexes, foreign currency, and futures.

Merton's Model

Merton's model extends the Black-Scholes model by treating continuous dividends as a negative interest rate. In Chapter 13 we saw how dividends reduce the value of a call option, because they reduce the value of the stock that underlies the option. In effect, a continuous dividend implies a continuous leakage of value from the stock that equals the dividend rate. We let the Greek letter delta, δ, represent this rate of leakage.[1] Merton's adjustment to the Black-Scholes model for continuous dividends is:

$$c_t^M = e^{-\delta(T-t)}S_t N(d_1^M) - Xe^{-r(T-t)}N(d_2^M)$$

$$d_1^M = \frac{\ln\left(\dfrac{S_t}{X}\right) + (r - \delta + .5\sigma^2)(T - t)}{\sigma\sqrt{T - t}}$$

$$d_2^M = d_1^M - \sigma\sqrt{T - t}$$

(16.1)

where

δ = the continuous dividend rate on the stock

To adjust the regular Black-Scholes model, we replace the current stock price with the stock price adjusted for the continuous dividend. That is, we replace S_t with:

$$e^{-\delta(T-t)}S_t$$

(16.2)

Substituting this expression into the formulas for d_1 and d_2 gives d_1^M and d_2^M as shown earlier. Merton's adjusted put value is:

$$p_t^M = Xe^{-r(T-t)}N(-d_2^M) - Se^{-\delta(T-t)}N(-d_1^M)$$

(16.3)

When $\delta = 0$, Merton's model reduces immediately to the Black-Scholes model.

We can determine the price of options on stock indexes, foreign currency, and futures if we can determine the correct term to substitute for expression 16.2 in the Black-Scholes model.

The Binomial Model

In Chapter 13, we saw that the price at time t of a European call, c_t, and a European put, p_t, could be expressed as follows under the terms of the binomial model.

$$c_t = \frac{\sum_{j=m}^{n} \left(\frac{n!}{j!(n-j)!}\right)(\pi_U{}^j \pi_D{}^{n-j})[U^j D^{n-j} S_t - X]}{R^n} \qquad (16.4)$$

$$p_t = \frac{\sum_{j=0}^{n} \left(\frac{n!}{j!(n-j)!}\right)(\pi_U{}^j \pi_D{}^{n-j}) \mathrm{MAX}[0, \, X - U^j D^{n-j} S_t]}{R^n} \qquad (16.5)$$

where:

U = 1 + percentage increase in a period if the stock price rises
D = 1 − percentage decrease in a period if the stock price falls
R = 1 + risk-free rate per period
π_U = probability of a price increase in any period
π_D = probability of a price decrease in any period

These pricing models apply for any time span divided into n periods, where m is the minimum number of price increases to bring the call into-the-money at expiration.

To apply the binomial model to options on goods paying a continuous dividend, we need to adjust the binomial parameters to reflect the continuous leakage of value from the stock that the dividend represents and to accurately reflect the price movements on the stock. For Merton's model for European options on a stock paying a continuous dividend, we saw that the adjustment largely involved subtracting the continuous dividend rate, δ, from the risk-free rate, r. This is exactly the adjustment required for the binomial model. For options on a good paying a continuous dividend δ, the U, D, and π_U factors are:

$$U = e^{\sigma\sqrt{\Delta t}}$$

$$D = \frac{1}{U} \qquad (16.6)$$

$$\pi_U = \frac{e^{(r-\delta)\Delta t} - D}{U - D}$$

We can apply this binomial model to options on stock indexes, foreign currency, or futures by determining the appropriate δ and the correct price of the instrument to take the place of S_t in the binomial model.

Options on Stock Indexes

The Merton model and the binomial model apply directly to pricing options on stock indexes. Because a stock index merely summarizes the performance of some set of stocks, we may think of the stock index as representing a portfolio of stocks, some of which pay dividends. Because we are pricing an option on this portfolio of stocks, we are concerned only with the dividends on the entire portfolio – we need to consider the dividend on individual stocks only insofar as they determine the overall dividend for the portfolio. Almost all individual stocks pay periodic discrete dividends (usually following a quarterly payment pattern). However, for stock indexes, including many stocks, the assumption of a continuous dividend payment is fairly realistic. In general, the greater the number of stocks represented in a stock index, the more realistic the assumption of continuous dividends.[2]

To illustrate the application of Merton's model to pricing options on stock indexes, consider a stock index that has a current value of 350.00. The standard deviation of returns for the index is .2, the risk-free rate is 8 percent, and the continuous dividend rate on the index is 4 percent. European call and put options on this stock index expire in 150 days and have a striking price of 340.00. Therefore, the dividend rate of 4 percent takes the role of δ in the Merton model and the index value of 350.00 takes the role of S_t. For these data, we find the value of the call and put in index units as follows:

$$d_1^M = \frac{\ln\left(\frac{350}{340}\right) + [.08 - .04 + .5(.2)(.2)]\left(\frac{150}{365}\right)}{.2\sqrt{\frac{150}{365}}}$$

$$= \frac{.028988 + .024658}{0.128212} = .418413$$

$$d_2^M = .418413 - .2\sqrt{\frac{150}{365}} = .290201$$

$N(d_1^M) = N(.418413) = .662177$; $N(d_2^M) = N(.290201) = .614169$; $N(-d_1^M) = N(-.418413) = .337823$, and $N(-d_2^M) = N(-.290201) = .385831$. Therefore, the call and put are worth:

$$c_t^M = 350.00e^{-.04(150/365)}(.662177) - 340.00\ e^{-.08(150/365)}(.614169) = \$25.92$$

$$p_t^M = 340.00e^{-.08(150/365)}(.385831) - 350.00\ e^{-.04(150/365)}(.337823) = \$10.63$$

For a five-period binomial model price on the same options, the call is worth $26.37, while the put is worth $11.08. With 200 periods, the call price is $25.94, and the put price is $10.65. (The calculations for the binomial model are not shown here, but similar calculations for other options appear later in this chapter.)

Options on Foreign Currency

We now explore the application of the Merton model to pricing options on a foreign currency. We assume that we are looking at the issues from the point of view of a U.S. option trader. In terms of the Merton model, the dollar value of the foreign currency takes the role of the stock price, S_t, and the foreign interest rate takes the role of the continuous dividend rate, δ. The standard deviation in the Merton model is that of the underlying asset, so the correct standard deviation to use in the model is the standard deviation of the foreign currency.

As an example, consider a European call and a European put option on the British pound. The pound is currently worth $1.40, and has a standard deviation of .5, reflecting difficulties in the European Monetary System (EMS). The current British risk-free rate is 12 percent, while the U.S.

rate is 8 percent. The call and put both have a striking price of $1.50 per pound, and they both expire in 200 days.

According to the Merton model, the call is worth $.1452, while the put value is $.2700. Both of these prices are the dollar price for an option on a single British pound. We illustrate the computation of the price of the currency options using a five-period binomial model. The binomial parameters are:

$$U = e^{\sigma\sqrt{\Delta t}} = e^{.5\sqrt{.1096}} = 1.1800$$

$$D = \frac{1}{U} = .847452$$

$$\pi_U = \frac{e^{(r-\delta)\Delta t} - D}{U - D} = .445579$$

The one-period discount factor is $e^{-.08(40/365)} = .9913$. Figure 16.1 shows the five-period binomial lattice for the foreign currency price, while Figure 16.2 shows the lattices for the call and the put. The price of the call is $.1519, and the put is worth $.2766. For a 200-period lattice, the call is worth $.1454 and the put is worth $.2702. These 200-period binomial estimates are extremely close to the values from the Merton model.

A Five-Period Binomial Lattice for the British Pound   **Figure 16.1**

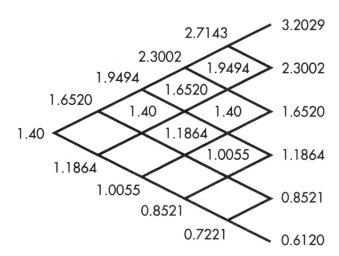

Figure 16.2	The Five-Period Lattices for Foreign Currency Call and Put Prices

Call tree

```
                                                     1.1919          1.7029
                                       .7666
                                               .4370                 .8002
                              .4649
                                       .2299
                      .2701
                               .1178           .0671                 .1520
              .1519                    .0296
                                               0.00                  0.00
                      .0592
                               .0131
                                                                     0.00
                                       0.00
                                               0.00                  0.00
```

Put tree

```
                                                     0.00            0.00
                                       0.00
                                               0.00                  0.00
                              .0521
                                       .0947
                      .1511
                               .2330           .1723                 0.00
              .2766                    .3479
                                               .4946                 .3136
                      .3818
                               .5075
                                                                     .6479
                                       .6439
                                               .7742                 .8880
```

Options on Futures

Consider a good such as gold that has a large stock relative to consumption, is easily storable, does not have a seasonal production pattern (like wheat), and does not have a seasonal consumption pattern (like gasoline). Further, assume that it is possible to sell gold short and to obtain the use of the proceeds from the short sale.[3] When these conditions hold, the futures price at time t, F_t, for delivery of the good at time T is given by:

$$F_t = \text{SPOT}_t e^{r(T-t)} \tag{16.7}$$

If this relationship between the spot, or cash, price and the futures price did not prevail, there would be immediate arbitrage opportunities, as we have seen in Chapter 3. In general, all precious metals (gold, silver, platinum, and palladium) and all financial instruments (equities and debt) conform almost perfectly to this relationship. To the degree that a commodity fails to conform to the cost-of-carry model, the pricing techniques discussed in this chapter do not pertain to pricing futures options on that commodity.

In terms of the Merton model, the rate at which the spot price grows, r, takes the place of δ, and the futures price takes the place of the stock price in Equation 16.1. In other words, for futures on commodities that conform to the cost-of-carry model, $\delta = r$.[4] When we make this substitution in Equation 16.1, the formula becomes considerably simpler due to the equivalence of δ and r. For European futures options, the price of the futures call, c_t^F, and put, p_t^F, are:

$$c_t^F = e^{-r(T-t)}[F_t N(d_1^F) - X N(d_2^F)]$$

$$p_t^F = e^{-r(T-t)}[X N(-d_2^F) - F_t N(-d_1^F)] \tag{16.8}$$

$$d_1^F = \frac{\ln\left(\dfrac{F_t}{X}\right) + (.5\sigma^2)(T-t)}{\sigma\sqrt{T-t}}$$

$$d_2^F = d_1^F - \sigma\sqrt{T-t}$$

Equation 16.8 employs the standard deviation of the futures price.[5]

The binomial model also applies to options on futures, and the parameters of Equations 16.4 and 16.5 can be applied directly. Notice that the probability of a futures price increase becomes:

$$\pi_U = \frac{e^0 - D}{U - D} = \frac{1 - D}{U - D}$$

As an example, consider European options on a stock index futures that expire in one year. The current cash market price of the index is 480.00, and the risk-free rate is 7 percent. Therefore, according to the cost-of-carry model, the futures price must be:

$$F_t = 480.00 e^{.07(365/365)} = 514.80$$

European call and put options on this futures contract have an exercise price of 500.00, and the standard deviation of the futures price is .2. The price of the call and put according to the Merton/Black model must be:

$$d_1^F = \frac{\ln\left(\dfrac{514.80}{500.00}\right) + .5(.2)(.2)}{.2} = .245852$$

$$d_2^F = .245852 - .2 = .045852$$

$N(d_1^F) = .597102$, and $N(d_2^F) = .518286$. Therefore, the call and put prices are:

$$c_t^F = e^{-.07}[514.80(.597102) - 500.00(.518286)] = \$44.98$$

$$p_t^F = e^{-.07}[500.00(.481714) - 514.80(.402898)] = \$31.18$$

For a binomial model with five periods, the call and put prices are \$46.49 and \$32.69, respectively. With 200 periods the binomial model gives prices of \$44.95 and \$31.15 for the call and put, respectively.

Options on Futures versus Options on Physicals

For some goods, such as foreign currencies, options trade on the futures contract and on the good itself. For example, in Chapter 10 we saw that the Philadelphia Stock Exchange trades options on foreign currencies, while the Chicago Mercantile Exchange trades options on foreign currency futures. The difference between options on futures and options on the underlying good itself depends critically on whether the option is a European or an American option.

At the expiration of a futures contract, the futures price must equal the spot price. This is necessary to avoid arbitrage. For example, in the gold market if the spot price is \$400 per ounce and the futures contract is at expiration, the futures contract price must also be \$400. If it were not, there is a simple and immediate arbitrage opportunity. If the futures price at expiration exceeds the spot price, a trader would buy the physical good and deliver it in the futures market to capture the higher futures price. By contrast, if the futures price is below the spot price, the arbitrageur would buy a futures contract, take delivery of gold, and sell the gold for the higher spot price. To avoid both of these potential arbitrage plays, the spot price and the futures price must be equal at the expiration of the futures contract.

The no-arbitrage condition has important implications for pricing European futures options. Because a European option can be exercised only at expiration, a European futures option can be exercised only when the futures price and the spot price are identical. This restriction on exercise means that the payoffs on European futures options and options on physicals are identical. Therefore, the price of a European futures option and a European option on the physical must always be identical.

For American options, the analysis is more complex, because the trader can exercise an American option at any time. The relationship between prices of American options on futures and physicals depends on the relationship between the futures price and the spot price prevailing at a given time prior to expiration. For precious metals and financials, the futures price before expiration almost always exceeds the spot price. In the markets for some commodities, the spot price often exceeds the futures price. This happens in markets for industrial metals such as copper, in markets for agricultural goods, and in the energy market. While a complete explanation for why these price relationships arise lies beyond the scope of this book, we offer a very brief explanation. In essence, the futures price will lie above the spot price if supplies of the underlying good are large relative to consumption, if the underlying good is easily storable and transportable, if the market for the underlying good is well developed, if supply of and demand for the underlying good are free of seasonal fluctuations, and if it is easy and cheap to effect short sales for the underlying good. These conditions prevail for precious metals and financials. By contrast, industrial metals, agricultural commodities, and energy products are strongly affected by supply and demand seasonalities, by poorly developed cash markets, and by costly transportation and storage. These factors allow the spot price to exceed the futures price on occasion.[6]

Without regard to the economic factors that cause the futures price or the spot price to be higher, the relationship between the futures and spot price determines the relationship between prices for

American futures options and American options on the physical. When the futures price exceeds the spot price, the price of an American futures call must exceed the price of an American call on the physical, and the price of an American futures put must be less than the price of an American put on the physical. When the spot price exceeds the futures price, the price of an American futures call must be below the price of an American call on the physical and the price of an American futures put must exceed the price of an American put on the physical.

OPTION SENSITIVITIES

In Chapter 14 we considered the sensitivity of option prices to changes in the underlying parameters. Our exploration focused on the Merton model and we analyzed the DELTA, GAMMA, THETA, VEGA, and RHO of European calls and puts. In this section, we extend that analysis to options on stock indexes, options of foreign currencies, and options on futures. The principles are virtually identical, but we must make slight substitutions in the definitions of the sensitivities to account for differences in the underlying instruments. Tables 16.1 and 16.2 present the call and put sensitivities for the Merton model. These are the same tables discussed in Chapter 14, and these same sensitivities apply to options on stock indexes, options on foreign currencies, and options on futures with the following substitutions:

Sensitivities of Options on Stock Indexes. Interpret S_t as the price of the stock index, and interpret δ as the continuous dividend yield on the stock index. Adjust the computation of d_1 and d_2 by making these same substitutions.

Call Sensitivities for the Merton Model	Table 16.1

Name	Sensitivity
DELTA$_c$	$\dfrac{\partial c}{\partial S} = e^{-\delta(T-t)}N(d_1^M)$
THETA$_c$	$-\dfrac{\partial c}{\partial(T-t)} = -\dfrac{SN'(d_1^M)\sigma e^{-\delta(T-t)}}{2\sqrt{T-t}}$ $+ \delta SN'(d_1^M)e^{-\delta(T-t)} - rXe^{-r(T-t)}N(d_2^M)$
VEGA$_c$	$\dfrac{\partial c}{\partial \sigma} = S\sqrt{T-t}N'(d_1^M)e^{-\delta(T-t)}$
RHO$_c$	$\dfrac{\partial c}{\partial r} = X(T-t)e^{-r(T-t)}N(d_2^M)$
GAMMA$_c$	$\dfrac{\partial \text{DELTA}_c}{\partial S} = \dfrac{\partial^2 c}{\partial S^2} = \dfrac{N'(d_1^M)e^{-\delta(T-t)}}{S\sigma\sqrt{T-t}}$
Note:	$N'(d_1^M) = \dfrac{1}{\sqrt{2\pi}}e^{.5(d_1^M)^2}$

Table 16.2	Put Sensitivities for the Merton Model
Name	**Sensitivity**
DELTA$_p$	$\dfrac{\partial p}{\partial S} = e^{-\delta(T-t)}[N(d_1{}^M) - 1]$
THETA$_p$	$-\dfrac{\partial p}{\partial(T-t)} = -\dfrac{SN'(d_1{}^M)\sigma e^{-\delta(T-t)}}{2\sqrt{T-t}}$ $- \delta SN'(-d_1{}^M)e^{-\delta(T-t)} + rXe^{-r(T-t)}N(-d_2{}^M)$
VEGA$_p$	$\dfrac{\partial p}{\partial \sigma} = S\sqrt{T-t}N'(d_1{}^M)e^{-\delta(T-t)}$
RHO$_p$	$\dfrac{\partial p}{\partial r} = X(T-t)e^{-r(T-t)}N(-d_2{}^M)$
GAMMA$_p$	$\dfrac{\partial DELTA_p}{\partial S} = \dfrac{\partial^2 p}{\partial S^2} = \dfrac{N'(d_1{}^M)e^{-\delta(T-t)}}{S\sigma\sqrt{T-t}}$
Note:	$N'(d_1{}^M) = \dfrac{1}{\sqrt{2\pi}}e^{-.5(d_1{}^M)^2}$

Sensitivities of Options on Foreign Currency. Interpret S_t as the price of the foreign currency, and interpret δ as the continuous interest rate on the foreign risk-free instrument. Adjust the computation of d_1 and d_2 by making these same substitutions.

Sensitivities of Options on Futures. Interpret S_t as the price of the futures contract, and interpret δ as being equal to the risk-free rate, so that $r - \delta = 0$. Adjust the computation of d_1 and d_2 by making these same substitutions.

Because these sensitivities are so similar, we illustrate all with an example of a European option on the British pound. The current value of a British pound is $1.56. The U.S. risk-free rate of interest is 8 percent, while the risk-free rate on the British pound is 11 percent. The standard deviation of the British pound is .25, and the option expires in 90 days. The exercise price of the options we consider is $1.50. In terms of the Merton model, our inputs would be $S = \$1.56$, $X = \$1.50$, $\sigma = .25$, $T - t = 90$ days, $\delta = .11$, and $r = .08$. With these values a European call is worth $.1002, and a European put is worth $.0526. Table 16.3 shows the sensitivity values for this option.

PRICING AMERICAN OPTIONS

Chapter 15 explored the pricing of American stock options. There we saw that exact solutions for pricing American style options are generally not available. Further, we noted that the key feature that made American call option pricing distinct from European call option pricing was the payment of dividends by the underlying good. In this section, we explore the pricing of American options on stock indexes, foreign currency, and futures.

Foreign Currency Option Sensitivities	Table 16.3

	Merton Model	
	Call	**Put**
Option Prices	$.1002	$.0526
DELTA	.6082	−.3650
THETA	−.1085	−.1578
VEGA	.2859	.2859
RHO	.2093	−.1534
GAMMA	1.9058	1.9058

$S = \$1.56$; $X = \$1.50$; $\sigma = .25$; $T - t = 90$ days; $r = .08$; $\delta = .11$

As we have discussed earlier in this chapter, we may regard futures, foreign currencies, and stock indexes as goods that pay continuous dividends. This makes them particularly well-suited to analysis by the Barone-Adesi and Whaley analytic approximation. Therefore, we begin our analysis of American options on stock indexes, foreign currency, and futures by applying the analytic approximation to these instruments.

The binomial model also applies to these instruments, and we consider it in detail later in this chapter. The binomial model has special applicability to options on stock indexes, because stock indexes actually have dividend payment patterns that are discrete. As we will see later in this chapter, there are certain periods of the year when stocks tend to pay dividends. This seasonality in dividend payments from stocks implies that stock indexes will also exhibit a seasonal dividend pattern. The binomial model is particularly well suited to handling this type of dividend pattern.

Analytical Approximations

As we discussed in Chapter 15, we may analyze the value of an American option as consisting of the value of a corresponding European option, plus an early exercise premium. The value of an American option must always be at least the amount of its immediately available exercisable proceeds. For a call:

$$C_t \geq S_t - X$$

If a trader owns the American option, she has a choice between the exercisable proceeds or the value of the European call. Which is preferable depends upon how deep-in-the-money the option is, the dividend rate on the stock, δ, the interest rate, r, and the time remaining until the option expires, $T - t$. If the stock price reaches a critical level, S^*, such that:

$$S_t^* - X = c(S^*, X, T - t\} + \text{Early exercise premium} \qquad (16.9)$$

the owner of an American call option is indifferent about exercising. If the stock price exceeds S^*, she will exercise immediately to capture the exercise proceeds $S_t - X$. If the stock price is below S^*, she will not exercise. At the critical stock price, S^*, the European call is worth exactly $S^* - X$. For any stock price greater than S^*, the European call will be worth less than the exercisable proceeds for the American call. This explains why the owner of the American call is indifferent about exercise at a stock price of S^*; at that stock price the American and European calls are worth the same – $S^* - X$. For higher stock prices, the value of the European call falls below that of the American, and the value of the American call becomes equal to its exercisable proceeds. Thus, the owner of the American call should exercise to capture the quantity $S - X$. Those funds can then be invested from the exercise date to the expiration date to earn a return that will be lost if the option is not exercised.

A similar argument applies to American put options. As the stock price falls well below the exercise price, there comes a point at which:

$$X - S^{**} = p(S^{**}, X, T - t) + \text{Early exercise premium} \tag{16.10}$$

S^{**} is the critical stock price for an American put. If the stock price falls below S^{**}, the American put should be exercised to capture the exercised proceeds of $X - S_t$. From Chapter 15, the analytic approximation for an American call on a stock is:

$$C_t = c_t + A_2\left(\frac{S_t}{S^*}\right)^{q_2} \quad \text{if } S_t < S^* \tag{16.11}$$

$$= S_t - X \quad \text{if } S_t \geq S^*$$

where:

$$A_2 = \frac{S^*[1 - e^{-\delta(T-t)}N(d_1)]}{q_2}$$

and S^* is the solution to:

$$S^* - X = c_t(S^*, X, T - t) + \{1 - e^{-\delta(T-t)}N(d_1)\}(S^*/q_2) \tag{16.12}$$

$N(d_1)$ and $p(S^*, X, T - t)$ are evaluated at S^*. To find S^* requires an iterative search for the value that makes the equation balance. Other terms are:

$$q_2 = \frac{1 - n + \sqrt{(n-1)^2 + 4k}}{2}, \quad n = \frac{2(r - \delta)}{\sigma^2}, \quad k = \frac{2r}{\sigma^2(1 - e^{-r(T-t)})}$$

For an American put, the analytic approximation is:

$$P_t = p_t + A_1\left(\frac{S_t}{S^{**}}\right)^{q_1} \quad \text{if } S_t > S^{**} \tag{16.13}$$

$$= X - S_t \quad \text{if } S_t \leq S^{**}$$

where:

$$A_1 = \frac{S^{**}[1 - e^{-\delta(T-t)}N(-d_1)]}{q_1}$$

$$q_1 = \frac{1 - n - \sqrt{(n-1)^2 + 4k}}{2}$$

S^{**} is found by an iterative search to make the following equation hold:

$$X - S^{**} = p_t(S^{**}, X, T - t) - [1 - e^{-\delta(T-t)}N(-d_1)](S^{**}/q_1) \qquad (16.14)$$

$N(-d_1)$ and $p_t(S^{**}, X, T - t)$ are evaluated at the critical stock price S^{**}. We now consider how this model can apply to options on stock indexes, foreign currency, and futures.

The Analytic Approximation for Options on Stock Indexes. To apply the Barone-Adesi and Whaley model to options on stock indexes, we merely need to reinterpret certain parameters in the model. Specifically, we interpret S in the model to indicate the price of the stock index in question, and we interpret δ as the aggregate dividend rate on all of the stocks represented in the index. S^* and S^{**} are the critical levels of the stock index that would trigger exercise.

As an example, assume that a stock index has a current value of 400.00, that the risk-free rate of interest is 7 percent, that the continuous dividend rate on the stocks comprising the index is 3.5 percent, that the standard deviation of the stock index is .18, that the time to expiration is 140 days, and that the exercise price is 380.00. For these values, the Barone-Adesi and Whaley model gives a call price $C = 32.14$ and a put price $P = 7.41$, where these option values are expressed in index units. For the call, the critical price is $S^* = 822.31$, while for the put the critical price is $S^{**} = 328.50$. Because the current index value is below S^* and above S^{**}, there is no incentive to exercise. **OPTION!** solves for the critical stock index value and the price of American calls and puts on stock indexes using this analytic approximation. It also can graph the value of American options as a function of the underlying parameter values.

The Analytic Approximation for Options on Foreign Currencies. As with options on stock indexes, we can apply the Barone-Adesi and Whaley model to American options on foreign currencies by reinterpreting Equations 16.11 and 16.13. To apply these equations to options on foreign currency, we interpret S as the current value of the foreign currency. The dividend rate, δ, is interpreted as the risk-free rate of interest on the foreign currency.

Earlier in this chapter, we considered an example of a British pound in the context of the Merton model. In that example, the pound was currently worth $1.40 and had a standard deviation of .5. The British risk-free rate is 12 percent, while the U.S. rate is 8 percent. The exercise price for both a call and a put is $1.50, and the two options expire in 200 days. Using the Merton model, we found that the European option values would be $c = \$.1452$ and $p = \$.2700$. For these same parameter values, American options would be worth: $C = \$.1498$ and $P = \$.2718$. The critical prices are $S^* = \$2.52$ and $S^{**} = \$.69$. Thus, it would be unwise to exercise either the call or the put. These values were found by letting the spot value of the pound ($1.40) take on the role of S in the analytic approximation formula, while the British interest rate (12 percent) played the role of the dividend, δ. **OPTION!** can compute and graph American foreign currency option values under the Barone-Adesi and Whaley model.

The Analytic Approximation for Options on Futures. The Barone-Adesi and Whaley model applies with equal facility to options on futures. In Equations 16.11 to 16.13, we interpret S as the futures price, and we assume that the rate of return on the underlying asset equals the risk-free rate. That is, we assume that $r = \delta$. This assumption is valid if the futures contract is a financial asset or a precious metal.

To apply this model to futures, consider an American call and put on platinum. The cost-of-carry model holds very well for this precious metal, justifying our assumption that $r = \delta$. Assume that the current spot price of platinum is \$500.00 per ounce, that the risk-free rate of interest is 11 percent, that an American futures call and put expire in 75 days, and that the two options have an exercise price of \$500.00. If platinum conforms to the cost-of-carry, the futures price must be:

$$F = Se^{r(T-t)} = \$500e^{.11(75/365)} = \$511.43$$

The volatility of the futures price is .25. In applying Equation 16.11 to 16.13, we replace S with the futures price of \$511.43, and replace δ with the risk-free rate of 11 percent. For these data, the American option prices are $C = \$28.5323$ and $P = \$17.2875$, with critical futures prices $S^* = \$622.98$ and $S^{**} = \$401.2984$. For the corresponding European options, the prices are: $c = \$28.37$ and $p = \$17.1955$. The early exercise premium on the call is about \$.16, and for the put the premium is about \$.09.

Earlier we noted that the value of an American call on a futures would be higher than the value of an American call on the physical good if the futures price exceeded the spot price. We also said that the American put on the futures would be worth less than the corresponding American put on the physical if the futures price exceeded the cash price. This example confirms that point, because the prices of options on physical platinum (given the spot price of \$500 and assuming the same standard deviation of .25 pertains to the futures price and to the spot price) are: $C = \$22.09$ and $P = \$22.09$. Thus, the call price on the physical good is lower and the put price on the physical good is higher than the corresponding option on the futures.[7]

Summary. In this section, we have seen that the Barone-Adesi and Whaley analytical approximation applies not only to options on stocks, but to options on stock indexes, options on foreign currency, and options on futures. To apply the model to these disparate instruments, we merely need to reinterpret some of the parameters in the model in the way we have explored in this section.

It is worth emphasizing that the Barone-Adesi and Whaley model assumes that the underlying good in each case pays at a continuous rate, whether it be dividends on a stock index, the foreign interest rate for foreign currency options, or the cost-of-carry rate on the good underlying a futures contract. This assumption is virtually without flaw for options on foreign currency and options on futures, and it is quite reasonable for options on stock indexes. However, we must note that the dividend flow from stock indexes is not really continuous. To deal with discontinuous dividend flows, we now turn to a consideration of the binomial model and its applications to options on stock indexes, foreign currency, and futures.

The Binomial Model

In Chapter 15 we considered the application of the binomial model to pricing American options when the underlying good paid no dividend, a continuous dividend, a known dividend yield, or a known dollar dividend. Because this chapter considers options on stock indexes, foreign currency, and futures, we are most interested in applying the binomial model to a dividend payment stream that is continuous or that pays known dividends. As Chapter 15 has already shown how to apply the binomial model to the nondividend case and to the case of known dividend yields, we focus on the dividend patterns of greatest interest, continuous dividends and known dollar dividends.

Review of the Basic Strategy for the Binomial Model. As we have seen in Chapters 13 and 15, we follow a common strategy for computing option prices under the binomial model. For options on stocks with dividends, we applied the binomial model by creating a lattice for the stock that reflected the timing and amount of dividend payments that the stock would make. These adjustments affected the distribution of possible stock values at the expiration date. We then computed the option values in the usual way by working from the exercise date back to the present.

To apply the binomial model for American options, we follow the same basic valuation strategy, with one important difference. For the option lattice for an American option, the option value is set equal to the maximum of:

1. The expected option value in one period discounted for one period at the risk-free rate.
2. The immediate exercise value of the option, $S_t - X$ for a call, or $X - S_t$ for a put.

Except for this treatment of each node in the lattice for an American option, the binomial model for an American option is applied in exactly the same way as it is for a European option. As we work back through the tree, discounting the next period's expected option values, we must ask at every node whether the immediate exercise value or the computed present value is greater. The value at the node is the maximum of those two quantities. Further, we may note that the stock tree is unaffected by whether the option we are analyzing is an American or a European option.

Review of the Binomial Model and Continuous Dividends. In Chapter 13 we explored Merton's model, which adjusts the Black-Scholes model to price European options on stocks that pay a continuous dividend. We also showed how to use the binomial model to price European options on stocks that pay continuous dividends. There we saw that the parameters for the binomial model for a stock paying a continuous dividend were:

$$U = e^{\sigma\sqrt{\Delta t}}$$

$$D = \frac{1}{U}$$

$$\pi_U = \frac{e^{(r-\delta)\Delta t} - D}{U - D}$$

(16.15)

As we have discussed in this chapter, the stock price tree is identical whether we are pricing European or American options. Therefore, these parameters apply to generating the binomial tree of stock prices for American options on stocks paying a continuous dividend. As an examination of these parameters shows, the stock price tree will be identical in both cases. However, the probability of a stock price increase varies inversely with the level of the continuous dividend rate, δ.

Review of the Binomial Model and Known Dollar Dividends. To apply the binomial model to options on goods with known dollar dividends, the first step is to generate the tree describing the potential stock price movements. As we saw in Chapter 13 when we considered the pricing of European options on stock with known dollar dividends, there can be a problem with the tree failing to recombine after the dividend has been paid. In this situation, the number of nodes can increase dramatically, particularly when there are many periods and several dividends. (For details on why the tree fails to recombine, see Chapter 13.)

We can solve this problem as we did in Chapter 13 by making a simplifying assumption. We assume that the stock price reflects the dividend, which is known with certainty, and all other factors that might affect the stock price, which are uncertain. We then adjust the uncertain component of the stock price for the impending dividends and model the uncertain component of the stock price with the binomial tree adding back the present value of all future dividends at each node. Specifically, we follow these steps:

1. Compute the present value of all dividends to be paid during the life of the option as of the present time = t.
2. Subtract this present value from the current stock price to form $S_t' = S_t -$ PV of all dividends.
3. Create the binomial tree by applying the up and down factors in the usual way to the initial stock price S_t'.
4. After generating the tree, add to the stock price at each node the present value of all future dividends to be paid during the life of the option.
5. Compute the option values in the usual way by working through the binomial tree.

These were exactly the steps we used in Chapter 13 to resolve this difficulty.

The application of this procedure to American options is exactly the same as with European options, with a single exception. In working through the tree to generate the option price tree, we must compare the present value of the next period's expected option value with the exercise value of the option. The option price at the node is the higher of the present value or the exercise value. The computation of the value at a node is exactly the same as in other cases we have already considered.

The Binomial Model for Options on Stock Indexes. As we have just discussed, the binomial model can apply to options on stock indexes for both a continuous dividend on the stock index and specific dividends at certain times. Stock indexes in fact tend to pay dividends in a discrete manner, with higher dividend payments coming at certain times of the year. Figure 16.3 shows the typical dividend pattern on the S&P 500 index, and is a function of the tendency of firms to pay dividends at the end of each calendar quarter.

In this section, we explore how to apply the binomial model to options on stock indexes with discrete dividend patterns of the type shown in Figure 16.3. Later in this chapter, we show how to apply the binomial model to continuous payments on futures options and foreign currency.

To make the discussion more concrete, let us consider a stock index with a current value of 1,200.00. An American call and put option on the index expire in 125 days and have a common exercise price of 1,250.00. The volatility of the index is .2. The current risk-free interest rate is 8 percent. During the life of these options, the index will pay two dividends. The first dividend occurs on day 15 and will be 15 index units, while the second falls on day 120 and will be 20 index units. The present value of the two dividends at the present date is:

$$PV = 15.00e^{-.08(15/365)} + 20.00e^{-.08(120/365)} = 34.4316$$

The Seasonal Pattern of Dividends on the S&P 500 Stock Index   **Figure 16.3**

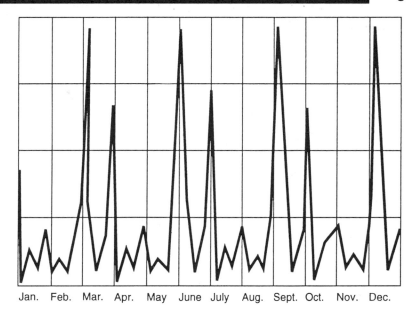

Jan. Feb. Mar. Apr. May June July Aug. Sept. Oct. Nov. Dec.

Source: From Chicago Mercantile Exchange, 1988. Reprinted by permission.

The next step is to subtract this value from the current index to form $S_t' = 1200.00 - 34.4316 = 1165.5684$.

We now compute the up and down factors and apply them to S_t' to form the stock index tree. We will form a tree with five periods, so each period consists of 25 days.

$$\Delta t = \frac{25}{365} = .0685 \text{ years}$$

$$U = e^{\sigma\sqrt{\Delta t}} = e^{.2\sqrt{.0685}} = 1.0537$$

$$D = \frac{1}{U} = .9490$$

$$\pi_U = \frac{e^{r\Delta t} - D}{U - D} = \frac{e^{.08(.0685)} - .9490}{1.0537 - .9490} = .5396$$

The upper panel in Figure 16.4 shows the stock index lattice for this example. However, we must still adjust this lattice by adding to each node the present value of all dividends to be received from that point to the expiration date of the option. The nodes occur at 0, 25, 50, 75, 100, and 125 days from the present. The first dividend occurs in 15 days, so it will affect only the node representing the present. The second dividend occurs in 120 days, so it will affect all nodes, except those at expiration. The lower panel of Figure 16.4 shows the stock index lattice adjusted for the present value

| Figure 16.4 | The Five-Period Stock Index Price Lattice |

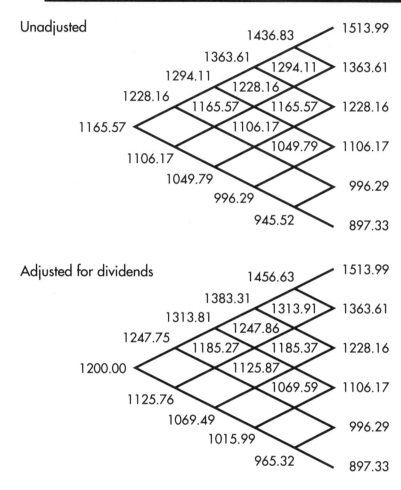

of the dividends. For the present, we already know that the present value of the both dividends is 34.43. All later periods occur after the first dividend, so we need to consider only the second dividend for subsequent nodes. At period 1, which is 25 days from now, the present value of the final dividend is:

$$20.00e^{-.08(120-25)/365} = 19.59$$

The other present values (19.70, 19.80, and 19.91) are found similarly, and are included in the stock index lattice in the bottom panel of Figure 16.4.

To compute the price of an option, we create a parallel lattice, starting at the expiration date. Figure 16.5 shows the call and put lattices for the American options we are considering. For the

The Five-Period Lattice for an American Call and Put on the Stock Index   Figure 16.5

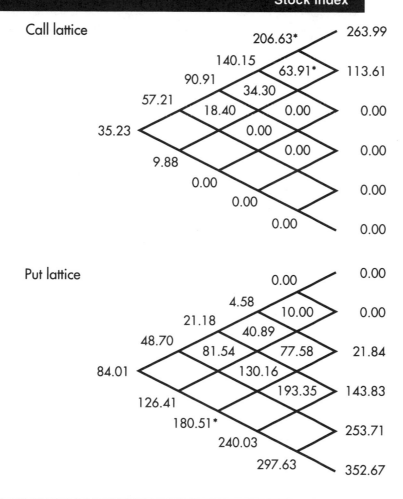

Call lattice

263.99
206.63*
140.15
90.91   63.91*   113.61
57.21   34.30
18.40   0.00   0.00
35.23   0.00
9.88   0.00   0.00
0.00   0.00
0.00
0.00   0.00

Put lattice

0.00   0.00
4.58
21.18   10.00   0.00
48.70   40.89
81.54   77.58   21.84
84.01   130.16
126.41   193.35   143.83
180.51*
240.03   253.71
297.63   352.67

option, the value at expiration is simply the intrinsic value of the option at that point. We then consider the nodes representing one period before expiration, and compute the expected value of the payoffs one period later and discount that expected payoff for one period. For example, if the stock index value falls in four periods, it will be at 996.29 at expiration, while if it falls every period, it will be at 897.33. For a put at expiration, the payoffs will be 253.71 and 352.67, respectively, as the adjusted lattice for the stock index shows. One period earlier, the discounted expected value of these two payoffs is:

$$\{.5396(253.71) + .4604(352.67)\} \times .9945 = 297.63$$

In terms of the adjusted lattice for the stock index, this corresponds to a stock index price at time four of 965.32.

Because we are working with American options, the holder of the put has the right to exercise at any time. At the fourth period, if the stock index price is 965.32, the immediate exercise value is $1250.00 - 965.32 = 284.68$. The holder of the put faces the following choice at the node we are considering. She may exercise the option for an immediate cash inflow of 284.68 index units, or continue to hold the put, with its expected present value of 297.63 index units. A rational trader would hold at this point. The node in the put lattice that we are considering must have the maximum of the immediate exercise value (284.68) or the discounted expected value of the payoffs in one period (297.63). Thus, the node in the put lattice in Figure 16.5 has the value 297.63. Asterisks in the option lattices indicate an entry resulting from an exercise. For example, if the stock price falls in both of the first two periods, the put holder should exercise. Figure 16.5 shows that the value of an American call on the stock index would be 35.23 index units, while the American put is worth 84.01 index units. As the figure also shows, early exercise of either option is unlikely.

The Binomial Model for Options on Foreign Currency. We now illustrate how the binomial model applies to options on foreign currency by considering the binomial model with continuous dividends. This continuous dividends approach applies to stock index options and options on futures as well.

We illustrate the application of the binomial model to American options on foreign currency with the same example considered earlier in this chapter, except we now allow the option to be an American option. Earlier, we analyzed a European call and put option on the British pound. The pound is currently worth $1.40, and has a standard deviation of .5. The current British risk-free rate is 12 percent, while the U.S. rate is 8 percent. The call and put both have a striking price of $1.50 per pound, and they both expire in 200 days.

With a five-period binomial model, we found that the parameters were $U = 1.1800$; $D = .847452$; and $\pi_U = .445579$. The one-period discount factor is $e^{-.08(40/365)} = .9913$. All of these values are the same whether the option under consideration is European or American. Consequently, the lattice for the foreign currency remains the same as well. As we saw for the European options, the five-period lattice gave a call price of $.1519 and a put price of $.2766. For a 200-period lattice the call was $.1454 and the put was $.2702. For comparison, the Merton model gave a call price of $.1452 and a put price of $.2700.

To compute the price of American options on the foreign currency, we apply our familiar technology of constructing and evaluating lattices for the call and the put. For each node we compute the expected value of the payoffs one period later and discount them for one period. Because we are now analyzing American options, we must check each node to determine whether the intrinsic value or our discounted expected value is greater. The node in question takes on the maximum of these two values.

Figure 16.6 gives the call and put lattices for these American options. An asterisk indicates a node at which early exercise is optimal. Because early exercise is optimal in some instances for both the call and the put, the price of these American options must be greater than the European counterpart. The price of the American call is $.1565, and the American put is $.2773. This gives an early exercise premium of $.0046 on the call and $.0007 for the put.

The Binomial Model for Options on Futures. We now apply the binomial model to options on futures. Generally, the goods underlying futures contracts may be thought of as paying a rate of return that equals the cost-of-carry. Earlier we saw that this rate must equal the risk-free rate of interest to

The Five-Period Lattice for an American Call and Put on the British Pound — **Figure 16.6**

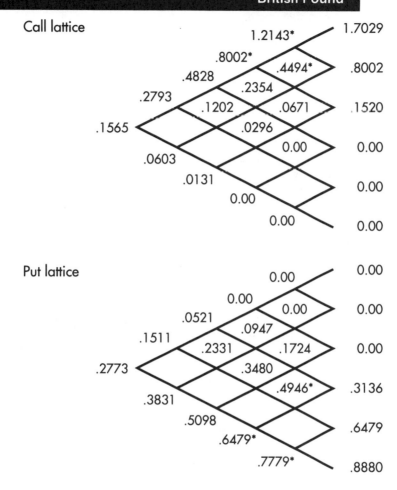

Call lattice

Put lattice

avoid arbitrage – at least if markets were sufficiently perfect. Equation 16.6 gave the parameters for the binomial model as it applies to options on goods paying a continuous return. For futures, we assume that $r = \delta$. The parameters for the binomial model are the same whether we consider a European or an American option.

As an example, we consider again the option on the stock index futures contract that we analyzed previously. A stock index stands at 480.00 and the risk-free rate of interest is 7 percent. A call and a put on the stock index futures contract expire in one year. Therefore, the futures prices must be 514.80, as we saw earlier. If the standard deviation of the futures contract is .2 and the exercise price on both the call and put is 500.00, we saw that the five-period binomial prices for the European call and put were 46.49 and 32.69, respectively.

For these options, the binomial parameters are:

$$U = e^{\sigma\sqrt{\Delta t}} = e^{.2\sqrt{.2}} = 1.0936$$

$$D = \frac{1}{U} = .9144$$

$$\pi_U = \frac{e^{(r-\delta)\Delta t} - D}{U - D} = .4777$$

The discount factor per period is .9861. Figure 16.7 shows a five-period binomial lattice for the futures price. At the end of one year, the futures price will range between $329.11 and $805.25. Figure 16.8 shows the American call and put lattices for options on this futures contract. The asterisks indicate nodes at which the exercise value was substituted for the computed present value of the next period's expected payoffs. As we saw earlier in this chapter, the five-period binomial price for European options was $46.49 and $32.69 for the call and put, respectively. As Figure 16.8 shows, the American option prices from a five-period binomial analysis are $47.28 and $33.28 for the call and put, respectively.

CONCLUSION

This chapter has applied familiar ideas to new instruments – options on stock indexes, options on foreign currency, and options on futures contracts. We considered both European and American

Figure 16.7 **The Five-Period Lattice for the Platinum Futures Price**

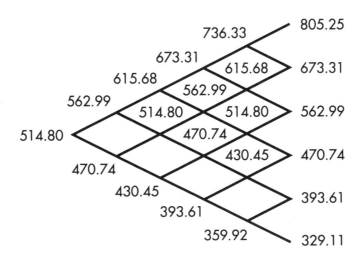

The Five-Period Lattice for the American Call and Put Futures Options

Figure 16.8

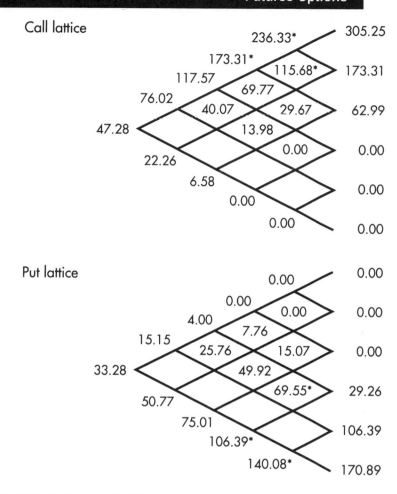

Call lattice

236.33*   305.25

173.31*

117.57   115.68*   173.31

76.02   69.77

40.07   29.67   62.99

47.28   13.98

0.00   0.00

22.26

6.58   0.00   0.00

0.00

0.00   0.00

Put lattice

0.00   0.00

0.00

4.00   0.00   0.00

15.15   7.76

25.76   15.07   0.00

33.28   49.92

69.55*   29.26

50.77

75.01   106.39

106.39*

140.08*   170.89

options. For European options on stock indexes, foreign currency, and futures, we saw that they can be priced by the Merton model or by the binomial model. For American options we analyzed the analytic approximation of Barone-Adesi and Whaley, and we considered the binomial model.

In essence, the Merton model applies directly, given a slight reinterpretation of the parameters of the model. The reinterpretation requires that we substitute the stock index value, the foreign currency value, or the futures price for the stock price in the Merton model. We also substitute the dividend rate on the stock index, the foreign interest rate on the foreign currency, or the cost-of-carry on the futures, which we presume to equal the risk-free rate. With these substitutions, we can apply the Merton model to price the options considered in this chapter. The binomial model applies in a straightforward way to European stock index options, options on foreign currency, and options on futures.

For American options, we saw that both the Barone-Adesi and Whaley model and the binomial model are well suited to analyzing the options considered in this chapter. It is extremely reasonable to regard foreign currencies and futures as paying a continuous yield, and it is a reasonable assumption for stock indexes as well. Thus, the analytic approximation works quite well for the types of options considered in this chapter.

The binomial model applies to all of the American options discussed in this chapter as well. It is particularly well suited to pricing options on stock indexes. While it may be reasonable to assume that stock indexes pay a continuous dividend, we saw that there are significant discontinuities in the dividend stream for many real-world stock indexes. The binomial model is ideal for pricing options on goods that pay discrete dividends.

QUESTIONS AND PROBLEMS

1. Explain why interest payments on a foreign currency can be treated as analogous to a dividend on a common stock.
2. Why do we assume that the cost-of-carry for a futures is the same as the risk-free rate?
3. Explain how to adjust a price lattice for an underlying good that makes discrete payments.
4. If a European and an American call on the same underlying good have different prices when all of the terms of the two options are identical, what does this difference reveal about the two options? What does it mean if the two options have identical prices?
5. Consider an option on a futures contract within the context of the binomial model. Assume that the futures price is 100.00, that the risk-free interest rate is 10 percent, that the standard deviation of the futures is .4, and that the futures expires in one year. Assuming that a call and a put on the futures also expire in one year, compute the binomial parameters U, D, and π_U. Now compute the expected futures price in one period. What does this reveal about the expected movement in futures prices?
6. For a call and a put option on a foreign currency, compute the Merton model price, the binomial model price for a European option with three periods, the Barone-Adesi and Whaley model price, and the binomial model price with three periods for American options. Data are as follows: The foreign currency value is 2.5; the exercise price on all options is 2.0; the time until expiration is 90 days; the risk-free rate of interest is 7 percent; and the foreign interest rate is 4 percent; and the standard deviation of the foreign currency is .2.
7. Consider a call and a put on a stock index. The index price is 500.00, and the two options expire in 120 days. The standard deviation of the index is .2, and the risk-free rate of interest is 7 percent. The two options have a common exercise price of 500.00. The stock index will pay a dividend of 20.00 index units in 40 days. Find the European and American option prices according to the binomial model, assuming two periods. Be sure to draw the lattices for the stock index and for all of the options that are being priced.
8. Consider two European calls and two European put options on a foreign currency. The exercise prices are $.90 and $1.00, giving a total of four options. All options expire in one year. The current risk-free rate is 8 percent, the foreign interest rate is 5 percent, and the standard deviation of the foreign currency is .3. The foreign currency is priced at $.80. Find all four option prices according

to the Merton model. Compare the ratios of the option prices to the ratio of the exercise prices. What does this show?

NOTES

[1] Again, this is not the same as capital delta, Δ, which stands for the sensitivity of the call option price to a change in the stock price.

[2] Even large indexes, such as the S&P 500, exhibit a distinct seasonal pattern in their index payments. Therefore, continuous dividends for a stock index represents something of an assumption.

[3] When these conditions are not met, the pricing relationships discussed in this section do not hold. Slight deviations from these idealized conditions lead to slight pricing discrepancies, while some commodities do not obey the pricing rule at all. This issue was discussed in Chapter 3 of this text. For more details, see R. Kolb, *Understanding Futures Markets,* 5e, Malden: MA, Blackwell Publishing Company, 1997, Chapters 1–3.

[4] Notice that this equivalence of δ and r implies that the expected change in the futures price is zero. As the futures requires no investment and we are employing risk-neutrality arguments, the expected payoff from all investments is the risk-free rate. The risk-free rate applied to zero investment gives a zero expected profit.

[5] The application of this model to options on futures was first presented in Fischer Black, ''The Pricing of Commodity Contracts,'' *Journal of Financial Economics,* 3, March 1976, pp. 167–79.

[6] For a detailed explanation of these pricing relationships, see Chapter 3 of *Understanding Futures Markets,* 5e, Malden, MA: Blackwell Publishing Company, 1997.

[7] Notice that the call and put on the physical have the same price of $22.09. This will always be the case if the price of the spot good equals the exercise price.

THE OPTIONS APPROACH TO CORPORATE SECURITIES

OVERVIEW

In this chapter we apply the concepts developed in this book to the analysis of corporate securities such as stocks and bonds. We will see that virtually all securities have option features, and the options approach to corporate securities can help us understand these securities more fully.

Since the Black-Scholes model first appeared in the early 1970s, research on options has expanded rapidly. Option theory has given insight into several areas of finance, one of the most fruitful being corporate finance. In this chapter, we explore the insights that option theory brings to understanding corporate securities. By thinking of corporate securities as embracing options, we can build a deeper understanding of the value of securities such as stocks and bonds.[1]

The chapter begins by considering a firm with a simple capital structure of equity and a single pure discount bond. We show that the equity of the firm can be regarded as a call option on the entire firm with an exercise price equal to the obligation to the bondholders. Similarly, we can analyze the bond as involving an option as well. For this simple case, we show that the corporate bond can be regarded as consisting of a risk-free bond plus a short position in a put option. Of course, most firms have a more complex financial structure, but considering this simple case introduces the option dimension of most corporate securities.

In more realistic situations, the options embedded in corporate securities are more complex. In many firms, some debt is subordinated to more senior debt, meaning that the firm pays on the junior debt only after the senior debt claims have been satisfied. We show that the options approach to junior and senior debt analyzes these bonds as involving different exercise prices. When a firm has equity and coupon bonds, the analysis of the equity shows that the stock owners have a series of options. As another example, convertible debt includes a specific option – the option to convert the debt instrument into shares of the firm. The option to convert debt to equity is an option purchased by and held by the bond owner. Most corporate bonds are callable, so the issuer of the bond is entitled to retire the bond under specified circumstances. This call feature gives the issuer of the bond options with specified exercise prices. Understanding the option features of these different debt instruments gives a clearer understanding of their pricing. As we will see, these option features of corporate bonds have value, and they definitely affect the value of the bonds in which they are embedded.

A **warrant** is a security that gives the owner the option to convert the warrant into a new share of the issuing firm by paying a stated exercise price. This definition shows that a warrant is very similar to an option. However, there is an important difference. An option has an existing share as its underlying good. By contrast, the exercise of a warrant requires that the firm issue a new share of stock. As we will see, this difference leads to a slight difference in the valuation of options and warrants.

EQUITY AND A PURE DISCOUNT BOND

We begin our analysis of corporate securities by focusing on a firm with an extremely simple capital structure. This firm has common stock and a single bond for its financing. The bond is a pure discount bond that matures in one year. In this section, we want to understand these securities from the option's point of view.

Common Stock as a Call Option

For this firm financed by common stock and a single pure discount bond, we assume the bond issue is a pure discount bond, with face value FV. Let the current time be $t = 0$ and let the maturity date of the bond be $t = m$. Between the present and $t = m$, the firm operates, generating cash flows. We further assume that the firm is operated by agents of the shareholders for the benefit of the shareholders. Also, during this period, new information about the prospects of the firm becomes available. At any time, the value of the firm equals the present value of the firm's future cash flows. The firm value also equals the total value of its outstanding securities. At $t = 0$, the firm's value, V_0, is:

$$V_0 = S_0 + B_0 \qquad (17.1)$$

where:

S_0 = entire value of all stocks outstanding at time zero
B_0 = entire value of all bonds outstanding at time zero

The value of the bonds equals the present value of the face value, discounted at the appropriate risky discount rate r' for m periods.

$$B_0 = FVe^{-r'm} \qquad (17.2)$$

When the bond matures, the firm can either pay the indebtedness, FV, or default. If the firm defaults, the bondholders take over the firm to salvage whatever they can. If the firm has a value greater than its indebtedness, FV, the firm will pay the bondholders and the firm will then belong entirely to the stockholders. Thus, the stockholders' payoff at $t = m$, S_m, is either zero (if they default) or the value of the firm minus the debt to the bondholders ($V_m - FV$). In other words, the stock is just like a European call, with a payoff that equals:

$$S_m = MAX(0, V_m - FV) \qquad (17.3)$$

Therefore, the stock is a call option on the firm with an exercise price equal to the debt obligation, FV. Figure 17.1 shows the position of the stockholders. If the firm value at expiration is less than or equal to FV, then the stockholders do not have enough to pay the bondholders. Accordingly, they default and receive nothing. If the firm value exceeds FV, the stockholders pay the bondholders and keep any excess value.

From our analysis of stock options, we know the call value must equal or exceed the stock price minus the present value of the exercise price. Applying that principle to our treatment of stock itself as an option, we have:

$$S_0 \geq V_0 - FVe^{-rt} \tag{17.4}$$

This formula emphasizes another principle of option pricing. We know that call prices increase for higher risk in the underlying good. In analyzing common stock as an option on the value of the firm, we see that increasing the risk of the firm will make the stock more valuable. This is true even if the increasing risk does not increase the expected value of the firm at the expiration of the bond. The reason for this increase in value is the same that we saw for stock options. The stockholders have an incentive to increase risk. If the higher risk pays off, the stockholders keep all the benefits. If the risk does not pay off, the limited liability feature of stock protects the stockholders from losing more than their investment. Therefore, increasing risk gives a better chance for a very positive outcome for the stockholders, while the option protects against very negative outcomes. However, increasing the risk of the firm without increasing its expected value cannot increase the value of the firm as a whole. The increase in the value of the stock must come at the expense of the bondholders. Increasing

Common Stock Analyzed as a Call Option   **Figure 17.1**

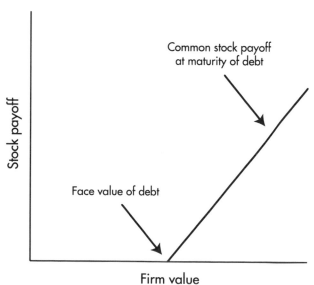

the risk of the firm without increasing the firm's expected value transfers wealth from bondholders to stockholders. Bondholders are aware of this incentive for the stockholders. As a result, bond covenants often prevent the borrower from increasing the risk of the firm.

The Option Analysis of Corporate Debt

Let us now examine the same simple firm from the perspective of the debtholder. The stockholders have promised to pay FV to the debtholders at $t = m$. However, the stockholders will pay only if the firm's value exceeds FV at the maturity of the debt. Otherwise, they will let the bondholders have the firm. Therefore, the payoff for the bondholders at $t = m$, B_m, will be the lesser of the firm's value or FV. Figure 17.2 graphs the payoffs that the bondholders receive. As the figure shows, the bondholders receive the entire value of the firm if the firm value at the maturity of the debt is less than the debt obligation, FV. However, the bondholders never receive more than the promised payment of FV. Thus, the payoff to the bondholders, B_m, is the lesser of the firm's value, V_m, or FV.

$$B_m = \mathrm{MIN}(V_m, \mathrm{FV}) \qquad (17.5)$$

We have already seen the payoff to the stockholders at $t = m$ and we know that the value of the bonds and stocks must equal the value of the firm. Therefore:

$$B_m = V_m - \mathrm{MAX}(0, V_m - \mathrm{FV}) \qquad (17.6)$$

Figure 17.2   **The Option Analysis of Corporate Debt**

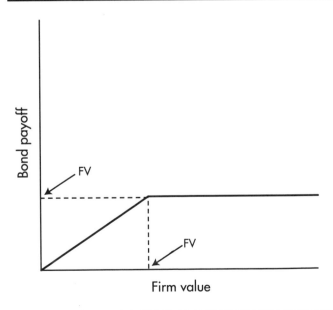

This equation shows that the bondholders have effectively purchased the entire firm and written a European call option to the stockholders. The call option is on the entire firm. The face value of the debt, FV, is the exercise price. This conclusion exactly complements our analysis of the stock as a call option on the value of the firm.

A closer analysis of Figure 17.2 shows that it has the same payoff shape that we studied in Chapter 11. In essence, the bondholders' payoff consists of two embedded positions. The general shape matches that of a short position in a put. However, the entire position can never be worth less than zero. The bondholders effectively hold a short position in a put with an exercise price of FV, in addition to a long position in a risk-free bond paying FV. To see why this is so, assume that the firm's value at maturity exactly matches the obligation to the bondholders, $V_m = \text{FV}$. From Figure 17.2, we see that the bondholders receive FV for this terminal firm value. With $V_m = \text{FV}$, the put option the bondholders issued expires worthless.

Now consider any lower value for the firm at maturity. If the firm value is lower than FV, the stockholders exercise their put option, forcing the firm upon the bondholders. Now the bondholders receive their risk-free payment of FV, but they lose an amount equal to the shortfall in the firm's value below FV. In our notation, the bondholders receive FV. They also lose either zero, if the firm's value exceeds FV, or they lose $\text{FV} - V_m$ if the debt obligation exceeds the value of the firm:

$$B_m = \text{FV} - \text{MAX}(0, \text{FV} - V_m) \tag{17.7}$$

As this equation shows, the bondholders receive a payoff equal to a long position in a riskless bond and a short position in a put with an exercise price of FV.

Thus, we have seen that we can analyze the position of the bondholders in two ways:

1. The bond consists of ownership of the entire firm with a short position in a call on the entire firm given to the shareholders. The exercise price of the call possessed by the shareholders is FV.
2. The bond consists of a risk-free bond paying FV combined with a short position in a put option sold to the shareholders, which allows the shareholders to put the entire firm to the bondholders for an exercise price of FV.

From our exploration of put-call parity in Chapter 11, we know that the following relationship must hold:

$$S_t - c_t = Xe^{-r(T-t)} - p_t \tag{17.8}$$

We can apply put-call parity to our present situation by recalling that the value of the entire firm, V_0, plays the role of the stock and that the exercise price equals the promised payment to the bondholders, FV.

$$V_0 - S_0 = B_0 \qquad \text{or} \qquad V_0 - c_t = \text{FV}e^{-r(T-t)} - p_t \tag{17.9}$$

In Equation 17.9, notice that the promised payment on the bond, FV, is discounted at the risk-free rate of interest, r, not the risky rate of interest r'. This difference reflects the analysis of the risky bond as consisting of a risk-free bond with a promised payment of FV plus a short position in the put option on the entire firm. The difference in price between the risk-free and risky bond equals the short position in the put.

SENIOR AND SUBORDINATED DEBT

Many firms have two or more debt issues in their capital structure. Thus, we now consider a firm with three securities: stock, senior debt, and subordinated debt. Subordinated debt is a bond issue that receives payment only after the firm fully meets senior debt obligations. Let the two debt issues be pure discount bonds that both mature at $t = m$. The face values on the two obligations are FV_s for the senior debt and FV_j for the junior or subordinated debt. We want to analyze the subordinated debt in option terms.

The holders of the subordinated debt receive payment only after the firm fully meets the claims of the senior debtholders. Therefore, for any firm value V_m that is less than FV_s, the junior debtholders receive zero. If the firm value exceeds FV_s, the junior debtholders receive at least some payment. The subordinated debtholders receive full payment if the firm's value equals or exceeds the entire amount due on both debt issues, $V_m \geq FV_s + FV_j$. Figure 17.3 shows the payoffs for the senior and junior debt. The payoffs on the junior debt match a portfolio of a long call with a striking price of FV_s and a short call with a striking price of FV_j, as Figure 17.4 shows. The stockholders in this firm own a call on the value of the firm with a striking price equal to $FV_s + FV_j$. For the call option represented by the stock to come into the money, the value of the firm must exceed the total payoff of the two debt issues. Therefore, the payoff on the call in this situation is:

$$S_m = \text{MAX}[0, V_m - (FV_s + FV_j)]$$

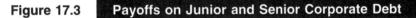

| **Figure 17.3** | **Payoffs on Junior and Senior Corporate Debt** |

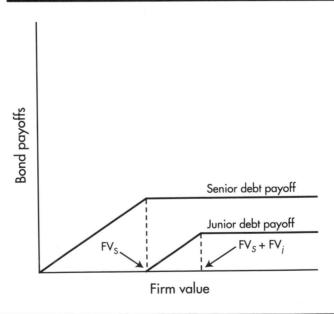

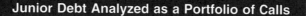

Junior Debt Analyzed as a Portfolio of Calls   **Figure 17.4**

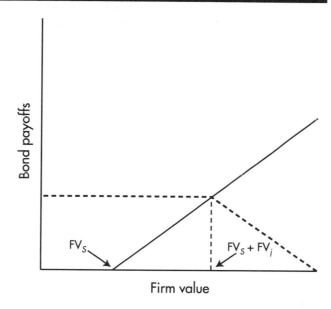

As always, the value of the firm must equal the value of all outstanding securities. However, the different classes of securities offer different ways to create various options and provide different divisions of the corporate pie when the bonds mature.

CALLABLE BONDS

The typical corporate bond is a callable bond. A **callable bond** is a bond that can be redeemed at the will of the issuer by the payment of a specified amount. Usually, the bond is not callable until a specified number of years after its issuance. Thereafter, the issuer may call the bond at any time. As an example, a firm might issue a bond today that is callable in five years (and thereafter), with a required payment equal to 110 percent of the face value of the bond. Typical call provisions allow this required payment to decline in subsequent years. In some cases, the bond is callable only on certain dates.

The issuer of the bond has an incentive to call the bond if the coupon rate exceeds the current market rate of interest. For example, if the callable bond were issued at 11 percent and current rates for similar debt are 6 percent, the issuer might wish to call the 11 percent bond and issue new debt at the prevailing market rate of 6 percent.

When it issues a callable bond, the firm itself retains a valuable option to require the bondholder to surrender the bond in return for the payment of a certain amount. Therefore, the call feature of a corporate bond means that the issuing firm has a call option on the outstanding bond. The exercise price of this call option is the call price that the firm must pay to call the bond.

For the bondholder, a callable bond is less desirable than a bond with no call feature. The bondholder knows that the issuer will exercise the call feature only when it benefits the issuing firm.

In our example, the bondholder receiving an 11 percent coupon payment in a 6 percent interest rate environment certainly would prefer that the issuer not call the bond. Therefore, in accepting a callable bond, the bondholder realizes that he is implicitly buying a (noncallable) bond and selling a call option on the bond to the issuer. As we have seen, this call option held by the issuer has greater value when market rates of interest lie below the coupon rate on the bond.

The value of the noncallable bond varies inversely and smoothly with interest rates over the entire range of rates. By contrast, the value of a callable bond parallels the value of the noncallable bond for higher interest rates. For low interest rates, however, the value of the callable bond remains constant at a lower level.

To understand the difference in the values of callable and noncallable bonds, consider the following example of two similar bonds. One is noncallable while the other is callable on a single date in five years at a call price of $1,100.[2] We assume that both bonds have an initial maturity of 30 years and that both have an 8 percent coupon and a $1,000 face value. We further assume that the noncallable bond has an 8 percent yield at issuance, so it is priced at its face value of $1,000. The callable bond is identical in its promised coupon payments and maturity and differs from the noncallable bond only in its call feature. As we have seen, this means that the buyer of the callable bond grants the issuer a call option which has some value. Therefore, we know that the price of the callable bond at issuance must be less than the otherwise identical noncallable bond.

Figure 17.5 illustrates the values of the two bonds five years after issuance, when both bonds have 25 years remaining until maturity. If market rates of interest are 8 percent, the noncallable bond will still be worth $1,000. The callable bond will be priced below $1,000 because of the call feature. If interest rates are higher, at 10 percent for example, the price of the noncallable bond will be $817,

Figure 17.5   **Callable versus Noncallable Bonds**

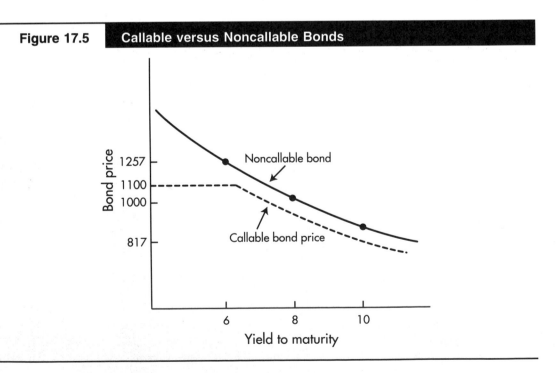

and the price of the callable bond will still be somewhat lower. If interest rates are substantially lower than 8 percent, say, 6 percent, the price of the noncallable bond will be $1,257. At this point we can see that there will be a substantial divergence between the prices of the callable and noncallable bond. The call price for the bond of $1,100 is effectively the upper bound on the price of the callable bond, even in a low interest rate environment. Investors will not be willing to pay more than $1,100 for the callable bond, because they know it can be called away from them at that price.

The issuing firm holds a call option on the bond and a short position in the underlying bond. If interest rates fall, the value of bonds will rise in general. However, the callable bond is a single security, meaning that the bond and the call option on the bond are inextricably bound together. To capture the value of the call option, the issuer must exercise the call feature of the bond. This union of the call and the underlying bond in a single security helps explain why the value of the callable bond cannot rise significantly above its call price. The resulting pricing is depicted in Figure 17.5. Summarizing, for prices at or below the call price on the callable bond, the two bonds will behave similarly. However, the callable bond will always be worth somewhat less than an otherwise similar bond due to the presence of the call feature. For higher prices on the noncallable bond, the price of the callable bond will be capped at or near the call price of the bond.

Figure 17.5 does not show the exact price of the callable bond, because it does not attempt to exactly price the call that is embedded in the callable bond. However, we know that the price of the embedded call will depend on the time until expiration, the prevailing interest rate, the price of the otherwise similar bond, the call price, and the volatility of the price of the otherwise similar bond.

CONVERTIBLE BONDS

Many corporate bonds are convertible into shares of the issuing firm. The holder of the bond has the option to convert the bond into shares under the terms specified in the bond indenture. For example, a firm might issue a $1,000 face value convertible bond with a 20-year maturity and a coupon rate of 9 percent. The bond could be converted into eight shares of stock by surrendering the bond.[3] We assume that a share of the issuing firm was worth $100 at the time of issuance. We can analyze this type of convertible bond as consisting of two elements: a regular bond with no conversion feature, plus a call option on eight shares of stock with the exercise price of the option being the value of the bond. The number of shares received for the bond upon conversion is the **conversion ratio**. Because the purchase of a convertible bond receives a call option on the shares of the issuing firm, the convertible bond sells for more than an otherwise similar nonconvertible bond. This means that the issuing firm can issue a convertible bond at a lower interest rate than an otherwise similar nonconvertible bond. However, the firm gives a call option to secure this lower interest rate.

At any time during its life, the bond must be worth at least its conversion value. In our example, we assume that the conversion ratio was eight shares, so the bond must be worth at least eight times the current share price. If this condition were not met, there would be an immediate arbitrage opportunity because a trader could buy the bond, exercise the conversion feature to secure the shares, and sell the shares for more than the price of the bond. Of course, the bond can sell for more than its conversion value, because the bond always has all of the features of a straight bond.

At the maturity of the bond, the bond will pay its face value, the bond will be converted, or the firm will default. The firm will default if the face value exceeds the value of the firm. In the case of default, the owners of the convertible bond will take over the entire firm. Assuming the firm does not default, the convertible bond will be worth the maximum of the face value or the conversion ratio times the stock price.

In many instances, the bond indenture prohibits the issuing firm from paying a dividend during the life of the convertible bond. In this case, the bond will not be converted prior to its maturity date. This is clear by analogy to a call. Exercising a call or converting a convertible bond on a nondividend stock terminates the option in favor of its intrinsic value. As we saw for a call, the owner is better off selling the call and buying the stock in the open market. Similarly, the holder of a convertible bond on a nondividend stock will not exercise, because doing so discards the excess value of the call option over and above its intrinsic value.

Some convertible bonds are also callable. For convertible callable bonds, both the issuer and the bondholder hold an option associated with the bond. As we have seen, the issuer has a call option on the underlying bond, and the owner of a convertible bond has a call option on the firm's shares. Consider a convertible bond that could be profitably converted, and assume that the underlying shares pay no dividend. As we have just seen, the bondholder will not willingly convert prior to the maturity of the bond, because converting the bond discards the time value that is inherent in the option. However, the issuer would like the holder of the convertible to convert as soon as possible for the same reason. Therefore, the issuer of a convertible callable bond can force conversion by calling the bond. As soon as the convertible callable bond can be converted, the issuer should call the bond to force conversion. This is clear, because if it behooves the bondholder to delay conversion, it must benefit the issuer to force conversion. After all, the bond is an asset to the bondholder, but a liability to the issuer. Therefore, forcing conversion eliminates the time premium associated with the conversion option.

WARRANTS

A typical warrant allows the owner to surrender the warrant and pay a stated price for a share of common stock of the firm that issues the warrant. Usually, warrants are created with three to seven years to expiration. As such, a warrant is very much like a call option on the stock of the issuing firm. However, a call option has as its underlying instrument an existing share. By contrast, the exercise of a warrant requires the issuing firm to create a new share and deliver it to the exerciser of the warrant. Therefore, the exercise of a warrant involves a dilution of ownership because a new share is created. Warrants are often attached to bonds as a "sweetener" to make the bonds more saleable. Often these warrants are detachable and can even trade in a separate market. However warrants are issued, they are valuable instruments with all of the features of a call option, except for the fact that they command a newly created share upon exercise rather than an existing share.

At the expiration date of the warrant, exercise would make sense only if the resulting share value from exercise exceeds the exercise price. Let V_B = the share price before exercise, X = the exercise price of the warrant, n = the number of shares outstanding before exercise, and q = the number of warrants. The value of the firm after exercise will be $nV_B + qX$, because the total exercise price on the warrants is qX, and the firm's value increases by the influx of cash from the exercise of the warrants. There will be $n(1 + q/n)$ shares outstanding after exercise. Therefore, the value of a share after exercise will be:

$$\frac{nV_B + qX}{n + q} \qquad (17.10)$$

As an example, consider a firm with 100 outstanding shares priced at $48 per share, and assume that the shares pay no dividend. The firm has warrants for 10 shares outstanding with an exercise price on the warrants of $50. If the warrants are exercised, the firm will be worth $5,300, the present value of the firm plus the $500 exercise price of the warrants. The firm will then have 110 shares outstanding after it issues the 10 shares to meet the exercise of the warrants. Consequently, each share after exercise would be worth $48.18. With an exercise price of $50 and a post-exercise share price of $48.18, exercise is not feasible. Thus, exercise will only be feasible if the stock price equals or exceeds the exercise price.

As with a call option, a warrant should not be exercised until expiration. The reasoning is the same – early exercise discards the time premium associated with the option. Instead of exercising the call or warrant, the owner should sell the call or warrant and purchase the underlying good.

The value of a European warrant equals the value of a parallel European call after adjustment for the dilution of ownership caused by the exercise of the warrant. If q warrants are exercised and n shares are outstanding before exercise, there will be $n(1 + q/n)$ shares outstanding after exercise. The European warrant gives title to one of those shares. Therefore, the value of a European warrant at time t, W_t, must be:

$$W_t = \frac{c_t}{1 + \dfrac{q}{n}}$$

In other words, the value of a European warrant equals the value of a European call option divided by one plus the proportion of shares created in response to the exercise of the warrant.

CONCLUSION

In this chapter we have explored how various corporate securities can be analyzed in terms of the option concepts developed throughout this book. We began by considering an extremely simple firm drawing its capital only from common stock and a single pure discount bond. For such a firm, we saw that the common stock can be treated as a call option on the entire firm. In this case, the call option has an exercise price equal to the payment promised to the bondholders and the expiration date for the option is the maturity of the bond.

The bond itself can be analyzed in option terms as well. We used put-call parity to show that the bond can be analyzed in two equivalent ways. First, the bond represents ownership of the entire firm coupled with a short position in a call on the entire firm given to the shareholders. The exercise price of the call possessed by the shareholders is the payment promised to the bondholders. As a second and equivalent analysis, the bond consists of a risk-free bond paying the face value of the bond combined with a short position in a put option sold to the shareholders, which allows the shareholders to put the entire firm to the bondholders for an exercise price of the face value of the bond.

We next considered a firm with stock, senior debt, and subordinated debt in its capital structure. The stock owners have essentially the same position as in the simplest case. They own a call on the entire firm and the exercise price of the call is the total set of payments promised to both the senior and subordinated debtholders. The subordinated debtholder essentially holds a long call on the firm with an exercise price equal to the payment promised to the senior bondholders coupled with a short call on the entire firm with an exercise price equal to the payment promised to the junior bondholders. If the shareholders decide not to exercise their call, it will be because the value of the firm is less than the exercise price that the stockholders face – the payments promised to the junior and senior debtholders. The junior debtholders can then claim the firm by exercising their call on the senior debtholders; they merely must pay the senior debtholders as promised. However, the junior debtholders have also issued a call, because the stockholders may call the firm away from them by making the promised payment.

Both callable and convertible bonds have options imbedded in them. As we saw, a callable bond consists of a straight bond, but the issuer of the bond retains a call option on the bond. Thus, the issuer is long this call and the bondholder has sold the call to the issuer. This call gives the issuer of the bond the right to purchase the bond and avoid any further payments by paying the call price. In a bond convertible into common stock, the owner of the bond has a call option on the shares of the firm. The bondholder in this case can convert a bond into shares by surrendering the bond and paying the stipulated price to acquire the shares permitted by the bond covenant. In the case of both the callable bond and the convertible bond, the imbedded options have value, and this value can be a considerable proportion of the total value of the bond.

Finally, we considered the pricing of warrants. We noted that a warrant is similar to a call option. However, a call option gives the holder the right to buy an existing share, while a warrant gives the holder the right to buy a newly issued share from the firm. Therefore, the exercise of the warrant involves a dilution of ownership in the firm, and a warrant is, therefore, slightly less valuable than an otherwise similar call option.

QUESTIONS AND PROBLEMS

1. Explain why common stock is itself like a call option. In the option analysis of common stock, what plays the role of the exercise price and what plays the role of the underlying stock?
2. Consider a firm that issues a pure discount bond that matures in one year and has a face value of $1,000,000. Analyze the payoffs that the bondholders will receive in option pricing terms, assuming the only other security in the firm is common stock.
3. Consider a firm with common stock and a pure discount bond as its financing. The total value of the firm is $1,000,000. There are 10,000 shares of common stock priced at $70 per share. The bond matures in ten years and has a total face value of $500,000. What is the interest rate on the bond, assuming annual compounding? Would the interest rate become higher or lower if the volatility of the firm's cash flows increases?
4. A firm has a capital structure consisting of common stock and a single bond. The managers of the firm are considering a major capital investment that will be financed from internally generated funds. The project can be initiated in two ways, one with a high fixed cost component and the other with a low fixed cost component. Although both technologies have the same expected value, the high fixed cost approach has the potential for greater payoffs. (If the product is successful, the high fixed cost approach gives much lower total costs for large production levels.) What does option theory suggest about the choice the managers should make? Explain.
5. In a firm with common stock, senior debt, and subordinated debt, assume that both debt instruments mature at the same time. What is the necessary condition on the value of the firm at maturity for each security holder to receive at least some payment? With two classes of debt, does option theory counsel managers to increase the riskiness of the firm's operations? Would there be any

difference on this point between a firm with a single debt issue and two debt issues? Which bondholders would tend to be more risk averse as far as choosing a risk level for the firm's operations? Explain.

6. Consider a firm financed solely by common stock and a single callable bond issue. Assume that the bond is a pure discount bond. Is there any circumstance in which the firm should call the bond before the maturity date? Would such an exercise of the firm's call option discard the time premium? Explain.

7. Consider a firm financed only by common stock and a convertible bond issue. When should the bondholders exercise? Explain. If the common shares pay a dividend, could it make sense for the bondholders to exercise before the bond matures? Explain by relating your answer to our discussion of the exercise of American calls on dividend paying stocks.

8. Warrants are often used to compensate top executives in firms. Often these warrants cannot be exercised until a distant expiration date. This form of compensation is used to align the manager's incentives with the maximization of the shareholders' wealth. Explain how the manager's receiving warrants might thwart the efforts to change his or her incentives.

NOTES

[1] Of course the original Black-Scholes paper, "The Pricing of Options and Corporate Liabilities," *Journal of Political Economy,* 81, 1973, pp. 637–59, already focused on the option characteristics of stocks and bonds.

[2] Generally, bonds are not callable until their first call date, and they are then callable at any time thereafter.

[3] Other features are possible. For example, some bonds can be converted to preferred stock. Some convertible bonds can be converted only by surrendering the bond and making a cash payment. Some convertible bonds can be converted only on certain dates. Further, some convertible securities are preferred stock that can be converted into common stock.

EXOTIC OPTIONS

OVERVIEW

In recent years, financial engineers have created a variety of complex options that are collectively known as **exotic options**. The payoffs on these options are considerably more diverse than the payoffs on the straightforward options that we have considered to this point. For example, the payoff on a **lookback call option** depends on the minimum stock price experienced during some past period. Other exotic options have different and more complicated payoff structures. This chapter explores the pricing and uses of these exotic options.

We approach these exotic options by contrasting them with the plain vanilla options explored earlier in this book. For a **plain vanilla option**, the value of an option at any particular moment depends only upon the current price of the underlying good, the exercise price, the risk-free rate of interest, the volatility of the underlying good, the time until expiration, and the dividend rate on the underlying good. Further, there is a fixed underlying good, a fixed and stated exercise price, a known time to expiration, and no special conditions on any of the option parameters.

With respect to the price of the underlying good, it is import to emphasize that the price of a plain vanilla option depends only on the current price of the underlying good, so the price of the option is independent of the price path followed by the underlying good. As we will see in this chapter, many exotic options exhibit **path dependence** – the price of the option today depends on the previous or future price path followed by the underlying good. For example, the price of a lookback call option depends on the minimum price reached by the underlying good over some past period. Further, the price of an average price option depends upon the future average price of the underlying good. Thus, to price a path-dependent option, it is not enough to know the current price of the underlying good. Instead, we must have information about the previous path that the price of the underlying good traversed.[1]

This chapter considers nine classes of exotic options: forward-start options, compound options, chooser options, barrier options, binary options, lookback options, average price options, exchange options, and rainbow options. Because of the complexity of these options, we focus on European options, emphasizing cases in which closed-form solutions are available. Thus, all of the exotic options are analyzed as extended instances of the Merton continuous dividend model. In their working paper, "Exotic Options," Mark Rubinstein and Eric Reiner have presented a unified and comprehensive treatment of these exotic options, and this chapter relies largely on this excellent work. We also refer to other studies and original contributions for each of the types of exotic options.

This chapter explores each type of exotic option in a separate section that discusses the payoff structure of the option, presents the valuation formula for the option, and shows a calculation example. The **OPTION!** software that accompanies this book can compute the value of all of the exotic options discussed in this chapter.

ASSUMPTIONS OF THE ANALYSIS AND THE PRICING ENVIRONMENT

In this chapter we focus exclusively on European exotic options for which closed-form solutions exist. For most American exotic options, and for some European exotic options, there is no exact pricing formula. For these options, simulation or approximation methods must be used to estimate the price, a process that adds considerable complexity. By focusing on European exotic options with closed-form solutions, we can gain a rich understanding of exotic options, while avoiding much mathematical complexity.

In our analysis, we make the usual assumptions underlying the Black-Scholes model and the Merton model. Particularly, we assume that the price of the asset underlying the exotic option follows a lognormal random walk, that there are no arbitrage opportunities, and that the price of the underlying asset is expected to appreciate at the risk-free rate of interest, less any payouts from the asset such as dividends. These assumptions allow us to evaluate options in a risk-neutral framework. As we explored in Chapter 13, these assumptions lead to the Black-Scholes model and the Merton model. Because we will refer to it often in this chapter, we repeat the Merton model here for convenience:

$$c_t^M = e^{-\delta(T-t)}S_t N(d_1^M) - Xe^{-r(T-t)}N(d_2^M)$$

$$p_t^M = Xe^{-r(T-t)}N(-d_2^M) - e^{-\delta(T-t)}S_t N(-d_1^M)$$

$$d_1^M = \frac{\ln\left(\dfrac{S_t}{X}\right) + (r - \delta + .5\sigma^2)(T - t)}{\sigma\sqrt{T - t}} \tag{18.1}$$

$$d_2^M = d_1^M - \sigma\sqrt{T - t}$$

FORWARD-START OPTIONS

In a **forward-start option**, the price of the option is paid at the present, but the life of the option starts at a future date. Further, the exercise price is typically specified to be the current price at the beginning of the option's life, that is, the option contract specifies that the option will be at-the-money when the option's life begins. Forward-start call options are often used in executive compensation packages. An executive might receive a forward-start call option on the firm's shares with an exercise price to equal the firm's share price at the time the option life starts.

For a forward-start option, there are three dates to consider: the valuation date, t, the date that the option life begins (which is called the **grant date**), tg, and the date when the option eventually expires, T. Thus, it must be the case that:

$$t \leq tg \leq T$$

Accordingly, the time until the option's life begins will be $tg - t$, and when the option's life begins, the time until expiration will be $T - tg$.

The value of a forward-start option is simply the value of an option with the current stock price, an exercise price equal to the current stock price, and a time to expiration of $T - tg$, with this value being discounted by the dividend rate on the underlying good over the period until the option is granted, $tg - t$:

$$\text{Forward-Start Call} = e^{-\delta(tg-t)}C_{tg}^{M} \qquad (18.2)$$
$$\text{Forward-Start Put} = e^{-\delta(tg-t)}P_{tg}^{M}$$

where C_{tg}^{M} and P_{tg}^{M} are the values of the call and put options, respectively, according to the Merton model, with a time to expiration of $T - tg$. The idea here is that the price of the underlying good and the exercise price on the forward-start option will change proportionally. (For a forward-start option specified to be at-the-money on the grant date, the stock and exercise price at that time will be equal.) Therefore, a forward-start option today is essentially a deferred granting of an option with a stock and exercise price equal to today's stock price and a time to expiration that equals the period from the grant date to the final expiration date.[2]

To illustrate the value of these forward-start options more fully, consider the following data:

$$S = 100$$
$$X = 100$$
$$T - t = 1 \text{ year}$$
$$\sigma = 0.2$$
$$r = 0.1$$
$$\delta = 0.05$$
$$tg = 0.5 \text{ years}$$

Using these data we will price a call option. Notice that the time to expiration as of the grant date is $T - tg = 0.5$ years, so this is the time to expiration that will be used in the Merton model. We first compute d_1^M and d_2^M:

$$d_1^M = \frac{\ln\left(\frac{100}{100}\right) + [0.1 - 0.05 + 0.5(0.2)(0.2)](0.5)}{0.2\sqrt{0.5}} = 0.247487$$

$$d_2^M = 0.247487 - 0.141421 = 0.106066$$

With these values for d_1^M and d_2^M, $N(d_1^M) = 0.597734$ and $N(d_2^M) = 0.542235$. So the value of the underlying call option is:

$$c_{tg}^{M} = e^{-\delta(T-tg)}S_t N(d_1^M) - Xe^{-r(T-tg)}N(d_2^M)$$

$$= e^{-0.05(0.5)}100(0.597734) - 100e^{-0.1(0.5)}(0.542235)$$

$$= 6.7186$$

The value of the forward-start call is:

$$\text{Forward-Start Call} = e^{-\delta(tg-t)}C_{tg}{}^M = e^{-0.05(0.5)}6.7186 = 6.5527$$

With the same input values, the forward-start put is worth 4.2042.

COMPOUND OPTIONS

A **compound option** is an option on an option; in other words when one option is exercised, the underlying good is another option. In this section we consider the pricing of the four types of possible compound European options: a call on a call, a call on a put, a put on a call, and a put on a put. For example, consider the owner of a call on a call. The owner of the compound call has until the expiration date of the compound option (the call on a call) to decide whether to exercise the compound option. If so, she will receive the underlying call option with its own exercise price and time until expiration. If that underlying option is exercised, she will receive the underlying good.

For the underlying option, we will use our familiar notation, letting X be the exercise price, and letting T be the expiration date. For the compound option, let x be the exercise price and let te be the time at which the compound option expires. Because these are European options, the owner of the compound option cannot exercise until the expiration date of the compound option, te. If she exercises the compound option she will immediately receive the underlying call in the case we are considering. Therefore, when the compound option is at expiration, the choice is really very simple: pay x and receive the underlying option or do nothing and allow the option to expire worthless. Thus, when the compound option reaches expiration, the trader will exercise the compound call if the price of the underlying call is worth more than the exercise price of the compound option, x. At the expiration date of the compound option, the underlying call (or underlying put) can be priced according to the Merton model with inputs S_{te} for the price of the underlying good, X for the exercise price, $T - te$ for the time remaining until expiration, σ for the volatility of the underlying good, r for the risk-free rate, and δ for the dividend rate on the underlying good.

Before the expiration date of the compound option, that is, from t until te, the value of the compound option depends on the value of the underlying good in a compound manner. First, the value of the underlying option is largely a function of the value of the underlying good, as we have studied throughout this book. Secondly, the value of the compound option also depends on the price of its underlying good, which is the option underlying the compound option.

The valuation of these compound options is highly analogous to the valuation of an American option with a dividend payment between the valuation date and the expiration date that we studied in Chapter 15. There we saw that the value depends on the critical stock price, S^*, that made the owner of the underlying call indifferent between exercising and allowing the option to expire worthless. In the case of an option on an underlying call, the critical stock price will be the stock price that leaves the owner of the underlying call indifferent between exercising or not. Therefore, for a compound option on an underlying call, the critical price is the stock price at which the value of the underlying call equals the cost of acquiring it, which is x. Thus, the critical stock price for an underlying call (a call on a call or a put on a call) is the value of S^* that makes the following equation hold:

$$S^*e^{-\delta(T-te)}N(z) - Xe^{-r(T-te)}N(z - \sigma\sqrt{T - te}) - x = 0 \qquad (18.3)$$

where:

$$z = \frac{\ln\left(\dfrac{S*}{X}\right) + (r - \delta + 0.5\sigma^2)(T - te)}{\sigma\sqrt{T - te}}$$

For a compound option on an underlying put (a call on a put or a put on a put), the critical stock price satisfies the following relationship:

$$-S*e^{-\delta(T-te)}N(-z) + Xe^{-r(T-te)}N(-z + \sigma\sqrt{T - te}) - x = 0 \qquad (18.4)$$

Before we can write the valuation formula for a call on a call, we must define three additional variables:

$$w_1 = \frac{\ln\left(\dfrac{S}{S*}\right) + (r - \delta + 0.5\sigma^2)(te - t)}{\sigma\sqrt{te - t}}$$

$$w_2 = \frac{\ln\left(\dfrac{S}{X}\right) + (r - \delta + 0.5\sigma^2)(T - t)}{\sigma\sqrt{T - t}}$$

and

$$\rho = \sqrt{\frac{te - t}{T - t}}$$

With these definitions, the value of a call on a call, CC_t, is:

$$CC_t = Se^{-\delta(T-t)}N_2(w_1; w_2; \rho) - Xe^{-r(T-t)}N_2(w_1 - \sigma\sqrt{te - t}; w_2 - \sigma\sqrt{T - t}; \rho) \qquad (18.5)$$
$$- xe^{-r(te-t)}N(w_1 - \sigma\sqrt{te - t})$$

In equation 18.5, the three terms correspond to the key factors that determine the value of the compound option, S, k, and K. The function N_2 is the bivariate normal cumulative probability already discussed in Chapter 15.[3]

To apply this formula, consider the following data:

$S = 100$
$\sigma = 0.2$
$r = 0.1$
$\delta = 0.05$
$X = 100$ (the exercise price on the underlying option)
$x = 8$ (the exercise price on the compound option)
$T - t = 1$ year (the expiration date of the underlying option)
$te = .25$ years (the expiration date of the compound option)

With these data, we must first find the critical value that would make the option owner indifferent between exercising the compound option and allowing it to expire. The critical price depends on the value of z, which in turn depends on S^*. This means that the values of S^* and z must be solved simultaneously. This can be done by an iterative search over potential values of S^*, which is best done by computer. For these data, the critical value is 99.235871. This can be verified by computing z and the resulting value of zero in the equation for finding S^*.

Having found S^*, the values of w_1 and w_2 are given by:

$$w_1 = \frac{\ln\left(\dfrac{100}{99.235871}\right) + [0.1 - 0.05 + .5(0.2)(0.2)](0.25)}{0.2\sqrt{0.25}}$$

$$= \frac{0.007671 + 0.0175}{0.1}$$

$$= 0.251706$$

$$w_2 = \frac{\ln\left(\dfrac{100}{100}\right) + [0.1 - 0.05 + 0.5(0.2)(0.2)](1.0)}{0.2(1.0)} = \frac{0 + 0.07}{0.2} = 0.35$$

The correlation coefficient is:

$$\rho = \sqrt{\frac{0.25}{1.0}} = 0.5$$

With these values of w_1, w_2, and ρ, we can compute all of the values for the unit and bivariate cumulative normal probabilities:

$$N_2(w_1; w_2; \rho) = N_2(0.251706; 0.35; 0.5) = 0.458898$$

$$N_2(w_1 - \sigma\sqrt{te - t}; w_2 - \sqrt{T - t}; \rho) = N_2(0.151706; 0.15; 0.5) = 0.395366$$

$$N(w_1 - \sigma\sqrt{te - t}) = N(0.251706 - 0.1) = 0.560291$$

These probabilities can be found and verified by using **OPTION!**. We can now use these intermediate results to compute the value of our compound option:

$$CC_t = 100e^{-0.05(1.0)}(0.458898) - 100e^{-0.1(1.0)}(0.395366) - 8e^{-0.1(0.25)}(0.560291)$$

$$= 3.5059$$

This result can also be verified by using these input values and the **OPTION!** software.

Using the appropriate definition for the critical stock price (given in equation 18.3 for compound calls or equation 18.4 for compound puts), the following formulas give the value of a call-on-a-put (CP_t), a put-on-a-call (PC_t), and a put-on-a-put (PP_t):

$$CP_t = -Se^{-\delta(T-t)}N_2(-w_1; -w_2; \rho) + Xe^{-r(T-t)}N_2(-w_1 + \sigma\sqrt{te - t}; -w_2 + \sigma\sqrt{T - t}; \rho) \quad (18.6)$$
$$- xe^{-r(te-t)}N(-w_1 + \sigma\sqrt{te - t})$$

$$PC_t = -Se^{-\delta(T-t)}N_2(-w_1; -w_2; -\rho) + Xe^{-r(T-t)}N_2(-w_1 + \sigma\sqrt{te - t}; w_2 - \sigma\sqrt{T - t}; -\rho) \quad (18.7)$$
$$+ xe^{-r(te-t)}N(-w_1 + \sigma\sqrt{te - t})$$

$$PP_t = Se^{-\delta(T-t)}N_2(w_1; -w_2; -\rho) - Xe^{-r(T-t)}N_2(w_1 - \sigma\sqrt{te - t}; -w_2 + \sigma\sqrt{T - t}; -\rho) \quad (18.8)$$
$$+ xe^{-r(te-t)}N(w_1 - \sigma\sqrt{te - t})$$

With the same input values used for the call-on-a-call, the resulting compound option values are: $CP_t = 0.6490$; $PC_t = 1.3675$; and $PP_t = 3.1498$.

Figure 18.1 shows how compound option values vary as a function of the underlying stock price. Panels A–D correspond to call-on-a-call, call-on-a-put, put-on-a-call, and put-on-a-put compound options respectively. For each graph, we use the same parameters as our example calculation. As Figure 18.1A shows, the value of a call-on-a-call is an increasing function of the stock price, while

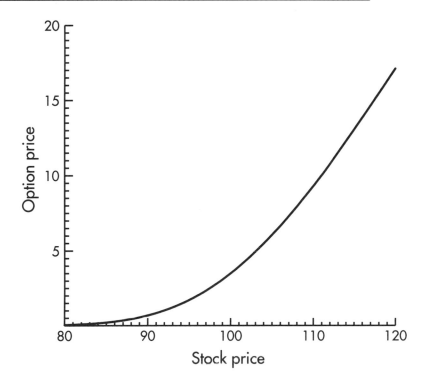

Call-on-a-Call Price as a Function of the Stock Price   **Figure 18.1A**

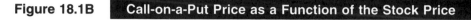

Figure 18.1B **Call-on-a-Put Price as a Function of the Stock Price**

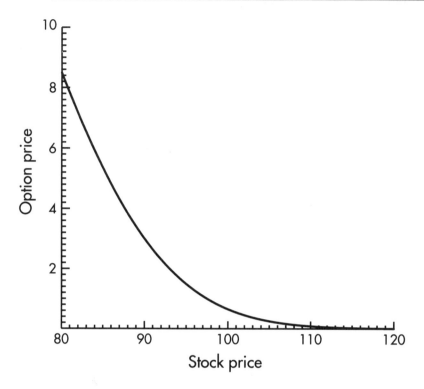

Figure 18.1B shows that the value of a call-on-a-put is a decreasing function of the stock price. Both of these compound calls vary in price, as would the price of the underlying options. However, as Figures 18.1C–D show, the value of a put-on-a-call is a decreasing function of the stock price, while the price of a put-on-a-put increases with an increasing stock price.

CHOOSER OPTIONS

The owner of a **chooser option** has the right to determine whether the chooser option will become a call or a put option by a specified choice date. After the choice date, the option becomes a plain vanilla call or put, depending on the owner's choice. Chooser options are also known as **as-you-like-it options**. Bankers Trust offers several types of chooser options in the over-the-counter market.[4] Chooser options are useful for hedging a future event that might not occur. For example, while Congress considered the North American Free Trade Agreement (NAFTA) in 1993, there was considerable uncertainty about the bill's passage. Passage was expected to be beneficial to the value of the Mexican peso; rejection of the bill was expected to send the peso tumbling. Traders could hedge this uncertainty with a chooser option on the Mexican peso. If NAFTA passed, one could choose to let the option be a call; if the bill failed, the owner could choose to let the option be a put.[5]

Put-on-a-Call Price as a Function of the Stock Price | **Figure 18.1C**

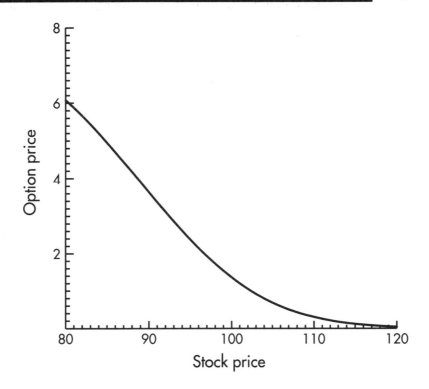

In considering chooser options, there are three dates to consider: the valuation date, t; the choice date, when the owner of the chooser must choose for the option to be a call or put, tc; and the expiration of the option, T. The dates must have the following relative values:

$$t \leq tc \leq T$$

The problem is to evaluate the option at time t, before the choice date. After the choice date, the value of the option will simply be the value of the plain vanilla call or put given by the Merton model. In our treatment of chooser options, we will focus on simple chooser options, in which the potential put and call have a common exercise price and expiration date. Complex choosers allow the potential call and put to have different exercise prices, different expiration dates, or both different exercise prices and expiration dates.

For a simple chooser, there are two extreme values for the choice date, tc, to consider. If the choice must be made immediately, $t = tc$, then the owner of the chooser will choose that the option be a call or a put, whichever has a greater value:

$$\text{If } t = tc, \text{ then Chooser}_t = \text{MAX}\begin{Bmatrix} C(S, X, T - t, \sigma, r, \delta) \\ P(S, X, T - t, \sigma, r, \delta) \end{Bmatrix}$$

Figure 18.1D   **Put-on-a-Put Price as a Function of the Stock Price**

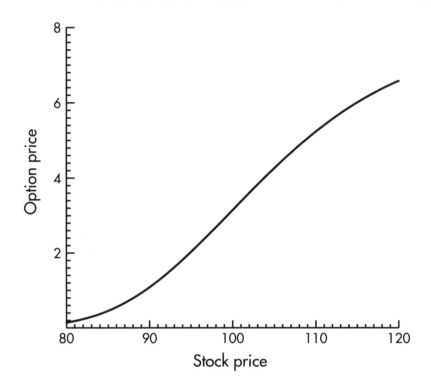

If the choice date is at the expiration of the option, $tc = T$, then the chooser is really a straddle. Viewed from the valuation date, T, the value of the straddle is the value of the call and the put:

$$\text{If } t = T, \text{ then Chooser}_t = C(S, X, T - t, \sigma, r, \delta) + P(S, X, T - t, \sigma, r, \delta)$$

Thus, these extreme values for the choice date determine the upper and lower bounds for the value of a simple chooser. If the choice date is now, $t = tc$, then the chooser value is at the lower bound and equals the maximum of the call or put value. If the choice can be deferred until the expiration date, $tc = T$, then the value of the chooser is the same as a straddle and equals the combined value of the plain vanilla call plus the plain vanilla put.

In the normal event, when the choice date, tc, is after t but before T, one will not want to choose whether the option is a call or put until the choice date. Therefore, the payoff on a chooser comes on the choice date, and it will be:

$$\text{Chooser}_{tc} = \text{MAX}\begin{Bmatrix} C(S_{tc}, X, T - tc, \sigma, r, \delta) \\ P(S_{tc}, X, T - tc, \sigma, r, \delta) \end{Bmatrix}$$

Applying put-call parity, the value of the Chooser at *tc* is:

$$\text{Chooser}_{tc} = \text{MAX}\left\{ \begin{array}{l} C(S_{tc},\, X,\, T - tc,\, \sigma,\, r,\, \delta) \\ C(S_{tc},\, X,\, T - tc,\, \sigma,\, r,\, \delta) + Xe^{-r(T-tc)} - S_{tc}e^{-\delta(T-tc)} \end{array} \right\}$$

This is equivalent to:

$$\text{Chooser}_{tc} = C(S_{tc},\, X,\, T - tc,\, \sigma,\, r,\, \delta) + \max\{0,\, Xe^{-r(T-tc)} - S_{tc}e^{-\delta(T-tc)}\}$$

Viewed from the present valuation date, *t*, this payoff at *tc* means that the value of the chooser will be the same as the following portfolio:

$$C(S,\, X,\, T - t,\, \sigma,\, r,\, \delta) + P(Se^{-\delta(T-tc)},\, Xe^{-r(T-tc)},\, tc - t,\, \sigma,\, \delta)$$

Therefore, the value of a simple chooser at time *t* is:

$$\text{Chooser}_t = Se^{-\delta(T-t)}N(w_1) - Xe^{-r(T-t)}N(w_1 - \sigma\sqrt{T - t}) + Xe^{-r(T-t)}N(-w_2 + \sigma\sqrt{tc - t}) - Se^{-\delta(T-t)}N(-w_2)$$

$$\tag{18.9}$$

where the values of w_1 and w_2 are:

$$w_1 = \frac{\ln\left(\dfrac{S}{X}\right) + (r - \delta + 0.5\sigma^2)(T - t)}{\sigma\sqrt{T - t}}$$

$$w_2 = \frac{\ln\left(\dfrac{S}{X}\right) + (r - \delta)(T - t) + 0.5\sigma^2(tc - t)}{\sigma\sqrt{tc - t}}$$

In equation 18.9, the value of the chooser has two parts. The first portion, with the form $S - X$, corresponds to the value of the potential call, while the second portion, with the form $X - S$, corresponds to the value of the potential put.

As a calculation example, consider the following data:

$$S = 100$$
$$X = 100$$
$$T - t = 1 \text{ year}$$
$$\sigma = 0.25$$
$$r = 0.10$$
$$\delta = 0.05$$
$$tc = 0.5 \text{ years}$$

With these values, we first compute w_1 and w_2, finding that $w_1 = 0.3250$ and $w_2 = 0.371231$. The cumulative normal values required are:

$$N(w_1) = N(0.3250) = 0.627409$$

$$N(-w_2) = N(-0.371231) = 0.355233$$

$$N(w_1 - \sigma\sqrt{T - t}) = N(0.3250 - 0.25) = 0.529893$$

$$N(-w_2 + \sigma\sqrt{tc - t}) = N(-0.371231 + 0.17678) = 0.422910$$

Applying these values to equation 18.9, we find:

$$\begin{aligned}
\text{Chooser}_t = &\ 100(0.951229)(0.627409) - 100(0.904837)(0.529893) \\
&+ 100(0.904837)(0.422910) - 100(0.951229)(0.355233) \\
= &\ 16.2100
\end{aligned}$$

We can verify that the value of this chooser lies between the lower and upper bounds by computing the value of the corresponding plain vanilla call and put. With the same parameter values, the call is worth 11.7343 and the put is worth 7.0951. We noted that the lower bound for the price of the chooser would be the maximum value of either the plain vanilla call or the put. The upper bound for the price of the chooser is the combined value of the call and put, which is equivalent to the straddle:

$$\text{MAX\{plain vanilla call or put\}} \leq \text{Chooser} \leq \text{plain vanilla call} + \text{plain vanilla put}$$
$$\text{MAX\{11.7343, 7.0951\}} \leq \text{Chooser} \leq 11.7343 + 7.0951$$
$$11.7343 \leq \text{Chooser} = 16.21 \leq 18.8294$$

Figure 18.2 shows how the value of a chooser option varies with the stock price by using the same parameter values as our example chooser and allowing the stock price to vary. The parabolic shape of the graph reflects the characteristic graph of a straddle, such as that shown in Figure 5.20. Figure 18.3 shows more specifically how the value of our example chooser will vary with the time until the choice must be made. If the choice must be made immediately, Figure 18.3 shows that the value of the chooser will be 11.73, which equals the value of the plain vanilla call. If the choice can be deferred until expiration, Figure 18.3 shows that the value of the chooser is the same as the value of the straddle, which is 18.83.

BARRIER OPTIONS

Barrier options can be "in" options or "out" options. An "in" barrier option has no value until the price of the underlying good touches a certain barrier price. When that happens, the option becomes a plain vanilla option. Accordingly, an "out" option is initially like a plain vanilla option, except if the price of the underlying good penetrates the stated barrier, the option immediately expires worthless. Barrier options can be either calls or puts, permitting eight types of barrier options:

The Price of a Simple Chooser Option as a Function of the Stock Price	**Figure 18.2**

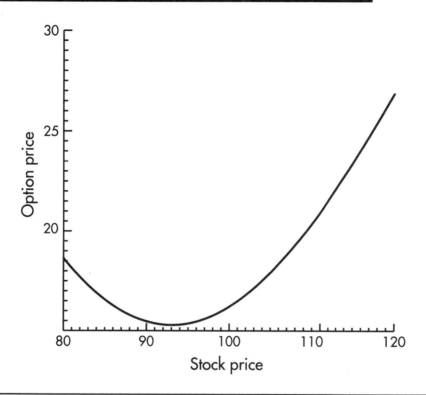

Down-and-in call
Up-and-in call
Down-and-in put
Up-and-out put
Down-and-out call
Up-and-out call
Down-and-out put
Up-and-out put

Barrier options may also pay a rebate, which is a booby prize. For an "out" barrier option, the rebate is paid immediately when the barrier is hit and the option passes out of existence. For an "in" barrier option, the rebate is paid if the option expires without ever hitting the barrier price. Barrier options, also known as **knock-in** and **knock-out** options, exhibit path dependence. The value of a barrier option at the present depends on the previous sequence of stock prices, particularly on whether the stock price has already hit the barrier for an "in" option. The current price of a barrier option can

Figure 18.3 **Price of a Chooser Option as a Function of the Days Until the Choice Date**

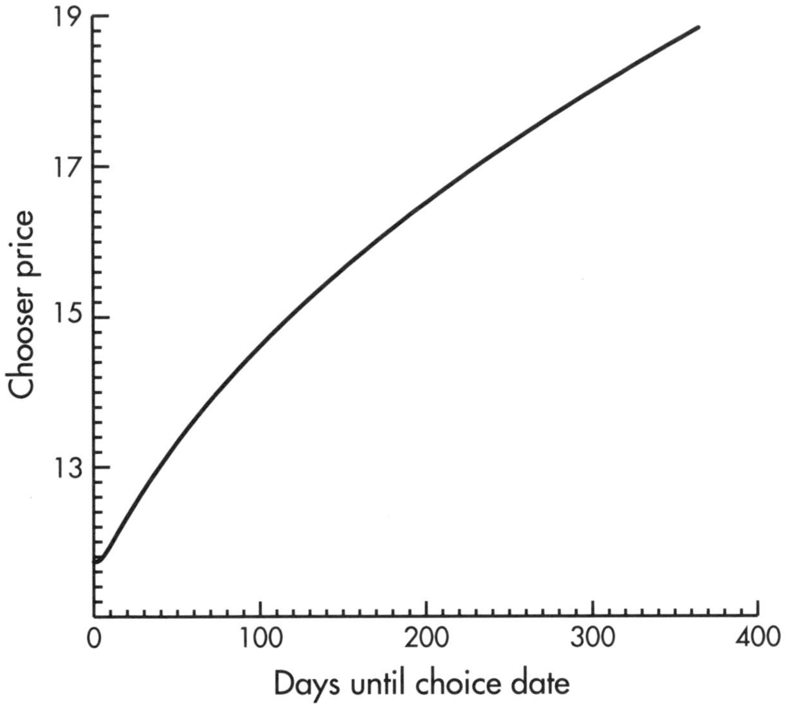

also depend on the future price path of the underlying stock – will the price hit the barrier between now and expiration?

Barrier options may be viewed as conditional plain vanilla options. "In" barrier options become plain vanilla options if the barrier is hit. "Out" barrier options are plain vanilla options, with the condition that they may pass out of existence if the barrier is hit. These conditions make barrier options inferior to unconditional plain vanilla options, so barrier options will be cheaper than otherwise identical plain vanilla options. This cheapness gives barrier options a special usefulness in hedging applications. For example, a portfolio manager may expect the value of her portfolio to increase but wish to protect against the possibility of a large drop in value. Accordingly, she might buy a put option with an exercise price slightly below the present price of the portfolio. As we saw in Chapter 11, this is essentially a portfolio insurance strategy. By buying a down-and-in put instead of a plain vanilla put, the portfolio manager can get the same protection, but at a cheaper price.

Figure 18.4 shows how payoffs arise for a down-and-in option. As mentioned earlier, the stock price must be above the barrier for such an option to be interesting. If the stock price is below the barrier, the barrier has been touched and the barrier option has already become a plain vanilla option. Thus, the initial stock price will exceed the barrier, but the exercise price may be either higher or

Alternative Stock Price Paths for Down-and-In Barrier Options   Figure 18.4

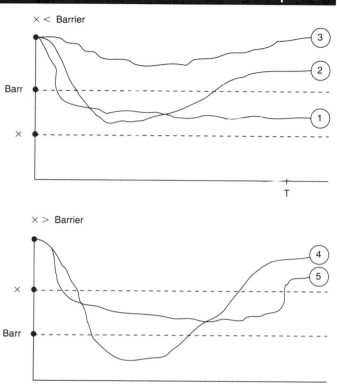

lower than the barrier. The top panel of Figure 18.4 shows a situation in which the barrier, BARR, exceeds the exercise price, X. Three stock price paths are shown in this panel. First, the stock price may penetrate the barrier and terminate above the exercise price but below the barrier. Second, the stock price may penetrate the barrier, and the terminal price might exceed the barrier. (We distinguish these two cases, because the probabilities associated with these two price paths are different, even though they have the same payoff.) Third, the stock price may never penetrate the barrier and the payoff is the rebate amount, REBATE. The bottom panel shows a similar situation, except in this case the exercise price exceeds the barrier. In price path 4, the stock price penetrates the barrier, but terminates above the exercise price. Finally, in price path 5, the barrier is never hit so the payoff is REBATE. As Figure 18.4 pertains only to down-and-in options, we must also consider down-and-out options, particularly the fact that the rebate is paid immediately upon the barrier being pierced. This gives a sixth payoff possibility.

   As an example, we focus on the payoffs from a down-and-in call. For this option, there are three possible payoff outcomes: if the barrier is never touched, the payoff is REBATE; if the barrier is touched, and $S_T > X$, the payoff is $S_T - X$; and if the barrier is touched, and $S_T \leq X$, the payoff is 0. There are alternative ways that these various payoffs may be earned, particularly when we realize it is possible for the exercise price to be either above or below the barrier price. To price a down-and-in call, we must consider these five price paths and their associated payoffs, for a stock price at expiration of S_T:

1. BARRIER $\geq S_T \geq X$; payoff is $S_T - X$
2. $S_T \geq$ BARRIER $\geq X$, and the barrier was touched; payoff is $S_T - X$
3. $S_T \geq$ BARRIER $\geq X$, and the barrier was never touched; payoff is REBATE
4. $S_T \geq X \geq$ BARRIER, and the barrier was touched; payoff is $S_T - X$
5. $S_T \geq X \geq$ BARRIER, and the barrier was never touched; payoff is REBATE

The value of a down-and-in call is the present expected value of these payoffs. In addition, for an "out" option there is a sixth price path and payoff to consider, which is presented later. For each type of option, we need expressions for these possible payoffs and price paths.

We define some intermediate values prior to considering the six payoff/probability expressions that cover both "in" and "out" barrier options:

$$\lambda = \frac{r - \delta + 0.5\sigma^2}{\sigma^2}$$

$$\mu = r - \delta - 0.5\sigma^2$$

$$a = \frac{\mu}{\sigma^2} \qquad b = \frac{\sqrt{\mu^2 + 2r\sigma^2}}{\sigma^2}$$

Letting BARR indicate the barrier price, we define:

$$w_1 = \frac{\ln\left(\dfrac{S}{X}\right)}{\sigma\sqrt{T-t}} + \lambda\sigma\sqrt{T-t}$$

$$w_2 = \frac{\ln\left(\dfrac{S}{\text{BARR}}\right)}{\sigma\sqrt{T-t}} + \lambda\sigma\sqrt{T-t}$$

$$w_3 = \frac{\ln\left(\dfrac{\text{BARR}^2}{SX}\right)}{\sigma\sqrt{T-t}} + \lambda\sigma\sqrt{T-t}$$

$$w_4 = \frac{\ln\left(\dfrac{\text{BARR}}{S}\right)}{\sigma\sqrt{T-t}} + \lambda\sigma\sqrt{T-t}$$

$$w_5 = \frac{\ln\left(\dfrac{BARR}{S}\right)}{\sigma\sqrt{T-t}} + b\sigma\sqrt{T-t}$$

Tables 18.1 through 18.4 present expressions for the present values of payoffs resulting from particular price paths with their associated probabilities. Table 18.5 shows the value of each possible barrier option in terms of the expressions in Tables 18.1 through 18.4.

As an example, let us consider a down-and-in call with the exercise price lying above the barrier ($X > BARR$). According to Table 18.1, the value of this call will be DC4 + DC5. This analysis corresponds to the bottom panel of Figure 18.4. The value of this down-and-in call (given that $X > BARR$) is the present value of the two payoffs, $S_T - X$ or REBATE, multiplied by their associated probabilities.[6]

Pursuing this same example, we will compute the value of a down-and-in call (with $X > BARR$) using the following data:

$$S = 100$$
$$X = 100$$
$$T - t = 1 \text{ year}$$
$$\sigma = 0.2$$
$$r = 0.1$$
$$\delta = 0.05$$
$$BARR = 97$$
$$REBATE = 2$$

where BARR is the barrier price and REBATE is the rebate amount. The value of this down-and-in call will be DC4 + DC5, so we will need the intermediate values of λ, w_2, w_3, and w_4. These values

Valuation Expressions for Down Calls	Table 18.1

DC1
$$Se^{-\delta(T-t)}N(w_1) - Xe^{-r(T-t)}N(w_1 - \sigma\sqrt{T-t})$$

DC2
$$Se^{-\delta(T-t)}N(w_2) - Xe^{-r(T-t)}N(w_2 - \sigma\sqrt{T-t})$$

DC3
$$Se^{-\delta(T-t)}\left(\frac{BARR}{S}\right)^{2\lambda}N(w_4) - Xe^{-r(T-t)}\left(\frac{BARR}{S}\right)^{2\lambda-2}N(w_4 - \sigma\sqrt{T-t})$$

DC4
$$Se^{-\delta(T-t)}\left(\frac{BARR}{S}\right)^{2\lambda}N(w_3) - Xe^{-r(T-t)}\left(\frac{BARR}{S}\right)^{2\lambda-2}N(w_3 - \sigma\sqrt{T-t})$$

DC5
$$REBATE\,e^{-r(T-t)}\left\{N(w_2 - \sigma\sqrt{T-t}) - \left(\frac{BARR}{S}\right)^{2\lambda-2}N(w_4 - \sigma\sqrt{T-t})\right\}$$

DC6
$$REBATE\left\{\left(\frac{BARR}{S}\right)^{a+b}N(w_5) + \left(\frac{BARR}{S}\right)^{a-b}N(w_5 - 2b\sigma\sqrt{T-t})\right\}$$

Table 18.2	Valuation Expressions for Down Puts
DP1	$Xe^{-r(T-t)}N(-w_1 + \sigma\sqrt{T-t}) - Se^{-\delta(T-t)}N(-w_1)$
DP2	$Xe^{-r(T-t)}N(-w_2 + \sigma\sqrt{T-t}) - Se^{-\delta(T-t)}N(-w_2)$
DP3	$Xe^{-r(T-t)}\left(\dfrac{\text{BARR}}{S}\right)^{2\lambda-2} N(w_4 - \sigma\sqrt{T-t}) - Se^{-\delta(T-t)}\left(\dfrac{\text{BARR}}{S}\right)^{2\lambda} N(w_4)$
DP4	$Xe^{-r(T-t)}\left(\dfrac{\text{BARR}}{S}\right)^{2\lambda-2} N(w_3 - \sigma\sqrt{T-t}) - Se^{-\delta(T-t)}\left(\dfrac{\text{BARR}}{S}\right)^{2\lambda} N(w_3)$
DP5	$\text{REBATE}\,e^{-r(T-t)}\left\{ N(w_2 - \sigma\sqrt{T-t}) - \left(\dfrac{\text{BARR}}{S}\right)^{2\lambda-2} N(w_4 - \sigma\sqrt{T-t}) \right\}$
DP6	$\text{REBATE}\left\{ \left(\dfrac{\text{BARR}}{S}\right)^{a+b} N(w_5) + \left(\dfrac{\text{BARR}}{S}\right)^{a-b} N(w_5 - 2b\sigma\sqrt{T-t}) \right\}$

Table 18.3	Valuation Expressions for Up Calls
UC1	$Se^{-\delta(T-t)}N(w_1) - Xe^{-r(T-t)}N(w_1 - \sigma\sqrt{T-t})$
UC2	$Se^{-\delta(T-t)}N(w_2) - Xe^{-r(T-t)}N(w_2 - \sigma\sqrt{T-t})$
UC3	$Se^{-\delta(T-t)}\left(\dfrac{\text{BARR}}{S}\right)^{2\lambda} N(-w_4) - Xe^{-r(T-t)}\left(\dfrac{\text{BARR}}{S}\right)^{2\lambda-2} N(-w_4 + \sigma\sqrt{T-t})$
UC4	$Se^{-\delta(T-t)}\left(\dfrac{\text{BARR}}{S}\right)^{2\lambda} N(-w_3) - Xe^{-r(T-t)}\left(\dfrac{\text{BARR}}{S}\right)^{2\lambda-2} N(-w_3 + \sigma\sqrt{T-t})$
UC5	$\text{REBATE}\,e^{-r(T-t)}\left\{ N(-w_2 + \sigma\sqrt{T-t}) - \left(\dfrac{\text{BARR}}{S}\right)^{2\lambda-2} N(-w_4 + \sigma\sqrt{T-t}) \right\}$
UC6	$\text{REBATE}\left\{ \left(\dfrac{\text{BARR}}{S}\right)^{a+b} N(-w_5) + \left(\dfrac{\text{BARR}}{S}\right)^{a-b} N(-w_5 + 2b\sigma\sqrt{T-t}) \right\}$

are: $\lambda = 1.75$; $w_2 = 0.502296$; $w_3 = 0.045408$; and $w_4 = 0.197704$. The needed cumulative normal values are:

$$N(w_3) = 0.518109$$
$$N(w_2 - \sigma\sqrt{T-t}) = 0.618787$$
$$N(w_3 - \sigma\sqrt{T-t}) = 0.438571$$
$$N(w_4 - \sigma\sqrt{T-t}) = 0.499084$$

	Valuation Expressions for Up Puts	Table 18.4

UP1
$$Xe^{-r(T-t)}N(-w_1 + \sigma\sqrt{T-t}) - Se^{-\delta(T-t)}N(-w_1)$$

UP2
$$Xe^{-r(T-t)}N(-w_2 + \sigma\sqrt{T-t}) - Se^{-\delta(T-t)}N(-w_2)$$

UP3
$$Xe^{-r(T-t)}\left(\frac{BARR}{S}\right)^{2\lambda-2} N(-w_4 + \sigma\sqrt{T-t}) - Se^{-\delta(T-t)}\left(\frac{BARR}{S}\right)^{2\lambda} N(-w_4)$$

UP4
$$Xe^{-r(T-t)}\left(\frac{BARR}{S}\right)^{2\lambda-2} N(-w_3 + \sigma\sqrt{T-t}) - Se^{-\delta(T-t)}\left(\frac{BARR}{S}\right)^{2\lambda} N(-w_3)$$

UP5
$$REBATE\,e^{-r(T-t)}\left\{ N(-w_2 + \sigma\sqrt{T-t}) - \left(\frac{BARR}{S}\right)^{2\lambda-2} N(-w_4 + \sigma\sqrt{T-t}) \right\}$$

UP6
$$REBATE\left\{ \left(\frac{BARR}{S}\right)^{a+b} N(-w_5) + \left(\frac{BARR}{S}\right)^{a-b} N(-w_5 + 2b\sigma\sqrt{T-t}) \right\}$$

	Valuation of Barrier Options	Table 18.5

	$X > BARR$	$X < BARR$
Down-and-In Call (DIC)	DC4 + DC5	DC1 − DC2 + DC3 + DC5
Up-and-In Call (UIC)	UC1 + UC5	UC2 − UC4 + UC3 + UC5
Down-and-In Put (DIP)	DP2 + DP3 − DP4 + DP5	DP1 + DP5
Up-and-In Put (UIP)	UP1 − UP2 + UP3 + UP5	UP4 + UP5
Down-and-Out Call (DOC)	DC1 − DC4 + DC6	DC2 − DC3 + DC6
Up-and-Out Call (UOC)	UC6	UC1 − UC2 − UC3 + UC4 + UC6
Down-and-Out Put (DOP)	DP1 − DP2 − DP3 + DP4 + DP6	DP6
Up-and-Out Put (UOP)	UP2 − UP3 + UP6	UP1 − UP4 + UP6

With these intermediate values, we can compute the values of DC4 and DC5 from Table 18.1:

$$DC4 = 100(0.951229)\left(\frac{97}{100}\right)^{3.5}(0.518109) - 100(0.904837)\left(\frac{97}{100}\right)^{1.5}(0.438571)$$

$$= 44.300383 - 37.911247$$

$$= 6.389136$$

$$DC5 = 2(0.904837)\left\{ 0.618787 - \left(\frac{97}{100}\right)^{1.5}(0.499084) \right\} = 0.256960$$

The value of the down-and-in call with an exercise price above the barrier, $DIC_{X>BARR}$, is the sum of the two portions, DC4 for the present value of the $S_T - X$ payoff, plus DC5 for the present value of the rebate payoff, where the payoffs are weighted by the probability that it will be received:

$$DIC = DC4 + DC5 = 6.3891 + 0.2570 = 6.6461$$

Figure 18.5 shows how our sample down-and-in call price varies as a function of the barrier price. If the barrier price is 50, the option is worth little, because the stock price stands at 100 and the chance of its falling to 50 within the next year is small. By contrast, if the barrier is near 100, the chance of hitting the barrier is much greater, so the barrier option price is closer to that of a plain vanilla call. With these same parameter values, a plain vanilla call would be worth 9.94.

For our particular barrier option, with BARR = 97 and REBATE = 2, the computed price was 6.6461. Only 0.26 of this price was attributable to the barrier, which was DC5. For the same barrier option with BARR = 97 and REBATE = 0, the price of the option is 6.3891. By focusing on this same option, but assuming that REBATE = 0, we can see how the price of the barrier option approaches the price of a plain vanilla call as the barrier is set closer to the current stock price of 100. Assuming that REBATE = 0, our option would be worth 6.39 with BARR = 97; 7.46 with BARR = 98; 8.64 with BARR = 99; and 9.94 (the same as the plain vanilla call) with BARR = 99.9999.

Figure 18.5	Down-and-In Call Price as a Function of the Barrier Price

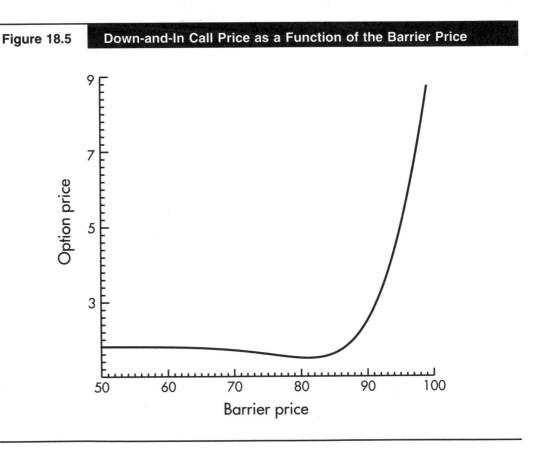

BINARY OPTIONS

Binary options have payoffs that are discontinuous, either paying nothing or a considerable amount depending on the satisfaction of some condition. For example, a **cash-or-nothing** call is a type of binary option that pays a fixed cash amount if the stock price terminates above the exercise price or pays nothing if the terminal stock price is below the exercise price. Other types of binary options that we will consider in this section are **asset-or-nothing options**, **gap options**, and **supershares**. These binary options are also known as **digital options**, a name that reflects the all-or-nothing character of their payoffs.[7]

Cash-or-Nothing Options

A cash-or-nothing call pays a fixed cash amount, Z, if the terminal stock price, S_T, exceeds the exercise price, X; otherwise the call pays nothing. Similarly, a cash-or-nothing put pays a fixed cash amount, Z, if the terminal stock price is below the exercise price. These options require no payment of an exercise price. Instead, the exercise price merely determines whether the option owner receives a payoff. Viewed from the perspective of the valuation date, t, the value of a cash-or-nothing call will simply be the present value of the fixed cash payoff multiplied by the probability that the terminal stock price will exceed the exercise price. Let $CONC_t$ and $CONP_t$ indicate cash-or-nothing calls or puts, respectively.

From the Merton model, the probability of the option finishing in the money is d_2^M. The present value of the fixed cash payoff, Z, is $Ze^{-r(T-t)}$. Therefore, the value of a cash-or-nothing call is:

$$CONC_t = Ze^{-r(T-t)}N(d_2^M) \qquad (18.10)$$

By analogous reasoning, the value of a cash-or-nothing put is:

$$CONP_t = Ze^{-r(T-t)}N(-d_2^M) \qquad (18.11)$$

Consider now a cash-or-nothing call and put with the following parameter values:

$$S = 100$$
$$X = 105$$
$$T - t = 0.5 \text{ years}$$
$$\sigma = 0.2$$
$$r = 0.1$$
$$\delta = 0.05$$
$$Z = 100$$

where Z is the fixed cash amount that the option owner receives if the option finishes in-the-money. For these values:

$$d_2^M = \dfrac{\ln\left(\dfrac{S_t}{X}\right) + (r - \delta + .5\sigma^2)(T - t)}{\sigma\sqrt{T - t}} - \sigma\sqrt{T - t}$$

$$= \dfrac{\ln\left(\dfrac{100}{105}\right) + [0.1 - 0.05 + 0.5(0.2)(0.2)](0.5)}{0.2\sqrt{0.5}} - 0.2\sqrt{0.5}$$

$$= -0.238933$$

and $N(d_2^M) = N(-0.238933) = 0.405579$. For the put $N(-d_2^M) = N(0.238933) = 0.594421$. The values of the two options are:

$$\text{CONC}_t = Ze^{-r(T-t)}N(d_2^M) = 100e^{-0.1(0.5)}(0.405579) = 38.5799$$

$$\text{CONP}_t = Ze^{-r(T-t)}N(-d_2^M) = 100e^{-0.1(0.5)}(0.594421) = 56.5431$$

Notice that a portfolio consisting of a cash-or-nothing call and put (with the same payoff and term to expiration) has a certain payoff. Specifically, the portfolio will pay the common amount, Z. Therefore:

$$\text{CONC}_t + \text{CONP}_t = Ze^{-r(T-t)}, \text{ for a common expiration and a common } Z$$

Figure 18.6 shows how the values of these options vary as a function of the stock price. The value of the two options together equals the present value of Z no matter what the stock price might be.

Asset-or-Nothing Options

Asset-or-nothing options are similar to cash-or-nothing options, with one major difference. Instead of paying a fixed cash amount as cash-or-nothing options do, the payoff on an **asset-or-nothing** option is the underlying asset. If the terminal asset price exceeds the exercise price, the owner of a call receives the asset, but if the terminal asset price is below the exercise price, the call expires worthless. For a put, if the terminal asset price is less than the exercise price, the put owner receives the asset, but if the terminal asset price exceeds the exercise price, the put expires worthless. As with cash-or-nothing options, the exercise price is never paid. Instead, the value of the asset relative to the exercise price determines whether the option pays off or is worthless.

For an asset-or-nothing call (AONC), the value is simply the present value of the asset, depreciated for dividends between the present and expiration, multiplied by the probability that the terminal asset price will exceed the exercise price. Similarly, the asset-or-nothing put (AONP) is worth the present value of the asset, discounted for the dividends between the present and expiration, multiplied by the probability that the terminal asset price will be below the exercise price. Thus, the values of the options are:

$$\text{AONC}_t = e^{-\delta(T-t)}S_t N(d_1^M) \qquad\qquad (18.12)$$

$$\text{AONP}_t = e^{-\delta(T-t)}S_t N(-d_1^M)$$

The Value of Cash-or-Nothing Options as a Function of the Stock Price | Figure 18.6

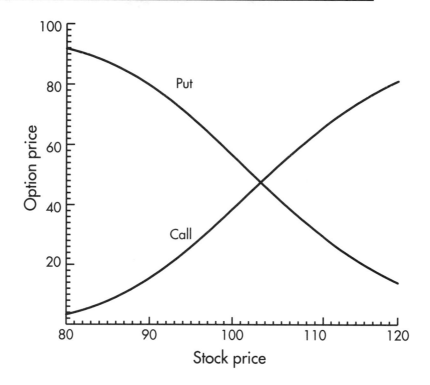

A portfolio of an asset-or-nothing call and put, with the same term to expiration and underlying asset, is worth the present value of the asset discounted for the dividends to be paid over the life of the option:

$$AONC_t + AONP_t = e^{-\delta(T-t)}S_t N(d_1^M) + e^{-\delta(T-t)}S_t N(-d_1^M)$$
$$= e^{-\delta(T-t)}S_t [N(d_1^M) + N(-d_1^M)]$$
$$= e^{-\delta(T-t)}S_t$$

As an example, consider asset-or-nothing options with the following parameters:

$S = 100$
$X = 90$
$T - t = 0.5$ years
$\sigma = 0.2$
$r = 0.1$
$\delta = 0.05$

With these values: $d_1^M = 0.992499$; $N(d_1^M) = N(0.992499) = 0.839523$; and $N(-d_1^M) = N(-0.992499) = 0.160477$. The option values with these parameters are:

$$AONC_t = e^{-\delta(T-t)}S_tN(d_1^M) = e^{-.05(0.5)}100(0.839523) = 81.8795$$

$$AONP_t = e^{-\delta(T-t)}S_tN(-d_1^M) = e^{-.05(0.5)}100(0.160477) = 15.6515$$

Figure 18.7 graphs the value of our two sample options as a function of the stock price. Notice that the shape of the value curves in this figure are quite similar to those for the cash-or-nothing options in Figure 18.6. When the stock price is high, say around 120, the asset-or-nothing put is worth very little, reflecting the slight chance that the terminal stock price will be below the exercise price of 90. With a high stock price, the call is worth very nearly the same as the stock. For example, with a stock price of 100, the call is worth 81.88, as we have seen, and the present value of the asset is 97.53, so the call is worth 83.95 percent of the asset. For a stock price of 120, with a present value of 117.04, the call is worth 115.72, or 98.87 percent of the present value of the asset. Finally, if the stock is at 150, the call is worth 146.29, which equals the present value of the stock.

Figure 18.7   **The Value of Asset-or-Nothing Options as a Function of the Stock Price**

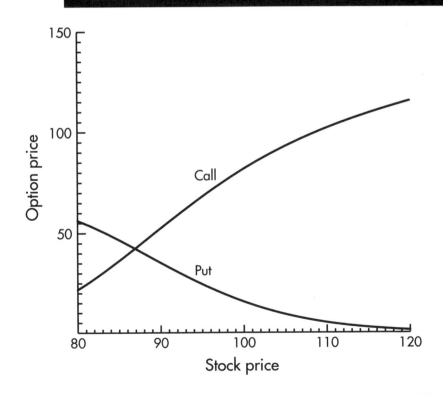

Gap Options

Gap options are similar to plain vanilla options, except the payoff is determined as a function of the exercise price. The payoff on a gap option depends on the usual factors in a plain vanilla option, but it is also affected by the gap amount, which may be negative or positive. Letting the value of the gap be indicated by g, the value of a gap call $(GAPC_t)$ and a gap put $(GAPP_t)$ are:

$$GAPC_t = e^{-\delta(T-t)}S_t N(d_1^M) - (X + g)e^{-r(T-t)}N(d_2^M) \tag{18.13}$$

$$GAPP_t = (X + g)e^{-r(T-t)}N(-d_2^M) - e^{-\delta(T-t)}S_t N(-d_1^M)$$

These formulas are very similar to those for plain vanilla options according to the Merton model, with the values for d_1^M and d_2^M being identical to those from the Merton model. In the valuation formulas, the gap amount is added to the exercise price so the quantity $X + g$ replaces X in the valuation formulas (but not in the formulas for d_1^M and d_2^M).

As an example of gap options, consider the following parameters:

$$S = 100$$
$$X = 90$$
$$T - t = 0.5 \text{ years}$$
$$\sigma = 0.3$$
$$r = 0.1$$
$$\delta = 0.05$$

With these values we will compute the value of a gap call with a positive gap $g = 5$ and a gap put with a negative gap, $g = -5$. Both options have common values for d_1^M and d_2^M:

$$d_1^M = \frac{\ln\left(\dfrac{100}{90}\right) + [0.1 - 0.05 + 0.5(0.3)(0.3)](0.5)}{0.3\sqrt{0.5}} = 0.720591$$

$$d_2^M = d_1^M - \sigma\sqrt{T - t} = 0.720591 - 0.3\sqrt{0.5} = 0.508459$$

Corresponding cumulative values are $N(d_1^M) = 0.764420$, $N(d_2^M) = 0.694434$, $N(-d_1^M) = 0.235580$, and $N(-d_2^M) = 0.305566$. With $g = +5$ for the gap call and $g = -5$ for the gap put, the option values are:

$$GAPC_t = 100e^{-0.05(0.5)}0.764420 - (90 + 5)e^{-0.1(0.5)}0.694434$$

$$= 11.8008$$

$$GAPP_t = (90 - 5)e^{-0.1(0.5)}0.305566 - 100e^{-0.05(0.5)}0.235580$$

$$= 1.7300$$

Figure 18.8 focuses on the gap call of this example, in which the call had a positive gap of 5. As Equation 18.13 makes clear, a positive gap for a call effectively increases the exercise price,

Figure 18.8   **Gap Call Prices as a Function of the Stock Price**

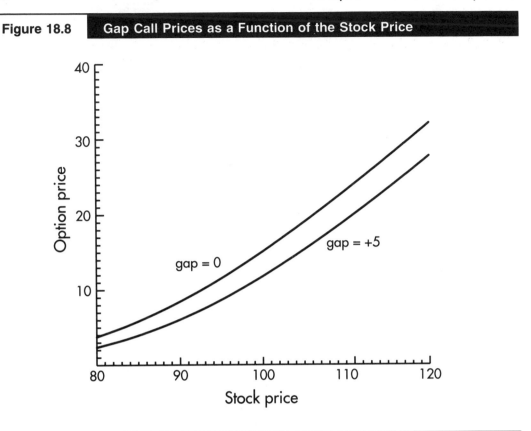

which is a liability from the point of view of the call's owner. Therefore, a positive gap for a call decreases the value of the call relative to an otherwise identical plain vanilla call. In Figure 18.8, the lower line graphs the value of the gap call of our computational example. The upper line graphs the value of the otherwise similar call with a zero gap, $g = 0$. When $g = 0$, the gap option becomes a plain vanilla option.

Supershares

A **supershare** is a financial instrument whose value depends on an underlying portfolio of other financial assets. A supershare represents a contingent claim on a fraction of the underlying portfolio. The contingency is that the value of the underlying portfolio must lie between a lower and an upper bound on a certain future date. If the value of the underlying portfolio lies between the bounds, the supershare is worth a proportion of the portfolio. If the value of the portfolio lies outside the bounds, the supershare expires worthless.[8]

    The basic idea behind supershares is the creation of a financial intermediary that holds a portfolio of securities and issues two kinds of claims against that portfolio. The first kind of claim is a supershare, which has an uncertain payoff depending on the performance of the portfolio. The second kind of claim is a purchasing power bond that pays a given rate of real interest. In our analysis, we are concerned with the claim that has an uncertain payoff – the supershare.

Letting X_L indicate the lower bound and X_U represent the upper bound, the payoffs for the supershare on the expiration date, T, are as follows:

$$S_T/X_L \text{ if } X_L \leq S_T \leq X_H; 0 \text{ otherwise}$$

A supershare is essentially like a portfolio of two asset-or-nothing calls, in which the owner of a supershare purchases an asset-or-nothing call with an exercise price of X_L and sells an asset-or-nothing call with an exercise price of X_H. This is quite similar to the bull spread with calls that we considered in Chapter 11. As such the price of a supershare is:

$$SS = \frac{Se^{-\delta(T-t)}}{X_L}[N(w_L) - N(w_H)] \tag{18.14}$$

where:

$$w_L = \frac{\ln\left(\dfrac{S}{X_L}\right) + (r - \delta + 0.5\sigma^2)(T - t)}{\sigma\sqrt{T - t}}$$

and:

$$w_H = \frac{\ln\left(\dfrac{S}{X_H}\right) + (r - \delta + 0.5\sigma^2)(T - t)}{\sigma\sqrt{T - t}}$$

As a calculation example, consider the following data:

$$S = 100$$
$$X_L = 100$$
$$X_H = 105$$
$$T - t = 0.5 \text{ years}$$
$$\sigma = 0.2$$
$$r = 0.1$$
$$\delta = 0.05$$

With these input values, $w_L = 0.247487$, $w_H = -0.097511$, $N(w_L) = 0.597735$, and $N(w_H) = 0.461160$. The value of this supershare is:

$$SS = \frac{100e^{-0.05(0.5)}}{100}[0.599735 - 0.461160] = 0.1352$$

Figure 18.9 shows how the price of this supershare varies with the stock price. The higher, more sharply curved line in the figure is the graph of our example supershare. Notice that the price of the supershare is 13.52 when the stock price is 100. The value of the supershare reaches its highest value for stock prices in the neighborhood of 100–105. This neighborhood is exactly the range of the lower and upper bounds that determine the payoff. Notice also that the shape of this line is quite similar to that of a short position in a strangle as in Figure 5.16.

The flatter curve in Figure 18.9 is for the same supershare, except it assumes that the underlying stock has a standard deviation of 0.4. With a higher standard deviation, there is less chance that the terminal stock price will fall in the range of 100–105, so the supershare written on a higher risk stock has a lower value.

LOOKBACK OPTIONS

For a plain vanilla option, the payoff depends only on the terminal stock price, not the price at any other time. For a **lookback option**, the exercise price and the option's payoff are functions of the price of the underlying good up to the expiration of the option. For lookback calls, the exercise price is the minimum stock price experienced over the life of the option. For lookback puts, the exercise

Figure 18.9   **Supershare Prices as a Function of the Stock Price**

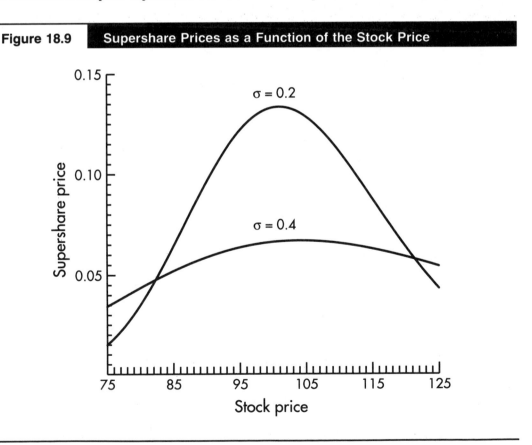

price is the maximum stock price over the same period. Thus, it is said of lookback options that they allow the option owner to "buy at the low and sell at the high." Of course, this opportunity will be priced in a rational market.

Consider the decision to purchase a lookback at time t with expiration at time T. The payoffs on the lookback call (LBC) and put (LBP) would be:

$$\text{LBC: } \max\{0, S_T - \min[S_t, S_{t+1}, \ldots, S_T]\}$$
$$\text{LBP: } \max\{0, \max[S_t, S_{t+1}, \ldots, S_T] - S_T\}$$

In effect, a lookback call allows the purchaser to acquire the asset at its minimum price over the life of the option, while the lookback put allows the owner to sell the asset at its maximum price over the relevant interval. Of course, the option to make these transactions has considerable value. Notice that lookbacks should always be exercised. For a call, the terminal stock price will always exceed some price experienced on the asset during its life. For a put, the terminal stock price will always be less than some stock price during the interval. Lookback options are clearly path dependent options, because the value ultimately depends on the minimum or maximum stock price reached over the life of the option, not merely on the terminal price when the option expires.[9]

Assuming that the stock price is observed continuously, the value of a lookback call is:

$$\text{LBC} = Se^{-\delta(T-t)} - \text{MINPRI}e^{-r(T-t)}N\left(\frac{b + \mu(T - t)}{\sigma\sqrt{T - t}}\right)$$
$$+ \text{MINPRI}e^{-r(T-t)}\lambda e^{b(1-1/\lambda)}N\left(\frac{-b + \mu(T - t)}{\sigma\sqrt{T - t}}\right) \quad (18.15)$$
$$- Se^{-\delta(T-t)}(1 + \lambda)N\left(\frac{-b - \mu(T - t) - \sigma^2(T - t)}{\sigma\sqrt{T - t}}\right)$$

where MINPRI = the minimum price of the underlying asset experienced during the life of the option and:

$$b = \ln\left(\frac{S}{\text{MINPRI}}\right); \qquad \mu = r - \delta - 0.5\sigma^2; \qquad \lambda = \frac{0.5\sigma^2}{r - \delta}$$

$$\text{LBP} = -Se^{-\delta(T-t)} + \text{MAXPRI}e^{-r(T-t)}N\left(\frac{-b - \mu(T - t)}{\sigma\sqrt{T - t}}\right)$$
$$- \text{MAXPRI}e^{-r(T-t)}\lambda e^{b(1-1/\lambda)}N\left(\frac{b - \mu(T - t)}{\sigma\sqrt{T - t}}\right) \quad (18.16)$$
$$+ Se^{-\delta(T-t)}(1 + \lambda)N\left(\frac{b + \mu(T - t) + \sigma^2(T - t)}{\sigma\sqrt{T - t}}\right)$$

where MAXPRI is the maximum price experienced during the life of the option. The variables λ and μ are the same as defined for the lookback call, but the definition of b for the lookback put is:

$$b = \ln\left(\frac{S}{\text{MAXPRI}}\right)$$

As an example of lookback call pricing, consider the following values:

$$S = 100$$
$$\text{MINPRI} = 90$$
$$T - t = 0.5 \text{ years}$$
$$\sigma = 0.3$$
$$r = 0.1$$
$$\delta = 0.05$$

Using these data, we will compute the value of the lookback call. The intermediate values we need are:

$$b = \ln\left(\frac{100}{90}\right) = 0.105361$$

$$\lambda = \frac{0.5(0.3)(0.3)}{0.10 - 0.05} = 0.9$$

$$\mu = [0.1 - 0.05 - 0.5(0.3)(0.3)] = 0.005$$

The value for the lookback call, taking into account all of the discounting and showing the value of the arguments for the cumulative normal function, is:

$$\text{LBC} = 97.5310 - 85.6106N(0.508462)$$
$$+ 85.6106 \; 0.9e^{0.105361(-0.1111)}N(-0.484891)$$
$$- 97.5310(1.9)N(-0.720594)$$

Thus, the value of the lookback call is:

$$\text{LBC} = 97.5310 - 59.4510 + 23.9027 - 43.6551 = 18.3275$$

Because lookbacks offer cheap exercise prices for calls and high payoffs for puts, lookbacks are worth considerably more than their plain vanilla counterparts. For a plain vanilla call with the same parameters, including the exercise price of 90, the price would be 15.10. Thus, the lookback call has a price that is 3.23 higher than the corresponding plain vanilla call. The difference could be even more severe. For example, consider the same input values used for the lookback call, but assume that the minimum price to date is 100. The price of this lookback would be 16.4920. The corresponding plain vanilla call, with $X = 100$, would be 9.3970.

Figure 18.10 graphs our sample option using the same parameters. The upper line of Figure 18.10 shows the value of the lookback call. The lower line shows the value of an otherwise similar plain vanilla call option with an exercise price $X = 90$. Notice that the volatility of these options is $\sigma = 0.3$. For higher volatility stocks, both the value of the lookback call and the plain vanilla call

The Value of a Lookback Call and a Plain Vanilla Call as a Function of the Stock Price   **Figure 18.10**

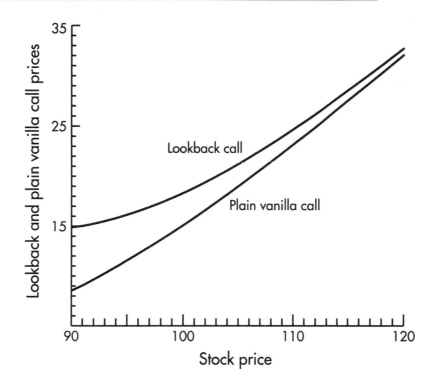

will be higher. Figure 18.11 shows the value of a lookback call and a corresponding plain vanilla call with the same parameter values as our sample option, except the volatility of the options is $\sigma = 0.9$. Comparing Figures 18.10 and 18.11 shows that the higher the volatility of the underlying stock, the greater will be the difference between the lookback and plain vanilla calls. The large percentage difference in the price of the lookback and plain vanilla calls emphasizes the costliness of lookbacks.

The high premiums on lookback options has hindered their popularity in actual markets. This limitation has led to the creation of **partial lookback options**. These partial lookbacks restrict the minimum or maximum used in computing the payoff in some way.[10]

AVERAGE PRICE OPTIONS

An **Asian option** is an option whose payoff depends on the average of the price of the underlying good or the average of the exercise price. (These options are called "Asian options" because Bankers Trust was the first to offer such products, and they offered them initially in their Tokyo office.[11]) In this section, we consider one type of Asian option, an average price option. In an average price

Figure 18.11	**The Value of a Lookback Call and a Plain Vanilla Call as a Function of the Stock Price**

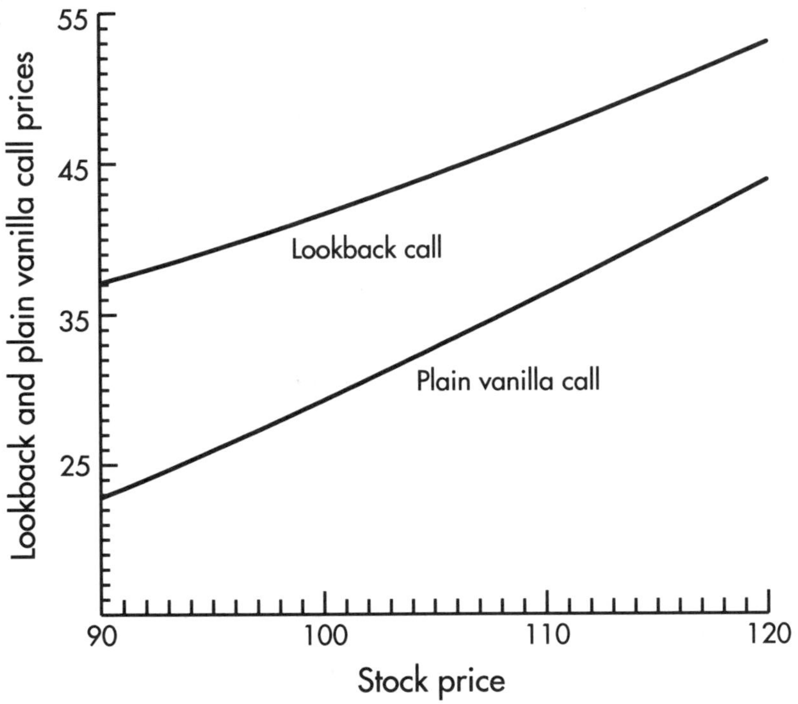

option, the average price of the underlying good essentially takes the place of the terminal price of the underlying good in determining the payoff.

Asian options are extremely useful in combating price manipulations. For example, consider a corporate executive given options on the firm's shares as part of her compensation. If the option payoff were determined by the price of the firm's shares on a particular day, the executive could enrich herself by manipulating the price of her shares for that single day. However, if the payoff of the option depended upon the average closing price of the shares over a six-month period, it would be much more difficult for her to profit from a manipulation. Asian options were first used in this kind of application. As a further example, commodity-linked bonds have two forms of payoffs, the payoffs from a straight bond plus an option on the average price of the linked commodity. By making the payoff depend on the average price of the commodity, such as oil, the chance of a manipulation is lessened.[12]

The average price may be computed as either a geometric average or as an arithmetic average. Unfortunately, there is no closed-form solution for the price of an arithmetic average price option, even though most actual average price options are based on an average price. These options must be valued by simulation techniques. It is possible, however, to compute the value of a geometric average price option, and this section focuses exclusively on a geometric average price call option.

A fundamental concern is the frequency with which the price will be observed over the averaging period. If the price is observed at the close each day, then the geometric average price will be computed by multiplying the available n daily price observations together and then taking the nth root of the product. An average price option may exist with some of the averaging period already under way. Alternatively, the time for averaging may lie in the future. Therefore, there are three time variables to consider:

t_0 = the time until the averaging period begins
t_1 = the time since the averaging period began
t_2 = the time remaining for averaging

It is typical for the averaging period to last until the option expires, and this typical case is assumed in this analysis. Therefore, $t_2 = T - t$, when the option expires at time T and the option is being valued at time t. Thus, there are three possibilities to consider:

1. The averaging period has already begun prior to the present time t
   In this case, $t_0 = 0$ and $t_1 > 0$.
2. The averaging period begins immediately at time t
   In this case, $t_0 = t_1 = 0$.
3. The averaging period will begin sometime later, after time t but before time T
   In this case, $t_0 > 0$ and $t_1 = 0$.

If the averaging period has already started, there is an average price A available to compute. If the averaging period starts in the future, the average price, AVGPRI, is one.

We begin the presentation of the pricing formula by defining several intermediate variables:

$$W = A^{\left(\frac{t_1}{t_1+t_2+h}\right)} S^{\left(\frac{t_2+h}{t_1+t_2+h}\right)}$$

$$M = \left(t_0 + t_2\frac{t_2 + h}{2(t_1 + t_2 + h)}\right)[r - \delta - 0.5\sigma^2]$$

$$\Sigma^2 = t_0 + \left(\frac{t_2(t_2 + h)(2t_2 + h)}{6(t_1 + t_2 + h)^2}\right)\sigma^2$$

$$w_1 = \frac{\ln\left(\frac{W}{X}\right) + M}{\Sigma} + \Sigma$$

where h is the frequency of price observations used to compute the average price. For example, if the price is observed daily, $h = 1/365$ years. The price of the geometric average price call, AVGPRI, is:

$$AVGPRI = We^{-r(T-t)}e^{(M+0.5\Sigma^2)}N(w_1) - Xe^{-r(T-t)}N(w_1 - \Sigma) \tag{18.17}$$

As a calculation example, consider a geometric average price option for which averaging has been under way for one-half year and the option expires in one-half year. For this option, the price is observed daily to compute the average price. The data are:

$S = 100$
$X = 90$
$\sigma = 0.2$
$r = 0.1$
$\delta = 0.05$
$t_0 = 0.0$
$t_1 = 0.5$ years
$t_2 = 0.5$ years
h = each day or $1/365$ years
$A = 95$

For these data, we have: $W = 97.474774$; $M = 0.00376$; $\Sigma^2 = 0.001671$; and $w_1 = 2.084497$. The value of the option is:

$$\text{AVGPRI} = (97.474774)e^{-0.1(0.5)}e^{[0.00376+0.5(0.001671)]}(0.981443) - 90e^{-0.1(0.5)}(0.979504)$$

$$= 91.419406 - 83.855912$$

$$= 7.5634$$

Figure 18.12 shows the relationship between the value of our example average price call and the average price of the underlying good.

EXCHANGE OPTIONS

We now consider an option to exchange one asset for another. Upon exercising, the owned asset is exchanged for the acquired asset. The valuation of an exchange option depends upon the usual parameters for the individual assets – price, risk, and dividend rate. In addition, the time until expiration and the correlation of returns between the assets are important. We will treat the owned asset as asset 1 and the asset to be acquired as asset 2. Thus, an exchange option may be regarded as a call on asset 2 with the exercise price being the future value of asset 1.

Although exchange options were first priced in 1978, these options have existed for quite some time in the form of incentive fee arrangements, margin accounts, exchange offers, and standby commitments.[13] As an example, consider an example from the merger market. A target firm is offered the opportunity to exchange shares from the target firm for shares in the acquiring firm. The shareholders in the target firm now hold an exchange option to exchange their shares for those of the acquirer. The value of this option can range from zero to the quite valuable. To know how valuable this kind of option is, we need a pricing formula.

The value of a European exchange option is:

$$\text{EXOPT} = S_2 e^{-\delta_2(T-t)}N(w_1) - S_1 e^{-\delta_1(T-t)}N(w_2) \tag{18.18}$$

The Price of an Average Price Call as a Function of the Average Stock Price   **Figure 18.12**

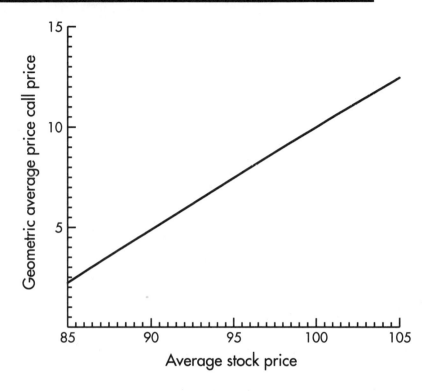

where:

$$\Sigma^2 = \sigma_1^2 + \sigma_2^2 - 2\rho\sigma_1\sigma_2$$

$$w_1 = \frac{\ln\left(\dfrac{S_2}{S_1}\right) + (\delta_1 - \delta_2 + 0.5\Sigma^2)(T - t)}{\Sigma\sqrt{T - t}}$$

$$w_2 = \frac{\ln\left(\dfrac{S_2}{S_1}\right) + (\delta_1 - \delta_2 - 0.5\Sigma^2)(T - t)}{\Sigma\sqrt{T - t}}$$

This formula is quite similar to the Merton model, except the volatility of the portfolio of the two assets, Σ, takes the place of the volatility of the underlying stock, σ, and the price of the asset to be sacrificed, S_1, takes the place of the exercise price, X. As a computational example, consider the following data:

$$S_1 = 100$$
$$S_2 = 100$$
$$\sigma_1 = 0.3$$
$$\sigma_2 = 0.2$$
$$\delta_1 = 0.05$$
$$\delta_2 = 0.05$$
$$T - t = 0.5 \text{ years}$$
$$\rho = 0.5$$

According to our convention, asset 1 is the owned asset that may be exchanged for asset 2. With these values we have: $\Sigma^2 = 0.07$; $w_1 = 0.093541$; $w_2 = -0.093541$; $N(w_1) = 0.537262$; and $N(w_2) = 0.462737$. The value of the option to exchange asset 1 for asset 2 is:

$$\text{EXOPT} = 100e^{-0.05(0.5)}0.537263 - 100e^{-0.05(0.5)}0.462737$$
$$= 52.399840 - 45.131198$$
$$= 7.2687$$

For our sample exchange option, Figure 18.13 shows how the price of the option varies with the volatilities of the individual assets. The bottom line shows how the value of the option varies with the volatility of asset 1, while the upper line pertains to the volatility of asset 2. Each line shows the sensitivity of the option's value to changes in the volatility of one asset, holding the volatility of the other asset constant. For our example option, $\sigma_1 = 0.3$ and $\sigma_2 = 0.2$. The bottom line shows that the option is worth 6.04 at that level of volatility. As σ_1 varies (and σ_2 remains constant), the value of the exchange option varies directly. The upper line shows the same relationship for asset 2. For the same sample exchange option, Figure 18.14 shows that the value of the option varies inversely with the correlation between the two assets.

RAINBOW OPTIONS

This section considers a class of exotic options known as **rainbow options**. The discussion here is limited to "two-color" rainbow options – options on two risky assets, where the number of risky assets is the number of colors in the rainbow. This section distinguishes and analyzes five types of two-color rainbow options: the best of two risky assets and a fixed cash amount, the better of two risky assets, the worse of two risky assets, the maximum of two risky assets, and the minimum of two risky assets. We consider each of these in turn, starting with an option on the best of two risky assets and cash. As we will see, the other rainbow options can be understood largely in terms of this first option.

As an example of a two-color rainbow option, consider a zero-coupon bond that pays a stated rate of interest, but allows the owner of the bond to choose the currency in which the interest is paid. The value of the bond upon maturity will differ depending on the exchange rate. The right to choose the currency of repayment gives the holder of the bond a call on the maximum of two assets – the repayment in one currency or another. By contrast, consider the same type of bond, but assume that instead the firm may choose the currency of repayment.[14]

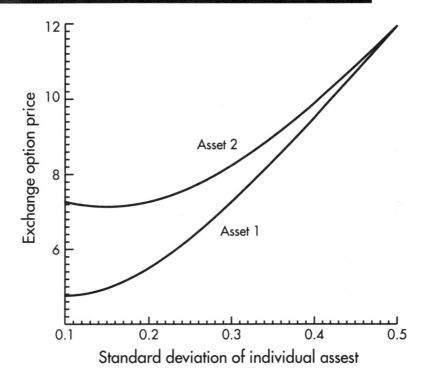

The Value of an Exchange Option as a Function of Individual Asset Volatilities

Figure 18.13

Call on the Best of Two Risky Assets and Cash

The owner of this option has a choice among three payoffs at expiration: risky asset 1, risky asset 2, or a fixed cash amount. There is no exercise price. Letting S_{1T} be the terminal value of asset 1, S_{2T} be the terminal value of asset 2, and X be the fixed cash amount, the present value of each payoff is:

Q1. $e^{-r(T-t)}E(S_{1T})$, conditional on $S_{1T} > S_{2T}$ and $S_{1T} > X$
Q2. $e^{-r(T-t)}E(S_{2T})$, conditional on $S_{2T} > S_{1T}$ and $S_{2T} > X$
Q3. $e^{-r(T-t)}X$, conditional on $X > S_{1T}$ and $X > S_{2T}$

Prior to exercise, the value of the option will equal the sum of the present value of these expected payoffs. Thus, the evaluation of the option turns on assessing how high the stock prices are likely to go, and which asset is likely to have the highest price at expiration. The performance of the two assets will depend in part on the degree to which they are correlated.

To present the pricing formula, we begin with some preliminary variable definitions:

Figure 18.14   **Value of an Exchange Option as a Function of the Correlation Between Assets**

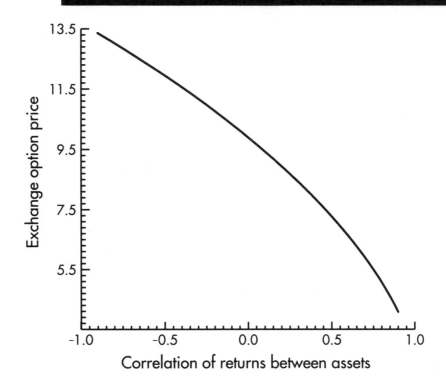

$$\Sigma^2 = \sigma_1{}^2 + \sigma_2{}^2 - 2\rho\sigma_1\sigma_2$$

$$\rho_1 = \frac{\rho\sigma_2 - \sigma_1}{\Sigma}$$

$$\rho_2 = \frac{\rho\sigma_1 - \sigma_2}{\Sigma}$$

$$w_1 = \frac{\ln\left(\dfrac{S_1}{X}\right) + (r - \delta_1 + 0.5\sigma_1{}^2)(T - t)}{\sigma_1\sqrt{T - t}}$$

$$w_2 = \frac{\ln\left(\dfrac{S_2}{X}\right) + (r - \delta_2 + 0.5\sigma_2{}^2)(T - t)}{\sigma_2\sqrt{T - t}}$$

$$w_3 = \frac{\ln\left(\dfrac{S_1}{S_2}\right) + (\delta_2 - \delta_1 + 0.5\Sigma^2)(T - t)}{\Sigma\sqrt{T - t}}$$

$$w_4 = \frac{\ln\left(\dfrac{S_2}{S_1}\right) + (\delta_1 - \delta_2 + 0.5\Sigma^2)(T - t)}{\Sigma\sqrt{T - t}}$$

With these preliminary definitions, the value of each potential payoff is:

Q1. $S_1^{-\delta_1(T-t)}\{N(w_3) - N_2(-w_1; w_3; \rho_1)\}$

Q2. $S_2^{-\delta_2(T-t)}\{N(w_4) - N_2(-w_2; w_4; \rho_2)\}$ (18.19)

Q3. $Xe^{-r(T-t)}N_2(-w_1 + \sigma_1\sqrt{T - t}; -w_2 + \sigma_2\sqrt{T - t}; \rho)$

The value of a call on the best of two risky assets and cash, BEST3, equals the sum of these three quantities:

$$\text{BEST3} = Q1 + Q2 + Q3 \qquad (18.20)$$

As a computational example, consider the following data:

$S_1 = 100$
$S_2 = 95$
$X = 110$
$T - t = 1$ year
$\sigma_1 = 0.2$
$\sigma_2 = 0.3$
$r = 0.08$
$\delta_1 = 0.04$
$\delta_2 = 0.03$
$\rho = 0.4$

Since the owner of the option will receive the best of two assets or the cash payment, the value should be at least the present value of the largest quantity, which is the cash payment of 110. However, there is also a chance that one of the two assets will exceed 110 when the option expires in one year, so we must take into account the potential payoff of these other assets.

With our sample data, we have the following intermediate results:

$$\Sigma^2 = 0.082; \quad \rho_1 = -0.279372; \quad \rho_2 = -0.768273$$

$$w_1 = -0.176551; \quad w_2 = -0.172012; \quad w_3 = 0.287381; \quad w_4 = -0.001024$$

$$N(w_3) = 0.613090; \quad N(w_4) = 0.499591$$

$N_2(-w_1; w_3; \rho_1) = 0.307309; \quad N_2(-w_2; w_4; \rho_2) = 0.147242; \quad N_2(-w_1 + \sigma_1; -w_2 + \sigma_2; \rho) = 0.496938$

Using these intermediate results, the three partial results for asset 1, asset 2, and the fixed cash payment are:

Q1. $100e^{-0.04}(0.305781) = 29.3787$
Q2. $95e^{-0.03}(0.352349) = 32.4833$
Q3. $110e^{-0.08}(0.496938) = 50.4605$

The value of the option, BEST3, equals the sum of these three parts:

$$\text{BEST3} = \text{Q1} + \text{Q2} + \text{Q3} = 29.3787 + 32.4833 + 50.4605 = 112.3224$$

Figure 18.15 shows how the value of this sample option varies inversely with the correlation between the two risky assets.

Figure 18.15   **The Value of a Call on the Best of Two Risky Assets and Cash as a Function of the Correlation Between the Two Risky Assets**

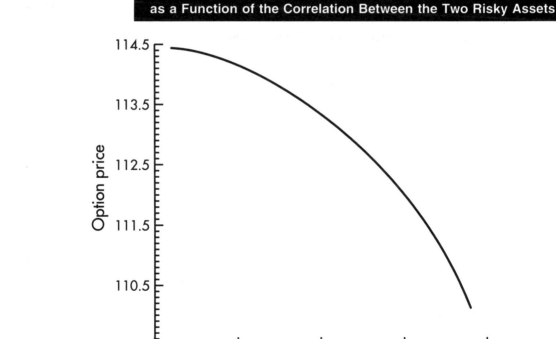

Call on the Maximum of Two Risky Assets

In this section, we consider calls on the maximum of two risky assets. This is similar to the option on the maximum of two risky assets and cash that we just considered. However, for this option there is no potential cash payoff. Further, these options have an exercise price. To exercise the call, the owner pays the exercise price and selects the better of the two risky assets.

   The valuation of this option is quite straightforward once we have valued a call on the maximum of two assets and cash. The payoff on a call on the maximum of two assets is the same as that of a call on two risky assets and cash minus the payment of the exercise price:

$$MAX(S_{1T}, S_{2T}, X) - X$$

As we have already seen in the preceding section, the value of an option with payoffs of $max(S_{1T}, S_{2T}, X)$ is simply BEST3 = Q1 + Q2 + Q3. The future liability X has a present value of $Xe^{-r(T-t)}$. Therefore, the value of a call on the maximum of two risky assets, CMAX, is:

$$CMAX = BEST3 - Xe^{-r(T-t)} = Q1 + Q2 + Q3 - Xe^{-r(T-t)} \qquad (18.21)$$

Using the same data from the previous section, the value of this option will be:

$$BEST3 - Xe^{-r(T-t)} = 112.3224 - 110e^{-0.08(1)} = 10.7796$$

Later in this chapter we will see how to value a put on the maximum of two risky assets.

   Figure 18.16 shows that the value of the option on the maximum of two assets varies inversely with the correlation between the two assets. A comparison of Figures 18.15 and 18.16 shows that the value of a call on the best of two risky assets and cash and a call on the maximum of the same two assets have exactly the same sensitivity to the correlation between the two assets.

Call on the Better of Two Risky Assets

A call on the better of two risky assets, CBETTER, is a special case of a call on two risky assets and cash. To form the special case, we merely need to specify that the exercise price is zero, $X = 0$. The call on two risky assets and cash is now just a call on two risky assets. With $X = 0$, w_1 and w_2 become arbitrarily large. Therefore:

$$CBETTER = BEST3, \text{ given that } X = 0 \qquad (18.22)$$

Using the same inputs as those for a call on two risky assets and cash, the value of this call is CBETTER = 104.9635.

Put on the Maximum of Two Risky Assets

The valuation of a put on the maximum of two risky assets can be derived as a function of the value of the options we have just been studying. To exercise a put on the maximum of two risky assets,

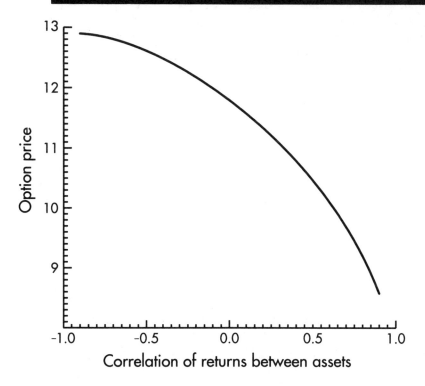

Figure 18.16   The Value of a Call on the Maximum of Two Risky Assets as a Function of the Correlation Between the Two Risky Assets

the owner surrenders the more valuable of the two risky assets and receives the exercise price. Thus, the payoff on this put is:

$$MAX[0, X - MAX(S_{1T}, S_{2T})]$$

This payoff can be replicated by the following portfolio:

Replicating Portfolio
Lend the present value of the exercise price
Buy a call on the maximum of the two risky assets with exercise price X
Sell a call on the better of the two risky assets

At Expiration (assume asset 1 is more valuable than asset 2)
Receive X as loan matures

If Asset 1 is Worth More than X
Exercise option on the maximum, pay *X*, and receive asset 1
Deliver asset 1
   Net Result: 0

If X *is Greater Than Value of Asset 1*
Let call on the maximum expire worthless
Purchase asset 1 in market
   Net result: $X - S_{1T}$

Thus, the payoff from this portfolio will be exactly like the put on the maximum of two risky assets. Since the put and this portfolio must have the same value, the value of a put on the maximum of two assets, PMAX, is:

$$PMAX = CMAX - CBETTER + Xe^{-r(T-t)} \tag{18.23}$$

Using the data given earlier in the rainbow option section, we have:

$$PMAX = 10.7796 - 104.9635 + 101.5428 = 7.3589$$

Figure 18.17 shows that the value of our sample put varies directly with the correlation between the two assets. Comparing Figures 18.16, for a call on the maximum of our two sample assets, and 18.17 shows that calls vary inversely with the correlation, while puts vary directly.

Call on the Minimum of Two Risky Assets

A call on the minimum of two risky assets pays the value of the inferior risky asset upon payment of the exercise price *X*. This call has the following payoff:

$$\text{Call payoff: MAX}[0, \text{MIN}(S_{1T}, S_{2T}) - X]$$

This call can be replicated by a portfolio of three options we have considered already:

Buy a plain vanilla option on the first asset with exercise price *X*
Buy a plain vanilla option on the second asset with exercise price *X*
Sell a call on the maximum of the two assets with exercise price *X*

Upon expiration, the portfolio owner exercises the call on the more valuable asset and uses this asset to satisfy the call on the maximum that was sold to form the portfolio. These transactions have a net zero cash flow, because the portfolio owner receives *X* and pays *X*. The portfolio owner still holds the call on the inferior asset. If the inferior asset is worth *X* or less, the option expires worthless. If the inferior asset is worth more than *X*, the portfolio owner exercises for a profit equal to the difference. Therefore, the value of a call on the minimum of two assets, CMIN, with exercise price *X* equals:

$$CMIN = C_t^M(S_1) + C_t^M(S_2) - CMAX \tag{18.24}$$

Figure 18.17 | **The Value of a Put on the Maximum of Two Risky Assets as a Function of the Correlation Between the Two Risky Assets**

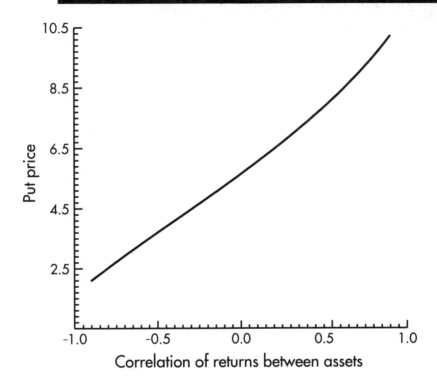

where $C_t^M(S_j)$ indicates a plain vanilla call on asset S_j. Using our data we have:

$$C_t^M(S_1) = 5.4369$$
$$C_t^M(S_2) = 7.4635$$
$$\text{CMAX} = 10.7796 \text{ (as solved earlier)}$$

Therefore, the value of a call on the minimum of two assets is:

$$\text{CMIN} = 5.4369 + 7.4635 - 10.7796 = 2.1208$$

We show how to price a put on the minimum of two assets below.

Call on the Worse of Two Risky Assets

A call on the worse of two risky assets has a payoff equal to the inferior asset, but without the payment of any exercise price. In this case, $X = 0$, so the payoff is:

Call payoff: $MAX[0, MIN(S_{1T}, S_{2T}) - 0] = MIN(S_{1T}, S_{2T})$

We have already seen that CBETTER is the same as CMAX, if $X = 0$. Therefore, we can find the value of a call on the worse of two risky assets, CWORSE, by finding the value of plain vanilla calls with $X = 0$ for the two assets and subtracting the value of CBETTER.

$$CWORSE = C_t^M(S_1) + C_t^M(S_2) - CBETTER, \text{ given that } X = 0 \qquad (18.25)$$

Using the same example values:

$$C_t^M(S_1) = 96.0789, \text{ if } X = 0$$

$$C_t^M(S_2) = 92.1923, \text{ if } X = 0$$

$$CBETTER = 104.9635, \text{ as calculated earlier}$$

$$CWORSE = 96.0789 + 92.1923 - 104.9635 = 83.3077$$

Put on the Minimum of Two Risky Assets

A put on the minimum of two risky assets pays X and requires the delivery of the inferior asset. Therefore, the payoff on this put is:

Put payoff: $MAX[0, X - MIN(S_{1T}, S_{2T})]$

To value this put, we create a replicating portfolio:

Replicating Portfolio
Buy call on the minimum of two risky assets with exercise price X
Sell call on the worse of two risky assets
Lend the present value of the exercise price X

At Expiration (assume asset 2 has the lower value)
Receive X

   If $S_{2T} \geq X$
   Exercise call on minimum, paying X
   Deliver inferior asset to complete obligation on sale of call on the worse of two assets
      Net Result: 0

   If $S_{2T} < X$
   Buy inferior asset in market
   Deliver inferior asset to complete obligation on sale of call on the worse of two assets
      Net Result: $X - S_{2T}$

As this portfolio exactly replicates the payoffs on the put, it must have the same value as the put on the minimum of two risky assets, PMIN. Therefore:

$$\text{PMIN} = \text{CMIN} - \text{CWORSE} + Xe^{-r(T-t)} \tag{18.26}$$

From our previous solutions we have:

$$\text{CMIN} = 2.1201$$
$$\text{CWORSE} = 83.3077$$

Therefore:

$$\text{PMIN} = 2.1201 - 83.3077 + 101.5428 = 20.3552$$

CONCLUSION

In this chapter, we have explored a large variety of exotic options. The analysis focused on European options for which closed-form solutions exist. As we have seen, many of these exotic options can be understood in terms of the familiar plain vanilla options priced in the Merton model.

This chapter considered nine classes of exotic options: forward-start options, compound options, chooser options, barrier options, binary options, lookback options, average price options, exchange options, and rainbow options. For each of these options, the payoffs are more complicated than those of plain vanilla options. We have seen that these specialized payoffs can be used to manage risks or to shape a speculative position more exactly. Many of these options exhibit path dependence, with the price of the option at a given time depending upon the price history or the price future of the underlying asset.

The **OPTION!** software that accompanies this text can compute the value of all of the exotic options discussed in this chapter and can price all of the example options considered in this chapter.

QUESTIONS AND PROBLEMS

For all of the following problems, compute the answers by hand, being sure to show intermediate results. After making the computation, use **OPTION!** to check the accuracy of your computations.

1. Using the following parameter values, find the price of a forward-start put: $S = 100$; $X = 100$; $T - t = 1$ year; $\sigma = 0.2$; $r = 0.1$; $\delta = 0.05$; $tg = 0.5$.
2. Price all four types of compound options assuming the following parameter values: $S = 100$; $\sigma = 0.4$; $r = 0.1$; $\delta = 0.05$; $X = 100$; $x = 8$; $T = 1$ year; $te = 0.25$ years.
3. Price a simple chooser option based on the following parameter values: $S = 100$; $X = 100$; $T = 1$ year; $\sigma = 0.5$; $r = 0.1$; $\delta = 0.05$; $tc = 0.5$ years. By comparing this result with that of the example chooser in the sample text, what can you conclude about the influence of the stock's risk on the value of the chooser?
4. Find the value of a down-and-in put with: $S = 100$; $X = 100$; $T - t = 1$ year; $\sigma = 0.3$; $r = 0.1$; $\delta = 0.05$; BARR = 97; and REBATE = 2.
5. Consider a cash-or-nothing call and put, with common parameter values: $S = 100$; $X = 110$; $T - t = 0.5$ years; $\sigma = 0.4$; $r = 0.1$; $\delta = 0.0$; and $Z = 200$. What is the value of each option? What is the value of a long position in both options? Which items of information given above are not needed to value the portfolio of the two options?

6. Consider an asset-or-nothing call and put, with common parameter values: $S = 100$; $X = 110$; $T - t = 0.5$ years; $\sigma = 0.4$; $r = 0.1$; and $\delta = 0.0$. What is the value of each option? What is the value of a long position in both options? Which items of information given above are not needed to value the portfolio of the two options?

7. Value a gap call with: $S = 100$; $X = 100$; $T - t = 0.5$ years; $\sigma = 0.5$; $r = 0.1$; $\delta = 0.03$; and $g = 7$.

8. Value a supershare with: $S = 100$; $X_L = 95$; $X_H = 110$; $T - t = 0.5$ years; $\sigma = 0.2$; $r = 0.1$; $\delta = 0.05$. By comparing this calculation with the sample supershare of the text, what can you conclude about the value of supershares and the value $X_H - X_L$?

9. Find the value of a lookback call and put with the common parameters: $S = 110$; $T - t = 1$ year; $\sigma = 0.25$; $r = 0.08$; and $\delta = 0.0$. For the call, MINPRI = 80. For the put, MAXPRI = 130.

10. Find the value of an average price option with these common parameters: $S = 100$; $X = 90$; $\sigma = 0.2$; $r = 0.1$; $\delta = 0.05$; $t_0 = 0.0$; $t_1 = 0.5$; $t_2 = 0.5$; and $A = 95$. Compute the value of the option with observations every two days, $h = 2/365$. Now compute the value of the option assuming continuous observation, that is, $h = 0$. Compare these results with the sample option of the chapter. What does this suggest about the value of the option and the frequency of observation?

11. Consider an exchange option with the following common parameter values: $S_1 = 100$; $S_2 = 100$; $\sigma_1 = 0.3$; $\sigma_2 = 0.2$; $\delta_1 = 0.05$; $\delta_2 = 0.05$; $T - t = 0.5$ years. Compute the value of this exchange option with $\rho = 0.0$ and $\rho = 0.7$. Compare your results with those for the sample exchange option in the chapter. What do these results suggest about the value of exchange options as a function of the correlation between the two assets?

For rainbow options, consider these parameter values: $S_1 = 100$; $S_2 = 100$; $X = 95$; $T - t = 0.5$ years; $\sigma_1 = 0.4$; $\sigma_2 = 0.5$; $r = 0.06$; $\delta_1 = 0.02$; $\delta_2 = 0.03$; and $\rho = 0.2$. (Interpret $X = 95$ as the exercise price or as the cash payment depending on the type of option.) Use this information for problems 12–18.

12. Find the value of an option on the best of two assets and cash.
13. Find the value of an option on the better of two assets.
14. Find the value of a call on the maximum of two assets.
15. Find the value of a put on the maximum of two assets.
16. Find the value of a call on the minimum of two assets.
17. Find the value of a call on the worse of two assets.
18. Find the value of a put on the minimum of two assets.

NOTES

[1] For a good introduction to the idea of path dependence in option pricing, see W. Hunter and D. Stowe, "Path-Dependent Options: Valuation and Applications," *Economic Review*, Federal Reserve Bank of Atlanta, July/August 1992, pp. 30–43.

[2] For more on the pricing and applications of forward start options, see Mark Rubinstein, "Pay Now, Choose Later," *Risk*, February 1991; Mark Rubinstein and Eric Reiner, "Exotic Options," Working Paper, University of California at Berkeley, 1995; and Peter G. Zhang, *Exotic Options: A Guide to the Second-Generation Options*, World Scientific Press, 1996.

[3] For the original paper on pricing compound options, see R. Geske, ''The Valuation of Compound Options,'' *Journal of Financial Economics,* 7, March 1979, pp. 63–81. See also Mark Rubinstein, ''Double Trouble,'' *Risk,* December 1991–January 1992; Mark Rubinstein and Eric Reiner, ''Exotic Options,'' Working Paper, University of California at Berkeley, 1995; Alan Tucker, ''Exotic Options,'' Working Paper, Pace University, New York, 1995; and Peter G. Zhang, *Exotic Options: A Guide to the Second-Generation Options,* World Scientific Press, 1996.

[4] See Mark Rubinstein, ''Options for the Undecided,'' *Risk,* April 1991, and Mark Rubinstein and Eric Reiner, ''Exotic Options,'' Working Paper, University of California at Berkeley, 1995.

[5] This peso example is drawn from Peter G. Zhang, *Exotic Options: A Guide to the Second-Generation Options,* World Scientific Press, 1996. For pricing of chooser options see also Alan Tucker, ''Exotic Options,'' Working Paper, Pace University, New York, 1995.

[6] For more detailed discussion of the pricing of barrier options, see Mark Rubinstein, ''Breaking Down the Barriers,'' *Risk,* September 1991; Mark Rubinstein and Eric Reiner, ''Exotic Options,'' Working Paper, University of California at Berkeley, 1995; Alan Tucker, ''Exotic Options,'' Working Paper, Pace University, New York, 1995; and Peter G. Zhang, *Exotic Options: A Guide to the Second-Generation Options,* World Scientific Press, 1996.

[7] For a discussion of the pricing of binary options, see Mark Rubinstein, ''Unscrambling the Binary Code,'' *Risk,* October 1991; Mark Rubinstein and Eric Reiner, ''Exotic Options,'' Working Paper, University of California at Berkeley, 1995; Alan Tucker, ''Exotic Options,'' Working Paper, Pace University, New York, 1995; Peter G. Zhang, *Exotic Options: A Guide to the Second-Generation Options,* World Scientific Press, 1996.

[8] Supershares were created by Nils Hakansson, ''The Purchasing Power Fund: A New Kind of Financial Intermediary,'' *Financial Analysts Journal,* November/December 1976.

[9] The first paper on lookback options appeared in 1979, long before such options actually existed. See Barry Goldman, Howard Sosin, and Mary Ann Gatto, ''Path Dependent Options: Buy at the Low, Sell at the High,'' *Journal of Finance,* 34, December 1979, pp. 1111–27. The results of Goldman, Sosin, and Gatto were generalized to embrace a dividend paying underlying asset by Mark Garman, in his paper, ''Recollection in Tranquility,'' *Risk,* March 1989, pp. 16–18. For more on the pricing of lookbacks, see also Mark Rubinstein and Eric Reiner, ''Exotic Options,'' Working Paper, University of California at Berkeley, 1995; Alan Tucker, ''Exotic Options,'' Working Paper, Pace University, New York, 1995; and Peter G. Zhang, *Exotic Options: A Guide to the Second-Generation Options,* World Scientific Press, 1996.

[10] For a discussion of partial lookback options, see Peter G. Zhang, *Exotic Options: A Guide to the Second-Generation Options,* World Scientific Press, 1996.

[11] Peter G. Zhang, *Exotic Options: A Guide to the Second-Generation Options,* World Scientific Press, 1996.

[12] For a discussion of Asian options, see A. Kemna and A. Vorst, ''A Pricing Method for Options Based on Average Asset Values,'' *Journal of Banking and Finance,* 14, March 1990, pp. 113–29; Mark Rubinstein and Eric Reiner, ''Exotic Options,'' Working Paper, University of California at Berkeley, 1995; S. Turnbull and L. Wakeman, ''A Quick Algorithm for Pricing European Average Options,'' *Journal of Financial and Quantitative Analysis,* 26, September 1991, pp. 377–89; Alan Tucker, ''Exotic Options,'' Working Paper, Pace University, New York, 1995; and Peter G. Zhang, *Exotic Options: A Guide to the Second-Generation Options,* World Scientific Press, 1996. Kemna and Vorst give examples of several commodity-linked bonds.

[13] The first paper on exchange options was by William Margrabe, ''The Value of an Option to Exchange One Asset for Another,'' *Journal of Finance,* March 1978. Margrabe distinguished the four applications just mentioned. For additional insights on pricing exchange options, see Mark Rubinstein, ''One for

Another,'' *Risk,* July 1991; Mark Rubinstein and Eric Reiner, ''Exotic Options,'' Working Paper, University of California at Berkeley, 1995; Alan Tucker, ''Exotic Options,'' Working Paper, Pace University, New York, 1995; and Peter G. Zhang, *Exotic Options: A Guide to the Second-Generation Options,* World Scientific Press, 1996.

[14] The original paper on rainbow options was by Rene Stulz, ''Options on the Minimum or the Maximum of Two Risky Assets,'' *Journal of Financial Economics,* 10, July 1982, pp. 161–85. Thus, Stulz was pricing two-color rainbow options. Stulz's work was extended to multicolored rainbow options by Herb Johnson, ''Options on the Maximum or the Minimum of Several Assets,'' *Journal of Financial and Quantitative Analysis,* 22, September 1987, pp. 277–83. The name ''rainbow option'' was originated by Mark Rubinstein, ''Somewhere Over the Rainbow,'' *Risk,* November 1991. For additional discussion of rainbow options, see Mark Rubinstein, ''Return to Oz,'' *Risk,* November 1994; Mark Rubinstein and Eric Reiner, ''Exotic Options,'' Working Paper, University of California at Berkeley, 1995; Alan Tucker, ''Exotic Options,'' Working Paper, Pace University, New York, 1995; and Peter G. Zhang, *Exotic Options: A Guide to the Second-Generation Options,* World Scientific Press, 1996.

THE SWAPS MARKET: INTRODUCTION

OVERVIEW

This chapter provides a basic introduction to the swaps market. As we will see, the swaps market has grown rapidly in the last few years because it provides firms that face financial risks with a flexible way to manage that risk. We will explore the risk management motivation that has led to this phenomenal growth in some detail.

Essentially, swaps are agreements between two parties to exchange sequences of cash flows over a certain period. At least one sequence of cash flows is uncertain when the swap agreement is initiated. The change in value for the uncertain sequence of cash flows that occurs during the life of the swap agreement benefits one party financially. However, both parties may benefit by reducing financial uncertainty. In addition to the participants in the swap agreement, the industry includes swap facilitators, those agents who bring together the actual participants. This chapter explores the exact nature of these agreements more fully and shows how the industry is organized to provide a vibrant speculative arena and, even more important, a powerful financial business tool for shaping and transforming financial risk.

SWAPS

A **swap** is an agreement between two or more parties to exchange sets of cash flows over a period in the future. For example, Party A might agree to pay a fixed rate of interest on $1 million each year for five years to Party B. In return, Party B might pay a floating rate of interest on $1 million each year for five years. The parties that agree to the swap are known as **counterparties**. The cash flows that the counterparties make are generally tied to the value of debt instruments or to the value of foreign currencies. Therefore, the two basic kinds of swaps are **interest rate swaps** and **currency swaps**.

A significant industry has arisen to facilitate swap transactions. This section considers the role of **swap facilitators** – economic agents who help counterparties identify each other and help the counterparties consummate swap transactions. Swap facilitators, who are either brokers or dealers, may function as agents that identify and bring prospective counterparties into contact with each other. Alternatively, swap dealers may actually transact for their own account to help complete the swap.

By taking part in swap transactions, swap dealers expose themselves to financial risk. This risk can be serious, because it is exactly the risk that the swap counterparties are trying to avoid. The swap dealer has two key problems. First, the swap dealer must price the swap to provide a reward for his services in bearing risk. Second, the swap dealer essentially has a portfolio of swaps that results from his numerous transactions in the swap market. Therefore, the swap dealer has the problem of managing a swap portfolio. This chapter explores how swap dealers price their swap transactions and manage the risk inherent in their swap portfolios.

The origins of the swap market can be traced to the late 1970s, when currency traders developed currency swaps as a technique to evade British controls on the movement of foreign currency. The first interest rate swap occurred in 1981 in an agreement between IBM and the World Bank. Since that time, the market has grown rapidly. Table 19.1 shows the amount of swaps outstanding at year end for 1987–1995. By 1995, interest rate swaps with $10.6 trillion in underlying value were outstanding, and currency swaps totaled another $993 billion. The total swaps market exceeded a principal amount of $11.5 trillion, with about 90 percent of the swaps being interest rate swaps and the remaining 10 percent being currency swaps. Of these swaps, about 50 percent involved the U.S. dollar. The growth in this market has been phenomenal; in fact, it has been the most rapid for any financial product in history. With more than $11 trillion in outstanding principal, the figures in the swap market rival the U.S. federal debt, and the swap market is growing even faster than the federal debt.[1]

THE SWAPS MARKET

In this section we consider the special features of the swaps market. For purposes of comparison, we begin by summarizing some of the key features of futures and options markets. Against this background, we focus on the most important features of the swap product. The section concludes with a brief summary of the development of the swaps market.

Table 19.1	Value of Outstanding Swaps ($ Billions of Principal)	
Year	Total Interest Rate Swaps	Total Currency Swaps
1987	$ 682.9	$182.8
1988	1,010.2	316.8
1989	1,539.3	434.8
1990	2,311.5	577.5
1991	3,065.1	807.2
1992	3,850.8	860.4
1993	6,177.8	899.6
1994	8,815.6	914.8
1995	10,617.4	993.6

Source: From International Swaps and Derivatives Association. Reprinted by permission.

Review of Futures and Options Market Features

In Chapters 2–18 we explored the futures and options markets. We noted that futures contracts trade exclusively in markets operated by futures exchanges and regulated by the Commodity Futures Trading Commission (CFTC). In our discussion of options, we focused primarily on exchange-traded options. Again, this portion of the options market is highly formalized with the options exchanges playing a major role in the market, and the options exchanges are regulated by the Securities Exchange Commission (SEC).

Futures markets trade highly standardized contracts, and the options traded on exchanges also have highly specified contract terms that cannot be altered. For example, the S&P 500 futures contract is based on a particular set of stocks, for a particular dollar amount, with only four fixed maturity dates per year. In addition, futures and exchange-traded options generally have a fairly short horizon. In many cases, futures contracts are listed only about one to two years before they expire. Even when it is possible to trade futures for expiration in three years or more, the markets do not become liquid until the contract comes much closer to expiration. For exchange-traded stock options, the longest time to maturity is generally less than one year. These futures and options cannot provide a means of dealing with risks that extend farther into the future than the expiration of the contracts that are traded. For example, if a firm faces interest rate risk for a ten-year horizon associated with a major building project, the futures market allows risk management only for the horizon of futures contracts currently being traded, which is about three years.

Characteristics of the Swaps Market

On futures and options exchanges, major financial institutions are readily identifiable. For example, in a futures pit, traders will be able to discern the activity of particular firms, because traders know who represents which firm. Therefore, exchange trading necessarily involves a certain loss of privacy. In the swaps market, by contrast, only the counterparties know that the swap takes place. Thus, the swaps market affords a privacy that cannot be obtained in exchange trading.[2]

We have noted that the futures and options exchanges are subject to considerable government regulation. By contrast, the swaps market has virtually no government regulation. As we will see later, swaps are similar to futures. The swaps market feared that the CFTC might attempt to assert regulatory authority over the swaps market on the grounds that swaps are really futures. However, the CFTC has formally announced that it will not seek jurisdiction over the swaps market. This means that the swaps market is likely to remain free of federal regulation for the foreseeable future. For the most part, participants in the swaps market are thankful to avoid regulation.

The swaps market also has some inherent limitations. First, to consummate a swap transaction, one potential counterparty must find a counterparty that is willing to take the opposite side of a transaction. If one party needs a specific maturity, or a certain pattern of cash flows, it can be very difficult to find a willing counterparty. Second, because a swap agreement is a contract between two counterparties, the swap cannot be altered or terminated early without the agreement of both parties. Third, for futures and exchange-traded options, the exchanges effectively guarantee performance on the contracts for all parties. By its very nature, the swaps market has no such guarantor. As a consequence, parties to the swap must be certain of the creditworthiness of their counterparties.

As we will see later in this chapter, the swaps market has developed mechanisms to deal with these three limitations. The problem of potential default is perhaps the most important. Assessing the financial credibility of a counterparty is difficult and expensive. Therefore, participation in the swaps market is effectively limited to firms and institutions that either engage in frequent swap transactions or have access to major swap facilitators that can advise on creditworthiness. In effect, the swaps market is virtually limited to firms and financial institutions, and there are few or no individual transactors in the market.

PLAIN VANILLA SWAPS

In this section we analyze the different kinds of swaps that are available, and we show how swaps can help corporations manage various types of risk exposure. We begin by considering the mechanics of the simplest kinds of swaps. A **plain vanilla swap**, the simplest kind, can be an interest rate swap or a foreign currency swap.

Interest Rate Swaps

In a plain vanilla interest rate swap, one counterparty has an initial position in a fixed rate debt instrument, while the other counterparty has an initial position in a floating rate obligation. In this initial position, the party with the floating rate obligation is exposed to changes in interest rates. By swapping this floating rate obligation, this counterparty eliminates exposure to changing interest rates. For the party with a fixed rate obligation, the interest rate swap increases the interest rate sensitivity. (Later, we explore the motivation that these counterparties might have for taking their respective positions. First, however, we need to understand the transactions.)

To see the nature of the plain vanilla interest rate swap most clearly, we use an example. We assume that the swap covers a five-year period and involves annual payments on a $1 million principal amount. Let us assume that Party A agrees to pay a fixed rate of 12 percent to Party B. In return, Party B agrees to pay a floating rate of LIBOR + 3 percent to Party A. LIBOR stands for ''London Interbank Offered Rate,'' and it is a base rate at which large international banks lend funds to each other. Floating rates in the swaps market are most often set as equaling LIBOR plus some additional amount. Figure 19.1 shows the basic features of this transaction. Party A pays 12 percent of $1 million, or $120,000 each year to Party B. Party B makes a payment to Party A in return, but the actual amount of the payments depends on movement in LIBOR.

Conceptually, the two parties also exchange the principal amount of $1 million. However, actually making the transaction of sending each other $1 million would not make practical sense. As a consequence, principal amounts are generally not exchanged. Instead, the principal plays a conceptual role in determining the amount of the interest payments. Because the principal is not actually exchanged, it is called a **notional principal**, an amount used as a base for computations, but not an amount that

Figure 19.1   A Plain Vanilla Interest Rate Swap

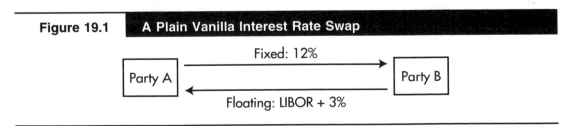

is actually transferred from one party to another. In our example, the notional principal is $1 million, and knowing that amount lets us compute the actual dollar amount of the cash flows that the two parties make to each other each year.

Let us assume that the LIBOR is 10 percent at the time of the first payment. This means that Party A will be obligated to pay $120,000 to Party B. Party B will owe $130,000 to Party A. Offsetting the two mutual obligations, Party B owes $10,000 to Party A. Generally, only the **net payment**, the difference between the two obligations, actually takes place. Again, this practice avoids unnecessary payments.[3]

Foreign Currency Swaps

In a currency swap, one party holds one currency and desires a different currency. The swap arises when one party provides a certain principal in one currency to its counterparty in exchange for an equivalent amount of a different currency. For example, Party C may have German marks and be anxious to swap those marks for U.S. dollars. Similarly, Party D may hold U.S. dollars and be willing to exchange those dollars for German marks. With these needs, Parties C and D may be able to engage in a currency swap.

A plain vanilla currency swap involves three different sets of cash flows. First, at the initiation of the swap, the two parties actually do exchange cash. The entire motivation for the currency swap is the actual need for funds denominated in a different currency. This differs from the interest rate swap in which both parties deal in dollars and can pay the net amount. Second, the parties make periodic interest payments to each other during the life of the swap agreement. Third, at the termination of the swap, the parties again exchange the principal.

As an example, let us assume that the current spot exchange rate between German marks and U.S. dollars is 2.5 marks per dollar. Thus, the mark is worth $.40. We assume that the U.S. interest rate is 10 percent and the German interest rate is 8 percent. Party C holds 25 million marks and wishes to exchange those marks for dollars. In return for the marks, Party D would pay $10 million to Party C at the initiation of the swap. We also assume that the term of the swap is seven years and the parties will make annual interest payments. With the interest rates in our example, Party D will pay 8 percent interest on the 25 million marks it received, so the annual payment from Party D to Party C will be 2 million marks. Party C received $10 million dollars and will pay interest at 10 percent, so Party C will pay $1 million each year to Party D. In this example, the two parties pay a fixed rate of interest on their respective currencies.[4]

In actual practice, the parties will make only net payments. For example, assume that at year 1 the spot exchange rate between the dollar and mark is 2.2222 marks per dollar, so the mark is worth $.45. Valuing the obligations in dollars at this exchange rate, Party C owes $1 million and Party D owes $900,000 (2 million marks times $.45). Thus, Party C would pay the $100,000 difference. At other times, the exchange rate could be different, and the net payment would reflect that different exchange rate.

At the end of seven years, the two parties again exchange principal. In our example, Party C would pay $10 million and Party D would pay 25 million marks. This final payment terminates the currency swap. Figure 19.2 shows the first element of the swap, which is the initial exchange of principal. Figure 19.3 represents the payment of interest, and in our example there would be seven of these payments, one for each year of the swap. Finally, Figure 19.4 shows the second exchange of principal that completes the swap.

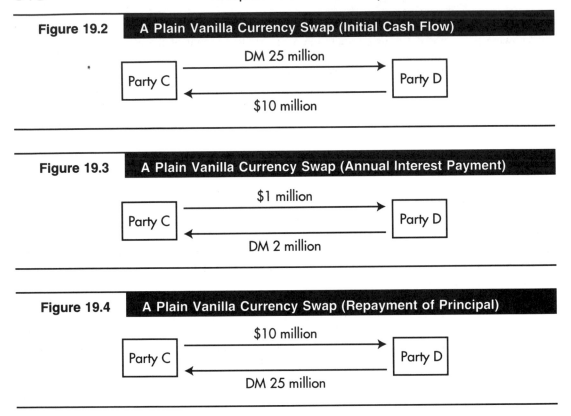

Figure 19.2   **A Plain Vanilla Currency Swap (Initial Cash Flow)**

Party C — DM 25 million → Party D

Party C ← $10 million — Party D

Figure 19.3   **A Plain Vanilla Currency Swap (Annual Interest Payment)**

Party C — $1 million → Party D

Party C ← DM 2 million — Party D

Figure 19.4   **A Plain Vanilla Currency Swap (Repayment of Principal)**

Party C — $10 million → Party D

Party C ← DM 25 million — Party D

Summary

In this section we considered the transactions involved in plain vanilla interest rate and currency swaps. As we saw for an interest rate swap, the essential feature is the transformation of a fixed rate obligation to a floating rate obligation for one party, and a complementary transformation of a floating rate obligation to a fixed rate obligation for the other party. In a currency swap, the two parties exchange currencies to obtain access to a foreign currency that better meets their business needs. To this point, we have only focused on the elementary transactions involved in simple swaps, but we have not considered the motivation that leads to swap agreements.

MOTIVATIONS FOR SWAPS

In our example of a plain vanilla swap, we saw that one party begins with a fixed rate obligation and seeks a floating rate obligation. The second party exchanges a floating rate for a fixed rate obligation. For this swap to occur, the two parties have to be seeking exactly the opposite goals.

There are two basic motivations that we consider in this section. First, the normal commercial operations of some firms naturally lead to interest rate and currency risk positions of a certain type. Second, some firms may have certain advantages in acquiring specific types of financing. Firms can borrow in the form that is cheapest and use swaps to change the characteristics of the borrowing to one that meets the firm's specific needs. In this section we consider several simple examples of motivations for swaps.

Commercial Needs

As an example of a prime candidate for an interest rate swap, consider a typical savings and loan association. Savings and loan associations accept deposits and lend those funds for long-term mortgages. Because depositors can withdraw their funds on short notice, deposit rates must adjust to changing interest rate conditions. Most mortgagors wish to borrow at a fixed rate for a long time. As a result, the savings and loan association can be left with floating rate liabilities and fixed rate assets. This means that the savings and loan is vulnerable to rising rates. If rates rise, the savings and loan will be forced to increase the rate it pays on deposits, but it cannot increase the interest rate it charges on the mortgages that have already been issued.

To escape this interest rate risk, the savings and loan might use the swaps market to transform its fixed rate assets into floating rate assets or transform its floating rate liabilities into fixed rate liabilities. Let us assume that the savings and loan wishes to transform a fixed rate mortgage into an asset that pays a floating rate of interest. In terms of our interest rate swap example, the savings and loan association is like Party A – in exchange for the fixed rate mortgage that it holds, it wants to pay a fixed rate of interest and receive a floating rate of interest. Engaging in a swap as Party A did will help the association resolve its interest rate risk.

To make the discussion more concrete, we extend our example of the plain vanilla interest rate swap. We assume that the savings and loan association has just loaned $1 million for five years at 12 percent with annual payments, and we assume that the savings and loan pays a deposit rate that equals LIBOR plus 1 percent. With these rates, the association will lose money if LIBOR exceeds 11 percent, and it is this danger that prompts the association to consider an interest rate swap.

Figure 19.5 shows our original plain vanilla interest rate swap with the additional information about the savings and loan that we have just elaborated. In the figure, Party A is the savings and loan association, and it receives payments at a fixed rate of 12 percent on the mortgage. After it enters the swap, the association also pays 12 percent on a notional principal of $1 million. In effect, it receives mortgage payments and passes them through to Party B under the swap agreement. Under the swap agreement, Party A receives a floating rate of LIBOR plus 3 percent. From this cash inflow, the association pays its depositors LIBOR plus 1 percent. This leaves a periodic inflow to the association of 2 percent, which is the spread that it makes on the loan.

In our example, the association now has a fixed rate inflow of 2 percent, and it has succeeded in avoiding its exposure to interest rate risk. No matter what happens to the level of interest rates, the association will enjoy a net cash inflow of 2 percent on $1 million. This example clarifies how the savings association has a strong motivation to enter the swaps market. From the very nature of the savings and loan industry, the association finds itself with a risk exposure to rising interest rates. However, by engaging in an interest rate swap, the association can secure a fixed rate position.

Comparative Advantage

In many situations, one firm may have better access to the capital market than another firm.[5] For example, a U.S. firm may be able to borrow easily in the United States, but it might not have such

Figure 19.5 Motivation for the Plain Vanilla Interest Rate Swap

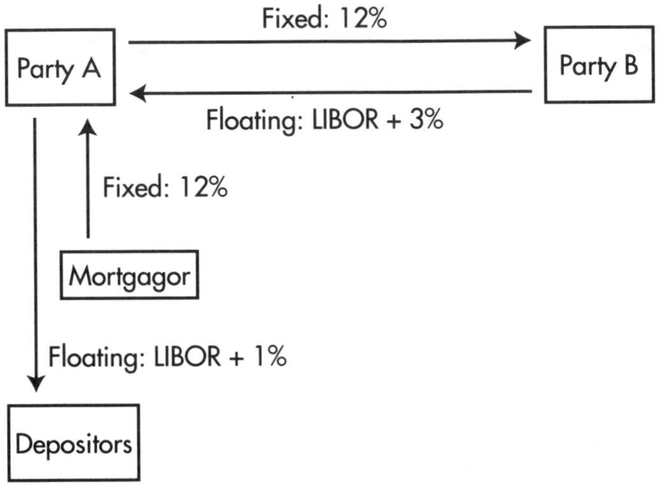

favorable access to the capital market in Germany. Similarly, a German firm may have good borrowing opportunities domestically but poor opportunities in the United States.

Table 19.2 presents borrowing rates for Parties C and D, the firms of our plain vanilla currency swap example. In the plain vanilla example, we assumed that, for each currency, both parties faced the same rate. We now assume that Party C is a German firm with access to marks at a rate of 7 percent, while the U.S. firm, Party D, must pay 8 percent to borrow marks. On the other hand, Party D can borrow dollars at 9 percent, while the German Party C must pay 10 percent for its dollar borrowings.

As the table shows, Party C enjoys a comparative advantage in borrowing marks and Party D has a comparative advantage in borrowing dollars. These rates raise the possibility that each firm can exploit its comparative advantage and share the gains by reducing overall borrowing costs. This possibility is shown in Figures 19.6–19.8, which parallel Figures 19.2–19.4.

Figure 19.6 resembles Figure 19.2, but it provides more information. In Figure 19.6, Party C borrows 25 million marks from a third party lender at its borrowing rate of 7 percent, while Party D borrows $10 million from a fourth party at 9 percent. After these borrowings, both parties have the funds to engage in the plain vanilla currency swap that we have already analyzed. To initiate the swap, Party C forwards the 25 million marks it has just borrowed to Party D, which reciprocates

Table 19.2 Borrowing Rates for Two Firms in Two Currencies

Firm	U.S. Dollar Rate	German Mark Rate
Party C	10%	7%
Party D	9%	8%

A Plain Vanilla Currency Swap (Initial Cash Flow with Lenders)   **Figure 19.6**

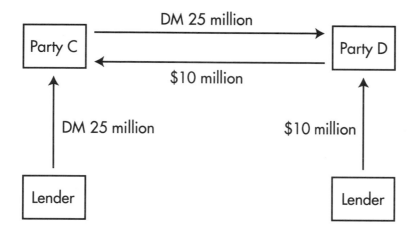

with the $10 million it has borrowed. In effect, the two parties have made independent borrowings and then exchanged the proceeds. For this reason, currency swaps are also known as an **exchange of borrowings**.

Figure 19.7 shows the same swap terms we have already analyzed. Party C pays interest payments at a rate of 10 percent on the $10 million it received from Party D, and Party D pays 2 million marks interest per year on the 25 million marks it received from Party C. Notice that these rates are the same ones that the two firms could obtain from other sources. However, Figure 19.7 also shows the interest payments that Parties C and D must make on their borrowings. Party C pays 1.75 million marks interest annually, but it receives 2 million marks from Party D. For its part, Party D receives $1 million from Party C, from which it pays interest of $900,000.

Now we can clearly see how the swap benefits both parties. Party C gets the use of $10 million and pays out 1.75 million marks. Had it borrowed dollars on its own, it would have paid a full 10 percent, or $1 million per year. At current exchange rates of 2.5 marks per dollar, Party C is effectively paying $700,000 annual interest on the use of $10 million. This is an effective rate of 7 percent. Party D pays $900,000 interest each year and receives the use of 25 million marks. This is equivalent to paying 2,250,000 marks annual interest ($900,000 times 2.5 marks per dollar) for the use of 25 million marks, or a rate of 9 percent. By using the swap, both parties achieve an effective borrowing rate that is much lower than they could have obtained by borrowing the currency they needed directly. By engaging in the swap, both firms can use the comparative advantage of the other to reduce their borrowing costs. Figure 19.8 shows the termination cash flows for the swap, when both parties repay the principal.

Summary

In this section we have explored two motivations for engaging in swaps: commercial needs and comparative borrowing advantages. The first led to an interest rate swap, while the second motivated

Figure 19.7 A Plain Vanilla Currency Swap (Interest Payments with Lenders)

$1 million
Party C
Party D
DM 2 million
DM 1.75 million
$900,000
Lender
Lender

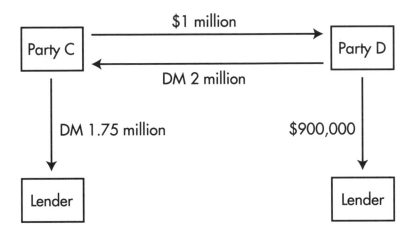

Figure 19.8 A Plain Vanilla Currency Swap (Repayment of Principal with Lenders)

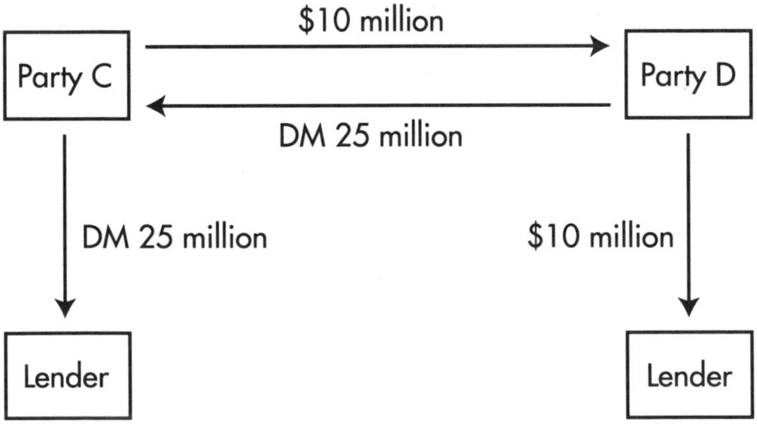

$10 million
Party C
Party D
DM 25 million
DM 25 million
$10 million
Lender
Lender

a currency swap. Both swaps that we analyzed were plain vanilla swaps. While swaps can become much more complex, they are generally motivated by the considerations we explored in this section.

SWAP FACILITATORS

As we mentioned earlier, a swap facilitator is a third party who assists in the completion of a swap. When a swap facilitator acts strictly as an agent, without taking any financial position in the swap transaction, the facilitator acts as a **swap broker**. In some instances, a swap facilitator may actually transact for its own account to help complete the swap. In this case, the swap facilitator acts as a **swap dealer**. Both swap brokers and swap dealers are known as swap banks, so a **swap bank** is equivalent to a swap facilitator. This section explores the role of swap brokers and dealers.

Swap Brokers

For a swap transaction to occur, two counterparties with matching needs must find each other. As we have seen, a firm with a short-term and fairly standard risk exposure might use futures or exchange-traded options to manage that risk. Special risk exposures often lead firms to look beyond futures and exchange-traded options to the swaps market for the management of that special exposure. For example, even with the plain vanilla interest rate and currency swaps examples that we considered, the risks faced by the parties could not be managed completely with futures or exchange-traded options. As the risk exposure goes beyond the plain vanilla variety, futures and exchange-traded options are even less adequate for managing these more complex risks.

For a potential swap participant with a specific need, finding a counterparty can be very difficult. In the previous example of a plain vanilla currency swap, Party C must find another firm that meets a number of conditions. The firm that will act as a counterparty to Party C must have: preferential borrowing access to $10 million, a need for German marks, a requirement that matches Party C in size ($10 million versus 25 million marks), a time horizon of seven years, a willingness to transact at the time desired by Party C, and an acceptable credit standing. For Party C to find this potential counterparty is a daunting task.

The difficulty of finding counterparties creates an opportunity for a swap broker. A swap broker has a number of firms in her client base and stands ready to search for swap counterparties upon demand. In the example of the plain vanilla currency swap, Party C might approach a swap broker and seek assistance in finding a counterparty. In effect, Party C would rely on the swap broker's specialized knowledge of the swap needs of many firms.

After Party C solicits the assistance of a swap broker, the broker contacts potential counterparties. Generally, a firm like Party C will desire privacy, so the broker will not identify Party C until she finds a very likely counterparty. (This is another reason that firms use swap brokers. By having a swap broker conduct the search, Party C in our example can preserve its anonymity.) Once the swap broker finds a suitable counterparty, which turns out to be Party D in our plain vanilla currency swap example, the broker brings the two parties together. The broker then helps negotiate and complete the swap contract. For her services, the swap broker receives a fee from each of the counterparties.

In summary, the swap broker serves as an information intermediary. The broker uses her superior knowledge of potential swap participants to find the right counterparty. The broker exercises discretion by protecting the identity of the potential counterparties until the swap partners are found. Notice that the swap broker is not a party to the swap contract. As a broker, the swap facilitator does not bear financial risk, but merely assists the two counterparties in completing the swap transaction.

Swap Dealers

A swap dealer fulfills all of the functions of a swap broker. In addition, a swap dealer also takes a risk position in the swap transaction by becoming an actual party to the transaction. Just because the swap dealer may take a risk position to complete a swap transaction does not mean that the swap dealer is a speculator. Instead, the swap dealer accepts a risk position in order to complete the transaction for the initial counterparty. The swap transaction may leave the swap dealer with a risk position, but the swap dealer will then try to offset that risk. The swap dealer functions as a financial intermediary, earning profits by helping complete swap transactions. If completing a swap results in a risk position for the swap dealer, the dealer will then try to minimize that risk by its own further transactions.

To explore the functions served by the swap dealer, we assume that the dealer begins with its optimal set of investments. In other words, the swap dealer has financial assets, but they are invested in a way that the swap dealer finds optimal. Therefore, if the swap dealer takes part in a swap transaction and has his financial position altered as a result of that transaction, we assume that the change in the swap dealer's position represents an unwanted risk that the dealer accepted only to help complete the swap transaction and thereby to earn profits. Against this background, we return to our example of a plain vanilla interest rate swap to explore the additional role performed by the swap dealer.

In the plain vanilla interest rate swap example, we noted that Party A was a savings and loan association that paid a floating rate of LIBOR + 1 percent to its depositors and made a five-year fixed rate mortgage loan at 12 percent. This initial business position left Party A exposed to rising interest rates, and Party A wanted to avoid this risk by converting the fixed rate it received on its mortgage loan to a floating rate. Party A's ability to complete this swap depended on finding a suitable counterparty with a matching need, such as Party B in our example.

If a firm like Party B cannot be found, Party A is left unable to complete the swap. Often a swap broker will be unable to find a suitable counterparty, or the swap broker can find only a partial match. In many instances, the swap broker may be able to find a potential counterparty that will take only a portion of the swap that the initial counterparty wants to complete, or the potential counterparty does not want to transact at the time the initial counterparty desires.

To complete the swap transaction for Party A, the swap dealer may act as a counterparty. Figure 19.9 shows the plain vanilla interest rate swap example as before, except the swap dealer acts as the counterparty to Party A. As a result, we see that the swap gives the swap dealer the same cash flows that Party B had in Figure 19.5.

As a result of this transaction, the swap dealer now has an undesired risk position. Over the next five years the dealer is obligated to pay a floating rate of LIBOR + 3 percent and to receive a fixed rate of 12 percent on a notional amount of $10 million. The swap dealer must believe that he can make money by acting as a counterparty to Party A. To do so, the swap dealer wants to offset the risk that he has undertaken, but he needs to offset that risk on better terms than he undertook as a counterparty to Party A.

Let us assume that the dealer knew of a potential party in the swaps market, Party E, that was willing to pay a floating rate of LIBOR + 3.1 percent in exchange for a fixed rate of 12 percent on

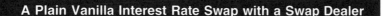

A Plain Vanilla Interest Rate Swap with a Swap Dealer   Figure 19.9

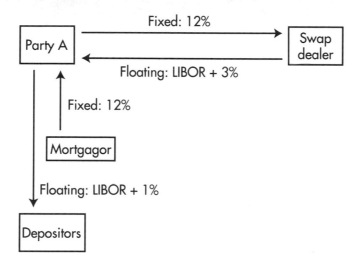

a notional amount of $10 million. However, Party E is willing to accept a term of only three years, not the five years that Party A desires. Given a knowledge of this client, the swap dealer decides to act as a counterparty to Party A. By also transacting with Party E, the swap dealer is able to offset a substantial portion of the risk he accepts by transacting with Party A. Figure 19.10 shows the transactions involving Parties A and E and the swap dealer. After completing these transactions, we see that the swap dealer has some profits to show for his efforts. Specifically, the dealer is making 10 basis points on the floating rate side of the transaction because he receives LIBOR + 3.1 percent and pays LIBOR + 3 percent. However, the swap dealer still has considerable risk as a result of the transaction.

Table 19.3 shows the swap dealer's cash flows resulting from the swap. The first two columns of Table 19.3 show the cash flows that result from the swap dealer's transactions with Party A. To serve the needs of Party A, the swap dealer has agreed to receive a 12 percent fixed rate payment in exchange for paying LIBOR + 3 percent on a $10 million notional amount. Based on the portion of the transaction with Party A, the swap dealer will receive $1.2 million each year and pay LIBOR + 3 percent on $10 million each year. Which set of cash flows is better is uncertain because the future course of interest rates is not known. For example, if LIBOR stays constant at 8 percent over the five years, the swap dealer will profit handsomely, making 1 percent per year for five years on $10 million. However, if LIBOR jumps to 11 percent and remains constant, the swap dealer will be paying 14 percent on $10 million each year. As a result, the swap dealer will receive $1.2 million but must pay $1.4 million each year, for an annual net loss of $200,000. Thus, the riskiness of acting as a counterparty to Party A is clear.

Table 19.3 also shows the swap dealer's cash flows that result from transacting with Party E. For each of the first three years, the dealer will pay a fixed interest rate of 12 percent on $10,000,000,

Figure 19.10   **The Swap Dealer as Intermediary in a Plain Vanilla Interest Rate Swap**

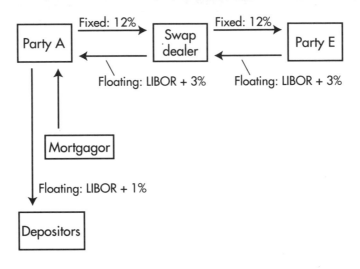

Table 19.3		The Swap Dealer's Cash Flows		
Year	**From Party A**	**To Party A**	**From Party E**	**To Party E**
1	$1,200,000	LIBOR + 3%	LIBOR + 3.1%	$1,200,000
2	$1,200,000	LIBOR + 3%	LIBOR + 3.1%	1,200,000
3	$1,200,000	LIBOR + 3%	LIBOR + 3.1%	1,200,000
4	$1,200,000	LIBOR + 3%	0	0
5	$1,200,000	LIBOR + 3%	0	0

or $1,200,000. In addition, the dealer will receive a rate of LIBOR + 3.1 percent on a notional amount of $10,000,000.

The swap dealer's net cash flows are as follows:

Year	Dealer's Net Cash Flow
1	$10,000
2	10,000
3	10,000
4	$1,200,000 − LIBOR + 3%
5	$1,200,000 − LIBOR + 3%

For the first three years, the swap dealer has achieved a perfect match in cash flows, receiving $1.2 million from Party A and paying it to Party E. The dealer has a net zero cash flow on this part of the transaction. During the first three years, the dealer also receives LIBOR + 3.1 percent from Party E and pays LIBOR + 3 percent to Party A, both on notional amounts of $10 million. On this portion of the transaction, the dealer receives a net spread of 10 basis points on a $10 million notional amount. Taking all of the dealer's cash flows during the first three years into account, we see that the dealer has a net cash inflow of $10,000 per year.

Even after transacting with both Parties A and E, the swap dealer has a residual risk that is evident from the total cash flows. In years four and five, the dealer will receive $1.2 million from Party A, but he must pay LIBOR + 3 percent. Whether this will create a profit or loss for the dealer depends on future interest rates. However, in Table 19.3 we can see that the dealer has substantially reduced his risk position by trading with Party E.

Swap Dealers as Financial Intermediaries

Table 19.3 also shows that the swap dealer is making a profit as a financial intermediary. Because of his superior knowledge of the market, the dealer was able to find Party E. By transacting with Party E, instead of just transacting with Party A, the swap dealer secures a 10 basis point spread on the notional amount for three years. In addition to earning a profit on the spread, the dealer's transaction with Party E offsets a substantial portion of the risk inherent in acting as a counterparty to Party A in the initial swap transaction.

In our example of the swap dealer's transactions, we assumed that the swap dealer had an initial portfolio of assets that met his needs in terms of risk and diversification. By acting as a counterparty to Party A, the swap dealer assumed a risk in pursuit of profit. The dealer could have taken this position as a speculation on interest rates. However, the swap dealer preferred to act as a financial intermediary, making a profit by providing informational services. In our example, the swap dealer was able to capture a spread of 10 basis points and reduce risk by transacting with Party C. Ideally, the swap dealer acting as a financial intermediary would also like to avoid the remaining risk exposure in years four and five. Being able to do so requires that the dealer find another swap partner. We explore the ways in which swap dealers manage the risks associated with acting as counterparties later in this chapter.

Summary

In this section we have seen that swap facilitators or swap banks may act as either brokers or dealers. A swap broker facilitates swap transactions by bringing potential counterparties together, but the broker does not take a risk position in the swap. By contrast, a swap dealer acts as a counterparty in the swap, in addition to providing the informational assistance provided by a broker. Notice that the same firm can act as a swap broker in some transactions and as a swap dealer in others. Calling a firm a swap broker or swap dealer refers to the function that the firm fulfills in a particular transaction.

By taking a position in a swap transaction, a swap dealer accepts a risk position. The firm that accepts this risk position could approach the transaction as a speculator or as a swap dealer. Functioning as a swap dealer, the firm accepts the position with the idea of avoiding as much of the risk exposure as possible. Specifically, the firm acting as a financial intermediary will attempt to offset the initial risk and will be satisfied to make a profit by acting as a conduit between other swap parties. When the swap dealer acts as a counterparty, the dealer intends to be only a temporary substitute for an unavailable counterparty.

PRICING OF SWAPS

In this section we explore the principles that underlie swap pricing. To simplify the discussion, we focus on plain vanilla interest rate swaps, and we assume that the swap dealer wishes to act as a pure financial intermediary. That is, the swap dealer does not want to assume a risk position with respect to interest rates. The principles apply, however, to swaps of all types.

Factors That Affect Swap Pricing

The swap dealer must price swaps to reflect a number of factors. These include the creditworthiness of the potential swap partner, the availability of other swap opportunities that will allow the swap dealer to offset the risk of an initial swap, and the term structure of interest rates.[6] We discuss each of these in turn.

Creditworthiness. The swap dealer must appraise the creditworthiness of the swap partner. As we have seen earlier in this chapter, there is no clearinghouse in the swaps market to guarantee performance on a contract if one of the counterparties defaults. If the swap dealer suffers a default by one of its counterparties, the dealer must either absorb the loss or institute a lawsuit to seek recovery on the defaulted obligation.

In most swaps, the timings of cash flows between the counterparties are matched fairly closely. For example, in the plain vanilla interest rate swap of Figure 19.10, the fixed and floating cash flows occur at similar times, and we noted that only the net amount is actually exchanged. Thus, default on a swap seldom could involve failure to pay the notional amount or even an entire periodic payment. In this sense, default on a swap is not as critical as default on a corporate bond, in which an investor might lose the entire principal. Instead, a swap default would generally imply a loss of the change in value due to shifting interest rates. While this amount can be quite significant, such a default would not be as catastrophic as a bond default in which the entire principal could be lost.

As we saw in Figure 19.10 and as we explore in more detail later in this chapter, the swap dealer seeks to build a swap portfolio in which the risks of individual swaps offset each other. In Figure 19.10, the risks in the swap with Party A are largely offset by the risks in the swap with Party E. When a swap dealer suffers a default, the elaborate structure of offsetting risks can be upset. This leaves the swap dealer in a riskier position, and the dealer must struggle to re-establish the risk control that was upset by the default.

Because of the potential costs associated with default, the swap dealer will adjust the pricing on swaps to reflect the risk of default. Parties that have a high risk of default are likely to be excluded from the market. For example, airlines under bankruptcy protection probably have very limited access to the swaps market. As we noted earlier, the swaps market is mainly a market for financial institutions and corporations due to the importance of default considerations and the need for one party to be able to confirm the creditworthiness of a prospective counterparty.[7]

Availability of Additional Counterparties. Because we are assuming that the swap dealer wishes to act only as a financial intermediary, the swap dealer will be very concerned about how the risk involved in a prospective swap can be offset by participating in other swaps. For example, in the dealer's swap of Figure 19.10, the willingness of the swap dealer to enter the transaction with Party A may well depend on the dealer's knowledge of Party E. If the dealer considers transacting with Party A and does not know of Party E, the dealer may require more favorable terms to transact with

Party A. However, if the dealer knows about Parties A and E from the outset, the dealer may accept less favorable terms because he knows he can offset some of the risk of acting as Party A's counterparty by engaging in a second swap with Party E.

As we noted, the swap dealer faces the net cash flows in the last column of Table 19.3 after engaging in the two interest rate swaps with Parties A and E. Assume now that another potential swap participant, Party F, is available to swap the cash flows in years four and five. In other words, Party F would be willing to pay a floating rate on a $10 million notional amount for years four and five and to receive a fixed rate of 12 percent. The swap dealer would find Party F to be a very attractive counterparty. The dealer might be quite willing to swap with Party F on even terms ($1,200,000 versus LIBOR + 3%) just to offset the risk that remained after swapping with Parties A and E. In sum, the swap dealer will be very pleased to create a structure of swaps that leaves no interest rate risk and still provides a decent profit.

The Term Structure of Interest Rates. The term structure of interest rates is an important feature in bond pricing. Not surprisingly, the market for interest rate swaps must reflect the term structure that prevails in the bond market. If the swaps market did not reflect the term structure, traders would find ready arbitrage opportunities, and they could quickly discipline swap traders to pay attention to the term structure. For example, if the term structure is rising, the swap dealer must charge a higher yield on swaps of longer maturity. The next section illustrates these considerations from the term structure.

The Indication Swap Pricing Schedule

In the early to mid-1980s, swap banks were often able to charge a **front-end** fee for arranging a swap. As the market has matured, that ability has been competed away. (For some very complicated swaps that require substantial analysis, front-end fees are still charged, however.) Therefore, the swap dealer today generally receives his total compensation by charging a spread between the rates he is willing to pay and the rate he demands on swap transactions. With a maturing market, this spread has also narrowed. Whereas in the mid-1980s spreads might have been 50 basis points, a 10 basis point spread is much more common today. This tightening spread reflects the increasing liquidity, sophistication, and pricing efficiency of a maturing financial market.

Table 19.4 shows a sample indication pricing schedule for an interest rate swap. The table assumes that the customer of the swap bank will offer LIBOR flat, that is, a rate exactly equal to LIBOR without any yield adjustment. There are two important features of Table 19.4. First, the rate the bank pays or receives increases with the maturity in question. This increase reflects the upward sloping term structure revealed by the column of current T-note yields. Second, the swap bank makes a gross profit that equals the spread between what the bank pays and what it receives. Consequently, the spread ranges from 10 basis points for a two-year horizon to 22 basis points for a ten-year horizon. This increasing spread for more distant maturities reflects the lower liquidity of longer term instruments.

As an example of how the pricing schedule in Table 19.4 functions, assume that the customer wishes to pay a floating rate and receive a fixed rate for seven years. Based on the pricing schedule of Table 19.4, the customer would pay the LIBOR rate on the notional amount in each period and would receive a fixed rate from the swap bank that equals the seven-year T-note rate of 8.14 percent plus 82 basis points for a total rate of 8.96 percent. By contrast, if the customer wishes to pay a fixed rate for a seven-year horizon, the customer would pay the seven-year T-note rate of 8.14 percent plus

Table 19.4	Sample Swap Indication Pricing		
Bank's Fixed Rates: (T-Note Rate Plus Indicated Basis Points)			
Maturity (years)	Bank Pays	Bank Receives	T-Note Yields
2	18	28	7.40
3	34	45	7.66
4	52	68	7.84
5	70	89	8.05
7	82	102	8.14
10	88	110	8.20

Source: From J. Marshall and K. Kapner, *The Swaps Market* (Miami: Kolb Publishing, 1993). Reprinted by permission.

102 basis points for a rate of 9.16 percent. In return, the bank would pay the customer the LIBOR rate in each period.[8] As the swap market has developed in recent years, it has become much more competitive and the spread available to swap dealers has dwindled.[9]

SWAP PORTFOLIOS

In this section we briefly consider the principal risks that a swap dealer faces in managing a swap portfolio. These risks range from default risk to interest rate risk. We then illustrate how the swap dealer can manage some of these risks.

Risks in Managing a Swap Portfolio

In managing a portfolio of many swaps, the swap dealer faces a number of different risks. First, there is the risk that one of its counterparties might default, as we discussed earlier. Second, the bank faces **basis risk** – the risk that the normal relationship between two prices might change. To illustrate this risk, assume that a bank engages in an interest rate swap agreeing to receive the T-note rate plus some basis points and to pay LIBOR. After this agreement is reached, assume that market disturbances in Europe cause LIBOR to rise relative to the T-note rate. The swap dealer must still pay LIBOR, but this rate is now higher than the swap dealer anticipated when it initiated the swap. Therefore, the swap dealer suffers a loss due to basis risk as the normal relationship between LIBOR and the T-note rate has changed.

The swap dealer also faces mis-match risk. When he acts as a counterparty in a swap, the swap dealer accepts a risk position that he is anxious to offset by engaging in other swaps. **Mis-match risk** refers to the risk that the swap dealer will be left in a position that he cannot offset easily through another swap. This arises if there is a mis-match in the needs between the swap dealer and other participants. In Table 19.3, for example, the two swaps with Parties A and E left the swap dealer with a residual risk position, due to the mis-match between the needs of Parties A and E.

One of the most serious risks that the swap dealer faces is interest rate risk. For example, the swap dealer may have promised to pay a floating rate and to receive a fixed rate. If the general level of interest rates rises, the swap dealer's cash outflows will rise as well. However, the dealer continues to receive the stipulated fixed rate. The swap dealer incurs a loss due to a shift in interest rates. In Table 19.3, for example, the swap dealer is left to receive $1.2 million annually and to pay LIBOR + 3% on a notional principal of $10 million in years four and five. If rates rise, the payments that the dealer must make will increase, while the dealer's cash inflows will remain the same. Such a rise in interest rates would generate a loss for the swap dealer, so the dealer faces interest rate risk.

Managing Mis-Match and Interest Rate Risk in a Swap

We illustrate how swap dealers can manage mis-match and interest rate risk by considering the swap dealer's transactions with Parties A and E, as shown in Table 19.3. We have already noted that the swap dealer accepts a risk position by acting as a counterparty in a swap. Because we assume that the swap dealer wishes to function strictly as a financial intermediary and not as a speculator, the dealer is anxious to avoid any risk that it might have temporarily undertaken to complete the swap.

In our discussion of Table 19.3, for example, we saw that the dealer participated in a swap with Party A and was able to offset part of the risk by engaging in another swap with Party E. As Table 19.3 shows, however, some residual risk remains. Specifically, the swap bank is still committed to receiving $1.2 million and paying LIBOR + 3% on a notional amount of $10 million in years four and five.

This residual risk position reflects both mis-match risk and interest rate risk. The mis-match risk occurs because the dealer was unable to offset the risks associated with the swap with Party A. The transaction with Party E offset most of the risk arising from the swap with Party A, but some risk remains due to the mis-match between the needs of Parties A and E. The transactions of Table 19.3 also reflect a continuing interest rate risk. As we noted, if rates rise, the dealer suffers a loss as it must pay the higher floating rates that result.

As a consequence, the swap dealer will be anxious to avoid these two remaining risks associated with his commitments in periods four and five in Table 19.3. Ideally, the dealer would arrange a third swap, in addition to those with Parties A and E, to offset this risk. For example, the dealer would like to swap to receive floating and pay fixed for years four and five. Such a transaction would avoid both the mis-match and the interest rate risk. However, such swaps are not always immediately available to the dealer. As a consequence, the swap dealer will seek other means to control this risk.

When the swap dealer faces a risk such as that in Table 19.3, he can use the futures market as a temporary means of offsetting the risk. For example, the swap dealer might sell Eurodollar futures with a distant expiration. Eurodollar rates are highly correlated with LIBOR. With this transaction, the swap dealer offsets a considerable portion of the risk that remains in Table 19.3. When the swap dealer executes the futures transaction properly, he will be left only with an obligation to pay a fixed amount.

However, even after this transaction, some risk remains. Eurodollar futures may be a close substitute for the unavailable swap, but they are unlikely to provided a perfect substitute. In our example, the dealer will probably not be able to match the futures expiration with the four and five year cash flows, there is likely to be some imperfection in setting the quantity of futures to trade, and there is still some basis risk between the LIBOR rate of the cash flows in years four and five and the rate on the Eurodollars.

Because of these imperfections in substituting for the unavailable swap, the swap dealer will likely continue to seek a swap that meets the risk needs exactly. However, until that is available, the Eurodollar futures position can act as an effective risk-reducing position.

CONCLUSION

This chapter introduced the swaps market. From origins in the late 1970s and early 1980s, the swaps market has grown to enormous proportions, with notionals approaching $3 trillion. Most of the market is concentrated in interest rate swaps, but there are also billions of dollars of foreign currency swaps outstanding as well. Of all swaps, about 40 to 50 percent involve the U.S. dollar.

In contrast with futures and exchange-traded options, we noted that swap agreements are extremely flexible in amount, maturity, and other contract terms. As further points of differentiation between futures and exchange-traded options versus swaps, the swaps market does not utilize an exchange and is virtually free of governmental regulation.

The chapter also analyzed plain vanilla interest rate and currency swaps. We saw that an interest rate swap essentially involves a commitment by two parties to exchange cash flows tied to some principal, or notional, amount. One party pays a fixed rate, while the second party pays a floating rate. In a foreign currency swap, both parties acquire funds in different currencies and exchange those principal amounts. Each party pays interest to the other in the currency that was acquired, with these interest payments taking place over the term of the swap agreement. To terminate the agreement, the parties again exchange foreign currency. Motivations for swaps arise from a desire to avoid financial risk or a chance to exploit some borrowing advantage.

Swap brokers and dealers are two kinds of swap facilitators. A swap broker helps counterparties complete swaps by providing introduction and guidance in the negotiation of the swap, but the swap broker does not take a risk position in the swap. By contrast, a swap dealer provides the services of the swap broker, but will also act as a counterparty in a swap. For the swap dealer, we considered the factors that influence pricing, and we discussed the techniques that swap dealers use to manage the risk associated with their portfolios of swaps.

QUESTIONS AND PROBLEMS

1. Explain the differences between a plain vanilla interest rate swap and a plain vanilla currency swap.
2. What are the two major kinds of swap facilitators? What is the key difference between the roles they play?
3. Assume that you are a financial manager for a large commercial bank and that you expect short-term interest rates to rise more than the yield curve would suggest. Would you rather pay a fixed long-term rate and receive a floating short rate, or the other way around? Explain your reasoning.
4. Explain the role that the notional principal plays in understanding swap transactions. Why is this principal amount regarded as only notional? (Hint: What is the dictionary definition of "notional"?)
5. Consider a plain vanilla interest rate swap. Explain how the practice of net payments works.
6. Assume that the yield curve is flat, that the swaps market is efficient, and that two equally creditworthy counterparties engage in an interest rate swap. Who should pay the higher rate, the party that pays a floating short-term rate or the party that pays a fixed long-term rate? Explain.

7. In a currency swap, counterparties exchange the same sums at the beginning and the end of the swap period. Explain how this practice relates to the custom of making interest payments during the life of the swap agreement.
8. Explain why a currency swap is also called an "exchange of borrowings."
9. Assume that LIBOR stands today at 9 percent and the seven-year T-note rate is 10 percent. Establish an indication pricing schedule for a seven-year interest rate swap, assuming that the swap dealer must make a gross spread of 40 basis points.
10. Explain how basis risk affects a swap dealer. Does it affect a swap broker the same way? Explain.
11. Assume a swap dealer attempts to function as a pure financial intermediary avoiding all interest rate risk. Explain how such a dealer may yet come to bear interest rate risk.

NOTES

[1] Catharina J. Hooyman, "The Use of Foreign Exchange Swaps by Central Banks," *International Monetary Fund Staff Papers*, 41:1, May 1994, pp. 149–62, reports that central banks have used foreign exchange swaps in the conduct of monetary policy, although that practice seems now to be losing favor.

[2] This does not mean to imply that exchange trading sacrifices all anonymity. However, traders watch the activities of major institutions. When these institutions initiate major transactions, it is not possible to maintain complete privacy. It is somewhat ironic that individual traders can trade on futures and options markets with a discretion that is not available to multi-billion dollar financial institutions.

[3] The practice of net payments and not actually exchanging principal also protects each counterparty from default by the other. For example, it would be very unpleasant for Party A if it paid the principal amount of $1 million in our example and Party B failed to make its payment to Party A. Making only net payments greatly reduces the potential impact of default.

[4] Some authors consider the plain vanilla currency swap to be an arrangement in which one party pays a fixed rate while the other pays a floating rate, thus creating a fixed-for-floating currency swap. Our example is a fixed-for-fixed currency swap. Chapter 20 considers some of the various types of currency swaps in more detail.

[5] This discussion of comparative advantage draws on the excellent analysis by K. Kapner and J. Marshall in *The Swaps Handbook*, New York: New York Institute of Finance, 1990.

[6] The swap dealer will also consider some other issues in setting final pricing terms. If the swap is very complicated, the swap dealer may charge a higher price than otherwise. Similarly, if the swap is to involve cross-border currency flows, the dealer may be concerned with regulatory constraints that might impede the flow of funds.

[7] The problem of default risk is receiving active attention. See, for example, Eric H. Sorensen and Thierry F. Bollier, "Pricing Swap Default Risk," *Financial Analysts Journal*, 50:3, May/June 1994, pp. 23–33 for a model of swap default risk. Some swap agreements allow a party to terminate a swap agreement if a counterparty receives a credit downgrade. Douglas J. Lucas explores this issue in his paper, "The Effectiveness of Downgrade Provisions in Reducing Counterparty Credit Risk," *Journal of Fixed Income*, 5:1, June 1995, pp. 32–41.

[8] In actual market practice, the participants must carefully consider the actual way in which yields are calculated on Treasury securities versus the money market computations that govern LIBOR. We abstract from these technicalities.

[9] See Keith C. Brown, W. V. Harlow, and Donald J. Smith, ''An Empirical Analysis of Interest Rate Swap Spreads,'' *Journal of Fixed Income*, 3:4, March 1994, pp. 61–78. These authors find that the spreads have narrowed considerably.

CHAPTER
20

THE SWAPS MARKET: REFINEMENTS

OVERVIEW

This chapter extends our discussion of swaps to more sophisticated swap structures and applications. In addition, the chapter revisits both options and futures to highlight some of the connections among futures, options, and swaps.

The discussion begins by considering some more complex types of swaps. Both interest rate and foreign currency options have a number of variations that make swaps an even more flexible financial instrument. In addition, emerging equity and commodity swaps promise to bring the swap market into corporate equity financing and into trade in physical commodities.

The chapter also considers extensions to swaps by showing how they can be extended to incorporate option features. A **swaption**, for example, is an option on a swap. In addition, we will see that an interest rate swap can be analyzed as a portfolio of interest rate futures contracts, when the expiration dates on the futures contracts match the payment dates on a swap.

As these swap structures become more complicated, they become more difficult to evaluate. Accordingly, the chapter considers a general technique that allows the potential swap user to compare alternative financial arrangements to find the best overall terms. This technique is called the **all-in-cost**.

BEYOND PLAIN VANILLA SWAPS[1]

In Chapter 19 we focused on plain vanilla interest rate and currency swaps. In this section we explore the additional features that swaps may possess to make them more varied, more flexible, and more efficiently designed for particular risk management situations. Currently, there is a bewildering variety of swap structures being used in the market, and new features are constantly being created. Therefore, the catalog of this section is incomplete, but it provides some insight into the basic enhancements that can extend swaps beyond the plain vanilla structure that we have explored. We consider interest rate swaps and foreign currency swaps in turn.

635

Flavored Interest Rate Swaps

A plain vanilla interest rate swap has a constant notional principal for the life of the swap. Further, each interest payment on the fixed side is for the same amount, being calculated on the same notional principal at the same rate of interest. While the floating payment may vary due to fluctuating interest rates, it is computed on the same notional principal in each period. It is possible to extend interest rate swaps beyond the plain vanilla structure by altering the characteristics of the notional principal or the payments derived from that principal.

In an **amortizing swap**, the notional principal is reduced over time. This means that the fixed interest payment becomes smaller during the life of the swap, and the floating payment does as well, at least if interest rates are stable. An amortizing swap is particularly useful for swaps designed to manage the risks associated with mortgage debt. Because mortgage principal is generally amortized, an amortizing swap provides a useful instrument for managing the interest rate risk associated with mortgages.

While the notional principal diminishes in an amortizing swap, it can also be scheduled to increase. In an **accreting swap**, the notional principal becomes larger during the life of the swap. This kind of swap matches the cash flows often encountered in construction finance. For example, consider a construction project in which the builder will draw down $10 million of additional financing at the end of each of the seven years of the life of a particular building project as interim construction objectives are achieved. Typically, this kind of financing is committed at the outset of the project, and the additional loans are promised at a floating rate. These flows could be converted to a fixed rate through an accreting swap designed with a principal that increases $10 million each year and a fixed interest rate.

By combining features of amortizing and accreting swaps, it is possible to create interest rate swaps with quite variable notional principals that increase and decrease over the life of the swap. In a **seasonal swap**, the notional principal varies according to a fixed plan. This kind of swap can be useful in matching the financing needs of retailers. For example, the swap could be structured on a seasonal basis to match the typically heavy fourth quarter cash needs of retailing firms. When the swap has radically fluctuating notional principal amounts, the swap is called a **roller coaster swap**. Thus, the notional principal can be structured to conform to any financing or risk management need.

In addition to allowing the notional principal of an interest rate swap to vary, swaps can be created with variations on coupon payments. In a plain vanilla swap, the fixed and floating payments are established at the prevailing rates when the swap is initiated. For example, consider a five-year swap with annual payments on a notional principal of $25 million initiated when the yield curve is flat at 8 percent. In this situation, one might create an **off-market swap** by setting the fixed payment at 9 percent and the floating payment equal to the LIBOR rate. In this example, the fixed payor has agreed to pay a higher rate over the life of the swap. To compensate for this series of extra payments, the floating rate payor must make an additional cash payment to the fixed rate payor. With a fixed rate of interest at 1 percent above the market on a notional principal of $25 million, the fixed payor will be paying an excess $250,000 each year. With the yield curve flat at 8 percent, the appropriate payment from the floating to fixed payor would be the present value of those five payments of $250,000 discounted at 8 percent, which is $998,178.

In this example, the fixed payor receives $998,178 at the initiation of the swap and pays $2,250,000 annually. The floating rate payor pays at a floating rate on a notional principal of $25 million. Thus, this example includes features of a loan and an interest rate swap, with the floating rate payor providing approximately $1 million of financing to the fixed rate payor as part of the swap agreement.

As we have seen for a plain vanilla interest rate swap, one party pays a fixed rate of interest, while the second pays a floating rate. In a **basis swap**, both parties pay a floating rate of interest, but the payments are computed on different indexes. Let us assume that the three-month LIBOR currently stands at 6 percent, while the three-month T-bill rate is 5.25 percent. In a basis swap with a notional principal of $100 million based on these two rates, one party might pay the T-bill rate plus 75 basis points, while the second party would pay LIBOR. Although the T-bill rate and LIBOR tend to move together, the spread between the two rates does change with the perceived differential in default risk between Eurocurrencies and U.S. treasuries.

If the rate widens, the party paying the T-bill rate plus 75 basis points will win; if the rate narrows, the party paying LIBOR will win. For example, assuming annual payments on the $100 million notional principal, both parties expect to pay $6 million annually. If rates rise, but LIBOR rises more due, perhaps, to political unrest, rates might change to a T-bill rate of 5.50 percent and a LIBOR rate of 6.40 percent. With these new rates, the LIBOR payment would be $6,400,000, while the T-bill payor would be obligated for $6,250,000, leaving a net payment of $150,000 per year from the LIBOR payor.

Another kind of basis swap is a yield curve swap. In a **yield curve swap**, both parties pay a floating rate, but the indexes differ in yields. For example, one party might pay based on the three-month T-bill rate, while the other party might pay based on a 30-year bellwether bond. Assuming that long-term rates are initially above short-term rates, a flattening yield curve would benefit the party paying based on the 30-year bond, while a steepening yield curve would benefit the payor basis payment on the short-term index.

This kind of yield curve swap is a technique that might appeal to financial institutions, particularly those with long-term assets and short-term liabilities, such as a savings and loan association. For example, assume that a savings and loan holds short-term deposits and long-term assets. Such an institution is subject to losses if short-term rates rise relative to long-term rates. The savings and loan might enter a yield curve swap in which it makes payments based on a long-term index and receives payments based on a short-term index. This swap arrangement could help protect the institution from the yield curve risk that it faces in its core S&L business.

Flavored Currency Swaps

The plain vanilla currency swap calls for the two parties to make a series of fixed payments denominated in two currencies. For example, one party might pay $1 million annually, while the other party might pay DM 1.8 million. In addition, there is generally an exchange of principal amounts at the outset and at the conclusion of the swap. Currency swaps are subject to many of the same elaborations as those we have considered for interest rate swaps.

As we observed in discussing interest rate swaps, more complicated swap structures can be created by allowing the notional principal to vary over the tenor of the swap. In the context of interest rate swaps, we considered amortizing, accreting, seasonal, and roller coaster swaps based on pre-negotiated changes in the notional principal. Currency swaps are subject to the same variations. For example, a U.S. firm might import clothes from Hong Kong, with much higher imports in the winter, and pay for these in Hong Kong dollars. The firm might structure a currency swap with a seasonal notional amount to match its greater anticipated need for funds in winter months.

As with interest rate swaps, more complex currency swaps also can be created by creating variations in the interest payments. In Chapter 19 we considered an example of a plain vanilla currency swap in which each party paid interest at a fixed rate. This was a **fixed-for-fixed currency swap**. It is also possible to create a **fixed-for-floating currency swap**.[2] In this type of swap, parties typically exchange principal at the outset of the swap, but one party pays a fixed rate of interest on the foreign currency it receives, while the other pays a floating rate on the currency it receives.

As an example of a fixed-for-floating currency swap, consider a swap arranged between a German and a Japanese firm, assuming that one mark is worth 60 yen. Let the notional amount be DM 10,000,000 and ‡60,000,000, with a tenor of four years based on annual payments. The German four-year interest rate is 7 percent, and the Japanese firm promises to pay this fixed rate. For its part, the German firm promises to pay a floating Japanese rate, which is currently 5 percent. Assuming no change in rates, Table 20.1 shows the anticipated cash flows.

Two fixed-for-floating swaps can be combined to create a fixed-for-fixed currency swaps. A **circus swap** is a fixed-for-fixed currency swap created by arranging a pair of fixed-for-floating swaps. As an example, consider a firm that has entered into a fixed-for-floating swap to receive fixed French franc payments and to pay in U.S. dollars based on LIBOR. By pairing this swap with another fixed-for-floating agreement, the firm can create a fixed-for-fixed swap. For example, assume that the second swap agreement obligates the firm to make fixed payments in German marks and to receive floating payments in U.S. dollars. Figure 20.1 shows the two fixed-for-floating swaps.

As Figure 20.1 shows, the firm both makes and receives floating U.S. dollar payments. Thus, assuming equal notional principal amounts for the two swaps, these payments offset each other. Figure 20.2 shows the net cash flows resulting from this circus swap for the firm. Given the offset of the U.S. dollar flows, the firm is left receiving fixed French franc payments and paying fixed German mark payments.

COMMODITY SWAPS

In a **commodity swap** the counterparties make payments based on the price of a specified amount of a commodity, with one party paying a fixed price for the good over the tenor of the swap, while

Table 20.1	A Fixed-for-Floating Currency Swap

Outset
    German firm pays DM 10,000,000
    Japanese firm pays ¥60,000,000

Annual Interest Payments (assuming no fluctuations in rates)
    German firm pays ¥3,000,000 (at a floating rate of 5 percent)
    Japanese firm pays DM 700,000 (at a fixed rate of 7 percent)

Termination
    German firm pays ¥60,000,000
    Japanese firm pays DM 10,000,000

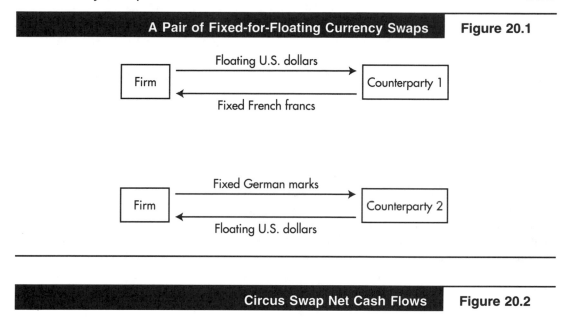

A Pair of Fixed-for-Floating Currency Swaps — **Figure 20.1**

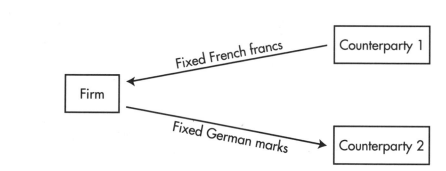

Circus Swap Net Cash Flows — **Figure 20.2**

the second party pays a floating price. In general, the commodity is not actually exchanged, and the parties make only net payments. Chase Manhattan Bank created the first commodity swap in 1986.[3]

As an example, consider a rice farmer producing 200 tons of rice annually. The farmer is anxious to avoid the price fluctuations of the spot rice market, particularly as import restrictions in Japan and Korea wax and wane. However, the farmer is uncomfortable trying to use the futures market in rice due to its low liquidity and uncertain future. Therefore, the farmer seeks a swap arrangement in which she receives a fixed payment per ton for each of the next five years and pays the actual market price of rice each year. Figure 20.3 shows the cash flows associated with this swap agreement. Each year, the farmer pays the actual price of rice based on the nominal amount of 200 tons, while the counterparty pays a fixed price negotiated when the swap agreement was established. With this arrangement, the farmer knows that she will receive a certain price for her rice for each of the next five years.

Figure 20.3   **A Commodity Swap for Rice**

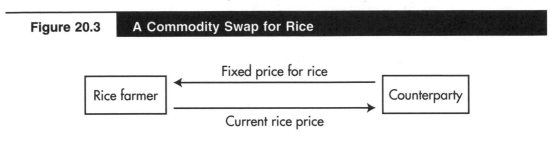

If we consider a single annual crop, this swap agreement has a structure that is very similar to the classic hedging example with agricultural futures. In the classic short hedge, the farmer anticipates a harvest and sells futures to establish a fixed price for her crop. In fact, a commodity swap is so similar to a futures contract that the Commodity Futures Trading Commission (CFTC) restricted the permissible range of commodity swap agreements to ensure that they remained sufficiently distinct from the futures contracts that the Commission regulates. Specifically, the CFTC stipulated that such agreements cannot be canceled by one party alone, that they are not supported by a system of margins or marking-to-market, that the agreements be related to the parties' normal line of business, and that the transactions be restricted to commercial firms and not the retail trade.[4]

The form of a commodity swap is very similar to that of an interest rate swap. Neither type of swap employs an exchange of notionals. In a commodity swap, one party pays a fixed rate while the second pays a floating rate, just as in an interest rate swap. Further, only net payments are actually made, as in interest rate swaps. The basic difference is simply that the underlying good in an interest rate swap is cash, while the underlying good in a commodity swap is some physical good.

EQUITY SWAPS

In an **equity swap**, the counterparties exchange payments based on a notional principal specified as a stock portfolio. Like a commodity swap, the equity swap is quite similar to an interest rate swap, because there is an underlying notional principal, a fixed tenor, and one party paying a fixed rate while the other pays a floating rate.

Consider an institutional investor with a $100 million portfolio of stocks invested in an index fund that tracks the S&P 500. If the manager of this portfolio becomes bearish, she has several choices for avoiding the risk of a stock market decline. She could sell the stocks in the portfolio, hedge the stock market risk in the futures market, or hedge the risk by using index options. She could also use an equity swap.

For her situation, the portfolio manager could enter an equity swap agreement in which she pays the S&P 500 return each period and receives a fixed percentage payment, with both payments being based on the $100 million notional principal of her portfolio. For example, each quarter the portfolio manager might pay the total return earned by the S&P 500 and receive a quarterly payment of 2.5 percent, both payments being based on the $100 million notional principal. Figure 20.4 illustrates these cash flows. This arrangement would insulate the value of the portfolio against any drop in the stock market and guarantee the portfolio manager a quarterly return of 2.5 percent.

For example, if the S&P 500 enjoyed a return of 3 percent in a given quarter, her undisturbed portfolio would rise in value by 3 percent and she would pay this to the counterparty, so this would

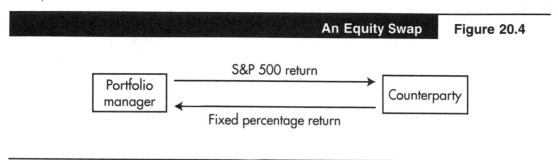

An Equity Swap | **Figure 20.4**

leave the portfolio value unchanged. However, the portfolio manager would also receive a payment of 2.5 percent. If the S&P 500 had a return of −5 percent, the portfolio manager would make no payment and would receive a payment of 7.5 percent. This inflow of 7.5 percent, combined with the drop in the value of the portfolio of 5 percent, would still give a net return on the portfolio of 2.5 percent.

As with the other swap structures we have considered in this chapter, the equity swap can be elaborated by allowing variations in the notional principal or the periodic payment. For example, one variant of the equity swap might be for one counterparty to pay the S&P 500 return and receive the Russell 2000 return, creating a swap agreement to speculate on the differential return between large and small stocks.

FORWARD AND EXTENSION SWAPS[5]

A **forward swap** is a swap agreement in which the parties agree that the cash flows will begin at a date in the future and that they may be interest rate, currency, commodity, or equity swaps. For example, two counterparties might agree to exchange LIBOR for a fixed rate beginning in two years, with the tenor of the swap being five years from that date. If the contractual rates are based on the forward rate for the two instruments at the planned initiation date, there should be no exchange of cash at the initiation of the agreement. If the rates specified do not conform to the forward rates for the planned inception of the cash flows, then the swap is an off-market swap and one party will be obligated to pay the other.

An **extension swap** is a swap agreement designed to extend the tenor of an existing swap. As such, an extension swap is a special type of forward swap. For example, in the middle of the tenor of an interest rate swap in which one party pays LIBOR plus 50 basis points and receives the two-year T-note rate, the parties might agree to extend the tenor of the swap by an additional three years. If the agreement is initiated based on the forward rates for the date of inception (i.e., at the termination of the current swap agreement), there should be no payment at the time the agreement is made.

SWAPTIONS

A **swaption** is an option on a swap. Like all options, there are call swaptions and put swaptions, and they may be either American or European in form. The owner of a call swaption has the right to buy a swap by paying the exercise price, while the seller of a call swaption is obligated to sell a swap for the exercise price. (The buyer of an interest rate swap pays a fixed rate of interest and receives a floating rate.) The owner of a put swaption has the right to sell a swap at the exercise price, while the seller of a put swaption is obligated to sell a swap at the exercise price. For all of these options, there is some stated expiration date.

To understand these features more clearly, consider a call swaption. The purchaser of the call will pay an agreed premium to the seller at the inception of the transaction. Usually the premium is stated as some number of basis points on the notional principal of the swap underlying the option. It is typical for this premium to lie in the range of 20–40 basis points, but the premium depends upon the exercise price, the time to expiration, and the volatility of the underlying rates.[6] The exercise price of the swaption is a fixed rate specified in the swaption agreement. Assuming the swaption is European, the owner will exercise the call swaption if the contractual fixed rate (the exercise price) is lower than the fixed rate prevailing in the open market for swaps with the same tenor as that underlying the swaption.

As an example, consider a European call swaption on a five-year swap with annual payments and a notional principal of $10,000,000. Let us assume that the fixed rate specified in the swap agreement is 8 percent and the floating rate is LIBOR plus 50 basis points. For such a call swaption, the premium might be 30 basis points. With a principal of $10,000,000, the premium would then be $30,000. Six months after contracting, at the expiration date of the option, the owner of the call swaption can either exercise or let the option expire worthless. The owner will exercise if the market rate for the fixed payor on this type of option is less than 8 percent. The benefit for the call holder is the present value of the cash flows due to the difference between the contractual rate of 8 percent and the fixed rate available in the open market, say 7.60 percent. The call holder benefits if the market rate for fixed payments is less than 8 percent, because by exercising the option, the call owner will secure a swap agreement in which he receives a fixed payment of 8 percent over the tenor of the swap. Without the call swaption, the trader would receive only the currently available fixed rate of 7.60 percent. In virtue of the swaption, the trader receives an additional 40 basis points over the tenor of the swap.

Swaptions offer the same kinds of speculative and hedging opportunities of all other options, as we have studied in previous chapters. As an example, consider a firm that has issued a callable bond. We may analyze a bond with a call provision as consisting of a noncallable bond plus the purchase of a call option on the bond. From the issuing firm's point of view, the firm has paid for the option by promising a higher coupon rate for the callable bond than the rate necessary for a noncallable bond.

Now assume that the firm has determined that it will not wish to call the bond. Having made this determination, the call feature on the bond has no value to the firm, yet the option still has value in the marketplace. The bond-issuing firm could then sell a call swaption with terms that match the call feature of the bond. In effect, this transaction would unwind the call feature inherent in the original bond. The firm bought a call swaption from the bondholders with its original issuance, and by selling a call swaption, it recaptures the remaining value in the call feature that the firm no longer desires.

If rates do not fall sufficiently to engender exercise of the call swaption against the firm, the firm merely keeps the option premium, and this cash inflow offsets the value of the call feature inherent in the callable bond. On the other hand, if the owner of the call swaption exercises against the firm, it will have done so because fixed rates are below the currently available fixed rate on a swap. If this exercise is reasonable, the issuer of the callable bond now has an incentive to exercise its call option against its own bondholders, and it should not lose on the exercise.

AN INTEREST RATE SWAP AS A PORTFOLIO OF FORWARD CONTRACTS

In this section we analyze an interest rate swap in terms of a portfolio of interest rate forward contracts.[7] Consider a forward contract on an interest rate instrument that calls for the purchaser to receive delivery of a three-month money market instrument on the expiration date in exchange for a payment determined when the forward contract is negotiated. The purchaser of the forward contract will gain from the transaction when the yield implied by the forward contract is lower than the yield prevailing on three-month instruments at the expiration of the forward contract. In effect, the forward contract requires the exchange of a fixed payment for a floating payment, with the gain or loss being realized at the expiration date.

To make this example more concrete, assume that today is December 15, 1997, and a party buys a forward contract to mature on December 15, 1998, that calls for the purchase of $1,000,000 face value of three-month Eurodollar deposits at a yield of 9 percent. This contract essentially establishes the payment of a fixed rate of 9 percent for these instruments. If the actual yield on these instruments at the expiration date is lower than 9 percent, say 8 percent, then the purchaser of the forward contract has a gain. For a three-month zero coupon instrument and typical money market yield conventions, this 1 percent interest rate differential would be worth $2,500, reflecting a $25 per basis point value.

In essence, this forward contract is similar to one of the payments in an interest rate swap agreement. An interest rate swap agreement is a portfolio of such payments. Therefore, we may analyze an interest rate swap as a portfolio of forward contracts with successive expiration dates.

As we learned in Chapter 2, futures contracts are a type of forward contract with specific additional institutional features. A futures is distinguished from other forward contracts by the margining and daily resettlement feature along with the presence of exchange trading and clearinghouse guarantees. Aside from these institutional considerations, an interest rate futures contract is essentially like an interest rate forward contract. Therefore, an interest rate swap can be viewed as a portfolio of successively maturing interest rate futures contracts. In terms of our earlier example, we might think of an interest rate swap as being similar to a strip of interest rate futures contracts. As we noted in Chapter 6, a **strip** is a sequence of futures contracts with successive expirations. Because interest rate swap agreements so often use LIBOR as the floating rate in the contract, a strip of Eurodollar futures contracts is highly analogous to an interest rate swap agreement.

One of the main reasons for the development of the swap market was the need for custom-tailored instruments with a tenor that exceeded the maturities available in the futures market. Typically, futures contract maturities do not extend for more than two years or so, but swap agreements can have a considerably longer tenor. Further, most futures contracts have very limited volume and open interest in the more distant maturities. As we have seen in Chapter 19, a swap dealer who participates in an interest rate swap may be left with a risk position that is undesired. As we saw in our earlier discussion, the swap dealer accepts this risk position to complete the swap agreement and earn a fee, but the dealer would typically like to avoid this risk.

If a strip of futures contracts could be regarded as a substitute for an interest rate swap, the swap dealer might be able to use Eurodollar strips to hedge unwanted interest rate risk that arises in the swap business. However, such a strategy would require an active market in distant Eurodollar maturities. In the earlier days of the swaps market, the Eurodollar futures contract certainly did not possess the depth or liquidity to allow Eurodollar strips to serve this roll. For example, at the end of 1986, total open interest in all Eurodollar contract expirations was 214,000 and the most distant listed Eurodollar futures was the December 1988 contract, which was only two years distant. Figure 20.5 shows recent quotations for the Eurodollar contract with an extremely high level of open interest and with contract expirations extending for many years. This extended maturity range and deep liquidity is unparalleled for any other futures contract of any type. The main reason for these special features is the interest of swap dealers in using Eurodollar strips to offset risk inherent in the interest rate swap positions that they undertake.

CREATING SYNTHETIC SECURITIES WITH SWAPS

In earlier chapters, we saw that certain securities could be synthesized from combinations of derivatives. For example, in Chapter 11 we explored the put-call parity relationship that shows how any three of four instruments (a put, a call, the underlying good, a risk-free bond) can synthesize the fourth instrument. In this section, we explore some similar relationships using swaps. This idea is already familiar; as we have just seen in the preceding section, a swap is, in effect, a portfolio of forward contracts.

Figure 20.5   Quotations for Eurodollar Futures

EURODOLLAR (CME)-$1 million; pts of 100%

	Open	High	Low	Settle	Chg	Yield Settle	Chg	Open Interest
May	94.54	94.55	94.54	94.55	....	5.45	....	17,564
June	94.56	94.56	94.53	94.55	....	5.45	....	380,507
July	94.50	94.51	94.49	94.50	− .01	5.50	+ .01	2,130
Sept	94.40	94.41	94.35	94.38	− .01	5.62	+ .01	358,468
Dec	94.14	94.15	94.10	94.14	− .01	5.86	+ .01	344,217
Mr97	93.94	93.97	93.91	93.96	− .01	6.04	+ .01	239,138
June	93.81	93.81	93.75	93.79	− .01	6.21	+ .01	201,494
Sept	93.67	93.67	93.62	93.66	− .02	6.34	+ .02	174,671
Dec	93.51	93.52	93.48	93.52	− .01	6.48	+ .01	134,625
Mr98	93.48	93.48	93.43	93.47	− .01	6.53	+ .01	108,682
June	93.40	93.40	93.36	93.40	− .01	6.60	+ .01	86,446
Sept	93.32	93.32	93.29	93.33	− .01	6.67	+ .01	72,242
Dec	93.21	93.22	93.19	93.22	− .01	6.78	+ .01	57,318
Mr99	93.17	93.18	93.15	93.18	− .01	6.82	+ .01	46,463
June	93.10	93.12	93.10	93.13	....	6.87	....	42,479
Sept	93.05	93.07	93.04	93.08	....	6.92	....	33,776
Dec	92.96	92.98	92.96	92.99	....	7.01	....	29,290
Mr00	92.93	92.95	92.93	92.96	....	7.04	....	28,475
June	92.88	92.91	92.87	92.91	+ .01	7.09	− .01	25,174
Sept	92.83	92.86	92.82	92.86	+ .01	7.14	− .01	20,800
Dec	92.75	92.78	92.74	92.78	+ .01	7.22	− .01	17,609
Mr01	92.73	92.76	92.72	92.76	+ .01	7.24	− .01	13,037
June	92.68	92.71	92.68	92.72	+ .02	7.28	− .02	6,775
Sept	92.64	92.67	92.64	92.67	+ .01	7.33	− .01	6,122
Dec	92.56	92.59	92.56	92.59	+ .01	7.41	− .01	5,846
Mr02	92.56	92.59	92.56	92.59	+ .01	7.41	− .01	6,343
June	....	....	....	92.54	+ .01	7.46	− .01	4,331
Sept	....	....	....	92.49	+ .01	7.51	− .01	5,070
Dec	92.40	92.43	92.39	92.42	+ .01	7.58	− .01	5,301
Mr03	....	....	....	92.43	+ .01	7.57	− .01	4,744
June	....	....	....	92.39	+ .01	7.61	− .01	3,683
Sept	....	....	....	92.35	+ .01	7.65	− .01	4,346
Dec	....	....	....	92.28	+ .01	7.72	− .01	3,517
Mr04	....	....	....	92.30	+ .01	7.70	− .01	2,027
June	....	....	....	92.27	+ .01	7.73	− .01	3,032
Sept	....	....	....	92.23	+ .01	7.77	− .01	3,516
Dec	....	....	....	92.16	+ .01	7.84	− .01	3,787
Mr05	....	....	....	92.18	+ .01	7.82	− .01	2,364
June	....	....	....	92.14	+ .01	7.86	− .01	1,762
Sept	....	....	....	92.10	+ .01	7.90	− .01	1,208
Dec	....	....	....	92.03	+ .01	7.97	− .01	785
Mr06	....	....	....	92.05	+ .01	7.95	− .01	613

Est vol 236,592; vol Mn 293,690; open int 2,509,777, +5,561.

Source: *The Wall Street Journal,* April 24, 1996.

Synthetic Fixed Rate Debt

Consider a firm with an existing floating rate debt obligation that wishes to eliminate the uncertainty inherent in floating debt. A firm in this position could create a synthetic fixed rate debt instrument by combining its existing floating rate obligation with an interest rate swap. Assume a firm has an outstanding issue of $50,000,000 on which it pays a floating rate annual coupon and that the debt matures in six years. The firm wishes to transform this obligation into a fixed rate instrument with the same maturity.

Figure 20.6 shows the firm's existing obligation in the upper time line. To transform this existing obligation into a fixed rate instrument, the firm can engage in a swap agreement to receive a floating rate and pay a fixed rate, with a tenor and payment timing to match its existing debt, as shown in the bottom time line of Figure 20.6. The combination of the existing debt and the pay fixed/receive floating interest rate swap gives the firm a synthetic fixed rate obligation instead of its current floating rate debt.

Elements of Synthetic Fixed-Rate Debt   **Figure 20.6**

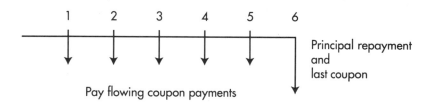

Synthetic Floating Rate Debt

An existing fixed rate obligation can be transformed into floating rate debt by reversing the technique used to create synthetic fixed rate debt. Assume a firm has an existing fixed rate debt obligation with a maturity of six years that requires annual interest rate payments. The upper time line of Figure 20.7 shows the cash flows associated with this obligation. (This example parallels that of Figure 20.6, except the initial obligation has fixed rate coupons.)

By combining this fixed rate obligation with an interest rate swap to pay a fixed rate and receive a floating rate, the instrument can be transformed from a fixed rate to a synthetic floating rate obligation. The lower time line of Figure 20.7 shows the cash flows on an interest rate swap to pay fixed and receive floating. By combining this swap with the existing obligation, the firm transforms its existing fixed rate obligation into a synthetic floating rate debt with the same maturity.

Synthetic Callable Debt

Consider a firm with an outstanding fixed rate obligation that possesses no call feature. The issuing firm would like to be able to call this debt in three years but does not want the obligation to retire

Figure 20.7	**Elements of Synthetic Floating-Rate Debt**

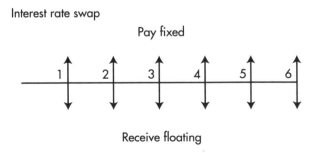

the issue. In essence, the firm wishes that the existing noncallable debt had a call provision allowing a call in three years.

When a firm calls an existing debt instrument, it repays the debt. We may view that repayment as creating a new financing need that the firm will meet from floating rate obligations. After all, in calling the debt, it retired the existing fixed rate obligation. From this perspective we may see that the decision to call an existing fixed rate obligation is like creating a synthetic floating rate debt obligation using a call. As we have just seen, a fixed rate debt obligation, combined with an interest rate swap to receive fixed payments and pay floating, transforms the fixed rate instrument into a floating rate obligation.

However, in the present instance, the issuer wishes to have the option, but not the obligation, to make this transformation. Therefore, the firm can create a synthetic callable bond by using a swaption. Because the firm wants to possess the call option, we know that the firm must purchase a swaption, because only buying an option gives that flexibility. The swap must allow the firm to receive fixed and pay a floating rate; therefore, the firm needs the option to sell a swap. (Recall that purchasing a swap means to pay fixed and receive floating.) Consequently, the firm needs to purchase a put swaption with a maturity of three years. The exercise price on the put swaption will play the role of the call price on a callable bond. Thus, by combining a noncallable fixed rate debt obligation with the purchase of a put swaption, the firm can transform its initial obligation into a callable bond.

Synthetic Noncallable Debt

A firm with outstanding callable debt can use interest rate swaps to eliminate the call feature. When it issued the callable debt, the firm essentially purchased a call option from the bondholders. If the firm is sure that it will not wish to call the debt, it may wish to recapture the value represented by that call option.

If the issuance of callable debt involves the sale of a call option to the bondholders, this can be "unwound" by now selling a call swaption with the correct characteristics – the same characteristics possessed by the option that the firm purchased from its bondholders. Specifically, the call swaption that the firm now decides to sell should have maturity and exercise incentives that match those inherent in the original callable debt. Measured from the expiration date of the swaption, the swap should have a tenor that matches the remaining life of the bond from that date.

Once it sells the call swaption, two outcomes are possible. The option can expire worthless or the option can be exercised against the issuing firm. If the option is never exercised, the firm merely continues to pay the fixed rate of interest for the full life of the bond and the original call feature on the bond never comes into play. The first line of Table 20.2 shows the firm's position if the swaption is never exercised. If the swaption is not exercised against the firm, the firm will simply not exercise the call provision in the bonds it has issued, and the firm will in effect have a straight debt obligation.

If interest rates fall sufficiently, the owners of the call swaption will exercise that option against the firm. However, the firm will then exercise the call provision of the bond it has issued. In effect, when the firm suffers the exercise, it passes that exercise through to its own bondholders, and the firm remains unaffected by the exercise of the call against it. As the second line of Table 20.2 indicates, the issuer continues to enjoy a position that is effectively similar to having issued noncallable straight debt initially.

Table 20.2	Transforming Callable into Noncallable Debt		
Call Date Scenario	**Swap**	**Issuer**	**Result**
Interest rates higher.	Swaption not exercised.	Does not call the bond.	Issuer has fixed rate financing.
Interest rates lower.	Swaption exercised. Issuer pays fixed and receives floating for remainder of bond's life.	Calls the bond and funds floating for remainder of bond's life.	Issuer has fixed rate financing.

Source: From L. S. Goodman, "Capital Market Applications of Interest Rate Swaps," in C. R. Beidleman, *Interest Rate Swaps,* 1991, p. 155. Reprinted by permission of Irwin Professional, Burr Ridge, Illinois.

Synthetic Dual-Currency Debt[8]

A **dual currency bond** has principal payments denominated in one currency, with coupon payments denominated in a second currency. For example, a firm might borrow dollars and pay coupon payments on the instrument in German marks. When the bond expires, the firm would repay its principal obligation in dollars. This dual currency bond can be synthesized from a regular single currency bond with all payments in dollars (a dollar-pay bond) combined with a fixed-for-fixed currency swap.

The upper time line in Figure 20.8 shows the cash flows from owning a typical dollar-pay bond from the point of view of the bond owner. The purchaser of the bond invests at the outset and then receives coupon inflows and the return of principal upon maturity. Thus, the down arrows indicate outflows, while the up arrows represent cash inflows. The second time line in Figure 20.8 shows the cash flows for a fixed-for-fixed foreign currency swap in which the party receives fixed German mark inflows and pays fixed dollar amounts. Notice that there is no exchange of borrowings in this swap. The amount of the cash flows in the currency swap are constructed to equal the coupon payments.

Figure 20.9 shows the effect of combining the dollar-pay bond with the foreign currency swap. The dollar coupon payments on the dollar-pay bond and the dollar payments on the fixed-for-fixed currency swap perfectly offset each other. This leaves German mark inflows from the swap which take the place of the coupon payments. As Figure 20.9 shows, the principal payment and repayment are in dollars; all of the coupon cash flows are in German marks. Thus, a dollar-pay bond combined with the appropriate fixed-for-fixed currency swap with no exchange of borrowings produce a dual-currency bond.

THE ALL-IN COST

As we have seen in the preceding section, it is possible to use swaps to create a variety of synthetic securities. In a perfect market without taxes, all securities with the same cash flow should have the same value. However, it must also be acknowledged that an early impetus to the development of the swaps market was the difference in net costs of various financial structures that were equivalent in

Elements of Synthetic Dual-Currency Debt   **Figure 20.8**

Dollar-pay bond

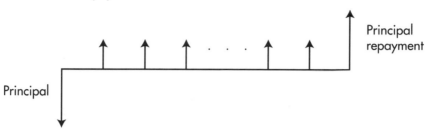

Principal repayment

Principal

Fixed-for-fixed currency swap

Receive German marks

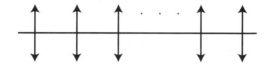

Pay U.S. dollars

Cash Flows on Synthetic Dual-Currency Debt   **Figure 20.9**

German mark coupon

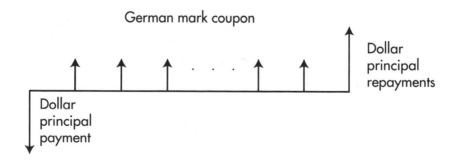

Dollar principal repayments

Dollar principal payment

terms of their underlying cash flows. These cost differences emerged from various market imperfections and inefficiencies. These market imperfections included taxes, transaction costs, illiquidity in some markets, and similar factors. In the early development of the swaps market, it may also have been possible to exploit inefficiencies in the market when instruments with the same cash flows sold for different prices. According to considerable anecdotal evidence, these inefficiencies resulted from investor ignorance of techniques for creating synthetic securities and from a failure to recognize that various securities had synthetic equivalents.

In a financial market that functions well, the same asset must sell for the same price in two different locations. For example, in Chapter 1 we considered a hypothetical example of a share of IBM trading at two different prices on the New York Stock Exchange and the Pacific Stock Exchange. Clearly, a single share of stock is such a simple security that all parties recognize that it should have a single price on two exchanges. However, when securities become more complex and cash flows are extended in time, these equivalences may not be so obvious. Therefore, a tool to compare financing alternatives can be quite useful.

The **all-in cost** is the Internal Rate of Return (IRR) for a given financing alternative. It is called the all-in cost because it includes all costs associated with the alternative being evaluated, such as flotation costs and administrative expenses, as well as the actual cash flows for the instrument being evaluated. As such, the all-in cost represents an effective annual percentage cost and provides an effective basis for comparing different financing alternatives.

We illustrate the concept of the all-in cost by comparing two financing alternatives available to the firm that are different in structure but that have the same actual cash flows. The first instrument is a ten-year semiannual payment bond with a principal amount of $40 million and a coupon rate of 7 percent. This instrument is priced at par.

$$P = \sum_{t=1}^{M} \frac{C_t}{(1 + r)^t} \qquad (20.1)$$

where:

   M = maturity date of the bond
   C_t = the cash flow from the bond at time t, which could be principal or interest
   r = yield to maturity on the bond

In Equation 20.1, r is the yield on the bond, which is also the IRR that equates the price and the present value of the cash flows associated with the bond. Therefore, the yield to maturity meets the definition of the all-in cost for this bond. Because the bond pays a coupon of 7 percent and is priced at par, the yield on the bond is also 7 percent and the all-in cost is also 7 percent. Therefore, the firm can secure its fixed rate financing at an all-in cost of 7 percent by issuing a straight bond.

As a second financing alternative, the firm can borrow $40 million for ten years at a floating rate of LIBOR plus 30 basis points, with the rate being reset each six months. LIBOR currently stands at 6.5 percent. Because the floating rate is currently 6.8 percent, it looks attractive compared to the 7 percent fixed rate financing vehicle. However, the firm has determined to secure fixed rate financing. As we saw earlier in this chapter, issuing a floating rate bond combined with an interest rate swap to pay fixed and receive floating is equivalent to a fixed rate bond. Upon inquiry, the firm learns that it can secure an interest rate swap to pay fixed and receive floating. The payment will be fixed at

6.8 percent, while the floating cash inflow on the swap will be LIBOR plus 30 basis points. However, the fee for arranging the swap and the associated administrative costs is an immediate payment of $400,000.

In summary of this second financing alternative, the firm would borrow $40 million at a floating rate of LIBOR plus 30 basis points, and it would enter a swap agreement to pay 6.8 percent and receive LIBOR plus 30 basis points. The firm must also pay a $400,000 fee for the swap, so it will net only $39,600,000 of actual financing. The two financing alternatives have very similar cash flows and both imply a fixed rate financing of about $40 million. The choice of financing, therefore, reduces to comparing the all-in costs of the two deals. Figure 20.10 shows the net cash flow line for the second financing alternative, reflecting the effect of the swap. The firm receives $39.6 million at inception, makes 20 semiannual payments of $1.36 million, and repays the principal of $40 million at the end of ten years. The all-in cost for the second alternative is simply the IRR that equates the present cash inflow of $39.6 million with all of the cash outflows. For these flows the IRR is 0.034703 on a semiannual basis, or 0.069406 in annual terms. This is slightly lower than the 7 percent IRR on the straight bond financing, so the firm prefers the floating rate instrument coupled with the interest rate swap. Being able to compute the IRR on the two deals and compare the all-in costs leads to the correct decision.

CONCLUSION

This chapter has considered some important refinements in understanding the swaps market that go beyond the plain vanilla interest rate and currency swaps explored in Chapter 19. A plain vanilla interest rate swap has a fixed notional principal and a fixed coupon rate that is constant at the market level of yields prevailing when the swap is initiated. An interest rate swap can be enriched by allowing the notional principal and the coupon rate to vary over the life of the instrument. For example, we saw that the notional principal can be amortized or increased over the life of the swap. Similarly, the coupon rate can be adjusted to reflect the slope of the yield curve. Foreign currency swaps are subject to similar adjustments. While these vehicles are more complicated than their plain vanilla cousins, they allow more exacting risk management.

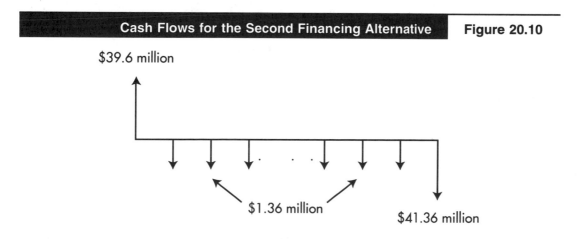

Cash Flows for the Second Financing Alternative   **Figure 20.10**

$39.6 million

$1.36 million

$41.36 million

Commodity and equity swaps go beyond plain vanilla interest rate and currency swaps by changing the underlying notional instrument. In a commodity swap, one party makes fixed payments, and the counterparty makes floating payments tied to the physical commodity that underlies the agreement. An equity swap is essentially like a commodity swap, except that the underlying ''commodity'' is a stock market index of some sort. Swaps can also be extended beyond plain vanilla in other ways. Forward swaps are normal swap agreements, but the initiation of the payments occurs in the future. An extension swap tacks on a longer period to an existing swap.

This chapter also considered swaptions, which are options on swaps. These instruments combine the features of both swaps and options. Similarly, this chapter showed that a swap agreement can be viewed as a portfolio of forward contracts. Thus, an interest rate swap agreement is essentially a portfolio of interest rate forward contracts collected into a single instrument. Given the intimate connection between swaps and forward contracts, it is not surprising that swaps can be used to create synthetic securities. For example, we showed how an interest rate swap agreement can be used to create either synthetic fixed rate or synthetic floating rate debt.

Given the complexities of these instruments and the relationships among forwards, futures, options, options on futures, and swaps, there is often more than one combination of instruments that can achieve a given risk management objective. Thus, some basis for comparing these alternatives is essential. We showed that the all-in cost provides a useful analytical technique for making these comparisons. By analyzing all of the cash flows from competing strategies, the all-in cost finds the strategy with the lowest internal rate of return as the cheapest solution to the particular risk management problem.

QUESTIONS AND PROBLEMS

1. What is the difference between a seasonal and a roller coaster swap?
2. Compare and contrast an accreting and an amortizing swap.
3. Generally, political unrest in Europe is accompanied by an increase in the yield differential between Eurocurrency deposit rates and U.S. T-bill rates. Explain how to construct a basis swap to profit from such a development. Explain how this might be related to a TED spread in futures.
4. Using interest rate swaps based on U.S. Treasury instruments, explain how to create a yield curve swap that will profit if the yield curve has an upward slope and the curve steepens. Explain how this might be related to the NOB spread in futures.
5. Explain how two foreign currency swaps might be combined to create a fixed-for-fixed foreign currency swap.
6. ''An equity swap is nothing but a commodity swap!'' Do you agree or disagree with this statement? Explain.
7. Consider two interest rate swaps to pay fixed and receive floating. The two swaps require the same payments each semiannual period, but one swap has a tenor of five years, while the second has a tenor of ten years. Assume that you buy the ten-year swap and sell the five-year swap. What kind of instrument do these transactions create? Explain.
8. ''A swaption is essentially a portfolio of options on futures or options on forwards.'' Is this statement correct? Explain.
9. Explain how an interest rate swap can be analyzed as a strip of futures.
10. Assume you can borrow at a fixed rate for ten years for 11 percent or that you can borrow at a floating rate of LIBOR plus 40 basis points for ten years. Assume also that LIBOR stands at

10.60 percent. Under these circumstances, your financial advisor states: ''The all-in cost is the same on both deals – 11 percent. Therefore, the two are equivalent and one should be indifferent between these two financing alternatives.'' How would you react? Explain.

NOTES

[1] This section draws on an article by Peter A. Abken, ''Beyond Plain Vanilla: A Taxonomy of Swaps,'' Federal Reserve Bank of Atlanta, *Economic Review*, March/April 1991. Reprinted in R. Kolb, *The Financial Derivatives Reader*, Miami: Kolb Publishing, 1993.

[2] Some authors regard the fixed-for-floating currency swap as the archetypal plain vanilla currency swap.

[3] J. Marshall and K. Kapner, *The Swaps Market*, 2e, Miami: Kolb Publishing, 1993, p. 120.

[4] K. R. Kapner and J. F. Marshall, *The Swaps Handbook*, New York: New York Institute of Finance, 1990, pp. 288–89.

[5] This section draws on an article by Peter A. Abken, ''Beyond Plain Vanilla: A Taxonomy of Swaps,'' Federal Reserve Bank of Atlanta, *Economic Review*, March/April 1991. Reprinted in R. Kolb, *The Financial Derivatives Reader*, Miami: Kolb Publishing, 1993.

[6] See P. A. Abken, ''Beyond Plain Vanilla: A Taxonomy of Swaps,'' Federal Reserve Bank of Atlanta, *Economic Review*, March/April 1991. Reprinted in R. Kolb, *The Financial Derivatives Reader*, Miami: Kolb Publishing, 1993.

[7] See I. G. Kawaller, ''Interest Rate Swaps versus Eurodollar Strips,'' *Financial Analysts Journal*, September/October 1989, for a discussion of the relationship between swaps and strips.

[8] This example is adapted from John F. Marshall and Kenneth R. Kapner, *The Swaps Market*, 2e, Miami: Kolb Publishing, 1993, pp. 143–46.

OPTION! Installation and Quick Start

OVERVIEW

OPTION! software is included with each copy of this text. **OPTION!** operates on virtually any IBM PC or compatible, and it can compute virtually all of the option values and relationships discussed in the text. If the computer has a graphics capability, **OPTION!** can graph many of the option pricing relationships explained in this text. The program can save hundreds of hours of tedious computations, and it can be used as an effective learning tool to illustrate and explore the option pricing relationships discussed in the text.

The program has been written for easy use. This chapter does not attempt to explain all of the features of **OPTION!**. Instead, it explains the architecture of the program and illustrates how to install and use the software. All of the modules operate similarly, and the text explains the meaning of all the calculations that **OPTION!** can perform.

FEATURES OF **OPTION!** SOFTWARE

OPTION! can calculate virtually all of the option prices and relationships covered in the text. Figure 1 shows the main menu from the software and the nine modules that constitute the program. This section briefly considers each module.

Module A, Option Values and Profits at Expiration, computes the outcome for various option strategies that are held to expiration of the options. From this module, you can view or print a report summarizing the results of the strategy you are considering. In this module you can select up to three calls plus three puts and the underlying stock. Given your choice of strategies, you can then see how the strategy will perform for various stock prices at expiration. You can also graph these outcomes.

Module B, Option Values and Profits Before Expiration, is similar in structure and spirit to Module A. However, Module B allows you to price the options in your portfolio by using the Black-Scholes and Merton models. You may then see how changing stock prices will affect the current value of your strategy. You may view or print a report, and you may graph the outcomes from your strategy as a function of the stock price.

Figure 1   **The Main Menu for OPTION!**

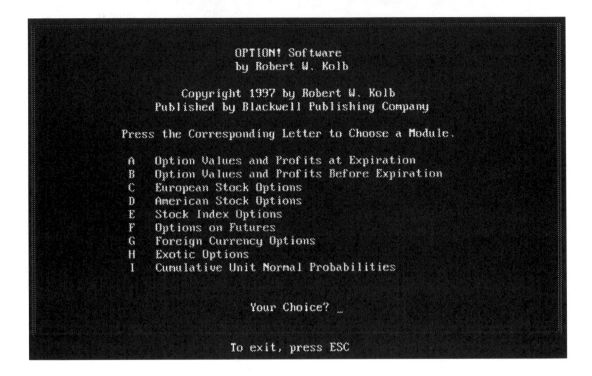

```
              OPTION! Software
              by Robert W. Kolb

           Copyright 1997 by Robert W. Kolb
        Published by Blackwell Publishing Company

     Press the Corresponding Letter to Choose a Module.

        A   Option Values and Profits at Expiration
        B   Option Values and Profits Before Expiration
        C   European Stock Options
        D   American Stock Options
        E   Stock Index Options
        F   Options on Futures
        G   Foreign Currency Options
        H   Exotic Options
        I   Cumulative Unit Normal Probabilities


                   Your Choice? _


                 To exit, press ESC
```

In Module C, European Stock Option Pricing, there are six submodules, identified by the letters A–F. These cover the binomial model with specified price movements (submodule A), the Black-Scholes model (submodule B), Implied Volatility according to the Black-Scholes and Merton models (submodule C), Simulation of Stock and Option Prices consistent with the Black-Scholes model (submodule D), the Binomial Approximation of the Black-Scholes model using stock price movements consistent with a Black-Scholes framework (submodule E), and Dividend Adjustments for European Options (submodule F). Many of these submodules allow extensive graphical analysis of pricing relationships, as we explore later.

Module D, American Stock Option Pricing, consists of five submodules that cover virtually all dimensions of pricing American options on individual stocks. Submodule A can compute the exact price of an American call option on a stock with one dividend prior to the expiration of the option. Submodule B uses the analytic approximation devised by Barone-Adesi and Whaley to price American calls and puts written on a stock paying a continuous dividend. Submodule C applies the binomial model to American options on stocks paying proportional dividends. Submodule D applies the binomial model to a stock paying periodic dividend yields, while submodule E applies the binomial model to stocks paying periodic cash dividends. Submodules A and B are accompanied by extensive graphical choices. In submodules C–D, you can specify the number of periods to be used in the binomial model.

Modules E, F, and G cover Stock Index Options, Options on Futures, and Foreign Currency Options, respectively. They are similar in their operation. Each computes the value of call and put options according to the Black-Scholes model, the Merton model, the analytic approximation for American options, the binomial model for a European option, and the binomial model for an American option. Each of these three modules also provides graphical analysis for both the European and American options.

Module H deals with exotic options. As the text explains, there are many different types of exotic options, including forward start options, compound options, chooser options, binary options, barrier options, lookback options, average price options, exchange options, and rainbow options. For some of these types of exotic options, there are several subspecies. **OPTION!** can price all of these exotic options and graph the price of the option as a function of the key input parameters. The program focuses on exotic European options, as these are the options for which closed-form pricing formulas exist.

The last module, Module I, Cumulative Unit Normal Probabilities, computes univariate and bivariate cumulative probabilities. It is included as a useful utility to avoid tables of these values and interpolations. For example, for computing $N(d_1)$, you can provide the value of d_1, and this module will compute the value of $N(d_1)$ to six decimal place accuracy.

INSTALLATION

The installation of **OPTION!** is extremely easy. The program can operate from a floppy disk drive, or it can be installed onto a hard disk. We strongly recommend using **OPTION!** from a hard disk to save time.

Installation on a Floppy Drive System

1. Make a back-up copy of the original **OPTION!** diskette.
2. Place the original diskette in a safe location.
3. Place the working copy of **OPTION!** in drive A: and make drive A: the logged drive by giving the following command: ''A:''.
4. Installation is complete. You may run the program by typing ''OPTION!'' and pressing return.

Installation on a Hard Drive System

1. Make a directory to hold the files for **OPTION!**. Assuming the system has a hard disk named drive C: and you want to install the software in a subdirectory called ''OPTION,'' use the Make Directory command as follows:

   ''MD C:\OPTION''

2. Place the original diskette for **OPTION!** in the A: drive.
3. Copy all the files from the original diskette to the subdirectory on the hard disk created in step 1 by using the following command:

"COPY A:*.* C:\OPTION"

4. To run **OPTION!**, be sure that the logged drive and subdirectory hold the **OPTION!** files. To do this you can use the following two commands:

"C:" and "CD\OPTION"

5. Installation is complete. Place the original diskette in a safe location. You may start the program with the following command: "OPTION!" and press return.

QUICK START

Great care has been taken to ensure that all of the modules in **OPTION!** function similarly. This section shows how to use the software by going step-by-step through a comprehensive example.

To use **OPTION!**, be sure that the logged drive or subdirectory is the location for all of the **OPTION!** files. To start the program, type "OPTION!" and press ENTER. The program then shows the main menu of Figure 1. The program contains nine modules, lettered A–I. To start a given module from the main menu, press the corresponding letter. To exit a given screen at any time, press ESC. Pressing ESC when the main menu is showing exits the program and returns to DOS. From any screen, pressing ESC repeatedly will exit the program.

In general, the modules function by allowing you to enter data and then press a function key to perform some analysis. For example, the program uses the F1 key to request solution. F2 is the key for graphics. Watch the bottom line of the screen for special instructions.

For our illustrative problem, we are going to find the value of a European call option according to the famous Black-Scholes model. (The text examines the mathematics and economics of the Black-Scholes model in detail.) From the main menu shown in Figure 1, we select the module for European Stock Options by pressing "C". Figure 2 shows that there are six submodules for European Stock Option Pricing lettered A–F. Because we want to apply the Black-Scholes model, we now select submodule B by pressing "B".

This brings us to the screen shown in Figure 3. On this screen we can now enter the data necessary to solve our problem. As the text explains, the Black-Scholes model expresses the value of a European option as a function of five underlying variables: the stock price, the exercise price, the time until the option expires, the volatility of the underlying stock, and the risk-free rate of interest. For our problem we consider a stock that currently trades at $100. The option has an exercise price of $90, and there are 55 days until expiration. The standard deviation of returns for the stock is 0.3, and the risk-free rate of interest is 7 percent.

To enter these values we navigate from one data entry block to the next by using the up and down arrow keys. If you make a mistake in entering a number, you can delete the last entry by pressing DEL, the delete key. Figure 4 shows these values entered in the screen in the appropriate positions. (We leave the dividend at zero, because the stock has no dividend.)

We are now ready to solve the problem. Notice the line of instructions at the bottom of the screen:

Press F1 for option results, F2 to graph, or ESC to exit.

The Menu for European Stock Option Pricing | **Figure 2**

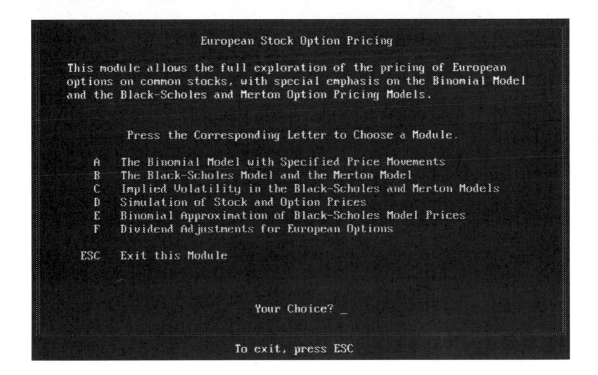

```
                European Stock Option Pricing

This module allows the full exploration of the pricing of European
options on common stocks, with special emphasis on the Binomial Model
and the Black-Scholes and Merton Option Pricing Models.


        Press the Corresponding Letter to Choose a Module.

    A    The Binomial Model with Specified Price Movements
    B    The Black-Scholes Model and the Merton Model
    C    Implied Volatility in the Black-Scholes and Merton Models
    D    Simulation of Stock and Option Prices
    E    Binomial Approximation of Black-Scholes Model Prices
    F    Dividend Adjustments for European Options

  ESC    Exit this Module




                Your Choice? _


            To exit, press ESC
```

Function key F1 is always used to solve a problem, and F2 is always used to bring up the graphics menu. ESC (the escape key) is always used to exit a current screen and return to a previous screen. After we press F1, the screen will appear as in Figure 5, which shows the solution to our problem.

We now decide that we would like to graph some of the option relationships that are explored in the text. Accordingly, we now select F2, which brings up the graphics menu shown in Figure 6. There we have six different options (no pun intended), and we decide to graph the call price as a function of the price of the underlying stock. Therefore, from the graphics menu in Figure 6, we press "A".

This presents another menu, shown in Figure 7. Because we want to graph the price of the call option as a function of the stock price, we now press "A". Figure 8 shows the resulting graph. The curved line in the graph shows the value of the call as a function of the stock price. The lower straight line shows the value of the call at expiration. As we would expect, the price of the call option is an increasing function of the stock price. Also, from the graph we note that the call price approaches its intrinsic value for higher stock prices. Notice that the graph shows stock prices from $80 to $120 on the x-axis. The computer program automatically selects the most appropriate range of x-values based on the particular problem you have specified.

Figure 3   **The Data Screen for the Black-Scholes Model**

```
                Black-Scholes and Merton Option Pricing Models

     Use this screen to find put and call prices according to the Black-Scholes
     and Merton Option Pricing Models.  The program computes put and call values
     with no dividends (Black-Scholes) or with continuous dividends (Merton).

        Stock Price                                                  0.0000
        Exercise Price                                               0.0000
        Days Until Expiration                                        0.0000
        Volatility (standard deviation per year, e.g., 0.30)         0.0000
        Risk-Free Rate per Year (e.g., 0.06)                         0.0000
        Annualized Dividend Yield (e.g., 0.03)                       0.0000

                                 OUTPUT AREA




             Press F1 for option results, F2 to graph, or ESC to exit.
```

We now assume that you would like to print the graph. With **OPTION!** you can save any graph to a computer file for printing through almost any word processing program. To save the graph, press F7. The screen gives a quick blink and writes the graphics file to the current directory. When you press F7, **OPTION!** creates the graphics file as a PCX file. This is an extremely popular and general graphical format. Most word processing programs (such as Word and WordPerfect) can print these files. The program assigns sequential file names to the graphs that you save. The first PCX file saved to a directory is given the name "KPGRF001.PCX". Subsequent graphs are saved to files with the next unused number in the file name. Figure 8 was saved in this manner and printed through WordPerfect. (To save time and avoid running out of space when saving a graph, it is best to operate **OPTION!** from a hard drive.) If the program is being run under Windows, it is possible to transfer graphs to other programs using the Windows clipboard. Consult the Windows manual for your particular system for instructions on using the clipboard.

At this point, with our graph on screen, we are at the innermost layer of the **OPTION!** program. After viewing the graph, we press ESC, which returns us to the graphics menu for the sensitivity of the option price to the input parameters (Figure 7). We can select another graph choice, or press ESC again. If we press ESC, we return to the graphics menu for the Black-Scholes model (Figure 6). Pressing ESC again returns us to the data entry screen with our data still in place (Figure 5). Here

The Data for the Sample Problem	Figure 4

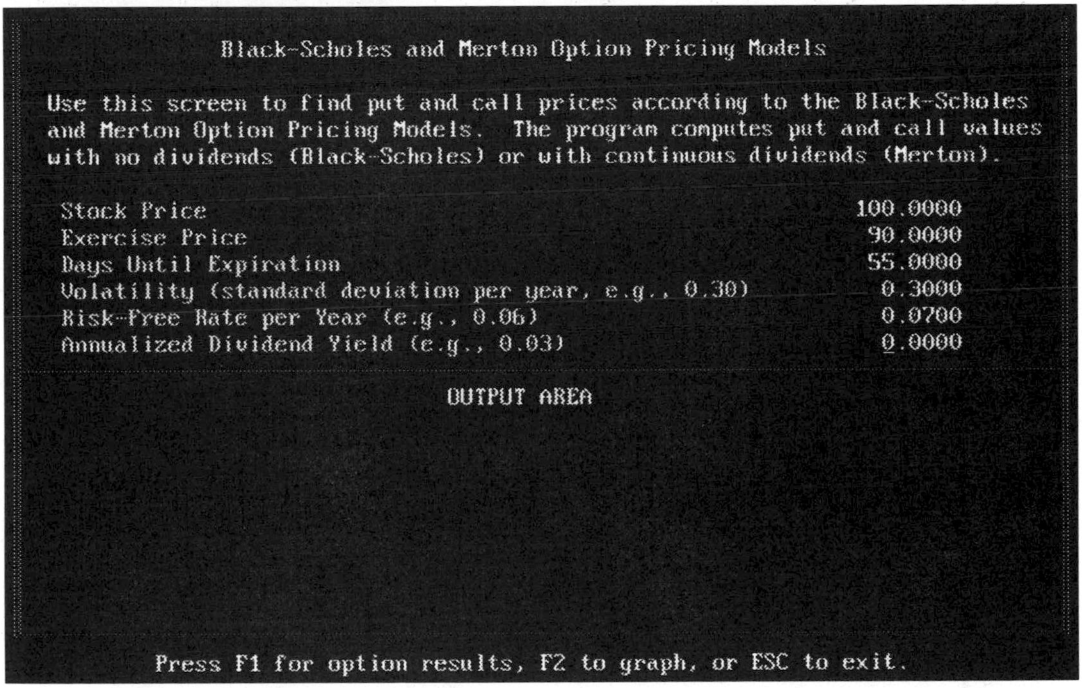

Black-Scholes and Merton Option Pricing Models

Use this screen to find put and call prices according to the Black-Scholes
and Merton Option Pricing Models. The program computes put and call values
with no dividends (Black-Scholes) or with continuous dividends (Merton).

Stock Price	100.0000
Exercise Price	90.0000
Days Until Expiration	55.0000
Volatility (standard deviation per year, e.g., 0.30)	0.3000
Risk-Free Rate per Year (e.g., 0.06)	0.0700
Annualized Dividend Yield (e.g., 0.03)	0.0000

OUTPUT AREA

Press F1 for option results, F2 to graph, or ESC to exit.

we can enter new values for another problem, or press ESC to return to the menu for the European Stock Option submodule (Figure 2). From the menu for the submodule, pressing ESC again returns us to the main menu (Figure 1). From the main menu, pressing ESC terminates the program and returns us to the operating system.

SUMMARY AND OPERATING TIPS

1. Be sure that you operate **OPTION!** from the logged drive or subdirectory.
2. Use the delete key, DEL, to erase erroneous data entries.
3. Use the cscape key, ESC, to leave any screen and return to a previous screen.

Standard key assignments are:

F1 = Solve for an option value after data are entered.
F2 = Proceed to the graphics menu.
F3 = Choose a report.
F7 = Save the graph on screen to a file in the current directory with a name of the form KPGRFnnn.PCX.
ESC = Leave the current screen and return to the previous screen.
DEL = When entering data, delete the last key stroke.

Figure 5   **The Solution to the Sample Problem**

```
              Black-Scholes and Merton Option Pricing Models

Use this screen to find put and call prices according to the Black-Scholes
and Merton Option Pricing Models.  The program computes put and call values
with no dividends (Black-Scholes) or with continuous dividends (Merton).

    Stock Price                                         100.0000
    Exercise Price                                       90.0000
    Days Until Expiration                                55.0000
    Volatility (standard deviation per year, e.g., 0.30) 0.3000
    Risk-Free Rate per Year (e.g., 0.06)                 0.0700
    Annualized Dividend Yield (e.g., 0.03)               0.0000

                           OUTPUT AREA
    Call Option                         Put Option
        Price      11.8671                  Price       0.9228
        Delta       0.8540                  Delta      -0.1460
        Theta     -13.9970                  Theta      -7.7631
        Gamma       0.0197                  Gamma       0.0197
        Vega        8.8905                  Vega        8.8905
        Rho        11.0796                  Rho        -2.3398


        Press F1 for option results, F2 to graph, or ESC to exit.
```

The Graphics Menu for the Black-Scholes Model   **Figure 6**

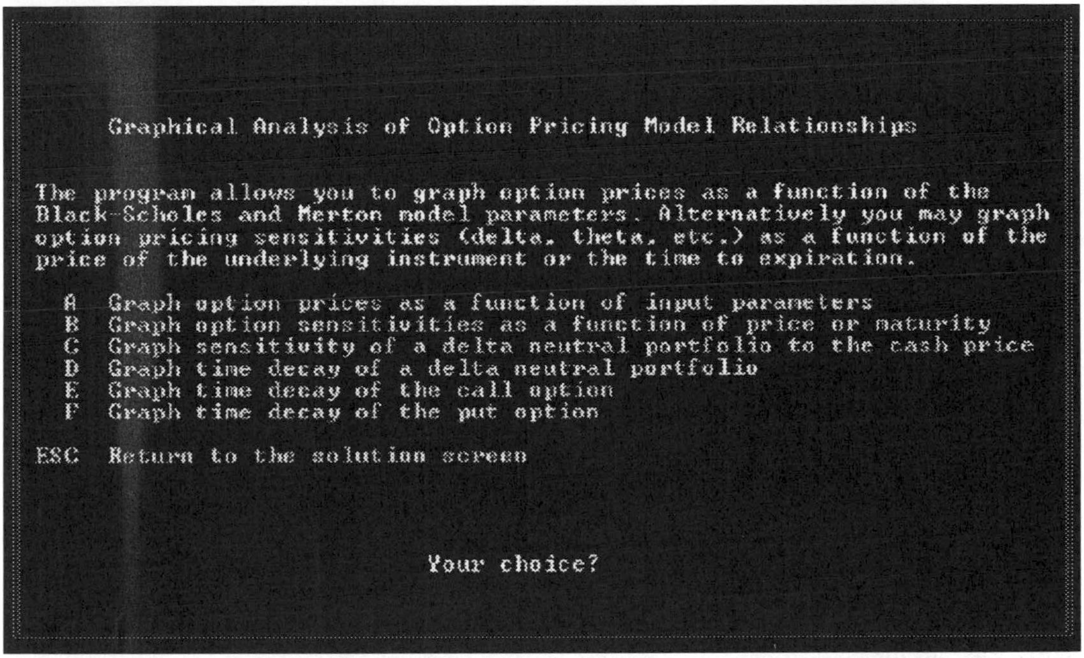

```
        Graphical Analysis of Option Pricing Model Relationships


The program allows you to graph option prices as a function of the
Black-Scholes and Merton model parameters. Alternatively you may graph
option pricing sensitivities (delta, theta, etc.) as a function of the
price of the underlying instrument or the time to expiration.

    A   Graph option prices as a function of input parameters
    B   Graph option sensitivities as a function of price or maturity
    C   Graph sensitivity of a delta neutral portfolio to the cash price
    D   Graph time decay of a delta neutral portfolio
    E   Graph time decay of the call option
    F   Graph time decay of the put option

ESC   Return to the solution screen



                        Your choice?
```

Figure 7   **The Graphics Menu for European Option Prices as a Function of the Input Parameters**

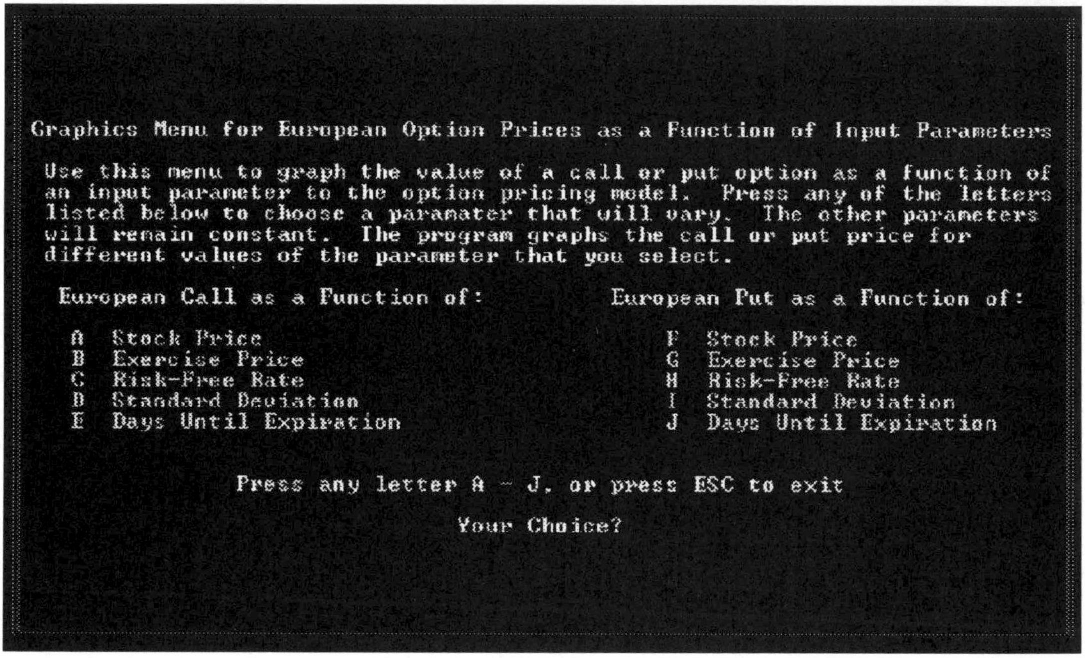

```
Graphics Menu for European Option Prices as a Function of Input Parameters

Use this menu to graph the value of a call or put option as a function of
an input parameter to the option pricing model.  Press any of the letters
listed below to choose a parameter that will vary.  The other parameters
will remain constant.  The program graphs the call or put price for
different values of the parameter that you select.

    European Call as a Function of:          European Put as a Function of:

    A   Stock Price                          F   Stock Price
    B   Exercise Price                       G   Exercise Price
    C   Risk-Free Rate                       H   Risk-Free Rate
    D   Standard Deviation                   I   Standard Deviation
    E   Days Until Expiration                J   Days Until Expiration


              Press any letter A - J. or press ESC to exit

                           Your Choice?
```

The Call Price as a Function of the Stock Price in the Sample Problem | **Figure 8**

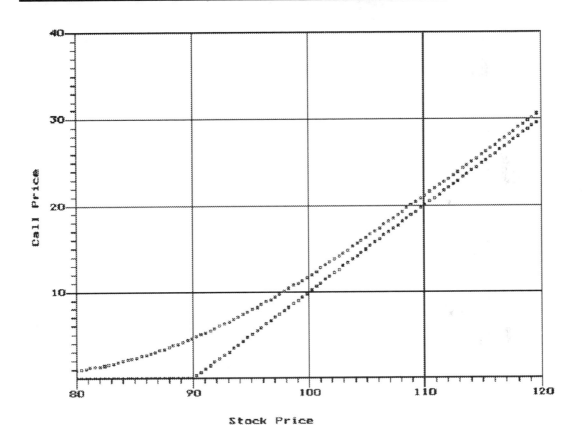

EXERCISES FOR OPTION!

1. Consider a call and a put option on the same underlying stock. Both options have an exercise price of $75. The call costs $5, and the put costs $4. If you buy both the call and the put, what is the position called? Complete the following table showing the value and profits and losses at expiration. Complete an **OPTION!** graph showing both the value of the position at expiration and the profits and losses on the position at expiration.

Stock Price at Expiration	Position Value at Expiration	Position Profit at Expiration
$50		
$65		
$70		
$75		
$80		
$85		
$90		

2. Consider a call and a put on the same underlying stock. Both options have the same exercise price of $50. The stock currently sells for $50. If you buy the stock, sell the put for $3, and buy the call for $4, complete the following table showing the value of the entire position and the profits and losses on the position at expiration.

Stock Price at Expiration	Position Value at Expiration	Position Profit at Expiration
$35		
$40		
$45		
$50		
$55		
$60		
$65		

3. Consider two calls on the same underlying stock. The calls have the same expiration date and exercise prices of $80 and $90. If the calls cost $12 and $4, respectively, complete the following table showing the value of and profits on a bull spread at expiration using these two calls. Prepare an **OPTION!** graph showing the profits and losses at expiration.

Stock Price at Expiration	Position Value at Expiration	Position Profit at Expiration
$70		
$75		
$80		
$85		
$90		
$95		
$100		
$105		
$110		

4. Consider two puts on the same underlying stock. The puts have the same expiration date and exercise prices of $80 and $90. If the puts cost $4 and $12, respectively, complete the following table showing the value of and profits on a bull spread at expiration using these two puts. Prepare an **OPTION!** graph showing the profits and losses at expiration.

Stock Price at Expiration	Position Value at Expiration	Position Profit at Expiration
$70		
$75		
$80		
$85		
$90		
$95		
$100		
$105		
$110		

5. Consider two calls on the same underlying stock. The calls have the same expiration date and exercise prices of $80 and $90. If the calls cost $12 and $4, respectively, complete the following table showing the value of and profits on a bear spread at expiration using these two calls. Prepare an **OPTION!** graph showing the profits and losses at expiration.

Stock Price at Expiration	Position Value at Expiration	Position Profit at Expiration
$70		
$75		
$80		
$85		
$90		
$95		
$100		
$105		
$110		

6. Consider two puts on the same underlying stock. The puts have the same expiration date and exercise prices of $80 and $90. If the puts cost $4 and $12, respectively, complete the following table showing the value of and profits on a bear spread at expiration using these two puts. Prepare an **OPTION!** graph showing the profits and losses at expiration.

Stock Price at Expiration	Position Value at Expiration	Position Profit at Expiration
$70		
$75		
$80		
$85		
$90		
$95		
$100		
$105		
$110		

7. For the same underlying stock, three calls with the same expiration date have exercise prices of $30, $35, and $40. For a long butterfly spread, complete the following table showing the value of and profits on the position at expiration. Prepare an **OPTION!** graph showing the profits and losses on the position at expiration assuming initial call prices of $11, $8, and $5 for the calls.

Stock Price at Expiration	Position Value at Expiration	Position Profit at Expiration
$20		
$25		
$30		
$35		
$40		
$45		
$50		

8. For the same underlying stock, two calls with the same expiration date have exercise prices of $30 and $40 and cost $11 and $8, respectively. Using these options, create two bull ratio spreads, one with a 2:1 ratio and the other with a 3:1 ratio. Complete the following table for the profits on the two spreads. For each spread, prepare an **OPTION!** graph showing the profits and losses on the positions at expiration.

Stock Price at Expiration	Profits on 2:1 Ratio Spread	Profits on 3:1 Ratio Spread
$20		
$25		
$30		
$35		
$40		
$45		
$50		

9. A stock now sells at $70 and a put on this stock with an exercise price of $70 costs $4. Using these instruments, create an insured portfolio and complete the following table.

Stock Price at Expiration	Profits on Stock Alone	Profits on Insured Portfolio
$50		
$55		
$60		
$65		
$70		
$75		
$80		
$85		
$90		

10. A stock sells at $100, and a call and a put on this stock both expire in one year and have the same exercise price of $100. The risk-free rate of interest is 9 percent. For a position that is long

the call, short the stock, and long a bond that pays $100 in one year, complete the following table. What can you infer from the table?

Stock Price at Expiration	Value of Combined Position	Value of Call – Put
$80		
$85		
$90		
$95		
$100		
$105		
$110		
$115		
$120		

11. Consider a call option that expires in one year and has an exercise price of $100. The underlying stock price is $150, and the risk-free rate of interest is 10 percent. From these facts alone, what can you say about the current price of the call option? Using these values in the Black-Scholes model, complete the following table. Draw a graph showing the price of this call as a function of the standard deviation using the values in the table. What does this show about the no-arbitrage bounds for the price of a call option?

Standard Deviation	Call Price
.9	
.8	
.7	
.6	
.5	
.4	
.3	
.2	
.1	
.01	

12. Consider a put option that expires in one year and has an exercise price of $150. The underlying stock price is $100, and the risk-free rate of interest is 10 percent. From these facts alone, what can you say about the current price of the put option? Using these values in the Black-Scholes model, complete the following table. Draw a graph showing the price of this put as a function of the standard deviation using the values in the table. What does this show about the no-arbitrage bounds for the price of a put option?

Standard Deviation	Put Price
.9	
.8	
.7	
.6	
.5	
.4	
.3	
.2	
.1	
.01	

13. A put option has an exercise price of $100 and expires in one year. The risk-free rate of interest is 10 percent, and the standard deviation of the underlying stock is .2. Complete the following table. Explain what the table shows about the value of European versus American put options. Prepare a graph showing the put price and the intrinsic value of the put as a function of the stock price using the values in the table below.

Stock Price	Black-Scholes European Put Price	Intrinsic Value of Put
$80		
$85		
$90		
$95		
$100		
$105		
$110		
$115		
$120		

14. A put option has an exercise price of $100 and the underlying stock is worth $80. The risk-free rate of interest is 10 percent, and the standard deviation of the underlying stock is .2. Complete the following table. Explain what the table shows about the value of European versus American put options.

Days Until Expiration	Black-Scholes European Put Price	Intrinsic Value of Put
5		
10		
30		
90		
180		
270		
365		

15. Consider two call options on the same underlying stock. The calls have exercise prices of $80 and $90 and both expire in 150 days. The risk-free rate of interest is 8 percent, and the stock price is $100. Using the Black-Scholes model, complete the following table. What principle does the table illustrate regarding boundary conditions on call options?

Standard Deviation	Call Price $X = \$80$	Call Price $X = \$90$	Price Difference
.9			
.8			
.7			
.6			
.5			
.4			
.3			
.2			
.1			
.01			

16. Consider a call option with an exercise price of $80 that expires in 150 days. The risk-free rate of interest is 8 percent, and the stock price is $80. Using the Black-Scholes model, complete the following table. What principle does the table illustrate regarding the pricing of call options? Prepare a graph using the data in the table expressing the value of the call option as a function of the standard deviation.

Standard Deviation	Call Price
.9	
.8	
.7	
.6	
.5	
.4	
.3	
.2	
.1	
.01	

17. Consider two put options on the same underlying stock, with a standard deviation of .3. The puts have exercise prices of $80 and $90 and both expire in 150 days. The risk-free rate of interest is 8 percent, and the stock price is $60. Using the Black-Scholes model, complete the following table. What principle does the table illustrate regarding boundary conditions on put options?

Standard Deviation	Put Price X = $80	Put Price X = $90	Price Difference
.9			
.8			
.7			
.6			
.5			
.4			
.3			
.2			
.1			
.01			

18. Consider two put options on the same underlying stock. The stock trades for $100. One put has an exercise price of $80, while the other has an exercise price of $120. The standard deviation of the stock is .3, and the risk-free rate of interest is 11 percent. Complete the following table. What does the completed table indicate about the influence of the time until expiration on the pricing of puts? Explain the difference in the price patterns for the two puts. Would call options exhibit the same kind of price pattern? Explain.

Days Until Expiration	Put Price X = $80	Put Price X = $120
100		
120		
140		
160		
180		
200		
220		
240		
260		

19. A call option expires in one period and has an exercise price of $100. The underlying stock price is also $100. The stock price can rise or fall by 10 percent over the period. Using the one-period binomial model, complete the following table. How is the probability of a stock price increase related to the interest rate? Explain why this relationship makes sense. Explain why the call price varies with the interest rate as it does.

Interest Rate	Call Price	Probability of a Stock Price Increase
0.01		
0.02		
0.03		
0.04		
0.05		
0.06		
0.07		
0.08		
0.09		

20. A stock currently trades at $140 and a call option on the stock has an exercise price of $150 and expires in one year. The standard deviation of the stock price is .3, and the risk-free rate of interest is 12 percent. What is the Black-Scholes price for this call option? Complete the following table using the multiperiod binomial model. What is the relationship between prices from the binomial model and the Black-Scholes model? Explain.

Periods	Binomial Model Price
1	
2	
5	
10	
25	
50	
100	
150	
200	

21. A stock currently trades at $140 and a call option on the stock has an exercise price of $150 and expires in one year. The call price is $11.00, and the risk-free rate of interest is 12 percent. What is the standard deviation of the underlying stock? Complete the following table using the Black-Scholes model to find each price, and show the price to four decimals. What does the completed table show about the technique necessary to find the volatility when the other parameters are known?

Standard Deviation	Call Price	Error
0.01		
0.2		
0.1		
0.15		
0.125		
0.13		
0.1275		
0.1285		
0.1282		

22. A stock trades for $75 and is expected to pay a dividend of $2 in 30 days. European call and put options on this stock expire in 90 days and have an exercise price of $75. The risk-free rate of interest is 7 percent, and the standard deviation of the stock is .3. Find the price of these options according to the Black-Scholes model, ignoring dividends. What are the values of these European options according to the adjustments to the Black-Scholes model for known dividends? Verify your answer by showing your own calculations.

23. A stock trades at $40 and has a standard deviation of .4. The risk-free rate is 8 percent. A European call and put on this stock expire in 90 days. The exercise price for the call is $35, and the exercise price for the put is $45. Using the Merton model, complete the following table. What does the completed table show about the influence of dividends on call and put prices?

Continuous Dividend Rate	Call Price	Put Price
0.005		
0.01		
0.02		
0.03		
0.05		
0.075		
0.1		
0.125		
0.15		

24. A stock pays a continuous dividend of 3 percent and currently sells for $80. The risk-free rate of interest is 7 percent, and the standard deviation on the stock is .25. A European call and put on this stock both have an exercise price of $75 and expire in 180 days. Find the price of these options according to the Black-Scholes model (i.e., ignoring the dividend) and the Merton model. Find the price of these options according to the binomial model with 5, 25, 50, 100, and 200 periods.

25. A stock pays a proportional dividend equal to 2 percent of its value in 150 days. The current stock price is $120, the risk-free rate is 9 percent, and the standard deviation of the stock is .2. A European call and put option on this stock both expire in 270 days and both have an exercise price of $120. Find the price of these options according to the Black-Scholes model (i.e., ignoring the dividend) and the Merton model. Find the price of these options according to the binomial model with 5, 25, 50, 100, and 200 periods.

26. A stock will pay a cash dividend of $1.75 in 150 days. The current stock price is $120, the risk-free rate is 9 percent, and the standard deviation of the stock is .2. A European call and put option on this stock both expire in 270 days and both have an exercise price of $120. Find the price of these options according to the Black-Scholes model (i.e., ignoring the dividend) and the Merton model. Find the price of these options according to the binomial model with 5, 25, 50, 100, and 200 periods.

27. A stock trades at $80 and has a standard deviation of .4. The risk-free rate of interest is 6 percent. A European call and put both expire in 100 days and have the same exercise price of $80. Complete the following table for the sensitivities of the two options.

Stock	DELTA	THETA	VEGA	RHO	GAMMA
$60					
$65					
$70					
$75					
$80					
$85					
$90					
$95					
$100					

28. A stock trades at $80 and has a standard deviation of .4. The stock pays a continuous dividend of 3 percent. The risk-free rate of interest is 6 percent. A European call and put both expire in 100 days and have the same exercise price of $80. Complete the following table for the sensitivities of the two options.

Stock	DELTA	THETA	VEGA	RHO	GAMMA
$60					
$65					
$70					
$75					
$80					
$85					
$90					
$95					
$100					

29. Two stocks have the same standard deviation of .4, but Stock A is priced at $110, and Stock B trades for $100. The risk-free rate is 11 percent. Consider two call options written on these two stocks that both expire in 90 days. Call A has an exercise price of $110, while Call B has an exercise price of $100. Find the DELTAs for these two options. What is unusual about the result, and how can it be explained?

30. A stock trades for $50 and has a standard deviation of .4. A call on the stock has an exercise price of $40 and expires in 55 days. The risk-free rate is 8 percent. Find the DELTA for the call, and explain how to create a delta-neutral portfolio. (Assume that you are short one call.) Complete the following table.

Stock Price	Call Price	Portfolio Value
$45		
$46		
$47		
$48		
$49		
$50		
$51		
$52		
$53		
$54		
$55		

31. A stock trades for $50 and has a standard deviation of .4. A call on the stock has an exercise price of $40 and expires in 55 days. The risk-free rate is 8 percent. Find the DELTA for the call, and explain how to create a delta-neutral portfolio. (Assume that you are short one call.) Complete the following table showing how the value of the delta-neutral portfolio changes over time. Assume the stock price does not change. How do you account for the change in the value of the delta-neutral portfolio?

Days Until Expiration	Call Price	Portfolio Value
55		
50		
45		
40		
35		
30		
25		
20		
15		
10		
5		

32. A stock trades for $100 and has a standard deviation of .3. A call on the stock has an exercise price of $100 and expires in 77 days. The risk-free rate is 8 percent. Find the DELTA for the call, and form a delta-neutral portfolio assuming that you are short one call. What is the GAMMA for the stock and for the call? Does the portfolio have a positive or negative GAMMA? Complete the following table. How do these values illustrate the GAMMA of the portfolio?

Stock Price	Call Price	Portfolio Value
$80		
$85		
$90		
$95		
$100		
$105		
$110		
$115		
$120		

33. A stock with a standard deviation of .5 now trades for $100. Two calls on this stock both expire in 70 days and have exercise prices of $90 and $100. The risk-free rate is 10 percent. Find the

DELTA and GAMMA for both calls. Construct a portfolio that is long one share of stock and that is both delta-neutral and gamma-neutral. For the portfolio, complete the following table.

Standard Deviation	Portfolio Value
.3	
.35	
.45	
.5	
.55	
.6	
.65	
.7	

34. A stock sells for $70, has a standard deviation of .3, and pays a 2 percent continuous dividend. The risk-free rate is 11 percent. Three calls on this stock all expire in 100 days and have exercise prices of $65, $70, and $75. Using these calls, construct a long position in a butterfly spread. What does the spread cost? Complete the following table for the profitability of the spread as a function of the stock price for the current time and for the expiration date. For the long position, is time decay beneficial or detrimental? Explain.

Stock Price	Profit with $T - t = 100$	Profit at Expiration
$50		
$55		
$60		
$65		
$70		
$75		
$80		
$85		
$90		

35. Consider a long position in a straddle with an exercise price of $50. The stock price is $80, and the standard deviation of the stock is .4. The risk-free rate is 6 percent, and the options expire in 180 days. What is the current price of the two options? Prepare a graph of the current value of the straddle as a function of the stock price. On the same axes, graph the value of the straddle at expiration. Let the range of stock prices range from $30 to $70. As a first step to preparing the graph, complete the following table.

Stock Price	Current Straddle Price	Straddle Price at Expiration
$30		
$35		
$40		
$45		
$50		
$55		
$60		
$65		
$70		

36. A stock trades at $50 and has a standard deviation of .3. The risk-free rate is 7 percent. An American and a European call on this stock both have an exercise price of $55, and both expire in 100 days. The stock will pay a dividend in 50 days, but the amount is uncertain. For the different possible dividend amounts shown in the table below, compute the exact American option price and the Black-Scholes model price with the known dividend adjustment. What kind of systematic difference do you notice in the pricing from the two models, if any?

Dividend Amount	Exact American	Black-Scholes Adjusted for Known Dividends
$.01		
$.05		
$.10		
$.25		
$.50		
$1.00		
$1.50		
$2.00		
$3.00		

37. A stock trades for $150 and has a standard deviation of .4. The risk-free rate of interest is 7 percent. Two dividends are expected. The first, due in 30 days, is for $1.50, while the second, due in 150 days, is for $2.00. Find the pseudo-American option price for a call that expires in 200 days with an exercise price of $140. Also, find the option price according to the Black-Scholes model adjusted for known dividends.

38. A stock with a standard deviation of .33 trades for $75. The risk-free rate is 6 percent. The stock pays a continuous dividend of 2 percent. An American call and put on this stock have an exercise price of $70 and both expire in 100 days. Find the price of these options using the analytic approximation of the American option price. What are the critical values for the call and the put? Using the Merton model, find the price of both options.

39. A stock has a current price of $80 and a standard deviation of .3. The stock pays a continuous dividend of 3 percent. The risk-free rate is 7 percent. An American and a European call on this stock both expire in 200 days, and both have an exercise price of $70. Find the price of the American call according to the analytic approximation formula, and find the price of the European option according to the Merton model. What is the critical price for the American call? Complete the following table for the two options using the two respective models. Graph the price of the two options as a function of the stock price over the range from $60 to $100. Explain any particularly important features of the graph.

Stock Price	American Call According to the Analytic Approximation	European Call According to the Merton Model
$60		
$65		
$70		
$75		
$80		
$85		
$90		
$95		
$100		

40. A stock has a current price of $70 and a standard deviation of .3. The risk-free rate is 7 percent. An American and a European put on this stock both expire in 200 days, and both have an exercise price of $80. Find the price of the American put according to the analytic approximation formula, and find the price of the European option according to the Merton model. What is the critical price for the American put? Complete the following table for the two options using the two respective models. Graph the price of the two options as a function of the stock price over the range from $60 to $100. Explain any particularly important features of the graph.

Stock Price	American Put According to the Analytic Approximation	European Put According to the Merton Model
$60		
$65		
$70		
$75		
$80		
$85		
$90		
$95		
$100		

41. A stock has a current price of $80 and a standard deviation of .3. The risk-free rate is 7 percent. An American and a European call on this stock both expire in 200 days, and both have an exercise price of $70. The stock pays a continuous dividend of 3 percent. Find the price of the American call according to the analytic approximation formula, and find the price of the European option according to the Merton model. Complete the following table for the two options using the two respective models. How can you explain the price differentials reported in the table?

Stock Price	American Call According to the Analytic Approximation	European Call According to the Merton Model
$60		
$65		
$70		
$75		
$80		
$85		
$90		
$95		
$100		

42. A stock has a current price of $80 and a standard deviation of .3. The risk-free rate is 7 percent. An American and a European call on this stock both expire in 200 days, and both have an exercise price of $70. If the stock is to pay a dividend it will be at a continuous rate, but the rate is uncertain. Alternative dividend rates are given in the table below. Find the price of the American call according to the analytic approximation formula, and find the price of the European option according to the Merton model for each dividend rate in the table. What do the price differentials in the table indicate about the importance of dividends for call pricing? For any of these dividend rates, should the American option be exercised now? If so, for which dividend rates?

Dividend Rate	American Call According to the Analytic Approximation	European Call According to the Merton Model
0.001		
0.005		
0.01		
0.02		
0.03		
0.04		
0.05		

43. A stock sells for $110 and has a standard deviation of .2. The risk-free rate is 7 percent. An American put on this stock has an exercise price of $120 and expires in 200 days. Using the

binomial model for an American put and a European put, complete the following table. Should the American put be exercised now? Explain.

Number of Periods	American Put Price	European Put Price
1		
2		
5		
10		
25		
50		
100		
200		

44. A stock sells for $110 and has a standard deviation of .2. The risk-free rate is 7 percent. An American put on this stock has an exercise price of $120 and expires in 200 days. Using the binomial model with 100 periods for an American put and a European put, complete the following table. From the table alone, what can you say about the correct exercise policy for the American put? Using the binomial model with 100 periods, find the exact stock price below which the American put should be exercised. Explain.

Stock Price	American Put Price	European Put Price
$90		
$95		
$100		
$105		
$110		
$115		
$120		
$125		
$130		

45. The HOT100 stock index stands at 4000.00 and has a standard deviation of .20. The continuous dividend rate on the HOT100 is 3 percent, and the risk-free rate of interest is 5 percent. Using the Merton model, find the prices for the calls and puts shown in the table below.

Index Value	Call X = 4000.0 T − t = 180 days	Call X = 3750.0 T − t = 90 days	Put X = 4000.0 T − t = 180 days	Put X = 3750.0 T − t = 90 days
3500.0				
3750.0				
4000.0				
4250.0				
4500.0				

46. The HOT100 stock index stands at 4000.00 and has a standard deviation of .20. The continuous dividend rate on the HOT100 is 3 percent, and the risk-free rate of interest is 5 percent. Using the Merton model, complete the table below for a call option with 180 days until expiration and an exercise price of $4000.0.

Index Value	DELTA	THETA	VEGA	RHO	GAMMA
4500.0					
4250.0					
4000.0					
3750.0					
3500.0					

47. The HOT100 stock index stands at 4000.00 and has a standard deviation of .20. The continuous dividend rate on the HOT100 is 3 percent, and the risk-free rate of interest is 5 percent. Using the Merton model, complete the table below for a put option with 180 days until expiration and an exercise price of $4000.0.

Index Value	DELTA	THETA	VEGA	RHO	GAMMA
4500.0					
4250.0					
4000.0					
3750.0					
3500.0					

48. The current dollar value of a German mark is $.6100, and the standard deviation of the mark is .25. The U.S. risk-free rate is 8 percent, while the German rate is 5 percent. European call and put options on the mark have an exercise price of $.6000 and expire in 250 days. What are these options worth today? If the German interest rate falls from 5 to 4 percent, what happens to the value of the options? Explain.

49. The current dollar value of a German mark is $.6100, and the standard deviation of the mark is .25. The U.S. risk-free rate is 8 percent, while the German rate is 5 percent. Consider an American and a European call on the mark with an exercise price of $.6000 that expires in 250 days. What are these options worth today? Should the American option be exercised now? If the German

interest rate falls from 5 to 4 percent, what happens to the value of the options? Does it change the exercise decision? Explain.

50. Options now trade on the well-known widget futures contract. The current widget price is $100.0 per widget, and the futures price is $107.50. The futures contract expires in two years. The widget market is well known for its strict adherence to cost-of-carry principles. The standard deviation of the futures price is .25. A European and an American call option on this futures have an exercise price of $105.00. What are the two options worth according to the Merton model and the analytic approximation for the American option? What would an American and European put be worth, assuming they have the same contract terms?

51. The text has assumed that the cost-of-carry equals the risk-free rate. Explain how **OPTION!** could be used to value a futures option if the cost-of-carry were less than or greater than the risk-free rate.

52. Using **OPTION!**, complete the following table for forward-start call and put options. $S = 80$; $X = 75$; $T - t = 350$ days; $\sigma = 0.4$; $r = 0.08$; and $\delta = 0.03$. As the table indicates, the day of the grant, tg, varies. Taking the call as an example, what do the values in the table indicate about how the option price varies with tg?

tg in Days	Forward-Start Call	Forward-Start Put
50		
100		
150		
200		
250		
300		
349		

53. Complete the following table for the compound options shown below. Common parameters are: $S = 100$; $\sigma = 0.3$; $r = 0.01$; $\delta = 0.04$; $X = 100$; $te = 100$ days; and $T - t = 365$ days. As the table indicates, the exercise price of the compound option varies.

Exercise Price of Compound Option	Call-on-Call	Call-on-Put	Put-on-Call	Put-on-Put
5				
10				
15				
20				
25				
30				
35				

54. Complete the following table for the compound options shown below. Common parameters are: $S = 100$; $\sigma = 0.3$; $r = 0.01$; $\delta = 0.04$; $X = 100$; $x = 10$; and $T - t = 365$ days. As the table indicates, the expiration date of the compound option varies.

Expiration Date of Compound Option in days	Call-on-Call	Call-on-Put	Put-on-Call	Put-on-Put
50				
100				
150				
200				
250				
300				
350				

55. Consider a European straddle with the following parameters: $S = 50$; $X = 50$; $T - t = 365$ days; $\sigma = 0.5$; $r = 0.06$; and $\delta = 0.03$. What is the value of the straddle? Now consider a chooser option with the same parameters, but a varying choice date. Complete the table shown below. What does the table illustrate about the relationship between chooser prices and straddle prices?

Choice Date, tc, in Days	Chooser Value
0	
1	
50	
100	
150	
200	
250	
300	
350	
355	
360	
364	

56. Consider a European call and a European put with parameter values of: $X = 70$; $T - t = 180$ days; $\sigma = 0.25$; $r = 0.1$; and $\delta = 0.0$. What is the value of the call and put if $S = 80$? Now consider a down-and-in call and a down-and-in put, with BARR = 80 and REBATE = 0.0. Using these data, complete the following table. What do these results suggest about the value of barrier options relative to plain vanilla options?

Stock Price	Down-and-In Call	Down-and-In Put
120		
100		
90		
85		
83		
82		
81		
80.10		
80.01		

57. Consider an up-and-out call and an up-and-out put with the following common parameter values: $T - t = 180$ days; $\sigma = 0.2$; $r = 0.1$; $\delta = 0.03$; BARR = 100; and REBATE = 0. Complete the following table. What can you conclude from the completed table?

Stock Price	Up-and-Out Call $X = 80$	Up-and-Out Put $X = 100$
99		
95		
90		
85		
80		
75		
70		

58. Consider an up-and-out call and an up-and-out put with the following common parameter values: $S = 98$; $\sigma = 0.2$; $r = 0.1$; $\delta = 0.03$; BARR = 100; and REBATE = 0. Complete the following table, and interpret the results.

$T - t$ in Days	Up-and-Out Call $X = 80$	Up-and-Out Put $X = 100$
1		
2		
5		
10		
20		
50		
100		
300		

59. A supershare is written with the following parameters: $S = 100$; $T - t = 365$ days; $\sigma = 0.4$; $r = 0.1$; and $\delta = 0.06$. Complete the following table for this supershare, assuming the varying upper and lower bounds in the table. What does the table illustrate about the influence of the bounds on the prices of supershares?

X_L	X_H	Supershare
70	80	
80	90	
90	100	
95	105	
100	110	
110	120	
120	130	

60. Consider two lookback calls with the following common parameters: $S = 100$; $T - t = 90$ days; $r = 0.06$; and $\delta = 0.0$. As the table indicates, the two calls are the same except one has MINPRI = 50, while the other has MINPRI = 95. Complete the following table and explain the differences in the prices of the two options.

Standard Deviation	Lookback Call MINPRI = 50	Lookback Call MINPRI = 95
0.1		
0.2		
0.3		
0.4		
0.5		
0.6		
0.9		

61. Consider an option to exchange one asset for another with $S_1 = 100$; $S_2 = 200$; $\delta_1 = 0.01$; $\delta_2 = 0.01$; $T - t = 90$ days; and $\rho = 0.0$. Complete the following table and interpret your results.

$\sigma_1 = \sigma_2$	Price of Exchange Option
0.5	
0.4	
0.3	
0.2	
0.1	
0.05	

62. A call on the maximum of two assets has the following parameters: $S_1 = 100$; $S_2 = 100$; $T - t =$ 365 days; $r = 0.08$; $\delta_1 = 0.0$; $\delta_2 = 0.0$; $\rho = 0.0$. Complete the following table and interpret your results.

$\sigma_1 = \sigma_2$	Call Price	Put Price
0.5		
0.4		
0.3		
0.2		
0.1		
0.05		
0.01		
0.001		
0.0001		

FUTURES DATA GUIDE

INTRODUCTION

Futures price data accompany this text to facilitate data analysis projects. All files have the same format, showing the date and the settlement price for a particular contract. These data can be used for a variety of exercises: to study volatility, to compute percentage price changes as a measure of returns, to consider intracommodity and intercommodity spreads, and so on. The data are just a small sample of the actual data generated by the market, but they are useful in providing an opportunity for data exploration. The remainder of this description explains the kinds of data included in the data set and the format in which the data are stored.

THE DATASET

Each file contains a sequence of dates and corresponding settlement prices for a single futures contract. Each file name has the same format:

XXYYMM.PRN

"XX" is a two-letter code identifying the commodity, as explained in Table 1. "YY" is the year of the contract's expiration, while "MM" indicates the month of the contract's expiration. The "PRN" extension indicates that the file is in ASCII format. For example SP9303.PRN is the S&P 500 futures contract expiring in March 1993. Table 1 shows the commodity codes for the commodity futures included on the data diskette.

As the table indicates, there are 20 commodities represented on the data diskette, with an initial total of 45 contract expirations. By the time you read this, more may have been added. Therefore, please see if there is a file on the diskette named "README." If there is, please use your word processor or editor to review this file.

DATA FORMATS

All of the files have the same data format. A typical line in a data file might appear as follows:

930602 433.22

The first column of numbers is the date in YYMMDD format. Thus, 930602 is the date June 2, 1997. The second number is the settlement price for the given futures contract on that date in the format indicated in Table 1. Data may be accessed for analysis in several ways:

1. Data can be imported into any spreadsheet program.
2. Data can be read by almost any statistical package.
3. Data can be read by any programming language (C, C++, BASIC, Pascal, etc.)
4. Data can be manipulated by any word processor or editor.

Probably the easiest and most powerful way to explore these data is by using a spreadsheet program.

Table 1	Commodity Codes and Method of Price Quotations	
Identifier	Commodity	Market and Price Quotation
AG	Silver	(COMEX) Cents per troy ounce
AU	Gold	(COMEX) U.S. dollars per troy ounce
BP	British Pound	(CME) U.S. dollars per pound
CC	Corn	(CBOT) Cents per bushel
CL	Crude Oil	(NYME) U.S. dollars per 42 gal. barrel
DM	Deutschemark	(CME) U.S. dollars per mark
ED	Eurodollar	(CME) IMM Index
HO	Heating Oil	(NYME) U.S. dollars per gallon
JY	Japanese Yen	(CME) Cents per yen
MM	Major Market Index	(CBOT; CME) Index units
PL	Platinum	(NYME) U.S. dollars per troy ounce
SB	Soybeans	(CBOT) Cents per bushel
SF	Swiss franc	(CME) U.S. dollars per franc
SM	Soymeal	(CBOT) U.S. dollars per ton
SO	Soyoil	(CBOT) Cents per pound
SP	S&P 500 Index	(CME) Index units
TB	Treasury Bill	(CME) IMM Index
UN	Unleaded Gas	(NYME) U.S. dollars per gallon
US	Treasury Bond	(CBOT) Points and 32nds of par
WH	Wheat	(CBOT) Cents per bushel

APPENDIX

Cumulative Distribution Function
for the Standard Normal Random Variable

	.00	.01	.02	.03	.04	.05	.06	.07	.08	.09
0.0	.5000	.5040	.5080	.5120	.5160	.5199	.5239	.5279	.5319	.5359
0.1	.5398	.5438	.5478	.5517	.5557	.5596	.5636	.5675	.5714	.5753
0.2	.5793	.5832	.5871	.5910	.5948	.5987	.6026	.6064	.6103	.6141
0.3	.6179	.6217	.6255	.6293	.6331	.6368	.6406	.6443	.6480	.6517
0.4	.6554	.6591	.6628	.6664	.6700	.6736	.6772	.6808	.6844	.6879
0.5	.6915	.6950	.6985	.7019	.7054	.7088	.7123	.7157	.7190	.7224
0.6	.7257	.7291	.7324	.7357	.7389	.7422	.7454	.7486	.7517	.7549
0.7	.7580	.7611	.7642	.7673	.7704	.7734	.7764	.7794	.7823	.7852
0.8	.7881	.7910	.7939	.7967	.7995	.8023	.8051	.8078	.8106	.8133
0.9	.8159	.8186	.8212	.8238	.8264	.8289	.8315	.8340	.8365	.8389
1.0	.8413	.8438	.8461	.8485	.8508	.8531	.8554	.8577	.8599	.8621
1.1	.8643	.8665	.8686	.8708	.8729	.8749	.8770	.8790	.8810	.8830
1.2	.8849	.8869	.8888	.8907	.8925	.8944	.8962	.8980	.8997	.9015
1.3	.9032	.9049	.9066	.9082	.9099	.9115	.9131	.9147	.9162	.9177
1.4	.9192	.9207	.9222	.9236	.9251	.9265	.9279	.9292	.9306	.9319
1.5	.9332	.9345	.9357	.9370	.9382	.9394	.9406	.9418	.9429	.9441
1.6	.9452	.9463	.9474	.9484	.9495	.9505	.9515	.9525	.9535	.9545
1.7	.9554	.9564	.9573	.9582	.9591	.9599	.9608	.9616	.9625	.9633
1.8	.9641	.9649	.9656	.9664	.9671	.9678	.9686	.9693	.9699	.9706
1.9	.9713	.9719	.9726	.9732	.9738	.9744	.9750	.9756	.9761	.9767
2.0	.9772	.9778	.9783	.9788	.9793	.9798	.9803	.9808	.9812	.9817
2.1	.9821	.9826	.9830	.9834	.9838	.9842	.9846	.9850	.9854	.9857
2.2	.9861	.9864	.9868	.9871	.9875	.9878	.9881	.9884	.9887	.9890
2.3	.9893	.9896	.9898	.9901	.9904	.9906	.9909	.9911	.9913	.9916
2.4	.9918	.9920	.9922	.9925	.9927	.9929	.9931	.9932	.9934	.9936
2.5	.9938	.9940	.9941	.9943	.9945	.9946	.9948	.9949	.9951	.9952
2.6	.9953	.9955	.9956	.9957	.9959	.9960	.9961	.9962	.9963	.9964
2.7	.9965	.9966	.9967	.9968	.9969	.9970	.9971	.9972	.9973	.9974
2.8	.9974	.9975	.9976	.9977	.9977	.9978	.9979	.9979	.9980	.9981
2.9	.9981	.9982	.9982	.9983	.9984	.9984	.9985	.9985	.9986	.9986
3.0	.9987	.9987	.9987	.9988	.9988	.9989	.9989	.9989	.9990	.9990
3.1	.9990	.9991	.9991	.9991	.9992	.9992	.9992	.9992	.9993	.9993
3.2	.9993	.9993	.9994	.9994	.9994	.9994	.9994	.9995	.9995	.9995
3.3	.9995	.9995	.9995	.9996	.9996	.9996	.9996	.9996	.9996	.9997
3.4	.9997	.9997	.9997	.9997	.9997	.9997	.9997	.9997	.9997	.9998

INDEX